Microsoft® Office Access™ 2007

ILLUSTRATED

COMPLETE

Lisa Friedrichsen

COURSE TECHNOLOGY
CENGAGE Learning

Australia • Brazil • Japan • Korea • Mexico • Singapore • Spain • United Kingdom • United States

COURSE TECHNOLOGY
CENGAGE Learning™

Microsoft® Office Access™ 2007—
Illustrated Complete
Lisa Friedrichsen

Senior Acquisitions Editor: Marjorie Hunt

Senior Product Manager: Christina Kling Garrett

Associate Product Manager: Rebecca Padrick

Editorial Assistant: Michelle Camisa

Senior Marketing Manager: Joy Stark

Marketing Coordinator: Jennifer Hankin

Contributing Author: Elizabeth Eisner Reding

Developmental Editor: Lisa Ruffolo

Production Editor: Jill Klaffky

Copy Editor: Gary Michael Spahl

Proofreader: Kathy Orrino

Indexer: Alexandra Nickerson

QA Manuscript Reviewers: Nicole Ashton,
   Jeff Schwartz, Danielle Shaw, Teresa Storch,
   Susan Whalen

Cover Designers: Elizabeth Paquin, Kathleen Fivel

Cover Artist: Mark Hunt

Composition: GEX Publishing Services

For product information and technology assistance, contact us at
Cengage Learning Customer & Sales Support, 1-800-354-9706
For permission to use material from this text or product, submit all requests online at **www.cengage.com/permissions**
Further permissions questions can be e-mailed to
permissionrequest@cengage.com

ISBN-13: 978-14239-0519-6
ISBN-10: 1-4239-0519-9

Course Technology
25 Thomson Place
Boston, MA 02210
USA

Trademarks:

Some of the product names and company names used in this book have been used for identification purposes only and may be trademarks or registered trademarks of their respective manufacturers and sellers.

Microsoft and the Office logo are either registered trademarks or trademarks of Microsoft Corporation in the United States and/or other countries. Course Technology is an independent entity from Microsoft Corporation, and not affiliated with Microsoft in any manner. Microsoft product screen shots reprinted with permission from Microsoft Corporation.

Cengage Learning is a leading provider of customized learning solutions with office locations around the globe, including Singapore, the United Kingdom, Australia, Mexico, Brazil, and Japan. Locate your local office at:
international.cengage.com/region

Cengage Learning products are represented in Canada by Nelson Education, Ltd.

For your lifelong learning solutions, visit **course.cengage.com**

Purchase any of our products at your local college store or at our preferred online store **www.ichapters.com**

Printed in the United States of America
4 5 6 7 8 11 10 09

About This Book

Welcome to *Microsoft Office Access 2007—Illustrated Complete*! Since the first book in the Illustrated Series was published in 1994, millions of students have used various Illustrated texts to master software skills and learn computer concepts. We are proud to bring you this new Illustrated book on the most exciting version of Microsoft Office ever to release.

As you probably have heard by now, Microsoft completely redesigned this latest version of Office from the ground up. No more menus! No more toolbars! The software changes Microsoft made were based on years of research during which they studied users' needs and work habits. The result is a phenomenal and powerful new version of the software that will make you and your students more productive and help you get better results faster.

Before we started working on this new edition, we also conducted our own research. We reached out to nearly 100 instructors like you who have used previous editions of this book and our Microsoft Office texts. Some of you responded to one of our surveys, others of you generously spent time with us on the phone, telling us your thoughts. Seven of you agreed to serve on our Advisory Board and guided our decisions.

As a result of all the feedback you gave us, we have preserved the features that you love, and made improvements that you suggested and requested. And of course we have covered all the key features of the new software. (For more details on what's new in this edition, please read the Preface.) We are confident that this book and all its available resources will help your students master Microsoft Office Access 2007.

Advisory Board

We thank our Advisory Board who enthusiastically gave us their opinions and guided our every decision on content and design from beginning to end. They are:

Kristen Callahan, Mercer County Community College

Paulette Comet, Assistant Professor, Community College of Baltimore County

Barbara Comfort, J. Sargeant Reynolds Community College

Margaret Cooksey, Tallahassee Community College

Rachelle Hall, Glendale Community College

Hazel Kates, Miami Dade College

Charles Lupico, Thomas Nelson Community College

Author Acknowledgments

Lisa Friedrichsen This book is dedicated to my students, and all who are using this book to teach and learn about Access. Thank you. Also, thank you to all of the professionals who helped me create this book.

Preface

Welcome to *Microsoft Office Access 2007—Illustrated Complete*. If this is your first experience with the Illustrated series, you'll see that this book has a unique design: each skill is presented on two facing pages, with steps on the left and screens on the right. The layout makes it easy to digest a skill without having to read a lot of text and flip pages to see an illustration.

This book is an ideal learning tool for a wide range of learners—the rookies will find the clean design easy to follow and focused with only essential information presented, and the hotshots will appreciate being able to move quickly through the lessons to find the information they need without reading a lot of text. The design also makes this a great reference after the course is over! See the illustration on the right to learn more about the pedagogical and design elements of a typical lesson.

What's New in This Edition

We've made many changes and enhancements to this edition to make it the best ever. Here are some highlights of what's new:

- **New Getting Started with Microsoft® Office 2007 Unit**—This unit begins the book and gets students up to speed on features of Office 2007 that are common to all the applications, such as the Ribbon, the Office button, and the Quick Access toolbar.

- **Real Life Independent Challenge**—The new Real Life Independent Challenge exercises offer students the opportunity to create projects that are meaningful to their lives, such as databases that track travel experiences, record geographic information, and maintain research on careers.

- **New Case Study**—A new case study featuring Quest Specialty Travel provides a practical and fun scenario that students can relate to as they learn

---

Each two-page spread focuses on a single skill.

Concise text introduces the basic principles in the lesson and integrates a real-world case study.

UNIT A
Access 2007

Editing Data

Updating existing information is another critical data management task. To change the contents of an existing record, click the field you want to change, then type the new information. You can delete unwanted data by clicking the field and using [Backspace] or [Delete] to delete text to the left or right of the insertion point. Other data-entry keystrokes are summarized in Table A-4. Mark Rock asks you to make some corrections to the records in the Tours table.

STEPS

1. **Double-click** Dance **in the TourName field of the TourID 10 record, and press the [Delete] key twice**
   You deleted both the word "Dance" and the extra space between "Dazzlers" and "Troupe." Access automatically saves new records and changes to existing data as soon as you move to another record or close the datasheet.

2. **Click after** Barilla **in the TourName field of TourID 12 record, and type** -Cavuto
   When you are editing a record, the **edit record symbol**, which looks like a small pencil, appears in the record selector box to the left of the current record, as shown in Figure A-6, to indicate you are in Edit mode.

3. **Double-click** Speech **in the TourID 15 record, and type** Debate
   You use the same editing techniques in an Access datasheet that you use in an Excel spreadsheet or Word document.

4. **Click the** TourStartDate **field in the TourID 22 record, click the** Calendar icon 📅**, then navigate to and click** August 27, 2010
   The **calendar picker**, a pop-up calendar from which you can choose dates for a date field, is a new feature for Access 2007. You can also type the date directly into the field as 8/27/2010.

QUICK TIP
The ScreenTip for the Undo button displays the action you can undo.

5. **Press** [Esc]
   Pressing [Esc] once removes the current field's editing changes, so the TourStartDate changes back to 7/16/2010. Pressing [Esc] twice removes all changes to the current record. Once you move to another record, the edits are saved, you return to Navigation mode, and you can no longer use [Esc] to remove editing changes to the current record. You can, however, click the Undo button 🔄 on the Quick Access toolbar to undo the last change you made.

6. **Click the record selector for the TourID 16 record, click the** Delete **button in the Records group on the Home tab, then click** Yes
   A message warns that you cannot undo a record deletion operation. Notice that the Undo button is dimmed, indicating that it cannot be used now.

7. **Click the** Close button ✕ **on the title bar to close both the Quest-A.accdb database and Access 2007**
   Because Access saves data as you work in a database, you are not prompted to save data when you close the database or the Access itself.

Resizing and moving datasheet columns

You can resize the width of a field in a datasheet by dragging the **column separator**, the thin line that separates the field names to the left or right. The pointer changes to ↔ as you make the field wider or narrower. Release the mouse button when you have resized the field. To adjust the column width to accommodate the widest entry in the field, double-click the column separator. To move a column, click the field name to select the entire column, then drag the field name left or right.

Hints as well as troubleshooting advice appear right where you need them—next to the step itself.

Clues to Use boxes provide concise information that either expands on the major lesson skill or describes an independent task that in some way relates to the major lesson skill.

Every lesson features large, full-color representations of what the screen should look like as students complete the numbered steps.

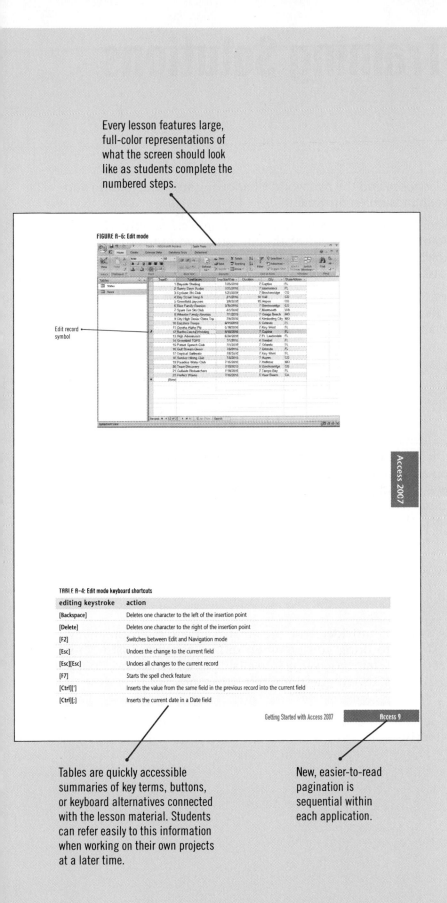

FIGURE A-6: Edit mode

Edit record symbol

TABLE A-4: Edit mode keyboard shortcuts

editing keystroke	action
[Backspace]	Deletes one character to the left of the insertion point
[Delete]	Deletes one character to the right of the insertion point
[F2]	Switches between Edit and Navigation mode
[Esc]	Undoes the change to the current field
[Esc][Esc]	Undoes all changes to the current record
[F7]	Starts the spell check feature
[Ctrl][']	Inserts the value from the same field in the previous record into the current field
[Ctrl][;]	Inserts the current date in a Date field

Getting Started with Access 2007

Access 9

Tables are quickly accessible summaries of key terms, buttons, or keyboard alternatives connected with the lesson material. Students can refer easily to this information when working on their own projects at a later time.

New, easier-to-read pagination is sequential within each application.

skills. This fictional company offers a wide variety of tours around the world.

- **Content Improvements**—All of the content in the book has been updated to cover Office 2007 and also to address instructor feedback. See the instructor resource CD for details on specific content changes for Access.

Assignments

The lessons use Quest Specialty Travel, a fictional adventure travel company, as the case study. The assignments on the light purple pages at the end of each unit increase in difficulty. Data files and case studies provide a variety of interesting and relevant business applications. Assignments include:

- **Concepts Reviews** consist of multiple choice, matching, and screen identification questions.

- **Skills Reviews** provide additional hands-on, step-by-step reinforcement.

- **Independent Challenges** are case projects requiring critical thinking and application of the unit skills. The Independent Challenges increase in difficulty, with the first one in each unit being the easiest. Independent Challenges 2 and 3 become increasingly open-ended, requiring more independent problem solving.

- **Real Life Independent Challenges** are practical exercises in which students create documents to help them with their every day lives.

- **Advanced Challenge Exercises** set within the Independent Challenges provide optional steps for more advanced students.

- **Visual Workshops** are practical, self-graded capstone projects that require independent problem solving.

v

Assessment & Training Solutions

SAM 2007

SAM 2007 helps bridge the gap between the classroom and the real world by allowing students to train and test on important computer skills in an active, hands-on environment.

SAM 2007's easy-to-use system includes powerful interactive exams, training, or projects on critical applications such as Word, Excel, Access, PowerPoint, Outlook, Windows, the Internet, and much more. SAM simulates the application environment, allowing students to demonstrate their knowledge and think through the skills by performing real-world tasks.

Designed to be used with the Illustrated series, SAM 2007 includes built-in page references so students can print helpful study guides that match the Illustrated textbooks used in class. Powerful administrative options allow instructors to schedule exams and assignments, secure tests, and run reports with almost limitless flexibility.

Student Edition Labs

Our Web-based interactive labs help students master hundreds of computer concepts, including input and output devices, file management and desktop applications, computer ethics, virus protection, and much more. Featuring up-to-the-minute content, eye-popping graphics, and rich animation, the highly interactive Student Edition Labs offer students an alternative way to learn through dynamic observation, step-by-step practice, and challenging review questions. Also available on CD at an additional cost.

Online Content   Blackboard

Blackboard is the leading distance learning solution provider and class-management platform today. Course Technology has partnered with Blackboard to bring you premium online content. Instructors: Content for use with *Microsoft Office Access 2007—Illustrated Complete* is available in a Blackboard Course Cartridge and may include topic reviews, case projects, review questions, test banks, practice tests, custom syllabi, and more.

Course Technology also has solutions for several other learning management systems. Please visit *www.course.com* today to see what's available for this title.

Instructor Resources

The Instructor Resources CD is Course Technology's way of putting the resources and information needed to teach and learn effectively into your hands. With an integrated array of teaching and learning tools that offer you and your students a broad range of technology-based instructional options, we believe this CD represents the highest quality and most cutting edge resources available to instructors today. Many of these resources are available at *www.course.com*. The resources available with this book are:

- **Instructor's Manual**—Available as an electronic file, the Instructor's Manual includes detailed lecture topics with teaching tips for each unit.

- **Sample Syllabus**—Prepare and customize your course easily using this sample course outline.

- **PowerPoint Presentations**—Each unit has a corresponding PowerPoint presentation that you can use in lecture, distribute to your students, or customize to suit your course.

- **Figure Files**—The figures in the text are provided on the Instructor Resources CD to help you illustrate key topics or concepts. You can create traditional overhead transparencies by printing the figure files. Or you can create electronic slide shows by using the figures in a presentation program such as PowerPoint.

- **Solutions to Exercises**—Solutions to Exercises contains every file students are asked to create or modify in the lessons and end-of-unit material. Also provided in this section, there is a document outlining the solutions for the end-of-unit Concepts Review, Skills Review, and Independent Challenges. An Annotated Solution File and Grading Rubric accompany each file and can be used together for quick and easy grading.

- **Data Files for Students**—To complete most of the units in this book, your students will need Data Files. You can post the Data Files on a file server for students to copy. The Data Files are available on the Instructor Resources CD, the Review Pack, and can also be downloaded from *www.course.com*. In this edition, we have included a lesson on downloading the Data Files for this book, see page xvi.

Instruct students to use the Data Files List included on the Review Pack and the Instructor Resources CD. This list gives instructions on copying and organizing files.

- **ExamView**—ExamView is a powerful testing software package that allows you to create and administer printed, computer (LAN-based), and Internet exams. ExamView includes hundreds of questions that correspond to the topics covered in this text, enabling students to generate detailed study guides that include page references for further review. The computer-based and Internet testing components allow students to take exams at their computers, and also saves you time by grading each exam automatically.

CourseCasts—Learning on the Go. Always Available...Always Relevant.

Want to keep up with the latest technology trends relevant to you? Visit our site to find a library of podcasts, CourseCasts, featuring a "CourseCast of the Week," and download them to your mp3 player at *http://coursecasts.course.com*.

Our fast-paced world is driven by technology. You know because you're an active participant—always on the go, always keeping up with technological trends, and always learning new ways to embrace technology to power your life.

Ken Baldauf, a faculty member of the Florida State University Computer Science Department, is responsible for teaching technology classes to thousands of FSU students each year. He knows what you know; he knows what you want to learn. He's also an expert in the latest technology and will sort through and aggregate the most pertinent news and information so you can spend your time enjoying technology, rather than trying to figure it out.

Visit us at *http://coursecasts.course.com* to learn on the go!

Contents

ACCESS 2007 **Unit G: Enhancing Forms** **161**

ACCESS 2007 **Unit H: Analyzing Data with Reports** **185**

ACCESS 2007 **Unit I: Importing and Exporting Data** **209**

ACCESS 2007 **Unit J: Analyzing Database Design Using Northwind** **233**

Unit K: Creating Advanced Queries   261

Unit L: Creating Advanced Reports   289

Unit M: Managing Database Objects   313

Read This Before You Begin

Frequently Asked Questions

What are Data Files?

A Data File is a partially completed Access database, or another type of file that you use to complete the steps in the units and exercises to create the final document that you submit to your instructor. Each unit opener page lists the Data Files that you need for that unit.

Where are the Data Files?

Your instructor will provide the Data Files to you or direct you to a location on a network drive from which you can download them. Alternatively, you can follow the instructions on page xvi to download the Data Files from this book's Web page.

What software was used to write and test this book?

This book was written and tested using a typical installation of Microsoft Office 2007 installed on a computer with a typical installation of Microsoft Windows Vista. The browser used for any steps that require a browser is Internet Explorer 7.

If you are using this book on Windows XP, please see the "Important Notes for Windows XP Users" on the next page. If you are using this book on Windows Vista, please see the appendix at the end of this book.

Do I need to be connected to the Internet to complete the steps and exercises in this book?

Some of the exercises in this book assume that your computer is connected to the Internet. If you are not connected to the Internet, see your instructor for information on how to complete the exercises.

What do I do if my screen is different from the figures shown in this book?

This book was written and tested on computers with monitors set at a resolution of 1024 × 768. If your screen shows more or less information than the figures in the book, your monitor is probably set at a higher or lower resolution. If you don't see something on your screen, you might have to scroll down or up to see the object identified in the figures.

The Ribbon (the blue area at the top of the screen) in Microsoft Office 2007 adapts to different resolutions. If your monitor is set at a lower resolution than 1024 × 768, you might not see all of the buttons shown in the figures. The groups of buttons will always appear, but the entire group might be condensed into a single button that you need to click to access the buttons described in the instructions. For example, the figures and steps in this book assume that the Editing group on the Home tab in Word looks like the following:

If your resolution is set to 800 × 600, the Ribbon in Word will look like the following figure, and you will need to click the Editing button to access the buttons that are visible in the Editing group.

1024 × 768 Editing Group

Editing Group on the Home Tab of the Ribbon at 1024 × 768

800 × 600 Editing Group

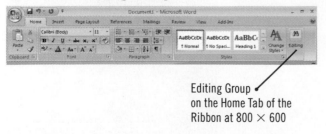

Editing Group on the Home Tab of the Ribbon at 800 × 600

800 × 600 Editing Group Clicked

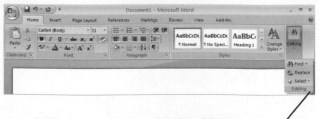

Editing Group on the Home Tab of the Ribbon at 800 × 600 is selected to show available buttons

Important Notes for Windows XP Users

The screen shots in this book show Microsoft Office 2007 running on Windows Vista. However, if you are using Microsoft Windows XP, you can still use this book because Office 2007 runs virtually the same on both platforms. There are a few differences that you will encounter if you are using Windows XP. Read this section to understand the differences.

Dialog boxes

If you are a Windows XP user, dialog boxes shown in this book will look slightly different than what you see on your screen. Dialog boxes for Windows XP have a blue title bar, instead of a gray title bar. However, beyond this difference in appearance, the options in the dialog boxes across platforms are the same.

Alternate Steps for Windows XP Users

Nearly all of the steps in this book work exactly the same for Windows XP users. However, there are a few tasks that will require you to complete slightly different steps. This section provides alternate steps for a few specific skills.

Starting a program

1. Click the **Start button** on the taskbar
2. Point to **All Programs**, point to **Microsoft Office**, then click the application you want to use

FIGURE 1: Starting a program

Saving a file for the first time

1. Click the **Office button**, then click **Save As**
2. Type a name for your file in the File name text box
3. Click the **Save in list arrow**, then navigate to the drive and folder where you store your Data Files
4. Click **Save**

FIGURE 2: Save As dialog box

Opening a file

1. Click the **Office button**, then click **Open**
2. Click the **Look in list arrow**, then navigate to the drive and folder where you store your Data Files
3. Click the file you want to open
4. Click **Open**

FIGURE 3: Open dialog box

Downloading Data Files for This Book

In order to complete many of the lesson steps and exercises in this book, you are asked to open and save Data Files. A **Data File** is a partially completed Word document, Excel workbook, Access database, PowerPoint presentation, or another type of file that you use as a starting point to complete the steps in the units and exercises. The benefit of using a Data File is that it saves you the time and effort needed to create a file; you can simply open a Data File, save it with a new name (so the original file remains intact), then make changes to it to complete lesson steps or an exercise. Your instructor will provide the Data Files to you or direct you to a location on a network drive from which you can download them. Alternatively, you can follow the steps below to download the Data Files from this book's Web page.

1. Start Internet Explorer, type www.cengage.com/coursetechnology/ in the address bar, then press [Enter]

2. Click in the Enter ISBN Search text box, type 9781423905196, then click Search

3. When the page opens for this textbook, click the About this Product link for the Student, point to Student Downloads to expand the menu, and then click the Data Files for Students link

4. If the File Download – Security Warning dialog box opens, click Save. (If no dialog box appears, skip this step and go to Step 6)

5. If the Save As dialog box opens, click the Save in list arrow at the top of the dialog box, select a folder on your USB drive or hard disk to download the file to, then click Save

6. Close Internet Explorer and then open Computer and display the contents of the drive and folder to which you downloaded the file

7. Double-click the file 9781423905196.exe in the drive or folder, then, if the Open File – Security Warning dialog box opens, click Run

8. In the WinZip Self-Extractor window, navigate to the drive and folder where you want to unzip the files to, then click Unzip

9. When the WinZip Self-Extractor displays a dialog box listing the number of files that have unzipped successfully, click OK, click Close in the WinZip Self-Extractor dialog box, then close Computer

    The Data Files are now unzipped in the folder you specified in Step 8 and ready for you to open and use.

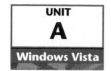

Getting Started with Windows Vista

Microsoft Windows Vista, or **Windows**, is an **operating system**—software that manages the complete operation of your computer. When you start a computer, Windows sets it up for use and then displays the **desktop**—a graphical user interface (GUI) that you use to interact with Windows and the other software on your computer. The Windows desktop displays **icons**, or small images, that represent items such as the Recycle Bin and Computer. When you open a program or document, Windows displays the program or document in a rectangular-shaped work area known as a **window**. Windows helps you organize **files** (collections of stored electronic data, such as text, pictures, video, music, and programs) in **folders** (containers for files) so that you can easily find them later. Windows also keeps all the computer hardware and software working together properly. As a new Oceania tour guide for Quest Specialty Travel (QST), you need to develop basic Windows skills to keep track of all the tour files on your company laptop computer.

OBJECTIVES

Start Windows Vista

Use a pointing device

Start a program

Move and resize windows

Use menus, toolbars, and
   keyboard shortcuts

Use dialog boxes

Use scroll bars

Use Windows Help and Support

End a Windows Vista session

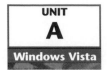
Starting Windows Vista

When you start your computer, Windows steps through a process called **booting** to get the computer up and running. During this time, you might need to select your user account and enter your password. This information identifies you to Windows as an authorized user of the computer and helps keep your computer secure. After booting is complete, Windows displays the Windows desktop. The desktop, shown in Figure A-1, provides a way for you to interact with Windows Vista and to access its tools. The desktop appears with preset, or **default**, settings; however, you can change these settings to suit your needs. The image that fills the desktop background is called **wallpaper**. The desktop contains an icon for the Recycle Bin, which stores deleted files and folders. The desktop also displays **gadgets** (mini-programs for performing everyday tasks, such as a Clock) on the **Sidebar**. The **taskbar**, the horizontal bar at the bottom of the screen, displays information about open programs, folders, and files. You click the **Start button** on the left side of the taskbar to start programs, find and open files, access Windows Help and Support, and more. The **Quick Launch toolbar**, located on the taskbar, includes buttons for showing the desktop when it is not currently visible, switching between windows (the work areas for open programs), and starting the Internet Explorer Web browser. Table A-1 identifies the default icons and elements found on a desktop. Your supervisor, Nancy McDonald, Oceania's tour developer, asks you to become familiar with Windows Vista and its features before your upcoming tour.

STEPS

1. **If your computer and monitor are turned off, press the** Power button **on the front of the system unit, then press the** Power button **on the monitor**

   After your computer starts, you see either a **Welcome screen** with icons for each user account on the computer or the Windows desktop. If you see the Welcome screen, continue with Step 2. If you see the Windows desktop, compare it to the one shown in Figure A-1, then continue with Step 4.

2. **If necessary, click the icon for your user account**

   If you use a password with your user account, Windows prompts you for the password. If not, continue with Step 4.

   TROUBLE
   If you don't know your password, ask your instructor or technical support person. If you don't use a password, leave the Password box empty and click the Next button

3. **If prompted for a password, type your password in the Password box, then click the** Next button

   After Windows verifies your password, you see the Windows desktop. See Figure A-1. Your Windows desktop may look slightly different.

4. **If the Welcome Center opens, click the** Close button **⊠ in the upper-right corner of the Welcome Center window**

TABLE A-1: Common desktop components

desktop element	icon	allows you to
Recycle Bin	🗑	Store folders and files you delete from your hard drive(s) and restore them
Windows Sidebar (or Sidebar)		View the current time on a clock, view a slide show, and more
Taskbar		Switch between open programs, folders, and files; and resize windows
Notification area		Check the time, adjust the volume of your speakers, connect to the Internet, check problems identified by Windows Vista, and more
Quick Launch toolbar		Show the desktop, switch between windows, and open the Internet Explorer Web browser
Start button	🔵	Start programs, search for files, open documents, view pictures, listen to music, play games, get help, and more

FIGURE A-1: Windows Vista desktop

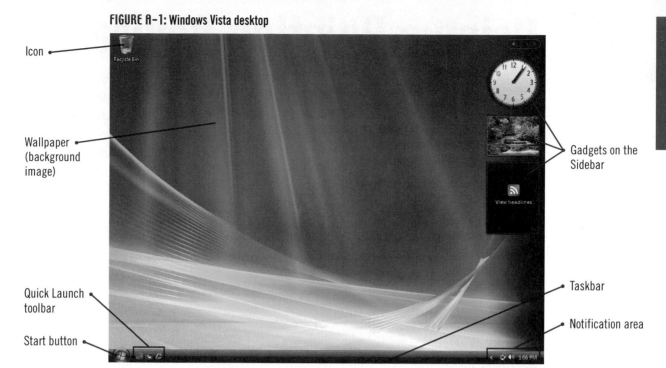

Icon

Wallpaper (background image)

Quick Launch toolbar

Start button

Gadgets on the Sidebar

Taskbar

Notification area

Using Windows Vista with Aero

Some editions of Windows Vista support **Windows Aero**, a new graphical user-interface feature that enhances the transparency (referred to as **translucency**) of the Start menu, taskbar, windows, and dialog boxes, as shown in Figure A-2. These transparency features also enable you to locate content by seeing through one window to the next window. **Windows Flip** allows you to display a set of thumbnails or miniature images of all open windows. **Windows Flip 3D** allows you to

display stacked windows at a three-dimensional angle to see even more of the content of all open windows. Likewise, **live taskbar thumbnails** display the content within open, but not visible, windows, including live content such as video. These features provide three different ways to quickly view, locate, and select windows with the content you need. To view these effects, your version of Windows Vista and your computer's hardware must support the use of Windows Aero.

FIGURE A-2: Windows Aero features

Translucent Start menu

Translucent window frame and borders

Live thumbnail

Live taskbar thumbnail for a minimized window

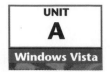

Using a Pointing Device

The most common way to interact with your computer and the software you are using is with a **pointing device**, such as a mouse, trackball, touch pad, or pointing stick, as shown in Figure A-3. If touch input is available on your computer, you can also use an onscreen **touch pointer** to perform pointing operations with a finger. As you move your pointing device, a small arrow or other symbol on the screen, called a **pointer**, moves in the same direction. Table A-2 illustrates common pointer shapes and their functions. You press the left and right buttons on the pointing device to select and move objects (such as icons and desktop windows); open programs, windows, folders, and files; and select options for performing specific tasks, such as saving your work. Table A-3 lists the five basic ways in which you can use a pointing device. Pointing devices can work with your computer through a cable or through a wireless connection that transmits data using radio waves. ▰▰▰ You'll practice using your pointing device so you can work more efficiently.

STEPS

1. **Locate the pointer on the desktop, then move your pointing device**

   The pointer moves across the Windows desktop in the same direction as you move your pointing device.

2. **Move the pointer so the tip is directly over the Recycle Bin icon 🗑**

   Positioning the pointer over an item is called **pointing**. The Recycle Bin icon is highlighted and a **ToolTip**, or label, identifies its purpose.

3. **With the pointer over 🗑, press and release the left button on your pointing device**

   Pressing and releasing the left button, called **clicking** or **single-clicking**, selects an icon on the desktop or in a window and selects options and objects within a program. In this case, the Recycle Bin icon is selected.

4. **With 🗑 still selected, press and hold down the left button on your pointing device, move your pointing device to another location on the desktop, then release the left button**

   A copy of the Recycle Bin icon moves with the pointer. When you release the left button on your pointing device, the Recycle Bin is placed on the desktop in a different location. You use this technique, called **dragging**, to move icons and windows.

5. **Drag 🗑 back to its original desktop location**

6. **Position the pointer over 🗑, then press and release the right button on your pointing device**

   This action, called **right-clicking**, opens a shortcut menu, as shown in Figure A-4. A **shortcut menu** lists common commands for an object. A **command** is an instruction to perform a task, such as renaming an object. If a command is dimmed, such as "Empty Recycle Bin," it is not currently available for you to use.

7. **Click the desktop background**

   The shortcut menu closes and Windows selects the desktop background.

8. **Point to 🗑, then quickly press the left button on your pointing device twice and release it**

   Quickly clicking the left button twice is called **double-clicking**, which opens a window or a program. In this case, the Recycle Bin window opens to display any folders and files deleted from the hard disk.

9. **Click the Close button ✕ in the upper-right corner of the Recycle Bin window**

   The Recycle Bin window closes. Every window has a Close button; clicking it is the fastest way to close a window.

FIGURE A-3: Common pointing devices

Mouse

Trackball

Touch pointer

Touchpad

Pointing stick

FIGURE A-4: Shortcut menu

Selected object

Dimmed command is unavailable

Command

Shortcut menu

TABLE A-2: Common pointer shapes

shape	name	description
⬉	Normal Select	Points to an object and chooses a command
○	Busy	Indicates that Windows or another program is busy and you must wait before continuing
⬉○	Working in Background	Indicates that Windows or another program is busy and the computer's response time is slower, but you can still perform other operations
I	Text Select (also called I-Beam)	Identifies where you can type, select, insert, or edit text
⬆	Link Select	Identifies a link you can click to jump to another location, such as a Help topic or a Web site

TABLE A-3: Basic pointing device techniques

technique	what to do
Pointing	Move the pointing device to position the tip of the pointer over an object, option, or item
Clicking	Quickly press and release the left button
Double-clicking	Quickly press and release the left button twice
Dragging	Point to an object, press and hold the left button, move the object to a new location, then release the left button
Right-clicking	Point to an object, then quickly press and release the right button

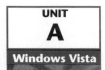
Starting a Program

From the Start menu, you can open programs or software products on your computer. In addition to other software that you purchase and install on the computer, Windows Vista includes a variety of programs, such as Windows Calendar, Windows Mail, Windows Movie Maker, and Windows Photo Gallery. Windows also comes with **accessories**, which are simple programs to perform specific tasks, such as the Windows Calculator accessory for performing quick calculations. Table A-4 describes the organization of the Start menu. ██████ Because you need to develop QST tour proposals and brochures with photographs of exotic Pacific islands, you want to try the Windows Photo Gallery.

STEPS

> **QUICK TIP**
> You can also press the Windows logo key to open or close the Start menu.

1. **Click the Start button 🔵 on the taskbar**

   The Start menu opens, as shown in Figure A-5. From the left pane, you can start programs installed on your computer. From the right pane, you can open specific folders, open Windows tools, change Windows settings, get Help and Support, and shut down Windows. Some of the options on your Start menu will differ.

2. **Point to All Programs**

   The All Programs menu opens in the left pane, with an alphabetical listing of the programs installed on your computer followed by groups of related programs, such as Accessories. See Figure A-6. Your list of programs will differ.

> **TROUBLE**
> If you see an Info Pane on the right side of the window, close it by clicking the Hide Info Pane button.

3. **Click Windows Photo Gallery on the All Programs menu**

   The Windows Photo Gallery window opens, displaying thumbnails of images in the Sample Pictures folder on your computer. See Figure A-7. A **thumbnail** is a smaller image of the actual contents of a file that contains a picture. Windows also displays a Windows Photo Gallery button on the taskbar for the now open Windows Photo Gallery.

4. **Leave the Photo Gallery window open for the next lesson**

TABLE A-4: Start menu components

component	description
Pinned Items List	Contains the two programs commonly used for a Web browser and e-mail: Internet Explorer and a version of Microsoft Outlook; you can change these two programs and you can add other programs to this list
Recently-opened Programs List	Lists programs you have recently opened so you can quickly return to them.
All Programs	Displays a list of programs installed on your computer
Search Box	Quickly locates programs, folders, and files, and shows the search results in the left pane of the Start menu
User Folders	Provides quick access to your Documents, Pictures, Music, and Games folders, plus the folder for your user account (your username at the top of the right pane)
Windows Tools	Search quickly locates programs, folders, and files Recent Items displays the names of up to 15 files you recently opened Computer opens a Windows Explorer window and shows the drives and other hardware on your computer Network provides access to computers and other hardware on your network Connect To shows your Internet and network connections
Settings & Help	Control Panel provides tools for viewing and changing Windows settings and installing hardware and software Default Programs lets you specify the programs and program settings you prefer to use Help and Support opens the Windows Help and Support Center to provide you with assistance and Help information
Power & Lock Buttons	Power button puts your computer to sleep (your computer appears off and uses very little power) Lock button locks your computer (a security measure for when you are not using the computer), and displays shut-down options

FIGURE A-5: Start menu

Pinned items list

Recently-opened programs

Power, Lock, and Lock menu buttons

User account icon

Your important folders

Windows tools, settings, and Help

FIGURE A-6: All Programs menu

Installed programs (your list will differ)

FIGURE A-7: Windows Photo Gallery window

Taskbar button for Windows Photo Gallery window

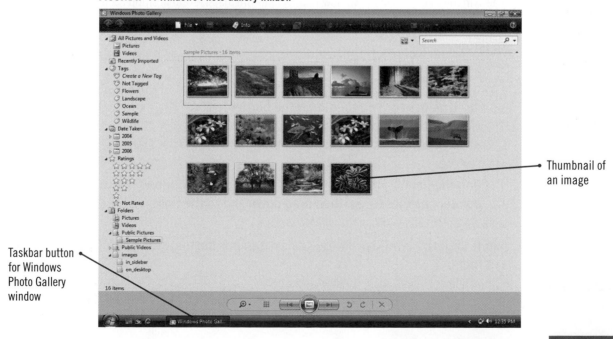

Thumbnail of an image

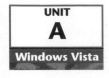
Moving and Resizing Windows

Each program you start opens in its own window. As you work, you will invariably need to move and resize windows so that you can see more of one window or view two or more windows at the same time. To resize a window, you use the **resizing buttons**—Maximize 🔲, Restore Down 🗗, and Minimize 🗕 —in the upper-right corner of the window. To adjust a window's height or width (or both), you drag a window border or window corner. To move a window, you drag its **title bar**—the area across the top of the window that displays the window name or program name. If you open more than one program at once, you are **multitasking**—performing several tasks at the same time—and each program appears in a different window. The **active window** is the window you are currently using. An **inactive window** is another open window that you are not currently using. As you examine photos for a new tour brochure, you need to move and resize the Windows Photo Gallery window.

STEPS

1. **If the Windows Photo Gallery window does not fill the desktop, click the Maximize button 🔲 in the upper-right corner of the Windows Photo Gallery window**

   The Windows Photo Gallery window is maximized. A **maximized window** fills your desktop and you cannot see its borders. After you maximize a window, the Maximize button changes to a Restore Down button.

2. **Click the Restore Down button 🗗 in the upper-right corner of the Windows Photo Gallery window**

   The Windows Photo Gallery window returns to its previous size and position on the desktop. The window borders are visible, and the Restore Down button changes to a Maximize button.

3. **Click the Minimize button 🗕 in the upper-right corner of the Windows Photo Gallery window**

   The Windows Photo Gallery window is still open, just not visible. See Figure A-8. A **minimized window** shrinks to a button on the taskbar. You can use this feature to hide a window that you are not currently using, but may use later.

4. **Click the Windows Photo Gallery taskbar button**

   The Windows Photo Gallery window returns to its original size and position on the desktop.

5. **Drag the title bar on the Windows Photo Gallery window to the upper-left corner of the desktop**

   The Windows Photo Gallery window is repositioned on the desktop.

6. **Position the pointer on the right border of the Windows Photo Gallery window until the pointer changes to ⇔, then drag the border left**

   The width of the Windows Photo Gallery window narrows. See Figure A-9. To widen the window, you drag the right window border to the right. To decrease or increase a window's height, you drag the bottom border up or down.

7. **Position the pointer on the lower-right corner of the Windows Photo Gallery window until the pointer changes to ⤡, then drag down and to the right**

   Both the height and width of the window change.

8. **Right-click the Windows Photo Gallery taskbar button, then click Close on the shortcut menu**

   The Windows Photo Gallery window closes.

FIGURE A-8: Minimized window

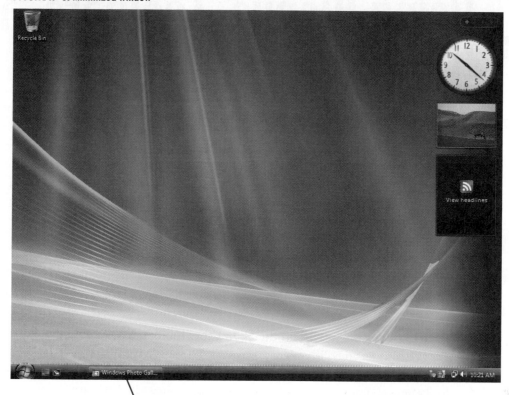

Windows Photo Gallery
is open, but not visible

FIGURE A-9: Restored down window being resized

Title bar

Close button

Maximize
button

Minimize
button

Side border
adjusts the
window's
width

Corner
adjusts the
window's
height and
width

Using Menus, Toolbars, and Keyboard Shortcuts

A **menu** displays a list of commands you use to accomplish a task. Menus organize commands into groups of related tasks. In some program windows, you open menus from a **menu bar** located below the window's title bar. At other times, you open menus from a **toolbar**, a set of buttons you can click to open menus or select common commands that may also be available from a menu bar. Some menu commands and toolbar buttons have a **keyboard shortcut**, which is a key or a combination of keys that you press to perform a command. 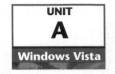 As you prepare for your first tour, Nancy recommends that you examine the Slide Show gadget and the Windows Photo Gallery.

STEPS

TROUBLE

If you don't see the Sidebar, click the Start button, point to All Programs, click Accessories, then click Windows Sidebar. If you still don't see the Sidebar, click the Windows Sidebar icon in the taskbar Notification area.

1. **Point to the Slide Show gadget on the Sidebar, resting the pointer on the displayed image**

   The Slide Show toolbar appears at the bottom of the slide show image, and the Slide Show gadget toolbar appears to the right of the Slide Show gadget. See Figure A-10. The left border of the Sidebar is now visible.

2. **Click the View button ⊡ on the Slide Show toolbar**

   The Windows Photo Gallery window opens and displays an enlarged view of the image displayed in the Slide Show gadget. The title bar identifies the filename of the image and the name of the open program. A toolbar appears below the title bar, with options for working with the image.

3. **Click the File button ⊡ File ▾ on the toolbar**

   The File menu lists commands related to working with the files. See Figure A-11. A keyboard shortcut appears to the right of some commands.

4. **Click Exit**

   The Windows Photo Gallery window closes.

5. **Point to the Slide Show gadget on the Sidebar, then click ⊡ on the Slide Show toolbar**

   The Photo Gallery Viewer window opens again.

6. **Click the Play Slide Show button ⊙ on the Slide Show toolbar at the bottom of the window**

   Windows Photo Gallery displays a full-screen slide show of each image in your Sample Pictures folder, one at a time.

QUICK TIP

"Esc," an abbreviation for "Escape," is a standard keyboard shortcut for canceling an operation or backing up a step.

7. **Press [Esc]**

   The slide show stops and you return to the Windows Photo Gallery window.

8. **Press and hold [Alt], press and release [F4], then release [Alt]**

   The Windows Photo Gallery window closes. The keyboard shortcut [Alt][F4] closes any active window.

FIGURE A-10: Windows Sidebar

Add Gadget button

Slide Show gadget

View button

FIGURE A-11: File menu

File button

Commands on File menu

Play Slide Show button

Toolbar

Keyboard shortcut

Dimmed command is unavilable

Exit command

Using keyboard shortcuts

Keyboard shortcuts allow you to work more quickly and efficiently because you can keep your hands on the keyboard rather than moving between the keyboard and your pointing device. Many programs use the same keyboard shortcuts for common operations, such as [Ctrl][O] for opening a file and [Ctrl][S] for saving a file. Taking the time to learn the keyboard shortcuts for the actions you perform frequently will improve your productivity. Keyboard shortcuts are shown on menus with a plus sign separating the keys you need to press at the same time, such as Ctrl+S for saving a file. Remember, you do not press the plus sign when you use a keyboard shortcut

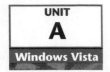

Using Dialog Boxes

When you select a command from a menu or toolbar, the program may perform the operation immediately. Or, it may open a **dialog box**, a type of window in which you specify how you want to complete the operation. Although dialog boxes are similar to a window, they do not contain Maximize, Minimize, and Restore Down buttons, and you usually cannot resize a dialog box. Figure A-12 shows a Print dialog box with two **tabs**—General and Options—that separate groups of settings into related categories. Dialog boxes provide different ways to select options. Table A-5 lists common types of options found in dialog boxes. ▬▬▬ You want to review the Sidebar default settings to determine whether they meet your needs while you work.

STEPS

1. **Right-click the background of the Sidebar under the last gadget, then click Properties**

   The Windows Sidebar Properties dialog box opens, as shown in Figure A-13. **Properties** are characteristics or settings of a component of the graphical user interface. The first setting in the dialog box is a check box for starting the Sidebar whenever Windows starts. A **check box** turns an option on (checked) or off (unchecked). You click the check box to change the option's status. As you can see from the check mark in the Start Sidebar when Windows starts check box, it is already turned on.

2. **Click the Sidebar is always on top of other windows check box**

   A check mark is added to the check box, which sets the Sidebar to remain visible when you open a window.

3. **In the Arrangement section, click the Left option button**

   You click one **option button** to select from several options. In this case, you clicked the option button to display the Sidebar on the left side of the desktop. You can select only one option button for a setting. The "Display Sidebar on monitor" button is a **drop-down list button** that you click to open a list that shows one or more options to choose. The **link** at the bottom of the Maintenance section opens a Help topic about how to customize the Sidebar. At the bottom of the dialog box are **command buttons**, which you click to complete or cancel any changes you make in the dialog box. Clicking OK closes the dialog box and applies the settings you selected. Clicking Apply applies the settings you selected, but keeps the dialog box open for additional changes. Clicking Cancel leaves the settings unchanged and closes the dialog box.

   QUICK TIP

   In a dialog box, pressing [Enter] is the same as clicking OK; pressing [Esc] is the same as clicking Cancel.

4. **Click Cancel**

   The dialog box closes without changing any of the settings for the Sidebar.

FIGURE A-12: Print dialog box

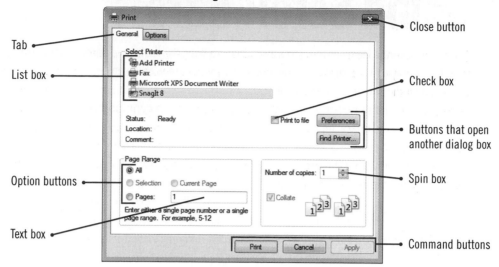

Tab

List box

Option buttons

Text box

Close button

Check box

Buttons that open another dialog box

Spin box

Command buttons

FIGURE A-13: Windows Sidebar Properties dialog box

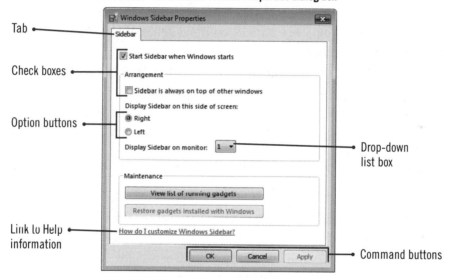

Tab

Check boxes

Option buttons

Link to Help information

Drop-down list box

Command buttons

TABLE A-5: Typical elements in a dialog box

element	description
Check box	A box that turns an option on when checked or off when unchecked
Collapse button	A button that shrinks a portion of a dialog box to hide some settings
Command button	A button that completes or cancels an operation
Drop-down list button	A button that displays a list of options from which you can choose
Expand button	A button that extends a dialog box to display additional settings
Link	A shortcut for opening a Help topic or a Web site
List box	A box that displays a list of options from which you can choose (you may need to adjust your view to see additional options in the list)
Option button	A small circle you click to select only one of two or more related options
Slider	A shape you drag along a bar to select a setting that falls within a range, such as between Slow and Fast
Spin box	A text box with up and down arrows; you can type a setting in the text box or click the arrows to increase or decrease a setting
Text box	A box in which you type text (such as a password)

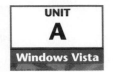

Using Scroll Bars

When you cannot see all of the items available in a window, list box, or drop-down list box, you must **scroll**, or adjust your view. Scrolling is similar to taking a picture with a camera. You move the camera to select a view of a landscape in front of you. If you move the camera to the right or left or up or down, you see a different part of that same landscape. When a window on your computer contains more items than it can display at once, scroll bars appear so you can adjust your view in the window. **Scroll bars** are vertical and horizontal bars that appear along the right and bottom sides of a window when there is more content than can be displayed within the window. At each end of a scroll bar are **scroll arrow buttons** for shifting your view in small increments in either direction. Within each scroll bar is a **scroll box** you can drag to display a different part of a window. You can also click in a scroll bar on either side of the scroll box to shift your view in larger increments. Instead of using a pointing device to scroll, you can also use keyboard shortcuts to scroll, which can be faster. Table A-6 summarizes different ways to scroll. ▓▓▓▓ For each QST tour, you work with a large variety of files. To locate your files, and to view different pages within each file, you use scroll bars. You will practice scrolling using a Windows Vista accessory called Paint—a graphics program.

STEPS

1. **Point to the Slide Show gadget on the Sidebar, then click the View button 🔍 on the Slide Show toolbar**

   An image from your Sample Pictures folder appears in the Windows Photo Gallery window.

2. **Click the Open button on the toolbar, then click Paint**

   The image opens in a Paint window for editing. Paint is one of the Windows Vista accessories.

> **TROUBLE**
> If you don't see scroll bars, drag the lower-right corner of the Paint window up and to the left until both scroll bars appear.

3. **If the Paint window fills the desktop, then click its Restore Down button 🗗**

   Because of the large size of the image, you can see only a portion of it within the window. However, Paint displays scroll bars on the right and bottom of the window so you can adjust your view. See Figure A-14. Your image and view may differ.

4. **Click the down scroll arrow in the vertical scroll bar**

   The window scrolls down to show another part of the image, and part of the image has now scrolled out of view.

5. **Drag the vertical scroll box slowly down the window to the bottom of the vertical scroll bar**

   The window view changes in larger increments, and the bottom part of the image is visible at the bottom of the window.

6. **Click the vertical scroll bar between the scroll box and the up scroll arrow**

   The view moves up approximately the height of one window.

7. **Click the right scroll arrow in the horizontal scroll bar three times**

   The window keeps scrolling right to show other views onto the image.

> **TROUBLE**
> If a dialog box opens asking if you want to save changes to the image, click Don't Save.

8. **Click the Close button ✖ on the Paint title bar**

   The Paint window closes.

9. **Click ✖ on the Windows Photo Gallery title bar**

   The Windows Photo Gallery window closes.

FIGURE A-14: Scroll bars

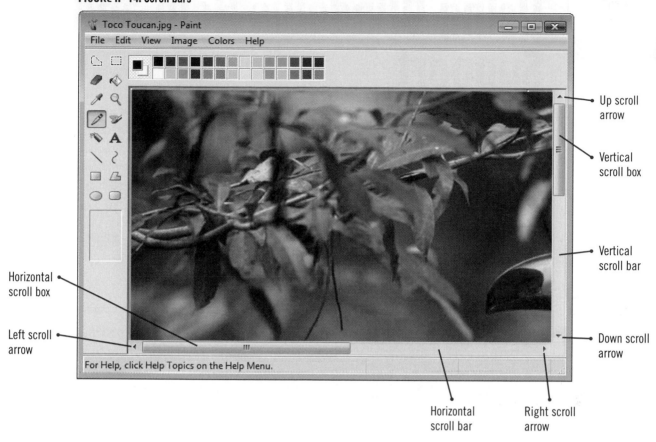

Up scroll arrow

Vertical scroll box

Vertical scroll bar

Down scroll arrow

Horizontal scroll box

Left scroll arrow

Horizontal scroll bar

Right scroll arrow

TABLE A-6: Using scroll bars

to	do this with the mouse
Move down a small increment or one line	Click the down scroll arrow at the bottom of the vertical scroll bar
Move up a small increment or one line	Click the up scroll arrow at the top of the vertical scroll bar
Move down about one window's height	Click between the scroll box and the down scroll arrow in the vertical scroll bar
Move up about one window's height	Click between the scroll box and the up scroll arrow in the vertical scroll bar
Move up a large distance	Drag the scroll box up the vertical scroll bar
Move down a large distance	Drag the scroll box down the vertical scroll bar
Move left or right a small distance	Click the left or the right scroll arrow in the horizontal scroll bar
Move to the left or right one window's width	Click between the scroll box and the left or right scroll arrow in the horizontal scroll bar
Move left or right a large distance	Drag the scroll box in the horizontal scroll bar to the left or right

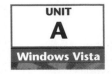
Using Windows Help and Support

When you need assistance or more information about how to use Windows, you can use Help and Support. After you open Help and Support, you can browse Help by first selecting a general category, such as "Windows Basics," then a narrower category, such as "Desktop fundamentals," and finally a specific Help topic, such as "The desktop (overview)." Or, you can select a topic from a table of contents. You can also search Help and Support using one or more descriptive words called **keywords**, such as "Windows Sidebar gadgets," to obtain a list of search results for all the Help topics that include the word or phrase. In certain places within Help and Support, you can use Windows Media Player to watch video clips called Windows Vista demos that provide an overview of Windows features and how to use them. 　　 Because you often use the Sidebar and Windows Photo Gallery as a tour guide, you decide to review the information in Windows Help and Support on these two Windows features.

STEPS

> **TROUBLE**
>
> If the Help and Support dialog box opens, asking you if you want to get the latest online content, click No. If a warning appears that you have lost your connection to the Windows Help and Support Web site, you are not connected to the Internet. Continue with the remaining steps.

1. **Click the Start button ⊕ on the taskbar, click Help and Support, then click the Maximize button ⬜ if the window doesn't fill the desktop**

   The Windows Help and Support window opens and fills the desktop. Figure A-15 identifies the various types of Help options. Table A-7 explains the purpose of the buttons on the Help toolbar in the upper-right corner of the window.

2. **Under Find an answer, click the Windows Basics icon**

   Windows Help and Support displays categories of Help topics about basic Windows features.

3. **Under Desktop fundamentals, click Windows Sidebar and gadgets (overview)**

   The Windows Sidebar and gadgets (overview) Help topic explains what the Sidebar is, how it works, why you would use it, and how to work with gadgets—including adding, removing, and organizing gadgets.

4. **Click in the Search Help text box, type edit my digital photos, then click the Search Help button 🔍**

   A list of search results appears for the keywords you specified. As shown in Figure A-16, the 30 best results for editing digital photos are listed.

> **QUICK TIP**
>
> If you click a topic under "In this article," the window automatically scrolls to that topic.

5. **Click Working with digital pictures in the list of Help topics**

   This Help topic explains how to get pictures from a camera into your computer—just what you need as a tour guide.

6. **In the second paragraph, click flash memory card (shown in green)**

   The definition of a flash memory card and how you can use this device appears.

7. **Click the Close button ❌ in the upper-right corner of the Windows Help and Support window**

   The Windows Help and Support window closes.

Using Windows Online Help

Windows Vista Help and Support provides answers on how to use basic and advanced Windows Vista features. You can get additional help from the Microsoft Windows Help and How-to Web site. On this Web site, you can find more information about basic and advanced Windows Vista features, view "how-to" videos, get help from other people in Windows Vista online discussion groups, read up-to-date articles on changes in Windows Vista, and get online support from Microsoft technical support staff. To open the Windows Online Help and Support Home page, click Windows Online Help in the Find an answer section of the Windows Help and Support window.

FIGURE A-15: Windows Help and Support window

Back button
Forward button
Help category
Home button

Options button
Ask button
Browse Help button
Print button
Online Help

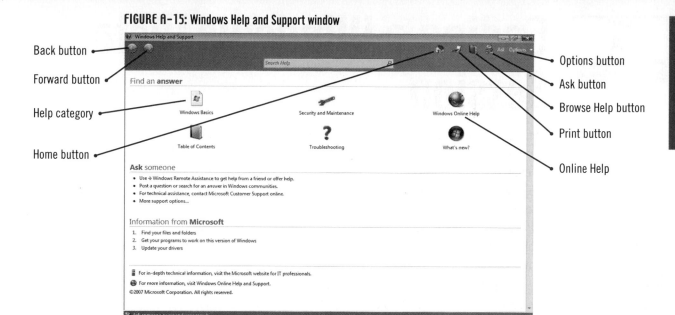

FIGURE A-16: Search results

Search keywords

Search Help button

Search Help text box

Search results

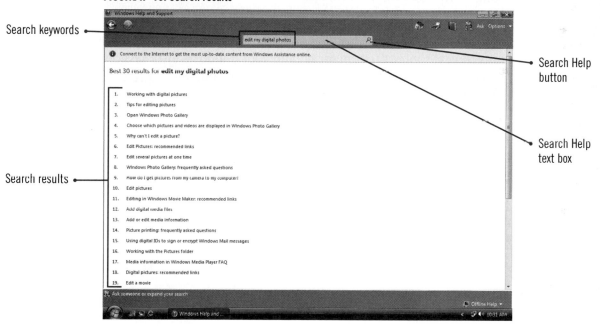

TABLE A-7: Windows Help and Support toolbar buttons

button icon	button name	purpose
←	Back	Takes you back to previous Help topic(s)
→	Forward	Returns you to Help topic(s) you just left (available only after you click the Back button)
	Home	Opens the Help and Support starting page
	Print	Prints a Help topic
	Browse Help	Displays a list of Help topics to browse
Ask	Ask	Provides additional resources and tools for finding Help information
Options ▼	Options	Lists options for printing, browsing Help, adjusting the Help text size, searching a Help topic page, and changing Help settings

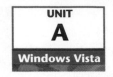
Ending a Windows Vista Session

When you finish working on your computer, you should save and close any open files, close any open programs, close any open windows, and shut down Windows. As shown in Table A-8, there are various options for ending your Windows sessions. Whichever option you choose, it's important to shut down your computer in an orderly manner. If you turn off the computer while Windows Vista is running, you could lose data or damage Windows Vista and your computer. If you are working in a computer lab, follow your instructor's directions and your lab's policies and guidelines for ending your Windows session. You have examined the basic ways in which you can use Windows Vista, so you are ready to end your Windows Vista session.

STEPS

1. **Click the Start button ⊕ on the taskbar**

   The Start menu has three buttons for ending a Windows session—the Power button, the Lock button, and the Lock menu button.

   > **QUICK TIP**
   > Some keyboards have Log Off and Sleep keys that you can press to perform these operations.

2. **Point to the Lock menu button ▶**

   The Lock menu lists all the shut-down options. See Figure A-17.

3. **If you are working in a computer lab, follow the instructions provided by your instructor or technical support person for ending your Windows Vista session; if you are working on your own computer, click Shut Down or the option you prefer for ending your Windows Vista session**

   After you shut down your computer, you may also need to turn off your monitor and other hardware devices, such as a printer, to conserve energy.

FIGURE A-17: Shut down Windows Vista options

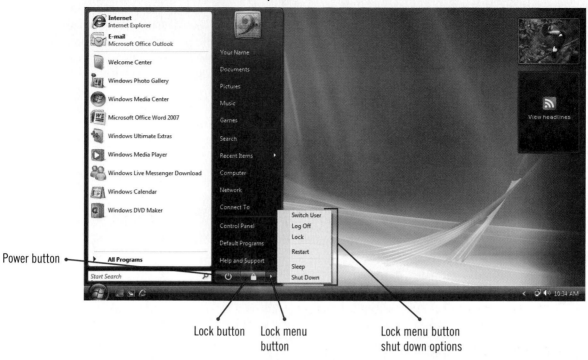

Power button

Lock button   Lock menu button   Lock menu button shut down options

TABLE A-8: Options for ending a Windows Vista session

option	description	click
Shut Down	Completely shuts down your computer.	Start button, Lock menu button, Shut Down
Log Off	Closes all windows, programs, and documents, then displays the Welcome screen.	Start button, Lock menu button, Log Off
Restart	Shuts down your computer, then restarts it.	Start button, Lock menu button, Restart
Switch User	Locks your user account and displays the Welcome screen so another user can log on.	Start button, Lock menu button, Switch User
Lock	Locks your user account, then displays the Welcome screen.	Start button, Lock button, OR Start button, Lock menu button, Lock
Sleep	Saves your work, turns off the monitor, then reduces power consumption to all hardware components in your computer so it appears off.	Start button, Power button, OR Start button, Lock menu button, Sleep
Hibernate	Saves your work, then turns off your computer.	Start button, Lock menu button, Hibernate

Practice

SAM

If you have a SAM user profile, you may have access to hands-on instruction, practice, and assessment of the skills covered in this unit. Log in to your SAM account (http://sam2007.course.com/) to launch any assigned training activities or exams that relate to the skills covered in this unit.

▼ CONCEPTS REVIEW

Identify each of the items labeled in Figure A-18.

FIGURE A-18

Match each statement with the term it describes.

12. A desktop object that displays buttons for open programs and windows
13. A desktop object that represents a program or Windows tool
14. A type of window that opens after you select a menu command so you can specify settings for completing the operation
15. A Windows component for adjusting your view within a window
16. The workspace within which you work with a program

a. dialog box
b. taskbar
c. scroll bar
d. window
e. icon

Select the best answer from the list of choices.

17. Operating system software is software that:
    a. Interferes with your use of a computer.
    b. Manages the operation of a computer.
    c. Performs a single task, such as connecting to the Internet.
    d. Creates documents, such as a resume.

18. When you right-click a pointing device such as a mouse, Windows:
    a. Opens a Windows tool or program.
    b. Moves an object, such as a desktop icon.
    c. Opens a shortcut menu.
    d. Deletes the object.

19. What portion of a window displays the name of the program you opened?

   a. Title bar   **c.** Toolbar

   b. Menu bar   **d.** Scroll bar

20. You use the Maximize button to:

   a. Restore a window to its previous size and location.   **c.** Temporarily hide a window.

   b. Expand a window to fill the entire desktop.   **d.** Scroll through a window.

21. When you put a computer to sleep, Windows:

   a. Completely shuts down the computer.   **c.** Restarts your computer.

   b. Provides an option for switching users.   **d.** Reduces power to the computer and its hardware.

▼ SKILLS REVIEW

1. Start Windows Vista and view the desktop.

   a. Turn on your computer, select your user account or enter your user name, then enter your password (if necessary).

   b. Identify and list as many components of the Windows Vista desktop as you can without referring to the lessons.

   c. Compare your results to Figure A-1 to make sure that you have identified all the desktop objects and icons.

2. Use a pointing device.

   a. Point to the Recycle Bin icon and display its ToolTip.

   b. Double-click the Recycle Bin icon, then restore down the Recycle Bin window if it is maximized.

   c. Drag the Recycle Bin window to the upper-left corner of the desktop, then close the window.

3. Start a program.

   a. Open the Start menu.

   b. Display a list of all programs.

   c. Start Windows Calendar.

4. Move and resize windows.

   a. If the Windows Calendar window is maximized, restore down the window.

   b. Adjust the height and width of the window in one operation.

   c. Maximize, minimize, then restore the Windows Calendar window.

5. Use menus, toolbars, and keyboard shortcuts.

   a. Open the View menu on the menu bar, then choose Month to display a calendar for the current month.

   b. Use the View button on the toolbar to display a calendar for the current day.

   c. In the mini-calendar in the Navigation pane on the left, click the date for the next day to view its schedule.

   d. Use the keyboard shortcut [Alt][F4] to close Windows Calendar.

6. Use dialog boxes.

   a. If you do not see the Sidebar on the desktop, open the Start menu, display the All Programs menu, and then choose Windows Sidebar from the Accessories menu (or click the Windows Sidebar icon in the Notification area).

   b. Right-click the Clock gadget, then click Options to view settings for the Clock gadget.

   c. Under the preview of a clock, use the Next button to advance through the eight options for viewing the Clock.

   d. Use the Previous button to return to the first (default) view for the Clock gadget.

   e. Click the Cancel button to close the Clock dialog box without making any changes to the settings.

7. Use scroll bars.

   a. From the Start menu, open Windows Help and Support and maximize the window (if necessary).

   b. Open the Windows Basics Help topic.

   c. Use the down scroll arrow in the vertical scroll bar to examine other Help topics.

   d. Use the up scroll arrow in the vertical scroll bar to view previously displayed Help topics.

   e. Use the scroll box in the vertical scroll bar to view the last Windows Basics Help topic.

8. Use Windows Help and Support.

   a. Open "The Start menu (overview)" Help topic.

   b. Read the information about the Start menu in the first two paragraphs (through the bulleted list).

   c. Use the Search Help box to locate help on gadgets.

    d. Open the Help topic entitled "Windows Sidebar and gadgets (overview)."

    e. Under "In this article," click "Adding and removing gadgets" to jump to this Help topic.

    f. Click "To add a gadget to Sidebar" (shown in blue) to view the steps for this process, then click the "To remove a gadget from Sidebar" (shown in blue) to view the single step for this process.

    g. Close the Windows Help and Support window.

9. End a Windows Vista session.

    a. If you are working in a computer lab, follow the instructions provided by your instructor for using the Start menu to log off the computer, restart the computer, put the computer to sleep, or shut down the computer completely. If you are working on your own computer, use the Start menu to choose the shut-down option you prefer.

▼ INDEPENDENT CHALLENGE 1

You work as a teacher for ABC Computer Mentors. You need to prepare a set of handouts that provide an overview of some of the new desktop features in Windows Vista for individuals enrolled in an upcoming class on Computer Survival Skills.

    a. Open Windows Help and Support, then open the Windows Basics Help topic.

    b. Open the **Using menus, buttons, bars, and boxes** Help topic under Desktop Fundamentals.

    c. Use the vertical scroll bar to read the entire Help topic.

    d. Prepare a handwritten list of 10 new features that you learned about working with menus, buttons, bars, and boxes. Use the following title for your list: **Using Menus, Buttons, Bars, and Boxes**

    e. Close Windows Help and Support, write your name on your list, and submit it to your instructor.

▼ INDEPENDENT CHALLENGE 2

You are a freelance photographer who takes photographs for magazine covers, articles, newsletters, and Web sites. You want to evaluate how the Windows Photo Gallery can be used to make simple changes to digital photos.

    a. Open Windows Help and Support and search for tips on editing pictures in Windows Photo Gallery.

    b. After reading the Tips for editing pictures Help topic, prepare a handwritten summary with the title **Tips for Editing Pictures**, listing the recommended workflow for editing pictures in Windows Photo Gallery. (*Hint*: Use the first figure in the Help topic on the recommended workflow in Photo Gallery to identify the four steps.)

    c. Use Windows Help and Support to search for information on how to remove red eye from a picture.

    d. Add to your summary a short paragraph that describes red eye and how you can correct this problem with Windows Photo Gallery.

    e. Close Windows Help and Support, write your name on your summary, and submit it to your instructor.

▼ INDEPENDENT CHALLENGE 3

As a marketing analyst for Expert AI Systems, Ltd., in Great Britain, you contact and collaborate with employees at an Australian branch of the company. Because your colleagues live in a different time zone, you want to add another clock to your Sidebar and customize it to show the time in Australia. This way, you can quickly determine when to reach these employees at a convenient time during their workday hours.

    a. If Windows does not display the Sidebar on the desktop, use the All Programs menu or the Windows Sidebar icon in the Notification area to display the Sidebar.

    b. Use Windows Help and Support to search for information on how to customize the Windows Sidebar and how to change an individual gadget's options.

    c. Use this Help information to view the settings for the Clock gadget on the Sidebar, then try each setting.

    d. Click Cancel to close the Clock dialog box without changing the settings.

▼ INDEPENDENT CHALLENGE 3 (CONTINUED)

Advanced Challenge Exercise

- Point to the Gadgets toolbar at the top of the Sidebar, then click the Add Gadget button.
- Double-click the Clock gadget in the Add Gadgets dialog box, then close the Add Gadgets dialog box.
- Drag the new copy of the Clock gadget and place it below the last gadget on the Sidebar.
- Right-click the new Clock gadget, then click Options on the shortcut menu to view settings for the new Clock.
- Choose a different view for the clock and, in the Clock name text box, type Australia.
- Click the Time Zone list arrow to display a list of different time zones, then click the time zone for Canberra, Melbourne, and Sydney. (*Hint:* You want the GMT+10:00 time zone near the bottom of the list of time zones.)
- Add a check mark to the "Show the second hand" check box to enable this feature.
- Click OK to close the Clock dialog box.
- Right-click the new Clock gadget, then click Close Gadget on the shortcut menu to restore your Sidebar to its original state.

e. Prepare a handwritten summary entitled Using Clock Gadgets that describes what settings you examined and how you might use them in your daily life.

f. Write your name on your summary and submit it to your instructor.

▼ REAL LIFE INDEPENDENT CHALLENGE

In preparation for an upcoming convention to present new products produced by your company, Continental Saunas, Inc., you decide to prepare a slide show using the Windows Photo Gallery.

a. Open Windows Help and Support, then search for Help information on viewing your pictures as a slide show.

b. Read the Help information, studying the features of the Slide Show Controls toolbar and slide show themes.

c. Open the Photo Gallery Viewer from the Slide Show gadget on the Sidebar.

d. Use the Play Slide Show button to view a slide show of the photos in your Pictures folder.

Advanced Challenge Exercise

Note: To view the Slide Show Controls toolbar as well as certain themes and transitions, your computer must have a graphics card capable of displaying these features and special effects.

- After the slide show starts, move your pointing device to display the Slide Show Controls toolbar.
- Use the Slide Show Controls toolbar to perform the following operations during the slide show. Note the default setting for specific buttons, which options you choose, and what they do so that you can prepare a short written summary for co-workers who might use the Windows Photo Gallery for slide shows.
- Use the Themes pop-up list button to select and view other themes (or presentation formats) for slide shows. Note the default theme, try at least three other themes, then restore the default theme.
- Use the Slide Show Settings button to change the slide show speed and examine the Shuffle and Loop options, then restore the default slide show speed and Shuffle or Loop option.
- Use the Previous and Next buttons to view the previous and next image.
- Use the Exit button to end the slide show.

e. Prepare a one-page handwritten summary titled Photo Gallery Slide Show that describes what you have learned about the Windows Photo Gallery and how you might use it in your daily life.

f. Write your name on the summary and submit it to your instructor.

▼ VISUAL WORKSHOP

After returning from a Quest Specialty Travel tour, you want to print a copy of a digital photo to promote an upcoming trip. Use the skills you have learned in this lesson to print a copy of a digital photo:

- Use Windows Help and Support to search for information on how to print a picture using Windows Photo Gallery.
- Use the Slide Show gadget to open the Windows Photo Gallery, then choose the option to print a 4 x 6 inch copy of the image on letter-size paper, as shown in Figure A-19.
- Write your name on the printed copy and submit it to your instructor.

FIGURE A-19

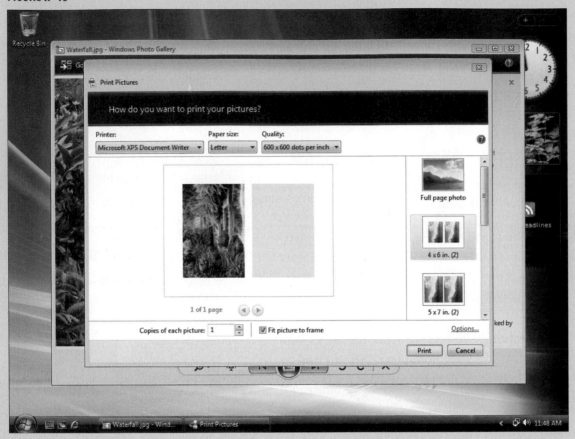

Getting Started with Windows Vista

Understanding File Management

Files You Will Need:

No files needed.

You use Windows Vista to access the drives where you store your folders and files. Each **drive** on your computer is a physical location for storing files. Most people store their files on the computer's hard disk drive and keep duplicate copies on other drives, such as a USB flash drive. The **hard disk** is a built-in, high-capacity, high-speed storage medium for all the software, folders, and files on a computer. When you create a document or other types of data with a program, you save the results in a file, which consists of stored electronic data such as text, a picture, a video, or music. Each file is stored in a folder, which is a container for a group of related files such as reports, correspondence, or e-mail contacts.  As a tour guide for Quest Specialty Travel (QST), you want to better understand how you can use Windows Vista to manage the files you need for proposing, planning, organizing, and documenting QST tours.

OBJECTIVES

Manage folders and files

Open the Computer window

Create and save documents

Open the Documents folder

Copy files

Open, edit, and print files

Move and rename files

Search for files

Delete and restore files

Managing Folders and Files

Most of the work you do on a computer involves using programs to create files, which you then store in folders. Over time, you create many folders and files and save them on different storage media. The process of organizing and finding your folders and files can become a challenge. It is helpful to develop a strategy for organizing your folders and files; these tasks are referred to as **file management**. Windows Vista provides a variety of file management tools to assist you in these tasks. ▦▦▦▦ As a QST tour guide for destinations in the South Pacific, you work with many types of files. You want to review how Windows can help you track and organize your files.

DETAILS

You can use Windows Vista to:

- **Create folders for storing and organizing files**

    Folders provide a location for your important files and help you organize them into groups of related files so that you can easily locate a file later. You give each folder you create a unique, descriptive **folder name** that identifies the files you intend to place in the folder. A folder can also contain other folders, called **subfolders**, to help organize files into smaller groups. This structure for organizing folders and files is called a **file hierarchy** because it describes the logic and layout of the folder structure on a disk. Windows Vista provides the Documents folder in which you create folders and subfolders for saving your files on your hard disk drive. Most programs automatically open and use the Documents folder when you save or open files. Figure B-1 illustrates how you might organize your tour folders and files within the Documents folder. Windows Vista provides other folders dedicated to specific types of files, such as the Pictures folder for image files; the Music folder for music or sound files; the Contacts folder for e-mail addresses and other contact information, including names, addresses, and phone numbers; and the Favorites folder for Internet shortcuts to your preferred Web sites. Figure B-2 shows the standard folders that Windows Vista creates for each user.

- **Rename, copy, and move folders and files**

    If you want to change the name of a folder or file, you can rename it. For example, you might change the name of the "French Polynesia Tour Proposal" file to "French Polynesia Tour" after your supervisor approves the tour. If you need a duplicate of a file, you can copy it. For example, you could make a copy of the "French Polynesia Tour" file, rename the copy to "Fiji Islands Tour Proposal," then modify the file's content for a new tour location. You can also move a folder or file to another folder or disk and physically change its location.

- **Delete and restore folders and files**

    Deleting folders and files you no longer need frees up storage space on your disk and helps keep your files organized. Folders and files deleted from your hard disk are moved to a Windows folder called the Recycle Bin. If you accidentally delete an important folder or file, or if you change your mind and want to restore a deleted folder or file, you can retrieve it from the Recycle Bin. Folders or files deleted from a removable disk, such as a USB flash drive, are permanently removed and cannot be retrieved with Windows.

- **Locate folders and files quickly using Instant Search**

    Instant Search helps you quickly locate a folder or file if you forget where you stored it. If you can provide part of the folder or file name—or some other fact about the item, such as the author's name—Instant Search can easily locate it and save you a lot of time and effort.

- **Use shortcuts to access frequently used files and folders**

    As your file structure becomes more complex, a file or folder you use often might be located several levels down the file hierarchy and require multiple steps to open. To save time, you can create shortcuts on your desktop to the files and folders you use frequently. A **shortcut** is a link that gives you quick access to a folder, file, or Web site. As shown in Figure B-2, Windows uses shortcuts to folders that contain sample files, such as pictures, music, and videos. Also, each program listed on the All Programs menu is a shortcut to the actual program stored elsewhere on your computer.

FIGURE B-1: Sample folder and file hierarchy

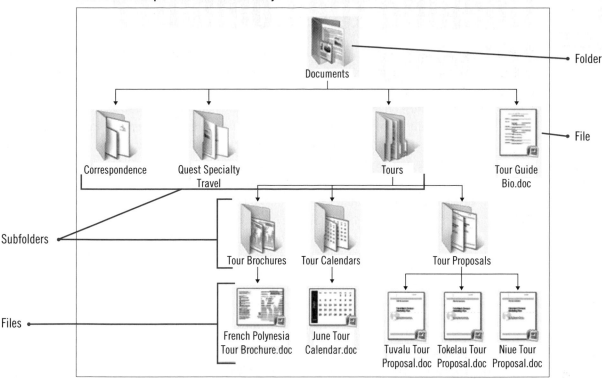

FIGURE B-2: Default user folders in Windows Vista

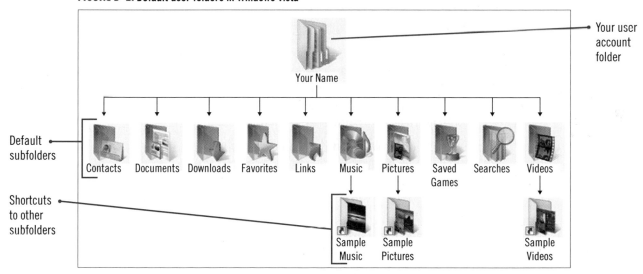

Organizing your folders and files efficiently

Good planning is essential for effective file management. First, identify the types of files you work with, such as images, music, and reports, then determine a logical system for organizing your files. The Pictures and Music folders are good places to store images and music. The Documents folder is the most common place to store all of your other files. Within each folder, use subfolders to better organize the files into smaller groups. For example, use subfolders in the Pictures folder to separate family photos from vacation photos, or to group them by year. In the Documents folder, you might group personal files in one subfolder and business files in another subfolder, then create additional subfolders to further distinguish sets of files. For example, your personal files might include subfolders for resumes, letters, and income tax returns, to name a few. Your business files might include subfolders for clients, projects, and invoices. You should periodically reevaluate your folder structure to ensure that it continues to meet your needs.

Opening the Computer Window

The **Computer window** shows the drives on your computer organized into two groups—Hard Disk Drives and Devices with Removable Storage. A **device** is a hardware component in your computer system. **Removable storage** refers to storage media that you can easily transfer from one computer to another, such as DVDs, CDs, or flash drives. **USB flash drives** (also called pen drives, jump drives, keychain drives, and thumb drives) are a popular removable storage device because of their ease of use and portability. When you attach a USB flash drive to a computer, a new drive icon appears under Devices with Removable Storage. To distinguish one drive from another, each drive has a unique **drive name** that consists of a letter followed by a colon, such as C: for the hard disk drive. Table B-1 lists examples of different drive types. Table B-2 lists commonly used terms to describe the storage capacities of different types of disks. Before you plan your next tour, you want to see what types of drives are available on your computer.

STEPS

1. **Start your computer and Windows Vista, logging onto your computer if necessary**

QUICK TIP

The **Navigation Pane** contains links to your personal folders, including the Documents, Pictures, and Music folders.

2. **Click the Start button 🟢 on the taskbar, click Computer on the right side of the Start menu, then click the Maximize button 🔲 if the Computer window does not fill the desktop**

   The Computer window opens, displaying icons for the hard disk drive and removable storage devices on your computer. Your computer may have more than one hard disk drive or other types of removable storage. You may also see icons for other types of hardware, such as a scanner or digital camera.

TROUBLE

If the Details Pane is hidden, click the Organize button on the toolbar, point to Layout, then click Details Pane.

3. **Under Hard Disk Drives, click the your hard disk drive icon**

   As shown in Figure B-3, the **Details Pane** at the bottom of the Computer window shows a friendly name for your hard disk drive (such as Local Disk), its actual drive name (C:), the total size or total storage capacity, the amount of free space, and a horizontal bar that shows the storage space already being used on the hard disk drive. When you select the hard disk drive (or some other drive), the options on the toolbar change to ones available for that drive.

4. **Click the Close button ❌ on the Computer window title bar**

   The Computer window closes.

TABLE B-1: Drive names and drive icons

drive type	drive icon	friendly name	drive name	referred to as
floppy disk drive		3½ Floppy	A:	drive A
hard disk drive		Local Disk	C:	drive C
CD drive		CD-RW Drive, CD-R Drive, or CD-ROM Drive	next available drive letter; for example, D:	drive D
DVD drive		DVD-RW Drive, DVD-R Drive, or DVD-ROM Drive	next available drive letter; for example, E:	drive E
USB flash drive		[varies with drive]	next available drive letter; for example, F:	drive F

FIGURE B-3: Computer window

Address Bar

Navigation Pane

Details Pane

Toolbar

Friendly name

Drive name

Drive icon

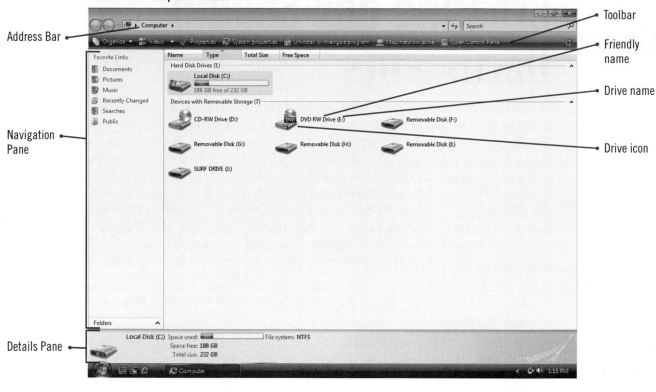

TABLE B-2: Disk storage capacity terms

term	equals approximately	example	storage space
byte	one character of storage space on disk or in RAM (memory)	A simple text file with the phrase *To-Do List*	10 bytes; count all the characters in the phrase including the hyphen and the blank space between the two words (10 characters = 10 bytes of storage space)
kilobyte (KB or K)	one thousand bytes	A file with a 10-page term paper (approximately 3500 characters per page)	35 KB (approximately 35,000 bytes)
megabyte (MB or M)	one million bytes (or one thousand kilobytes)	512 MB USB flash drive	512 MB (approximately 512 million bytes)
gigabyte (GB or G)	one billion bytes (or one thousand megabytes)	350 GB hard disk	350 GB (approximately 350 billion bytes)
terabyte (TB or T)	one trillion bytes (or one thousand gigabytes)	1 TB hard disk drive	1 TB (approximately one trillion bytes)

Displaying the Computer icon on the desktop

By default, the Computer icon does not appear on the desktop. You can display the Computer icon on the desktop so you can open the Computer window in one step rather than from the Start menu, which involves several steps. To add the Computer icon to your desktop, click the Start button, right-click Computer, then click Show on Desktop. You can now quickly open the Computer window by double-clicking the Computer icon on the desktop. You can repeat these steps to remove the Computer icon from the desktop.

Creating and Saving Documents

Windows comes with easy-to-use programs called Accessories. For example, you can use the WordPad Accessory to create simple text documents such as a letter or to-do list. Any document you create with WordPad (or another program) is temporarily stored in your computer's **RAM (random access memory)**. Anything stored in RAM is lost when you turn off your computer or the power fails unexpectedly. Before you close a document or exit WordPad, you must create a permanent copy of the document by saving it as a file on a disk. You can save files in the **Documents folder** on your local hard disk drive (drive C) or on a removable storage device such as a USB flash drive. When you name a file, choose a **filename** that clearly identifies the file contents. Filenames can be no more than 255 characters, including spaces and can include letters, numbers, and certain symbols. ▓▓▓▓ You want to use WordPad to create a to-do list for your next tour, then save the file to the Documents folder. The To-Do List is shown in Figure B-4.

STEPS

1. **Click the Start button ⊕ on the taskbar, point to All Programs, click Accessories, then click WordPad**

   The WordPad window opens with a new, blank document. Table B-3 identifies the components of the WordPad window. In the document window, a blinking **insertion point** indicates where the next character you type will appear.

QUICK TIP

If you make a typing mistake, press [Backspace] to delete the character to the left of the insertion point.

2. **Type To-Do List on the first line, then press [Enter] three times**

   Each time you press [Enter], WordPad inserts a new blank line and places the insertion point at the beginning of the line.

3. **Type the text shown in Figure B-4, pressing [Enter] at the end of each line**

4. **Click File on the menu bar, click Save As, then click the Browse Folders button in the Save As dialog box**

TROUBLE

If the Documents folder is not displayed, click Documents in the Navigation Pane.

   The Save As dialog box expands to show the contents of the Documents folder, as shown in Figure B-5.

5. **Click Document.rtf in the File name text box to select it, then type To-Do List**

TROUBLE

If a Confirm Save As dialog box asks if you want to replace a file with the same name, click Yes.

6. **Click Save in the Save As dialog box**

   WordPad saves the document in a file named "To-Do List" in the Documents folder and closes the Save As dialog box. The title bar displays "To-Do List.rtf"—the filename you entered followed by the file extension .rtf. A **file extension** identifies the type of file. Each program assigns a file extension to files you create, so you only need to enter a name for the file. Depending on how Windows is set up, you may not see the file extensions.

7. **Click the Close button ▩✕ on the WordPad title bar**

FIGURE B-3: Components of the WordPad window

component	used to
Title bar	Display the name of the open document and program
Menu bar	Display menu names with commands for performing operations on a document and its contents and for specifying program settings
Toolbar	Display buttons for common menu commands, such as saving and printing
Format bar	Display buttons for formatting, or enhancing, the appearance of a document
Ruler	Mark a document's width in ⅛ths of an inch (also shows one-inch marks)
Document window	Display all or part of the open document
Status bar	Display simple Help information and tips

FIGURE B-4: WordPad document

Temporary filename

Program name

Insertion point

Toolbar

Format bar

Ruler

Document window

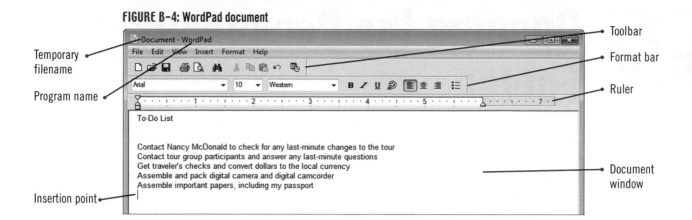

FIGURE B-5: Save As dialog box

Navigation Pane

Current folder

Folders in the current folder (yours will differ)

Temporary filename

Type of file

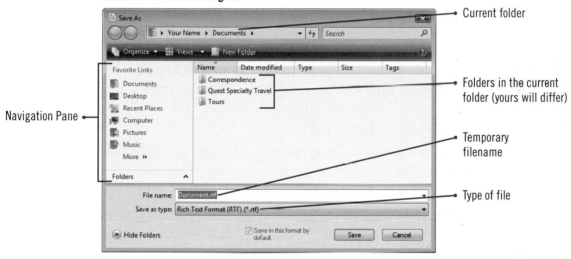

Using the Address Bar in the Save As dialog box

The **Address Bar** shows your current location in the computer's file hierarchy as a series of links separated by arrows. In Figure B-5, this series of links appears as an icon followed by "Your Name" (your user account folder name) then Documents. If you click the leftmost arrow in the Address Bar, you can use the drop-down list that opens to switch to the desktop, the Computer window, or other system folders. If you click the arrow after your user account name, you can use the list that opens to switch to any of your user account folders, such as Contacts, Music, Pictures, and Videos. If you click the arrow after Documents, you can use the list that opens to switch to a subfolder in the Documents folder, as shown in Figure B-6.

FIGURE B-6: Address Bar drop-down menu

Address Bar

Address Bar arrow displays a drop-down list of subfolders within the Documents folder

Subfolders in the Documents folder

Opening the Documents Folder

The Documents folder is the most common place to store files you create or receive from others. From the Documents folder, you can examine your files, organize them into subfolders, or perform other common file management tasks such as renaming, copying, moving, or deleting a folder or file. ▰▰▰ You store all your QST tour files in the Documents folder on your computer. You want to organize the files in your Documents folder before you copy them to a USB flash drive.

STEPS

1. **Click the Start button ⊕ on the taskbar, then click Documents**

   The Documents window opens and displays your folders and files, including the To-Do List.rtf file. Table B-4 identifies the components of the Documents window.

   TROUBLE
   If your view did not change, Windows Vista is already set to Large Icons view.

2. **Click the Views button arrow on the toolbar, then click Large Icons**

   Like some of the other views, Large Icons view displays folder icons with different icons for the types of files (such as a text document) contained in a folder or a **live view** of the actual content in files.

   QUICK TIP
   The Layout option on the Organize menu controls whether to display the Details, Preview, and Navigation panes.

3. **If you do not see the Preview Pane on the right side of the window, click the Organize button on the toolbar, point to Layout, then click Preview Pane**

   The **Preview Pane** shows the actual contents of the selected file, such as the WordPad file, without starting a program. Preview may not work for some types of files.

4. **Click the To-Do List.rtf file icon**

   The Preview Pane shows the actual contents of your To-Do List file, and the Details Pane lists information about the file itself, including the dates it was created and last modified, and its size. See Figure B-7.

5. **Leave the Documents window open for the next lesson**

TABLE B-4: Components of the Documents window

component	used to
Back button	Go back to previously viewed folders
Forward button	Return to the folders you just left
Address Bar	Display the name of the current folder and navigate to a different folder
Search box	Locate files or folders in the current folder
Toolbar	Perform common tasks on a folder or its contents (such as changing the view or e-mailing a file)
Navigation Pane	Navigate to another folder
File list	Display the subfolders and files in the current folder
Details Pane	View information about the folder or file you select in the File list
Preview Pane	View the actual content within some types of files

FIGURE B-7: Documents window

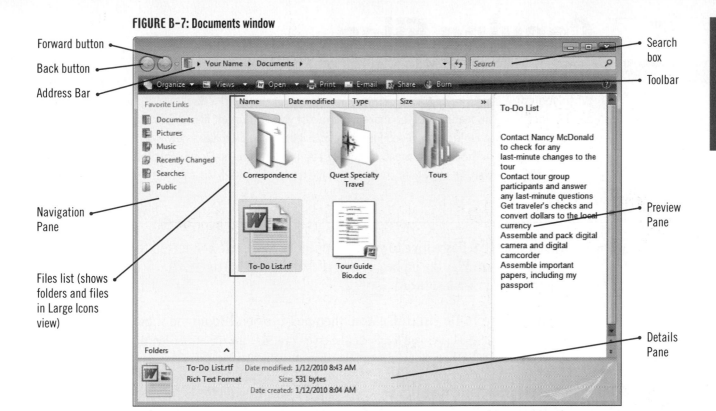

Forward button

Back button

Address Bar

Navigation Pane

Files list (shows folders and files in Large Icons view)

Search box

Toolbar

Preview Pane

Details Pane

Changing views in a window

The Views button provides seven ways to display the folders and files in a window. Extra Large Icons, Large Icons, and Medium Icons views display rows of folder and file icons at different sizes, with their names displayed under the icon. Small Icons view displays rows of even smaller folder and file icons with the folder or filename to the right of the icon. List view displays columns of very small folder or filename icons with the names to the right of the icon. Tiles view is similar to Small Icons view, but displays larger icons and also lists the type of folder or file and the file size. Details view is similar to List view, but displays columns with the folder or filename, the date and time that a folder or file was modified, the type of folder or file, the size of files, and any tags assigned to a file. A **tag** is a word or phrase that reminds you of a file's content. You can use the Views button slider bar to scale icons to your preferred size between Small Icons and Extra Large Icons.

Copying Files

You can copy a file, a group of files, or a folder from one disk drive to another or from one folder to another. When you **copy** a file, the original file stays in its current location and a duplicate of the file is created in another location. This feature lets you make a backup of your important files. A **backup** is a copy of a file that is stored in another location. If you lose the original file, you can make a new working copy from your backup. You can use the Send To menu to quickly copy a file from the Documents folder to another disk drive. ■■■■■ You want to copy your To-Do List.rtf file to your USB flash drive so you can work with the file as you travel.

If you are using a different storage device, insert the appropriate disk and substitute that device whenever you see USB flash drive in the steps.

1. **Attach your USB flash drive to your computer or to a cable connected to your computer, then, if the AutoPlay dialog box opens, click the** Close button ■X■
   Your USB flash drive is ready to use.

2. **Right-click the** To-Do List.rtf **file icon, then point to** Send To **on the shortcut menu**
   A list of the available drives and locations where you can copy the file appears on the shortcut menu, as shown in Figure B-8. The options on your Send To menu will differ.

If you hold down [Shift] while you click a Send To option, Windows moves the file to that disk; it does not make another copy

3. **Click the** USB flash drive **option**
   Windows copies the To-Do List.rtf file to your USB flash drive. There are now two copies of the same file stored in two different locations.

4. **Click the first** Address Bar arrow ▶ **on the Address Bar, as shown in Figure B-9, then click** Computer
   The contents of the Computer folder appear in the window.

5. **Double-click the** USB flash drive **icon**
   The contents of your USB flash drive, including the To-Do List.rtf file you copied to this disk, appear in the window. See Figure B-10.

6. **Click the** Close button ■X■ **on the Removable Disk window title bar**

Using the Send To menu

You can create a shortcut on the desktop to any folder or file you use frequently with the "Desktop (create shortcut)" option on the Send To menu. The Compressed (zipped) Folder option on the Send To menu creates a new compressed file using the same filename, but with the .zip file extension. For example, compressing To-Do List.rtf creates a new file named To-Do List.zip. Before you send a file by e-mail, especially a large file, it is a good idea to **compress** it, which makes the file smaller in size.

FIGURE B-8: Send To menu

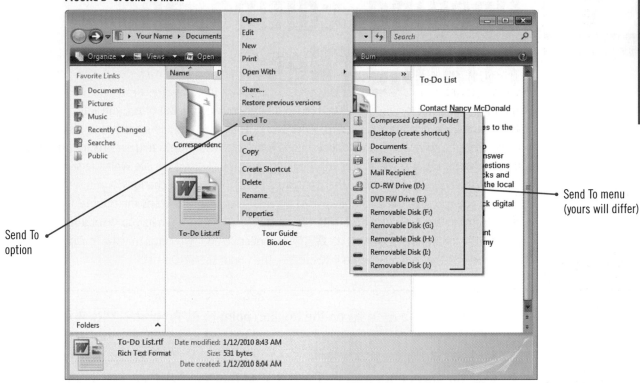

Send To option

Send To menu (yours will differ)

FIGURE B-9: Navigating with the Address Bar

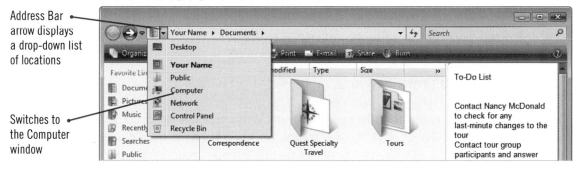

Address Bar arrow displays a drop-down list of locations

Switches to the Computer window

FIGURE B-10: Removable Disk window

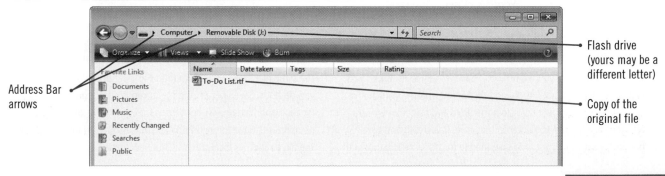

Address Bar arrows

Flash drive (yours may be a different letter)

Copy of the original file

Opening, Editing, and Printing Files

Sometimes you create new files, as you did in the previous lesson. But often, you want to change a file that you or someone else already created. After you open an existing file stored on a disk, you can **edit**, or make changes, to it. For example, you might want to add or delete text, or change the **formatting** or appearance of the text. After you finish editing, you usually save the file with the same filename, which replaces the file with a new copy that contains all your most recent changes. If you want to keep the original file, you can save the edited file with a different filename; this keeps the original file without the edits and creates a new copy of the file with the most recent changes. When you want a **hard copy**, or paper copy of the file, you need to print it. ▰▰▰ You need to add two items to your To-Do List, so you want to open and edit the file you created in WordPad, then print the To-Do List.

STEPS

1. **Click the Start button ⊕ on the taskbar, point to All Programs, click Accessories, then click WordPad**

   The WordPad program window opens.

2. **Click the Open button 🖝 on the WordPad toolbar, click Computer in the Navigation Pane, then double-click your USB flash drive icon**

   The Open dialog box displays the contents of your USB flash drive. See Figure B-11. You may see additional files.

   > **QUICK TIP**
   > You can also open a file by double-clicking it in the Open dialog box.

3. **Click To-Do List.rtf in the File list, then click Open in the Open dialog box**

   The Open dialog box closes and the To-Do List.rtf file appears in the WordPad window.

4. **Click at the beginning of the last blank line in the To-Do List, then type the two additional lines shown in Figure B-12, pressing [Enter] after each line**

5. **Click the Save button 🖫 on the WordPad toolbar**

   WordPad saves the edited To-Do List.rtf file under the same filename on your USB flash drive.

   > **QUICK TIP**
   > You should always use Print Preview before you print to save time and effort as well as toner ink and paper.

6. **Click the Print Preview button 🗅 on the WordPad toolbar**

   Print Preview displays a full-page view of your document, as shown in Figure B-13, so you can check its layout before you print. Dotted lines separate the area on the page reserved for the document and the blank space reserved for the left, right, top, and bottom margins. If you need to make additional edits, click the Close button on the Print Preview toolbar (not the title bar), make your changes, then use Print Preview to check the document again before printing.

7. **Click the Print button on the Print Preview toolbar**

   Print Preview closes and the Print dialog box opens, so you can verify the print settings.

8. **Click Print in the Print dialog box, then retrieve your printed copy from the printer**

9. **Click the Close button ▣ on the WordPad title bar**

   WordPad closes.

Comparing Save and Save As

The File menu has two save options—Save and Save As. When you first save a file, the Save As dialog box opens (whether you choose Save or Save As) so you can select the drive and folder where you want to save the file and enter its filename. If you edit and save a previously saved file, you can save the file to the same location with the same filename, you can change the location or filename, or you can do both. Save updates the file stored on disk using the same location and filename without opening the Save As dialog box. Save As opens the Save As dialog box so you can save an updated copy of the file to another location or with a new filename.

FIGURE B-11: Open dialog box

Address Bar arrows

Navigation Pane

Current drive (yours may be a different letter)

Open this file

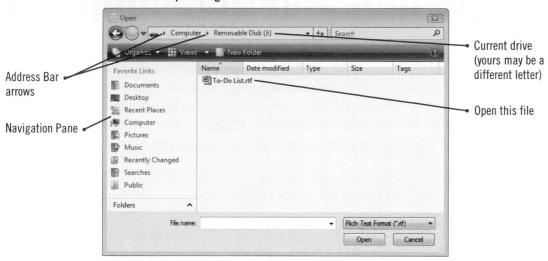

FIGURE B-12: Edited To-Do List file

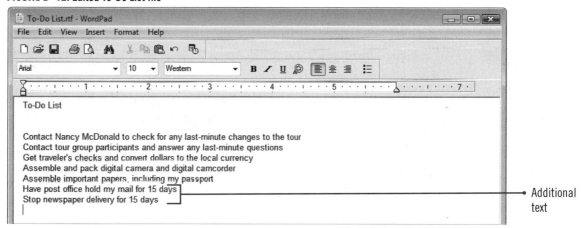

Additional text

FIGURE B-13: Print Preview

Closes Print Preview, but not the document

Closes the document and WordPad

Top margin

Right margin

Left margin

Bottom margin

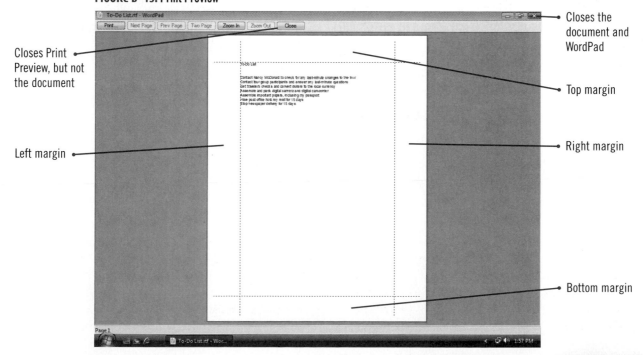

Moving and Renaming Files

You can move a file, a group of files, or a folder to another location such as a different folder on the same drive or a different drive. When you **move** a file, the original file is stored in a different location. One of the fastest ways to move a file is with **drag and drop** (which uses a pointing device to drag a file or folder to a new location). You may also need to rename a file, giving it a name that more clearly describes the file's contents and how you intend to use the file. ▰▰▰ You want to move the To-Do List.rtf file to a new folder and rename it so you can update the list for your next tour.

STEPS

1. **Click the** Start button 🏁 **on the taskbar, click** Computer, **then double-click your** USB flash drive icon

   The contents of your USB flash drive appear in the Computer window.

2. **Click the** Views button arrow **on the Computer window toolbar, then click** Large Icons

   The larger icons make it easier to work with folder and file icons as you move and rename files.

3. **Click the** Organize button **on the Computer window toolbar, then click** New Folder

   Windows creates a new folder named "New Folder," as shown in Figure B-14. The folder name is highlighted so you can type a more descriptive folder name.

TROUBLE

If you cannot type a name for the new folder, press [F2] (the Rename key), then repeat Step 4.

4. **Type** French Polynesia Tour **as the folder name, then press** [Enter]

   Windows changes the name of the folder.

5. **Click the** white background of the window, **point to the** To-Do List.rtf file, **press and hold the** left button **on your pointing device, drag the** To-Do List.rtf file **icon on top of the French Polynesia Tour folder, then pause**

   As shown in Figure B-15, a smaller transparent copy of the To-Do List.rtf file icon appears over the French Polynesia Tour folder and a ToolTip describes the type of operation.

6. **Release the** left button **on your pointing device**

   The To-Do List.rtf file moves into the French Polynesia Tour folder.

7. **Double-click the** French Polynesia Tour folder

   The Address Bar shows the name of the open folder, French Polynesia Tour. The To-Do List.rtf file appears in this folder.

8. **Click the** To-Do List.rtf file icon, **click the** Organize button, **then click** Rename

   The first part of the filename is highlighted so you can type a new name for the file.

9. **Type** Tour Preparation **as the new filename, then press** [Enter]

   Windows renames the file. See Figure B-16.

10. **Click the** Close button 🗙 **on the title bar**

FIGURE B-14: Creating a new folder

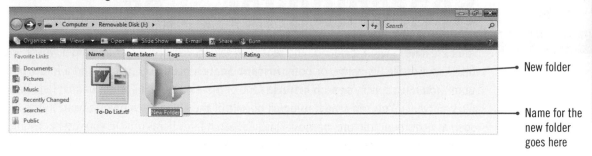

New folder

Name for the
new folder
goes here

FIGURE B-15: Moving a file using drag and drop

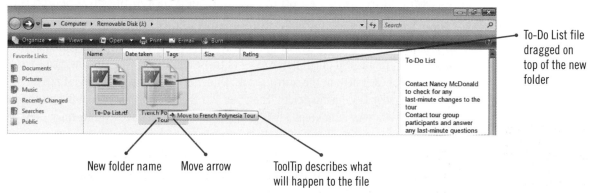

To-Do List file
dragged on
top of the new
folder

New folder name   Move arrow   ToolTip describes what
will happen to the file

FIGURE B-16: Renamed file

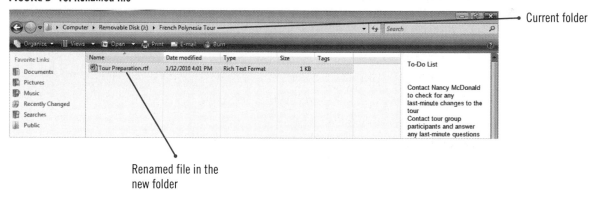

Current folder

Renamed file in the
new folder

Using drag and drop to copy and move files

If you drag and drop a file to a folder on the same drive, Windows
moves the file into that folder. However, if you drag and drop a file
to a folder on another drive, Windows copies the file instead. If you
want to move a file to another drive, hold down [Shift] while you
drag and drop. If you want to copy a file to another folder on the
same drive, hold down [Ctrl] while you drag and drop.

Searching for Files

After creating, saving, deleting, and renaming folders and files, you may forget where you stored a particular folder or file, its name, or both. **Instant Search** helps you quickly find a folder or file on your computer. You must specify **search criteria** (one or more pieces of information that help Windows identify the file you want). You can search using all or part of the filename, a unique word in the file, or the file type such as document, picture, or music. Instant Search finds items only in your user account, not in other user accounts on the same computer. The **Boolean filters** shown in Table B-5 allow you to specify multiple criteria so that you have a greater chance of finding what you need quickly. When you use the Boolean filters AND, OR, and NOT, you must type them in uppercase so they work properly. 🖐️ You want to quickly locate the copy of the To-Do List for your next tour.

STEPS

1. **Click the Start button ⊕ on the taskbar, then click in the Start Search box**

QUICK TIP

Searches are not case sensitive, so you can use uppercase or lowercase letters when you type search criteria.

2. **Type To**

The search results on the left side of the Start menu are organized by categories, as shown in Figure B-17. Your search results will differ; however, all of the search results will have the characters "To" somewhere in the name of each item in the search results. Under Files, you may see two listings for To-Do List.rtf. One is the file in your Documents folder. The other is a shortcut to the original file on the flash drive that you renamed. Windows Vista keeps a list of shortcuts to files you have used recently, even if that file no longer exists.

QUICK TIP

If you type "To-Do List" with quotation marks, Instant Search finds the To-Do List.rtf file and any shortcut or other files with the same name.

3. **Type -Do List after the word "To", then press [Spacebar]**

The additional text you typed narrows the search results, as shown in Figure B-18. Now you see documents with "To," "Do," and "List" in the filename.

4. **Under Files, click To-Do List.rtf**

The To-Do List.rtf file opens in Microsoft Word, WordPad, or another program that works with Rich Text Format files.

5. **Click the Close button ▣ in the program window's title bar**

TABLE B-5: Boolean filters

Boolean filter	example	how it works
AND	tour AND proposal	Finds all files that contain the word *tour* and the word *proposal*; the two words may or may not be located next to each other
OR	tour OR proposal	Finds all files that contain the word *tour* or the word *proposal* (or both)
NOT	tour NOT proposal	Finds all files that contain the word *tour* but not the word *proposal*
" " (quotation marks)	"tour proposal"	Finds all files that contain the exact phrase *tour proposal*

Understanding File Management

FIGURE B-17: Search results

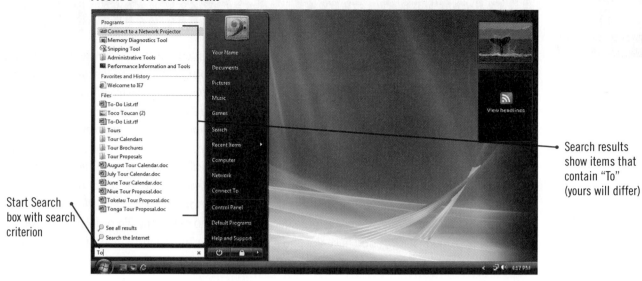

Start Search box with search criterion

Search results show items that contain "To" (yours will differ)

FIGURE B-18: Narrowed search results

Search found the file with the To-Do List

Search criteria

Search results (yours will differ)

Performing more advanced searches

If you want to search all your personal folders for a file, use the Start Search box on the Start menu. If you want to locate a file in a specific folder and all its subfolders (such as the Documents folder), open the folder and use the Search box in the folder. If you want to locate all files that have the same file extension (such as .rtf), type the file extension as your search criteria. If you want to locate files created by a certain person, use the first name, last name, or first and last name as your search criteria. If you want to locate files created on a certain date, type the date (for example, 7/9/2010) as your search criteria. If you remember the title in a document, type the title as your search criteria. If you have created e-mail contacts in your Contacts folder, you can type the person's name to find his or her e-mail address.

Deleting and Restoring Files

If you no longer need a folder or file, you can **delete** (or remove) it. If you delete a folder, Windows removes the folder as well as everything stored in it. Windows places folders and files you delete from your hard disk drive in the Recycle Bin. If you later discover that you need a deleted file or folder, you can restore it to its original location as long as you have not yet emptied the Recycle Bin. Emptying the Recycle Bin permanently removes the deleted folders and files from your computer. By deleting files and folders you no longer need and periodically emptying the Recycle Bin, you free up valuable storage space on your hard disk drive and keep your computer uncluttered. Be aware that files and folders you delete from a removable disk drive, such as a USB flash drive, are immediately and permanently deleted and cannot be restored by Windows. If you try to delete a file or folder that is too large for the Recycle Bin, Windows asks whether you want to permanently delete the file or folder. Choose Yes to delete the file or folder, or choose No to cancel the operation. ▰▰▰▰ You have the updated copy of the To-Do List.rtf file stored on your USB flash drive, so you want to delete the copy in the Documents folder.

STEPS

1. **Click the Start button ⊕ on the taskbar, click Documents, then click the To-Do List file in the Documents folder**

   After you select a folder or file, you can delete it.

QUICK TIP

You can also quickly delete a selected folder or file by pressing [Delete] or [Del].

2. **Click the Organize button on the toolbar, then click Delete**

   The Delete File dialog box opens so you can confirm the deletion, as shown in Figure B-19.

3. **Click Yes**

   The file moves from the Documents folder into the Recycle Bin.

4. **Click the Minimize button ▭ on the Documents window title bar and examine the Recycle Bin icon**

   The Recycle Bin icon contains wads of paper if the Recycle Bin contains deleted folders and files. If the Recycle Bin icon does not contain wads of paper, then it is empty and does not contain any deleted files or folders.

5. **Double-click the Recycle Bin icon 🗑**

   The Recycle Bin window opens and displays any deleted folders and files, including the To-Do List.rtf file, as shown in Figure B-20. Your Recycle Bin's contents may differ.

QUICK TIP

Windows keeps track of the original location of deleted subfolders and files so it can restore them later, recreating the original folder structure as needed.

6. **Click the To-Do List.rtf file to select it, then click the Restore this item button on the Recycle Bin toolbar**

   The file returns its original location and no longer appears in the Recycle Bin window.

7. **Click the Close button ☒ on the Recycle Bin title bar, then click the Documents taskbar button**

   The Recycle Bin window closes, and the Documents window opens. The Documents window contains the restored file. You decide to permanently delete this previous version of the To-Do List file.

8. **Click the To-Do List file, press [Delete], then click Yes in the Delete File dialog box**

   The To-Do List moves from the Documents folder to the Recycle Bin.

9. **Click the Close button ☒ on the Documents window title bar, then end your Windows session**

FIGURE B-19: Delete File dialog box

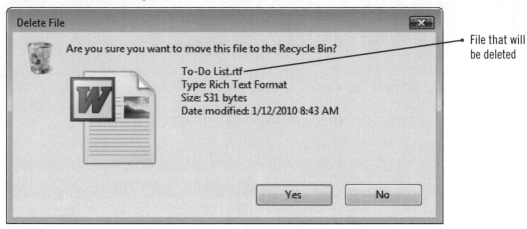

File that will
be deleted

FIGURE B-20: Recycle Bin folder

Deleted file

Emptying the Recycle Bin

If you are certain that you no longer need any of the deleted files and folders in your Recycle Bin, you can empty it. If the Recycle Bin folder is open, click the Empty the Recycle Bin button on the toolbar. If it is closed, right-click the Recycle Bin icon on the desktop, then click Empty Recycle Bin on the shortcut menu. In the Delete Multiple Items dialog box, choose Yes to confirm that you want to permanently delete all the items in the Recycle Bin, or choose No to cancel the operation.

Practice

▼ CONCEPTS REVIEW

Label each of the elements of the window shown in Figure B-21.

FIGURE B-21

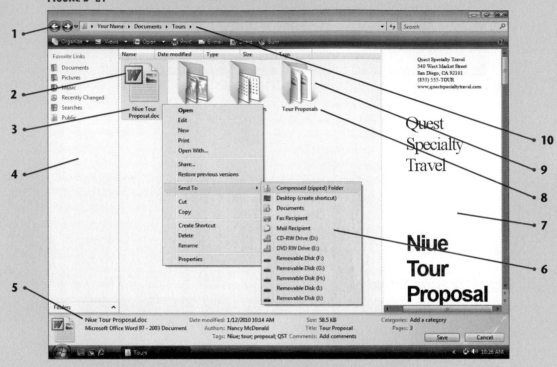

Match each statement with the term it best describes.

11. A container for related files

12. A link that provides quick access to a folder, file, or Web site

13. One or more pieces of information for locating a folder or file

14. Organizing and managing folders and files

15. The name that you assign to a file to identify its contents

a. file management
b. filename
c. folder
d. Search criteria
e. shortcut

Select the best answer from the list of choices.

16. One billion bytes of storage space on a disk is referred to as a:
   a. Kilobyte.
   b. Megabyte.
   c. Gigabyte.
   d. Terabyte.

17. To save a previously saved file with a new filename, you use the:
   a. Save command on the File menu.
   b. Save As command on the File menu.
   c. Save or Save As command on the File menu.
   d. Save button on the program's toolbar.

18. The blinking vertical bar in the WordPad application window is called the:
   a. Insertion point.
   b. Pointer.
   c. Ruler.
   d. Shortcut.

19. After you copy a file, you have:
   a. Only one copy of the file.
   b. A duplicate copy of the file in a different location.
   c. Moved the orginal file to a new location.
   d. Deleted the file.

20. After you move a file, you have:

    a. A backup copy of that file.

    b. A duplicate copy of the file in a different location.

    c. The orginal file in a different location.

    d. Deleted the file.

21. When you delete a file from your hard disk drive, Windows:

    a. Puts the deleted file in the Recycle Bin.

    b. Permanently deletes the file from the hard disk drive.

    c. Stores a duplicate copy of the file in the Recycle Bin..

    d. Moves the file to a removable disk.

▼ SKILLS REVIEW

1. Manage folders and files.

    a. Assume you manage a small travel agency. How would you organize your business files using a hierarchical file structure?

    b. What icon can you place on your desktop to quickly locate your flash drive where you store copies of important files?

    c. What shortcuts would you place on your desktop for easier access to your business files?

2. Open the Computer window. (If possible, use a different computer than you used for the lessons.)

    a. Attach your USB flash drive to your computer.

    b. Open the Computer window from the Start menu.

    c. Note the types of drives on this computer, their friendly names, and their actual drive names. Note the drive name assigned to your USB flash drive.

    d. Select the hard disk drive icon, then view the information in the Details Pane about the hard disk drive's total size and free space.

    e. Close the Computer window.

3. Create and save documents.

    a. Open WordPad from the All Programs menu.

    b. Type Oceania Tours as the title, followed by one blank line.

    c. Type your name, followed by two blank lines.

    d. Use WordPad to create the following list of current Oceania tours.

        Current Tours:

        1. French Poynesia

        2. Fiji Islands

        3. Pitcairn Islands

        4. Tonga

        5. Niue

        6. Tokelau

    e. Save the WordPad file with the filename Oceania Tours in the Documents folder.

    f. View the full filename in the WordPad title bar, then close WordPad.

4. Open the Documents folder.

    a. Open the Documents folder from the Start menu.

    b. If necessary, use the Views button to change the folder view to Large Icons.

    c. Click the Oceania Tours.rtf file.

    d. If necessary, use the Organize menu to display the Preview Pane.

    e. View the contents of the Oceania Tours.rtf file in the Preview Pane.

5. Copy files.

    a. Right-click the Oceania Tours.rft file, point to Send To on the shortcut menu, then send a copy of the WordPad file to your USB flash drive.

    b. Use the Address Bar to change to the Computer window, then to your USB flash drive window.

    c. Verify you successfully copied the Oceania Tours.rtf file to your USB flash drive, then close the USB flash drive window.

6. Open, edit, and print files.

    a. Open WordPad from the Start menu.

    b. Open the WordPad file named Oceania Tours.rtf from your USB flash drive (not from your Documents folder).

   c. Click at the beginning of the blank line after the last current tour, then add the names of two more tours on two separate lines: **Palau** and **Tuvalu**.

   d. Save the edited WordPad file.

   e. Use Print Preview to display a full-page view of the document.

   f. Print the Oceania Tours.rtf document and retrieve your printed copy from the printer, then close WordPad.

7. Move and rename files.

   a. Open a Computer window, then display the contents of your USB flash drive.

   b. If necessary, change your folder view to Large Icons.

   c. Use the Organize menu to create a new folder and name it **Oceania Tours**.

   d. Use drag and drop to move the Oceania Tours.rtf file into the new folder.

   e. Open the new folder and verify the move operation.

   f. Use the Organize menu to rename the moved WordPad file as **Current Oceania Tours**.

   g. Close the folder window.

8. Search for files.

   a. From the Start menu, enter **Oceania** in the Search box as the search criteria.

   b. Examine the Search results, then open the original Oceania Tours.rtf file.

   c. Close the program window.

9. Delete and restore files.

   a. Open the Documents folder from the Start menu.

   b. Select and delete your original WordPad file with the name **Oceania Tours.rtf**.

   c. Minimize the Documents window, then open the Recycle Bin.

   d. Select and restore the file named **Oceania Tours.rtf** that you just deleted, then close the Recycle Bin window.

   e. Use the Documents taskbar button to redisplay the Documents window.

   f. Verify Windows restored the file named Oceania Tours.rtf to the Documents folder.

   g. Select and delete this file again, then close the Documents window.

   h. Submit the printed copy of your revised WordPad document and your answers to Step 1 to your instructor.

▼ INDEPENDENT CHALLENGE 1

To meet the needs of high-tech workers in your town, you have opened an Internet café named Internet To-Go where your customers can enjoy a cup of fresh-brewed coffee and bakery goods while they check e-mail. To promote your new business, you want to develop a newspaper ad, flyers, and breakfast and lunch menus.

   a. Connect your USB flash drive to your computer, if necessary.

   b. Create a new folder named **Internet To-Go** on your USB flash drive.

   c. In the Internet To-Go folder, create three subfolders named **Advertising**, **Flyers**, and **Menus**.

   d. Use WordPad to create a short ad for your local newspaper that describes your business:

     • Use the name of the business as the title for your document.

     • Write a short paragraph about the business. Include a fictitious location, street address, and phone number.

     • After the paragraph, type your name.

   e. Save the WordPad document with the filename **Newspaper Ad** in the Advertising folder.

   f. Preview and then print your WordPad document.

▼ INDEPENDENT CHALLENGE 2

As a freelance writer for several national magazines, you depend on your computer to meet critical deadlines. Whenever you encounter a computer problem, you contact a computer consultant who helps you resolve the problem. This consultant asked you to document, or keep records of, your computer's current settings.

   a. Connect your USB flash drive to your computer, if necessary.

   b. Open the Computer window so that you can view information on your drives and other installed hardware.

▼ INDEPENDENT CHALLENGE 2 (CONTINUED)

c. Open WordPad and create a document with the title **My Hardware Documentation** and your name on separate lines.

d. List the names of the hard disk drive (or drives), devices with removable storage, and any other hardware devices, such as a digital camera, installed on the computer you are using. Also include the total size and amount of free space on your hard disk drive(s). (*Hint:* If you need to check the Computer window for this information, use the taskbar button for the Computer window to view your drives, then use the WordPad taskbar button to return to WordPad.)

e. Save the WordPad document with the filename **My Hardware Documentation** on your USB flash drive.

f. Preview your document, print your WordPad document, then close WordPad.

▼ INDEPENDENT CHALLENGE 3

As an adjunct, or part-time, instructor at Everhart College, you teach special summer classes for kids on how to use and create computer games, compose digital art, work with digital photographs, and compose digital music. You want to create a folder structure on your USB flash drive to store the files for each class.

a. Connect your USB flash drive to your computer, then open the Computer window to your USB flash drive.

b. Create a folder named **Computer Games**.

c. In the Computer Games folder, create a subfolder named **Class 1**.

Advanced Challenge Exercise

- In the Class 1 folder, create subfolders named **Class Outline** and **Hands-On Lab**.
- Rename the Class Outline folder to **Class Handouts**.
- Create a new folder named **Interactive Presentations** in the Class 1 subfolder.

d. Close the Class 1 folder window.

e. Use WordPad to create a document with the title **Photocopying** and your name on separate lines, and the following list of items that you need to photocopy for the first class:

Class 1:

Class 1 Topics & Resources

Hands-On Lab Assignment

On Your Own Exercise

Interactive Presentation Slides

f. Save the WordPad document with the filename **Photocopying** in the Class 1 folder. (*Hint:* After you switch to your USB flash drive in the Save As dialog box, open the Computer Games folder, then open the Class 1 folder before saving the file.)

g. Preview and print the Photocopying.rtf file, then close WordPad.

h. Draw a diagram of your new folder structure on the printed copy of your WordPad document.

▼ REAL LIFE INDEPENDENT CHALLENGE

This Real Life Independent Challenge requires an Internet connection. You want to open a small specialty shop for pottery, stained glass, handcrafts, and other consignments from local artists and craftspeople. First, you need to search for information on the Internet about preparing a business plan so that you can obtain financing from your local bank for the business.

a. Using the Start Search box on the Start menu, enter **Preparing a Business Plan** as the search criteria, then click the Search the Internet button in the Search Results pane.

b. From the list of Search results, locate a Web site that contains information on how to write a business plan.

c. Start WordPad and create a document in which you summarize in your own words the basic process for preparing a business plan. Include a title and your name in the document. At the bottom of your document, list the URL of the Web site or sites from which you prepared your WordPad document. (*Note*: You should not copy the exact content of a Web site, but instead summarize your findings in your own words because many sites copyright the content on their Web site. If you want to determine what content at a Web site is copyrighted and the conditions for using that content, scroll to the bottom of the Web site and click the link that covers copyright use and restrictions.)

d. Preview and print your WordPad document, then save the document on your USB flash drive.

As a technical support specialist at Advanced Robotic Systems, Ltd., in Great Britain, you need to respond to employee queries quickly and thoroughly. You decide that it is time to evaluate and reorganize the folder structure on your computer so you can quickly access the resources required for your job. Create the folder structure shown in Figure B-22 on your USB flash drive. As you work, use WordPad to prepare a simple outline of the steps you follow to create the folder structure. Include your name in the document, preview and print the document, then submit it to your instructor.

FIGURE B-22

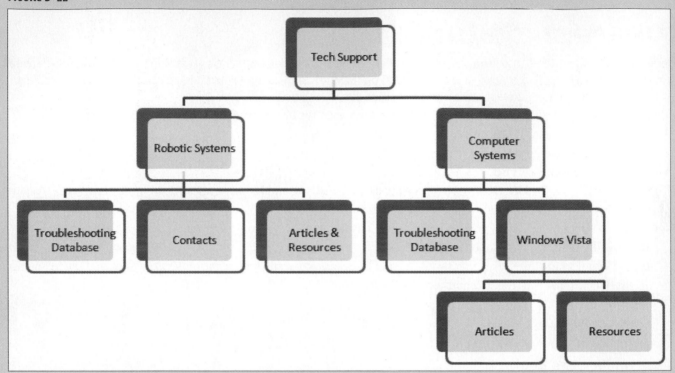

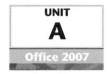

Getting Started with Microsoft Office 2007

Microsoft Office 2007 is a group of software programs designed to help you create documents, collaborate with co-workers, and track and analyze information. Each program is designed so you can work quickly and efficiently to create professional-looking results. You use different Office programs to accomplish specific tasks, such as writing a letter or producing a sales presentation, yet all the programs have a similar look and feel. Once you become familiar with one program, you'll find it easy to transfer your knowledge to the others. This unit introduces you to the most frequently used programs in Office, as well as common features they all share.

OBJECTIVES

Understand the Office 2007 Suite

Start and exit an Office program

View the Office 2007 user interface

Create and save a file

Open a file and save it with a
  new name

View and print your work

Get Help and close a file

Understanding the Office 2007 Suite

Microsoft Office 2007 features an intuitive, context-sensitive user interface, so you can get up to speed faster and use advanced features with greater ease. The programs in Office are bundled together in a group called a **suite** (although you can also purchase them separately). The Office suite is available in several configurations, but all include Word and Excel. Other configurations include PowerPoint, Access, Outlook, Publisher, and/or others. Each program in Office is best suited for completing specific types of tasks, though there is some overlap in terms of their capabilities.

DETAILS

The Office programs covered in this book include:

* **Microsoft Office Word 2007**

  When you need to create any kind of text-based document, such as memos, newsletters, or multi-page reports, Word is the program to use. You can easily make your documents look great by inserting eye-catching graphics and using formatting tools such as themes. **Themes** are predesigned combinations of color and formatting attributes you can apply, and are available in most Office programs. The Word document shown in Figure A-1 was formatted with the Solstice theme.

* **Microsoft Office Excel 2007**

  Excel is the perfect solution when you need to work with numeric values and make calculations. It puts the power of formulas, functions, charts, and other analytical tools into the hands of every user, so you can analyze sales projections, figure out loan payments, and present your findings in style. The Excel worksheet shown in Figure A-1 tracks personal expenses. Because Excel automatically recalculates results whenever a value changes, the information is always up-to-date. A chart illustrates how the monthly expenses are broken down.

* **Microsoft Office PowerPoint 2007**

  Using PowerPoint, it's easy to create powerful presentations complete with graphics, transitions, and even a soundtrack. Using professionally designed themes and clip art, you can quickly and easily create dynamic slideshows such as the one shown in Figure A-1.

* **Microsoft Office Access 2007**

  Access helps you keep track of large amounts of quantitative data, such as product inventories or employee records. The form shown in Figure A-1 was created for a grocery store inventory database. Employees use the form to enter data about each item. Using Access enables employees to quickly find specific information such as price and quantity, without hunting through store shelves and stockrooms.

Microsoft Office has benefits beyond the power of each program, including:

* **Common user interface: Improving business processes**

  Because the Office suite programs have a similar **interface**, or look and feel, your experience using one program's tools makes it easy to learn those in the other programs. Office documents are **compatible** with one another, meaning that you can easily incorporate, or **integrate**, an Excel chart into a PowerPoint slide, or an Access table into a Word document.

* **Collaboration: Simplifying how people work together**

  Office recognizes the way people do business today, and supports the emphasis on communication and knowledge-sharing within companies and across the globe. All Office programs include the capability to incorporate feedback—called **online collaboration**—across the Internet or a company network.

FIGURE A-1: Microsoft Office 2007 documents

Word document

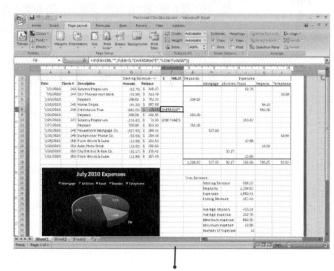

Excel worksheet

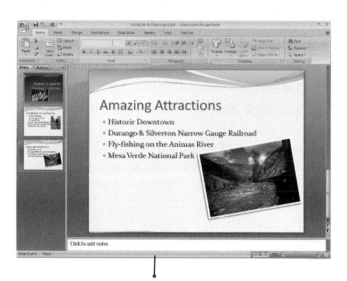

PowerPoint presentation

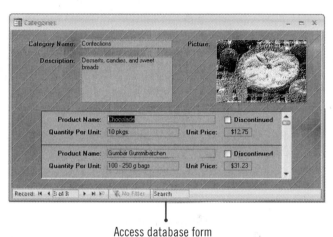

Access database form

Deciding which program to use

Every Office program includes tools that go far beyond what you might expect. For example, although Excel is primarily designed for making calculations, you can use it to create a database. So when you're planning a project, how do you decide which Office program to use? The general rule of thumb is to use the program best suited for your intended task, and make use of supporting tools in the program if you need them. Word is best for creating text-based documents, Excel is best for making mathematical calculations, PowerPoint is best for preparing presentations, and Access is best for managing quantitative data. Although the capabilities of Office are so vast that you *could* create an inventory in Excel or a budget in Word, you'll find greater flexibility and efficiency by using the program designed for the task. And remember, you can always create a file in one program, and then insert it in a document in another program when you need to, such as including sales projections (Excel) in a memo (Word).

Starting and Exiting an Office Program

The first step in using an Office program is of course to open, or **launch**, it on your computer. You have a few choices for how to launch a program, but the easiest way is to click the Start button on the Windows taskbar, or to double-click an icon on your desktop. You can have multiple programs open on your computer simultaneously, and you can move between open programs by clicking the desired program or document button on the taskbar or by using the [Alt][Tab] keyboard shortcut combination. When working, you'll often want to open multiple programs in Office, and switch among them throughout the day. Begin by launching a few Office programs now.

STEPS

> **QUICK TIP**
>
> You can also launch a program by double-clicking a desktop icon or clicking an entry on the Recent Items menu.

1. **Click the Start button 🪟 on the taskbar**

   The Start menu opens, as shown in Figure A-2. If the taskbar is hidden, you can display it by pointing to the bottom of the screen. Depending on your taskbar property settings, the taskbar may be displayed at all times, or only when you point to that area of the screen. For more information, or to change your taskbar properties, consult your instructor or technical support person.

2. **Point to All Programs, click Microsoft Office, then click Microsoft Office Word 2007**

   Microsoft Office Word 2007 starts and the program window opens on your screen.

> **QUICK TIP**
>
> It is not necessary to close one program before opening another.

3. **Click 🪟 on the taskbar, point to All Programs, click Microsoft Office, then click Microsoft Office Excel 2007**

   Microsoft Office Excel 2007 starts and the program window opens, as shown in Figure A-3. Word is no longer visible, but it remains open. The taskbar displays a button for each open program and document. Because this Excel document is **active**, or in front and available, the Microsoft Excel – Book1 button on the taskbar appears in a darker shade.

4. **Click Document1 – Microsoft Word on the taskbar**

   Clicking a button on the taskbar activates that program and document. The Word program window is now in front, and the Document1 – Microsoft Word taskbar button appears shaded.

> **QUICK TIP**
>
> If there isn't room on your taskbar to display the entire name of each button, you can point to any button to see the full name in a Screentip.

5. **Click 🪟 on the taskbar, point to All Programs, click Microsoft Office, then click Microsoft Office PowerPoint 2007**

   Microsoft Office PowerPoint 2007 starts, and becomes the active program.

6. **Click Microsoft Excel – Book1 on the taskbar**

   Excel is now the active program.

> **QUICK TIP**
>
> As you work in Windows, your computer adapts to your activities. You may notice that after clicking the Start button, the name of the program you want to open appears in the Start menu; if so, you can click it to start the program.

7. **Click 🪟 on the taskbar, point to All Programs, click Microsoft Office, then click Microsoft Office Access 2007**

   Microsoft Office Access 2007 starts, and becomes the active program.

8. **Point to the taskbar to display it, if necessary**

   Four Office programs are open simultaneously.

9. **Click the Office button 🪟, then click Exit Access, as shown in Figure A-4**

   Access closes, leaving Excel active and Word and PowerPoint open.

FIGURE A-2: Start menu

FIGURE A-3: Excel program window and Windows taskbar

Excel button
on taskbar

Word button
on taskbar

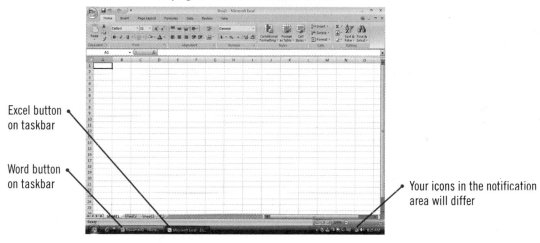

Your icons in the notification
area will differ

FIGURE A-4: Exiting Microsoft Office Access

Microsoft
Office button

Exit Access
button

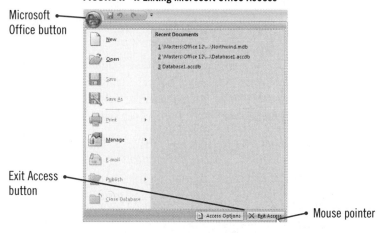

Mouse pointer

Using shortcut keys to move between Office programs

As an alternative to the Windows taskbar, you can use a keyboard shortcut to move among open Office programs. The [Alt][Tab] keyboard combination lets you either switch quickly to the next open program, or choose one from a palette. To switch immediately to the next open program, press [Alt][Tab]. To choose from all open programs, press and hold [Alt], then press and release [Tab] without releasing [Alt]. A palette opens on screen, displaying the icon and filename of each open program and file. Each time you press [Tab] while holding [Alt], the selection cycles to the next open file. Release [Alt] when the program/file you want to activate is selected.

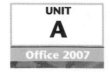

Viewing the Office 2007 User Interface

One of the benefits of using Office is that the programs have much in common, making them easy to learn and making it simple to move from one to another. Individual Office programs have always shared many features, but the innovations in the Office 2007 user interface mean even greater similarity among them all. That means you can also use your knowledge of one program to get up to speed in another. A **user interface** is a collective term for all the ways you interact with a software program. The user interface in Office 2007 includes a more intuitive way of choosing commands, working with files, and navigating in the program window. ▰▰▰▰ Familiarize yourself with some of the common interface elements in Office by examining the PowerPoint program window.

STEPS

QUICK TIP

In addition to the standard tabs on the ribbon, **contextual tabs** open when needed to complete a specific task; they appear in an accent color, and close when no longer needed.

1. **Click Microsoft PowerPoint – [Presentation1] on the taskbar**

    PowerPoint becomes the active program. Refer to Figure A-5 to identify common elements of the Office user interface. The **document window** occupies most of the screen. In PowerPoint, a blank slide appears in the document window, so you can build your slide show. At the top of every Office program window is a **title bar**, which displays the document and program name. Below the title bar is the **Ribbon**, which displays commands you're likely to need for the current task. Commands are organized into **tabs**. The tab names appear at the top of the Ribbon, and the active tab appears in front with its name highlighted. The Ribbon in every Office program includes tabs specific to the program, but all include a Home tab on the far left, for the most popular tasks in that program.

2. **Click the Office button** ⊙

    The Office menu opens. This menu contains commands common to most Office programs, such as opening a file, saving a file, and closing the current program. Next to the Office button is the **Quick Access toolbar**, which includes buttons for common Office commands.

TROUBLE

If you accidentally click the wrong command and an unwanted dialog box opens, press [Esc].

3. **Click** ⊙ **again to close it, then point to the Save button** 🖫 **on the Quick Access toolbar, *but do not click it***

    You can point to any button in Office to see a description; this is a good way to learn the available choices.

4. **Click the Design tab on the Ribbon**

    To display a different tab, you click its name on the Ribbon. Each tab arranges related commands into **groups** to make features easy to find. The Themes group displays available themes in a **gallery**, or palette of choices you can browse. Many groups contain a **dialog box launcher**, an icon you can click to open a dialog box or task pane for the current group, which offers an alternative way to choose commands.

QUICK TIP

Live Preview is available in many galleries and palettes throughout Office.

5. **Move the mouse pointer** ⌖ **over the Aspect theme in the Themes group as shown in Figure A-6, *but do not click the mouse button***

    Because you have not clicked the theme, you have not actually made any changes to the slide. With the **Live Preview** feature, you can point to a choice, see the results right in the document, and then decide whether you want to make the change.

QUICK TIP

If you accidentally click a theme, click the Undo button ↶ on the Quick Access toolbar.

6. **Move** ⌖ **away from the Ribbon and towards the slide**

    If you clicked the Aspect theme, it would be applied to this slide. Instead, the slide remains unchanged.

7. **Point to the Zoom slider** ▽ **on the status bar, then drag** ▽ **to the right until the Zoom percentage reads 166%**

    The slide display is enlarged. Zoom tools are located on the status bar. You can drag the slider or click the plus and minus buttons to zoom in/out on an area of interest. The percentage tells you the zoom effect.

8. **Drag the Zoom slider** ▽ **on the status bar to the left until the Zoom percentage reads 73%**

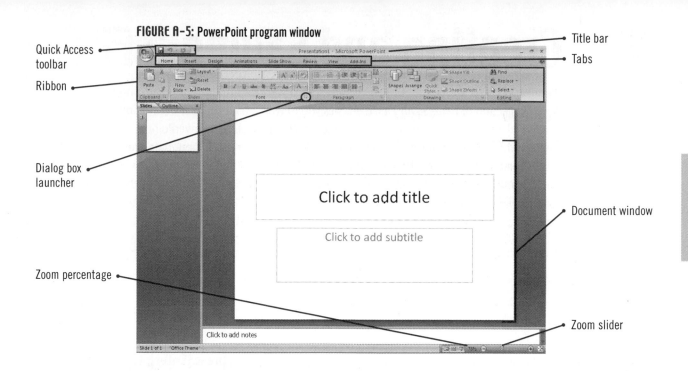

FIGURE A-5: PowerPoint program window

Quick Access toolbar

Ribbon

Dialog box launcher

Zoom percentage

Title bar

Tabs

Document window

Zoom slider

Click to add title

Click to add subtitle

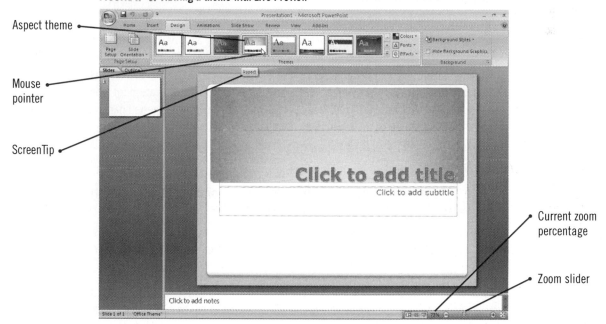

FIGURE A-6: Viewing a theme with Live Preview

Aspect theme

Mouse pointer

ScreenTip

Current zoom percentage

Zoom slider

Click to add title

Click to add subtitle

Customizing the Quick Access toolbar

You can customize the Quick Access toolbar to display your favorite commands. To do so, click the Customize Quick Access Toolbar button ▼ in the title bar, then click the command you want to add. If you don't see the command in the list, click More Commands to open the Customize tab of the Options dialog box. In the Options dialog box, use the Choose commands from list to choose a category, click the desired command in the list on the left, click Add to add it to the Quick Access toolbar, then click OK. To remove a button from the toolbar, click the name in the list on the right, then click Remove. To add a command to the Quick Access toolbar on the fly, simply right-click the button on the Ribbon, then click Add to Quick Access Toolbar on the shortcut menu. You can also use the Customize Quick Access Toolbar button to move the toolbar below the ribbon, by clicking Show Below the Ribbon, or to minimize the Ribbon so it takes up less space onscreen. If you click Minimize the Ribbon, the Ribbon is minimized to display only the tabs. When you click a tab, the Ribbon opens so you can choose a command; once you choose a command, the Ribbon closes again, and only the tabs are visible.

Creating and Saving a File

When working in a program, one of the first things you need to do is to create and save a file. A **file** is a stored collection of data. Saving a file enables you to work on a project now, then put it away and work on it again later. In some Office programs, including Word, Excel, and PowerPoint, a new file is automatically created when you start the program, so all you have to do is enter some data and save it. In Access, you must expressly create a file before you enter any data. You should give your files meaningful names and save them in an appropriate location, so they're easy to find. 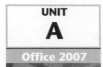 Use Microsoft Word to familiarize yourself with the process of creating and saving a document. First you'll type some notes about a possible location for a corporate meeting, then you'll save the information for later use.

STEPS

1. **Click** Document1 – Microsoft Word **on the taskbar**

2. **Type** Locations for Corporate Meeting, **then press [Enter] twice**

   The text appears in the document window, and a cursor blinks on a new blank line. The cursor indicates where the next typed text will appear.

3. **Type** Las Vegas, NV, **press [Enter],** type Orlando, FL, **press [Enter],** type Chicago, IL, **press [Enter] twice, then type your name**

   Compare your document to Figure A-7.

> **QUICK TIP**
>
> A filename can be up to 255 characters, including a file extension, and can include upper- or lowercase characters and spaces, but not ?, ", /, \, <, >, *, |, or :.

4. **Click the** Save button 🔲 **on the Quick Access toolbar**

   Because this is the first time you are saving this document, the Save As dialog box opens, as shown in Figure A-8. The Save As dialog box includes options for assigning a filename and storage location. Once you save a file for the first time, clicking 🔲 saves any changes to the file *without* opening the Save As dialog box, because no additional information is needed. In the Address bar, Office displays the default location for where to save the file, but you can change to any location. In the File name field, Office displays a suggested name for the document based on text in the file, but you can enter a different name.

> **QUICK TIP**
>
> You can create a desktop icon that you can double-click to both launch a program and open a document, by saving it to the desktop.

5. **Type** Potential Corporate Meeting Locations

   The text you type replaces the highlighted text.

6. **In the Save As dialog box, use the Address bar or Navigation pane to navigate to the drive and folder where you store your Data Files**

   Many students store files on a flash drive or Zip drive, but you can also store files on your computer, a network drive, or any storage device indicated by your instructor or technical support person.

> **QUICK TIP**
>
> To create a new blank file when a file is open, click the Office button, click New, then click Create.

7. **Click** Save

   The Save As dialog box closes, the new file is saved to the location you specified, then the name of the document appears in the title bar, as shown in Figure A-9. (You may or may not see a file extension.) See Table A-1 for a description of the different types of files you create in Office, and the file extensions associated with each. You can save a file in an earlier version of a program by choosing from the list of choices in the Save as type list arrow in the Save As dialog box.

TABLE A-1: Common filenames and default file extensions

File created in	is called a	and has the default extension
Excel	workbook	.xlsx
Word	document	.docx
Access	database	.accdb
PowerPoint	presentation	.pptx

FIGURE A-7: Creating a document in Word

Save button

Your name should appear here

Insertion point

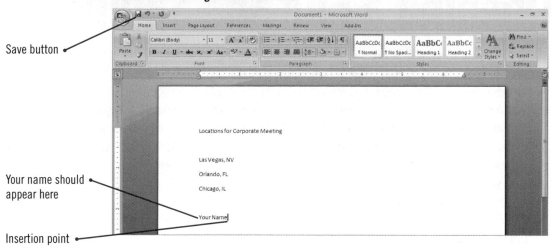

FIGURE A-8: Save As dialog box

Address bar

Navigation pane; your links and Folders setting may differ

File name field; your computer may not be set to display file extensions

Previous Locations list arrow

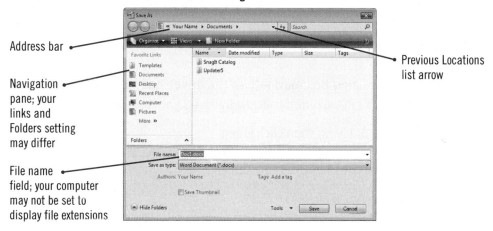

FIGURE A-9: Named Word document

Name appears in title bar

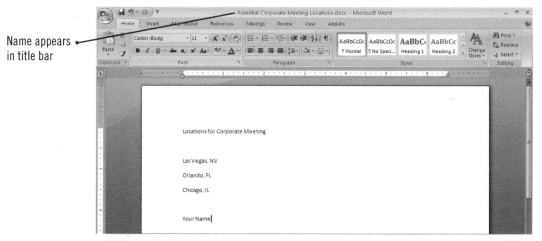

Office 2007

Using the Office Clipboard

You can use the Office Clipboard to cut and copy items from one Office program and paste them into others. The Clipboard can store a maximum of 24 items. To access it, open the Office Clipboard task pane by clicking the launcher in the Clipboard group in the Home tab. Each time you copy a selection, it is saved in the Office Clipboard. Each entry in the Office Clipboard includes an icon that tells you the program in which it was created. To paste an entry, click in the document where you want it to appear, then click the item in the Office Clipboard. To delete an item from the Office Clipboard, right-click the item, then click Delete.

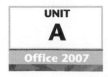

Opening a File and Saving it with a New Name

In many cases as you work in Office, you start with a blank document, but often you need to use an existing file. It might be a file you or a co-worker created earlier as a work-in-progress, or it could be a complete document that you want to use as the basis for another. For example, you might want to create a budget for this year using the budget you created last year; you could type in all the categories and information from scratch, or you could open last year's budget, save it with a new name, and just make changes to update it for the current year. By opening the existing file and saving it with the Save As command, you create a duplicate that you can modify to your heart's content, while the original file remains intact. ▰▰▰▰ Use Excel to open an existing workbook file, and save it with a new name so the original remains unchanged.

STEPS

1. **Click Microsoft Excel – Book1 on the taskbar, click the Office button ⊛, then click Open**

   The Open dialog box opens, where you can navigate to any drive or folder location accessible to your computer to locate a file.

2. **In the Open dialog box, navigate to the drive and folder where you store your Data Files**

   The files available in the current folder are listed, as shown in Figure A-10. This folder contains one file.

3. **Click OFFICE A-1.xlsx, then click Open**

   The dialog box closes and the file opens in Excel. An Excel file is an electronic spreadsheet, so it looks different from a Word document or a PowerPoint slide.

4. **Click ⊛, then click Save As**

   The Save As dialog box opens, and the current filename is highlighted in the File name text box. Using the Save As command enables you to create a copy of the current, existing file with a new name. This action preserves the original file, and creates a new file that you can modify.

5. **Navigate to the drive and folder where your Data Files are stored if necessary, type Budget for Corporate Meeting in the File name text box, as shown in Figure A-11, then click Save**

   A copy of the existing document is created with the new name. The original file, Office A-1.xlsx, closes automatically.

6. **Click cell A19, type your name, then press [Enter], as shown in Figure A-12**

   In Excel, you enter data in cells, which are formed by the intersection of a row and a column. Cell A19 is at the intersection of column A and row 19. When you press [Enter], the cell pointer moves to cell A20.

7. **Click the Save button ▣ on the Quick Access toolbar**

   Your name appears in the worksheet, and your changes to the file are saved.

Exploring File Open options

You might have noticed that the Open button on the Open dialog box includes an arrow. In a dialog box, if a button includes an arrow you can click the button to invoke the command, or you can click the arrow to choose from a list of related commands. The Open button list arrow includes several related commands, including Open Read-Only and Open as Copy. Clicking Open Read-Only opens a file that you can only save by saving it with a new name; you cannot save changes to the original file. Clicking Open as Copy creates a copy of the file already saved and named with the word "Copy" in the title. Like the Save As command, these commands provide additional ways to use copies of existing files while ensuring that original files do not get inadvertently changed.

FIGURE A-10: Open dialog box

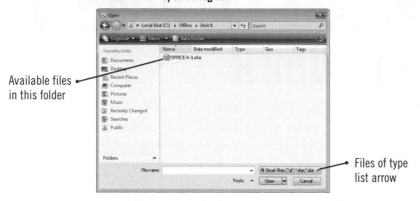

Available files
in this folder

Files of type
list arrow

FIGURE A-11: Save As dialog box

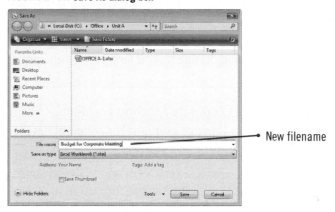

New filename

FIGURE A-12: Adding your name to the worksheet

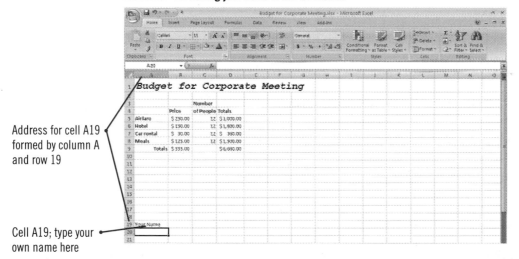

Address for cell A19
formed by column A
and row 19

Cell A19; type your
own name here

Working in Compatibility mode

Not everyone upgrades to the newest version of Office. As a general rule, new software versions are **backward-compatible**, meaning that documents saved by an older version can be read by newer software. The reverse is not always true, so Office 2007 includes a feature called Compatibility mode. When you open a file created in an earlier version of Office, "Compatibility Mode" appears in the title bar, letting you know the file was created in an earlier, but usable version of the program. If you are working with someone who may not be using the newest version of the software, you can avoid possible incompatibility problems by saving your file in

another, earlier format. To do this, click the Office button, point to the Save As command, then click a choice on the Save As submenu. For example, if you're working in Excel, click Excel 97-2003 Workbook format. When the Save As dialog box opens, you'll notice that the Save as type box reads "Excel 97-2003 Workbook" instead of the default "Excel Workbook." To see more file format choices, such as Excel 97-2003 Template or Microsoft Excel 5.0/95 Workbook, click Other Formats on the Save As submenu. In the Save As dialog box, click the Save as type button, click the choice you think matches what your co-worker is using, then click Save.

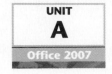

Viewing and Printing Your Work

If your computer is connected to a printer or a print server, you can easily print any Office document. Printing can be as simple as clicking a button, or as involved as customizing the print job by printing only selected pages or making other choices, and/or **previewing** the document to see exactly what a document will look like when it is printed. (In order for printing and previewing to work, a printer must be installed.) In addition to using Print Preview, each Microsoft Office program lets you switch among various **views** of the document window, to show more or fewer details or a different combination of elements that make it easier to complete certain tasks, such as formatting or reading text. You can also increase or decrease your view of a document, so you can see more or less of it on the screen at once. Changing your view of a document does not affect the file in any way, it affects only the way it looks on screen. ▨▨▨ Experiment with changing your view of a Word document, and then preview and print your work.

STEPS

1. **Click Potential Corporate Meeting Locations – Microsoft Word on the taskbar**

   Word becomes the active program, and the document fills the screen.

2. **Click the View tab on the Ribbon**

   In most Office programs, the View tab on the Ribbon includes groups and commands for changing your view of the current document. You can also change views using the View buttons on the status bar.

3. **Click Web Layout button in the Document Views group on the View tab**

   The view changes to Web Layout view, as shown in Figure A-13. This view shows how the document will look if you save it as a Web page.

> **QUICK TIP**
> You can also use the Zoom button in the Zoom group of the View tab to enlarge or reduce a document's appearance.

4. **Click the Zoom in button ⊕ on the status bar eight times until the zoom percentage reads 180%**

   Zooming in, or choosing a higher percentage, makes a document appear bigger on screen, but less of it fits on the screen at once; **zooming out**, or choosing a lower percentage, lets you see more of the document but at a reduced size.

5. **Drag the Zoom slider ▯ on the status bar to the center mark**

   The Zoom slider lets you zoom in and out without opening a dialog box or clicking buttons.

6. **Click the Print Layout button on the View tab**

   You return to Print Layout view, the default view in Microsoft Word.

7. **Click the Office button ⚇, point to Print, then click Print Preview**

   The Print Preview presents the most accurate view of how your document will look when printed, displaying the entire page on screen at once. Compare your screen to Figure A-14. The Ribbon in Print Preview contains a single tab, also known as a **program** tab, with commands specific to Print Preview. The commands on this tab facilitate viewing and changing overall settings such as margins and page size.

> **QUICK TIP**
> You can open the Print dialog box from any view by clicking the Office button, then clicking Print.

8. **Click the Print button on the Ribbon**

   The Print dialog box opens, as shown in Figure A-15. You can use this dialog box to change which pages to print, the number of printed copies, and even the number of pages you print on each page. If you have multiple printers from which to choose, you can change from one installed printer by clicking the Name list arrow, then clicking the name of the installed printer you want to use.

9. **Click OK, then click the Close Print Preview button on the Ribbon**

   A copy of the document prints, and Print Preview closes.

FIGURE A-13: Web Layout view

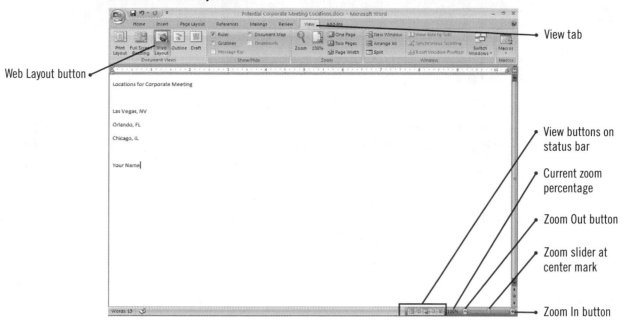

Web Layout button

View tab

View buttons on status bar

Current zoom percentage

Zoom Out button

Zoom slider at center mark

Zoom In button

FIGURE A-14: Print Preview screen

Print button

Orientation button

Zoom button

Close Print Preview button

FIGURE A-15: Print dialog box

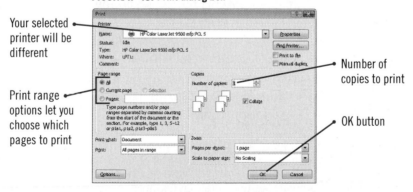

Your selected printer will be different

Print range options let you choose which pages to print

Number of copies to print

OK button

Using the Print Screen feature to create a screen capture

At some point you may want to create a screen capture. A **screen capture** is a snapshot of your screen, as if you took a picture of it with a camera. You might want to take a screen capture if an error message occurs and you want Technical Support to see exactly what's on the screen. Or perhaps your instructor wants to see what your screen looks like when you create a particular document. To create a screen capture, press [PrtScn]. (Keyboards differ, but you may

find the [PrtScn] button on the Insert key in or near your keyboard's function keys. You may have to press the [F Lock] key to enable the Function keys.) Pressing this key places a digital image of your screen in the Windows temporary storage area known as the **Clipboard**. Open the document where you want the screen capture to appear, click the Home tab on the Ribbon (if necessary), then click Paste on the Home tab. The screen capture is pasted into the document.

Getting Help and Closing a File

You can get comprehensive help at any time by pressing [F1] in an Office program. You can also get help in the form of a ScreenTip by pointing to almost any icon in the program window. When you're finished working in an Office document, you have a few choices regarding ending your work session. You can close a file or exit a program by using the Office button or by clicking a button on the title bar. Closing a file leaves a program running, while exiting a program closes all the open files in that program as well as the program itself. In all cases, Office reminds you if you try to close a file or exit a program and your document contains unsaved changes. 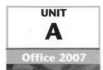 Explore the Help system in Microsoft Office, and then close your documents and exit any open programs.

STEPS

1. **Point to the Zoom button on the View tab of the Ribbon**

   A ScreenTip appears that describes how the Zoom button works.

   > **QUICK TIP**
   > If you are not connected to the Internet, the Help window displays only the help content available on your computer.

2. **Press [F1]**

   The Word Help window opens, as shown in Figure A-16, displaying the home page for help in Word. Each entry is a hyperlink you can click to open a list of related topics. This window also includes a toolbar of useful Help commands and a Search field. The connection status at the bottom of the Help window indicates that the connection to Office Online is active. Office Online supplements the help content available on your computer with a wide variety of up-to-date topics, templates, and training.

3. **Click the Getting help link in the Table of Contents pane**

   The icon next to Getting help changes and its list of subtopics expands.

   > **QUICK TIP**
   > You can also open the Help window by clicking the Microsoft Office Help button 🔘 to the right of the tabs on the Ribbon.

4. **Click the Work with the Help window link in the topics list in the left pane**

   The topic opens in the right pane, as shown in Figure A-17.

5. **Click the Hide Table of Contents button 📖 on the Help toolbar**

   The left pane closes, as shown in Figure A-18.

   > **QUICK TIP**
   > You can print the current topic by clicking the Print button 🖨 on the Help toolbar to open the Print dialog box.

6. **Click the Show Table of Contents button 📑 on the Help toolbar, scroll to the bottom of the left pane, click the Accessibility link in the Table of Contents pane, click the Use the keyboard to work with Ribbon programs link, read the information in the right pane, then click the Help window Close button**

7. **Click the Office button 🔵, then click Close; if a dialog box opens asking whether you want to save your changes, click Yes**

   The Potential Corporate Meeting Locations document closes, leaving the Word program open.

8. **Click 🔵, then click Exit Word**

   Microsoft Office Word closes, and the Excel program window is active.

9. **Click 🔵, click Exit Excel, click the PowerPoint button on the taskbar if necessary, click 🔵, then click Exit PowerPoint**

   Microsoft Office Excel and Microsoft Office PowerPoint both close.

FIGURE A-16: Word Help window

Help toolbar

Search field

Hide Table of
Contents
button

The colors
of your links
may differ

Connection status

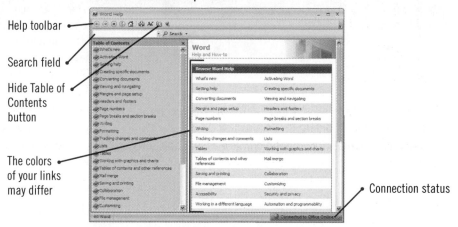

FIGURE A-17: Work with the Help window

Print button

Icon indicates
expanded topic

Work with
the Help
window link

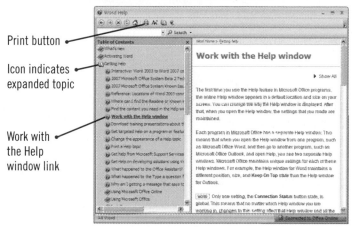

FIGURE A-18: Help window with Table of Contents closed

Show Table of
Contents button

Recovering a document

Sometimes while you are using Office, you may experience a power failure or your computer may "freeze," making it impossible to continue working. If this type of interruption occurs, each Office program has a built-in recovery feature that allows you to open and save files that were open at the time of the interruption. When you restart the program(s) after an interruption, the Document Recovery task pane opens on the left side of your screen displaying both original and recovered versions of the files that were open. If you're not sure which file to open (original or recovered), it's usually better to open the recovered file because it will contain the latest information. You can, however, open and review all versions of the file that were recovered and save the best one. Each file listed in the Document Recovery task pane displays a list arrow with options that allow you to open the file, save it as is, delete it, or show repairs made to it during recovery.

Office 2007

Practice

▼ CONCEPTS REVIEW

Label the elements of the program window shown in Figure A-19.

FIGURE A-19

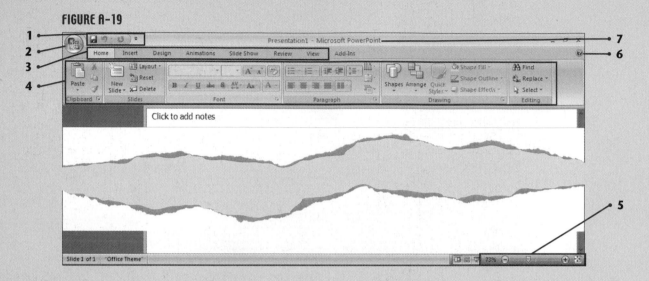

Match each project with the program for which it is best suited.

8. Microsoft Office PowerPoint
9. Microsoft Office Excel
10. Microsoft Office Word
11. Microsoft Office Access

a. Corporate expansion budget with expense projections
b. Business résumé for a job application
c. Auto parts store inventory
d. Presentation for Board of Directors meeting

▼ INDEPENDENT CHALLENGE 1

You just accepted an administrative position with a local car dealership that's recently invested in computers and is now considering purchasing Microsoft Office. You are asked to propose ways Office might help the dealership. You produce your proposal in Microsoft Word.

a. Start Word, then save the document as **Microsoft Office Proposal** in the drive and folder where you store your Data Files.

b. Type **Microsoft Office Word**, press [Enter] twice, type **Microsoft Office Excel**, press [Enter] twice, type **Microsoft Office PowerPoint**, press [Enter] twice, type **Microsoft Office Access**, press [Enter] twice, then type your name.

c. Click the line beneath each program name, type at least two tasks suited to that program, then press [Enter].

d. Save your work, then print one copy of this document.

Advanced Challenge Exercise

■ Press the [PrtScn] button to create a screen capture, then press [Ctrl][V].
■ Save and print the document.

e. Exit Word.

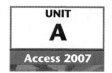

Getting Started with Access 2007

In this unit, you will learn the purpose, advantages, and terminology of Microsoft Office Access 2007, the relational database program in Microsoft Office 2007. You will create and modify tables, the basic building blocks of an Access relational database. You'll also navigate, enter, update, preview, and print data. Mark Rock is the tour developer for United States group travel at Quest Specialty Travel (QST), a tour company that specializes in cultural tourism and adventure travel. Mark uses Access to store, maintain, and analyze customer and tour information.

OBJECTIVES

Understand relational databases

Open a database

Enter data

Edit data

Create a database

Create a table

Create primary keys

Relate two tables

Print a datasheet

Understanding Relational Databases

Microsoft Office Access 2007 is relational database software that runs on the Windows operating system. You use **relational database software** to manage data that is organized into lists, such as information about customers, products, vendors, employees, projects, or sales. Many small companies track customer, inventory, and sales information in a spreadsheet program such as Microsoft Office Excel. While Excel does offer some list management features, Access provides many more tools and advantages, mainly due to the "relational" nature of the lists that Access manages. Table A-1 compares the two programs. 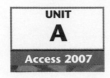 You and Mark Rock review the advantages of database software over spreadsheets for managing lists of information.

DETAILS

The advantages of using Access for database management include:

- **Duplicate data is minimized**

  Figures A-1 and A-2 compare how you might store sales data in a single Excel spreadsheet list versus three related Access tables. Note that with Access, you do not have to reenter information such as a customer's name and address or product description every time a sale is made, because lists can be linked, or "related," in relational database software.

- **Information is more accurate, reliable, and consistent because duplicate data is minimized**

  The relational nature of data stored in an Access database allows you to minimize duplicate data entry, which creates more accurate, reliable, and consistent information.

- **Data entry is faster and easier using Access forms**

  Data entry forms (screen layouts) make data entry faster and easier than entering data in a spreadsheet.

- **Information can be viewed and sorted in many ways using Access queries, forms, and reports**

  In Access, you can save queries (questions about the data), data entry forms, and reports, allowing you to use them over and over without performing extra work to re-create a particular view of the data.

- **Information is more secure using Access passwords and security features**

  Access databases can be password protected, and users can be given different privileges to view or update data.

- **Several users can share and edit information simultaneously**

  Unlike spreadsheets or word processing documents, Access databases are inherently multiuser. More than one person can be entering, updating, and analyzing data at the same time.

FIGURE A-1: Using a spreadsheet to organize sales data

	A	B	C	D	E	F	G	H	I	J	K	L	M	N	O	P
1	Cust No	First	Last	Street	City	State	Zip	Phone	Date	Invoice	Product No	Artist	Name	Format	Tracks	Cost
2	1	Kusong	Tse	222 Elm	Topeka	KS	66111	913-555-0000	8/1/2006	8111	11-222	Michael Smith	Always	CD	14	15
3	2	Paige	Denver	400 Oak	Lenexa	MO	60023	816-555-8877	8/1/2006	8112	11-222	Michael Smith	Always	CD	14	15
4	1	Kusong	Tse	222 Elm	Topeka	KS	66111	913-555-0000	8/2/2006	8113	22-333	Gold Flakes	Avalon	CD	13	14
5	3	Caitlyn	Baily	111 Ash	Ames	IA	50010	515-555-3333	8/3/2006	8114	22-333	Gold Flakes	Avalon	CD	13	14
6	2	Paige	Denver	400 Oak	Lenexa	MO	60023	816-555-8877	8/4/2006	8115	44-1111	Lungwort	Sounds	CD	15	13
7	3	Caitlyn	Baily	111 Ash	Ames	IA	50010	515-555-3333	8/4/2006	8116	44-1111	Lungwort	Sounds	CD	15	13
8	4	Max	Royal	500 Pine	Manilla	NE	55123	827-555-4422	8/5/2006	8117	44-1111	Lungwort	Sounds	CD	15	13
9																

Duplicate customer data is entered each time an existing customer makes an additional purchase

Duplicate product data is entered each time the same product is sold more than once

FIGURE A-2: Using a relational database to organize sales data

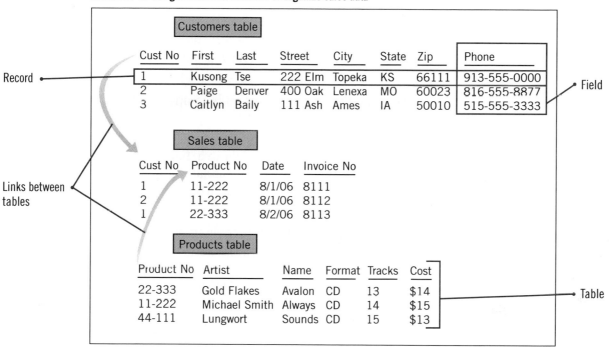

Record

Field

Links between tables

Table

TABLE A-1: Comparing Excel to Access

feature	Excel	Access
Layout	Provides a natural tabular layout for easy data entry	Provides a natural tabular layout as well as the ability to create customized data entry screens
Storage	Limited to approximately 65,000 records per sheet	Stores any number of records up to 2 GB
Linked tables	Manages single lists of information	Allows links between lists of information to reduce data redundancy
Reporting	Limited to the current spreadsheet arrangement of data	Creates and saves multiple presentations of data
Security	Limited to file security options such as marking the file "read-only" or protecting a range of cells	Allows users to access only the records and fields they need
Multiuser capabilities	Does not easily allow multiple users to simultaneously enter and update data	Allows multiple users to simultaneously enter and update data
Data entry	Provides limited data entry screens	Provides the ability to create extensive data entry screens called forms

Opening a Database

You can start Access from the Start menu, which opens when you click the Start button on the Windows taskbar, or from an Access shortcut icon on the desktop. Access opens to the Getting Started with Microsoft Office Access page, which shows different ways to work with Access. To open a specific database in Access, you can click a database in the Open Recent Database list or click the More link to navigate to a different database. You can also start Access and open a database at the same time by opening the database directly from a My Computer or Windows Explorer window. [image] Mark Rock has entered some tour information in a database called Quest-A. He asks you to start Access and review this database.

STEPS

TROUBLE
If a Security Warning bar appears below the Ribbon, click the Options button, click Enable this content, then click OK.

1. **Start Access**

   Access starts and opens the Getting Started with Microsoft Office Access page, shown in Figure A-3, which helps you create a new database from a template, create a new blank database, or open an existing database.

2. **Click the More link in the Open Recent Database list, navigate to the drive and folder where you store your Data Files, click the Quest-A.accdb database file, click Open, then click the Maximize button [] if the Access window is not already maximized**

   The Quest-A database contains two tables of data named States and Tours.

TROUBLE
If the Navigation Pane is not open, click the Shutter Bar Open/Close button [>>] to open it and view database table names.

3. **In the Navigation Pane, double-click the Tours table to open it, then click [] on the Tours table**

   The Tours table opens in Datasheet View, as shown in Figure A-4. **Tables** are the fundamental building blocks of a relational database because they store all of the data. **Datasheet View** displays the data in a table in a spreadsheet-like view of fields and records called the **datasheet**. The Tours datasheet contains six fields and 21 records. **Field names** are listed at the top of each column. Important database terminology is summarized in Table A-2.

QUICK TIP
For more information on using features of the Access window that are new to Microsoft Office 2007, see the unit "Getting Started with Office 2007."

4. **In the Navigation Pane, double-click the States table to open it**

   The States table contains only two fields, StateAbbreviation and StateName, and four records. By using a separate States table, you only need to enter full state names such as Colorado and Florida once, rather than every time you enter a record for a particular state in the Tours table. The Tours and States tables are linked together via the common StateAbbreviation field. Later in this unit, you learn more about how multiple lists of information, defined as tables in Access, are linked to create relational databases.

FIGURE A-3: Getting Started with Microsoft Office Access page

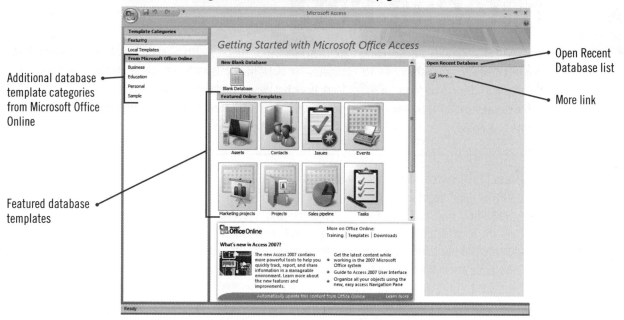

Additional database template categories from Microsoft Office Online

Featured database templates

Open Recent Database list

More link

FIGURE A-4: Tours table

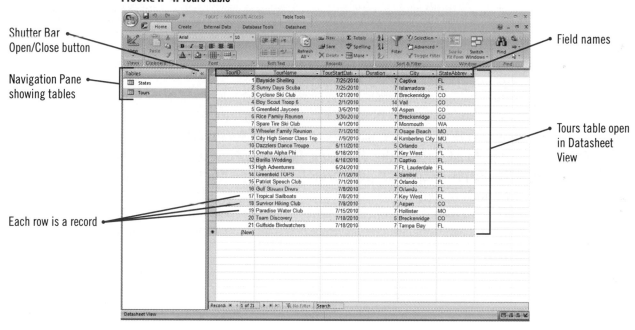

Shutter Bar Open/Close button

Navigation Pane showing tables

Each row is a record

Field names

Tours table open in Datasheet View

TABLE A-2: Important database terminology

term	description
Field	The smallest unit of data organization; consists of a specific category of data such as a customer's name, city, state, or phone number
Record	A group of related fields that describe a person, place, or thing
Key field	A field that contains unique information for each record, such as a customer number for a customer
Table	A collection of records for a single subject
Database	A collection of tables associated with a general topic
Relational database	An Access database with multiple tables that are linked together by a common field
Objects	The parts of an Access database that help you view, edit, manage, and analyze the data, such as **tables, queries, forms, reports, macros,** and **modules**

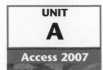

Entering Data

Your skill in navigating and entering data is a key to your success with a relational database. You use either mouse or keystroke techniques to navigate the data in the table's datasheet, which displays fields as columns and records as rows. ▨▨▨▨▨ Mark Rock has developed some new tours for Quest Specialty Travel, and asks you to add this tour information by entering new records in the States and Tours tables of the Quest-A database.

STEPS

1. **Press [Tab] twice, then press [Enter] twice**

    Both the [Tab] and [Enter] keys move the focus to the next field. The **focus** refers to which data you would edit if you started typing. The field name and record selector button for the field and record that have the focus are highlighted with a different color. When you navigate to the last field of the record, pressing [Tab] or [Enter] advances the focus to the first field of the next record. You can also use the Next record ▶ and Previous record ◀ **navigation buttons** on the navigation bar in the lower-left corner of the datasheet to navigate the records. The **Current Record** text box on the navigation bar tells you the number of the current record as well as the total number of records in the datasheet.

2. **Click the StateAbbrev field below WA to position the insertion point to enter a new record**

    You can also use the New (blank) record button ▶✱ on the navigation bar to move to a new record. You enter new records at the end of the datasheet. You learn how to sort and reorder them later. A complete list of navigation keystrokes is shown in Table A-3.

3. **Type CA, press [Tab], then type California**

    Access saves data automatically as you move among records or within the database. With the California record entered in the States table, you're ready to enter a new tour record in the Tours table.

4. **Double-click the Tours table in the Navigation Pane, click (New) in the last row, press [Enter] to advance to the TourName field, type Perfect Waves, press [Enter], type 7/16/10, press [Enter], type 5, press [Enter], type Hunt Beach, press [Enter], type CA, then press [Enter]**

    The new tour record you entered is shown in Figure A-5. The TourID field is an **AutoNumber** field, which means that Access automatically enters the next consecutive number into the field as it creates the record.

Changing from Navigation mode to Edit mode

If you navigate to another area of the datasheet by clicking with the mouse pointer instead of pressing [Tab] or [Enter], you change from **Navigation mode** to Edit mode. In **Edit mode**, Access assumes that you are trying to make changes to the current field value, so keystrokes such as [Ctrl][End], [Ctrl][Home], [←], and [→] move the insertion point *within* the field. To return to Navigation mode, press [Tab] or [Enter] (thus moving the focus to the next field), or press [↑] or [↓] (thus moving the focus to a different record).

FIGURE A-5: New record in the Tours table

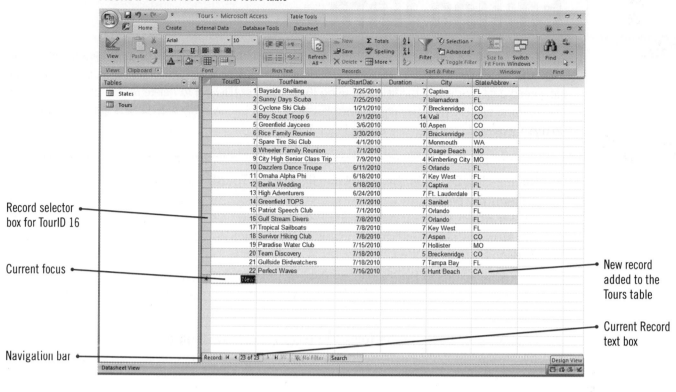

Record selector box for TourID 16

Current focus

Navigation bar

New record added to the Tours table

Current Record text box

TABLE A-3: Navigation mode keyboard shortcuts

shortcut key	moves to the
[Tab], [Enter], or [→]	Next field of the current record
[Shift][Tab] or [←]	Previous field of the current record
[Home]	First field of the current record
[End]	Last field of the current record
[Ctrl][Home] or [F5]	First field of the first record
[Ctrl][End]	Last field of the last record
[↑]	Current field of the previous record
[↓]	Current field of the next record

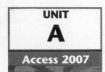
Editing Data

Updating existing information is another critical data management task. To change the contents of an existing record, click the field you want to change, then type the new information. You can delete unwanted data by clicking the field and using [Backspace] or [Delete] to delete text to the left or right of the insertion point. Other data-entry keystrokes are summarized in Table A-4. ⬛⬛⬛ Mark Rock asks you to make some corrections to the records in the Tours table.

STEPS

1. **Double-click Dance in the TourName field of the TourID 10 record, and press the [Delete] key twice**

   You deleted both the word "Dance" and the extra space between "Dazzlers" and "Troupe." Access automatically saves new records and changes to existing data as soon as you move to another record or close the datasheet.

2. **Click after Barilla in the TourName field of TourID 12 record, and type -Cavuto**

   When you are editing a record, the **edit record symbol**, which looks like a small pencil, appears in the record selector box to the left of the current record, as shown in Figure A-6, to indicate you are in Edit mode.

3. **Double-click Speech in the TourID 15 record, and type Debate**

   You use the same editing techniques in an Access datasheet that you use in an Excel spreadsheet or Word document.

4. **Click the TourStartDate field in the TourID 22 record, click the Calendar icon 🗒, then navigate to and click August 27, 2010**

   The **calendar picker**, a pop-up calendar from which you can choose dates for a date field, is a new feature for Access 2007. You can also type the date directly into the field as 8/27/2010.

QUICK TIP
The ScreenTip for the Undo button displays the action you can undo.

5. **Press [Esc]**

   Pressing [Esc] once removes the current field's editing changes, so the TourStartDate changes back to 7/16/2010. Pressing [Esc] twice removes all changes to the current record. Once you move to another record, the edits are saved, you return to Navigation mode, and you can no longer use [Esc] to remove editing changes to the current record. You can, however, click the Undo button 🔄 on the Quick Access toolbar to undo the last change you made.

6. **Click the record selector for the TourID 16 record, click the Delete button in the Records group on the Home tab, then click Yes**

   A message warns that you cannot undo a record deletion operation. Notice that the Undo button is dimmed, indicating that it cannot be used now.

7. **Click the Close button ✕ on the title bar to close both the Quest-A.accdb database and Access 2007**

   Because Access saves data as you work in a database, you are not prompted to save data when you close the database or the Access itself.

Resizing and moving datasheet columns

You can resize the width of a field in a datasheet by dragging the **column separator**, the thin line that separates the field names to the left or right. The pointer changes to ⟷ as you make the field wider or narrower. Release the mouse button when you have resized the field. To adjust the column width to accommodate the widest entry in the field, double-click the column separator. To move a column, click the field name to select the entire column, then drag the field name left or right.

FIGURE A-6: Edit mode

Edit record symbol

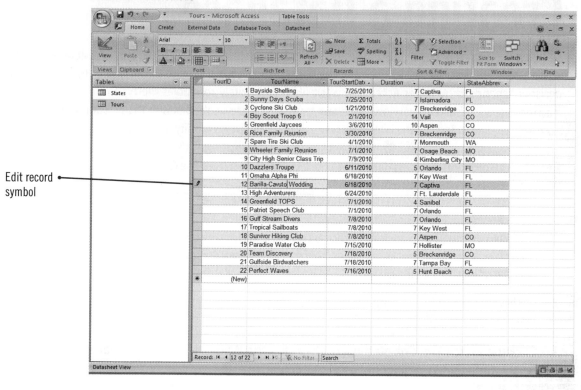

TABLE A-4: Edit mode keyboard shortcuts

editing keystroke	action
[Backspace]	Deletes one character to the left of the insertion point
[Delete]	Deletes one character to the right of the insertion point
[F2]	Switches between Edit and Navigation mode
[Esc]	Undoes the change to the current field
[Esc][Esc]	Undoes all changes to the current record
[F7]	Starts the spell check feature
[Ctrl][']	Inserts the value from the same field in the previous record into the current field
[Ctrl][;]	Inserts the current date in a Date field

Access 2007

Creating a Database

You can create a new database using an Access **template**, a sample database provided within the Microsoft Access program, or you can start with a blank database to create a database from scratch. Your decision depends on whether Access has a template that closely resembles the type of data you plan to manage. If it does, building your own database from a template might be faster than creating the database from scratch. Regardless of which method you use, you can always modify the database later, tailoring it to meet your specific needs. ▓▓▓▓ Mark Rock wants to organize Quest's clients, prospects, and vendors, and asks you to create an Access database to track contacts. You'll use the Contacts template to get started.

STEPS

QUICK TIP
To create a new blank database, use the Blank Database icon.

TROUBLE
If an Access Help window or Security Warning bar opens, close it. If a Microsoft Office Genuine Advantage dialog box opens, click Continue.

1. **Start Access**

   The "Getting Started with Microsoft Office Access" page opens, which you can use to create a database from a template. Some templates are stored on your computer when you install Access, and others are available from Microsoft Office Online.

2. **In the Featured Online Templates pane click Contacts, then click Download in the lower-right corner**

3. **Click the Watch This link on the left, then click the Watch this >> link to watch a short video on the Contact Management Database template**

   A short video plays explaining some of the features of the Microsoft Contact Management Database template. Note how to use the Options button to enable content.

4. **Close the Microsoft Office Online window, the Access Help window, and the Getting Started window**

   The Contact List form opens, as shown in Figure A-7.

5. **Click the Options button, click the Enable this content option button, click OK, close the Getting Started window if it opens again, enter your own name and e-mail address for the first record, use school information for the Business Phone and Company field, use Student for the Job Title field, then press [↓]**

   Although you are entering this record in an **Access form** (an easy-to-use data entry screen) instead of directly in a table, the data is stored in the underlying table. Forms and tables are database objects, and are displayed in the Navigation Pane. The **Navigation Pane** provides a way to move between objects (tables, queries, forms, and reports) in the database. Tables are the most important objects because they physically store all of the data. Table A-5 defines the four primary Access objects—tables, queries, forms, and reports— and the icon that identifies each in the Navigation Pane. When you created this database, the Contacts template not only created the Contact List form you used to enter your name, but also the Contact Details form and two reports, Directory and Phone Book.

TROUBLE
If the Phone Book report still shows your last name instead of "Johnson," close the report by right-clicking its tab and clicking Close, then double-click the report in the Navigation Pane to reopen it.

6. **Double-click the Contacts table in the Navigation Pane, double-click your last name in the Last Name field, type Johnson, then press [↓] to save the data**

   The Contacts table appears with the record you entered using the Contact List form. All data is physically stored in Access table objects when you move from record to record, even if the data is entered through a query or form.

7. **Double-click the Phone Book report in the Navigation Pane**

   All reports that depend on this data are automatically updated, as shown in Figure A-8.

8. **Click the Close button ✕ on the title bar to close both the Contacts database and Access 2007**

FIGURE A-7: Contact List form provided by the Contacts template

Shutter Bar
Open/Close
button

Form icon

Expand
button

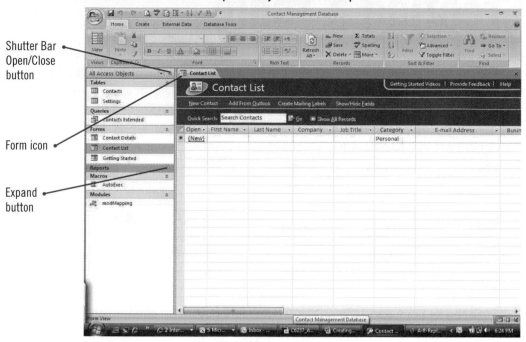

FIGURE A-8: Phone Book report provided by the Contacts template

Objects in
the Contact
database

Data edited in the
Contacts table is
updated in the
Phone Book report

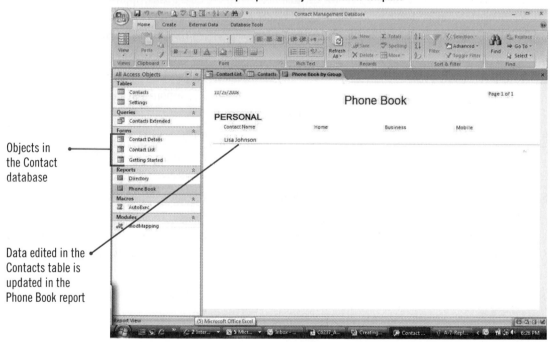

TABLE A-5: Access objects and their purpose

object	Navigation Pane icon	purpose
Table		Contains all of the raw data within the database in a spreadsheet-like view; tables are linked with a common field to create a relational database, which minimizes redundant data
Query		Allows the user to select a subset of fields or records from one or more tables; queries are created when a user has a question about the data
Form		Provides an easy-to-use data entry screen
Report		Provides a professional printout of data that can contain enhancements such as headers, footers, graphics, and calculations on groups of records

Creating a Table

After establishing your database, you often need to create a new table. You can use one of the table templates Access provides or you can create your own table from scratch. Creating a table consists of three essential tasks: meaningfully naming each field in the table, selecting an appropriate data type for each field, and naming the table itself. The **data type** determines what kind of data can be entered into a field, such as numbers, text, or dates. Data types are described in Table A-6. 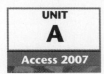 Mark Rock asks you to create a small table that lists the different types of tours Quest offers, such as Educational, Adventure, and Cultural. Because Access does not have a template for such a table, you'll create the table yourself.

1. **Reopen the Quest-A.accdb database, enable content if prompted, click the Create tab on the Ribbon, click the Table button, then click the Maximize button** ▭

   A new, blank table datasheet appears, as shown in Figure A-9, with one sample field named ID that has an AutoNumber data type. You don't need this sample field in the table, so you can rename the first field and use it to identify tour categories.

2. **Click the ID field name, then click the Rename button on the Datasheet tab**

   ID in the column header is highlighted, allowing you to enter a new field name.

3. **Type Category, then press [↓]**

   The new field, renamed Category, is now the first field. With the field named appropriately, the next step is to choose the correct data type for the field. Currently, the field has an AutoNumber data type, but because this field will store the name of each tour category, you need to change its data type to Text.

4. **Click the Data Type list arrow (which currently displays AutoNumber) on the Datasheet tab, then click Text**

   For this table, you want to create one more field called TourDescription that also has a Text data type because it will store text descriptions of each tour.

QUICK TIP

Widen the TourDescription field by dragging the resize pointer ↔ to resize the column.

5. **Double-click Add New Field, type TourDescription, then press [↓]**

   Because Text is the default data type for new fields, the TourDescription field has already been assigned with the correct data type.

6. **Click the blank cell below the Category field, type Adventure, then enter the remaining records as shown in Figure A-10**

   After naming the fields, assigning the data types, and entering the data, you save the table with an appropriate name. Table1 is the default name, but it is not very descriptive. You cannot rename a table that is open, so you'll close it and give it a descriptive name when prompted.

TROUBLE

The Close Window button for the table is on the Ribbon (not on the title bar). You can also click the Office button, then click Close to close the table.

7. **Click the Close Window button** ▨ **for the new table, click Yes, type TourCategories, then click OK**

FIGURE A-9: New blank table in Datasheet View

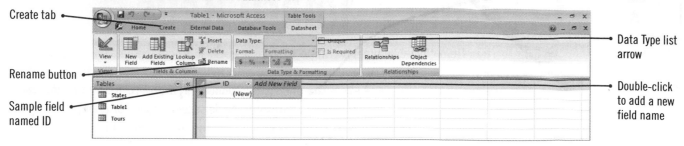

Create tab
Rename button
Sample field named ID

Data Type list arrow
Double-click to add a new field name

FIGURE A-10: Complete datasheet

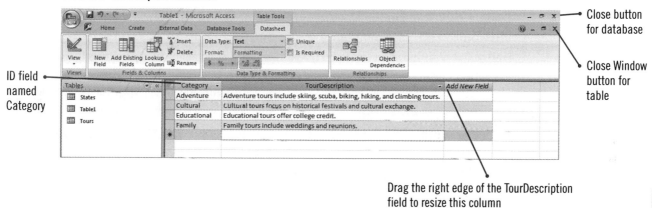

ID field named Category

Close button for database
Close Window button for table

Drag the right edge of the TourDescription field to resize this column

TABLE A-6: Data types

data type	description of data	size
Text	Text information or combinations of text and numbers, such as a street address, name, or phone number	Up to 255 characters
Memo	Lengthy text, such as comments or notes	Up to 65,535 characters
Number	Numeric information, such as quantities	Several sizes available to store numbers with varying degrees of precision
Date/Time	Dates and times	Size controlled by Access to accommodate dates and times across thousands of years (for example, 1/1/1850 and 1/1/2150 are valid dates)
Currency	Monetary values	Size controlled by Access; accommodates up to 15 digits to the left of the decimal point and four digits to the right
AutoNumber	Integers assigned by Access to sequentially order each record added to a table	Size controlled by Access
Yes/No	Only one of two values stored (Yes/No, On/Off, True/False)	Size controlled by Access
OLE Object	Office and Windows files that can be linked or embedded (OLE) such as pictures, sound clips, documents, or spreadsheets	Up to 2 GB
Attachment	Any supported file type including .jpg images, spreadsheets, and documents (new for Office 2007)	Up to 1 GB
Hyperlink	Web and e-mail addresses	Size controlled by Access

Creating Primary Keys

The **primary key field** of a table serves two important purposes. First, it contains data that uniquely identifies each record. No two records can have the exact same entry in the field designated as the primary key field. Secondly, the primary key field helps relate one table to another in a **one-to-many relationship**, where one record from one table is related to many records in the second table. For example, one state record in the States table might be related to many tours in the Tours table. In the States table, StateAbbreviation is the primary key field. This field is duplicated in the Tours table, providing the link between one state and many tours. The primary key field is always on the "one" side of a one-to-many relationship between two tables. Mark Rock asks you to check that a primary key field has been appropriately identified for each table.

STEPS

1. **Double-click Tours in the Navigation Pane, maximize the window, then click the Design View button on the Home tab**

   Design View, as shown in Figure A-11, is used to modify and define field properties that are not available in Datasheet View. You see many of a field's **properties** (characteristics that define a field) in the lower half of Design View. Some field properties, such as Field Name and Data Type, can be specified in either Datasheet View or Design View. Specifying the primary key field requires that you work in Design View.

2. **Click the TourID field if it is not already selected, then click the Primary Key button on the Design tab**

   A field designated as the primary key field for a table appears with the key icon, as shown in Figure A-12.

3. **Close and save the Tours table**

   Next, you'll use Design View to set the primary key fields for the other two tables.

4. **Double-click States in the Navigation Pane, click the Design View button, click StateAbbreviation if it is not already selected, click the Primary Key button, then close and save the States table**

   You'll use the Category field as the primary key field in the TourCategories table.

5. **Double-click TourCategories in the Navigation Pane, click the Design View button, make sure the Category field is the primary key, then close the TourCategories table**

   Now that each table has been modified to contain an appropriate primary key field, you no longer have to worry that two tour records in the Tours table could be assigned the same TourID, two states in the States table could be given the same StateAbbreviation, or two tour categories could be assigned to the same Category. In other words, assigning an appropriate primary key field to each table helps prevent you from entering incorrect and duplicate records. The second purpose of the primary key field is to help tie tables together in one-to-many relationships, which you learn about in the next lesson.

FIGURE A-11: Design View of the Tours table

Primary Key button

View button

Field Properties pane

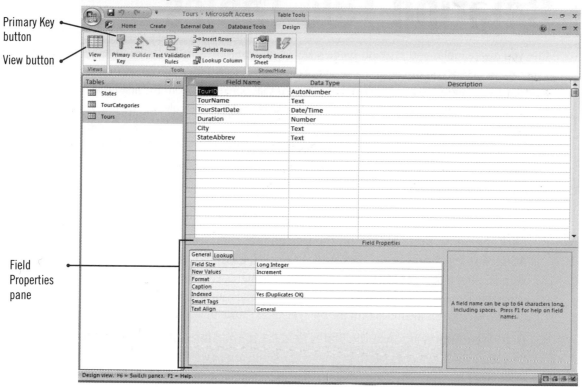

FIGURE A-12: TourID is set as the primary key field

Save button

Primary key field symbol

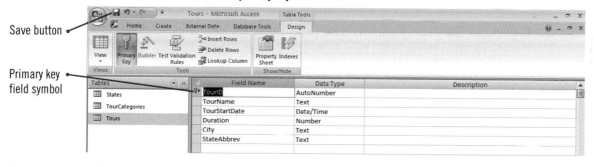

Learning about field properties

Properties are the characteristics that define the field. Two properties are required for every field: Field Name and Data Type. Many other properties, such as Field Size, Format, Caption, and Default Value, are defined in the Field Properties pane in the lower half of a table's Design View. As you add more property entries, you are generally restricting the amount or type of data that can be entered in the field, which increases data entry accuracy. For example, you might change the Field Size property for a State field to 2 in order to eliminate an incorrect entry such as FLL. Field properties change depending on the data type of the selected field. For example, there is no Field Size property for date fields, because Access controls the size of fields with a Date/Time data type.

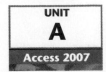

Relating Two Tables

After you create tables and establish primary key fields, you must link the tables together in one-to-many relationships before you can build queries, forms, or reports that display fields from more than one table. A one-to-many relationship between two tables means that one record from the first table is related to many records in the second table. You use a common linking field, which is always the primary key field in the table on the "one" side of the relationship, to establish this connection. ▄▄▄▟▟ Mark Rock mentions that he plans to create reports that include tour, category, and state information. To help in creating the reports, you define the one-to-many relationships between the tables of the Quest-A database.

STEPS

1. **Click the Database Tools tab on the Ribbon, then click the Relationships button**

2. **Click the Show Table button on the Design tab, click States, click Add, click Tours, click Add, click TourCategories, click Add, then click Close**

   With all three tables visible in the Relationships window, you're ready to link them together. Each table is represented by a small **field list** window that displays the names of the fields in the table. The primary key field in each table is identified with the key symbol, as shown in Figure A-13.

3. **Drag StateAbbreviation in the States field list to the StateAbbrev field in the Tours field list**

   Dragging a field from one table to another in the Relationships window links the two tables by the selected fields and opens the Edit Relationships dialog box, as shown in Figure A-14. **Referential integrity**, a set of Access rules that govern data entry, helps ensure data accuracy.

4. **Click the Enforce Referential Integrity check box in the Edit Relationships dialog box, then click Create**

   The **one-to-many line** shows the link between the StateAbbreviation field of the States table (the "one" side) and the StateAbbrev field of the Tours table (the "many" side, indicated by the **infinity symbol**). Similarly, you need to create a one-to-many relationship between the TourCategories table and the Tours table, so that one category can be associated with many tours. However, because these tables do not have a common field, you must establish one before you can join the tables.

5. **Right-click the Tours field list, click Table Design, click the cell below StateAbbrev, type Category, then press [Tab] to specify the default Text data type**

   A field added to the "many" table to help establish a one-to-many relationship is called the **foreign key field**. Now that you created the foreign key field for the link between the Tours and TourCategories, you can join the tables in a one-to-many relationship.

6. **Close and save the Tours table, drag the Category field from the TourCategories table to the Category field of the Tours table, then click Create in the Edit Relationships dialog box**

   The final Relationships window should look like Figure A-15. The relationship line between the Tours and TourCategories tables is also a one-to-many relationship, but the "one" and "many" symbols do not appear because you did not establish referential integrity on this relationship. The primary key field for the Tours table is TourID, but because it participates on the "many" side of two different one-to-many relationships, it contains two foreign key fields, StateAbbrev and Category.

7. **Close and save the Relationships window**

FIGURE A-13: Relationships window

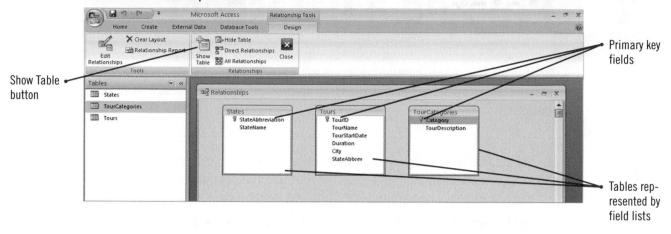

Show Table button

Primary key fields

Tables represented by field lists

FIGURE A-14: Edit Relationships dialog box

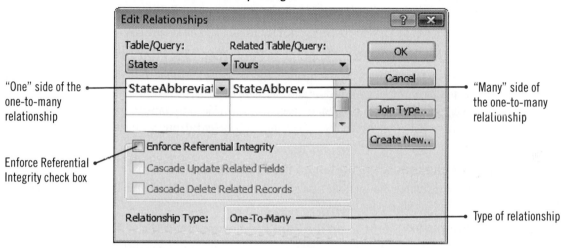

"One" side of the one-to-many relationship

Enforce Referential Integrity check box

"Many" side of the one-to-many relationship

Type of relationship

FIGURE A-15: Final Relationships window

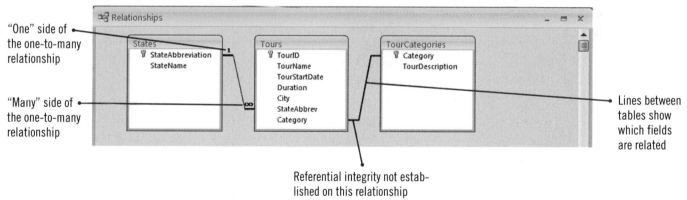

"One" side of the one-to-many relationship

"Many" side of the one-to-many relationship

Lines between tables show which fields are related

Referential integrity not established on this relationship

Enforcing referential integrity

Referential integrity is a set of rules that helps reduce invalid entries and orphan records. An **orphan record** is a record in the "many" table that doesn't have a matching entry in the linking field of the "one" table. With referential integrity enforced on a one-to-many relationship, you cannot enter a value in a foreign key field of the "many" table that does not have a match in the linking field of the "one" table. Referential integrity also prevents you from deleting a record in the "one" table if a matching entry exists in the foreign key field of the "many" table. You should enforce referential integrity on all one-to-many relationships if possible. If you are working with a database that already contains orphan records, you cannot enforce referential integrity on that relationship.

Printing a Datasheet

Printing and previewing Access data is similar to printing and previewing other types of Office documents. Previewing helps you see how the document will look when printed so you can make printing adjustments, such as changing the margins or page orientation, before printing it. 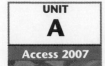 Mark Rock asks you to print the Tours datasheet.

1. **In the Navigation Pane, double-click the Tours table to open it in Datasheet View, then double-click each column separator to resize the columns to their best fit**

   One more new tour needs to be added to the list before you print it—a family reunion.

2. **Add a new record with your last name's Reunion in the TourName field, today's date in the TourStartDate field, 4 in the Duration field, your hometown in the City field, FL in the StateAbbrev field, and Family in the Category field**

   You decide to preview the datasheet before printing it to make sure it fits on one sheet of paper.

3. **Click the Office button 🔘, point to Print, then click Print Preview**

   The Tours table appears on a miniature page, as shown in Figure A-16, formatted as it will look when you print it. By previewing the datasheet, you realize that it is too wide to print on one page. (The Category and StateAbbrev fields do not appear on page 1.) You decide to try **landscape orientation** (11 inches wide by 8.5 inches tall) rather than the default **portrait orientation** (8.5 inches wide by 11 inches tall) to see if the printout fits on one page.

4. **Click the Landscape button on the Print Preview tab**

   The navigation buttons on the navigation bar in the lower-left corner in Figure A-17 are dim, indicating that the printout fits on one page.

   > **QUICK TIP**
   > Click the Close Print Preview button on the Print Preview tab to close the preview window and return to Datasheet View.

5. **Click the Print button on the Print Preview tab, then click OK**

   If you need to change printing options, you can use the Page Setup dialog box.

6. **Click the Close button ☒ on the title bar to close both the Quest-A.accdb database and Access 2007**

FIGURE A-16: Datasheet in print preview—portrait orientation

Landscape button

Not all seven fields appear on page 1

Active Next Page and Last Page buttons indicate this report contains more than one page

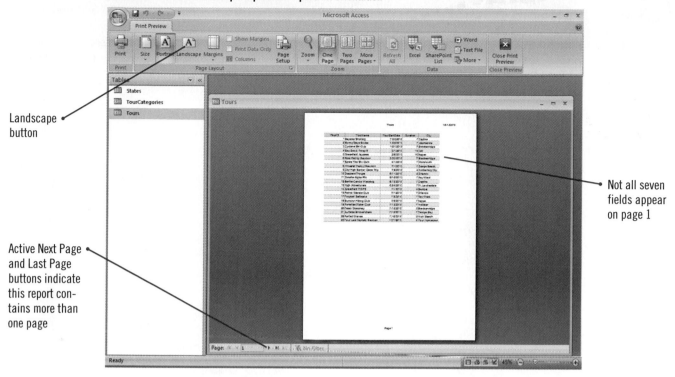

FIGURE A-17: Datasheet in print preview—landscape orientation

All fields now appear on page 1

Next Page and Last Page buttons are no longer active because the printout fits on one page

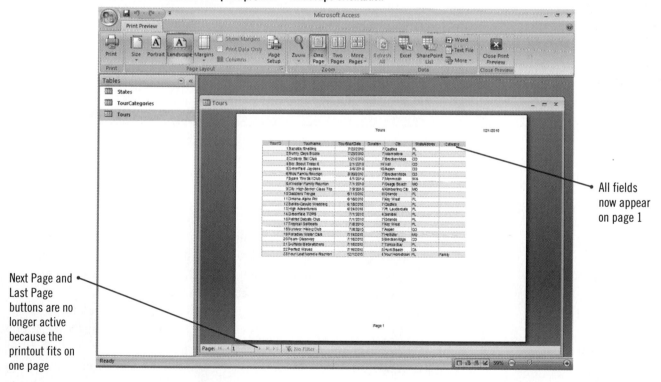

Access 2007

Practice

SAM

If you have a SAM user profile, you may have access to hands-on instruction, practice, and assessment of the skills covered in this unit. Log in to your SAM account (http://sam2007.course.com/) to launch any assigned training activities or exams that relate to the skills covered in this unit.

▼ CONCEPTS REVIEW

Label each element of the Access window shown in Figure A-18.

FIGURE A-18

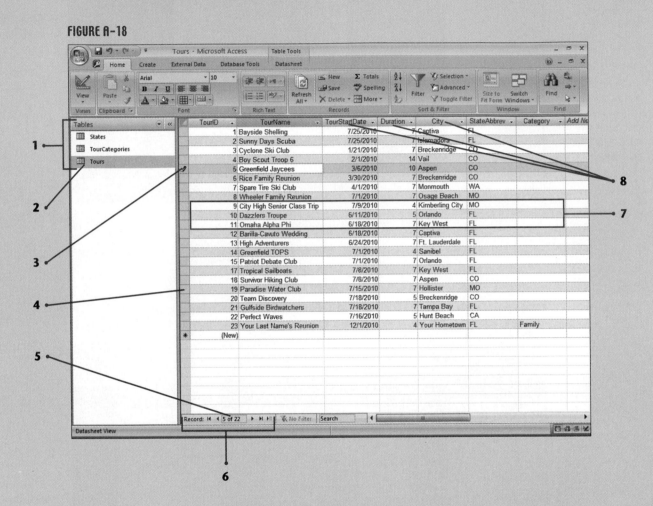

Match each term with the statement that best describes it.

9. Objects

10. Table

11. Record

12. Field

13. Datasheet

14. Form

15. Edit record symbol

a. Seven types of these are contained in an Access database and are used to enter, enhance, and use the data within the database

b. A collection of records for a single subject, such as all the customer records

c. A small pencil icon that appears in the record selector box

d. A spreadsheet-like grid that displays fields as columns and records as rows

e. A group of related fields for one item, such as all of the demographic information for one customer

f. A category of information in a table, such as a customer's name, city, or state

g. An Access object that provides an easy-to-use data entry screen

Select the best answer from the list of choices.

16. Which of the following is *not* a typical benefit of relational databases?
    - **a.** More accurate data
    - **b.** Automatic correction of data as it is entered
    - **c.** Faster information retrieval
    - **d.** Minimized duplicate data entry

17. Which of the following is *not* an advantage of managing data with relational database software such as Access versus spreadsheet software such as Excel?
    - **a.** Uses a single table to store all data
    - **b.** Reduces duplicate data entry
    - **c.** Provides greater security
    - **d.** Allows multiple users to enter data simultaneously

18. The object that creates a professional printout of data that includes headers, footers, and graphics is the:
    - **a.** Query.
    - **b.** Table.
    - **c.** Report.
    - **d.** Form.

19. The object that contains all of the database data is the:
    - **a.** Report.
    - **b.** Form.
    - **c.** Page.
    - **d.** Table.

20. What can you use to quickly create a new database?
    - **a.** Template
    - **b.** Object
    - **c.** Module
    - **d.** Form

▼ SKILLS REVIEW

1. **Understand relational databases.**
    - **a.** Identify five advantages of managing database information in Access versus using a spreadsheet.
    - **b.** Explain how a relational database organizes data to minimize redundant information. Use an example involving a database with two related tables, Customers and States, in your explanation.

2. **Open a database.**
    - **a.** Explain the relationship between a field, a record, a table, and a database.
    - **b.** Start Access.
    - **c.** Open the RealEstate-A.accdb database from the drive and folder where you store your Data Files. Enable content if a Security Warning message appears.
    - **d.** Open each of the three tables. On a sheet of paper, complete the following table:

table name	number of records	number of fields

3. **Enter data.**
    - **a.** Enter the following records into the Agents table, then print it. Tab through the AgentNo field as it is defined with an AutoNumber data type and it automatically increments as you enter the rest of the data in the record.

AgentNo	AgentFirst	AgentLast	AgentPhone	AgencyNo
(10)	(Your first name)	(Your last name)	555-888-9999	1
(11)	(Your instructor's first name)	(Your instructor's last name)	555-888-5555	3

b. Enter the following record into the Agencies table, then print it. Tab through the AgencyNo field because it is an AutoNumber field.

AgencyNo	AgencyName	Street	City	State	Zip	AgencyPhone
(4)	(Your last name) Realty	(Your school's street address)	(Your school's city)	(Your school's state)	(Your school's zip code)	555-888-4444

4. Edit data.

a. Open the Listings table datasheet.

b. Change the Area field for ListingNo 7 from Shell Knob to Ozark Mountain.

c. Change the SqFt field for ListingNo 14 from 3500 to 5500.

d. Delete the record for ListingNo 6. Resize the columns to their best fit. Your Listings table datasheet should look similar to the one in Figure A-19.

FIGURE A-19

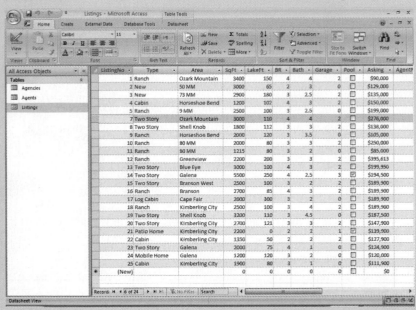

e. Enter one new record, using your own last name in the Area field, then print the first page only of the datasheet in landscape orientation. (*Hint:* Click the Pages option button in the Print dialog box, then enter 1 in both the From and To boxes.)

f. Close the RealEstate-A.accdb database and Access 2007.

5. Create a database.

a. Open Access 2007, then use the Student database template in the Education category to create a new database. This requires you to be connected to the Internet. Close any windows that open before the database does.

b. In the Student List form that opens, enter your first and last names. Use any valid entries for the E-mail Address, Business Phone, Company, and Job Title fields.

c. Print the record.

d. Expand the Navigation Pane, then use it to complete the following table on a sheet of paper to identify the number and names of the objects that were automatically created by the Students database template. The first row is completed for you.

object type	number created	names of the objects
Tables	2	Students, Guardians
Queries		
Forms		
Reports		

6. Create a table.

a. Create a new table called States with the following fields and data types:

StateName   Text

StateAbbreviation   Text

b. Enter your own state in the first record.

c. Close the States table, close the Students.accdb database, then exit Access 2007.

7. Create primary keys.

a. Open the **RealEstate-A.accdb** database used in earlier steps. Enable content if prompted.

b. Open the Agencies table in Design View, then set AgencyNo as the primary key field.

c. Open the Agents table in Design View, then set AgentNo as the primary key field.

d. Open the Listings table in Design View, then set ListingNo as the primary key field.

e. Save all your changes.

f. On another sheet of paper, answer the following questions:

Why is a field with an AutoNumber data type a good candidate for the primary key field for that table?

Why is a field with an AutoNumber data type *not* a good candidate for the foreign key field for a one-to-many relationship?

8. Relate two tables.

a. In the Relationships window, set a one-to-many relationship between the Agencies and Agents table, using the common AgencyNo field. Apply referential integrity to this relationship.

b. In the Relationships window, set a one-to-many relationship between the Agents and Listings table, using the common AgentNo field. Apply referential integrity to this relationship.

c. Click the Relationship Report button on the Design tab, then print the report that is created.

d. Close the Relationships report without saving changes, then close the Relationships window.

9. Print a datasheet.

a. Preview and print the Agencies table datasheet in landscape orientation.

b. Preview and print the Agents table datasheet in landscape orientation.

c. Close the RealEstate-A.accdb database, and exit Access 2007.

▼ INDEPENDENT CHALLENGE 1

Review the following twelve examples of database tables:

- Telephone directory
- College course offerings
- Restaurant menu
- Cookbook
- Movie listing
- Islands of the Caribbean

- Encyclopedia
- Shopping catalog
- International product inventory
- Party guest list
- Members of the U.S. House of Representatives
- Ancient wonders of the world

For each example, write a brief answer for the following.

a. What field names would you expect to find in each table?

b. Provide an example of two possible records for each table.

▼ INDEPENDENT CHALLENGE 2

You are working with several civic groups to coordinate a community-wide cleanup effort. You have started a database called Recycle-A that tracks the clubs, their trash deposits, and the trash collection centers that are participating.

a. Start Access, then open the **Recycle-A.accdb** database from the drive and folder where you store your Data Files.

b. Open each table's datasheet, and write the number of records and fields in each of the tables.

c. In the Centers table datasheet, modify the ContactFirst and ContactLast names for the Trash Can record to your name.

d. Preview the Centers table datasheet in landscape orientation, print the datasheet if your instructor requests it, then close the table.

e. Open the Relationships window and complete the following table on a sheet of paper:

type of relationship	table on the "one" side of the relationship	table on the "many" side of the relationship	linking field name in the "one" table	linking field name in the "many" table
One-to-many				
One-to-many				

Advanced Challenge Exercise

■ Open the datasheet for the Clubs table. Click the expand button to the left of each record (which looks like a small plus sign) to view related records from the Deposits table.

■ Close the datasheet for the Clubs table. Open the datasheet for the Centers table. Click the expand button to the left of each record to view related records from the Deposits table.

f. Close the Centers table, close the Recycle-A.accdb database, then exit Access.

▼ INDEPENDENT CHALLENGE 3

You are working for an advertising agency that provides advertising media for small and large businesses in the Midwestern United States. You have started a database called Media-A which tracks your company's customers.

a. Start Access and open the **Media-A.accdb** database from the drive and folder where you store your Data Files. Enable content as needed.

b. Add a new record to the Customers table, using your own first and last names, **$7,788.99** in the YTDSales field, and any reasonable entry for the rest of the fields.

c. Edit the Rocket Laboratory record. The Company name should be **Johnson County Labs**, and the Street value should be **2145 College St**.

d. Preview the Customers datasheet in landscape orientation, print the datasheet if your instructor requests it, then close the table.

e. Create a States table with two fields, **StateName** and **StateAbbreviation**, both with a Text data type.

f. Enter at least three records into the States table, making sure that all of the states used in the Customers datasheet are entered in the States table. This includes Kansas KS, Missouri MO, and any other state you entered in previous steps.

g. In Design View, set the StateAbbreviation field as the primary key field, then save and close the States table.

▼ INDEPENDENT CHALLENGE 3 (CONTINUED)

Advanced Challenge Exercise

- Open the Relationships window, add both table field lists to the window, then expand the size of the Customers field list so that all fields are visible.
- Drag the StateAbbreviation field from the States table to the State field of the Customers table, to create a one-to-many relationship between the two tables. Enforce referential integrity on the relationship. If you are unable to enforce referential integrity, it means that there is a value in the State field of the Customers table that doesn't have a match in the StateAbbreviation field of the States table. Open both datasheets, making sure every state in the Customers table is also represented in the States table, close all datasheets, and reestablish the one-to-many relationship between the two tables with referential integrity.
- Click the Relationship Report button on the Design tab, then print the report that is created.
- Close the Relationships report without saving changes, then close the Relationships window.

h. Close the Media-A.accdb database, then exit Access 2007.

▼ REAL LIFE INDEPENDENT CHALLENGE

This Independent Challenge requires an Internet connection.

Now that you've learned about Microsoft Access and relational databases, brainstorm how you might use an Access database in your daily life or career. Start by visiting the Microsoft Web site, and explore what's new about Access 2007.

a. Connect to the Internet, and use your browser to go to your favorite search engine. Use the keywords "benefits of a relational database" or "benefits of Microsoft Access" to find articles that discuss the benefits of organizing data in a relational database.

b. Read several articles about the benefits of organizing data in a relational database such as Access, identifying three distinct benefits. As you read the articles, list all of the terminology unfamiliar to you as well, identifying at least five items.

c. Using a search engine or a Web site that provides a computer glossary such as *www.whatis.com* or *www.webopedia.com*, look up the definition of the five or more new terms you have identified.

d. Using the research you have conducted on the Web, create a one-page document that lists the three benefits of using a relational database you identified in Step b as well as the five or more technical terms that you researched in Step c. In order to document the original sources of your information, be sure to list the Internet Web page addresses (URLs such as *www.microsoft.com*) for each source you reference for benefits and definitions.

e. Apply this research to a job you have had or would like to secure in the future. In one paragraph, describe the job and give at least one example of how Access might be used to manage data important to that job. In a second paragraph, discuss how the benefits of using a relational database might apply to this example.

▼ VISUAL WORKSHOP

Open the **Basketball-A.accdb** database from the drive and folder where you store your Data Files, then open the Players table datasheet. Modify the first three records in the existing Players table to reflect the changes shown in the First, Last, and Height fields of Figure A-20. Note that your name should be entered in the First and Last fields of the first record. Resize all columns to show all data, print the first page of the datasheet in landscape orientation, close the Players table, close the Basketball-A.accdb database, then exit Access.

FIGURE A-20

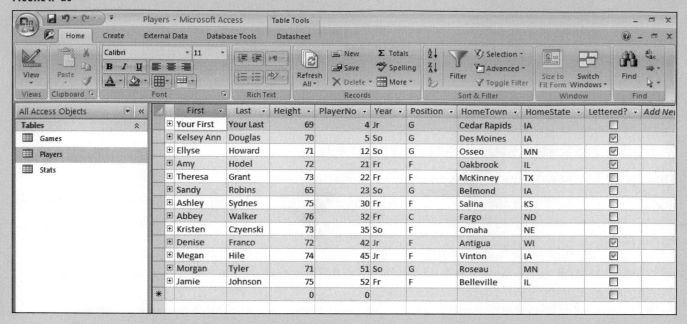

Building and Using Queries

Files You Will Need:

Quest-B.accdb

RealEstate-B.accdb

Vet-B.accdb

Membership-B.accdb

Recycle-B.accdb

Capitals-B.accdb

Basketball-B.accdb

You build queries in an Access database to ask "questions" about data, such as which adventure tours are scheduled for June or what types of tours take place in California. Queries present the answer in a datasheet, which you can sort, filter, and format. Because queries are stored in the database, they can be used multiple times. Each time a query is opened, it presents a current view of the latest updates to the database.  Mark Rock, tour developer for U.S. group travel at Quest Travel Services, has several questions about the customer and tour information in the Quest database. You'll develop queries to provide Mark with up-to-date answers.

OBJECTIVES

Create a query

Use Query Design View

Modify queries

Sort and find data

Filter data

Apply AND criteria

Apply OR criteria

Format a datasheet

Creating a Query

A **query** allows you to select a subset of fields and records from one or more tables and then present the selected data as a single datasheet. A major benefit of working with data through a query is that you can focus on the information you need to answer your questions, rather than navigating the fields and records from many large tables. You can enter, edit, and navigate data in a query datasheet just like a table datasheet. However, keep in mind that Access data is physically stored only in tables, even though you can view and edit it through other Access objects such as queries and forms. Because a query doesn't physically store the data, a query datasheet is sometimes called a **logical view** of the data. Technically, a query is a set of **SQL** (Structured Query Language) instructions, but because Access provides several easy-to-use query tools, knowledge of SQL is not required to build or use Access queries. ░░░ You use the Simple Query Wizard to build a query to display a few fields from the States and Tours tables in one datasheet.

STEPS

1. **Start Access, open the Quest-B.accdb database, then enable content, if prompted**

   Access provides several tools to create a new query. One way is to use the **Simple Query Wizard**, which prompts you for information needed to create a new query.

2. **Click the Create tab on the Ribbon, click the Query Wizard button, then click OK to start the Simple Query Wizard**

   The first Simple Query Wizard dialog box opens, prompting you to select the fields you want to view in the new query.

3. **Click the Tables/Queries list arrow, click Table: Tours, double-click TourName, double-click City, then double-click Category**

   So far, you've selected three fields from the Tours table for this query. You also want to add the full state name, a field stored only in the States table.

TROUBLE

Click the Remove Single Field button

` < ` if you need to remove a field from the Selected Fields list.

4. **Click the Tables/Queries list arrow, click Table: States, then double-click StateName**

   You've selected three fields from the Tours table and one from the States table for your new query, as shown in Figure B-1. Because the Tours and States tables are linked together in this database by a common field (StateAbbrev), you can create queries by selecting individual fields from each of the linked tables to present a datasheet with a subset of desired fields.

5. **Click Next, select Tours Query, type ToursByState in the text box, click Finish, then maximize the datasheet**

   The ToursByState datasheet opens, displaying three fields from the Tours table and the StateName field from the States table, as shown in Figure B-2.

FIGURE B-1: Selecting fields in the Simple Query Wizard

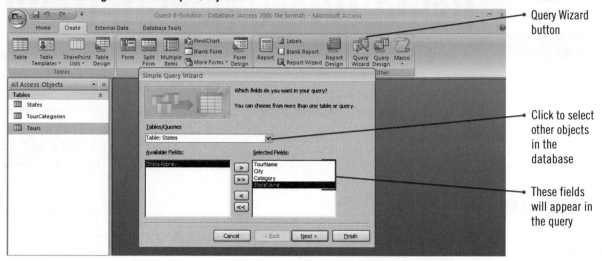

Query Wizard button

Click to select other objects in the database

These fields will appear in the query

FIGURE B-2: ToursByState query datasheet

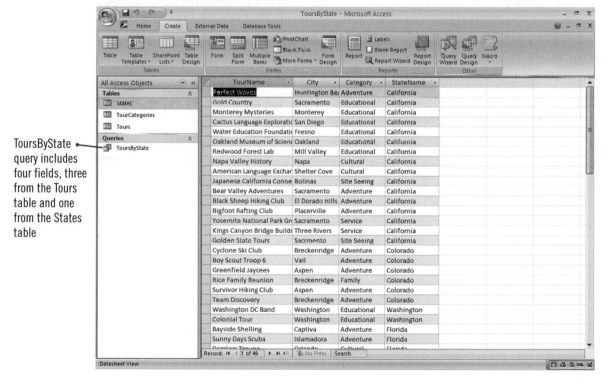

ToursByState query includes four fields, three from the Tours table and one from the States table

Using Query Design View

You use **Query Design View** to add, delete, or move the fields in an existing query, to specify sort orders, or to add **criteria** to limit the number of records shown in the resulting datasheet. (Criteria are limiting conditions you set in Query Design View.) You can also use Query Design View to create a new query from scratch. Query Design View presents the fields you can use for that query in small windows called **field lists**. If the fields of two or more related tables are used in the query, the relationship between two tables is displayed with a **join line** identifying which fields are used to establish the relationship. ▉▉▉▉▉ Mark Rock asks you to print a list of Adventure tours in Colorado. You use Query Design View to modify the existing ToursByState query to meet his request.

STEPS

1. **Click the** Home tab **on the Ribbon, then click the** Design View button **to switch to Query Design View for the ToursByState query**

   The Query Design View opens as shown in Figure B-3, showing the field lists for the States and Tours tables in the upper pane of the window, as well as the one-to-many relationship established between the two tables via the common StateAbbrev field. The four fields you previously requested for this query are displayed in the **query design grid** in the lower pane of the window.

   QUICK TIP
   Query criteria are not case sensitive.

2. **Click the** first Criteria cell **for the Category field, then type** adventure

   By adding the word "adventure" to the first Criteria cell for the Category field, only those records with this value in the Category field will be displayed in the datasheet.

3. **Click the** Datasheet View button **on the Design tab to switch to Datasheet View**

   The resulting datasheet lists the Adventure tours. To further narrow this list to tours in Colorado, you return to Query Design View and enter more criteria.

   TROUBLE
   If you see more than five records, return to Query Design View and make sure your criteria are on the same row.

4. **Click the** Design View button **on the Home tab, click the** first Criteria cell **for the StateName field, type** Colorado, **then click the** Datasheet View button **on the Design tab**

   Now only five records are displayed, as only five of the Adventure tours are in the state of Colorado, as shown in Figure B-4. You want to save this query with a different name.

5. **Click the** Office button ▣, **click** Save As, **type** ColoradoAdventures, **then click** OK

   Now two queries are included in the Queries list on the Navigation Pane: ToursByState and ColoradoAdventures.

FIGURE B-3: Query Design View of the TourByState query

Datasheet View button

Field list for States table

Query design grid

Field list for Tours table

Criteria cell for Category field

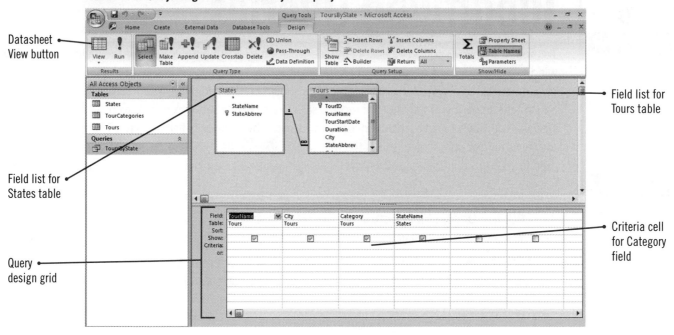

FIGURE B-4: ColoradoAdventures datasheet

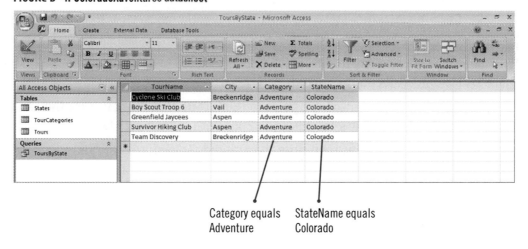

Category equals Adventure

StateName equals Colorado

Access 2007

Modifying Queries

To modify an existing query, you work in Query Design View. The upper pane of the Query Design View window shows the field lists for the tables used by the query. You use the lower pane of Query Design View to add, delete, or change the order of the fields shown on the datasheet. You also use the lower pane to add criteria to narrow the number of records selected, to define sort orders, and to build calculated fields. To delete or move a field in the query grid, you select it by clicking its field selector. The **field selector** is the thin gray bar above each field in the query grid. ▓▓▓▓▓ You want to add more fields and make other modifications to the ColoradoAdventures query. Use Query Design View to make the changes.

STEPS

1. **Click the Design View button on the Home tab**

   You want to move the StateName field to the third field position, immediately after the City field.

2. **Click the field selector for the StateName field to select it, then drag the StateName field selector one column to the left to position StateName between the City and Category fields**

   A black vertical line appears to help you visualize where you are repositioning the field. You also want to sort the records in ascending order based on the TourName field.

3. **Click the Sort cell for the TourName field, click the list arrow, then click Ascending**

   Defining the sort order in Query Design View allows you to permanently save the sort order with the query object so that every time you open the query, the specified sort is applied. Selecting an ascending sort order for the TourName field lists the query results in alphabetic order (A-Z) by TourName. You also want to add the TourStartDate and Duration fields to this query so they appear immediately after the TourName field.

4. **Drag the TourStartDate field from the Tours field list to the second column, then drag the Duration field from the Tours field list to the third column**

   The existing fields in the query grid move to the right to accommodate the addition of new fields to the grid, as shown in Figure B-5.

5. **Click the Datasheet View button on the Design tab to view the selected data**

   The datasheet is shown in Figure B-6. Note the order of the fields and sort order of the records.

6. **Change Discovery in the Team Discovery record to your last name, then save the ColoradoAdventures query**

7. **Click the Office button 🔘, point to Print, click Print Preview, click the Landscape button on the Print Preview tab, click the Print button, then click OK**

8. **Close Print Preview, then close the ColoradoAdventures query**

FIGURE B-5: Modified query in Design View

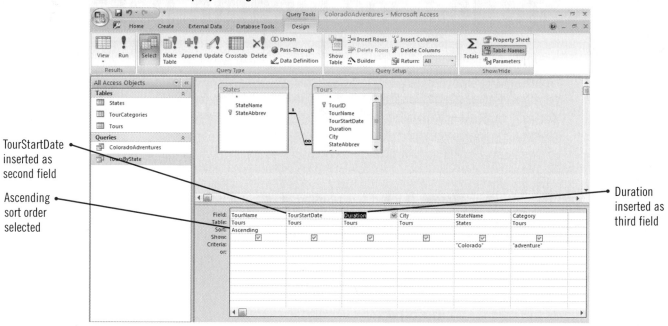

TourStartDate inserted as second field

Ascending sort order selected

Duration inserted as third field

FIGURE B-6: Modified datasheet

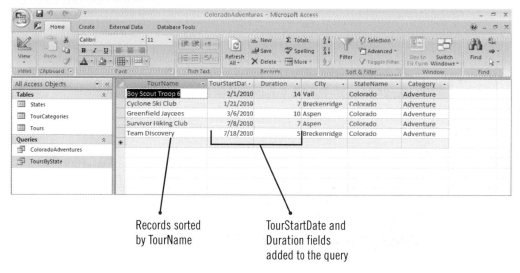

Records sorted by TourName

TourStartDate and Duration fields added to the query

Adding or deleting a table to a query

You might want to add a table's field list to the upper pane of Query Design View in order to select fields from that table for the query. To add a new table to Query Design View, click the Design tab on the Ribbon, click the Show Table button, then add the desired table(s). To delete an unneeded table from Query Design View, click its title bar, then press [Delete].

Sorting and Finding Data

The Access sort and find features are handy tools that help you quickly organize and find data. Table B-1 describes the Sort and Find buttons on the Home tab. Besides using these buttons, you can also click the list arrow on a datasheet's column heading, and then click a sorting option. Sorting and finding data works exactly the same way in table and query datasheets. ▰▰▰▰▰ Mark Rock asks you to provide a list of tours sorted by TourStartDate, and then by Duration. He also asks you to correct two tours by changing the entry of "Site Seeing" to "Cultural" in the Category field.

STEPS

QUICK TIP

Click the Navigation Pane list arrow, then make sure All Access Objects is checked to show all tables, queries, and other objects.

▶ 1. **Double-click Tours in the Navigation Pane to open the Tours datasheet, then maximize the window**

By default, records in a table datasheet are sorted on the primary key field. For the Tours table, the primary key field is the TourID field.

QUICK TIP

A sort arrow appears next to the field name by which the datasheet is sorted.

▶ 2. **Click any value in the TourStartDate field, then click the Ascending button ↑↓ on the Home tab**

The records are re-sorted based on the TourStartDate field. Notice that some tours start on the same date. You can specify a second sort order to further sort the records that have the same date in the TourStartDate field.

TROUBLE

To clear the current sort order, click the Clear All Sorts button ↕.

▶ 3. **Drag across the TourStartDate and Duration field selector buttons to select both columns, then click ↑↓**

The records are now listed in ascending order, first by TourStartDate, then by the values in the Duration field, as shown in Figure B-7. Sort orders always work left to right, so you might need to rearrange the fields before applying a sort order that uses more than one field. Your next task is to replace all occurrences of "Site Seeing" with "Cultural" in the Category field.

TROUBLE

If your find and replace did not work correctly, click the Undo button ↶ and repeat step 4.

▶ 4. **Click the Category column heading to select that field, click the Replace button on the Home tab, type Site Seeing in the Find What box, press [Tab], type Cultural in the Replace With box, click Find Next to find the first occurrence of Site Seeing, click Replace, click Replace again to replace the next occurrence of "Site Seeing," then click Cancel**

Access replaced two occurrences of "Site Seeing" with "Cultural" in the Category field, as shown in Figure B-8.

5. **Replace Rice in the TourID 26 record with your last name, then print the first page of the Tours datasheet**

6. **Save the Tours table**

If you close a datasheet without saving the changes, the records return to the original sort order based on the values in the primary key field. If you close a datasheet and save layout changes, the last sort order is saved.

FIGURE B-7: Tours datasheet sorted by TourStartDate and Duration fields

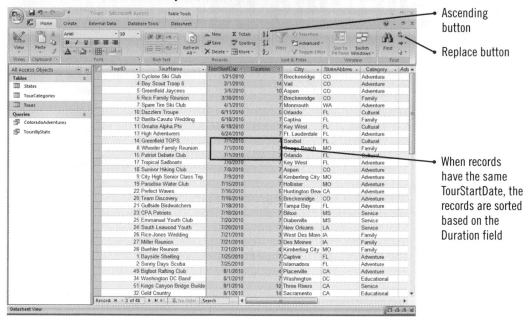

- Ascending button
- Replace button
- When records have the same TourStartDate, the records are sorted based on the Duration field

FIGURE B-8: "Site Seeing" replaced with "Cultural" in the Category field

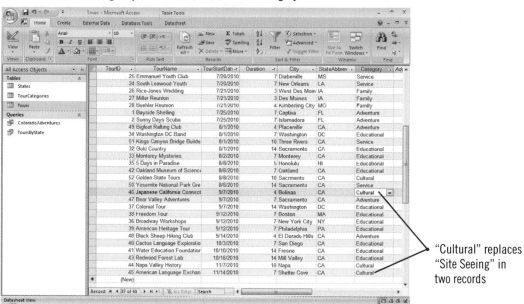

"Cultural" replaces "Site Seeing" in two records

TABLE B-1: Sort and Find buttons

name	button	purpose
Ascending		Sorts records based on the selected field in ascending order (0 to 9, A to Z)
Descending		Sorts records based on the selected field in descending order (Z to A, 9 to 0)
Clear All Sorts		Removes the current sort order
Find		Opens the Find and Replace dialog box, which allows you to find data in a single field or in the entire datasheet
Replace		Opens the Find and Replace dialog box, which allows you to find and replace data
Go To		Helps you navigate to the first, previous, last, or new record
Select		Helps you select a single record or all records in a datasheet

Filtering Data

Filtering a table or query datasheet temporarily displays only those records that match given criteria. Recall that criteria are limiting conditions you set. For example, you might want to show only those tours in the state of Florida, or those tours with a duration of less than seven days. While filters provide a quick and easy way to display a subset of records in the current datasheet, they are not nearly as powerful or flexible as queries. For example, a query is a saved object within the database, whereas filters are temporary. Filters are removed when the datasheet is closed, but if you want to apply a filter over and over again, you can save it as a query. Table B-2 compares filters and queries. ░░░░░ Mark Rock asks you to find all Adventure tours offered in the month of July. You can filter the Tours datasheet to provide this information.

STEPS

1. **Click any occurrence of Adventure in the Category field, click the Selection button 🐝 on the Home tab, then click Equals "Adventure"**

   Seventeen records are selected, as shown in Figure B-9. Filtering by a given field value, called **Filter By Selection**, is a fast and easy way to filter the records for an exact match. To filter for comparative data (for example, where TourStartDate is *equal to or greater than* 7/1/2010), you must use the **Filter By Form** feature. Filter buttons are summarized in Table B-3.

2. **Click the Advanced button 🖼 on the Home tab, then click Filter By Form**

   The Filter by Form window opens. The previous Filter By Selection criterion, "Adventure" in the Category field, is still in the grid. Access distinguishes between text and numeric entries by placing quotation marks around text criteria.

3. **Click the TourStartDate cell, then type 7/*/2010 as shown in Figure B-10**

   Filter by Form also allows you to apply two or more criteria at the same time. An asterisk (*) in the day position of the date criterion works as a wildcard, selecting any date in the month of July (the seventh month) in the year 2010.

4. **Click the Toggle Filter button 📊 on the Home tab**

   The datasheet redisplays all nine records that match both filter criteria, as shown in Figure B-11. Note that filter icons appear next to the TourStartDate and Category field names as both fields are involved in the filter.

5. **Change Bayside in TourID 1 to your last name, then print the filtered datasheet**

   To remove the current filter, you click the Toggle Filter button.

6. **Click 📊 to remove the filter, then save and close the Tours datasheet**

Using wildcard characters

To search for a pattern, you can use a **wildcard** character to represent any character in the criteria entry. Use a ? (question mark) to search for any single character and an * (asterisk) to search for any number of characters. Wildcard characters are often used with the Like operator. For example, the criterion Like "12/*/10" would find all dates in December of 2010, and the criterion Like "F*" would find all entries that start with the letter F.

FIGURE B-9: Filtering for Adventure records

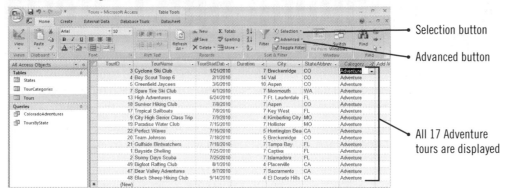

Selection button

Advanced button

All 17 Adventure tours are displayed

FIGURE B-10: Filter by Form window

Toggle Filter button

Adding a criterion to display records with a TourStartDate in July, 2010

"Adventure" criterion still in Category field

FIGURE B-11: Filtering for Adventure records in July, 2010

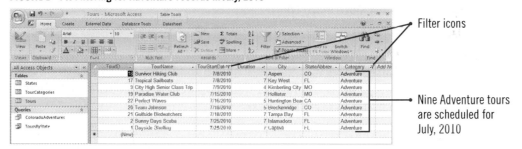

Filter icons

Nine Adventure tours are scheduled for July, 2010

TABLE B-2: Filters versus queries

characteristics	filters	queries
Are saved as an object in the database	No	Yes
Can be used to select a subset of records in a datasheet	Yes	Yes
Can be used to select a subset of fields in a datasheet	No	Yes
Resulting datasheet used to enter and edit data	Yes	Yes
Resulting datasheet used to sort, filter, and find records	Yes	Yes
Commonly used as the source of data for a form or report	No	Yes
Can calculate sums, averages, counts, and other types of summary statistics across records	No	Yes
Can be used to create calculated fields	No	Yes

TABLE B-3: Filter buttons

name	button	purpose
Filter		Provides a list of values in the selected field by which to customize a filter
Selection		Filters records that equal, do not equal, or are otherwise compared to the current value
Advanced		Provides advanced filter features such as Filter By Form, Save As Query, and Clear Grid
Toggle Filter		Applies or removes the current filter

Applying AND Criteria

As you have seen, you can limit the number of records that appear on a query datasheet by entering criteria into Query Design View. Criteria are tests, or limiting conditions, for which the record must be true to be selected for a datasheet. To create **AND criteria**, which means that *all* criteria must be true in order for the record to be selected, enter two or more criteria on the *same* Criteria row of the query design grid. Mark Rock asks you to provide a list of all educational tours in the state of California with a duration of greater than seven days. Use Query Design View to create the query with AND criteria to meet his request.

STEPS

QUICK TIP

Drag the bottom border of the Tours field list down to display all of the fields. The scroll bar disappears when all fields are displayed.

1. **Click the** Create tab **on the Ribbon, click the** Query Design button, **double-click** Tours, **click** Close **in the Show Table dialog box, then maximize the query window**
   You want to add four fields to this query.

2. **Double-click** TourName, **double-click** Duration, **double-click** StateAbbrev, **and double-click** Category **to add these fields to the query grid**
   Start by adding criteria to select only those records in California. Because you are using the StateAbbrev field, you need to use the two-letter state abbreviation for California, CA, as the Criteria entry.

3. **Click the** first Criteria cell **for the StateAbbrev field, type** CA, **then click the** Datasheet View button **on the Design tab**
   Querying for only those tours in the state of California selects 16 records. Next, you add criteria to select only those records in the Educational category.

4. **Click the** Design View button **on the Home tab to switch to Query Design View, click the** first Criteria cell **for the Category field, type** Educational, **then click the** Datasheet View button **on the Design tab**
   Criteria added to the same line of the query design grid are AND criteria. When entered on the same line, each criterion must be true for the record to appear in the resulting datasheet. Querying for both California and Educational tours selects six records. Every time you add AND criteria, you *narrow* the number of records that are selected because the record must be true for *all* criteria.

5. **Click the** Design View button **on the Home tab, click the** first Criteria cell **for the** Duration field, **then type** >7, **as shown in Figure B-12**
   Access assists you with **criteria syntax**, rules by which criteria need to be entered. Access automatically adds quotation marks around text criteria in Text fields and pound signs (#) around date criteria in Date/Time fields. The criteria in Number, Currency, and Yes/No fields are not surrounded by any characters. See Table B-4 for more information about comparison operators such as > (greater than).

TROUBLE

If your datasheet doesn't match Figure B-13, return to Query Design View and compare your criteria to that of Figure B-12.

6. **Click the** Datasheet View button **on the Design tab**
   The third AND criterion further narrows the number of records selected to three, as shown in Figure B-13.

7. **Click the** Save button 🖫 **on the Quick Access toolbar, type** CaliforniaEducational **as the query name, then click** OK
   The query is saved with the new name, CaliforniaEducational, as a new object in the Quest-B database.

Searching for blank fields

Is Null and **Is Not Null** are two other types of common criteria. The Is Null criterion finds all records where no entry has been made in the field. Is Not Null finds all records where there is any entry in the field, even if the entry is 0. Primary key fields cannot have a null entry.

Building and Using Queries

FIGURE B-12: Query Design View with criteria on one row (AND criteria)

Datasheet View button

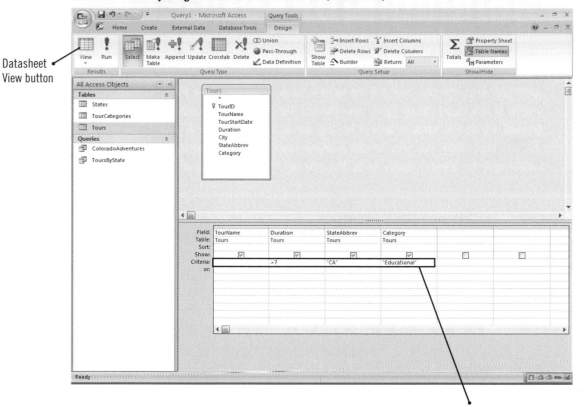

Criteria for displaying Educational tours in California that are longer than one week

FIGURE B-13: Datasheet of CaliforniaEducational query

Design View button

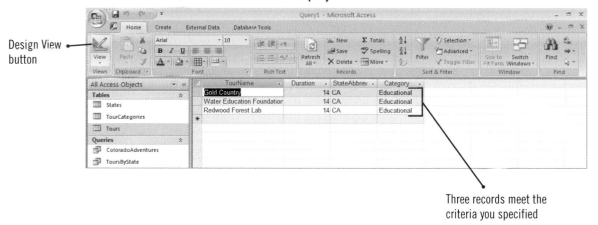

Three records meet the criteria you specified

TABLE B-4: Comparison operators

operator	description	expression	meaning
>	Greater than	>500	Numbers greater than 500
>=	Greater than or equal to	>=500	Numbers greater than or equal to 500
<	Less than	<"Braveheart"	Names from A to Braveheart, but not Braveheart
<=	Less than or equal to	<="Bridgewater"	Names from A through Bridgewater, inclusive
<>	Not equal to	<>"Fontanelle"	Any name except for Fontanelle

Applying OR Criteria

To create **OR criteria**, which means that *any one* criterion must be true in order for the record to be selected, enter two or more criteria on the *different* Criteria rows of the query design grid. To create OR criteria for the *same field*, enter the two criteria in the same Criteria cell separated by the OR operator. As you add rows of OR criteria to the query design grid, you *increase* the number of records selected for the resulting datasheet because the record needs to be true for *only one* of the criteria rows in order to be selected for the datasheet. Mark Rock asks you to add Cultural tours longer than seven days in duration from the state of California to the previous query. To do this, you can modify the query to employ OR criteria to add the records.

STEPS

1. **Click the** Design View button **on the Home tab, click the** second Criteria cell **in the Category field, type** cultural, **then click the** Datasheet View button **on the Design tab**

   The query added all of the tours with "Cultural" in the Category field to the datasheet, as specified by the second row of the query grid in Query Design View. Because each row of the query grid is evaluated separately, the fact that three criteria were entered in the first row is of no consequence to the second row. In order for the second row to also apply three criteria—Cultural, California, and duration of greater than 7—three criteria must be entered in the second row. In other words, the criteria in one row have no effect on the criteria of other rows.

2. **Click the** Design View button **on the Home tab, click the** second Criteria cell **in the Duration field, type** >7, **click the** second Criteria cell **in the StateAbbrev field, then type** CA

   Query Design View should look like Figure B-14.

3. **Click the** Datasheet View button **on the Design tab**

   Five records were selected that meet all three criteria as entered in row one OR row two of the query grid, as shown in Figure B-15.

4. **Edit the Gold Country record to be** your last name Country, **then save, print, and close the datasheet**

   Because the CaliforniaEducational query now selects both educational and cultural records, you rename it.

5. **Right-click** CaliforniaEducational **in the Navigation Pane, click** Rename **on the shortcut menu, type** CaliforniaEducationalCultural **to rename the query, then press** [Enter]

FIGURE B-14: Query Design View with criteria on two rows (OR criteria)

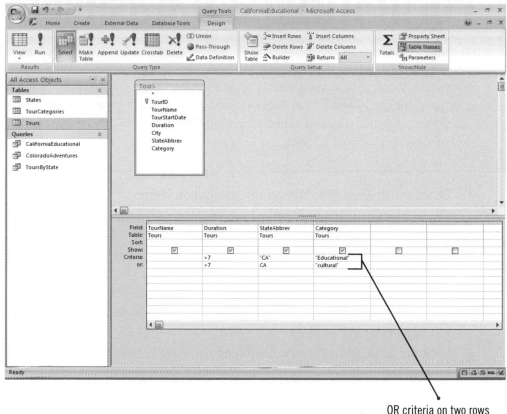

OR criteria on two rows
in the design grid

FIGURE B-15: Datasheet of CaliforniaEducationalCultural query

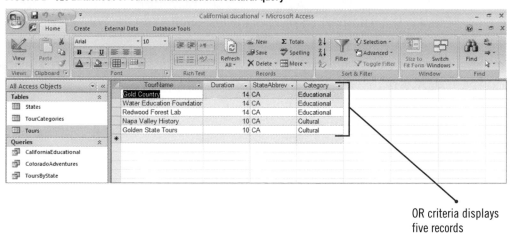

OR criteria displays
five records

Formatting a Datasheet

Although the primary Access tool to create professional printouts is the report object, you can print a datasheet as well. Although a datasheet printout does not allow you to add custom headers, footers, images, or subtotals as reports do, you can apply some formatting, such as changing the font size, font face, colors, and gridlines. ▰▰▰▰▰ Mark Rock has asked you to create a printout of the different tour categories and their descriptions, which is stored in the TourCategories table. You can format the TourCategories datasheet before printing it for Mark.

STEPS

1. **Double-click TourCategories in the Navigation Pane**

   The TourCategories datasheet opens. Before applying new formatting enhancements, you preview the default printout.

2. **Click the Office button** 🔘, **point to Print, click Print Preview, then click the top edge of the paper to zoom in**

   The preview window displays the layout of the printout, as shown in Figure B-16. By default, the printout of a datasheet contains the object name and current date in the header. The page number is in the footer. You decide to increase the size of the font and data before printing.

3. **Click the Close Print Preview button on the Print Preview tab, click the Font Size list arrow, then click 12**

   A larger font size often makes a printout easier to read. You also need to adjust the width of the Description column to its best fit.

4. **Double-click the column separator to the right of the Description field**

   Double-clicking the column (field) separator automatically adjusts the width of the column to the widest entry in the datasheet.

5. **Click the Alternate Fill/Back Color button arrow ▦▾ on the Home tab, then click Yellow**

   For datasheet printouts, alternating the background color of each row makes the printout easier to read, as shown in Figure B-17. You want to add one more new category, Sports, before printing the datasheet.

6. **Type Sports in the Category field for a new record, then type (any valid and unique description) for this category in the Description field**

7. **Preview the datasheet again, click the Print button on the Print Preview tab, then click OK in the Print dialog box**

8. **Save and close the TourCategories datasheet, close the Quest-B.accdb database, then exit Access**

FIGURE B-16: Default printout of a datasheet

Print Preview tab

Close Print Preview button

TourCategories datasheet in Print Preview

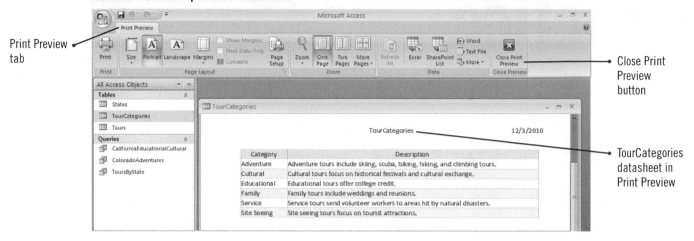

FIGURE B-17: Formatted datasheet

Font Size list arrow

Alternate Fill/Back Color button

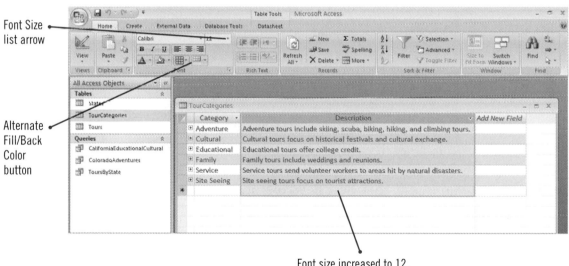

Font size increased to 12,
Description field resized, and
Yellow alternate color applied

Practice

▼ CONCEPTS REVIEW

Label each element of the Access window shown in Figure B-18.

FIGURE B-18

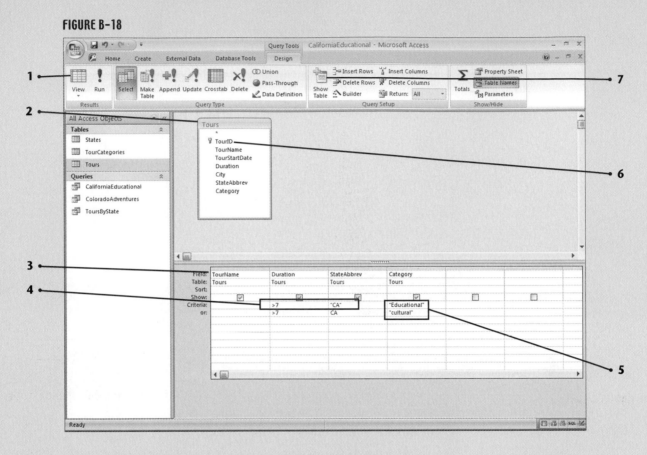

Match each term with the statement that best describes it.

8. **Query grid**

9. **Criteria**

10. **Filter**

11. **Syntax**

12. **Query**

13. **Sorting**

14. **Wildcard**

15. **Is Null**

a. Creates a datasheet of selected fields and records from one or more tables

b. Creates a temporary subset of records

c. Limiting conditions used to narrow the number of records that appear on a datasheet

d. Used to search for a pattern

e. Criterion that finds all records where no entry has been made in the field

f. The lower pane in Query Design View

g. Putting records in ascending or descending order based on the values of a field

h. Rules that determine how criteria is entered

Select the best answer from the list of choices.

16. The rules by which criteria need to be entered in the query grid are referred to as:

    a. Syntax.   **c.** Field lists.

    b. Hyperlink.   **d.** Formatting.

17. SQL stands for which of the following?

    a. Standard Query Language   **c.** Special Query Listing

    b. Structured Query Language   **d.** Simple Query Listing

18. A query is sometimes called a "logical view" of data because:

    a. You can create queries with the Logical Query Wizard.

    b. Queries contain logical criteria.

    c. Query naming conventions are logical.

    d. Queries do not store data, they only display a view of data.

19. Which of the following describes OR criteria?

    a. Using two or more rows of the query grid to select only those records that meet given criteria

    b. Selecting a subset of fields and/or records to view as a datasheet from one or more tables

    c. Reorganizing the records in either ascending or descending order based on the contents of one or more fields

    d. Using multiple fields in the query design grid

20. Which of the following is *not* true about a query?

    a. A query is the same thing as a filter.

    b. A query can be used to create calculated fields.

    c. A query can be used to create summary statistics.

    d. A query can be used to enter and edit data.

▼ SKILLS REVIEW

1. Create a query.

    a. Open the **RealEstate-B.accdb** database from the drive and folder where you store your Data Files. Enable content if you are prompted with a Security Alert message.

    b. Create a new query using the Simple Query Wizard. Select the AgentFirst and AgentLast names from the Agents table, and select the Type, SqFt, and Asking fields from the Listings table. Select all details, and title the query AgentListings.

    c. Choose any record with Michelle Litten's name and change it to your own. As soon as you save the changes by moving to another record, all three of Michelle's records update to your name. Although Michelle Litten was entered only once in the database, her agent number was linked to three different listings in the Listings table, which selects her name three times out of the Agents table for this query.

2. Use Query Design View.

    a. Open the AgentListings query in Query Design View.

    b. Enter criteria to display only homes with an Asking price of greater than $200,000. (*Hint*: Enter the value in the criterion as 200000 without a comma. Also, don't forget the greater than operator, >.) Display the datasheet.

    c. In Query Design View, sort the records in ascending order based on the AgentLast field, then display and print the datasheet.

    d. Save and close the AgentListings query.

3. Modify queries.

a. Open the ListingsMasterList query in Datasheet View.

b. Switch to Query Design View, then add the AgencyName field from the Agencies table to the first column in the query grid.

c. Add the AgentFirst field to the third column.

d. Add ascending sort orders to the AgentLast and AgentFirst fields, then display the datasheet.

e. Print, save, and close the ListingsMasterList query.

4. Sort and find data.

a. Open the Listings table datasheet.

b. Select both the SqFt and LakeFt fields, then sort the records in descending order.

c. In the Area field, find all occurrences of Shell Knob, replace them with **Shell City**, then close the Find and Replace dialog box.

d. Enter your own last name in the Area field of the first record, then print only the first page of the datasheet.

5. Filter data.

a. Filter the Listings datasheet for only those records where the Type field equals Two Story.

b. Apply an advanced filter by form to further narrow the records so that only the Two Story listings with an Asking Price of greater than or equal to $194,500 are selected.

c. Print the datasheet, then close the Listings datasheet without saving changes.

6. Apply AND criteria.

a. Open the ListingsMasterList query in Query Design View.

b. Enter criteria to select all of the listings in the Shell City area with three or more baths. Display the datasheet and save the changes.

c. Print the ListingsMasterList datasheet in landscape orientation.

7. Apply OR criteria.

a. Open the ListingsMasterList query in Query Design View.

b. In addition to the existing criteria, include criteria to select all listings in Kimberling City with three or more baths, so that both Shell City and Kimberling City records with three or more baths are selected. Display the datasheet, compare it to Figure B-19, and save the changes.

FIGURE B-19

AgencyName	AgentLast	AgentFirst	ListingNo	Type	Area	SqFt	BR	Bath	Asking
Camden and Camden Realtors	Fye	Donna	20	Two Story	Kimberling City	2700	3	3	$147,900
Camden and Camden Realtors	Fye	Donna	19	Two Story	Shell City	3200	3	4.5	$187,500
Camden and Camden Realtors	Pledge	Shari	18	Ranch	Kimberling City	2500	3	4	$189,900
Sun and Ski Realtors	StudentLast	StudentFirst	8	Two Story	Shell City	1800	3	3	$138,000
*			(New)						

The order of the records might differ, depending on your name

c. Print the ListingsMasterList datasheet in landscape orientation, then save and close the ListingsMasterList query.

8. Format a datasheet.

a. Open the Agents table datasheet and apply the Arial Narrow font and a 14-point font size.

b. Resize all columns so that all data and field names are visible.

c. Apply a Light Gray 2 alternate fill/back color.

d. Print the datasheet, then save and close the Agents datasheet.

e. Close the RealEstate-B.accdb database, then exit Access.

▼ INDEPENDENT CHALLENGE 1

You have built an Access database to track the veterinarians and clinics where they work in your area.

a. Start Access, open the **Vet-B.accdb** database from the drive and folder where you store your Data Files, enable content if prompted, then open the Vets table datasheet.

b. Open the Clinics datasheet, review the data in both datasheets, then close them.

c. Using the Simple Query Wizard, select the Last and First fields from the Vets table, and select the ClinicName and Phone fields from the Clinics table. Title the query **ClinicListing**, then view and maximize the datasheet.

d. Sort the records in ascending order by Last name, then First name. Review the values in the Last field, and determine if the First sort order was needed.

e. Find Cooper in the Last field, and replace it with **Chen**.

f. Find any occurrence of Leawood Animal Clinic in the ClinicName field, and change Leawood to **Emergency**.

g. In Query Design View, add criteria to select only Emergency Animal Clinic or Animal Haven in the ClinicName field.

h. Display the datasheet, change Vicki Kowalewski's name to your own, then save and print the ClinicListing datasheet.

i. Close the ClinicListing datasheet and the Vet-B.accdb database, and exit Access.

▼ INDEPENDENT CHALLENGE 2

You have built an Access database to track membership in a community service club. The database tracks member names and addresses as well as their status in the club, which moves from rank to rank as the members contribute increased hours of service to the community.

a. Start Access, open the **Membership-B.accdb** database from the drive and folder where you store your Data Files, enable content if prompted, open the Members and Status table datasheets to review the data, then close them.

b. In Query Design View, build a query with the following fields: LName and FName from the Members table, and StatusLevel from the Status table.

FIGURE B-20

c. View the datasheet, then return to Query Design View.

d. In Query Design View, add criteria to select only those members with a silver or gold StatusLevel. Apply an ascending sort order on the LName and FName fields, then view the datasheet.

e. Return to Query Design View, add an ascending sort order to StatusLevel, then rearrange the fields in the query grid so that the StatusLevel field is the first sort order, LName the second, and FName the third. View the datasheet.

f. Save the query with the name **GoldSilver**.

g. Return to Query Design View, then add the Phone field as the fourth field in the query. View the datasheet, shown in Figure B-20.

h. Enter your own name in the first record, widen all columns so that all data is visible, then print the datasheet.

i. Save and close the GoldSilver query, then close the Membership-B.accdb database, and exit Access.

▼ INDEPENDENT CHALLENGE 3

You have built an Access database to organize the deposits at a recycling center. Various clubs regularly deposit recyclable material, which is measured in pounds when the deposits are made.

a. Start Access, open the **Recycle-B.accdb** database from the drive and folder where you store your Data Files, then enable content if prompted.

b. Open the Clubs table datasheet to review this data, then close it. Open the Centers table datasheet to review this data, then close it.

c. Review the Deposits datasheet, then filter the datasheet for records where the Weight value is greater than or equal to 100.

d. Apply an alternate light gray fill/back color of your choice, print the datasheet, then save and close the Deposits datasheet.

e. Using either the Query Wizard or Query Design View, create a query with the following fields: Deposit Number, Deposit Date, and Weight from the Deposits table; Name from the Centers table; and Name from the Clubs table. Note that in the Simple Query Wizard's field list and in the query datasheet, when two fields from different tables have the same name, the fields are distinguished by adding the table name and a period before the field name.

f. Name the query **DepositList**. Sort the records in ascending order by Deposit Number.

g. Change any occurrence of "Adair" in the "Adair County Landfill" entry in the Centers.Name field to your last name, then print the datasheet.

h. Save and close the DepositList query.

Advanced Challenge Exercise

■ Compare the printout of the Deposits table datasheet and the DepositList query. In a document, answer the following questions:

- What common field links the Deposits table to the Centers table? (*Hint*: Use the Relationships window if the answer is not apparent from the printouts.)
- What common field links the Deposits table to the Clubs table? (*Hint*: Use the Relationships window if needed.)
- Why do you think that number fields are often used as the common field to link two tables in a one-to-many relationship, as opposed to text fields?
- How many times is each center name and each club name physically entered in the database?
- Why do many center names and club names appear many times on the DepositList query?

i. Close the Recycle-B.accdb database, then exit Access.

▼ REAL LIFE INDEPENDENT CHALLENGE

You can use an Access database to record and track your experiences, such as places you've visited. Suppose that your passion for travel includes a plan to visit the capitals of all 50 states. A database is provided with your Data Files that includes one table listing each state and capital, and another table of people from each state that you can contact for more information about state information.

a. Start Access, open the **Capitals-B.accdb** database from the drive and folder where you store your Data Files, then enable content if prompted.

b. Open both the Contacts and States datasheets to review their data, then close them.

c. In the States table, add a new field to track information about each state that you are personally interested in. Options include recording the current state population, state bird, primary tourist attraction, largest city, or any other fact about each state you choose.

d. Research and enter correct data for the new field you created in step c, for both your home state and another state that you are interested in, then print the States datasheet.

e. Using either Query Design View or the Simple Query Wizard, create a query with the following fields: StateName and Capital from the States table, and LName and FName from the Contacts table. Save the query as **StateContacts**, then display the datasheet.

f. Use Query Design View to add three ascending sort orders on these fields—StateName, then LName, then FName—then display the datasheet.

g. Use Query Design View to add a criterion to select only records from the state of New York, then display the datasheet.

h. Edit Ablany to correct the spelling of New York's state capital, Albany. Navigate to a new record so that the edit is saved in the database.

i. Format the datasheet to a 14-point font size, Times New Roman font face, and a Light Blue 1 alternate fill/back color.

j. Save the revised query with the name **NewYorkContacts**.

k. Change the name of the first record to your name, then print the datasheet.

Advanced Challenge Exercise

This Advanced Challenge Exercise requires an Internet connection.

- Use the Web to research state mottos.
- Create a Text field in the States table called Motto and enter the motto for at least five different states, including New York.
- In Query Design View of the NewYorkContacts query, add the Motto field as the fifth column of the query.
- View the datasheet, widen the motto field as necessary, as shown in Figure B-21, then print the NewYorkContacts query.
- Close the NewYorkContacts query without saving changes.

l. Close the Capitals-B.accdb database, then exit Access.

FIGURE B-21

Access 2007

▼ VISUAL WORKSHOP

Open the **Basketball-B.accdb** database from the drive and folder where you store your Data Files, and enable content if prompted. Create a query based on the Players, Stats, and Games tables as shown in Figure B-22. Criteria has been added so that only those records where the Reb-O (offensive rebounds) and Reb-D (defensive rebounds) field values are equal to or greater than 1, and the 3P (three pointer) field values are equal to or greater than 2. The records are also sorted. A Light Gray 1 alternate fill/back color has been applied. Change the name of Kelsey Douglas to your own name before printing, save the query with the name HighPerformers, then close the query, the Basketball-B.accdb database, and Access.

FIGURE B-22

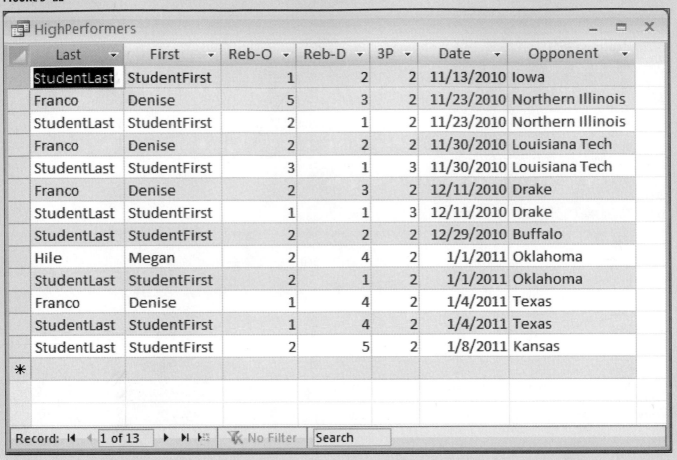

Using Forms

Files You Will Need:

Quest-C.accdb
RealEstate-C.accdb
Vet-C.accdb
Membership-C.accdb
Recycle-C.accdb
States-C.accdb
Basketball-C.accdb
QSTLogo.jpg
house.jpg
dog.jpg

Although you can enter and edit data on datasheets, most database designers develop and build forms as the primary method for users to interact with a database. In a datasheet, sometimes you have to scroll left or right to see all of the fields, which is inconvenient and time consuming. A form solves these problems by allowing you to organize the fields on the screen in any arrangement. A form also supports graphical elements such as pictures, buttons, and tabs, which make data entry faster and more accurate. Mark Rock, a tour developer at Quest Specialty Travel, asks you to create forms to make tour information easier to access, enter, and update in the Quest Access database.

OBJECTIVES

Create a form
Use Form Layout View
Use Form Design View
Add fields to a form
Modify form controls
Create calculations
Modify tab order
Insert an image

Creating a Form

A **form** is an Access database object that allows you to arrange the fields of a record in any layout so you can enter, edit, and delete records. A form provides an easy-to-use data entry and navigation screen. Forms provide many productivity and security benefits for the **user**, who is primarily interested in entering, editing, and analyzing the data in the database. As the **database designer**, the person responsible for building and maintaining tables, queries, forms, and reports, you also need direct access to all database objects, and use the Navigation Pane for this purpose. Users should not be able to access all the objects in a database—imagine how disastrous it would be if they accidentally deleted an entire table of data. You can prevent these types of problems by providing users with only the functionality they need in easy-to-use, well-designed forms. 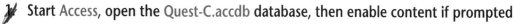 Mark Rock asks you to build a form to enter and maintain tour information.

STEPS

1. Start Access, open the Quest-C.accdb database, then enable content if prompted

You can use many methods to create a new form, but the Form Wizard is a popular way to get started. The **Form Wizard** is an Access tool that prompts you for information it needs to create a new form, such as the layout, style, title, and record source for the form.

2. Click the Create tab on the Ribbon, click the Tours table in the Navigation Pane, click the More Forms button, then click the Form Wizard

The Form Wizard starts, prompting you to select the fields for this form from the table you selected.

3. Click the Select All Fields button `>>`

You could now select more fields from other tables. In this case, you can base the new form only on the fields of the Tours table.

TROUBLE

Your field values might appear with a different color border, or no border at all.

4. Click Next, click the Columnar option button, click Next, click the Flow style, click Next, type Tours Entry Form as the title, click Finish, then maximize the form window

The Tours Entry Form opens in **Form View**, as shown in Figure C-1. The field names are shown as labels in the first column, and text boxes that display data from the underlying record source appear in the second column. You can enter, edit, find, sort, and filter records using Form View.

QUICK TIP

Always click a value in a field to identify which field you want to sort or filter before clicking the sort or filter buttons.

5. Click Cyclone Ski Club in the TourName text box, click the Ascending button `A↓` **on the Home tab, then click the Next record button** `▶` **on the navigation bar to move to the second record**

Numbers sort before letters in a Text field, so the tour named *5 Days in Paradise* appears before *American Heritage Tour*. Information about the current record number and total number of records appears in the navigation bar, just as it does in a datasheet.

6. Click the New (blank) record button `▶*` **on the navigation bar, then enter the record shown in Figure C-2**

Note that when you click in the TourStartDate text box, a small calendar icon appears to the right of the record. You can type a date directly into a date text box or click the **calendar icon** to select a date from a pop-up calendar. Similarly, when you work in the Category field, you can either type a value directly into the text box or click the list arrow to select an option from the drop-down list. Every item on the form, such as a label or text box, is called a **control**. Table C-1 summarizes the most common form controls as well as whether they are **bound** (display data) or **unbound** (do not display data).

FIGURE C-1: Tours Entry Form in Form View

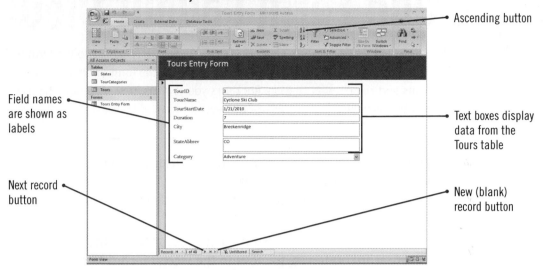

Field names are shown as labels

Text boxes display data from the Tours table

Next record button

New (blank) record button

Ascending button

FIGURE C-2: Adding a new record in the Tours Entry Form

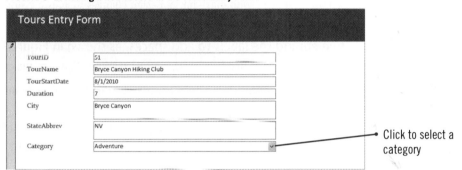

Click to select a category

TABLE C-1: Form controls

name	used to	bound	unbound
Label	Provide consistent descriptive text as you navigate from record to record; the label is the most common type of unbound control and can also be used as a hyperlink to another database object, external file, or Web page		x
Text box	Display, edit, or enter data for each record from an underlying record source; the text box is the most common type of bound control	x	
List box	Display a list of possible data entries	x	
Combo box	Display a list of possible data entries for a field, and provide a text box for an entry from the keyboard; combines the list box and text box controls	x	
Tab control	Create a three-dimensional aspect to a form		x
Check box	Display "yes" or "no" answers for a field; if the box is checked, it means "yes"	x	
Toggle button	Display "yes" or "no" answers for a field; if the button is pressed, it means "yes"	x	
Option button	Display a choice for a field	x	
Option group	Display and organize choices (usually presented as option buttons) for a field	x	
Bound object frame	Display data stored by an OLE (object linking and embedding) field, such as a picture	x	
Unbound object frame	Display a picture or clip art image that doesn't change from record to record		x
Line and Rectangle	Draw lines and rectangles on the form		x
Command button	Provide an easy way to initiate a command or run a macro		x

UNIT C

Access 2007

Using Form Layout View

Layout View, new to Access 2007, lets you make some design changes to the form while you are browsing the data. For example, you can add or delete a field to the form or change formatting characteristics such as fonts and colors. Mark Rock asks you to make several design changes to the Tours Entry Form. You can make these changes in Layout View.

STEPS

QUICK TIP
Click the Home tab on the Ribbon to display the frequently used View button.

1. **Click the TourID value, click the Ascending button on the Home tab, click the View button arrow, then click Layout View**
   In Layout View, you can move through the records, but you cannot enter or edit the data as you can in Form View.

2. **Click the First record button on the navigation bar to move to the first record, click the Next record button to move to the second record, click the TourID label to select it, then click between the words Tour and ID and press [Spacebar]**
   You often use Layout View to make minor design changes such as revising labels and changing formatting characteristics.

TROUBLE
Be sure to modify the *labels in the left column* instead of the text boxes on the right.

3. **Continue editing the labels to add spaces, as shown in Figure C-3**
   You also want to bold the first two labels, Tour ID and Tour Name, to make them more visible.

4. **Click the Tour ID label, click the Bold button on the Format tab, click the Tour Name label, then click**
   Often, you want to apply the same formatting enhancement to multiple controls. For example, you decide to narrow all of the text boxes. You select all the text boxes at the same time before applying the change.

TROUBLE
If you make an unintended change, click the Undo button on the Quick Access toolbar to undo your last action.

5. **Click the Tour ID text box (it currently displays 2), then press and hold [Shift] while clicking each of the other five text boxes and one combo box in that column**
   With all seven controls selected, any change you make to one control is made to all.

6. **Drag the right edge of the controls to the left to make them approximately half as wide**
   Your Layout View for the Tours Entry Form should look like Figure C-4.

FIGURE C-3: Using Layout View to modify form labels

Bold button

Spaces have been added between the words of each label

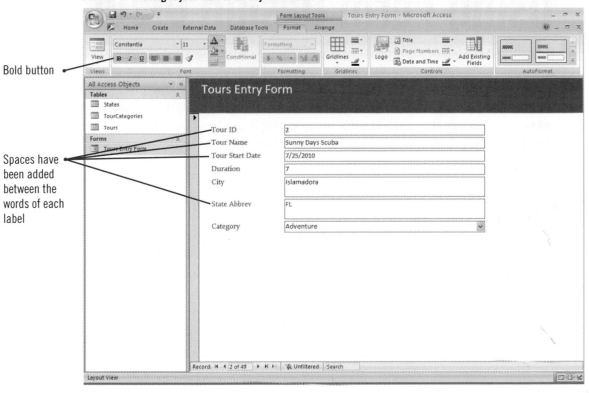

FIGURE C-4: Final Layout View for the Tours Entry Form

The first two labels are bold

The six text boxes and one combo box are resized

Combo box

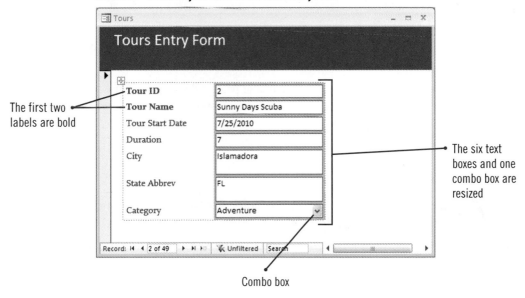

Using Form Design View

Design View of a form is devoted to working with the detailed structure of the form. Unlike Form View and Layout View, Design View displays no data, but rather provides full access to all of a form's structural and design modifications. In fact, Design View is the only place where you can modify certain structural elements such as the Form Header and Footer sections. ████ Mark Rock likes the design changes you've made so far, but asks that you add a title to the form that appears when it is printed. To do so, you add a title as a label in the Form Header section in Design View.

QUICK TIP

Another way to open an object in Design View is to right-click it in the Navigation Pane, then click Design View on the shortcut menu.

1. Click the View button arrow on the Home tab, then click Design View

In Design View, you can work with additional form sections such as the Form Header and Form Footer. The vertical and horizontal **rulers** help you position controls on the form. In Design View, you can add new controls to the form such as labels, combo boxes, and check boxes that are found on the Design tab of the Ribbon.

TROUBLE

If you do not see sizing handles on the Tours Entry Form label, click the label to select it.

2. Click the Label button on the Design tab, click below the Tours Entry Form label in the Form Header, type Quest Specialty Travel, then press [Enter]

With the label in position, as shown in Figure C-5, you change the font color and size so it is more visible. **Sizing handles**, small squares that surround the label, identify which control is currently selected.

3. With the Quest Specialty Travel label still selected, click the Font Color button arrow A, then click the white box

The white font color is more readable, but the label would be easier to read if it were larger, so you decide to increase the font size.

4. With the Quest Specialty Travel label still selected, click the Font Size list arrow [   ], click 18, then double-click a sizing handle to expand the label to automatically fit the entire entry

When you work with controls, the mouse pointer shape is very important. The shapes indicate whether dragging the mouse will select, move, or resize controls. Pointer shapes are summarized in Table C-2. With the Quest Specialty Travel label formatted appropriately, it's time to save your changes and review the form in Form View, where the users will work with it.

5. Click the Save button 🖫 on the Quick Access toolbar, then click the Form View button 🖃 on the Design tab

The updated Tours Entry Form is shown in Figure C-6.

FIGURE C-5: Modifying controls in Form Design View

Save button

Font Color button arrow

Form View button

Font Size button arrow

New label is selected in the Form Header section

Label button

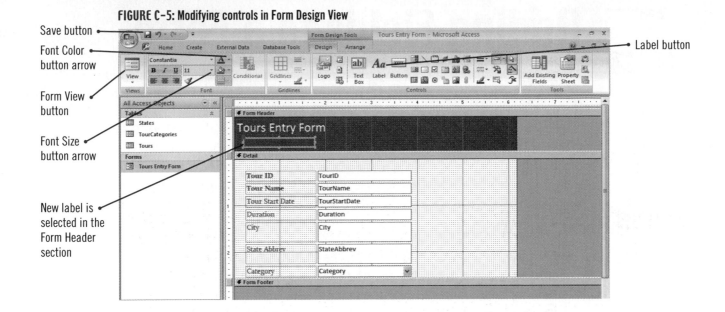

FIGURE C-6: Updated Tours Entry Form in Form View

New formatted label in the Form Header

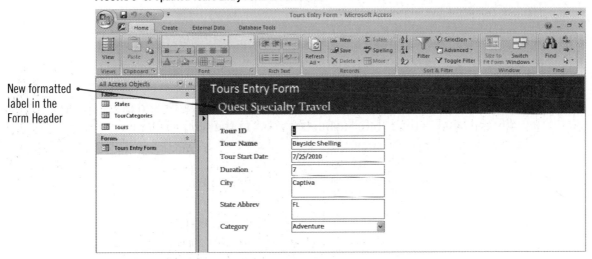

TABLE C-2: Mouse pointer shapes in Form Design View

shape	when does this shape appear?	action
⬂	When you point to any unselected control on the form (the default mouse pointer)	Single-clicking with this mouse pointer *selects* a control
✛	When you point to the edge of a selected control (but not when you are pointing to a sizing handle)	Dragging one control with this mouse pointer moves all selected controls
✛	When you point to the larger sizing handle in the upper-left corner of a selected control	Dragging the larger sizing handle moves *only the single control* where the pointer is currently positioned, not other controls that may also be selected
↕ ↔ ⤢ ⤡	When you point to any sizing handle (except the larger one in the upper-left corner)	Dragging with one of these mouse pointers *resizes* the control

Adding Fields to a Form

Adding and deleting fields to an existing form is a common activity. You can add or delete fields from a form in either Layout View or Design View using the Field List window. The **Field List** window lists the database tables and the fields they contain. To add a field to the form, drag it from the Field List to the desired location on the form. To delete a field on a form, click the field to select it, then press the [Delete] key. Deleting a field from a form does not delete it from the underlying table or have any effect on the data contained in the field. You can toggle the Field List on and off using the Add Existing Fields button. 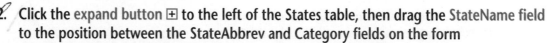 Mark Rock asks you to add the state name to the Tours Entry Form, as some of the users might not be familiar with all of the two-letter state abbreviations. You can use Layout View and the Field List window to accomplish this goal.

STEPS

TROUBLE
Click the Show all tables link at the bottom of the Field List if the States table is not visible in the Field List window.

1. **Click the Layout View button ▦ on the Home tab, click the Format tab if it is not already selected, then click the Add Existing Fields button**

   The Field List pane opens in Layout View, as shown in Figure C-7. Notice that the Field List is divided into an upper section, which shows the tables and fields within those tables that are used for the form, and the lower section, which shows related tables. The expand/collapse button to the left of the table names allows you to expand (show) the fields within the table or collapse (hide) them. The StateName field is in the States table in the lower section of the Field List.

2. **Click the expand button ⊞ to the left of the States table, then drag the StateName field to the position between the StateAbbrev and Category fields on the form**

   The form expands to accommodate the addition of the StateName label and text box by moving the Category label and text box down. When you add a new field to a form, two controls are generated: a label to describe the data that shows the field name, and a text box to display the contents of the field. With the field in place, you modify the label to be consistent with the other labels on the form.

3. **Click the StateName label to select it, click between the words and press [Spacebar] to modify the label to read State Name, then click to the right of Name: and press [Backspace] to delete the colon (:)**

   You also decide to delete the TourID field from the form. Because the TourID field has been defined as an AutoNumber field in the Tours table, it automatically increments as new tour records are entered and does not need to be displayed on this form.

4. **Click the text box that contains the TourID value, then press [Delete]**

   Deleting a field's text box automatically deletes its associated label control.

5. **Click the Save button ▦ on the Quick Access toolbar, then click the Form View button ▦ on the Design tab**

6. **Click the New (blank) record button ▦ in the navigation bar, then enter a new record in the updated form, as shown in Figure C-8**

   Note that after you enter MO in the StateAbbrev text box, the value in the StateName text box will automatically populate with the full state name, Missouri. Because the Tours table is related to the States table through the common State Abbrev field, the state name is automatically selected, or "pulled" out of the State table after you enter the state abbreviation into the Tour record.

FIGURE C-7: Adding controls in Form Layout View

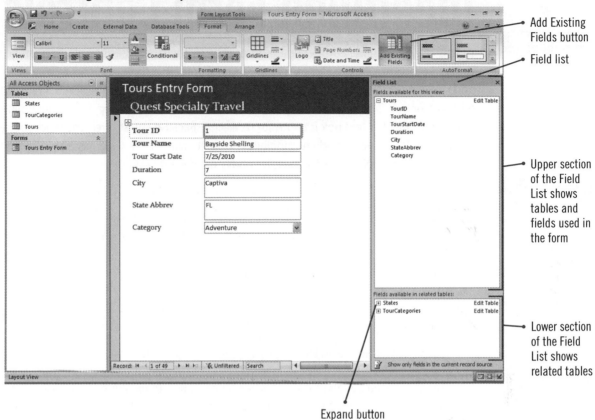

- Add Existing Fields button
- Field list
- Upper section of the Field List shows tables and fields used in the form
- Lower section of the Field List shows related tables
- Expand button

FIGURE C-8: Updated Tours Entry Form in Form View

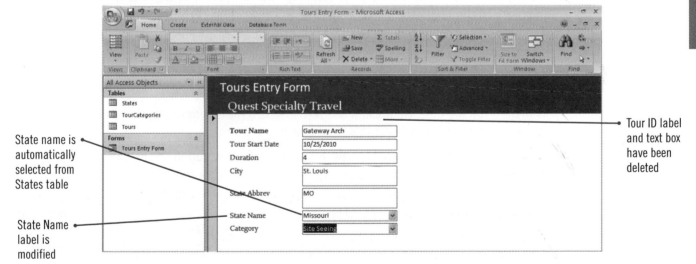

- State name is automatically selected from States table
- State Name label is modified
- Tour ID label and text box have been deleted

Bound versus unbound controls

Controls are said to be either bound or unbound. **Bound controls** are controls that display values from a field such as text boxes and combo boxes. **Unbound controls** do not display data, but rather serve to describe data or enhance the appearance of the form. Labels are the most common type of unbound control, but other types include lines, images, tabs, and command buttons. Another way to distinguish bound from unbound controls is to observe the form as you move from record to record. Because bound controls display data, their contents change as you move through the records, displaying the entry in the field of the current record. Unbound controls such as labels and lines do not change as you move through the records in a form.

Modifying Form Controls

You have already modified one type of form control, the label, by using the formatting buttons on the Ribbon to change font size and color. Some control properties, however, can only be viewed and modified using the control's **Property Sheet**, a comprehensive listing of all **properties** (characteristics) for the selected control. One such property is the **Control Source property**, which determines field **binding** (the field to which a text box is connected). 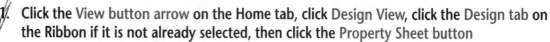 Because Quest offers more adventure tours than any other type of tour, you decide to modify the default value of the Category field to be "Adventure." You work with the control's Property Sheet to modify the default value.

STEPS

1. **Click the** View button arrow **on the Home tab, click** Design View, **click the** Design tab **on the Ribbon if it is not already selected, then click the** Property Sheet button

    The Property Sheet opens, showing you all of the properties for the selected item, which is currently the entire form. The Category field is bound to a **combo box**, which is a combination of a text box and a list of values commonly entered for that field.

2. **Click the** Category combo box, **click the** Data tab **in the Property Sheet, click the** Default Value box, **type** Adventure, **then press** [Enter]

    The Property Sheet should look like Figure C-9. Access often helps you with the rules, or syntax, of entering property values. In this case, it entered quotation marks around "Adventure" to indicate that the default entry is text. You can also use the Property Sheet window to modify the most important property of a text box, its Control Source property, to bind the text box to a field. In the Tours Entry Form, each text box and combo box is already bound to the field name shown in the control. To change this binding, use the Control Source property in the Property Sheet. In this case, you want to switch the order of the Duration and TourStartDate text boxes. You could either move the controls on the form or change their bindings.

> **QUICK TIP**
> If you know the field name, you can change a field's Control Source property by directly typing the field name into the text box on the form. You must know the exact field name to use this method.

3. **Click the** TourStartDate text box **to select it, click** TourStartDate **in the Control Source property of the Property Sheet, click the** list arrow, **then click** Duration

    At this point, you have two text boxes bound to the Duration field. Change the second one to bind it to the TourStartDate field.

> **TROUBLE**
> Be sure to modify the text boxes on the right, not the labels on the left. If the Expression Builder dialog box opens, click Cancel.

4. **Click the** second Duration text box **to select it, click** Duration **in the Control Source property of the Property Sheet, click the** list arrow, **then click** TourStartDate

    With the text boxes switched, you now also need to modify the descriptive labels on the left. The text displayed in a label is controlled by the Caption property.

5. **Click the** Tour Start Date label **to select it, click the** Format tab **in the Property Sheet, select** Tour Start Date **in the Caption property, type** Duration, **click the** Duration label **to select it, select** Duration **in the Caption property, type** Tour Start Date, **then press** [Enter]

    Don't be overwhelmed by the number of properties available for each control on the form or the number of ways to modify each property. Over time, you will learn about most of these properties, but at first you can make most property changes directly in Form or Layout View, rather than using the Property Sheet itself.

6. **Click the** Save button 🖫 **on the Quick Access toolbar, then click the** Form View button 🗐 **on the Design tab**

    The modified Tours Entry Form is shown in Figure C-10.

FIGURE C-9: Using the Property Sheet

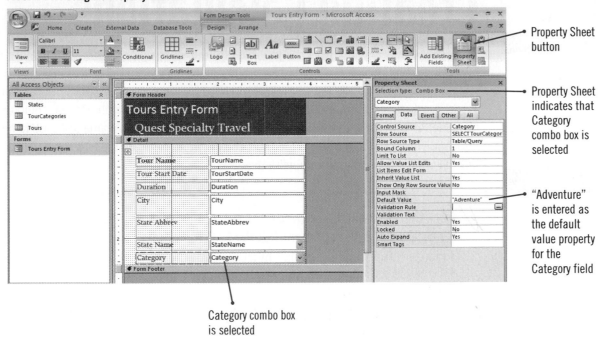

Property Sheet button

Property Sheet indicates that Category combo box is selected

"Adventure" is entered as the default value property for the Category field

Category combo box is selected

FIGURE C-10: Modified Tours Entry Form

Duration and Tour Start Date fields switched

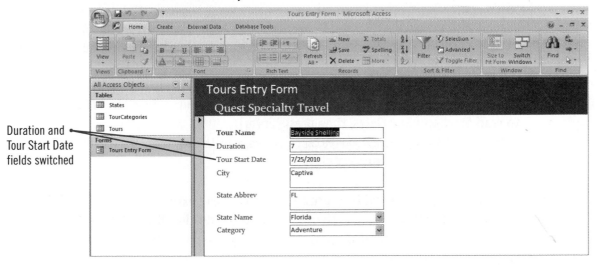

Creating Calculations

Text boxes are generally used to display data from underlying fields and are therefore *bound* to those fields. A text box control can also display a calculation. To create a calculation in a text box, you enter an **expression**, which consists of an equal sign and a combination of symbols that calculates a result. For example, you could use a text box to calculate sales tax or commission. Or, you could use a text box to combine, or concatenate, the values of two Text fields such as FirstName and LastName. Mark Rock asks you to add a text box to the Tours Entry Form to calculate the tour end date. You can add a text box in Form Design View to accomplish this.

STEPS

1. **Click the View button arrow on the Home tab, click Design View, click the Design tab if it is not already selected, then click the Property Sheet button to close the Property Sheet**

To add the calculation to determine the tour end date (the tour start date plus the duration), start by adding a text box to the form.

2. **Click the Text Box button on the Design tab, then click to the right of the TourStartDate text box on the form**

Adding a new text box automatically adds a new label to the left of the new text box. The form also widens to accommodate new controls. The number in the default caption of the label identifies how many controls you have previously added to the form. You don't need this label, so you can delete it.

> **TROUBLE**
> The number in your label might vary, based on previous work done to the form.

3. **Click the Text17 label to the left of the new text box, then press [Delete]**

> **QUICK TIP**
> You can resize controls one **pixel** (picture element) at a time by pressing [Shift] and an arrow key.

4. **Click the new text box to select it, click Unbound, type =[TourStartDate]+[Duration] , press [Enter] , then drag the middle-right sizing handle to the right far enough to view the entire expression, as shown in Figure C-11**

All expressions entered into a text box start with an equal sign (=). When referencing a field name within an expression, [square brackets]—(not parentheses) and not {curly braces}—surround the field name. In an expression, you must type the field name exactly as it was created in Table Design View, but you do not need to match the capitalization.

> **TROUBLE**
> Move the Start and End Dates label, the TourStartDate text box, and the calculated text box as necessary so that they do not overlap.

5. **Click the Tour Start Date label on the left to select it, click the Tour Start Date text, edit it to read Start and End Dates, then press [Enter]**

With the new calculation in place and the label modified, a final step before previewing the form is to align the top edges of the two text boxes that display dates.

6. **Click the TourStartDate text box, press [Shift] , click the expression text box to add it to the selection, click the Arrange tab on the Ribbon, then click the Align Top button**

Now the top edges of the text boxes are perfectly aligned. The Control Alignment buttons on the Layout tab (To Grid, Left, Right, Top, and Bottom) control alignment of two or more controls with respect to one another. Table C-3 shows techniques on how to select more than one control at the same time. The alignment buttons on the Design tab ▤, ▤, and ▤ align text within the edges of the control itself.

7. **Click the Save button ▤ on the Quick Access toolbar, click the Home tab on the Ribbon, click the Form View button ▤, then press [Page Down] to navigate to the Fullington Family Reunion tour, viewing the calculated field as you move through the records**

The updated Tours Entry Form with the tour date end calculation for the Fullington Family Reunion is shown in Figure C-12.

FIGURE C-11: Adding a text box to calculate a value

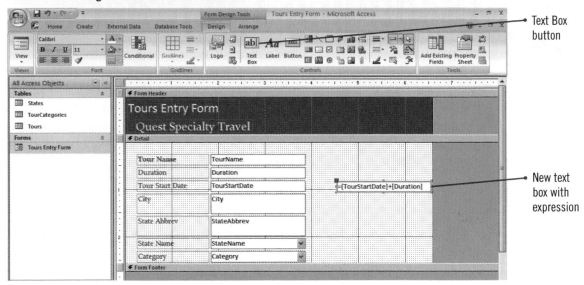

Text Box button

New text box with expression

FIGURE C-12: Displaying the results of a calculation in Form View

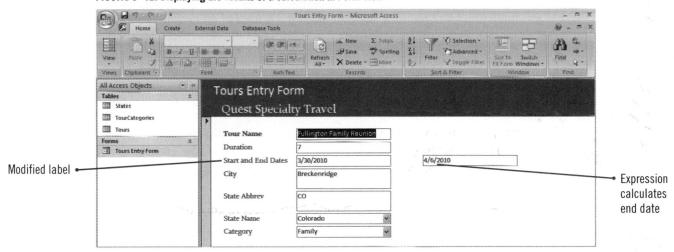

Modified label

Expression calculates end date

TABLE C-3: Selecting more than one control at a time

technique	description
Click, [Shift]+click	Click a control, then press and hold [Shift] while clicking other controls; each one is selected
Drag a selection box	Drag a selection box (an outline box you create by dragging the pointer in Form Design View); every control that is in or is touched by the edges of the box is selected
Click in the ruler	Click in either the horizontal or vertical ruler to select all controls that intersect the selection line
Drag in the ruler	Drag through either the horizontal or vertical ruler to select all controls that intersect the selection line as it is dragged through the ruler

Modifying Tab Order

After positioning all of the controls on the form, you should check the tab order and tab stops. A **tab stop** in Access refers to whether you can tab into a control when entering or editing data, in other words, whether the control can receive the focus. Recall that focus refers to which field would be edited if you started typing. **Tab order** is the order the focus moves as you press [Tab] in Form View. Controls that cannot be bound to fields such as labels and lines cannot have the focus in Form View because they are not used to enter or edit data. By default, all text boxes and combo boxes have a tab stop and are placed in the tab order. You plan to check the tab order of the Tours Entry Form, then change tab stops and tab order as necessary in Design View.

STEPS

1. **Click Fullington in the Tour Name text box, then press [Tab] eight times, watching the focus move through the bound controls of the form**

   Currently, focus moves through the first column to the tour end date text box and then to the next record. Because the tour end date text box is a calculated field, you don't want it to receive the focus, as this date is automatically calculated based on the tour start date plus the duration. To remove the tour end date text box from receiving the focus, you remove its tab stop. You also review the tab order before and after this change to observe the difference.

   > **TROUBLE**
   > If the order of your fields does not match those in Figure C-13, move a field by clicking the row selector and then dragging the field.

2. **Click the View button arrow on the Home tab, click Design View, click the Arrange tab, click the Tab Order button, then click Detail in the Section box**

   The Tab Order dialog box allows you to change the tab order of controls by dragging the **row selector**, the box to the left of the field name, up or down. Text17 in Figure C-13 is the name of the text box you added that contains the expression. It can appear anywhere in the list, depending on how you added the field.

3. **Click Cancel, click the new text box with the expression to select it, click the Design tab, then click the Property Sheet button to open the Property Sheet**

   The Other tab of the Property Sheet contains the properties you need to change the tab stop and tab order. The **Tab Stop** property determines whether the field accepts focus, and the **Tab Index** property indicates the tab order for the control on the form. Therefore, you can change the tab order property in either the Tab Order dialog box or in the Property Sheet.

   > **TROUBLE**
   > The name of the text box, Text17, might appear with a different number on your screen. The number identifies how many controls have been added to the form.

4. **Click the Other tab in the Property Sheet, then double-click the Tab Stop property to change the value from Yes to No**

   While working in this control's Property Sheet, you also decide to rename the text box from Text17 to something more descriptive so that when you reference this control, it also has a meaningful name.

5. **Double-click Text17 in the Name property box, then type TourEndDate**

   Your form should look like Figure C-14. With the tab stop modified for the TourEndDate calculation, you're ready to test the new form.

   > **QUICK TIP**
   > In Form Design View, press [Ctrl][.] to switch to Form View. In Form View, press [Ctrl][,] to switch to Form Design View.

6. **Click the Form View button** 🔲 **on the Design tab**

7. **Press [Tab] seven times, noticing that you no longer tab into the TourEndDate text box**

8. **Save the Tours Entry Form**

FIGURE C-13: Tab Order dialog box

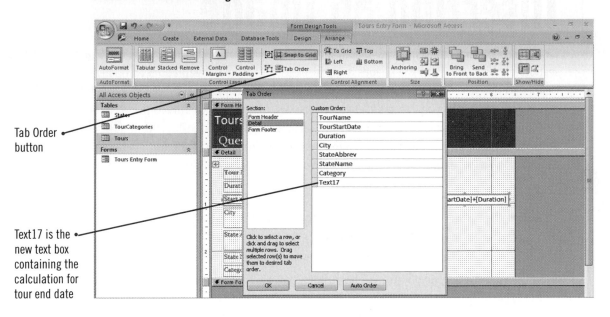

Tab Order button

Text17 is the new text box containing the calculation for tour end date

FIGURE C-14: Modifying tab properties for the selected field

Calculated field is selected on the form

New name for the calculated field

Tab Stop property set to No for the calculated field

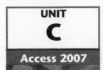

Inserting an Image

Graphic images, such as pictures, logos, or clip art, can add style and professionalism to a form. The form section in which you place the images is significant. For example, if you add a company logo to the Form Header section, the image appears at the top of the form in Form View as well as at the top of a printout. If you add the same image to the Detail section, it prints next to each record in a printout because the Detail section is printed for every record. Form sections are described in Table C-4. ████████ Mark Rock suggests that you add the Quest logo and a descriptive title to the top of the form. You plan to add the logo by inserting an unbound image control in the Form Header section.

1. **Click the View button arrow on the Home tab, click Design View, click the Design tab, close the Property Sheet, then click the Logo button**

   The Insert Picture dialog box opens, prompting you for the location of the image.

2. **Navigate to the drive and folder where you store your Data Files, then double-click QSTLogo.jpg**

   The Quest logo image is added to the left side of the Form Header. You need to move it to the right so that the two labels are still clearly visible.

3. **With the Quest logo still selected, drag the logo to the right, so that the labels and logo in the Form Header section are clearly visible, then drag a sizing handle on the logo to display it clearly**

   The Quest logo is inserted into the Form Header in an image control, as shown in Figure C-15. Table C-5 summarizes other types of multimedia controls that you can add to a form. With the form completed, you open it in Form View to observe the changes.

4. **Click the Save button 🖫 on the Quick Access toolbar, then click the Form View button 🔲 on the Design tab**

   You decide to add one more record.

5. **Enter the new record shown in Figure C-16, using your name in the TourName field**

   Now print only this new record.

6. **Click the Office button 🏢, click Print, click the Selected Record(s) option button, then click OK**

7. **Close the Tours Entry Form, close the Quest-C.accdb database, then exit Access**

FIGURE C-15: Adding an image to the Form Header section

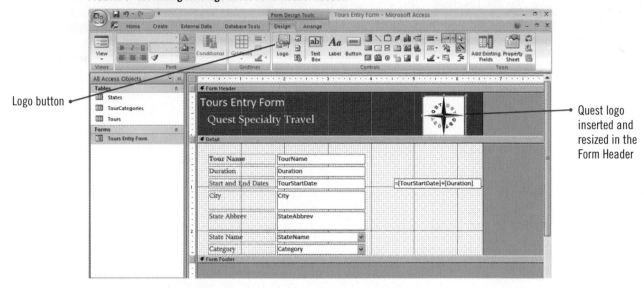

FIGURE C-16: Final Tours Entry Form

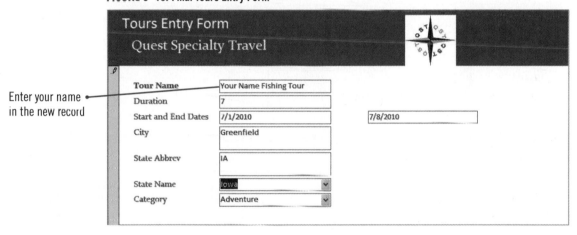

TABLE C-4: Form sections

section	description
Form Header	Controls placed in the Form Header section print only once at the top of the printout
Detail	Controls placed in the Detail section appear in Form View and print once for every record in the underlying table or query object
Form Footer	Controls placed in the Form Footer section print only once at the end of the printout

TABLE C-5: Multimedia controls

control	button	description
Image		Adds a single piece of clip art, a photo, or a logo to a form
Unbound object frame		Adds a sound clip, movie clip, document, or other type of unbound data (data that isn't stored in a table of the database) to a form
Bound object frame		Displays the contents of a field with an **OLE Object** (object linking and embedding) data type; an OLE Object field might contain pictures, sound clips, documents, or other data created by other software applications

Practice

If you have a SAM user profile, you may have access to hands-on instruction, practice, and assessment of the skills covered in this unit. Log in to your SAM account (http://sam2007.course.com/) to launch any assigned training activities or exams that relate to the skills covered in this unit.

▼ CONCEPTS REVIEW

Label each element of the Form View shown in Figure C-17.

FIGURE C-17

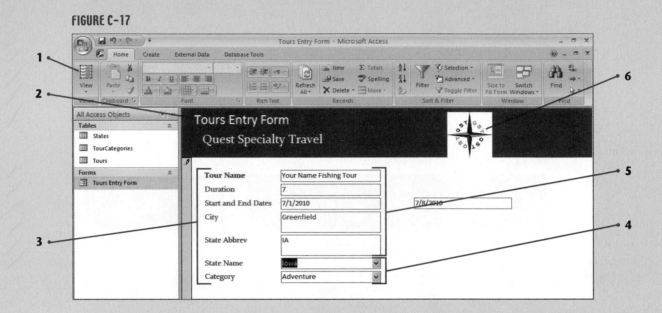

Match each term with the statement that best describes it.

7. **Bound control**
8. **Calculated control**
9. **Detail section**
10. **Form**
11. **Tab order**
12. **Form Footer section**

a. An Access database object that allows you to arrange the fields of a record in any layout and which is used to enter, edit, and delete records
b. The way the focus moves from one bound control to the next in Form View
c. Created by entering an expression in a text box
d. Controls placed here print once for every record in the underlying record source
e. Controls placed here print only once at the end of the printout
f. Used on a form to display data from a field

Select the best answer from the list of choices.

13. **Every element on a form is called a(n):**
    a. Property.
    b. Tool.
    c. Item.
    d. Control.

14. **Which of the following is probably *not* a graphic image?**
    a. Logo
    b. Calculation
    c. Clip art
    d. Picture

15. **The most common bound control is the:**
    a. Text box.
    b. List box.
    c. Combo box.
    d. Label.

16. **The most common unbound control is the:**
    a. Command button.
    b. Text box.
    c. Label.
    d. Combo box.

17. **Which view *cannot* be used to view data?**
    a. Layout
    b. Design
    c. Preview
    d. Datasheet

18. **Which property helps you bind a text box to a field?**
    a. Control Source
    b. Name
    c. Bindings
    d. Bound

19. **When you enter a calculation in a text box, the first character is a(n):**
    a. Equal sign, =
    b. Left parenthesis, (
    c. Left square bracket, [
    d. Asterisk, *

1. Create a form with the Form Wizard.

a. Start Access and open the RealEstate-C.accdb database from the drive and folder where you store your Data Files. Enable content if prompted.

b. Click the Create tab, then use the Form Wizard to create a form based on all of the fields in the Agents table. Use a Columnar layout and an Equity style. Title the form Agent Entry Form.

c. Add a new record with your name. Note that the AgentNo field is an AutoNumber field and automatically increments as you enter your first and last names. Enter your school's telephone number for the AgentPhone field value, and 4 as the AgencyNo field value.

2. Use Layout View.

a. Switch to Layout View.

b. Modify each of the labels in Layout View by adding a space between the words in the labels.

c. Modify the text color of the labels to be black.

d. Modify the font size of each label to be 14 points.

e. Save the form and view it in Form View.

3. Use Form Design View.

a. Open the Agent Entry Form in Design View.

b. Add a label with your name to the Form Header section, below the Agent Entry Form label.

c. Format both labels so that the font size is 22, the font color is white, and they are bold.

d. Resize the label with your name to display its complete text.

e. Position the labels so that the left edges are aligned and all text is clearly visible.

f. Save the form and view it in Form View.

4. Add fields to a form.

a. Open the form in Layout View.

b. Open the Field List window if it is not already displayed, then expand the field list for the Agencies table.

c. Drag the AgencyName field directly under the AgencyNo field on the form.

d. Delete the AgencyNo label and text box.

e. Modify the AgencyName: label to add a space between the words and to delete the colon.

f. Save the form and display it in Form View.

5. Modify form controls.

a. Open the form in Design View, then open the Property Sheet.

b. Change the order of the first three controls to AgencyName, AgentLast, and AgentFirst by using their Control Source properties. Change the Name property of the AgentLast text box to TemporaryName, change the Name property of the AgentFirst text box to AgentFirst, and then change the Name property of the AgentLast text box to AgentLast.

c. Change the text of the first three labels to Agency Name, Agent Last, and Agent First by using their Caption properties.

d. Save the form, then view it in Form View.

6. Create calculations.

a. Switch to Design View, then drag the top edge of the Form Footer down about 0.5 inch to make room for a new text box.

b. Add a text box to the Form Footer section, then delete the accompanying label.

c. Widen the text box to be almost as wide as the entire form, then enter the following expression into the text box, which will add the words "Agent information for" to the agent's first name, a space, and then the agent's last name.

="Agent information for "&[AgentFirst]&" "&[AgentLast]

d. Save the form, then view it in Form View.

7. Modify tab order.

a. Switch to Form Design View, then open the Property Sheet.

b. Select the new text box with the expression, change the Name property to AgentInfo and change the Tab Stop property to No.

c. Save the form and view it in Form View. Tab through the form to make sure that the tab order is sequential. Use the Tab Order button on the Arrange tab in Form Design View to modify tab order, if necessary.

8. Insert an image.

a. Switch to Form Design or Layout View, then close the Property Sheet.

b. Add the house.jpg image to the right side of the Form Header, then resize the image and labels as necessary.

c. Save, then display the form in Form View. It should look similar to Figure C-18. Display the record with your name in it, then print only that record.

d. Close the Agent Entry Form, close the RealEstate-C.accdb database, then exit Access.

FIGURE C-18

Access 2007

▼ INDEPENDENT CHALLENGE 1

As the office manager of a veterinary association, you need to create a data entry form for new veterinarians.

a. Start Access, then open the **Vet-C.accdb** database from the drive and folder where you store your Data Files. Enable content if prompted.

b. Using the Form Wizard, create a form that includes all the fields in the Vets table, using the Columnar layout and Solstice style. Title the form **Vet Entry Form**.

c. Add a record with your own name. Note that the VetNo field is an AutoNumber field and automatically increments. Add yourself to ClinicNo 1.

d. In Form Design View, add a label with your name to the Form Header, below the Vet Entry Form label, in a font color and size that is easily visible.

e. Right-align the text within the four labels in the Detail section so that they are closer to the text boxes they describe. (*Hint:* Use the Align Text Right button on the Design tab.)

f. Add the **dog.jpg** image to the Form Header section. Move and resize the image so that the entire image as well as both labels are clearly visible.

g. Save the form, then display it in Form View. Print only the record that includes your name, as shown in Figure C-19.

h. Close the Vet Entry Form, close the Vet-C.accdb database, then exit Access.

FIGURE C-19

▼ INDEPENDENT CHALLENGE 2

You have built an Access database to track membership in a community service club. The database tracks member names and addresses as well as their status in the club, which moves from rank to rank as the members contribute increased hours of service to the community.

a. Start Access, then open the **Membership-C.accdb** database from the drive and folder where you store your Data Files. Enable content if prompted.

b. Using the Form Wizard, create a form based on all of the fields of the Members table and only the DuesOwed field in the Status table.

c. View the data by Members, use a Columnar layout and a Trek style, then title the form **Membership Entry Form**.

d. Enter a new record with your name and the address of your school. Give yourself a StatusNo entry of **1**. In the DuesPaid field, enter **75**. DuesOwed automatically displays 100 because that value is pulled from the Status table and is based on the entry in the StatusNo field, which links the Members table to the Status table.

e. In Design View, expand the Detail section down about 0.5 inches, then add a text box below DuesOwed with an expression that calculates the balance between DuesOwed and DuesPaid. Change the label for the calculated field to **Balance**.

f. Right-align all of the labels.

g. Set the Tab Stop property for the calculated field to **No**, and enter **Balance** for the Name property.

Advanced Challenge Exercise

- Drag the top edge of the Form Footer down about 0.5 inch to make more room for the form's Detail section.
- Open the field list, then drag the Status field from the Status table in the field list to below the Balance field in the form. Edit the label to delete the colon (:).
- Check the tab order to make sure that the fields receive focus in a logical order.
- If the calculated field or Status text boxes or labels aren't sized or aligned similarly to the rest of the controls on the form, return to Layout or Design View to resize and align them. (*Hint*: Use the Size to Widest button on the Arrange tab to size several selected controls to the widest selection. Use the Align Left and Align Right buttons on the Arrange tab to align the edges of several selected controls.)
- View the form in Form View. It should look like Figure C-20.

h. Save the form, find the record with your name, then print only that record.

i. Close the Membership Entry Form, then close the Membership-C.accdb database and exit Access.

FIGURE C-20

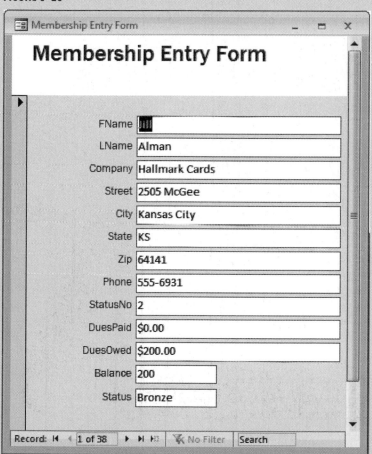

▼ INDEPENDENT CHALLENGE 3

You have built an Access database to organize the deposits at a recycling center. Various clubs regularly deposit recyclable material, which is measured in pounds when the deposits are made.

a. Open the **Recycle-C.accdb** database from the drive and folder where you store your Data Files. Enable content if prompted.

b. Using the Form Wizard, create a form based on all of the fields in the DepositList query. Use the Tabular layout and Urban style, then enter **Deposit List Form** as the title.

c. Bold each label. Resize the labels and text boxes to be sure they are all wide enough to accommodate all entries in the fields and display the entire label at the top of each column.

d. Modify the Centers_Name and Clubs_Name labels so they read Center Name and Club Name.

e. Continue to work in Layout View to drag the bottom edge of the text boxes up, so that they are tall enough to accommodate all of the entries, as shown in Figure C-21, but do not waste any vertical space.

f. In Form View, change any entry of Jaycees in the Clubs Name to your last name, then print the first page of the form.

Advanced Challenge Exercise

- Using Form View of the Deposit List Form, filter for all records with your name in the Clubs Name field.
- Using Form View of the Deposit List Form, sort the filtered records in ascending order on the Deposit Date field.
- Preview, then print the filtered and sorted records.

g. Save and close the Deposit List Form, close the Recycle-C.accdb database, then exit Access.

FIGURE C-21

Deposit Number	Deposit Date	Weight	Center Name	Club Name
1	1/5/2010	60	Trash Can	Boy Scouts #11
2	1/7/2010	90	Bachman Trash	Oak Hill Patriots
3	2/15/2010	50	Wilson County Landfill	Oak Hill Patriots
4	2/19/2010	30	Bachman Trash	Boy Scouts #11
5	2/22/2010	50	Johnson County Landfill	Girl Scouts #11
6	2/23/2010	100	Wilson County Landfill	Girl Scouts #11
7	3/1/2010	125	Bachman Trash	Lions
8	3/17/2010	60	Trash Can	Boy Scouts #11
9	4/5/2010	115	Trash Can	Lions
10	4/20/2010	105	Trash Can	Boy Scouts #11
11	5/20/2010	90	Bachman Trash	Boy Scouts #11
12	5/21/2010	80	Wilson County Landfill	Jaycees

Record: 1 of 100 — No Filter — Search

▼ REAL LIFE INDEPENDENT CHALLENGE

One way you can use an Access database on your own is to record and track your experiences, such as places you've visited. Suppose that your passion for travel includes a dream to visit all 50 states. A database with information about all 50 states is provided with your Data Files, and you can use it to develop a form to help you enter more travel information.

This Independent Challenge requires an Internet connection.

a. Start Access and open the **States-C.accdb** database from the drive and folder where you store your Data Files. Enable content if prompted.

b. Open the States table datasheet to view the existing information on each state.

c. Add a field to the States table with the name **Attractions** and a data type of Memo.

d. Create a form based on all of the fields of the States table. Title the form **State Entry Form**.

e. Using any search engine such as *www.google.com* or *www.yahoo.com*, research two states that you'd like to visit.

f. Make entries in the Attractions field of each of your two selected states to store information about the attractions that you'd like to visit in each of those states.

g. Make any other formatting embellishments on the State Entry Form that you desire, then print the record for each of the two states that you updated with information in the Attractions field.

h. Save and close the State Entry Form, close the States-C.accdb database, then exit Access.

▼ VISUAL WORKSHOP

Open the **Basketball-C.accdb** database, then use the Form Wizard to create the form as shown in Figure C-22 based on all of the fields in the Games table. Use a Columnar layout and a Foundry style. The label in the Form Header, Basketball Scores, is a font size of 22. The Margin of Victory label and calculation were added in Form Design View. The margin of victory is calculated as the Home Score minus the Opponent Score. Also notice that the labels are right-aligned. Enter the record shown in Figure C-22, using your name as the name of the school. Print only that record.

FIGURE C-22

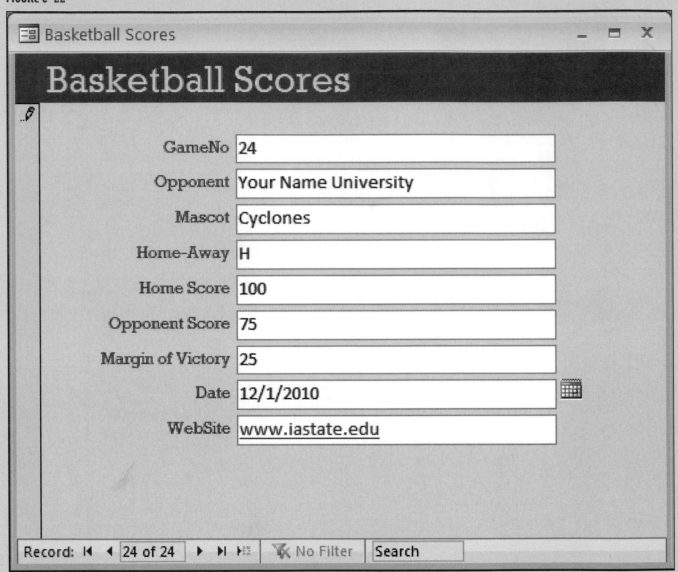

Using Reports

**Files You
Will Need:**

Quest-D.accdb

RealEstate-D.accdb

Vet-D.accdb

Membership-D.accdb

Recycle-D.accdb

States-D.accdb

Basketball-D.accdb

A **report** is an Access object used to create professional-looking printouts. Although you can print a datasheet or form, reports are the primary object you use to print database content because they provide many more data layout options. For example, a report might include formatting embellishments such as multiple fonts and colors, extra graphical elements such as clip art and lines, and multiple headers and footers. Reports are also very powerful data analysis tools. A report can calculate subtotals, averages, counts, or other statistics for groups of records. However, you cannot enter or edit data through a report. Mark Rock, a tour developer at Quest Specialty Travel, asks you to produce some reports to analyze data for Quest meetings.

OBJECTIVES

Preview a report

Use the Report Wizard

Use Report Design View

Use report sections

Add subtotals and counts

Resize and align controls

Format a report

Change page layout

Previewing a Report

When you want to communicate Access information at internal meetings or with customers, the report object helps you professionally format and summarize the data. Creating a report is similar to creating a form—you work with bound, unbound, and calculated controls in Report Design View just as you do in Form Design View. Reports, however, have more sections than forms. A **section** determines where and how often controls in that section print in the final report. Table D-1 shows more information on report sections. ▟▚▟▟ You and Mark Rock preview a completed report that illustrates many features of Access reports.

STEPS

1. **Start Access, open the Quest-D.accdb database, then enable content if prompted**

   The Quest-D database already contains two reports named Tour Descriptions and Tours By Category. You'll open the Tours By Category report in **Report View**, a view that maximizes the amount of data you can see on the screen.

TROUBLE

If you do not see any reports in the Navigation Pane, click the Reports button in the Navigation Pane.

2. **Double-click the Tours By Category report in the Navigation Pane, then double-click the title bar of the report to maximize it**

   The Tours By Category report appears in Report View, as shown in Figure D-1. The Tours By Category report shows all of the tours for each state within each category. In the Adventure category, four tours are in California and five tours are in Colorado.

3. **Double-click California in the State column, then attempt to type Oregon**

   Reports are **read-only** objects, meaning that they read and display data, but cannot be used to change (write to) data. Like forms, a report always displays the most up-to-date data that is stored in only one type of Access object, tables. Switching to **Print Preview** shows you how the report prints on a sheet of paper.

4. **Click the View button arrow on the Home tab, then click Print Preview**

   Print Preview shows you the report as it appears on a full sheet of paper, including margins. You can zoom in and out to increase or decrease the magnification of the image by clicking the report.

5. **Click the report once to view an entire sheet of paper, then click the Next Page button ▶ on the navigation bar to advance to the second page of the report**

   The second page of the Tours By Category report appears in Print Preview, as shown in Figure D-2. On the second page, you can clearly see how the records are grouped together by the value in the Category field, then by State, and finally sorted in ascending order on the Start Date field.

6. **Click the Close Print Preview button, then close the Tours By Category report**

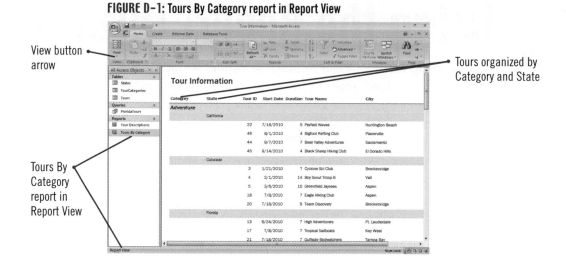

FIGURE D-1: Tours By Category report in Report View

View button arrow

Tours organized by Category and State

Tours By Category report in Report View

FIGURE D-2: Second page of the Tours By Category report in Print Preview

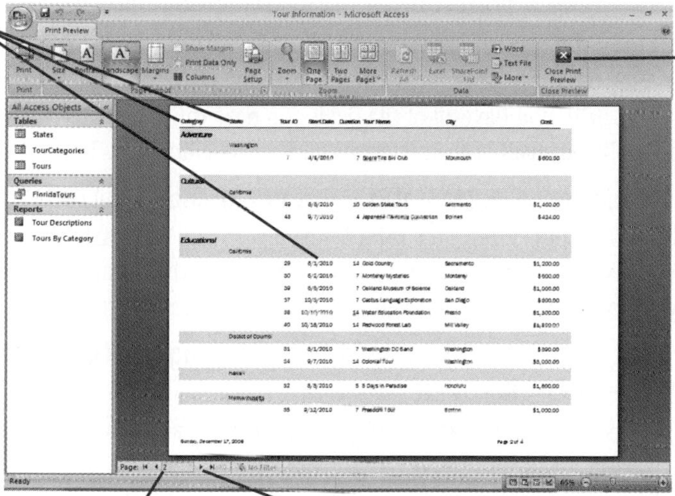

Report is grouped by Category, then State, and then sorted on Start Date

Close Print Preview button

Second page of the report

Next Page button

TABLE D-1: Report sections

section	where does this section print?	which controls are most commonly placed in this section?
Report Header	At the top of the first page of the report	Label controls containing the report title; can also include clip art, a logo image, or a line separating the title from the rest of the report
Page Header	At the top of every page (but below the Report Header on page one)	Text box controls containing a page number or date expression
Group Header	Before every group of records	Text box controls for the field by which the records are grouped
Detail	Once for every record	Text box controls for the rest of the fields in the recordset (the table or query upon which the report is built)
Group Footer	After every group of records	Text box controls containing calculated expressions, such as subtotals or counts, for the records in that group
Page Footer	At the bottom of every page	Text box controls containing a page number or date expression
Report Footer	At the end of the entire report	Text box controls containing expressions such as grand totals or counts that calculate a value for all of the records in the report

Using the Report Wizard

You can create reports in Access by using the **Report Wizard**, a tool that asks questions to guide you through the initial development of the report, similar to the Form Wizard. Your responses to the Report Wizard determine the record source, style, and layout of the report. The **record source** is the table or query that defines the fields and records displayed on the report. The Report Wizard also helps you sort, group, and analyze the records. ▓▓▓▓ You plan to use the Report Wizard to create a report similar to the Tours By Category report. This time, however, you want to group the tours by state.

1. **Click the Create tab on the Ribbon, then click the Report Wizard button**

The Report Wizard starts, prompting you to select the fields you want on the report. You can select fields from one or more tables or queries.

2. **Click the Tables/Queries list arrow, click Table: States, double-click the StateName field, click the Tables/Queries list arrow, click Table: Tours, click the Select All Fields button ⊡⊡, click StateAbbrev in the Selected Fields list, then click the Remove Field button ⊡**

By selecting the StateName field from the States table, and all fields from the Tours table except the StateAbbrev field, you have all of the fields you need for the report—including the full state name stored in the States table, instead of the two-letter state abbreviation used in the Tours table—as shown in Figure D-3.

3. **Click Next, then click by States if it is not already selected**

Choosing "by States" groups the records together within each state. In addition to record-grouping options, the Report Wizard asks if you want to sort the records within each group. You can use the Report Wizard to specify up to four fields to sort in either ascending or descending order.

> **TROUBLE**
> Click Back to review previous dialog boxes within a wizard.

4. **Click Next, click Next again to add no grouping levels, click the first sort list arrow, click TourName, then click Next**

The last questions in the wizard deal with report appearance and creating a report title.

> **TROUBLE**
> Depending on how you installed Access 2007, the appearance of your report might differ slightly.

5. **Click the Stepped option button, click the Portrait option button, click Next, click the Apex style, click Next, type Tours By State for the report title, click Finish, then maximize the Print Preview window**

The Tours By State report opens in Print Preview, as shown in Figure D-4. The records are grouped by state, the first state being California, and then sorted in ascending order by the TourName field within each state.

6. **Scroll down to see the second grouping section on the report for the state of Colorado, click the Close Print Preview button on the Print Preview tab, then save and close the report**

Closing Print Preview displays the report in either Report View, Layout View, or Design View, depending upon which view you used last.

FIGURE D-3: Selecting fields for a report using the Report Wizard

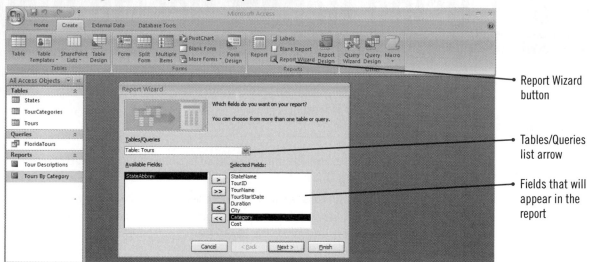

Report Wizard button

Tables/Queries list arrow

Fields that will appear in the report

FIGURE D-4: Tours By State report in Print Preview

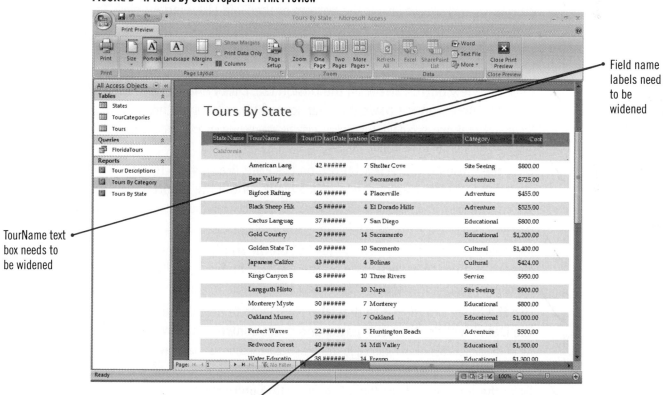

Field name labels need to be widened

TourName text box needs to be widened

TourStartDate text box needs to be widened

Using Report Design View

Like forms, reports have multiple views—including Report View, Layout View, Design View, and Print Preview—that you can use for various activities. Design View is the most complicated view because it allows you to make the most changes to the report. ▓▓▓▓ Mark Rock asks you to create a new report that lists all of the tours from Florida.

1. **Click the Create tab on the Ribbon, click the Report Design button, then maximize the window**

   Design View opens with a blank report design surface. When building a report from scratch in Report Design View, the first task is to select the object (table or query) on which to base the report. The **Record Source** property of the report determines the object that the report is based on, which provides the fields and records displayed on the report.

2. **Click the Property Sheet button on the Design tab, click the Data tab, click the Record Source list arrow, then click FloridaTours**

   The FloridaTours query contains all of the fields in the Tours table as well as criteria to select only those records from the state of Florida. By choosing this query for the Record Source property, the report will display only Florida tours. Now add the fields from the FloridaTours query to the report.

3. **Click the Add Existing Fields button on the Design tab, click the Show only fields in the current record source link at the bottom of the Field List window, click TourName, press and hold [Shift], click the Cost field, release [Shift], then drag the fields to the middle of the Detail section**

   Report Design View should look similar to Figure D-5.

4. **Click the View button arrow on the Design tab, click Print Preview, then click the Next Page button ▶ on the navigation bar several times to page through the report**

   Right now, only one record prints per page, making the report very long. You can return to Design View and modify the report to make it more compact.

5. **Click the Close Print Preview button on the Print Preview tab to return to Design View, close the Field List window, then click a blank spot in the report**

   You can save space by arranging the fields across the page in a row (instead of in a vertical column), with the field labels appearing above the text boxes.

6. **Right-click the TourName label, click Cut on the shortcut menu, right-click the Page Header section, then click Paste on the shortcut menu**

   Moving the TourName label to the Page Header section means it prints once per page.

7. **Use the Move pointer ✛ to drag the TourName text box under the TourName label in the Detail section, then cut, paste, and move controls as shown in Figure D-6**

   All of the labels are now positioned in the Page Header section so that they appear only once per page, and all of the text box controls are positioned in the Detail section.

8. **Drag the top edge of the Page Footer section up to the bottom edge of the text boxes, click the Save button ▤ on the Quick Access toolbar, type Tours In Florida, click OK, click the View button arrow on the Design tab, then click Print Preview**

   Because the Detail section prints once per record, eliminating blank space in this section removes extra blank space in the report overall.

9. **Click the Close Print Preview button on the Print Preview tab, then close the Tours In Florida report**

FIGURE D-5: Adding fields to Report Design View

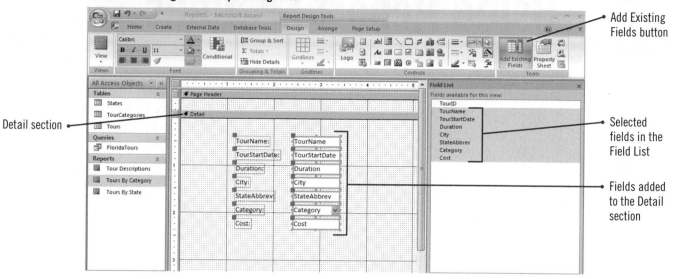

Detail section

Add Existing Fields button

Selected fields in the Field List

Fields added to the Detail section

FIGURE D-6: Redesigning a report in Report Design View

All of the labels are positioned in the Page Header section

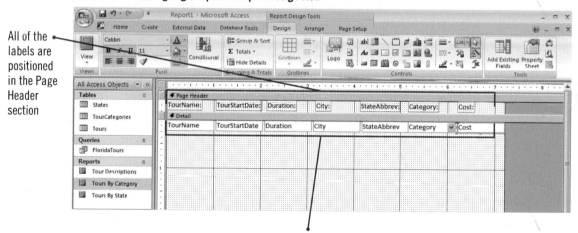

All of the text boxes are positioned in the Detail section

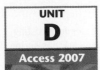

Using Report Sections

Grouping means to sort records in a particular order *plus* provide a header or footer section before or after each group. For example, if you group records by the State field, the grouping sections are called the State Header and State Footer. The State Header section appears once for each state in the report, immediately before the records in that state. The State Footer section also appears once for each state in the report, immediately after the records for that state. ▰▰▰▰▰ The records in the Tours By State report are currently grouped by state. Mark Rock asks you to further group the records by category within each state.

1. **Right-click the Tours By State report in the Navigation Pane, click Design View, then maximize the report**

   To change sorting or grouping options for a report, you need to work in Report Design View.

2. **Click the Design tab on the Ribbon if it is not already selected, then click the Group & Sort button**

   The Group, Sort, and Total pane opens, as shown in Figure D-7. Currently, the records are grouped by the StateAbbreviation field and further sorted by the TourName field. To add the Category field as a grouping field within each state, you work with the Group, Sort, and Total pane.

3. **Click the Add a group button in the Group, Sort, and Total pane; click the select field list arrow if the field list window doesn't automatically appear; then click Category**

   A Category Header section appears on the report. In addition to grouping the records by both the StateAbbreviation and Category fields, you want to count the number of records in each group later so that, as an example, you can find out how many Adventure tours are in California. You open the Category Footer section and then add an expression to calculate this information to the Category Footer section.

4. **Click the More button on the Group on Category bar, click the without a footer section list arrow, then click with a footer section**

   A Category Footer section is added to the report. You want to group the records by state, then category, and then sort them within each category by TourName. To accomplish this you need to switch the order of the TourName and Category fields in the Group, Sort, and Total pane.

5. **With the Group on Category bar still selected, click the Move up button ⬆**

   With the Category Header and Footer sections open and in correct position, you're ready to add controls to those sections to further enhance the report. First, move the Category text box to the Category Header section so that it displays once per new category, rather than once for every record.

6. **Right-click the Category combo box in the Detail section, click Cut on the shortcut menu, right-click the Category Header section bar, then click Paste**

7. **Save the report, click the View button arrow, then click Print Preview**

   The Tours By State report should look similar to Figure D-8. Notice that the values in the Category field now appear once per category, before the records in each category are listed.

FIGURE D-7: Group, Sort, and Total pane

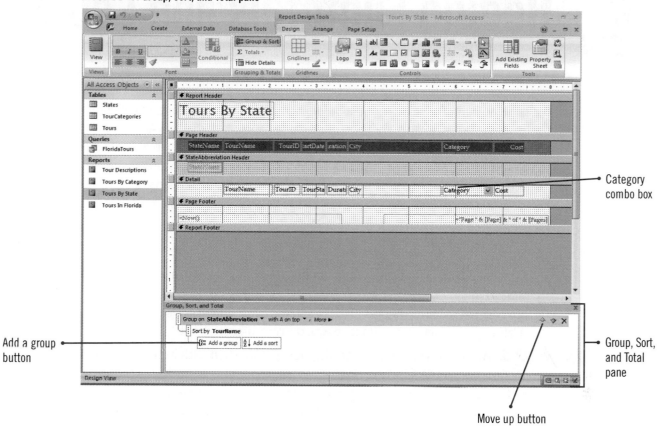

Add a group button

Category combo box

Group, Sort, and Total pane

Move up button

FIGURE D-8: Tours By State report with Category Header and Footer sections

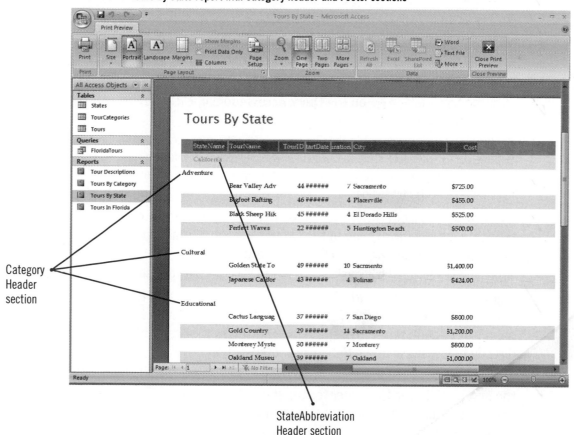

Category Header section

StateAbbreviation Header section

Adding Subtotals and Counts

In a report, you create a **calculation** by entering an expression into a text box. When a report is previewed or printed, the expression is evaluated and the resulting calculation is placed on the report. An **expression** is a combination of field names, operators (such as +, –, /, and *), and functions that result in a single value. A **function** is a built-in formula, such as Sum or Count, that helps you quickly create a calculation. Table D-2 lists examples of common expressions that use Access functions. Notice that every expression starts with an equal sign (=), and when it uses a function, the arguments for the function are placed in (parentheses). **Arguments** are the pieces of information that the function needs to create the final answer. When an argument is a field name, the field name must be surrounded by [square brackets]. ▓▓▓▓▓ Mark Rock asks you to add a calculation to the Tours By State report to count the number of records in each category within each state.

1. Click the Close Print Preview button on the Print Preview tab to return to Report Design View

Now you can add two controls to the Category Footer section—a label and a text box—to describe and calculate the total count of records within each category within each state.

QUICK TIP
To add only a descriptive label to the report, use the Label button *Aa* on the Design tab.

2. Click the Text Box button [abl] on the Design tab, then click in the Category Footer section below the City text box

Adding a new text box automatically adds a new label as well. First, you modify the label to identify the calculation you want to add to the text box, then you enter the appropriate expression to count the records in the text box.

TROUBLE
Depending on your activity in Report Design View, you may get a different number in the Text##: label. The number corresponds to the number of controls that have been added to this report.

3. Click the new Text19 label to select the label, double-click the Text19 entry to select the text, type Count of records, then press [Enter]

4. Click the Unbound text box in the Category Footer section to select it, click Unbound within the text box, type =Count([TourName]), then press [Enter]

The Count function counts the values in the TourName field, as shown in Figure D-9. To add numeric values in a Number or Currency field, you use the Sum function, as in =Sum([Price]).

5. Click the Save button [💾] on the Quick Access toolbar, click the View button arrow, then click Print Preview

The new label and calculation in the Category Footer section correctly identify how many records are in each category within each state. To calculate how many records are in each state, you can copy the controls from the Category Footer section to the StateAbbreviation Footer section. First, you need to open the StateAbbreviation Footer section.

6. Click the Close Print Preview button on the Print Preview tab; click the More button for the StateAbbreviation group in the Group, Sort, and Total pane; click the without a footer section list arrow; then click with a footer section

With the State Footer section open in Report Design View, you can now add controls to this section.

7. Right-click the text box with the Count expression in the Category Footer section, click Copy on the shortcut menu, right-click the StateAbbreviation Footer, click Paste, then press [→] enough times to position the controls in the StateAbbreviation Footer section directly below those in the Category Footer section

TROUBLE
Click the Next Page button [▶] to view page 2 if the footer for the state of California doesn't appear at the bottom of page 1.

8. Click [💾], click the View button arrow, click Print Preview, then scroll to the bottom of the first page to see the footer for the state of California

As shown in Figure D-10, 16 records were counted for the California group, but some of the data is not displayed correctly. You widen and align controls in the next lesson.

FIGURE D-9: Counting records in the Category Footer

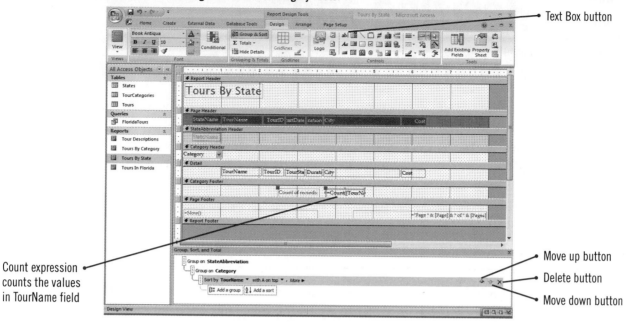

Text Box button

Count expression counts the values in TourName field

Move up button

Delete button

Move down button

FIGURE D-10: Previewing the new group footer calculations

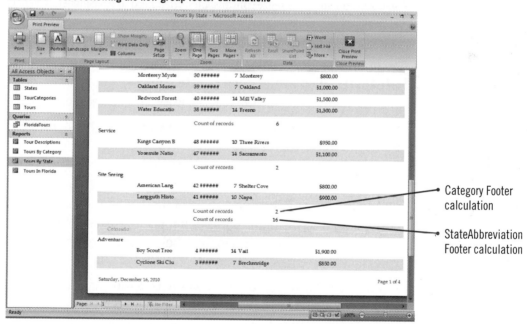

Category Footer calculation

StateAbbreviation Footer calculation

TABLE D-2: Sample Access expressions

sample expression	description
=Sum([Salary])	Uses the **Sum function** to add up the values in the Salary field
=[Price] * 1.05	Multiplies the Price field by 1.05 (adds 5% to the Price field)
=[Subtotal] + [Shipping]	Adds the value of the Subtotal field to the value of the Shipping field
=Avg([Freight])	Uses the **Avg function** to display an average of the values in the Freight field
=Date()	Uses the **Date function** to display the current date in the form of mm-dd-yy
="Page " &[Page]	Displays the word Page, a space, and the result of the [Page] field, an Access field that contains the current page number
=[FirstName]& " " &[LastName]	Displays the value of the FirstName and LastName fields in one control, separated by a space
=Left([ProductNumber],2)	Uses the **Left function** to display the first two characters in the ProductNumber field

Resizing and Aligning Controls

After you add information to the appropriate section of a report, you might also want to align the data on the report. Aligning controls in precise columns and rows makes the information easier to read. There are two different types of **alignment** commands. You can left-, right-, or center-align a control *within its own border* using the Align Text Left, ▤, Center ▤, and Align Text Right ▤ buttons on the Design tab. You can also align the edges of controls *with respect to one another* using the Align Left ▤, Align Right ▤, Align Top ▥, and Align Bottom ▥ buttons on the Arrange tab. ▰▰▰ You decide to widen and align several controls in the Category and State Footer sections to improve the readability of your report.

TROUBLE

If you make a mis-take, click the Undo button 🔄 on the Quick Access toolbar.

1. **Click the Close Print Preview button on the Print Preview tab to return to Design View, then use the ↔ pointer to widen the TourName and TourStartDate fields as shown in Figure D-11**

   When you add, move, or resize controls, they often need to be realigned. You decide to align the expressions that count records directly under the Cost text box.

TROUBLE

Be sure to select the text boxes that con-tain expressions, and not the labels.

2. **Click the Cost text box, press and hold [Shift], click the text box with the Count expression in the Category Footer as well as the text box with the Count expression in the StateAbbreviation Footer, then release [Shift]**

   With these three controls selected, you want to align the right edge of the controls *with respect to each other*.

3. **With the three controls still selected, click the Arrange tab on the Ribbon, then click the Align Right button ▤**

   With the expressions aligned, you want to move the labels in the footer sections below the City text box in the Detail section.

QUICK TIP

You can also click or drag through the horizontal or vertical rulers to select all controls that inter-sect with the selec-tion line.

4. **Point to the upper-left sizing handle of the Count of records label in the Category Footer, drag it to the right to position it just to the left of the expression it describes, then repeat this action to move the label in the StateAbbreviation Footer closer to the expression it describes**

TROUBLE

If the entire state name is not dis-played, return to Report Design View and widen the StateName field in the StateAbbreviation Header section.

5. **Click the Save button 🖫 on the Quick Access toolbar, click the Home tab, click the View button arrow, click Print Preview, then scroll to the bottom of the first page to see the footer for the state of California as shown in Figure D-12**

6. **Click the Close Print Preview button on the Print Preview toolbar, then close the Tours By State report**

FIGURE D-11: Widening controls

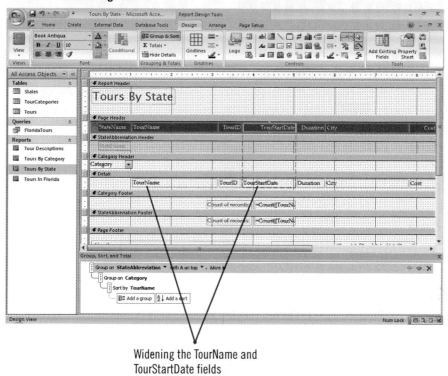

Widening the TourName and
TourStartDate fields

FIGURE D-12: Previewing the widened and aligned controls

TourName and
TourStartDate
fields are wide
enough to show
field values

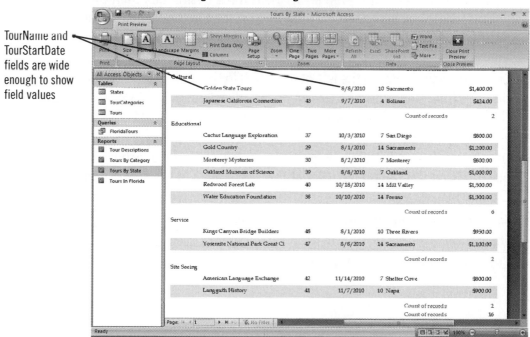

Precisely moving and resizing controls

You can move and resize controls using the mouse, but precise movements are often easier to accomplish using the keyboard. Pressing the arrow keys while holding [Ctrl] moves selected controls one **pixel** (picture element) at a time in the direction of the arrow. Pressing the arrow keys while holding [Shift] resizes selected controls one pixel at a time.

Formatting a Report

Formatting refers to enhancing the appearance of the information. Table D-3 lists several of the most popular formatting commands found on the Design tab. Although the Report Wizard automatically applies many formatting embellishments, you often want to improve the appearance of the report to fit your particular needs. ▆▆▆▆ When reviewing the Tour Descriptions report with Mark, you decide to format several sections to improve the appearance of the report.

1. Right-click the Tour Descriptions report in the Navigation Pane, click Print Preview, maximize the report, then click the report to zoom in

You decide to lighten the background of the Page Header section to the same shade as the Category Header section. You also want to darken the text color of the Page Header section to black. You can make some formatting changes in Layout View, which shows data, but Report Design View provides the best access to formatting and other design changes.

2. Click the Close Print Preview button on the Print Preview toolbar, right-click the Tour Descriptions report, click Design View, maximize the report, then click the Page Header section bar to select it

The **Back Color** property determines the color of the section background. It is represented as a hexadecimal number (which uses both numbers 0–9 and letters A–F) in the Back Color property on the Format tab of the property sheet, or you can modify it using the Fill/Back Color button on the Ribbon. Avoid relying too heavily on color formatting. Background shades often become solid black boxes when printed on a black-and-white printer or fax machine.

3. Click the Fill/Back Color button arrow ▨ on the Design tab, then click Aqua Blue 1 (the second to last box in the second from the top row) in the Standard Colors list

With the background color of the Page Header section lightened, the white labels in the Page Header section are now very difficult to read.

4. Click the vertical ruler to the left of the labels in the Page Header section to select them, click the Font Color button arrow ▨, then click Automatic

The report in Design View should look like Figure D-13. You also want to add a label to the Report Footer section to identify yourself.

5. Drag the bottom edge of the Report Footer down about 0.5 inches, click the Label button ▨ on the Design tab, click at the 1-inch mark in the Report Footer, then type Created by your name

6. Save, preview, then print the Tour Descriptions report

The final formatted Tour Descriptions report should look like Figure D-14.

7. Close Print Preview, then close the Tour Descriptions report

714-917-6030

FIGURE D-13: Formatting a report

Font color of labels in Page Header section has been changed to automatic (black)

Bottom edge of the Report Footer section

Label button

Back color of Page Header section has been changed to Aqua Blue 1

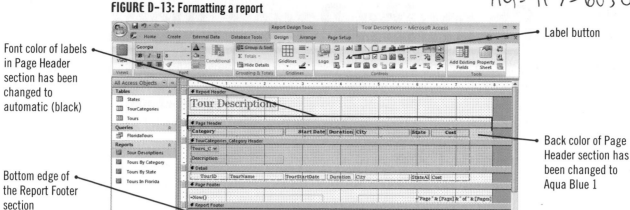

FIGURE D-14: Formatted Tour Descriptions report

Font color is automatic (black)

Back color is Aqua Blue 1

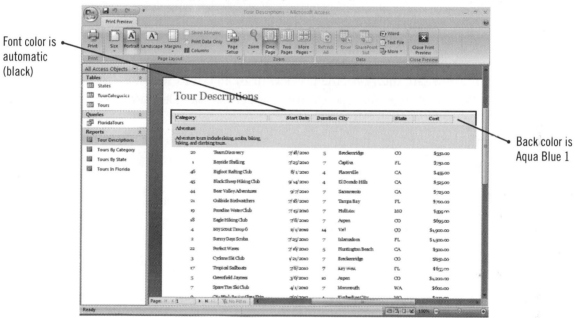

TABLE D-3: Useful formatting commands

button	button name	description
B	Bold	Toggles bold on or off for the selected control(s)
I	Italic	Toggles italics on or off for the selected control(s)
U	Underline	Toggles underline on or off for the selected control(s)
≡	Align Text Left	Left-aligns the selected control(s) within its own border
≡	Center	Centers the selected control(s) within its own border
≡	Align Text Right	Right-aligns the selected control(s) within its own border
◇	Fill/Back Color	Changes the background color of the selected control(s)
▦	Alternate Fill/Back Color	Changes the background color of alternate records in the selected section
A	Font Color	Changes the text color of the selected control(s)
✎	Line Color	Changes the border color of the selected control(s)
≡	Line Thickness	Changes the border style of the selected control(s)
▦	Line Type	Changes the special visual effect of the selected control(s)

Changing Page Layout

To fit all of the information on a report on a sheet of paper, you might need to change page layout options such as margins or page orientation. If a report contains many columns, for example, you might want to expand the print area by narrowing the margins. **Page orientation** refers to printing the report in either a **portrait** (8.5 inches wide by 11 inches tall) or **landscape** (11 inches wide by 8.5 inches tall) direction. Most of the page layout options such as paper size, paper orientation, and margins are accessible in Print Preview. ████████ Mark Rock asks you to print the Tours By State report. You preview it and make any page layout changes needed before printing it.

STEPS

1. **In the Navigation Pane, double-click the Tours By State report to open it in Report View, then maximize the report**

   In examining the report, you see that you need more horizontal space on the page to display all of the labels and field values properly. One way to provide more horizontal space on the report is to switch from portrait to landscape orientation.

2. **Click the View button arrow, click Print Preview, click the Landscape button on the Print Preview tab, then click the preview to zoom out to see an entire page**

   With the report in landscape orientation, you decide that wider margins would center the data to make it look better.

3. **Click the Margins button arrow on the Print Preview tab, then click Wide**

   Wide margins provide a one-inch top and bottom margin and at least a 0.75-inch left and right margin, as shown in Figure D-15.

4. **Close Print Preview, then switch to Report Design View**

   Carefully view the labels in the Page Header section, noting which ones need to be widened to display the entire entry.

5. **Use your moving, resizing, aligning, and previewing skills to make the report look like Figure D-16 in Print Preview**

   Your report doesn't have to look exactly like Figure D-16, but make sure that all of the labels are wide enough to display the text within them. To increase your productivity, use the [Shift] key to click and select more than one control at a time before you move, resize, or align them. You might need to move between Report Design View and Print Preview, making several adjustments before you are satisfied with your report.

QUICK TIP

If you want your name on the print-out, switch to Report Design View and add your name as a label to the Page Header section.

6. **When finished improving the layout, save it, click the Office button 🔘, click Print, click the From box, type 1, click the To box, type 1, then click OK**

7. **Close the Tours By State report, close the Quest-D.accdb database, then exit Access**

FIGURE D-15: Changing the margins of the Tours By State report

Landscape button

Margins button

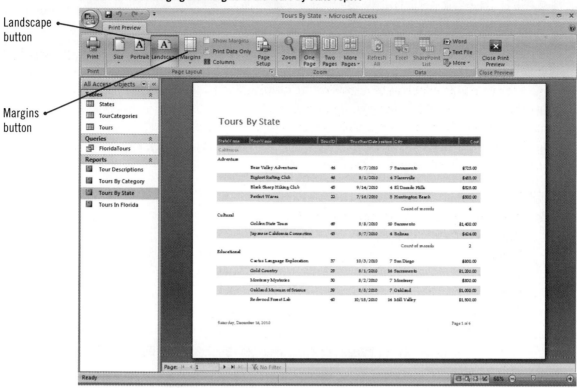

FIGURE D-16: Previewing the final Tours By State report

All labels and text boxes are widened to clearly see all values

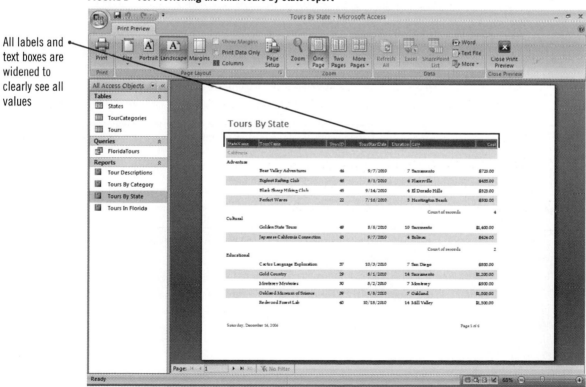

Practice

If you have a SAM user profile, you may have access to hands-on instruction, practice, and assessment of the skills covered in this unit. Log in to your SAM account (http://sam2007.course.com/) to launch any assigned training activities or exams that relate to the skills covered in this unit.

▼ CONCEPTS REVIEW

Label each element of the Report Design View window shown in Figure D-17.

FIGURE D-17

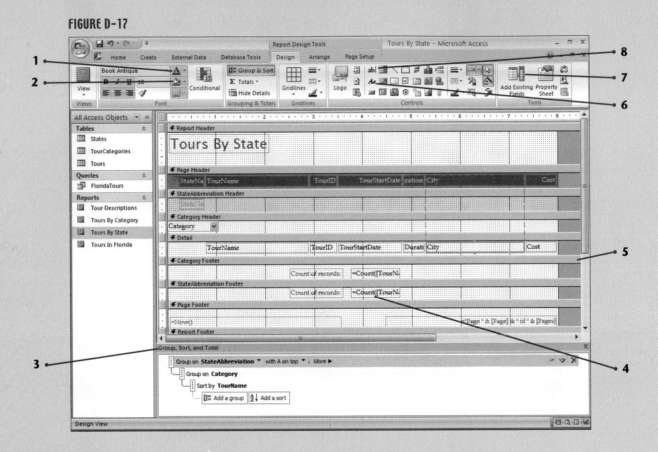

Match each term with the statement that best describes it.

9. **Expression**
10. **Section**
11. **Detail section**
12. **Record Source property**
13. **Formatting**
14. **Grouping**

a. Prints once for every record
b. Used to identify which fields and records are passed to the report
c. Enhancing the appearance of information displayed in the report
d. Sorting records *plus* providing a section
e. Determines where a control appears on the report and how often it prints
f. A combination of field names, operators, and functions that result in a single value before and after the group of records

Select the best answer from the list of choices.

15. You press and hold which key to select more than one control in Report Design View?
    a. [Alt]   c. [Shift]
    b. [Ctrl]   d. [Tab]

16. Which type of control is most commonly placed in the Detail section?
    a. Combo box   c. List box
    b. Label   d. Text box

17. Which type of control is most commonly placed in the Page Header section?
    a. Bound image   c. Command button
    b. Combo box   d. Label

18. A calculated expression is most often placed in which report section?
    a. Layout   c. Group Footer
    b. Formulas   d. Report Header

19. Which of the following would be the appropriate expression to count the number of records using the FirstName field?
    a. =Count([FirstName])   c. =Count(FirstName)
    b. =Count[FirstName]   d. =Count{FirstName}

20. To align the edges of several controls with respect to one another, you use the alignment commands on the:
    a. Formatting tab.   c. Print Preview ribbon.
    b. Design tab.   d. Arrange tab.

21. Which of the following *cannot* be changed in Print Preview?
    a. Font size   c. Paper orientation
    b. Margins   d. Paper size

Access 2007

▼ SKILLS REVIEW

1. Preview a report.

  a. Start Access and open the RealEstate-D.accdb database from the drive and folder where you store your Data Files. Enable content if prompted.

  b. Open the Agencies table and change A1 to your own last name in the A1 Realtors record, then close the Agencies table.

  c. Open the Agency Listings report in Print Preview, then print the report.

  d. On the printout, identify these sections:
  - Report Header
  - Page Header, Page Footer
  - Detail

  e. On the printout, identify the two Group Header sections as well as the field used to group the records. You can use Report Design View to confirm your answers, if needed.

  f. Close the Agency Listings report.

2. Use the Report Wizard.

  a. Use the Report Wizard to create a report based on the AgentLast and AgentPhone fields from the Agents table, and all the fields except the ListingNo, Pool, and AgentNo field from the Listings table.

  b. View the data by Agents, then group it by the Type field. (*Hint*: Click Type, then click the > button.) Sort the records in descending order by the Asking field.

  c. Use a Block layout and a Landscape orientation.

  d. Use a Solstice style and title the report Agent Listings by Type.

  e. Preview the first page of the new report. Notice which fields and field names are displayed completely and which need more space.

3. Use Report Design View.

  a. In Report Design View, widen the AgentLast label in the Page Header section to begin at the left edge of the page. This automatically widens the AgentLast text box in the Detail section.

  b. Modify the AgentLast label in the Page Header section to read Agent.

  c. Narrow the Bath label and corresponding text box to be half as wide as they currently appear.

  d. Switch between Print Preview and Report Design View to move and resize other labels in the Page Header section, so that the caption of each label is clearly visible. (*Hint*: If you make a mistake, click the Undo button.)

  e. Preview the first page of the new report, switching between Report Design View and Print Preview to size all controls in a way that makes all data visible. Do not design the report to exceed the width of one landscape sheet of paper.

  f. Save and close the Agent Listings by Type report, open the Agents table in Datasheet View, then enter your last name in place of Hughes in the Gordon Hughes record. Close the Agents table.

  g. Reopen the Agent Listings by Type report, then print the first page.

4. Use report sections.

  a. In Report Design View of the Agent Listings by Type report, expand the size of the Type Header section about 0.5 inches.

  b. Cut the Type field from the Detail section, then paste it in the Type Header section.

  c. Increase the font size of the Type text box to 14, then resize the control so that it is about three inches wide and tall enough for the larger text.

  d. Open the Group, Sort, and Total pane by clicking the Group & Sort button, and remove the AgentNo grouping level by clicking the Delete button on the right edge of the Group on AgentNo bar.

  e. Open a Group Footer section for the Type field.

  f. Close the Group, Sort, and Total pane, then preview the report.

5. Add subtotals and counts.

   a. In Report Design View, add a text box control to the Type Footer section, just below the Asking text box in the Detail section. Change the label to read **Subtotal of Asking Price:** and enter the expression **=Sum([Asking])** in the text box.

   b. Copy and paste the text box that contains the =Sum([Asking]) expression, so that two copies of the text box and accompanying label appear in the Type Footer section.

   c. Modify the second text box to read **=Avg([Asking])**, and the second label to read **Average Asking Price:**.

   d. Open the Property Sheet for the =Avg([Asking]) expression, and on the Format tab, change the Format property to Currency and the Decimal Places property to 0.

   e. Open the Property Sheet for the =Sum([Asking]) expression, and on the Format tab, change the Format property to Currency and the Decimal Places property to 0.

   f. Open the Property Sheet for the Asking text box in the Detail section, and on the Format tab, change the Format property to Currency and the Decimal Places property to 0.

   g. Preview the report to view the new subtotals in the Type Footer section.

6. Resize and align controls.

   a. In Report Design View, right-align the right edges of the Asking, the =Sum([Asking]), and the =Avg([Asking]) text boxes.

   b. Right-align the text within the labels to the left of the expression text boxes in the Type Footer section, and also align the right edges of the labels with respect to one another.

   c. Save and preview the report.

7. Format a report.

   a. Switch to Report Design View and change the font of the label in the Report Header to Freestyle Script, 36 points.

   b. Double-click a sizing handle on the label in the Report Header to expand it to accommodate the entire label. Be sure to double-click a sizing handle of the label, not the label itself, which opens the property sheet.

   c. Change the background color of the Page Header section to Light Gray 1 on the Fill/Back Color palette.

   d. Click the Detail section bar, and apply a Light Gray 1 background color using the Alternate Fill/Back Color palette.

   e. Save and preview the report.

8. **Change page layout.**

    a. Use Report Design View to move the text box in the Page Footer section that calculates the page number to the left, so that no controls on the page extend beyond the 9-inch marker on the horizontal ruler.

    b. Drag the right edge of the report to the left, so that it is no wider than nine inches.

    c. Save the report, then switch to Print Preview. The first page of the report should look like Figure D-18. Your fonts and colors might look different.

    d. Change the margins to Normal (.75-inch top and bottom, .35-inch left and right), then print the first page of the report.

    e. Close and save the Agent Listings by Type report.

    f. Close the RealEstate-D.accdb database, then exit Access.

FIGURE D-18

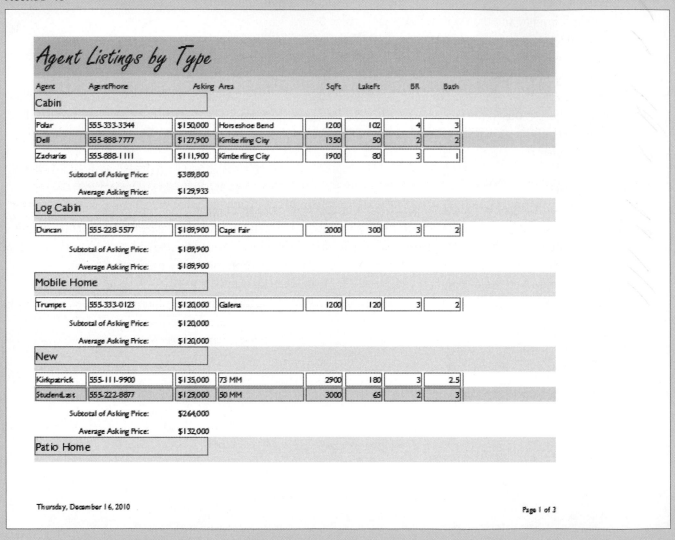

▼ INDEPENDENT CHALLENGE 1

As the office manager of a veterinary association, you need to create a report showing membership in the association.

a. Start Access, then open the **Vet-D.accdb** database from the drive and folder where you store your Data Files. Enable content if prompted.

b. Use the Report Wizard to create a report with the First and Last fields from the Vets table, and all the fields except for ClinicNo from the Clinics table.

c. View your data by Clinics, do not add any more grouping levels, and sort in ascending order by Last.

d. Use the Stepped layout, Portrait orientation, and Flow style.

e. Name the report **Clinic Membership**.

f. In Report Design View, expand the size of the Address1 label and text box to be about two inches wide. Be careful not to expand any controls beyond the 8-inch right edge of the report.

g. Open the Group, Sort, and Total pane, then add a ClinicNo Footer section.

h. Add a text box to the ClinicNo Footer section, just below the Last text box.

i. Modify the caption of the label to the left of the new text box in the ClinicNo Footer section to read **Count:**, move the label close to the text box, and right-align the text within the label.

j. Enter an expression in the new text box in the ClinicNo Footer section to count the values in the Last field, **=Count([Last])**, and left-align the values within the text box.

k. Add a label to the Report Header section to display your name. Format the label to be black text and 12 points, and expand the label to display your entire name as needed.

l. Using Report Design View to make modifications and Print Preview to review them, modify the controls as necessary to display all of the data clearly, then save the report and print the first page. Be careful not to expand beyond the 8-inch mark on the horizontal ruler in Report Design View, or the report will be wider than a sheet of paper in portrait orientation. The report should look similar to Figure D-19. Your fonts and colors might look different.

m. Close the Clinic Membership report, close the Vet-D.accdb database, then exit Access.

FIGURE D-19

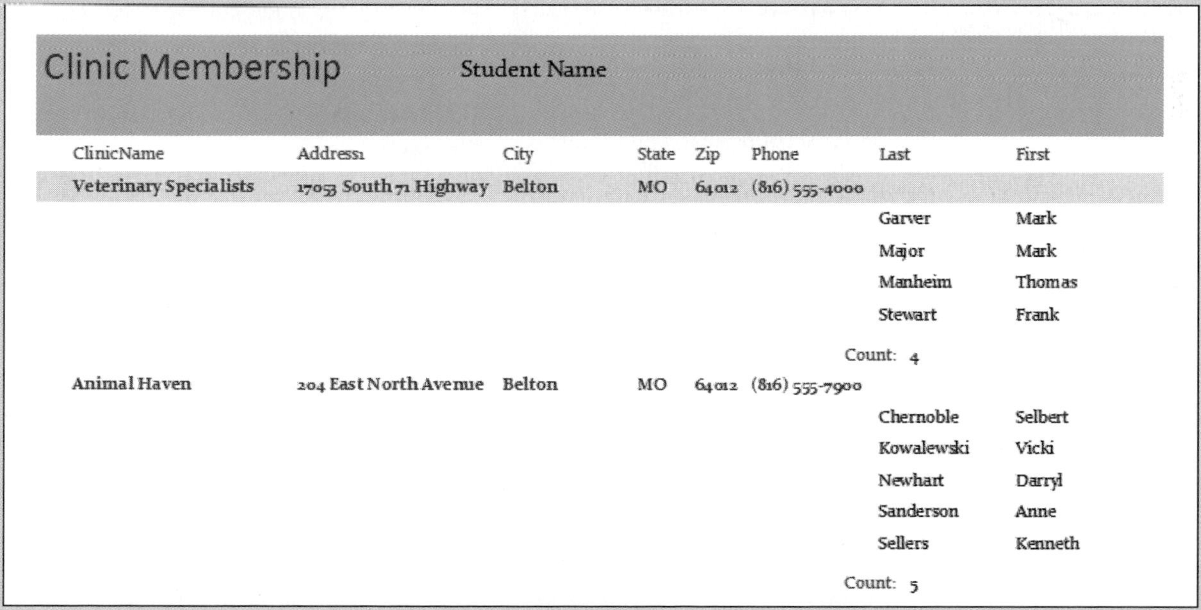

ClinicName	Address1	City	State	Zip	Phone	Last	First
Veterinary Specialists	17053 South 71 Highway	Belton	MO	64012	(816) 555-4000		
						Garver	Mark
						Major	Mark
						Manheim	Thomas
						Stewart	Frank
						Count: 4	
Animal Haven	204 East North Avenue	Belton	MO	64012	(816) 555-7900		
						Chernoble	Selbert
						Kowalewski	Vicki
						Newhart	Darryl
						Sanderson	Anne
						Sellers	Kenneth
						Count: 5	

Clinic Membership — Student Name

▼ INDEPENDENT CHALLENGE 2

You have built an Access database to track membership in a community service club. The database tracks member names and addresses as well as their status in the club, which moves from rank to rank as the members contribute increased hours of service to the community.

a. Start Access and open the Membership-D.accdb database from the drive and folder where you store your Data Files. Enable content if prompted.

b. Open the Members table and change the name of Traci Kalvert to your name, then close the Members table.

c. Use the Report Wizard to create a report using the Status and DuesOwed fields from the Status table, and the FName, LName, and DuesPaid fields from the Members table.

d. View the data by Status. Do not add any more grouping fields, and sort the records in ascending order by LName.

e. Use an Outline layout, Portrait orientation, and Civic style.

f. Title the report Dues Analysis, then preview the report.

g. In Report Design View, use the Group, Sort, and Total pane to open the StatusNo Footer section.

h. Add a text box to the StatusNo Footer section, just below the DuesPaid text box. Change the label to Count: and the expression in the text box to =Count([DuesPaid]).

i. Expand the StatusNo Footer section as necessary, and add a second text box to the StatusNo Footer section, just below the first. Change the label to Subtotal: and the expression in the text box to =Sum([DuesPaid]).

j. Apply two property changes to the =Sum([DuesPaid]) text box. The Format property should be set to Currency and the Decimal Places property should be set to 2.

Advanced Challenge Exercise

- Expand the StatusNo Footer section as necessary, and add a third text box to the StatusNo Footer section, just below the second. Change the label to Dues Owed Less Dues Paid:.
- Change the text box expression to =Count([DuesPaid])*[DuesOwed]–Sum([DuesPaid]).
- Apply two property changes to the new text box. The Format property should be set to Currency and the Decimal Places property should be set to 2.

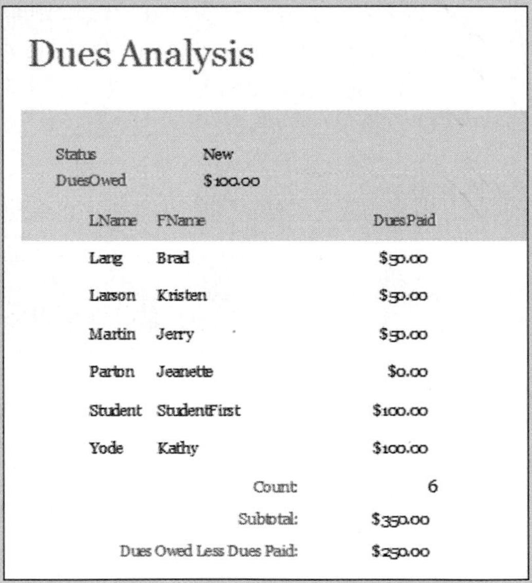

k. Align the right edges of the DuesPaid text box in the Detail section and all text boxes in the StatusNo Footer section. Also, right-align all data within these controls.

l. Align the right edges of the labels in the StatusNo Footer section.

m. Apply an Aqua Blue 1 Alternate Fill/Back color to the StatusNo Header, and a Dark Blue font color to the label in the Report Header.

n. Save, then preview the Dues Analysis report. The report should look similar to Figure D-20. Your fonts and colors might look different.

o. Print the first page of the Dues Analysis report, then close it.

p. Close the Membership-D.accdb database, then exit Access.

FIGURE D-20

Dues Analysis

Status	New	
DuesOwed	$100.00	
LName	FName	DuesPaid
Lang	Brad	$50.00
Larson	Kristen	$50.00
Martin	Jerry	$50.00
Parton	Jeanette	$0.00
Student	StudentFirst	$100.00
Yode	Kathy	$100.00

Count		6
Subtotal:		$350.00
Dues Owed Less Dues Paid:		$250.00

▼ INDEPENDENT CHALLENGE 3

You have built an Access database to organize the deposits at a recycling center. Various clubs regularly deposit recyclable material, which is measured in pounds when the deposits are made.

a. Start Access and open the **Recycle-D.accdb** database from the drive and folder where you store your Data Files. Enable content if prompted.

b. Open the Centers table, change Johnson in Johnson County Landfill to your own last name, then close the table.

c. Use the Report Wizard to create a report with the Name field from the Centers table, and the Deposit Date and Weight from the Deposits table.

d. View the data by Centers, do not add any more grouping levels, and sort the records in ascending order by Deposit Date.

e. Click the Summary Options button in the Report Wizard dialog box that also prompts for sort orders, and click the Sum check box for the Weight field.

f. Use a Stepped layout, a Portrait orientation, and a Flow style. Title the report **Deposit Totals**.

g. View the report in Print Preview, then switch to Report Design View and widen the Name text box. Switch between Print Preview and Report Design View to widen and then observe the Name text box. Widen it enough to make all trash center names visible.

h. In Report Design View, delete the long, top text box in the Center Number Footer section that starts with ="Summary.

i. Right-align the right edge of the Sum label in the Center Number Footer section with the Deposit Date text box in the Detail section.

j. Left-align the left edge of the =Sum([Weight]) text box in the Center Number Footer section with the Weight text box in the Detail section.

k. Save, preview, and then print the first page of the report. It should look similar to Figure D-21. Your fonts and colors might look different.

FIGURE D-21

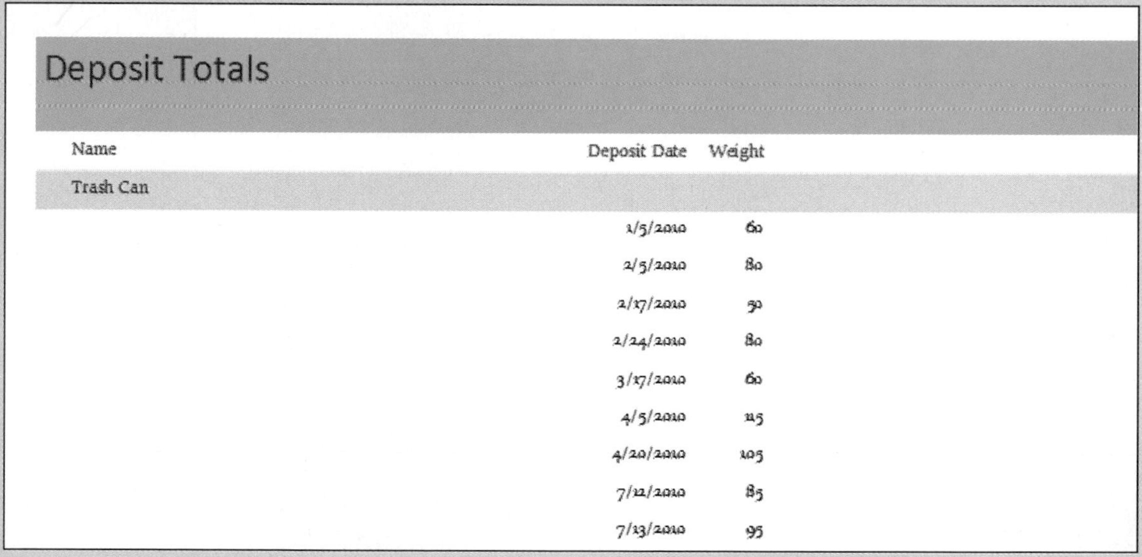

Deposit Totals

Name	Deposit Date	Weight
Trash Can		
	1/5/2010	60
	2/5/2010	80
	2/17/2010	50
	2/24/2010	80
	3/17/2010	60
	4/5/2010	115
	4/20/2010	105
	7/12/2010	85
	7/13/2010	95

▼ INDEPENDENT CHALLENGE 3 (CONTINUED)

Advanced Challenge Exercise

- In Report Design View, add Deposit Date as a grouping field, and move it above Deposit Date used as a sorting field.
- Open the Deposit Date Footer section, then change the by entire value option to by year.
- Add the Deposit Date field to the Deposit Date Header section, then change the Format property for the Deposit Date text box to **yyyy** (four-digit year format) and the Deposit Date label to **Year:**.
- Copy the controls from the Center Number Footer section, and paste them in the Deposit Date Footer section.
- Change the label in the Deposit Date Footer section from Sum to **Yearly Sum**. Change the label in the Center Number Footer section from Sum to **Center Sum**.
- Align the right edge of the label in the Deposit Date Footer section with the label in the Center Number Footer section, and the right edge of the text box in the Deposit Date Footer section with the right edge of the text box in the Center Number Footer section. Also, right-align the data within each of these four controls.
- Save and preview the report, then print the first page, a portion of which is shown in Figure D-22.

l. Close the Deposit Totals report, close the Recycle-D.accdb database, then exit Access.

FIGURE D-22

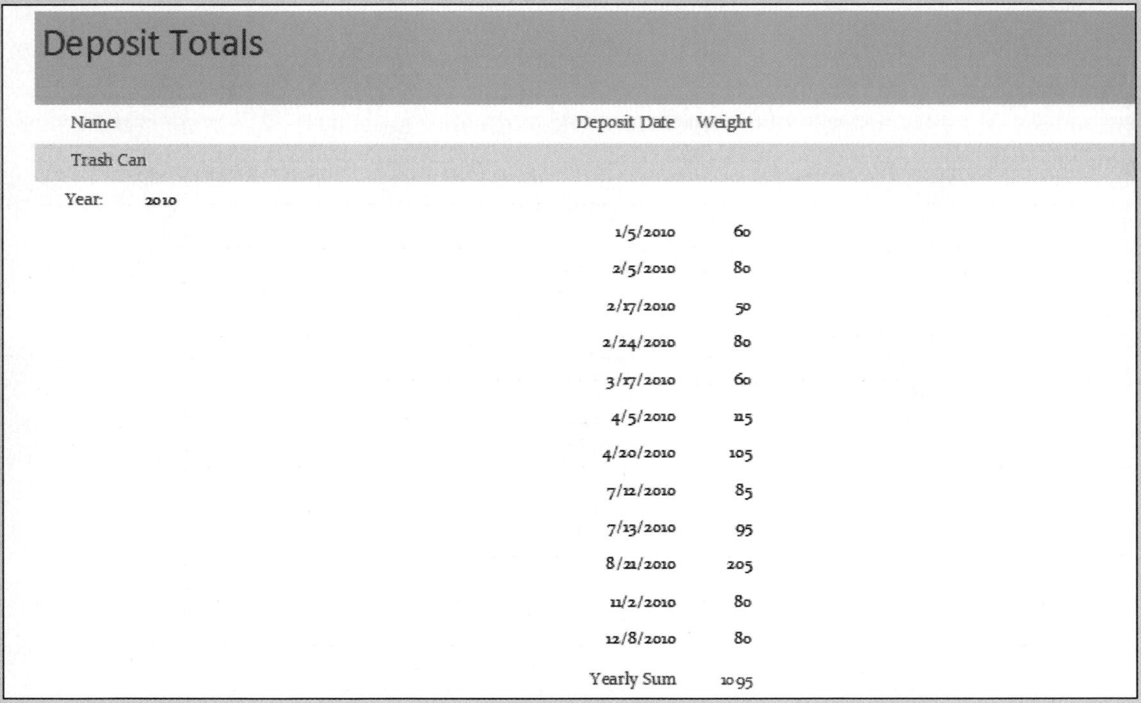

Deposit Totals

Name	Deposit Date	Weight
Trash Can		
Year: 2010		
	1/5/2010	60
	2/5/2010	80
	2/17/2010	50
	2/24/2010	80
	3/17/2010	60
	4/5/2010	115
	4/20/2010	105
	7/12/2010	85
	7/13/2010	95
	8/21/2010	205
	11/2/2010	80
	12/8/2010	80
	Yearly Sum	1095

▼ REAL LIFE INDEPENDENT CHALLENGE

One way you can use an Access database on your own is to help you study information. Suppose you have a passion for geography and want to memorize all 50 U.S. state capitals and mottos. A database with information about all 50 states is provided with your Data Files, and you can use it to develop a report to study this information.

    a. Start Access and open the States-D.accdb database from the drive and folder where you store your Data Files. Enable content if prompted.

    b. Use the Report Wizard to create a report that lists all four fields in the States table, sorted by StateName, using a Tabular layout, a Portrait orientation, and a None style. Title the report **State Trivia**.

    c. Widen all controls as necessary to display all of the data in each field, but do not extend the report beyond the width of the paper in portrait orientation.

    d. Add a line control to the top edge of the Detail section, just above the text boxes in the Detail section, to separate the states with a line, as shown in Figure D-23.

    e. Add your name as a label to the Report Header section.

    f. Save the report, then preview and print it.

    g. Close the State Trivia report, close the States.accdb database, then exit Access.

FIGURE D-23

State Trivia

StateName	StateAbbrev	Capital	Motto
Alabama	AL	Montgomery	We dare to defend our rights
Alaska	AK	Juneau	North to the future
Arizona	AZ	Phoenix	God enriches
Arkansas	AR	Little Rock	The people rule
California	CA	Sacramento	I have found it
Colorado	CO	Denver	Nothing without Providence
Connecticut	CT	Hartford	He who transplanted sustains
Delaware	DE	Dover	Liberty and independence
Florida	FL	Tallahassee	In God we trust
Georgia	GA	Atlanta	Wisdom, justice, and moderation
Hawaii	HI	Honolulu	The life of the land is perpetuated in righteousness
Idaho	ID	Boise	Let it be perpetual
Illinois	IL	Springfield	State sovereignty, national union

▼ VISUAL WORKSHOP

Open the **Basketball-D.accdb** database from the drive and folder where you store your Data Files and enable content if prompted. First, enter your own name instead of Heidi Harmon in the Players table. Your goal is to create the report shown in Figure D-24. Choose the First, Last, HomeTown, and HomeState fields from the Players table and the FG, 3P, and FT fields from the Stats table. View the data by Players, do not add any more grouping levels, and do not add any more sorting levels. When the Report Wizard prompts you for sort orders, click the Summary Options button and choose Sum for the FG, 3P, and FT fields. Use a Block layout, a Portrait orientation, a Solstice style, and title the report **Points per Player**. In Report Design View, delete the long text box calculation in the PlayerNo Footer section, and move and align the =Sum([FG]), =Sum([3P]), and =Sum([FT]) calculations in the PlayerNo Footer directly under the text boxes that they sum in the Detail section. Cut the First, Last, HomeTown, and HomeState text boxes from the Detail section, then paste them in the PlayerNoHeader section. Make sure that no Alternate Fill/Back color is applied to the Detail section. (Select the Detail section, then choose No Color for the Alternate Fill/Back color.) Move and resize all controls as needed.

FIGURE D-24

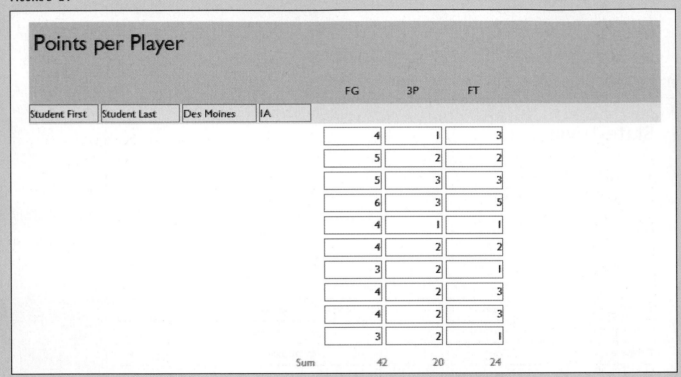

Modifying the Database Structure

In this unit, you refine a database by adding a new table to an existing database and linking tables using one-to-many relationships to create a relational database. You work with fields that have different data types, including Text, Number, Currency, Date/Time, and Yes/No, to define the data stored in the database. You create and use Attachment fields to store images. You also modify table and field properties to format and validate data. ▇▇▇▇ Working with Mark Rock, the tour developer for U.S. group travel at Quest Travel Services, you are developing an Access database to track the tours, customers, and sales for his division. The database consists of multiple tables that you can link, modify, and enhance to create a relational database.

OBJECTIVES

Examine relational databases
Design related tables
Create one-to-many relationships
Create Lookup fields
Modify Text fields
Modify Number and Currency fields
Modify Date/Time fields
Modify validation properties
Create Attachment fields

Examining Relational Databases

The purpose of a relational database is to organize and store data in a way that minimizes redundancy and maximizes your flexibility when querying and analyzing data. To accomplish these goals, a relational database uses related tables of data rather than a single large table. ▰▰▰▰ At one time, the Sales department at Quest Travel Services tracked information about their tour sales using a single Access table called Sales, shown in Figure E-1. You see a data redundancy problem because of the duplicate tour and customer information entered into a single table. You decide to study the principles of relational database design to help Quest Travel Services reorganize these fields into a correctly designed relational database.

DETAILS

To redesign a list into a properly structured relational database, follow these principles:

- **Design each table to contain fields that describe only one subject**

  Currently, the Sales table in Figure E-1 contains three subjects: tours, customers, and sales data. Putting multiple subjects in a single table creates redundant data. For example, the customer's name must be reentered every time that customer purchases a different tour. Redundant data causes extra data-entry work, a higher rate of data-entry inconsistencies and errors, and larger physical storage requirements. Moreover, it limits the user's ability to search for, analyze, and report on the data. These problems are minimized by implementing a properly designed relational database.

- **Identify a primary key field or key field combination for each table**

  A **primary key field** is a field that contains unique information for each record. An employee number field often serves this purpose in a table that stores employee data. A customer number field usually serves this purpose in a table that stores customer data. Although using the employee or customer's last name as the primary key field might work in a small database, it is generally a poor choice because it does not accommodate two employees or customers that have the same last name. A **key field combination** uses more than one field to uniquely identify each record.

- **Build one-to-many relationships between the tables of your database using a field common to each table**

  To tie the information from one table to another, a field must be common to each table. This linking field is the primary key field on the "one" side of the relationship and the **foreign key field** on the "many" side of the relationship. To create a one-to-many relationship between the tables, the primary key field contains a unique entry for each record in the "one" table, but the foreign key field can contain the same value in several records in the "many" table. Table E-1 describes common examples of one-to-many relationships. You are not required to give the linking field the same name in the "one" and "many" tables.

  The new design for the fields of the tour database is shown in Figure E-2. One customer can purchase many tours, so the Customers and Sales tables have a one-to-many relationship based on the linking CustNo field. One tour can have many sales, so the Tours and Sales tables also have a one-to-many relationship based on the common TourID field (named TourNo in the Tours table).

Using many-to-many relationships

As you design your database, you might find that two tables have a **many-to-many relationship**. To join them, you must establish a third table called a **junction table**, which contains two foreign key fields to serve on the "many" side of separate one-to-many relationships with the two original tables. The Customers and Tours tables have a many-to-many relationship because one customer can purchase many tours and one tour can have many customers purchase it. The Sales table serves as the junction table to link the three tables together.

Modifying the Database Structure

FIGURE E-1: Sales as a single table

TourName	City	StateAbbrev	SaleDate	FName	LName
American Heritage Tour	Philadelphia	PA	6/2/2010	Cynthia	Browning
American Heritage Tour	Philadelphia	PA	7/10/2010	Jan	Cabriella
American Heritage Tour	Philadelphia	PA	6/2/2010	Christine	Collins
American Heritage Tour	Philadelphia	PA	6/2/2010	Gene	Custard
American Heritage Tour	Philadelphia	PA	6/2/2010	John	Garden
Bayside Shelling	Captiva	FL	5/1/2010	Christine	Collins
Bayside Shelling	Captiva	FL	5/1/2010	Jim	Wilson
Bayside Shelling	Captiva	FL	5/1/2010	Kori	Yode
Bright Lights Expo	Branson	MO	7/10/2010	Jan	Cabriella
Bright Lights Expo	Branson	MO	7/9/2010	Denise	Camel
Bright Lights Expo	Branson	MO	7/8/2010	Christine	Collins
Bright Lights Expo	Branson	MO	7/10/2010	Gene	Custard

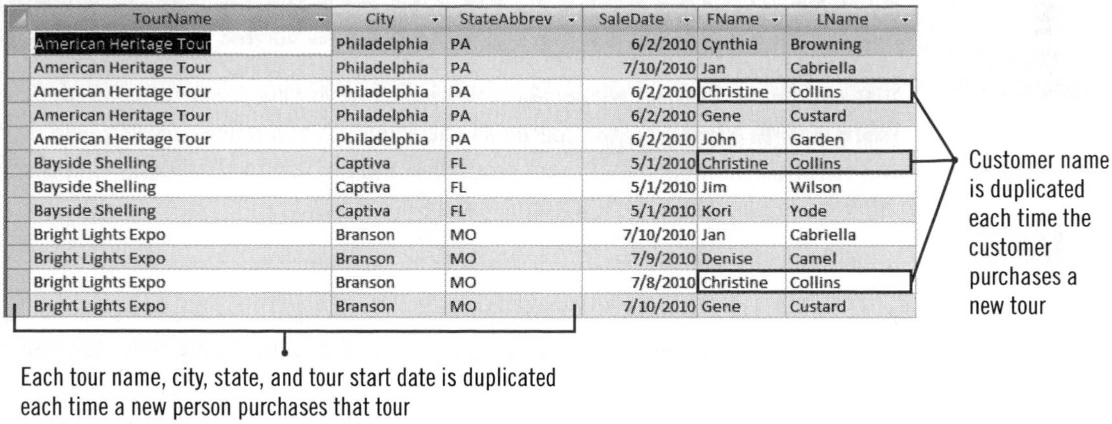

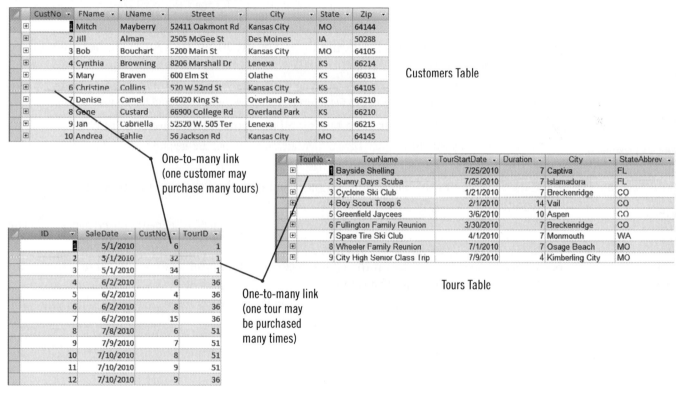

Customer name is duplicated each time the customer purchases a new tour
Each tour name, city, state, and tour start date is duplicated each time a new person purchases that tour

FIGURE E-2: Sales data split into three related tables

CustNo	FName	LName	Street	City	State	Zip
1	Mitch	Mayberry	52411 Oakmont Rd	Kansas City	MO	64144
2	Jill	Alman	2505 McGee St	Des Moines	IA	50288
3	Bob	Bouchart	5200 Main St	Kansas City	MO	64105
4	Cynthia	Browning	8206 Marshall Dr	Lenexa	KS	66214
5	Mary	Braven	600 Elm St	Olathe	KS	66031
6	Christine	Collins	520 W 52nd St	Kansas City	KS	64105
7	Denise	Camel	66020 King St	Overland Park	KS	66210
8	Gene	Custard	66900 College Rd	Overland Park	KS	66210
9	Jan	Cabriella	52520 W. 505 Ter	Lenexa	KS	66215
10	Andrea	Eahlie	56 Jackson Rd	Kansas City	MO	64145

Customers Table

TourNo	TourName	TourStartDate	Duration	City	StateAbbrev
1	Bayside Shelling	7/25/2010	7	Captiva	FL
2	Sunny Days Scuba	7/25/2010	7	Islamadora	FL
3	Cyclone Ski Club	1/21/2010	7	Breckenridge	CO
4	Boy Scout Troop 6	2/1/2010	14	Vail	CO
5	Greenfield Jaycees	3/6/2010	10	Aspen	CO
6	Fullington Family Reunion	3/30/2010	7	Breckenridge	CO
7	Spare Tire Ski Club	4/1/2010	7	Monmouth	WA
8	Wheeler Family Reunion	7/1/2010	7	Osage Beach	MO
9	City High Senior Class Trip	7/9/2010	4	Kimberling City	MO

Tours Table

ID	SaleDate	CustNo	TourID
1	5/1/2010	6	1
2	5/1/2010	32	1
3	5/1/2010	34	1
4	6/2/2010	6	36
5	6/2/2010	4	36
6	6/2/2010	8	36
7	6/2/2010	15	36
8	7/8/2010	6	51
9	7/9/2010	7	51
10	7/10/2010	8	51
11	7/10/2010	9	51
12	7/10/2010	9	36

Sales Table

One-to-many link (one customer may purchase many tours)
One-to-many link (one tour may be purchased many times)

TABLE E-1: Common one-to-many relationships

table on "one" side	table on "many" side	linking field	description
Products	Sales	ProductID	A ProductID field must have a unique entry in a Products table, but is listed many times in a Sales table as many copies of that item are sold
Students	Enrollments	StudentID	A StudentID field must have a unique entry in a Students table, but is listed many times in an Enrollments table as multiple classes are recorded for the same student
Employees	Promotions	EmployeeID	An EmployeeID field must have a unique entry in an Employees table, but is listed many times in a Promotions table as the employee is promoted over time

Designing Related Tables

After you develop a valid relational database design, you are ready to define the tables in Access. Using **Table Design View**, you can specify all characteristics of a table including field names, data types, field descriptions, field properties, lookup properties, and primary key field designations. ▓▓▓▓ Using the new database design, you are ready to create the Sales table.

STEPS

1. **Start Access, open the Quest-E.accdb database, then enable content if prompted**

The Customers, States, TourCategories, and Tours tables already exist in the database. You need to create the Sales table.

2. **Click the Create tab on the Ribbon, then click the Table Design button**

Table Design View opens, allowing you to enter field names and specify data types and field properties for the new table. Field names should be as short as possible, but long enough to be descriptive. The field name you enter in Table Design View is used as the default name for the field in all later queries, forms, and reports.

3. **Type SalesNo, press [Enter], click the Data Type list arrow, click AutoNumber, then press [Enter] twice to move to the next row**

The AutoNumber data type, which automatically assigns the next available integer in the sequence to each new record, works well for the SalesNo field because each sales number should be unique.

4. **Type the other field names, data types, and descriptions as shown in Figure E-3**

Field descriptions entered in Table Design View are optional, but are helpful in that they provide further information about the field.

5. **Click SalesNo in the Field Name column, then click the Primary Key button on the Design tab**

A **key symbol** appears to the left of SalesNo to indicate that this field is defined as the primary key field for this table.

6. **Click the Save button 🖫 on the Quick Access toolbar, type Sales in the Table Name text box, click OK, then close the table**

The Sales table is now displayed as a table object in the Quest-E database Navigation Pane, as shown in Figure E-4.

FIGURE E-3: Table Design View for the new Sales table

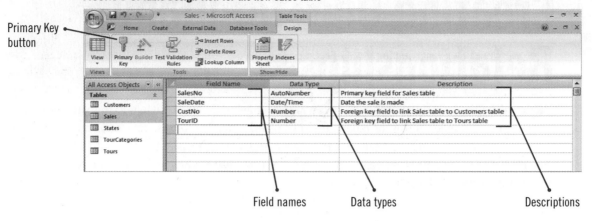

Primary Key button

Field names   Data types   Descriptions

FIGURE E-4: Sales table in the Quest-E database Navigation Pane

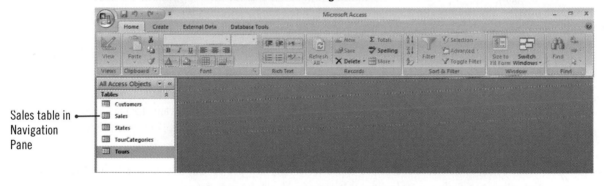

Sales table in Navigation Pane

Specifying the foreign key field data type

A foreign key field in the "many" table must have the same data type (Text or Number) as the primary key it is related to in the "one" table. An exception to this rule is when the primary key field in the "one" table has an AutoNumber data type. In this case, the linking foreign key field in the "many" table must have a Number data type. Also note that a Number field used as a foreign key field must have a Long Integer Field Size property to match the Field Size property of the AutoNumber primary key field.

Creating One-to-Many Relationships

After creating the tables you need, you link the tables together in appropriate one-to-many relationships before building queries, forms, or reports using fields from multiple tables. Your database design shows that the common CustNo field should link the Customers table to the Sales table, and that the TourID field should link the Tours table to the Sales table. ░░░░░ You are ready to define the one-to-many relationships between the tables of the Quest-E database.

STEPS

1. **Click the Database Tools tab on the Ribbon, then click the Relationships button**
   The States, Tours, and TourCategories table field lists appear in the Relationships window. The primary key fields are identified with a small key symbol to the left of the field name. You need to add the Customers and Sales table field lists to this window.

   QUICK TIP
   Drag the table's title bar to move the field list.

2. **Click the Show Table button on the Design tab, click Sales, click Add, click Customers, click Add, click Close, then maximize the window**
   With all of the field lists in the Relationships window, you're ready to link the Sales and Customers tables to the rest of the relational database.

   QUICK TIP
   Drag the bottom border of the field list to display all of the fields.

3. **Click TourNo in the Tours table field list, then drag it to the TourID field in the Sales table field list**
   Dragging a field from one table to another in the Relationships window links the two tables by the selected fields and opens the Edit Relationships dialog box, as shown in Figure E-5. Recall that referential integrity helps ensure data accuracy.

4. **Click the Enforce Referential Integrity check box in the Edit Relationships dialog box, then click Create**
   The **one-to-many line** shows the linkage between the TourNo field of the Tours table and the TourID field of the Sales table. The "one" side of the relationship is the unique TourNo value for each record in the Tours table. The "many" side of the relationship is identified by an infinity symbol pointing to the TourID field in the Sales table. The CustNo field should link the Customers table to the Sales table.

   QUICK TIP
   Right-click a relationship line, then click Delete if you need to delete a relationship and start over.

5. **Click CustNo in the Customers table field list, drag it to CustNo in the Sales table field list, click the Enforce Referential Integrity check box, then click Create**
   The updated Relationships window should look like Figure E-6.

   TROUBLE
   Click the Landscape button on the Print Preview tab if the report is too wide for portrait orientation.

6. **Click the Relationship Report button on the Design tab, click the Print button, then click OK**
   A printout of the Relationships window, called the Relationship report, shows how your relational database is designed and includes table names, field names, primary key fields, and one-to-many relationship lines. This printout is helpful as you later create queries, forms, and reports that use fields from multiple tables.

   QUICK TIP
   Add your name as a label to the Report Header section in Report Design View and reprint the report if you want your name on the printout.

7. **Click the Close Print Preview button on the Print Preview tab, close the Report Design View window, then click No when prompted to save the report**

8. **Close the Relationships window, then click Yes if prompted to save changes**

Modifying the Database Structure

FIGURE E-5: Edit Relationships dialog box

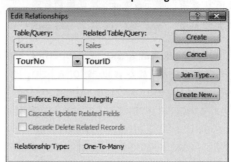

FIGURE E-6: Final Relationships window

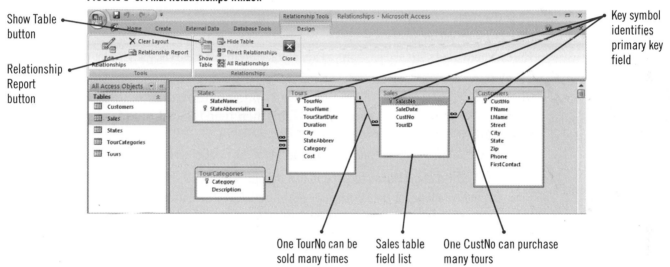

Show Table button

Relationship Report button

Key symbol identifies primary key field

One TourNo can be sold many times

Sales table field list

One CustNo can purchase many tours

More on enforcing referential integrity

Recall that referential integrity is a set of rules to help ensure that no orphan records are entered or created in the database. An orphan record is a record in the "many" table that doesn't have a matching entry in the linking field of the "one" table. (For example, an orphan record in the Quest database is a record in the Sales table that contains a TourID entry but has no match in the TourNo field of the Tours table, or a record in the Sales table that contains a CustNo entry but no match in the Customers table.) Referential integrity prevents orphan records in multiple ways. By enforcing referential integrity, you cannot allow a **null entry** (nothing) in a foreign key field nor can you make an entry in the foreign key field that does not match a value in the linking field of the "one" table (such as a Sales record with a TourID not included in the Tours table). Referential integrity also prevents you from deleting a record in the "one" table that has a matching entry in the foreign key field of the "many" table (such as a Customer record with a CustNo associated with a Sales record). You should enforce referential integrity on all one-to-many relationships if possible. Unfortunately, if you are working with a database that already contains orphan records, you cannot enforce this powerful set of rules.

Creating Lookup Fields

A **Lookup field** is a field that contains Lookup properties. **Lookup properties** are field properties that allow you to supply a drop-down list of values for a field. The values can be stored in another table or directly stored in the **Row Source** Lookup property of the field. Fields that are good candidates for Lookup properties are those that contain a defined set of appropriate values such as State, Gender, or Department. You can set Lookup properties for a field in Table Design View using the **Lookup Wizard**. 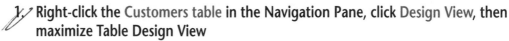 The FirstContact field in the Customers table identifies how the customer first made contact with Quest Specialty Travel such as being referred by a friend, finding the company through the Internet, or responding to a direct mail advertisement. You can use the Lookup Wizard to provide a set of defined values as a drop-down list for the FirstContact field.

1. **Right-click the Customers table in the Navigation Pane, click Design View, then maximize Table Design View**

   You access the Lookup Wizard from the Data Type list for the field in which you want to apply Lookup properties.

2. **Click the Text data type for the FirstContact field, click the Data Type list arrow, then click Lookup Wizard**

   The Lookup Wizard starts and prompts you for information about where you want the lookup column to get its values.

3. **Click the I will type in the values that I want option button, click Next, click the first cell in the Col1 column, type Friend, press [Tab], then type the rest of the values as shown in Figure E-7**

   These are the values to populate the lookup value list for the FirstContact field.

4. **Click Next, then click Finish to accept the default label and complete the Lookup Wizard**

   Note that the data type for the FirstContact field is still Text. The Lookup Wizard is a process for setting Lookup property values for a field, not a data type itself.

5. **Click the Lookup tab to observe the new Lookup properties for the FirstContact field as shown in Figure E-8**

   The Lookup Wizard helped you enter the correct Lookup properties for the FirstContact field, but you can always enter or edit them directly if you know what values you want to use for each property. The Row Source property stores the values that are provided in the drop-down list for a Lookup field.

6. **Click the View button on the Design tab, click Yes when prompted to save the table, press [Tab] eight times to move to the FirstContact field, click the FirstContact list arrow as shown in Figure E-9, then click Friend**

   The FirstContact field now provides a list of values that are valid for this field.

7. **Close the Customers table**

Creating multivalued fields

Multivalued fields allow you to make more than one choice from a drop-down list for a field. As a database designer, multivalued fields allow you to select and store more than one choice without having to create a more advanced database design. To create a multivalued field, use the Lookup Wizard and select the Allow Multiple Values check box for the question that asks "Do you want to store multiple values for this lookup?" This feature is only available for an Access database created or saved in Access 2007 file format.

FIGURE E-7: Entering a Lookup list of values

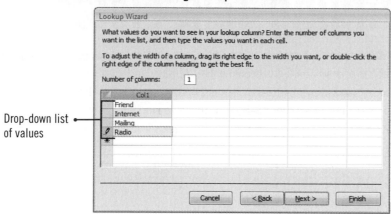

Drop-down list of values

FIGURE E-8: Viewing Lookup properties

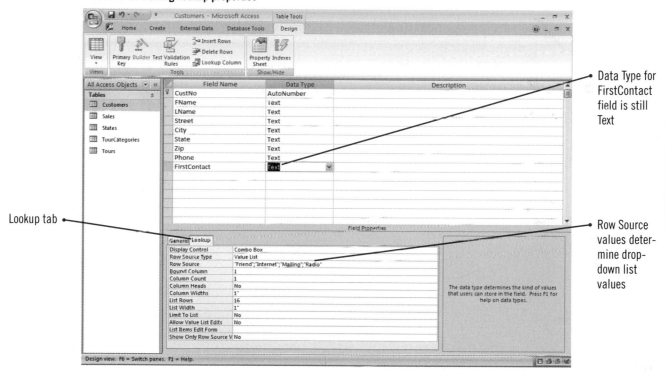

Data Type for FirstContact field is still Text

Lookup tab

Row Source values determine drop-down list values

FIGURE E-9: Using a Lookup field in a datasheet

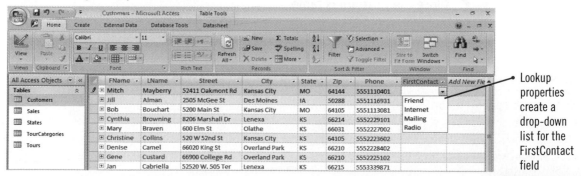

Lookup properties create a drop-down list for the FirstContact field

Access 2007

Modifying Text Fields

Field properties are the characteristics that apply to each field in a table, such as Field Size, Default Value, or Caption. These properties help ensure database accuracy and clarity because they restrict the way data is entered, stored, and displayed. You modify field properties in Table Design View. See Table E-2 for more information on Text field properties. ▰▰▰▰ After reviewing the Customers table with Mark Rock, you decide to make field property changes to several Text fields in that table.

STEPS

1. Right-click the Customers table in the Navigation Pane, then click Design View on the shortcut menu

The Customers table opens in Design View. The field properties appear on the General tab of the lower half of the Table Design View window and display the properties of the selected field. Field properties change depending on the field's data type. For example, when you select a field with a Text data type, the Field Size property is visible. However, when you select a field with a Date/Time data type, Access controls the Field Size property, so that property is not displayed. Many field properties are optional, but for those that require an entry, Access provides a default value.

2. Press [↓] to move through each field while viewing the field properties in the lower half of the window

The **field selector button** to the left of the field indicates which field is currently selected.

QUICK TIP

Because no entries in the FirstContact field are greater than 20 characters, you do not lose any data by making this property change.

3. Click the FirstContact field name, double-click 255 in the Field Size property text box, type 20, click the Save button 🖫 on the Quick Access toolbar, then click Yes

The maximum and the default value for the Field Size property for a Text field is 255. In general, however, you want to make the Field Size property for Text fields only as large as needed to accommodate the longest entry. You can increase the size later if necessary. In some cases, shortening the Field Size property helps prevent typographical errors. For example, you should set the Field Size property for a State field that stores two-letter state abbreviations to 2 to prevent errors such as TXX.

4. Change the Field Size property to 30 for the FName and LName fields, click 🖫, then click Yes

No existing entries are greater than 30 characters for either of these fields, so no data is lost. The **Input Mask** property provides a visual guide for users as they enter data. It also helps determine what types of values can be entered into a field.

TROUBLE

If the Input Mask Wizard is not installed on your computer, you can complete this step by typing !(999) 000-0000;;_ directly into the Input Mask property for the Phone field.

5. Click the Phone field name, click the Input Mask property text box, click the Build button ⋯ click the Phone Number input mask, click Next, click Next, then click Finish

Table Design View of the Customers table should look like Figure E-10, which shows the Input Mask property entered for the Phone field.

6. Click 🖫, click the View button on the Design tab, press [Tab] enough times to move to the Phone field for the first record, type 5554441234, then press [Enter]

The Phone Input Mask property creates an easy-to-use visual guide to facilitate accurate data entry.

7. Close the Customers table

FIGURE E-10: Changing Text field properties

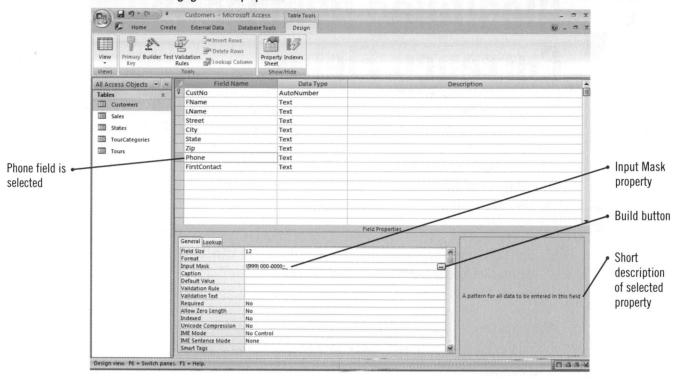

Phone field is selected

Input Mask property

Build button

Short description of selected property

TABLE E-2: Common Text field properties

property	description	sample field	sample property entry
Field Size	Controls how many characters can be entered into the field	State	2
Format	Controls how information will be displayed and printed	State	> (displays all characters in uppercase)
Input Mask	Provides a pattern for data to be entered	Phone	!(999) 000-0000;1;_
Caption	Describes the field in the first row of a datasheet, form, or report; if the Caption property is not entered, the field name itself is used to label the field	Emp#	Employee Number
Default Value	Displays a value that is automatically entered in the given field for new records	City	Kansas City
Required	Determines if an entry is required for this field	LastName	Yes

Exploring the Input Mask property

The Input Mask property provides a pattern for data to be entered, using three parts separated by semicolons. The first part provides a pattern for what type of data can be entered. For example, 9 represents an optional number, 0 a required number, ? an optional letter, and L a required letter. The second part determines whether all displayed characters (such as dashes in a phone number) are stored in the field. For the second part of the input mask, a 0 entry stores all characters such as 555-7722, and a 1 entry stores only the entered data, 5557722. The third part of the input mask determines which character Access uses to guide the user through the mask. Common choices are the asterisk (*), underscore (_), or pound sign (#).

Modifying Number and Currency Fields

Although some properties for Number and Currency fields are the same as the properties of Text fields, each data type has its own list of valid properties. Numeric and Currency fields have similar properties because they both contain numeric values. Currency fields store values that represent money, and Number fields store values that represent values such as quantities, measurements, and scores. ▰▰▰▰▰ The Tours table contains both a Number field (Duration) and a Currency field (Cost). You want to modify the properties of these two fields.

STEPS

1. Right-click the Tours table in the Navigation Pane, click Design View on the shortcut menu, click the Duration field name, then maximize Table Design View

The default Field Size property for a Number field is Long Integer. See Table E-3 for more information on the options for the Field Size property of a Number field. Access controls the size of Currency fields to control the way numbers are rounded in calculations, so the Field Size property isn't available for Currency fields.

2. Click Long Integer in the Field Size property text box, click the Field Size list arrow, then click Byte

Choosing a Byte value for the Field Size property allows entries from 0 to 255, so it greatly restricts the possible values and the storage requirements for the Duration field.

3. Click the Cost field name, click Auto in the Decimal Places property text box, click the Decimal Places list arrow, then click 0

Your Table Design View should look like Figure E-11. Because all of Quest's tours are priced at a round dollar value, you do not need to display cents in the Cost field.

> **QUICK TIP**
> The Property Update Options button ⧨ allows you to propagate field properties in the queries, forms, and reports that use the Cost field.

4. Save the table, then view the datasheet

Because none of the current entries in the Duration field is greater than 255, which is the maximum value allowed by a Number field with a Byte Field Size, you don't lose any data. You want to test the new property changes.

5. Press [Tab] three times to move to the Duration field for the first record, type 800, then press [Tab]

Because 800 is larger than the Byte Field Size property allows (0-255), an Access error message appears indicating that the value isn't valid for this field.

6. Press [Esc] twice to remove the inappropriate entry in the Duration field, then press [Tab] four times to move to the Cost field

The Cost field is set to display zero digits after the decimal point.

7. Type 750.25 in the Cost field of the first record, press [↓], then click $750 in the Cost field of the first record

Although the Decimal Places property for the Cost field dictates that entries in the field are *formatted* to display zero digits after the decimal point, 750.25 is the actual value stored in the field. Modifying the Decimal Places property does not change the actual data. Rather, the Decimal Places property only changes the way the data is *presented*.

8. Click the Undo button ⧨ on the Quick Access toolbar to restore the Cost entry to $750, then close the Tours table

FIGURE E-11: Changing Currency and Number field properties

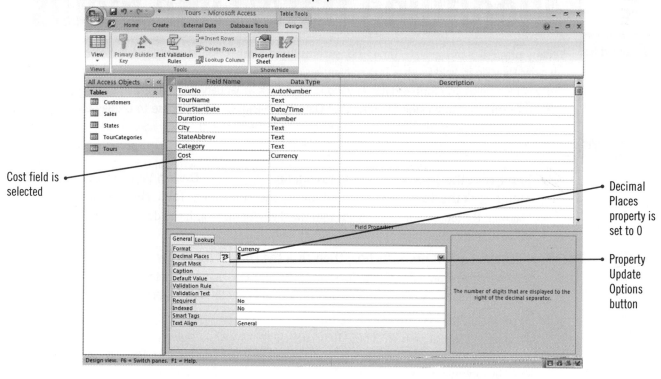

Cost field is selected

Decimal Places property is set to 0

Property Update Options button

TABLE E-3: Common Number field properties

property	description
Field Size	Determines the largest number that can be entered in the field, as well as the type of data (e.g., integer or fraction)
Byte	Stores numbers from 0 to 255 (no fractions)
Integer	Stores numbers from –32,768 to 32,767 (no fractions)
Long Integer	Stores numbers from –2,147,483,648 to 2,147,483,647 (no fractions)
Single	Stores numbers (including fractions with six digits to the right of the decimal point) times 10 to the –38th to +38th power
Double	Stores numbers (including fractions with over 10 digits to the right of the decimal point) in the range of 10 to the –324th to +324th power
Decimal Places	The number of digits displayed to the right of the decimal point

Modifying Date/Time Fields

Many properties of the Date/Time field, such as Input Mask, Caption, and Default Value, work the same way as they do in fields with a Text or Number data type. One difference, however, is the **Format** property, which helps you format dates in various ways such as January 25, 2006; 25-Jan-06; or 01/25/2006. 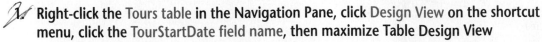 You want to change the format of Date/Time fields in the database to display two digits for the month and day values and four digits for the year, as in 05/05/2010.

STEPS

1. Right-click the Tours table in the Navigation Pane, click Design View on the shortcut menu, click the TourStartDate field name, then maximize Table Design View

You want the tour start dates to appear with two digits for the month and day, such as 07/05/2010, instead of the default presentation of dates, 7/5/2010.

QUICK TIP

Click any property box, then press F1 to open the Microsoft Access Help window to the page that describes that property.

2. Click the Format property box, then click the Format list arrow

Although several predefined Date/Time formats are available, none matches the format you want. To define a custom format, enter symbols that represent how you want the date to appear.

3. Type mm/dd/yyyy then press [Enter]

The updated Format property for the TourStartDate field shown in Figure E-12 sets the date to appear with two digits for the month, two digits for the day, and four digits for the year. The parts of the date are separated by forward slashes.

4. Save the table, display the datasheet, then click the New (blank) record button on the navigation bar

To test the new Format property for the TourStartDate field, you can add a new record to the table.

QUICK TIP

Access assumes that years entered with two digits from 30 to 99 refer to the years 1930 through 1999, and 00 to 29 refers to the years 2000 through 2029. To enter a year before 1930 or after 2029, enter all four digits of the year.

5. Press [Tab] to move to the TourName field, type Missouri Eagles, press [Tab], type 9/1/10, press [Tab], type 7, press [Tab], type Hollister, press [Tab], type MO, press [Tab], type a (for Adventure), press [Tab], then type 700

Your screen should look like Figure E-13. The new record is entered into the Tours table. The Format property for the TourStartDate field makes the entry appear as 09/01/2010, as desired.

FIGURE E-12: Changing Date/Time field properties

TourStartDate field is selected

Custom Format property

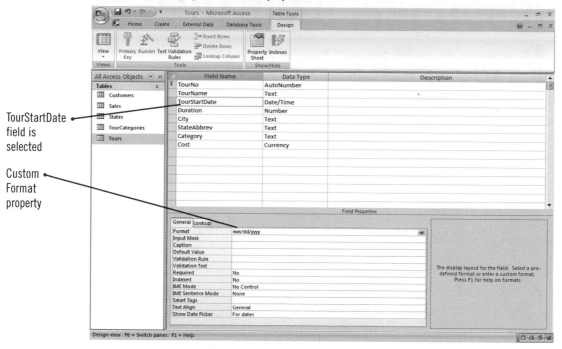

FIGURE E-13: Testing the Format property for the TourStartDate field

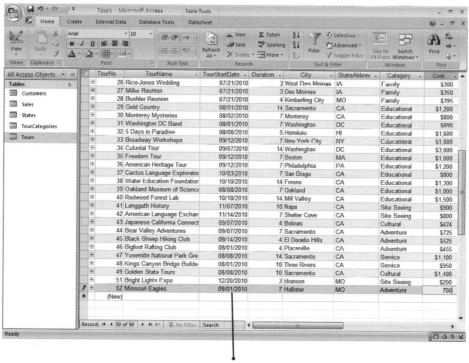

Custom mm/dd/yyyy
Format property

Using Smart Tags

The Property Update Options button ⧉ is an Access Smart Tag. **Smart Tags** are buttons that appear in certain conditions. They provide a small menu of options to help you work with the task at hand. Access provides the Property Update Options Smart Tag to help you quickly apply property changes to other objects of the database that use the field. The **Error Indicator button** ⧉ Smart Tag helps identify potential design errors. For example, if you are working in Form Design View and add a text box to the form but do not correctly bind it to an underlying field, the Error Indicator button appears by the text box to alert you to the problem.

Modifying Validation Properties

The **Validation Rule** property determines what entries a field can accept. For example, a Validation Rule for a Date/Time field might require date entries on or after 1/1/2010. A Validation Rule for a Currency field might indicate that valid entries fall between $0 and $1,500. You use the **Validation Text** property to display an explanatory message when a user tries to enter data that doesn't meet the criteria for a valid field entry established by the Validation Rule. Therefore, the Validation Rule and Validation Text field properties help you prevent unreasonable data from being entered into the database. 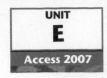 Mark Rock reminds you that Quest tours start no earlier than January 1, 2010. You can use the validation properties to establish this rule for the TourStartDate field.

STEPS

1. Click the View button **on the Home tab to return to Design View, click the** TourStartDate **field if it isn't already selected, click the** Validation Rule property box, **then type** >=1/1/2010

This entry forces all dates in the TourStartDate field to be greater than or equal to 1/1/2010. See Table E-4 for more examples of Validation Rule expressions. The Validation Text property provides a helpful message to the user when the entry in the field breaks the rule entered in the Validation Rule property.

2. Click the Validation Text box, **then type** Date must be on or after 1/1/2010

The Design View of the Tours table should now look like Figure E-14. Access modifies a property to include additional syntax by changing the entry in the Validation Rule property to >=#1/1/2010#. Pound signs (#) are used to surround date criteria.

3. Save the table, then click Yes **when asked to test the existing data with new data integrity rules**

Because no dates in the TourStartDate field are earlier than 1/1/2010, Access finds no date errors in the current data and saves the table. You now want to test that the Validation Rule and Validation Text properties work when entering data in the datasheet.

4. Click the View button **on the Design tab to display the datasheet, press [Tab] twice to move to the** TourStartDate **field, type** 1/1/06, **then press [Tab]**

Because you tried to enter a date that was not true for the Validation Rule property for the TourStartDate field, a dialog box opens and displays the Validation Text entry, as shown in Figure E-15.

5. Click OK **to close the validation message**

You now know that the Validation Rule and Validation Text properties work properly.

6. Press [Esc] to reject the invalid date entry in the TourStartDate **field**

7. Close the Tours **table**

FIGURE E-14: Entering validation properties

TourStartDate field is selected

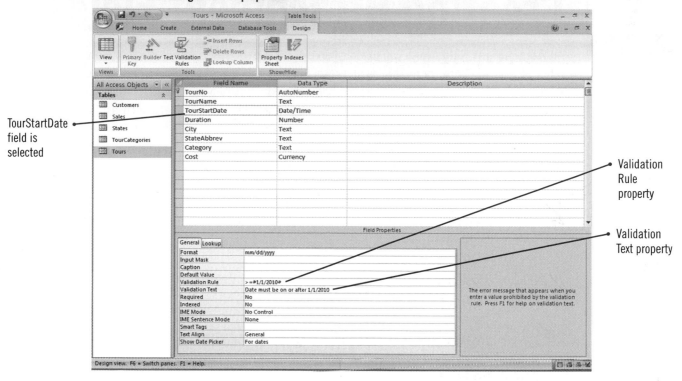

Validation Rule property

Validation Text property

FIGURE E-15: Validation Text message

Validation Text property

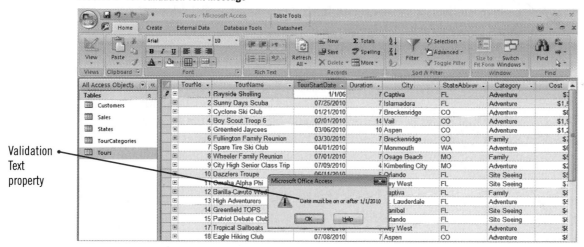

TABLE E-4: Validation Rule expressions

data type	validation rule expression	description
Number or Currency	>0	The number must be positive
Number or Currency	>10 And <100	The number must be between 10 and 100
Number or Currency	10 Or 20 Or 30	The number must be 10, 20, or 30
Text	"IA" Or "NE" Or "MO"	The entry must be IA, NE, or MO
Date/Time	>=#7/1/93#	The date must be on or after 7/1/1993
Date/Time	>#1/1/10# And <#1/1/12#	The date must be between 1/1/2010 and 1/1/2012

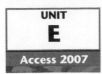

Creating Attachment Fields

An **Attachment field** allows you to attach an external file such as a Word document, PowerPoint presentation, Excel workbook, or image file to a record. Earlier versions of Access allowed you to link or embed external data using the **OLE** (object linking and embedding) data type. The Attachment data type is superior to OLE because it stores data more efficiently; stores more file formats, such as JPEG images; and requires no additional software to view the files from within Access. ▰▰▰▰▰ Mark Rock asks you to incorporate images on forms and reports to help describe and market each tour. You can use an Attachment field to store JPEG images that help illustrate each tour in the Tours table.

STEPS

1. **Right-click the Tours table in the Navigation Pane, click Design View, then maximize Table Design View**

You can add the new field below the Cost field.

2. **Click the Field Name cell below Cost, type Picture, press [Tab], click the Data Type list arrow, then click Attachment**

Now that you created the new Attachment field, you're ready to add data to it in Datasheet View.

3. **Click the Save button 🖫 on the Quick Access toolbar, click the View button on the Design tab to switch to Datasheet View, then press [Tab] enough times to move to the new Attachment field**

The Attachment field cell displays a small paper clip icon with the number of files attached to the field in parentheses, as shown in Figure E-16. You have not attached any files to this field yet, so each record shows zero (0) file attachments. You can attach files to this field directly from Datasheet View.

4. **Right-click the attachment icon for the first record, click Manage Attachments on the shortcut menu, click Add, navigate to the drive and folder where you store your Data Files, double-click Sunset.jpg, then click OK**

The Sunset.jpg file is now included with the first record, and the datasheet reflects that one (1) file is attached to the Picture field of the first record. You can add more than one file attachment to the same field, but good database practices encourage you to add only one piece of information per field. Therefore, if you want to also attach a Word document listing the trip itinerary to this record, good database practices encourage you to add a second Attachment field to handle this information. You can view all types of file attachments directly from the datasheet. You can also view images from a form or report that displays this information.

5. **Right-click the attachment icon for the first record, click Manage Attachments on the shortcut menu, then double-click Sunset.jpg to open it**

The image opens in the program that is associated with the .jpg extension on your computer. Figure E-17 shows the Sunset.jpg image as displayed by Windows Photo Gallery, but a different program on your computer might be associated with the .jpg file extension. **JPEG** is an acronym for Joint Photographic Experts Group, which defines the standards for the compression algorithms that allow image files to be stored in an efficient compressed format. Because the size requirements of JPEG images are minimized, the JPEG file format is ideal for storing large numbers of pictures in a database or for transporting images across a network.

6. **Close the window that displays the Sunset.jpg image, click Cancel in the Attachments dialog box, close the Tours table, close the Quest-E.accdb database, then exit Access**

FIGURE E-16: Attachment field in Datasheet View

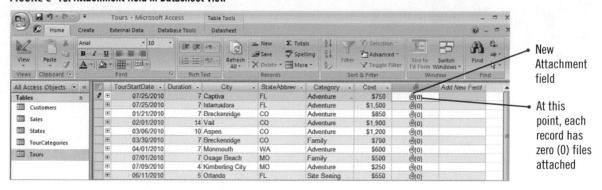

New Attachment field

At this point, each record has zero (0) files attached

FIGURE E-17: Viewing a JPEG image

This image appears in Windows Photo Gallery, but your image might appear in a different program

Recognizing database formats

When you create a new, blank database in Microsoft Office Access 2007, Access gives the file the .accdb extension and formats it as an Access 2007 database. Access 2007 displays the version of the current database file in the title bar when you first open the database. The **.accdb** file extension usually means the database is an Access 2007 format database, but note that Access 2007 format databases are *not* readable by earlier versions of Access such as Access 2000, Access 2002 (XP), or Access 2003. Some features such as multivalued fields and Attachment fields are only available when working on an Access 2007 database. In some cases, you might prefer to use Access 2007, but create or convert database files to an earlier Access format such as Access 2000 or Access 2002-2003. This option is helpful if you share the database with users who are still using earlier versions of Access. In Microsoft Office Access 2007, to save an existing database to a different version, use the Save As command on the Office button menu. Using this feature, Access 2000, 2002-2003 databases are given an **.mdb** file extension.

Practice

▼ CONCEPTS REVIEW

Identify each element of Table Design View shown in Figure E-18.

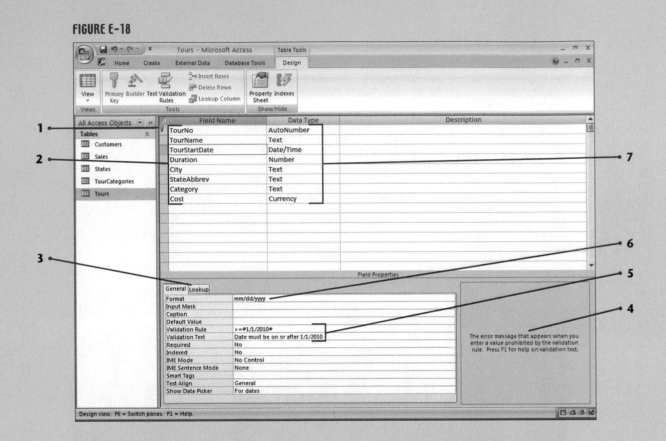

FIGURE E-18

Match each term with the statement that best describes it.

8. Primary key field
9. Validation properties
10. Table Design View
11. Row Source
12. Relational database
13. Input Mask
14. Lookup properties
15. Multivalued field
16. Attachment field

a. Field that allows you to store external files such as a Word document, PowerPoint presentation, Excel workbook, or image files

b. Field that allows you to make more than one choice from a drop-down list for a field

c. Field that holds unique information for each record in the table

d. Several tables linked together in one-to-many relationships

e. Field properties that allow you to supply a drop-down list of values for a field

f. Access window where all characteristics of a table, such as field names and field properties, are defined

g. Field properties that help you prevent unreasonable data entries for a field

h. Field property that provides a visual guide as you enter data

i. Lookup property that determines where the Lookup field gets its list of values

Select the best answer from the list of choices.

17. Which of the following problems most clearly indicates that you need to redesign your database?
  a. The Input Mask Wizard has not been used.
  b. Referential integrity is enforced on table relationships.
  c. Not all fields have Validation Rule properties.
  d. There is duplicated data in the field of several records of a table.

18. Which of the following is *not* defined in Table Design View?
  a. The primary key field
  b. Field Size properties
  c. Duplicate data
  d. Field data types

19. What is the purpose of enforcing referential integrity?
  a. To prevent incorrect entries in the primary key field
  b. To prevent orphan records from being entered
  c. To require an entry for each field of each record
  d. To force the application of meaningful validation rules

20. To create a many-to-many relationship between two tables, you must create:
  a. A junction table.
  b. Combination primary key fields in each table.
  c. A one-to-many relationship between the two tables, with referential integrity enforced.
  d. Foreign key fields in each table.

1. **Examine relational databases.**
   a. List the fields needed to create an Access relational database to manage membership information for a philanthropic club, community service organization, or international aid group.
   b. Identify fields that would contain duplicate values if all of the fields were stored in a single table.
   c. Group the fields into subject matter tables, then identify the primary key field for each table.
   d. Assume that your database contains two tables: Members and ZipCodes. If you did not identify these two tables earlier, regroup the fields within these two table names, then identify the primary key field for each table, the foreign key field in the Members table, and how the tables would be related using a one-to-many relationship.

2. **Design related tables.**
   a. Start Access 2007, then click the New Blank Database button.
   b. Type **Membership-E** in the File Name box, click the Folder icon to navigate to the drive and folder where you store your Data Files, click OK, then click Create.
   c. Use Table Design View to create a new table with the name **Members** and the field names and data types shown in Figure E-19.

   FIGURE E-19

field name	data type
FirstName	Text
LastName	Text
Street	Text
Zip	Text
Phone	Text
Birthdate	Date/Time
Dues	Currency
MemberNo	Text
MemberType	Text
CharterMember	Yes/No

   d. Specify MemberNo as the primary key field, save the Members table, then close it.
   e. Use Table Design View to create a new table named **ZipCodes** with the field names and data types shown in Figure E-20.

   FIGURE E-20

field name	data type
Zip	Text
City	Text
State	Text

   f. Identify Zip as the primary key field, save the ZipCodes table, then close it.
   g. Use Table Design View to create a third new table called **Activities** with the field names and data types shown in Figure E-21.

   FIGURE E-21

field name	data type
ActivityNo	AutoNumber
MemberNo	Text
ActivityDate	Date/Time
Hours	Number

   h. Identify ActivityNo as the primary key field, save the Activities table, then close it.

3. **Create one-to-many relationships.**

a. Open the Relationships window, double-click Activities, double-click Members, then double-click ZipCodes to add all three tables to the Relationships window. Close the Show Table dialog box.

b. Resize all field lists as necessary so that all fields are visible, then drag the Zip field from the ZipCodes table to the Zip field in the Members table to create a one-to-many relationship between the ZipCodes table and Members table, using the common Zip field.

c. Enforce referential integrity, and create the one-to-many relationship between ZipCodes and Members.

d. Drag the MemberNo field from the Members table to the MemberNo field in the Activities table to create a one-to-many relationship between the Members table and the Activities table, using the common MemberNo field.

e. Enforce referential integrity, and create the one-to-many relationship between Members and Activities. See Figure E-22.

f. Create a Relationship report for the Membership-E database, add your name as a label to the Report Header section of the report in Report Design View, then print the report.

g. Close the Relationship report without saving the report, then close the Relationships window. Save the changes to the Relationships window if prompted.

FIGURE E-22

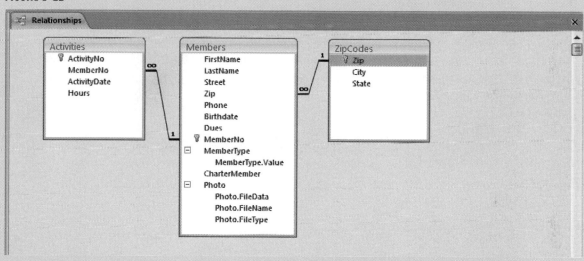

Access 2007

4. Create Lookup fields.

a. Open the Members table in Design View, then start the Lookup Wizard for the MemberType field.

b. Select the option that allows you to enter your own values, then enter **Active**, **Inactive**, **Teen**, **Adult**, and **Senior** as the values for the lookup column.

c. Use the default MemberType label, check the Allow Multiple Values check box, finish the Lookup Wizard, and confirm that you want to allow multiple values.

d. Save and close the Members table.

5. Modify Text fields.

a. Open the ZipCodes table in Design View.

b. Change the Field Size property of the State field to **2** then save the ZipCodes table and display it in Datasheet View.

c. Enter a record with the zip code, city, and state for your school. Try to enter more than two characters in the State field, then close the ZipCodes table.

d. Open the Members table in Design View. Use the Input Mask Wizard to create an Input Mask property for the Phone field. Choose the Phone Number Input Mask. Accept the other default options provided by the Input Mask Wizard. (*Hint*: If the Input Mask Wizard is not installed on your computer, type **!(999) 000-0000;;_** for the Input Mask property for the Phone field.) See Figure E-23.

e. Change the Field Size property of the FirstName, LastName, and Street fields to **30**. Save the Members table.

f. Open the Members table in Datasheet View and enter a new record with your name in the FirstName and LastName fields and your school's Street, Zip, and Phone field values. Note the effect of the Input Mask on the Phone field. Enter **1/1/1985** for the Birthdate field, **200** for Dues, and **1** for MemberNo. Choose both Active and Adult for the MemberType field, and do not check the CharterMember field.

FIGURE E-23

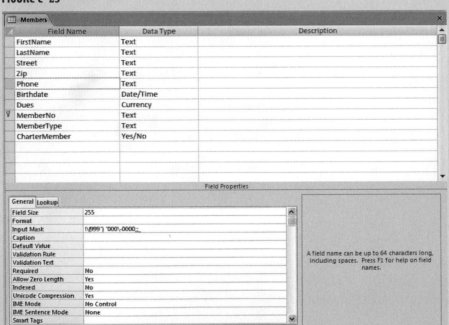

635-6232

6. Modify Number and Currency fields.

a. Open the Members table in Design View.

b. Change the Decimal Places property of the Dues field to 0. Save and close the Members table.

c. Open the Activities table in Design View.

d. Change the Field Size property of the Hours field to Byte. Save and close the Activities table.

7. Modify Date/Time fields.

a. Open the Members table in Design View.

b. Change the Format property of the Birthdate field to mm/dd/yyyy

c. Save and close the Members table.

d. Open the Activities table in Design View.

e. Change the Format property of the ActivityDate field to mm/dd/yyyy

f. Save and close the Activities table

8. Modify field validation properties.

a. Open the Members table in Design View.

b. Click the Birthdate field name, click the Validation Rule text box, then type <1/1/2000 (Note that Access automatically adds pound signs around date criteria in the Validation Rule property.)

c. Click the Validation Text box, then type Birthdate must be before 1/1/2000

d. Save and allow the changes, then open the Members table in Datasheet View.

e. Test the Validation Text and Validation Rule properties by tabbing to the Birthdate field and entering a date after 1/1/2000 such as 1/1/2001. Click OK when prompted with the Validation Text message, press [Esc] to return the Birthdate field value to 01/01/1985, then close the Members table.

Access 2007

9. Create Attachment fields.

a. Open the Members table in Design View, then add a new field with the field name Photo and an Attachment data type, as shown in Figure E-24. Save the table.

b. Display the Members table in Datasheet View, then attach the **Member1.jpg** file (provided in the drive and folder where you store your Data Files) to the new Photo field for the first record.

c. Close the Members table.

d. Use the Form Wizard to create a form based on all of the fields in the Members table. Use a Columnar layout, a Civic style, and title the form **Members Entry Form**.

e. Print the first page of the Members Entry Form that shows the picture stored in the Photo field, then close the form.

f. Close the Membership-E.accdb database, then exit Access.

FIGURE E-24

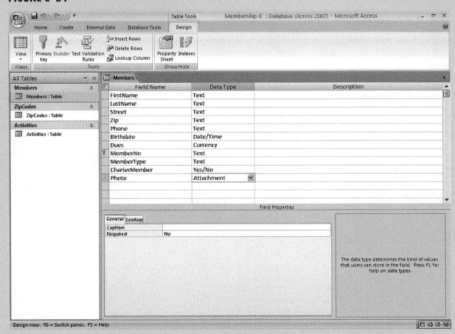

Modifying the Database Structure

▼ INDEPENDENT CHALLENGE 1

As the manager of a music store's instrument rental program, you decide to create a database to track rentals to schoolchildren. The fields you need to track are organized with four tables: Instruments, Rentals, Customers, and Schools.

a. Start Access, then create a new blank database called **MusicStore-E.accdb** in the folder where you store your Data Files.

b. Use Table Design View to create the four tables in the MusicStore-E database using the information shown in Figure E-25. The primary key field for each table is identified with bold text.

FIGURE E-25

table	field name	data type
Customers	FirstName	Text
	LastName	Text
	Street	Text
	City	Text
	State	Text
	Zip	Text
	CustNo	Text
	SchoolNo	Text
Instruments	Description	Text
	SerialNo	Text
	MonthlyFee	Currency
Schools	SchoolName	Text
	SchoolNo	Text
Rentals	**RentalNo**	AutoNumber
	CustNo	Text
	SerialNo	Text
	RentalDate	Date/Time

c. Enter >3/1/2010 as the Validation Rule property for the RentalDate field of the Rentals table. This change allows only dates later than 3/1/2010 to be entered into this field.

d. Enter **Dates must be after March 1, 2010** as the Validation Text property to the RentalDate field of the Rentals table. Note that Access adds pound signs (#) to the date criteria entered in the Validation Rule as soon as you enter the Validation Text property.

e. Save and close the Rentals table.

f. Open the Relationships window, add all four tables to the window, as shown in Figure E-26, and create one-to-many relationships as shown. Be sure to enforce referential integrity on each relationship.

g. Preview the Relationship report, add your name as a label to the Report Header section, then print the report, making sure that all fields of each table are visible.

h. Close the Relationship report without saving it. Close the Relationships window, then save the layout if prompted.

i. Close the MusicStore-E.accdb database, then exit Access.

FIGURE E-26

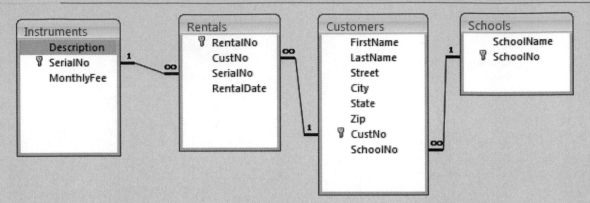

▼ INDEPENDENT CHALLENGE 2

You're a member and manager of a recreational baseball team and decide to create an Access database to manage player information, games, and batting statistics.

This Independent Challenge requires an Internet connection.

a. Start Access, then create a new database called Baseball-E.accdb in the drive and folder where you store your Data Files.

b. Create a Players table with fields and appropriate data types to record the player first name, last name, and uniform number. Make the uniform number field the primary key field.

c. Create a Games table with fields and appropriate data types to record an automatic game number, date of the game, opponent's name, home score, and visitor score. Make the game number field the primary key field.

d. Create an AtBats table with fields and appropriate data types to record hits, at bats, the game number, and the uniform number of the player. This table does not need a primary key field.

e. In the Relationships window, create a one-to-many relationship with referential integrity between the Games and AtBats table, using the common game number field.

f. In the Relationships window, create a one-to-many relationship with referential integrity between the Players and AtBats table, using the common uniform number field. The final Relationships window is shown in Figure E-27.

FIGURE E-27

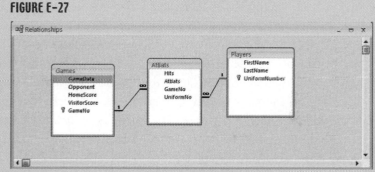

g. Use the Relationship Report button to create a report of the Relationships window, then print it. Close the Relationship report without saving it. Close the Relationships window, saving changes if prompted.

h. Using an Internet search tool, find the roster for a baseball team in your area, and enter nine players into the Players table. One of the players should have your name. Print the Players datasheet.

i. Research the games that this team has previously played, and enter one game record into the Games table.

j. Using the GameNo value of 1 and the UniformNo values from the Players table, enter nine records into the AtBats table to represent the batting statistics for the nine players for that game. Your entries do not need to represent a specific game, but they should be realistic. (*Hint*: Most players bat three or four times per game. A player cannot have more hits in a game than at bats.)

k. Print the AtBats datasheet.

l. Close the Baseball-E.accdb database, then exit Access.

▼ INDEPENDENT CHALLENGE 3

You want to create a database that documents blood bank donations by the employees of your company. Start by designing the database on paper, including the tables, field names, data types, and relationships. You want to track information such as employee name, department, blood type, date of donation, and the hospital that is earmarked to receive the donation. You also want to track basic hospital information, such as the hospital name and address.

a. On paper, create three balanced columns by drawing two vertical lines from the top to the bottom of the paper. Label the columns **Table**, **Field Name**, and **Data Type**, from left to right.

b. In the middle column, list all of the fields that need to be tracked to record the blood donations. When creating your field lists for each table, be sure to separate personal names into at least two fields, FirstName and LastName, so that you can easily sort, filter, and find data based on either part of a person's name.

c. In the first column, identify the table that contains this field. (*Hint*: In this case, you should identify three tables: Employees, Donations, and Hospitals.)

d. Identify the primary key field for each table by circling it. You might have to add a new field to each table if you do not have an existing field that naturally serves as the primary key field. (*Hint*: Each employee is identified with a unique EmployeeID, each hospital with a unique HospitalID, and each donation with a DonationID.)

e. In the third column, identify the appropriate data type for each field.

f. After identifying all field names, table names, and data types for each field, reorder the fields so that the fields for each table are listed together.

g. On a new sheet of paper, sketch the field lists for each table as they would appear in the Access Relationships window. Circle the primary key fields for each table. Include the one-to-many join lines as well as the "one" and "infinity" symbols to identify the "one" and "many" sides of the one-to-many relationship. To help determine how you should create the relationships between the tables, note that one employee can make several blood donations. One hospital can receive many donations. (*Hint*: When building a one-to-many relationship between two tables, one field must be common to both tables. To create a common field, you might need to return to your field lists in Step f and add a foreign key field to the table on the "many" side of the relationship in order to link the tables.)

Advanced Challenge Exercise

■ Build the database you designed in Access with the name **BloodDrive-E.accdb**. Don't forget to enforce referential integrity on the two one-to-many relationships in this database.

■ Print the Relationship report with your name added as a label to the Report Header section. Close the Relationship report without saving it, then close the Relationships window and save the layout changes.

■ Add Lookup properties to the blood type field to provide only valid blood type entries of **A–**, **A+**, **B–**, **B+**, **O–**, **O+**, **AB–**, and **AB+** for this field.

■ Close BloodDrive-E.accdb, then exit Access.

▼ REAL LIFE INDEPENDENT CHALLENGE

You want to document the books you've read by creating and storing the information in a relational database. You design the database on paper by identifying the tables, field names, data types, and relationships between the tables.

a. Complete Steps a through g as described in Independent Challenge 3, using the new case information. You like to read multiple books from the same author, so you should separate the author information into a separate table to avoid duplicate author name entries in the Books table. You also want to track information including the book title, category (such as Biography, Mystery, or Science Fiction), rating (a numeric value from 1–10 that indicates how much you liked the book), date you read the book, author's first name, and author's last name. When creating primary key fields, note that each book has an ISBN—International Standard Book Number—that is a unique number assigned to every book. To uniquely identify each author, use an AuthorNo field. Do not use the AuthorLastName field as the primary key field for the Authors table because it does not uniquely identify authors who have the same last names.

Advanced Challenge Exercise

- In Access, build the database you designed. Name the database **Books-E.accdb**, and save it in the drive and folder where you store your Data Files. Don't forget to enforce referential integrity on the one-to-many relationship in this database.
- Print the Relationship report with your name added as a label to the Report Header section. Close the Relationship report without saving it, then close the Relationships window and save the layout changes.
- Add Lookup properties to the field that identifies book categories. Include at least four types of book categories in the list.
- Add at least three records to each table and print them.
- Close Books-E.accdb, then exit Access.

▼ VISUAL WORKSHOP

Open the Training-E.accdb database, and create a new table called Vendors using the Table Design View shown in Figure E-28 to determine field names and data types. Make the following property changes: Change the Field Size property of the VState field to 2, the VZip field to 9, and VPhone field to 10. Change the Field Size property of the VendorName, VStreet, and VCity fields to 30. Apply a Phone Number Input Mask to the VPhone field. Be sure to specify that the VendorID field is the primary key field. Enter one record into the datasheet with your last name in the VendorName field and your school's contact information in the other fields. Print the datasheet in landscape orientation.

FIGURE E-28

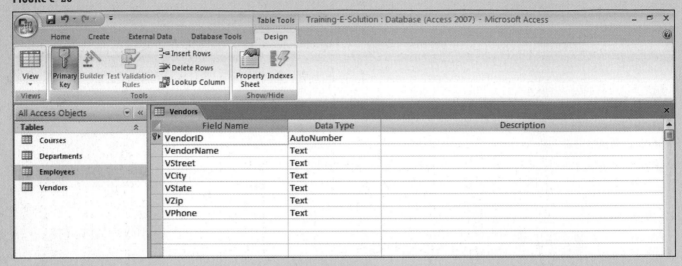

Creating Multiple Table Queries

Queries are database objects that organize fields from one or more tables into a single datasheet. A **select query**, the most common type of query, retrieves fields from related tables and displays records in a datasheet. Select queries are used to select only certain records from a database. They can also sort records, calculate new fields of data, or calculate statistics such as the sum or average of a given field. You can also present data selected by a query in Query PivotTable View or Query PivotChart View. These views display information about summarized groups of records in a crosstabular report or graph. ▰▰▰ The Quest database has been updated to contain more customers, tours, and sales. You help Mark Rock, a Quest tour developer for U.S. travel, create queries to analyze this information.

OBJECTIVES

Build select queries

Use multiple sort orders

Develop AND criteria

Develop OR criteria

Create calculated fields

Build summary queries

Build crosstab queries

Build PivotTables and PivotCharts

Building Select Queries

You can create select queries by using the **Simple Query Wizard** or by building the query in **Query Design View**. Creating a select query with the Simple Query Wizard is fast and easy, but learning how to use Query Design View gives you more flexibility and options when selecting and presenting information. When you open (or **run**) a query, the fields and records that you have selected for the query are presented as a datasheet in **Query Datasheet View**. Query Datasheet View does not present a duplicate copy of the data stored in the tables. Rather, it displays table data in a new arrangement, sometimes called a **logical view** of the data. If you edit data using a query datasheet, the changes are actually made to the underlying table as if you were working directly in a table datasheet. Mark Rock asks you to create a query to answer the question, "Who is purchasing our tours?" You can select fields from the Customers, Sales, and Tours tables using Query Design View to display a single datasheet that answers this question.

STEPS

1. **Start Access, open the Quest-F.accdb database from the drive and folder where you store your Data Files, then enable content if prompted**

2. **Click the Create tab on the Ribbon, then click the Query Design button**

   The Show Table dialog box opens and lists all the tables in the database. You use the Show Table dialog box to add the tables that contain the fields you want to view in the final query datasheet.

> **TROUBLE**
> If you add a table to Query Design View twice by mistake, click the title bar of the extra field list, then press [Delete].

3. **Double-click Customers, double-click Sales, double-click Tours, click Close, then maximize Query Design View**

   Recall that the upper part of Query Design View displays the fields for each of the three selected tables in **field lists**, with the name of the associated table shown in the field list title bar. Primary key fields are identified with a small key icon to the left of the field. To rearrange the field lists in Query Design View, drag the title bar of a field list to move it, or drag the edge of a field list to resize it. Relationships between tables are displayed with **one-to-many join lines** that connect the linking fields. You add the fields that you want the query to display in the columns in the lower part of Query Design View, known as the **query design grid**.

4. **Drag the FName field in the Customers table field list to the first column of the query design grid**

   The order in which you place the fields in the query design grid is the order they appear in the datasheet. When you drag a field to the query design grid, any existing fields move to the right to accommodate the new field.

> **TROUBLE**
> Drag the bottom edge of the Tours field list down to view all of the fields in that table.

5. **Double-click the LName field in the Customers field list, double-click the SaleDate field in the Sales field list, double-click the TourName field in the Tours field list, then double-click the Cost field in the Tours field list as shown in Figure F-1**

   If you add the wrong field to the query design grid, you can delete it by clicking the **field selector**, a thin gray bar above each field name, then pressing [Delete]. Deleting a field from the query design grid removes it from the logical view of this query's datasheet, but does not delete the field from the database. A field is defined and the field's contents are stored in a table object only.

6. **Click the View button on the Design tab to run the query and open the query datasheet**

   The resulting datasheet looks like Figure F-2. The datasheet shows the five fields selected in Query Design View: FName and LName from the Customers table, SaleDate from the Sales table, and TourName and Cost from the Tours table. The datasheet displays 40 records that represent 40 sales. The query has selected the name Christine Collins several times—even though this name is recorded only once in the Customers table—because she is related to many sales in the Sales table. The Bayside Shelling tour has been selected for the datasheet several times—though it is physically recorded only once in the Tours table—because it is related to many sales in the Sales table.

FIGURE F-1: Query Design View with five fields in the query design grid

View button

One-to-many join lines

Tours field list has been resized to show all fields

Field selectors

Resize bar

Query design grid

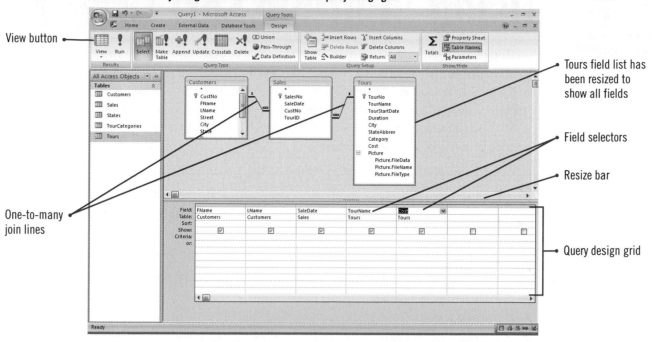

FIGURE F-2: Query datasheet showing related information from three tables

Fields from Customers table

Field from Sales table

Fields from Tours table

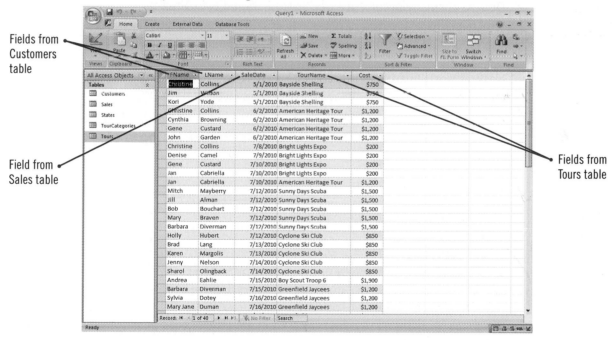

Resizing Query Design View

Drag the **resize bar**, a thin gray bar that separates the field lists from the query design grid, up or down to provide more room for the upper (field lists) or lower (query design grid) panes of Query Design View. By dragging the resize bar down, you can create enough room to resize each field list so that you can see all field names for each table.

Using Multiple Sort Orders

Sorting refers to reordering records in either ascending or descending order based on the values in a field. Queries allow you to specify more than one sort field in Query Design View. Sort orders are evaluated from left to right, meaning that the sort field farthest to the left is the primary sort field. Sort orders defined in Query Design View are saved with the query object. ▰▰▰▰ You want to list the records in alphabetical order based on the customer's last name. If the customer has purchased more than one tour, you decide to further sort the records by the sale date.

STEPS

1. **Click the View button on the Home tab to return to Query Design View**

   To sort the records by last name then by sale date, the LName field must be the primary sort field, and the SaleDate field must be the secondary sort field.

2. **Click the LName field Sort cell in the query design grid, click the Sort list arrow, click Ascending, click the SaleDate field Sort cell in the query design grid, click the Sort list arrow, then click Ascending**

   The resulting query design grid should look like Figure F-3.

QUICK TIP

You can resize the columns of a datasheet by pointing to the right column border that separates the field names, then dragging ◄╫► left or right to resize the columns. Double-click ◄╫► to automatically adjust the column width to fit the widest entry.

3. **Click the View button on the Design tab to see the query datasheet**

   The records of the datasheet are now listed in ascending order based on the values in the LName field. When the same value appears in the LName field, the records are further sorted by the date in the SaleDate field. Christine Collins purchased three tours, but she prefers to be called "Chris." You want to fix this error in the query datasheet.

4. **Double-click any occurrence of Christine, type Chris, then press [↓]**

   Because this name is physically stored only once in the Customers table (but selected three times for this query), all three records that contained the name "Christine" are automatically updated to "Chris," as shown in Figure F-4. In a properly designed relational database, editing any occurrence of a value in a table, query, or form automatically updates all other occurrences of that data in every other database object. You also need to update the price of the Sunny Days Scuba tour.

5. **Select any occurrence of $1,500 for the Cost field in one of the first three records, type 1400, click Sunny Days Scuba, click the Selection button, then click Equals "Sunny Days Scuba"**

   Because the Sunny Days Scuba tour is physically stored only once in the Tours table (but selected five times for this query), all occurrences of the price for the Sunny Days Scuba tour are now changed from $1,500 to $1,400, regardless of where they are sorted or if they are filtered in the datasheet. When Access saves a query object, it saves **Structured Query Language (SQL)** statements. You can view or work with SQL using Access query objects.

6. **Click the View button arrow on the Home tab, then click SQL View**

   The SQL statements determine what fields are selected, how the tables are joined, and how the resulting records are sorted. Fortunately, you do not have to be able to write or understand SQL to use Access. The easy-to-use Query Design View gives you a way to select and sort data from underlying tables without being an SQL programmer.

7. **Close the SQL window, click Yes when prompted to save the changes, type CustomerSales in the Query Name text box, then click OK**

   The query is now saved and listed as a query object in the Navigation Pane.

FIGURE F-3: Specifying multiple sort orders in Query Design View

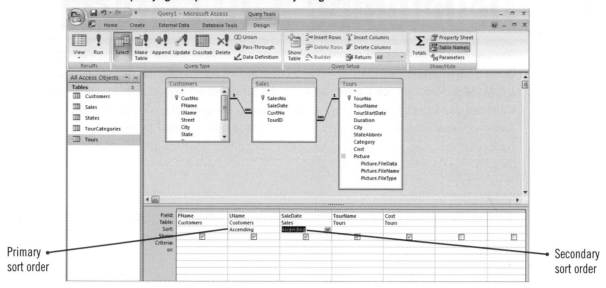

Primary sort order

Secondary sort order

FIGURE F-4: Records sorted by LName, then by SaleDate

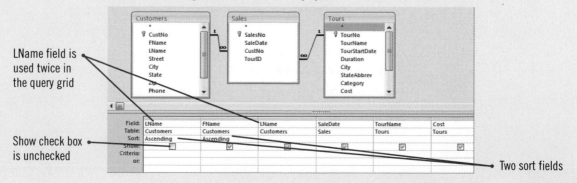

Primary sort order

Selection button

Secondary sort order

All three occurrences of Christine are changed to Chris

Specifying a sort order different from the field order in the datasheet

If your database has several customers with the same last name, you can include a secondary sort on the first name field to distinguish the customers. If you also want to display the fields in a first name, last name order, you can use the solution shown in Figure F-5. You can add a field to the query design grid twice and use the Show check box to sort the fields in one order (LName, FName), yet display the fields in the resulting datasheet in another order (FName, LName).

FIGURE F-5: Sorting on a field that is not displayed

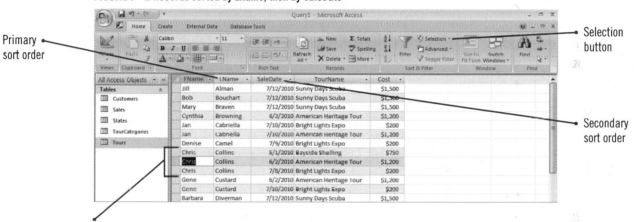

LName field is used twice in the query grid

Show check box is unchecked

Two sort fields

Creating Multiple Table Queries

Developing AND Criteria

You can limit the number of records that appear on the resulting datasheet by entering criteria in Query Design View. **Criteria** are tests, or limiting conditions, for which the record must be true to be selected for a datasheet. To create **AND criteria**, which means the query selects a record only if *all* criteria are true, enter two or more criteria on the same Criteria row of the query design grid. To create AND criteria for the *same field*, enter the two criteria in the same Criteria cell separated by the AND operator. ▰▰▰▰ Mark Rock predicts strong sales for adventure tours during the month of July. He asks you to create a list of the existing tour sales that meet those criteria.

STEPS

1. **Double-click CustomerSales in the Navigation Pane to open it in Datasheet View, click the View button arrow on the Home tab, click Design View, then maximize Query Design View**

   To query for adventure tours, you need to add the Category field and "Adventure" criterion for this field in the query grid.

2. **Double-click the Category field in the Tours field list to add it to the query grid, click the first Criteria cell for the Category field, then type adventure**

   To find all tours in the month of July for the year 2010, use the asterisk (*) **wildcard character** in the day portion of the SaleDate criterion.

QUICK TIP

Criteria are not case sensitive, so adventure, Adventure, and ADVENTURE are equivalent criteria entries.

3. **Click the first Criteria cell for the SaleDate field, type 7/*/2010, then press [↓]**

   As shown in Figure F-6, Access assists you with **criteria syntax**, rules by which criteria need to be entered. Access automatically adds quotation marks around text criteria in Text fields such as "adventure" in the Category field. The criteria in Number, Currency, and Yes/No fields are not surrounded by any characters. Access also adds the **Like operator** to the SaleDate field criterion because it includes the wildcard asterisk character. (Access uses the Like operator to find values in a field that match the pattern you specify.) See Table F-1 for more information on common Access comparison operators and criteria syntax.

4. **Click the Office button 🏢, click Save As, type JulyAdventure, then click OK**

   The query is saved with the new name, JulyAdventure, as a new object in the Quest-F.accdb database.

5. **Click the View button on the Design tab to view the query results**

   The query results are shown in Figure F-7.

6. **Close the JulyAdventure datasheet**

FIGURE F-6: Entering AND criteria on the same row

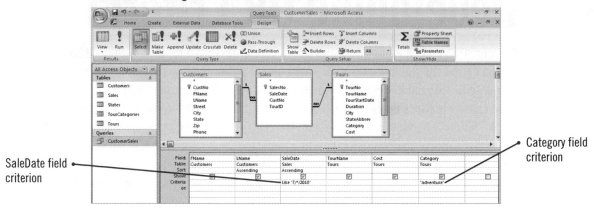

SaleDate field criterion

Category field criterion

FIGURE F-7: Datasheet for July Adventure records

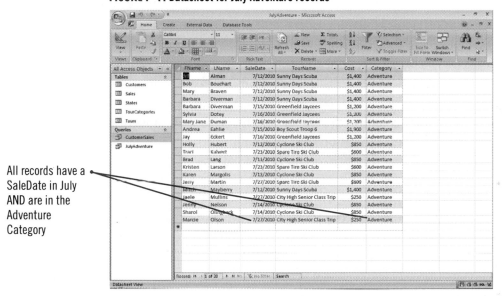

All records have a SaleDate in July AND are in the Adventure Category

TABLE F-1: Common comparison operators

operator	description	example	result
>	Greater than	>50	Value exceeds 50
>=	Greater than or equal to	>=50	Value is 50 or greater
<	Less than	<50	Value is less than 50
<=	Less than or equal to	<=50	Value is 50 or less
<>	Not equal to	<>50	Value is any number other than 50
Between...And	Finds values between two numbers or dates	Between #2/2/2006# And #2/2/2010#	Dates between 2/2/2006 and 2/2/2010, inclusive
In	Finds a value that is one of a list	In ("IA","KS","NE")	Value equals IA or KS or NE
Null	Finds records that have no entry in a particular field	Null	No value has been entered in a field
Is Not Null	Finds records that have any entry in a particular field	Is Not Null	Any value has been entered in a field
Like	Finds records that match the criterion	Like "A*"	Value starts with A
Not	Finds records that do not match the criterion	Not 2	Numbers other than 2

Developing OR Criteria

In a query, all criteria entries define which records are selected for the resulting datasheet. Whereas AND criteria *narrow* the number of records in the resulting datasheet by requiring that a record be true for multiple criteria, OR criteria *expand* the number of records that appear in the datasheet because a record needs to be true *for only one* of the criteria rows selected. You enter **OR criteria**, which means the query selects records where *any one* criterion is true, in the query design grid on different lines (criteria rows). Because each criteria row of the query design grid is evaluated separately, more OR criteria entries in the query grid produce more records for the resulting datasheet. ▓▓▓▓▓ Based on excellent July sales of adventure tours, Mark Rock inquires about July sales for educational tours. He asks you to modify the JulyAdventure query to expand the number of records to include sales for educational tours, too.

STEPS

1. **Right-click the** JulyAdventure **query in the Navigation Pane, click** Design View **on the shortcut menu, then maximize Query Design View**

   To add OR criteria, you have to enter criteria in the next available "or" row of the query design grid. By default, the query grid displays eight rows for additional OR criteria, but you can add even more rows using the Insert Rows button on the Design tab.

2. **In the Category column, click the** or Criteria cell **below "adventure", type** educational, **then click the** View button **on the Design tab**

   The datasheet expands from 20 records to 25 to include five tours in the Educational category. Because no date criterion is used in the SaleDate field, you see all Educational tour records instead of only those with a SaleDate in July. To select only those tours in July, you need to add more criteria to Query Design View.

3. **Click the** View button **on the Home tab to return to Query Design View, click the** next SaleDate Criteria cell, **type** 7/*/2010, **then press** [↓] **as shown in Figure F-8**

   Each criteria row is evaluated separately, which is why you must put the same date criterion for the SaleDate field in *both* rows of the query design grid if you want to select July records for both tour categories.

4. **Click the** View button **on the Design tab to return to Datasheet View**

   The resulting datasheet selects 21 records, as shown in Figure F-9. All of the records have a Category entry of Adventure or Educational and a SaleDate in July.

5. **Click the** Office button ⊚, **click** Save As, **type** JulyAdventureOrEducational, **then click** OK

   The JulyAdventureOrEducational query is saved as a new query object.

QUICK TIP
To rename an object from the Navigation Pane, right-click it, then choose Rename on the shortcut menu.

6. **Close the** JulyAdventureOrEducational **query**

   The Quest-F.accdb Navigation Pane displays the three queries you created.

FIGURE F-8: Entering OR criteria on different rows

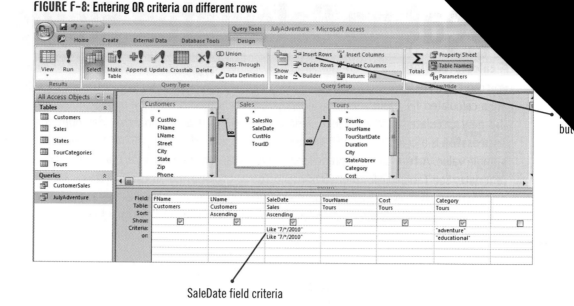

SaleDate field criteria

FIGURE F-9: OR criteria add more records to the datasheet

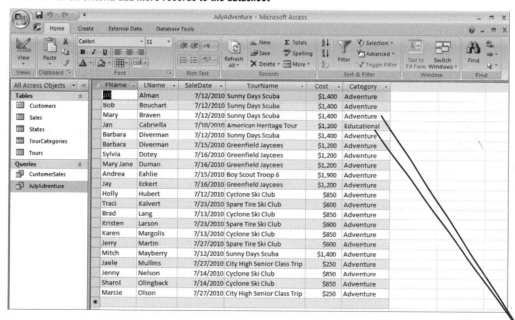

Adventure and Educational
tours with a SaleDate in July

Using wildcard characters in query criteria

To search for a pattern, use a wildcard character to represent any character in the criteria entry. Use a ? (question mark) to search for any single character and an * (asterisk) to search for any number of characters. Wildcard characters are often used with the Like operator.

For example, the criterion Like "10/*/2010" finds all dates in October of 2010, and the criterion Like "F*" finds all entries that start with the letter F.

ting Calculated Fields

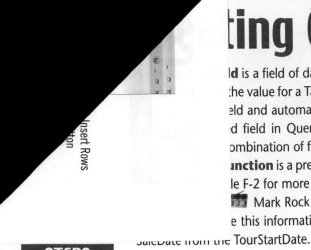

ld is a field of data that can be created based on the values of other fields. For example,
the value for a Tax field by multiplying the value of the Sales field by a percentage. To cre-
eld and automatically populate every record with the correct value for that field, define
d field in Query Design View using an expression that describes the calculation. An
mbination of field names, operators (such as +, −, /, and *), and functions that result in
nction is a predefined formula that returns a value such as a subtotal, count, or the cur-
le F-2 for more information on arithmetic operators and Table F-3 for more information
Mark Rock asks you to find the number of days between a sale and the tour's start
e this information, you can create a calculated field called LeadTime that subtracts the
SaleDate from the TourStartDate.

1. **Click the Create tab on the Ribbon, click the Query Design button, double-click Tours, double-click Sales, click Close in the Show Table dialog box, then maximize Query Design View**

   First you add the fields to the grid that you want to display in the query.

2. **Double-click the TourName field, double-click the TourStartDate field, double-click the Cost field, then double-click the SaleDate field**

   You create a calculated field in the Field cell of the design grid by entering a new descriptive field name followed by a colon, then an expression. Field names you use in an expression must be surrounded by square
   brackets.

   QUICK TIP
   To display a long entry in a field cell, you can also right-click the cell, then click Zoom.

3. **Click the blank Field cell in the fifth column, type LeadTime:[TourStartDate]-[SaleDate], then drag the ✛ pointer on the right edge of the fifth column selector to the right to display the entire entry as shown in Figure F-10**

4. **Click the View button on the Design tab to observe the calculated LeadTime field in the datasheet**

   The LeadTime field calculates correctly, showing the number of days between the TourStartDate and the
   SaleDate. You can create another calculated field to determine the commission paid on each sale, which is
   calculated as 10% of the Cost field.

   QUICK TIP
   You do not need to show the fields used in the expression (in this case, TourStartDate and Cost) in the query, but displaying them helps you determine if the expression is calculating correctly.

5. **Click the View button on the Home tab to return to Query Design View, click the blank Field cell in the sixth column, type Commission:[Cost]*0.1, then click the View button on the Design tab**

   The resulting datasheet, with two calculated fields, is shown in Figure F-11. Any change to a field value that
   is used in an expression for a calculated field automatically updates the calculation as well.

6. **Press [Tab], type 7/26/2010 in the TourStartDate field for the first record, press [Tab], type 800 in the Cost field for the first record, then press [↓]**

   The LeadTime and Commission calculated fields for the first three records of this query datasheet update
   automatically because the TourStartDate and Cost fields for the first three records are all based on the same
   tour, Bayside Shelling, which is physically entered in the database once in the Tours table.

7. **Click the Save button 🖫 on the Quick Access toolbar, type LeadTimesAndCommissions in the Save As dialog box, click OK, then close the datasheet**

   The query is saved as an object in the database.

Creating Multiple Table Queries

FIGURE F-10: Creating a calculated field

A colon (:) separates the field name from the expression

Lead time is the new calculated field name

Drag the column separator to widen the column

[TourStartDate]-[SaleDate] is the expression

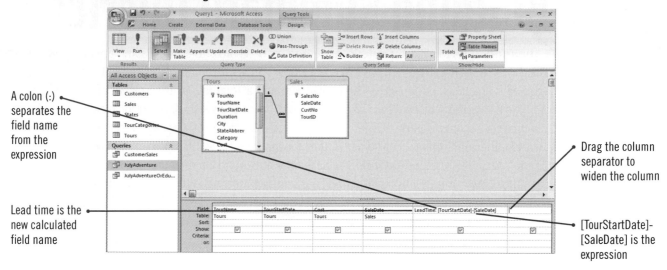

FIGURE F-11: Viewing and testing the calculated fields

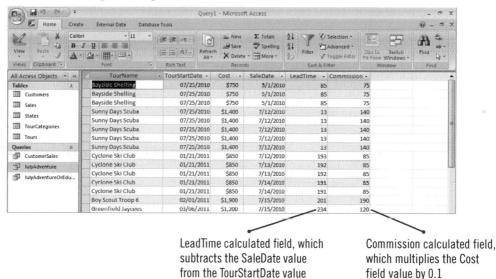

LeadTime calculated field, which subtracts the SaleDate value from the TourStartDate value

Commission calculated field, which multiplies the Cost field value by 0.1

TABLE F-2: Arithmetic operators

operator	description
+	Addition
–	Subtraction
*	Multiplication
/	Division
^	Exponentiation

TABLE F-3: Common functions

function	sample expression and description
DATE	DATE()-[BirthDate] Calculates the number of days between today and the date in the BirthDate field
PMT	PMT([Rate],[Term],[Loan]) Calculates the monthly payment on a loan where the Rate field contains the monthly interest rate, the Term field contains the number of monthly payments, and the Loan field contains the total amount financed
LEFT	LEFT([LastName],2) Returns the first two characters of the entry in the LastName field
RIGHT	RIGHT([Partno],3) Returns the last three characters of the entry in the Partno field
LEN	LEN([Description]) Returns the number of characters in the Description field

Access expressions are not case sensitive, so DATE()-[BirthDate] is equivalent to date()-[birthdate] and DATE()-[BIRTHDATE]. Therefore, use capitalization in expressions in any way that makes the expression easier to read.

Building Summary Queries

A **summary query** calculates statistics about groups of records. To create a summary query, you add the **Total row** to the query design grid to specify how you want to group and calculate the statistics using aggregate functions. In Access 2007, you can also add a Total row to the bottom of any table or query datasheet. **Aggregate functions** calculate a statistic such as a subtotal, count, or average on a given field in a group of records. Some aggregate functions, such as Sum or Avg (Average), can be used only on fields with Number or Currency data types. Other functions, such as Min (Minimum), Max (Maximum), or Count, can also be used on Text fields. Table F-4 provides more information on aggregate functions. A key difference between the statistics displayed by a summary query and those displayed by calculated fields is that summary queries provide calculations that describe a *group of records*, whereas calculated fields provide a new field of information for *each record*.  Mark Rock asks you to calculate total sales per tour category. You can use the Total row and build a summary query to provide these statistics.

STEPS

1. **Click the Create tab on the Ribbon, click the Query Design button, double-click Sales, double-click Tours, click Close in the Show Table dialog box, then maximize Query Design View**

   It doesn't matter in what order you add the field lists to Query Design View.

2. **Double-click the SalesNo field, double-click the Category field, double-click the Cost field, then click the View button on the Design tab to view the datasheet**

   Forty records are displayed, representing all 40 records in the Sales table. You can add a Total row to any datasheet.

   > **TROUBLE**
   > If the sum total is not completely displayed in the Cost field, widen the column to show the entire value.

3. **Click the Totals button on the Home tab, click the Total cell below the Cost field, click the Total list arrow, then click Sum**

   The Total row is added to the bottom of the datasheet and displays the sum total of the Cost field, $34,350. Other Total row statistics you can select include Average, Count, Maximum, Minimum, Standard Deviation, and Variance. To create subtotals per Category, you need to modify the query in Query Design View.

4. **Click the View button on the Home tab to return to Query Design View, click the Totals button on the Design tab, click Group By in the SalesNo column, click the list arrow, click Count, click Group By in the Cost column, click the list arrow, then click Sum**

   The Total row is added to the query grid below the Table row. To calculate summary statistics for each category, the Category field is the Group By field, as shown in Figure F-12.

5. **Click the View button on the Design tab to display the datasheet, widen each column as necessary to view all field names, click in the Total row for the SumOfCost field, click the list arrow, then click Sum**

   The Adventure category leads all others with a count of 23 sales totaling $22,650. The total revenue for all sales is $34,350, as shown in Figure F-13.

   > **QUICK TIP**
   > Because Access inserts the name of the query in the header of the datasheet printout, you can include your name or initials in the query name to uniquely identify a printout.

6. **Click the Save button 🖫 on the Quick Access toolbar, type CategorySummary, click OK, then close the datasheet**

Creating Multiple Table Queries

FIGURE F-12: Summary Query Design View

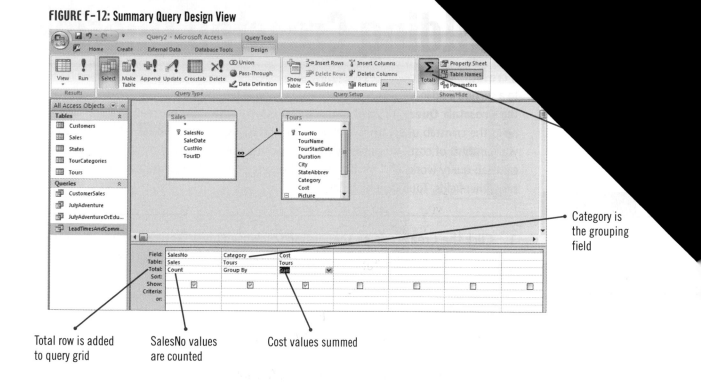

Category is the grouping field

Total row is added to query grid

SalesNo values are counted

Cost values summed

FIGURE F-13: Summarized and totaled records

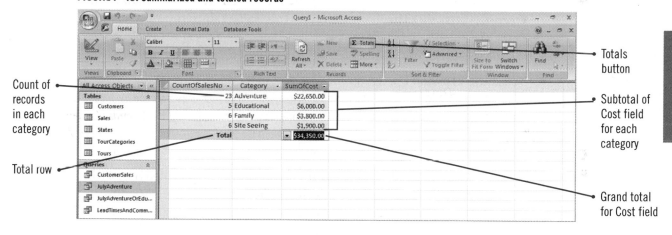

Count of records in each category

Total row

Totals button

Subtotal of Cost field for each category

Grand total for Cost field

TABLE F-4: Aggregate functions

aggregate function	used to find the
Sum	Total of values in a field
Avg	Average of values in a field
Min	Minimum value in a field
Max	Maximum value in a field
Count	Number of values in a field (not counting null values)
StDev	Standard deviation of values in a field
Var	Variance of values in a field
First	Field value from the first record in a table or query
Last	Field value from the last record in a table or query

ing Crosstab Queries

:alculates a statistic, such as a sum or average of a field, by grouping records according
column heading position and a third field used in a row heading position. You can use
y Wizard to guide you through the steps of creating a crosstab query, or you can
uery from scratch using Query Design View. Mark Rock asks you to continue
s per category by summarizing the cost values for each tour within each category. A
s well for this request because you want to subtotal the Cost field as summarized by
rName and Category.

---

te tab on the Ribbon, click the Query Design button, double-click Tours,
click Sales, click Close in the Show Table dialog box, then maximize Query
Design View

The fields you need for your crosstab query come from the Tours table, but you also need to include the Sales
table in this query to display the tour information for all 40 records in the Sales table.

2. **Double-click the TourName field, double-click the Category field, then double-click the Cost field**

The first step in creating a crosstab query is to create a select query with the three fields you want to use in
the crosstabular report.

3. **Click the View button on the Design tab to review the unsummarized datasheet of 40 records, then click the View button on the Home tab to return to Query Design View**

To summarize these 40 records in a crosstabular report, you need to change the current select query into a
crosstab query.

4. **Click the Crosstab button on the Design tab**

Note that two new rows are added to the query grid—the Total row and the Crosstab row. The Total row
helps you determine which fields group or summarize the records, and the **Crosstab row** identifies which
of the three positions each field takes in the crosstab report: Row Heading, Column Heading, or Value. The
Value field is typically a numeric field, such as Cost, that can be summed or averaged.

5. **Click Group By in the Total cell of the Cost field, click the list arrow, click Sum, click
the Crosstab cell for the TourName field, click the list arrow, click Row Heading, click the
Crosstab cell for the Category field, click the list arrow, click Column Heading, click
the Crosstab cell for the Cost field, click the list arrow, then click Value**

The completed Query Design View should look like Figure F-14. Note the choices made in the Total and
Crosstab rows of the query grid.

6. **Click the View button on the Design tab to review the crosstab datasheet**

The final crosstab datasheet is shown in Figure F-15. The datasheet summarizes all 40 sales records by the
Category field used as the column headings and by the TourName field used in the row heading position.
Although you can switch the row and column heading fields without changing the numeric information on
the crosstab datasheet, you should generally place the field with the most entries (in this case TourName) in
the row heading position so that the printout is taller (versus wider).

7. **Click the Save button on the Quick Access toolbar, type TourCrosstab as the query
name, click OK, then close the datasheet**

Crosstab queries appear with a crosstab icon to the left of the query name in the Navigation Pane.

FIGURE F-14: Query Design View of a crosstab query

Crosstab button

Total row

Crosstab row

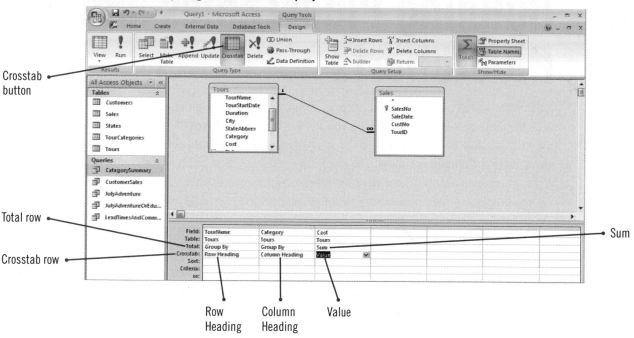

Sum

Row Heading

Column Heading

Value

FIGURE F-15: Crosstab query datasheet

Row Headings (values from the Category field)

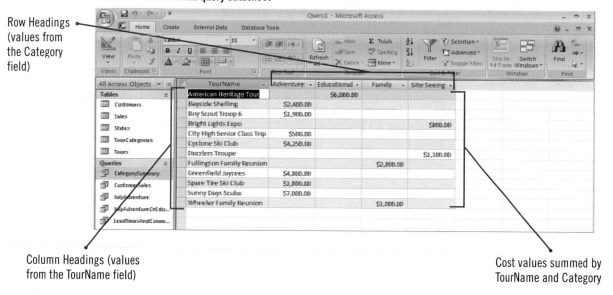

Column Headings (values from the TourName field)

Cost values summed by TourName and Category

Using Query Wizards

Four query wizards are available to help you build queries including the Simple (which creates a select query), Crosstab, Find Duplicates, and Find Unmatched Query Wizards. The **Find Duplicates Query Wizard** is used to determine whether a table contains duplicate values in one or more fields. The **Find Unmatched Query Wizard** is used to find records in one table that do not have related records in another table. To use the query wizards, click the Query Wizard button on the Create tab.

Access 2007

Building PivotTables and PivotCharts

A **PivotTable** calculates a statistic, such as a sum or average, by grouping records like a crosstab query with the additional benefit of allowing you to filter the data. A **PivotChart** is a graphical presentation of the data in the PivotTable. You build a PivotTable using **PivotTable View**. Similarly, you design PivotCharts in **PivotChart View**. The PivotChart and PivotTable Views are bound to one another so that when you make a change in one view, the other view is automatically updated. ▓▓▓▓ You use PivotChart View to graphically present summary information about the tours sold within each category.

TROUBLE
If this is the first time you are using PivotChart View, a dialog box might open indicating that Access is setting up a new feature.

1. **Double-click the Customers table to open its datasheet, then maximize the datasheet**
   You can view data of any existing table, query, or form in PivotTable and PivotChart views.

2. **Click the View button arrow on the Home tab, then click PivotChart View**
   In PivotChart View, you drag a field from the Chart Field List to a **drop area**, a position on the chart where you want the field to appear. The fields in the **Chart Field List** are the fields in the underlying object, in this case, the Customers table. The relationship between drop areas on a PivotChart, PivotTable, and crosstab query are summarized in Table F-5.

TROUBLE
To remove a field, drag it out of the PivotChart window.

3. **Drag FirstContact from the Chart Field List to the Drop Category Fields Here drop area**
   When you successfully drag a field to a drop area, the drop area displays a blue border. FirstContact field values now appear on the x-axis, also called the **category axis**.

TROUBLE
You might need to move or resize the Chart Field List title to see the Drop Series Fields Here drop area.

4. **Drag State from the Chart Field List to the Drop Series Fields Here drop area, then drag LName to the Drop Data Fields Here drop area as shown in Figure F-16**
   Because the LName field has a Text data type, when added to the Data Fields drop area, the field values are counted (rather than summed). Therefore, on this chart, the y-axis, also called the **value axis**, counts how many people from each state are added to the database for each FirstContact group displayed on the category axis. The colors of the bars represent state values, but are not identified until you add a legend.

5. **Click the Field List button to toggle it off, then click the Legend button on the Design tab to toggle it on**
   The legend now shows that the blue bars represent the state of Iowa (IA), the dark red bars represent Kansas (KS), and the green bars represent Missouri (MO). To view the information as a PivotTable, you change the view.

6. **Click the View button arrow on the Design tab, then click PivotTable View**
   The PivotTable appears showing the actual values for the data graphed in the PivotChart. PivotTables are very similar in structure to crosstab queries, but also allow you to move and filter the data. For example, if you want to analyze one state at a time, you might move the State field to the Filter Fields position and the City field to the Column Fields position.

QUICK TIP
The field's list arrow changes from black to blue if you use the field to filter the data.

7. **Drag the State field from the PivotTable to the Drop the Filter Fields Here position, drag the City field from the PivotTable Field List to the Drop Column Fields Here position, click the State list arrow, click the (All) check box to clear all check marks, click KS, then click OK**
   The filtered PivotTable should look like Figure F-17.

8. **Save and close the Customers table, close the Quest-F.accdb database, and exit Access**

FIGURE F-16: PivotChart View

Field List button

Legend button

Chart Field List

LName in Data area

State in Series area

Value axis

FirstContact in Category area

Category axis

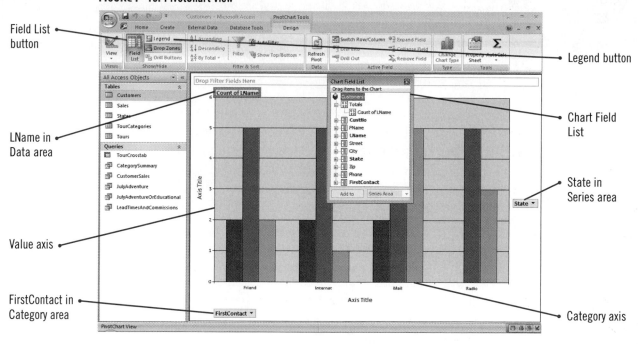

FIGURE F-17: Filtered PivotTable View

State field moved from PivotTable and filtered to display only Kansas records

City field provides column values

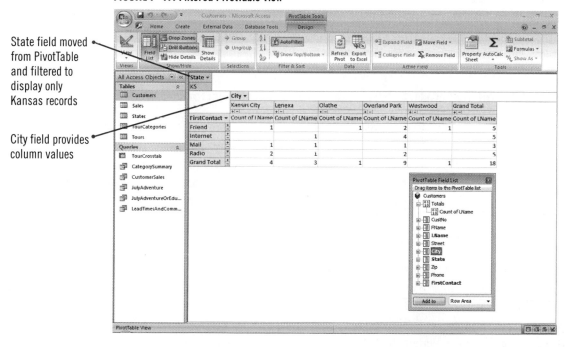

TABLE F-5: PivotTable and PivotChart drop areas

drop area on PivotTable	drop area on PivotChart	crosstab query field position
Filter Field	Filter Field	(NA)
Row Field	Category Field	Row Heading
Column Field	Series Field	Column Heading
Totals or Detail Field	Data Field	Value

Practice

▼ CONCEPTS REVIEW

Identify each element of the Query Design View shown in Figure F-18.

FIGURE F-18

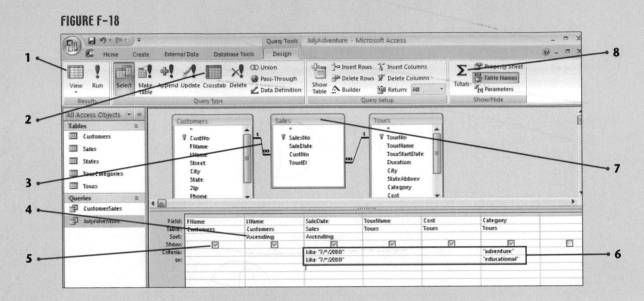

Match each term with the statement that best describes its function.

9. Select query

10. Wildcard character

11. AND criteria

12. Sorting

13. OR criteria

a. Entered on one row of the query design grid

b. Entered on more than one row of the query design grid

c. Asterisk (*) or question mark (?) used in query criteria

d. Retrieves fields from related tables and displays records in a datasheet

e. Placing the records of a datasheet in a certain order

Select the best answer from the list of choices.

14. The query datasheet can best be described as a:

   a. Duplication of the data in the underlying table's datasheet.

   b. Separate file of data.

   c. Logical view of the selected data from an underlying table's datasheet.

   d. Second copy of the data in the underlying tables.

15. Queries may *not* be used to:

   a. Calculate new fields of data.

   b. Set the primary key field for a table.

   c. Enter or update data.

   d. Sort records.

16. When you update data in a table that is also displayed in a query datasheet:

   a. The data is automatically updated in the query.

   b. You must relink the query to the table to refresh the data.

   c. You must also update the data in the query datasheet.

   d. You can choose whether to update the data in the query.

17. Which of the following is *not* an aggregate function available to a summary query?

a. Avg

b. Subtotal

c. Count

d. Max

18. The order in which records in a query are sorted is determined by:

a. The order in which the fields are defined in the underlying table.

b. The left-to-right position of the fields in the query design grid that contain a sort order choice.

c. The importance of the information in the field.

d. The alphabetic order of the field names.

19. The presentation of data in a crosstab query is most similar to:

a. Report Print Preview.

b. PivotChart View.

c. Table Datasheet View.

d. PivotTable View.

20. A crosstab query is generally constructed with how many fields?

a. 1

b. 3

c. Between 5 and 10

d. More than 10

21. In a crosstab query, which field is the most likely candidate for the Value position?

a. FName

b. Department

c. Cost

d. Country

▼ SKILLS REVIEW

1. Build select queries.

a. Start Access and open the **Membership-F.accdb** database from the drive and folder where you store your Data Files, and enable content if prompted.

b. Create a new select query in Query Design View using the Names and Zips tables.

c. Add the following fields to the query design grid in this order:

- First, Last, and Street from the Names table
- City, State, and Zip from the Zips table

d. In Datasheet View, replace the Last value in the Quentin Garden record with your last name.

e. Save the query as **AddressList**, print the datasheet, then close the query.

2. Use multiple sort orders.

a. Open the AddressList query in Query Design View.

b. Drag the First field from the Names field list to the third column in the query design grid to make the first three fields in the query design grid First, Last, and First.

c. Add the ascending sort criterion to the second and third fields in the query design grid, and uncheck the Show check box in the third column. The query is now sorted in ascending order by Last, then by First, though the order of the fields in the resulting datasheet still appears as First, Last.

d. Use Save As to save the query as **SortedAddressList**, view the datasheet, print the datasheet, then close the query.

3. Develop AND criteria.

a. Open the AddressList query in Design View.

b. Type **M*** (the asterisk is a wildcard) in the Last field Criteria cell to choose all people whose last name starts with M. Access assists you with the syntax for this type of criterion and enters Like "M*" in the cell when you click elsewhere in the query design grid.

c. Enter **KS** as the AND criterion for the State field. Be sure to enter the criterion on the same line in the query design grid as the Like "M*" criterion.

d. View the datasheet. It should select only those people from Kansas with a last name that starts with the letter M.

e. Enter a new value in the City field of the first record to uniquely identify the printout.

f. Use Save As to save the query as **KansasM**, then print and close the datasheet.

4. Develop OR criteria.

a. Open the KansasM query in Query Design View.

b. Enter **M*** in the second Criteria row (the or row) of the Last field.

c. Enter **IA** as the criterion in the second Criteria row (the or row) of the State field so that those people from IA with a last name that starts with the letter M are added to this query.

d. Use Save As to save the query as **KansasIowaM**, view and print the datasheet, then close the query.

5. Build calculated fields.

a. Create a new select query in Query Design View using only the Names table.

b. Add the following fields to the query design grid in this order: First, Last, Birthday.

c. Create a calculated field called Age in the fourth column of the query design grid by entering the expression: **Age: (Now()-[Birthday])/365** to determine the age of each person in years based on the information in the Birthday field.

d. Sort the query in descending order on the calculated Age field, then view the datasheet.

e. Return to Query Design View, right-click the calculated Age field, click Properties, then change the Format property to Standard and the Decimal Places property to 0. Close the Property Sheet.

f. Save the query with the name **AgeCalculation**, view the datasheet, print the datasheet, then close the query.

6. Build summary queries.

a. Create a new select query in Query Design View using the Names and Activities tables.

b. Add the following fields: First and Last from the Names table, Hours from the Activities table.

c. Add the Total row to the query design grid, then change the aggregate function for the Hours field from Group By to Sum.

d. Sort in descending order by Hours.

e. Save the query as **HoursSummary**, view the datasheet, print the datasheet, then close the query.

7. Build crosstab queries.

a. Create a select query with the City and State fields from the Zips table and the Dues field from the Names table. Save the query as **DuesCrosstab**, then view the datasheet.

b. Return to Query Design View, then click the Crosstab button to add the Total and Crosstab rows to the query design grid.

c. Specify City as the crosstab row heading, State as the crosstab column heading, and Dues as the summed value field within the crosstab datasheet.

d. View, print, then save and close the datasheet.

8. Build PivotTables and PivotCharts.

a. Create a select query with the State field from the Zips table and the CharterMember and Dues fields from the Names table. Save it as **DuesPivot**, then run the query.

b. Switch to PivotChart View, open the Chart Field List if it is not already visible, then drag the State field to the Drop Category Fields Here drop area, the CharterMember field to the Drop Series Fields Here drop area, and the Dues field to the Drop Data Fields Here drop area.

c. Close the field list, display the legend, then print the PivotChart, which should look similar to the one as shown in Figure F-19.

d. Switch to PivotTable View, close the field list, filter for only the states of Kansas (KS) and Missouri (MO), then print the PivotTable.

e. Save and close the DuesPivot query, close the Membership-F.accdb database, then exit Access.

FIGURE F-19

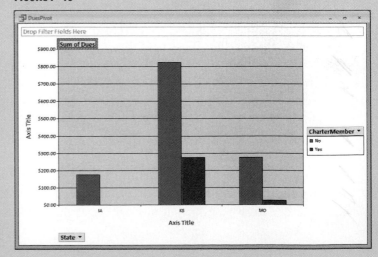

▼ INDEPENDENT CHALLENGE 1

As the manager of a music store's instrument rental program, you have created a database to track rentals to schoolchildren. Now that several rentals have been made, you want to query the database for several different datasheet printouts to analyze school information.

a. Start Access and open the **MusicStore-F.accdb** database from the drive and folder where you store your Data Files, and enable content if prompted.

b. In Query Design View, create a query with the following fields in the following order:
   - SchoolName field from the Schools table
   - Date field from the Rentals table
   - Description field from the Instruments table

(*Hint*: Although you don't use any fields from the Customers table, you need to add the Customers table to this query to make the connection between the Schools table and the Rentals table.)

c. Sort in ascending order by SchoolName, then in ascending order by Date.

d. Save the query as **SchoolRentals**, view the datasheet, replace Lincoln Elementary with your elementary school name, then print the datasheet.

e. Modify the SchoolRentals query by deleting the Description field. Use the Totals button to group the records by SchoolName and to count the Date field. Print the datasheet and use Save As to save the query as **SchoolCount**. Close the datasheet.

f. Create a crosstab query named **SchoolCrosstab** based on the SchoolRentals query. Remove the sort orders. Use Description as the row heading position and SchoolName in the column heading position. Count the Date field.

g. Save, view, print, and close the SchoolCrosstab query.

h. Modify the SchoolRentals query so that only those schools with the word Elementary in the SchoolName field are displayed. (*Hint*: You have to use wildcard characters in the criteria.)

i. Use Save As to save the query as **ElementaryRentals**, then view, print, and close the datasheet.

j. Close the MusicStore-F.accdb database, then exit Access.

▼ INDEPENDENT CHALLENGE 2

As the manager of a music store's instrument rental program, you have created a database to track rentals to schoolchildren. The database has already been used to answer several basic questions, and now that you've shown how easy it is to get the answers using queries, more questions are being asked. You can use queries to analyze customer and rental information.

a. Start Access and open the **MusicStore-F.accdb** database from the drive and folder where you store your Data Files, and enable content if prompted.

b. In Query Design View, create a query with the following fields in the following order:
   - Description and MonthlyFee fields from the Instruments table
   - LastName, Zip, and City fields from the Customers table

(*Hint*: Although you don't need any fields from the Rentals table in this query's datasheet, you need to add the Rentals table to this query to make the connection between the Customers table and the Instruments table.)

c. Add the Zip field to the first column of the query grid, and specify an ascending sort order for this field. Uncheck the Show check box for the first Zip field so that it does not appear in the datasheet.

d. Specify an ascending sort order for the Description field.

e. Save the query as **ZipAnalysis**.

f. View the datasheet, replace Johnson with your last name in the LastName field, then print and close the datasheet.

g. Modify the ZipAnalysis query by adding criteria to find the records where the Description is equal to **viola**.

h. Use Save As to save this query as **Violas**.

▼ INDEPENDENT CHALLENGE 2 (CONTINUED)

Advanced Challenge Exercise

- On a piece of paper, write how many records the Violas query contains.
- Modify the Violas query with AND criteria to further specify that the City must be **Ankeny**.
- Save this query as **AnkenyViolas**. On your paper, note how many records the AnkenyViolas query contains. Briefly explain how AND criteria affect this number.
- Modify the AnkenyViolas query with OR criteria that find all violas or violins, regardless of where they are located.
- Use Save As to save this query as **ViolasViolins**. On your paper, note how many records the Violas and Violins query contains. Briefly explain how OR criteria affect this number.
- In Query Design View, create a crosstab query that uses the Description field from the Instruments table for the column headings, the SchoolName field from the Schools table for the row headings, and that Sums the MonthlyFee field.
- Save the crosstab query as **RentalCrosstab**, preview the datasheet, then print the datasheet in landscape orientation so that it fits on one page.

i. Close the MusicStore-F.accdb database, then exit Access.

▼ INDEPENDENT CHALLENGE 3

As a real estate agent, you use an Access database to track residential real estate listings in your area. You can use queries to answer questions about the real estate and to analyze home values.

a. Start Access and open the **RealEstate-F.accdb** database from the drive and folder where you store your Data Files, and enable content if prompted.

b. In Query Design View, create a query with the following fields in the following order:
- AgencyName from the Agencies table
- AgentFirst and AgentLast from the Agents table
- SqFt and Asking from the Listings table

c. Sort the records in descending order by the Asking field.

d. Save the query as **AskingPrices**, view the datasheet, enter your own last name instead of Zacharias for the most expensive listing, then print the datasheet.

e. In Query Design View, modify the AskingPrices query by creating a calculated field that determines price per square foot. The new calculated field's name should be **SquareFootCost** and the expression should be the asking price divided by the square foot field, or **[Asking]/[SqFt]**.

f. Remove any former sort orders, sort the records in descending order based on the SquareFootCost calculated field, and view the datasheet.

g. Return to Query Design View, right-click the SquareFootCost field, click Properties, then change the Format property to **Currency** and the Decimal Places property to **2**.

h. Use Save As to save the query as **SquareFootCostAnalysis**, then view, print, and close the datasheet.

Advanced Challenge Exercise

- Open the SquareFootCostAnalysis query in Design View, then delete the AgentFirst, AgentLast, and SqFt fields.
- View the datasheet, then change the Sun and Ski Realtors agency name to your last name's Agency.
- In Design View, add the Total row, then Sum the Asking field and use the Avg (Average) aggregate function for the SquareFootCost calculated field. In Datasheet View, add the Total row and display the sum of the Asking Field.
- Print the query, save the query as **SummarizedSquareFootCostAnalysis** as shown in Figure F-20, then close it.

FIGURE F-20

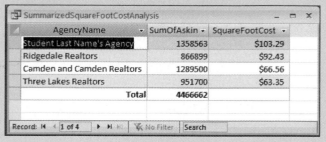

i. Close the RealEstate-F.accdb database, then exit Access.

▼ REAL LIFE INDEPENDENT CHALLENGE

One way to use Access in your real life is in a community service project. People in schools and nonprofit agencies often inherit databases created by others and need help extracting information from them. Suppose you're working with the local high school guidance counselor to help her with an Access database she inherited that is used to record college scholarship opportunities. You can help her keep the database updated and create several queries.

This Independent Challenge requires an Internet connection.

Access 2007

a. Start Access and open the **Scholarships-F.accdb** database from the drive and folder where you store your Data Files.

b. Conduct some research on the Internet to find at least five new scholarships. One of the five should be directed at business students; another should be directed at education majors. Add the five new records to the Scholarships table using the existing fields.

c. Create a query called **Business** that displays all the scholarship information except the ID for all scholarships with the word "business" anywhere in the Description field. (*Hint*: Use an appropriate wildcard character both before and after the word "business.")

d. Add OR criteria to the Business query to also select all scholarships that have the word "education" anywhere in the Description field. Save the query with the name **BusinessOrEducation**.

e. Create a query that selects the ScholarshipName, DueDate, and Amount from the Scholarships table, and sorts the records in ascending order by DueDate, then descending order by Amount. Name the query **ScholarshipMasterList**.

Advanced Challenge Exercise

- View the ScholarshipMasterList query in PivotTable view, then drag the Amount field to the Drop Totals or Detail Fields Here area, the ScholarshipName field to the Drop Row Fields Here area, and the DueDate By Month field to the Drop Filter Fields Here area.
- Filter the PivotTable for only those scholarships in the first quarter of the year 2010 as shown in Figure F-21.
- Save the query with the name **ScholarshipPivot**.

FIGURE F-21

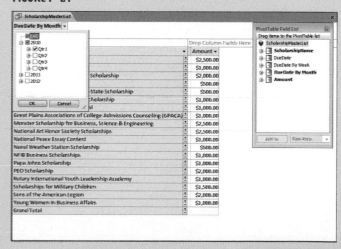

f. Save and close the ScholarshipPivot query, close the Scholarships-F.accdb database, then exit Access.

▼ VISUAL WORKSHOP

Open the Training-F.accdb database from the drive and folder where you store your Data Files, and enable content if prompted. In Query Design View, create a new select query with the Location field from the Employees table, the Cost and CourseID fields from the Courses table, and the Passed field from the Attendance table. Display the query in PivotChart View, then modify it as shown in Figure F-22. Note that the Passed field is in the Filter area. Filter the data for CourseIDs Access1 and Access2 and for the Passed value of Yes. Click the Show Legend button on the Design tab to display the legend below the Location field in the Series field area. Right-click the Axis Title for the x-axis, click Properties, click the Format tab, and add your name as the Caption. Save the query with the name **AccessGraduates**, then print it.

FIGURE F-22

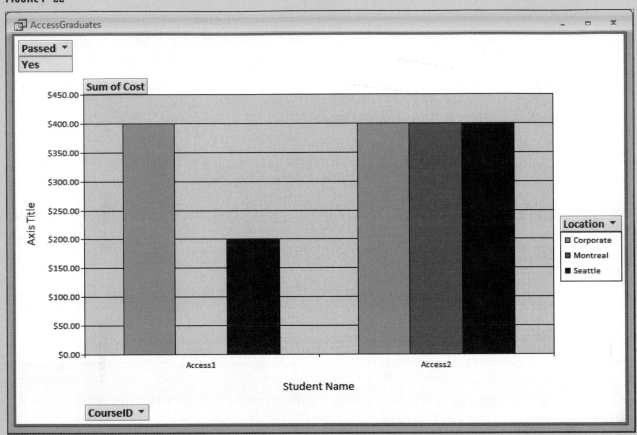

Enhancing Forms

A **form** is a database object designed to make data easy to find, enter, and edit. Forms are created by using **controls** such as labels, text boxes, combo boxes, and command buttons, which help you manipulate more quickly and reliably than working in a datasheet. A form that contains a **subform** allows you to work with related records in an easy-to-use screen arrangement. For example, a form/subform combination allows you to display customer data and all of the orders placed by that customer at the same time. Mark Rock wants to improve the usability of the forms in the Quest database. You will build and improve forms by working with subforms, split forms, combo boxes, option groups, and command buttons to enter, find, and filter data.

OBJECTIVES

Create subforms

Modify subforms

Create split forms

Add tab controls

Add a combo box for data entry

Add a combo box to find records

Add option groups

Add command buttons

Creating Subforms

A **subform** is a form within a form. The form that contains the subform is called the **main form**. A main form/subform combination displays the records of two tables that are related in a one-to-many relationship. The forms are linked by a common field, so only those records that are associated with the main form appear in the subform. For example, if a main form contains a customer record, the subform might contain all of the sales related to that customer. When you use the Form Wizard to create a form/subform combination, you create both the main form and the subform in one process. If the main form already exists, you can use the **Subform/Subreport control** 🔲 to start the Subform Wizard, which guides you through adding the subform to the main form in Form Design View. A form **layout** is the general way that the data and controls are arranged on the form. Columnar is the most popular layout for a main form, and datasheet is the most popular layout for a subform, but you can modify these choices by changing the form's **Default View property** in Form Design View. See Table G-1 for a description of form layouts. ▰▰▰▰ You decide to create a form/subform using the Form Wizard. The main form will display fields from the Tours table and the subform will display fields from the Sales and Customers tables to show the many sales for each tour.

STEPS

1. **Start Access, then open the** Quest-G.accdb **database from the drive and folder where you store your Data Files, then enable content if prompted**

2. **Click the** Create tab **on the Ribbon, click the** More Forms button, **then click** Form Wizard
   The Form Wizard starts and prompts you to select the fields of the main form/subform combination. You want the main form to display tour information, and the subform to display sales information including customer name. These fields come from three tables: Tours, Sales, and Customers.

3. **Click the** Tables/Queries list arrow, **click** Table: Tours, **click the** Select All Fields button [>>], **click the** Tables/Queries list arrow, **click** Table: Sales, **click** [>>], **click the** Tables/Queries list arrow, **click** Table: Customers, **double-click** FName, **double-click** LName, **then click** Next
   Because the Tours and Sales tables are linked in a one-to-many relationship in the Relationships window, the Form Wizard recognizes the opportunity to create a form/subform combination for the selected fields.

4. **Click by** Tours **as shown in Figure G-1 (if it is not already selected), then click** Next

5. **Click** Next **to accept the Datasheet layout, click** Aspect, **click** Next, **click** Finish **to accept the default names for the form and subform, then maximize the Tours form**
   By default, subforms are created with a Datasheet layout. The Tours form opens and includes the Sales subform in Datasheet layout, as shown in Figure G-2.

6. **Click the** Next record button ▶ **on the navigation bar for the main form several times to view the sales for each tour**
   The sales for each tour appear in the subform as you move through the records of the main form. Notice that the third tour, Cyclone Ski Club, has 10 sales because it has 10 sales in the subform. The fourth tour, Boy Scout Troop 6, has only two sales in the subform.

7. **Close the** Tours **form**
   When you close a main form, any subforms that it contains close as well.

FIGURE G-1: Form Wizard showing main form and subform

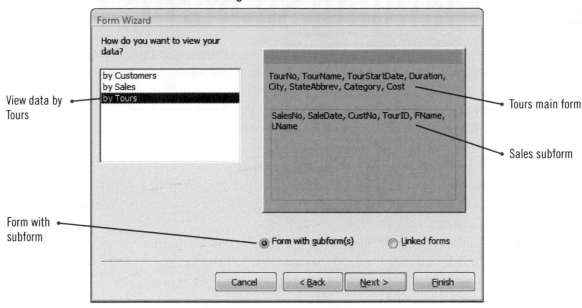

View data by Tours

Tours main form

Sales subform

Form with subform

FIGURE G-2: Tours main form with sales subform

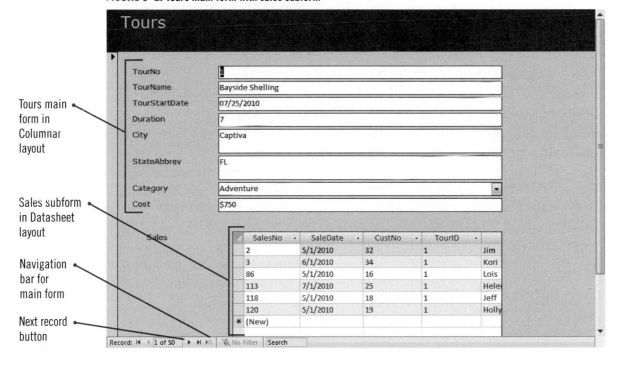

Tours main form in Columnar layout

Sales subform in Datasheet layout

Navigation bar for main form

Next record button

TABLE G-1: Form layouts

layout	description
Columnar	Each field appears on a separate row with a label to its left
Tabular	Each field appears as an individual column and each record is presented as a row
Datasheet	Fields and records are displayed as they appear in a table or query datasheet
PivotTable	Fields are organized in a PivotTable arrangement
PivotChart	Fields are organized in a PivotChart arrangement

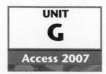

Modifying Subforms

You modify a subform, like any other form, in Form Design View. Often, however, it is easiest to work in Form Design View of the main form, as it allows you to modify both the main form and subform in the same view. To modify the fields that either the main form or subform contain, you work with the **Record Source** property of the forms. You want to change some of the fields in the subform and widen it to display all of the fields. Mark Rock also asks you to modify some of the labels in the main form.

STEPS

1. **Click the** Navigation list arrow ⊙ **in the Navigation Pane, click** Forms **(if not already selected), right-click** Tours, **click** Design View **on the shortcut menu, then maximize the Design View window**

   The Tours main form opens in Form Design View. First you'll modify the labels in the main form to display them more clearly.

2. **Click the** TourNo label **in the main form, edit it to read** Tour No, **then finish editing the labels in the main form as shown in Figure G-3**

   With the labels modified in the main form, you turn your attention to the subform. You decide that you don't really need the SalesNo field in the subform, but in addition to the name of the customer who purchased that tour, you want to see the customer's city in the City field. To modify the fields that a form displays, you work with the Record Source property of the form.

3. **Click the** edge of the subform **to select it, then double-click the** form selector button **to open the Property Sheet for the subform**

   The Property Sheet for the subform opens as shown in Figure G-4.

4. **Click the** Data tab **in the Property Sheet (if not already selected), click the** Record Source **property Build button** [...] **to open the Query Builder for the subform, delete the** SalesNo field **in the query grid, double-click the** City field **in the Customers field list, click the** Close button **on the Design tab, then click** Yes

   The Record Source property allows you to modify—add or delete—the fields that may be used on the form. Notice that the SalesNo field now displays an **error indicator**, a small green triangle in the upper-left corner of the SalesNo text box in the subform. You already know the reason for this error—the SalesNo field is no longer selected in the Record Source for this form. If you did not know the cause of the error, however, you could use the Error Checking Options button to get more information.

   TROUBLE
   You might have to scroll in the main form or subform to see all of the controls.

5. **Click the** Property Sheet button **on the Design tab to close it, click the** SalesNo text box, **press** [Delete], **click the** Add Existing Fields button, **then drag the** City field **from the Field List to just under the LName text box on the subform**

   The layout of the subform is datasheet, so the Cost field added to the bottom of the list of fields will appear as a new column on the right edge of the datasheet. You also need to widen the subform to display all of the fields it contains.

6. **Click the** edge of the subform **to select it, drag the** left edge of the subform **to the left to widen it, click the** Add Existing Fields button **to close the Field List, click the** Form View button 🖩 **on the Design tab, then resize the columns in the subform so that all of the fields are visible**

   The final form/subform should look like Figure G-5. Continue to make additional enchancements in Form Design View as desired.

7. **Save and close the** Tours **main form and** Sales **subform**

FIGURE G-3: Modifying the labels in the Tours main form

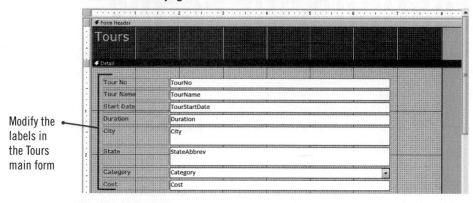

Modify the labels in the Tours main form

FIGURE G-4: Modifying the Record Source on the Sales subform

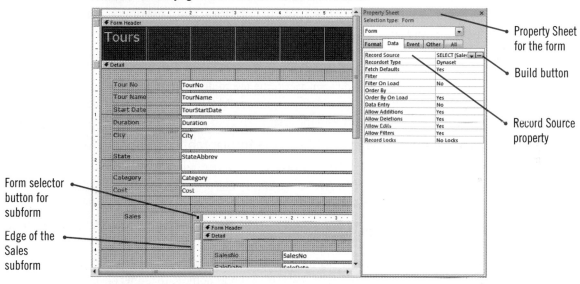

Property Sheet for the form

Build button

Record Source property

Form selector button for subform

Edge of the Sales subform

FIGURE G-5: Final form/subform

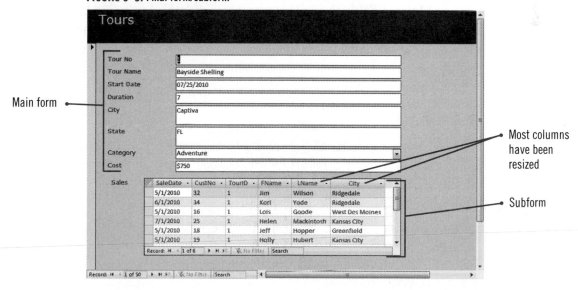

Main form

Most columns have been resized

Subform

Linking the form and subform

If the form and subform do not appear to be correctly linked, examine the subform's property sheet, paying special attention to the **Link Child Fields** and **Link Master Fields** properties on the Data tab. These properties tell you which field serves as the link between the main form and subform.

Creating Split Forms

A **split form** shows you two views of the same data at one time: a traditional form and a datasheet view. A split form is similar to a form/subform in that a split form contains a traditional form view on the top and a datasheet view of data on the bottom of the form. A split form is different, however, because it is only *one* form object instead of two used together as in a form/subform. A split form also shows two views of the *same* data at one time, whereas a form/subform shows two different (but related) sets of data in the main form and subform. You decide to create a split form to be able to productively find, view, and enter customer information.

1. **Click the Navigation list arrow ⊙ in the Navigation Pane, click Tables, click Customers, click the Create tab, click the Split Form button, then maximize the new form**

    The new Customers form appears in Layout View as shown in Figure G-6. Note that the same fields are used in the upper and lower portions of the window, but the layout shows only one record in the top portion, and organizes multiple records as a datasheet in the lower portion. Because the two views of a split form display the *same* data in two different views, the record displayed in the upper portion is also shown in the lower portion of the window. In this case, the record for Mitch Mayberry is displayed both ways. You can switch to Form View to work with the data.

2. **Click the Form View button 🖽 on the Format tab, then click the Next record button ▶ on the navigation bar several times**

    Observe that the record displayed in the upper portion of the split form matches the selected record in the lower datasheet view. You can use a split form, or any form, to sort and filter data.

3. **Click any occurrence of Kansas City in the datasheet portion of the form, click the Selection button on the Home tab, then click Equals "Kansas City"**

    The ten records with Kansas City in the City field of the datasheet are filtered in the lower portion of the split form, and the first record is displayed in the upper portion. To further organize the records, you can sort the filtered list in alphabetical order based on the LName field.

4. **Click any LName field value in the datasheet, click the Ascending button ↕↓ on the Home tab, then press [↓] to watch the record in the upper portion change based on the navigation of the datasheet**

    The Customers split form is both filtered and sorted as shown in Figure G-7. You can use the sort and filter buttons on a form just as you can in a datasheet. When sorting and filtering a split form, however, more than one record is visible in the datasheet portion of the form, which sometimes makes it easier to find the data you're looking for.

5. **Click the Save button 🖫 on the Quick Access toolbar, click OK, then close the Customers split form**

FIGURE G-6: Customers split form in Layout View

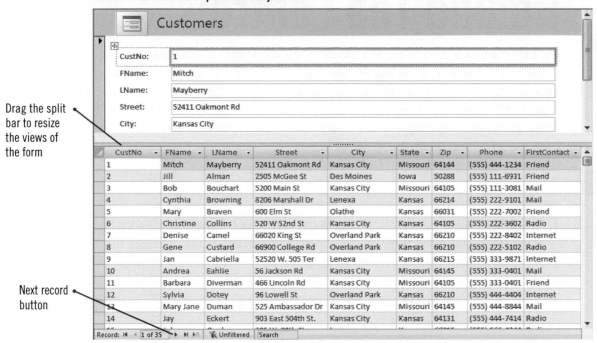

Drag the split bar to resize the views of the form

Next record button

FIGURE G-7: Filtering and sorting the Customers split form in Form View

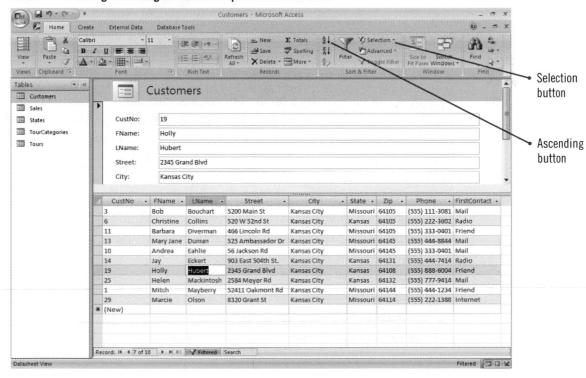

Selection button

Ascending button

Adding Tab Controls

The **tab control** is used to create a three-dimensional aspect to a form so that many controls can be organized and displayed by clicking the tabs. You have already used tab controls because many Access dialog boxes use tabs to organize information. For example, the Property Sheet uses tab controls to organize properties identified by categories: Format, Data, Event, Other, and All. ████████ You previously created a form used to update tour data called the Tour Update form. Mark Rock asks you to find a way to organize and present tour information based on three categories: General Info, Dates, and Costs. You decide to use tab controls.

1. **Click the** Navigation list arrow 🔽 **in the Navigation Pane, click** Forms, **right-click** Tour Update, **click** Design View **on the shortcut menu, then maximize the form**

   The Tour Update form appears in Design View. Currently, only two fields from the Tours table appear on the form, TourNo and TourName. You can add the tab control next.

2. **Click the** Tab Control button 🔲 **on the Design tab, then click** below the Tour No label **on the form**

   Your screen should look like Figure G-8. By default, the tab control you added has two pages with the default names of Page20 and Page21. You can change these to more descriptive names, but the default text refers to how many total controls have been added to the form over the life of the form.

   TROUBLE
   If the numbers of your pages are different, continue with the step as you revise these names anyway.

3. **Double-click** Page20 **to open its Property Sheet, click the** Other tab **(if it is not already selected), double-click** Page20 **in the Name property text box, type** General Info, **click the** Page21 tab **on the form, double-click** Page21 **in the Name text box of the property sheet, type** Dates, **then press** [Enter]

   The first two pages on the tab control now describe the information they will organize, but you need a third page named Costs before adding the appropriate controls to each page.

4. **Right-click the** Dates tab, **click** Insert Page, **double-click** Page22 **in the Name property text box, type** Costs, **then close the Property Sheet**

   With the pages in place on the tab control, you're ready to add controls to each page.

   TROUBLE
   In Form Design View you can undo many actions by clicking the Undo button 🔄 on the Quick Access toolbar.

5. **Click the** General Info page **on the tab control, click the** Add Existing Fields button **on the Design tab to display the Field List, click** City **in the Field List, press and hold** [Shift], **click** StateAbbrev **in the Field List, click** Category **in the Field List, release** [Shift], **then drag the** highlighted fields **to the top middle area of the General Info page**

   Your screen should look similar to Figure G-9. Three fields are added to the General Info page on the tab control.

   QUICK TIP
   A tab control becomes black when you are successfully adding controls to a page.

6. **Click the** Dates page **on the tab control, click** TourStartDate **in the Field List, press and hold** [Shift], **click** Duration **in the Field List, release** [Shift], **drag the** two highlighted fields **to the middle of the Dates page, click the** Costs page **on the tab control, then drag the** Cost field **to the middle of the Costs page**

   You can add any type of control, even a subform control, to a tab control page.

7. **Click the** Form View button 📄 **on the Design tab, click the** Dates tab, **click the** Costs tab, **click the** General Info tab, **then click the** Next record button ▶ **on the navigation bar to observe the tab control in Form View as shown in Figure G-10**

8. **Save and close the** Tour Update **form**

FIGURE G-8: Adding a tab control

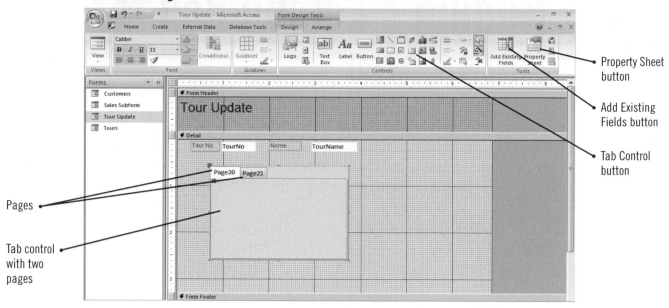

FIGURE G-9: Adding fields to a tab control in Form Design View

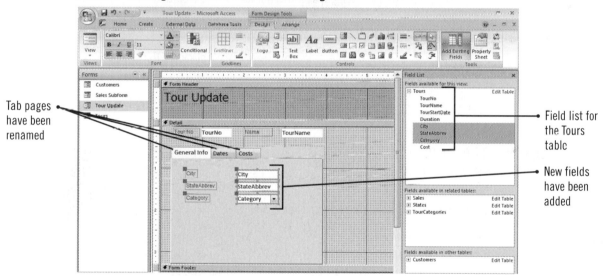

FIGURE G-10: Working with a tab control in Form View

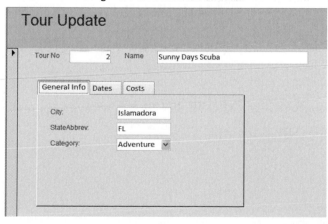

Adding a Combo Box for Data Entry

If a finite set of values can be identified for a field, using a combo box instead of a text box control on a form allows the user to select and enter data faster and more accurately. Both the **list box** and **combo box** controls provide a list of values from which the user can choose an entry. A combo box also allows the user to type an entry from the keyboard; therefore, it is a "combination" of the list box and text box controls. You can create a combo box by using the **Combo Box Wizard**, or you can change an existing text box or list box into a combo box. Fields with Lookup properties are automatically created as combo boxes on new forms. ▰▰▰ All Quest tours last 3, 4, 5, 7, 10, or 14 days. Because the Duration field contains a limited number of values, you decide to convert the existing Duration text box on the Tour Info form into a combo box.

1. **Right-click** Tour Update **in the Navigation Pane, click** Design View, **click the** Dates tab, **click the** Duration text box **to select it, right-click the** Duration text box, **point to** Change To, **then click** Combo Box

   Now that the control has been changed from a text box to a combo box, you are ready to populate the list with the appropriate duration values.

   QUICK TIP

   For more information on any property, click the property then press [F1].

2. **Click the** Property Sheet button **on the Design tab, click the** Data tab **in the Property Sheet, click the** Row Source Type property box, **click its** list arrow, **then click** Value List

   The **Row Source Type** property determines the source of the control's data—the source of the values in the combo box list. The three possible choices for the Row Source Type property include Table/Query, Value List, and Field List. They work hand-in-hand with the **Row Source** property, which specifies the actual table, values, or field used in the list.

   QUICK TIP

   The title bar of the property sheet identifies the name of the control that you are currently working with.

3. **Click the** Row Source property, **click the** Build button **⋯**, **then type the values for the list into the Edit List Items dialog box as shown in Figure G-11**

   The Edit List Items dialog box also allows you to specify a default value. Because the most common tour duration is 7 days, you'll set 7 as the default value.

4. **Click the** Default Value text box, **type** 7, **click** OK, **click the** Property Sheet button **to toggle it off, then click the** Form View button **▦** **on the Design tab**

   Access automatically created the Category field on the General Info tab as a combo box because it is assigned Lookup properties in the Tours Table Design View. The Duration combo box is on the Dates tab.

5. **Click** Dates tab, **click the** Duration list arrow, **then click** 10 **to change the duration for the first tour, Bayside Shelling, from 7 to 10 as shown in Figure G-12**

   Also note that you can add items to the combo box list in Form View by clicking the **Edit List Items button** ✍. To inactivate this feature, you change the combo box's **Allow Value List Edits** property to No in the combo box's property sheet. Another combo box property, the **Limit to List** property, controls whether a user can directly type an entry into the combo box that doesn't already appear on the list. To test the default value setting, you start entering a new record.

6. **Click the** New (blank) record button **▸⁕** **on the navigation bar to observe 7 as the default value for the Duration combo box**

FIGURE G-11: Creating a combo box for the Duration field

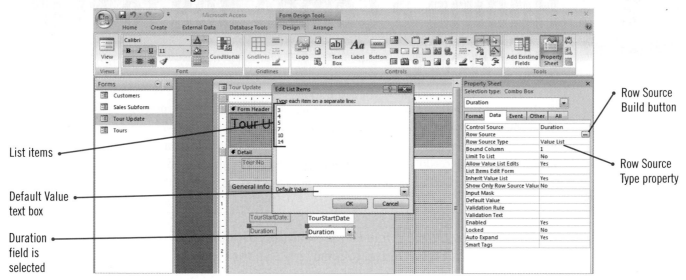

List items

Default Value text box

Duration field is selected

Row Source Build button

Row Source Type property

FIGURE G-12: Using the new Duration combo box

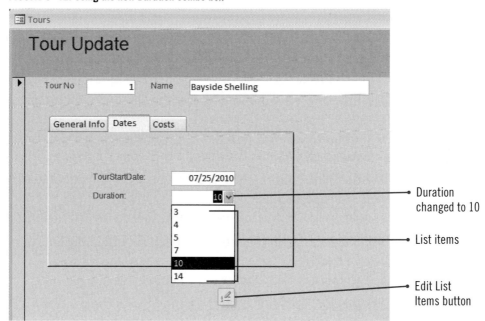

Duration changed to 10

List items

Edit List Items button

Choosing between a combo box and a list box

The list box and combo box controls are very similar, but the combo box is more popular for two reasons. While both provide a list of values from which the user can choose to make an entry in a field, the combo box also allows the user to make a unique entry from the keyboard (unless the Limit To List property is set to Yes). More importantly, however, most users like the drop-down list action of the combo box. A list box also provides a list of values through which the user scrolls and selects a choice, but has no "drop-down" action.

Adding a Combo Box to Find Records

Most combo boxes are used to enter data; however, you can also use the combo box control to find records. When you use a combo box to find data, you must carefully identify it as a tool for finding and retrieving records so that the user doesn't confuse the combo boxes used to enter data with one used to find a record. You decide to add a combo box to help quickly locate the desired tour on the Tour Update form. You will use the Combo Box Wizard to help guide your actions in building this new combo box.

STEPS

1. **Click the View button arrow on the Home tab, click Design View, click the TourName text box, then press [Delete] to remove it from the form**

   Instead of changing the existing TourName text box into a combo box, you'll add the TourName combo box back to the form using the Combo Box Wizard.

2. **Click the Combo Box button 📼 on the Design tab, then click just above the right edge of the tab control**

   The Combo Box Wizard opens as shown in Figure G-13. The first two options create a combo box used to enter data in a field. The difference between the two options determines the source of the data in the drop-down list. The third option corresponds to what you want to do now—use the combo box to find a record.

3. **Click the Find a record option button, click Next, double-click TourName, click Next, double-click the right edge of the TourName column to view all of the items in the list, click Next, type FIND A TOUR as the label for the combo box, then click Finish**

   You test the combo box in Form View.

4. **Click the Form View button 📼, click the FIND A TOUR list arrow, then click Greenfield Jaycees**

   The Greenfield Jaycees tour (Tour No 5) appears in the form, but you want to sort the combo box list values in ascending order. You must make this change in Form Design View.

5. **Click the View button arrow, click Design View, then double-click the new combo box to open its Property Sheet**

   To sort the values in ascending order, you work with the control's Row Source Property.

6. **Click the Data tab in the Property Sheet, click the Row Source property, then click the Build button [...]**

   The Query Builder opens, allowing you to modify the fields or sort order of the values in the combo box list.

7. **Click the Sort cell for the TourName field, click the list arrow, click Ascending, click the Close button on the Design tab, then click Yes when prompted to save the changes**

   Test the combo box in Form View.

8. **Click the Property Sheet button to close the Property Sheet, click 📼, click the FIND A TOUR list arrow, then scroll and click Gold Country**

   The form finds and displays Tour No 29 for the Gold Country tour in Sacramento, CA as shown in Figure G-14.

FIGURE G-13: Choices in the Combo Box Wizard

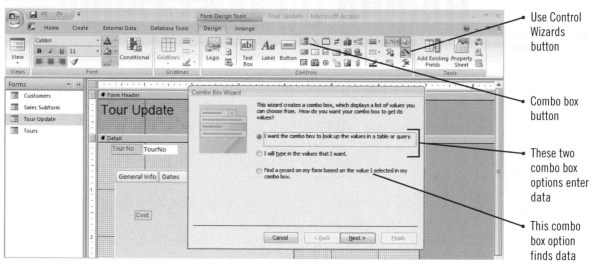

Use Control Wizards button

Combo box button

These two combo box options enter data

This combo box option finds data

FIGURE G-14: New combo box used to find tour names

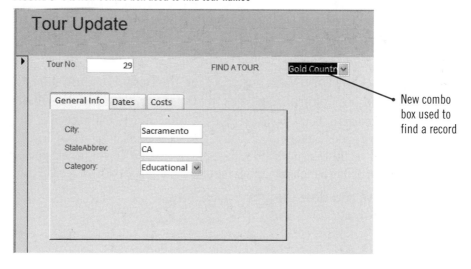

New combo box used to find a record

Access 2007

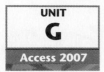

Adding Option Groups

An **option group** is a special type of bound control that is often used when only a few values are available for a field. You place **option button** controls within the option group to determine the value that is selected in the field. Each option button represents a different value that can be entered into the field bound to the option group. Option buttons within an option group are mutually exclusive; only one can be chosen at a time. ▓▓▓▓ Another way to select the data for the Duration field is to use option buttons within an option group. You can modify the Tour Update form to investigate this alternative.

STEPS

1. **Click the** View button arrow, **click** Design View, **click the** Dates tab, **click the** Duration combo box, **then press** [Delete]

   After deleting the Duration combo box and its associated label, you are ready to add the Duration field back to the form as an option group.

2. **Click the** Option Group button 🗒 **on the Design tab, then click** below the TourStartDate text box **on the tabbed control**

   The **Option Group Wizard** guides you as you develop an option group. The first question asks about label names for the option buttons. You'll enter all of the possible Quest tour durations.

3. **Type** 3 days, **press** [Tab], **then enter the options as shown in Figure G-15**

   The next question prompts you for the actual values associated with each option button.

4. **Click** Next, **click the** No, I don't want a default option button, **click** Next, **then enter the option values to correspond with their labels as shown in Figure G-16**

   The values are the actual data that are entered into the field and correspond with the **Option Value property** of each option button. The label names are just clarifying labels.

5. **Click** Next, **click the** Store the value in this field list arrow, **click** Duration, **click** Next, **click** Next **to accept** Option buttons **in an** Etched **style, click** Next, **type** Duration **as the caption, then click** Finish

   View the new option group in Form View.

6. **Click the** Form View button 🖼 **on the Design tab, use the** FIND A TOUR **list arrow to find the** Colonial Tour, **click the** Dates tab, **then click the** 10 days option button

   Your screen should look like Figure G-17. You changed the duration of this tour from 14 to 10 days. To add more option buttons to this option group later, work in Form Design View and use the Option Button button on the Design tab to add the new option button to the option group. Modify the value represented by that option button by opening the option button's property sheet and changing the Option Value property.

7. **Save and close the** Tour Update **form**

Protecting data

You may not want to allow all users who view a form to change all the data that appears on that form. You can design forms to limit access to certain fields by changing the Enabled and Locked properties of a control. The **Enabled property** specifies whether a control can have the focus in Form View. The **Locked property** specifies whether you can edit data in a control in Form View.

FIGURE G-15: Option Group Wizard

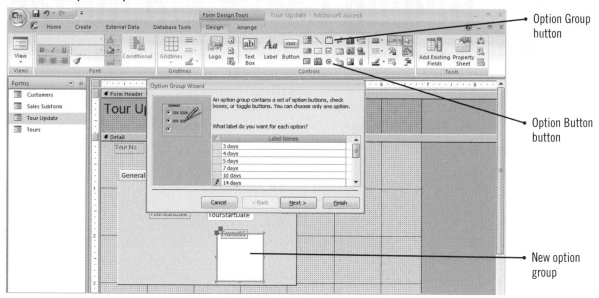

Option Group button

Option Button button

New option group

FIGURE G-16: Specifying the option button values

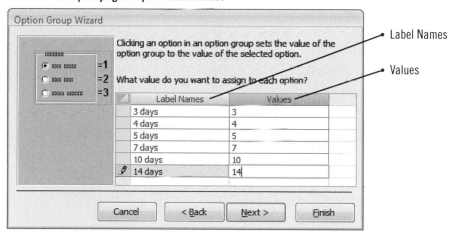

Label Names

Values

FIGURE G-17: Using an option group

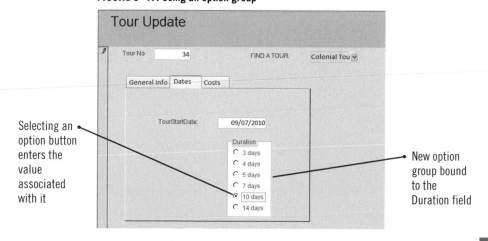

Selecting an option button enters the value associated with it

New option group bound to the Duration field

Adding Command Buttons

A **command button** is used to initiate a common action in Form View such as printing the current record, opening another form, or closing the current form. Command buttons are often added to the Form Header or Form Footer sections. **Sections** determine where controls appear on the screen and print on paper. See Table G-2 for more information on form sections. ▓▓▓ You add a command button to the Form Header section of the Tours form to help other Quest employees print only the current record.

1. **Double-click Tours in the Navigation Pane, then maximize the form**

   You plan to add the new command button to the right side of the Form Header section to print the current record.

2. **Click the View button arrow on the Home tab, click Design View, click the Button button on the Design tab, then click the right side of the Form Header section**

   The Command Button Wizard opens, listing over 30 of the most popular actions for the command button, organized within six categories as shown in Figure G-18.

3. **Click Record Operations in the Categories list, click Print Record in the Actions list, click Next, click Next to accept the default picture, type PrintCurrentRecord as the button name, then click Finish**

   Adding this command button to print only the current record helps avoid creating an unintended printout that prints every record. The **Display When property** of the Form Header determines when the controls in that section appear on screen and print.

4. **Double-click the Form Header section bar to open its Property Sheet, click the Format tab, click Always for the Display When property, click the Display When list arrow, click Screen Only, then click the Property Sheet button on the Design tab to toggle off the Property Sheet**

   Now the Print Record button appears on the screen when you are working in the form, but does not appear on printouts. You'll make one more modification to the form—to add your name as a label for identification purposes.

5. **Click the Label button on the Design tab, click to the right of the TourNo text box in the Detail section, type Created by your name, then press [Enter]**

   Save and test the form.

6. **Click the Save button 🔲 on the Quick Access toolbar, click the Form View button 🔲 on the Design tab, then click the Print button you added to the Form Header section to confirm that only one record prints and that the Form Header controls do not appear on the printout**

   The final Tours form should look like Figure G-19.

7. **Save and close the Tours form, then close the Quest-G.accdb database**

TABLE G-2: Form sections

section	description
Detail	Appears once for every record
Form Header	Appears at the top of the form and often contains command buttons or a label with the title of the form
Form Footer	Appears at the bottom of the form and often contains command buttons or a label with instructions on how to use the form
Page Header	Appears at the top of a printed form with information such as page numbers or dates
Page Footer	Appears at the bottom of a printed form with information such as page numbers or dates

Enhancing Forms

FIGURE G-18: Command Button Wizard

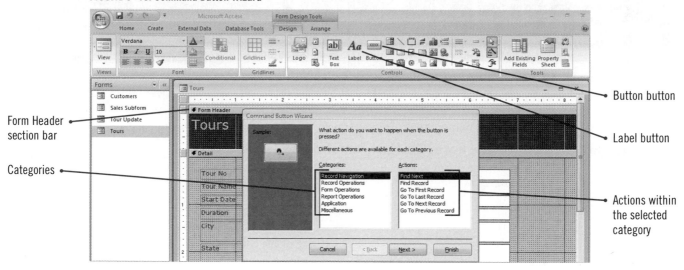

Form Header section bar

Categories

Button button

Label button

Actions within the selected category

FIGURE G-19: Final Tours form

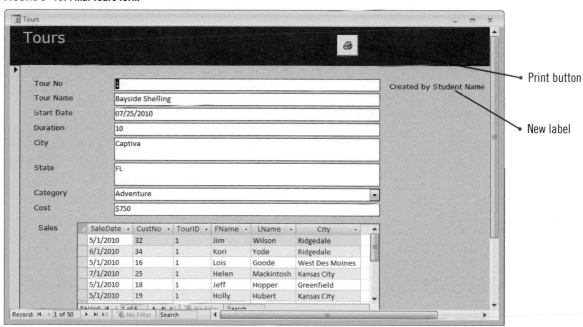

Print button

New label

Practice

▼ CONCEPTS REVIEW

Identify each element of the Form Design View shown in Figure G-20.

FIGURE G-20

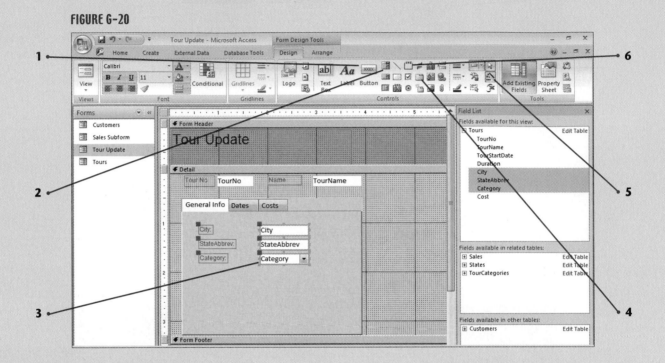

Match each term with the statement that best describes its function.

7. **Command button**
8. **Subform**
9. **Control**
10. **Option group**
11. **Combo box**

a. An element you add to a form such as a label, text box, or list box
b. A control that shows records that are related to one record shown in the main form
c. An unbound control that executes an action when it is clicked
d. A bound control that is really both a list box and a text box
e. A bound control that displays a few mutually exclusive entries for a field

Select the best answer from the list of choices.

12. **Which control works best to display three choices, 1, 2, or 3, for a Rating field?**
   a. Option group   c. Text box
   b. Label   d. Command button
13. **Which control would you use to initiate a print action?**
   a. Option group   c. Text box
   b. Command button   d. List box
14. **Which control would you use to display a drop-down list of 50 states?**
   a. Check box   c. Combo box
   b. Field label   d. List box

15. **To view many related records within a form, use a:**
   a. Link control.
   b. List box.
   c. Design template.
   d. Subform.

16. **Which of the following form properties defines the fields and records that appear on a form?**
   a. Default View
   b. Record Source
   c. Row Source
   d. List Items Edit Form

17. **Which is a popular layout for a main form?**
   a. Datasheet
   b. PivotTable
   c. Global
   d. Columnar

18. **Which is a popular layout for a subform?**
   a. Global
   b. PivotTable
   c. Columnar
   d. Datasheet

19. **Which Form Header property determines when the controls in that section appear on screen and print?**
   a. Display When
   b. Section Visible
   c. Special Effect
   d. Can Shrink

20. **Which control is most commonly used within an option group?**
   a. Option Button
   b. Toggle Button
   c. Command Button
   d. Check Box

▼ SKILLS REVIEW

1. **Create subforms.**
   a. Start Access and open the **Membership-G.accdb** database from the drive and folder where you store your Data Files. Enable content if prompted.
   b. Click the Database Tools tab, then click the Relationships button.
   c. Click the Relationship Report button.
   d. The Relationships for Membership-G appears as a report in Print Preview. In Report Design View, insert your name as a label in the Report Header section, then print the report.
   e. Close the Relationships report window without saving the report, and then close the Relationships window.
   f. Use the Form Wizard to create a form/subform combination based on the First, Last, and CharterMember fields in the Names table, and the ActivityDate and Hours fields in the Activities table. Use the printout of the relationships report to answer the Form Wizard question about how you want to view your data. The answer to this question determines which fields go in the main form, and which fields go in the subform. Use a Datasheet layout and an Origin style, and name the form **Names Main Form** and **Activities Subform**.

2. **Modify subforms.**
   a. In Form Design View, make the subform both wider and taller so that more records can be viewed at the same time.
   b. Open the Field List for the main form, and add the Birthday field between the Last text box and CharterMember check box.
   c. Save, then close the Names Main Form.

3. **Create split forms.**
   a. Click the Names table in the Navigation Pane, then use the Split Form button on the Create tab to create a split form based on the Names table.
   b. Maximize the form, filter for all members whose dues are $25, then sort the records in ascending order based on the Last field. Your screen should look like Figure G-21. (*Hint*: If all of the fields are not visible in the upper portion of the split form, drag the split bar that separates the two sections of the form.)
   c. Save the form as **Names Split Form**, then close it.

FIGURE G-21

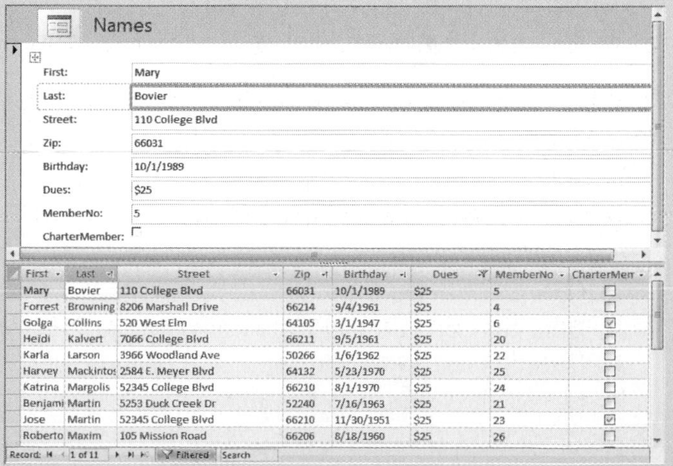

Access 2007

4. Add tab controls.

   a. Open Member Entry Form in Design View.

   b. Add a tab control and rename the two pages to be **Address** and **Activities**.

   c. Resize the tab control to fill the space available on the form under the existing controls.

   d. Open the Field List, then add the **Street** field from the Names table to the top of the Address page.

   e. Add the **Zip** field from the Names table to the bottom of the Address page.

   f. Add the **City** and **State** fields between the existing Street and Zip fields to the Address page from the Zips table in the Field List then close the Field List.

   g. Use your moving and alignment skills to order the fields top to bottom as: Street, City, State, and Zip. Right-align the right edges of these four new text boxes on the Address page and make the vertical spacing between the controls equal.

   h. Click the Activities page to bring it forward, then use the Subform/Subreport button on the Design tab to add the existing Activities Subform to that page. Use the rest of the defaults in the Subform Wizard, which helps you connect the main form and subform using the common MemberNo field.

   i. Resize the Activities Subform to fill the Activities page.

   j. Save and view the Member Entry Form in Form View. Sort the records in ascending order based on the MemberNo and move between the records of the main form observing the fields in both pages of the tab control. MemberNo 1, Micah Zecharius, should have an address in Shawnee, KS, and five activity records. Return to Design View and move or resize any controls that do not completely display the data they contain.

5. Add a combo box for data entry.

   a. Open the Member Entry Form in Design View, then right-click the Zip text box and change it to a combo box control.

   b. In the Property Sheet of the new combo box, click the Row Source property, then click the Build button.

   c. Select the Zips table only for the query, and then double-click the Zip field to add it as the only column of the query grid.

   d. Close the Query Builder window, and save the changes.

   e. Close the Property Sheet, then save and view the Member Entry Form in Form View.

   f. In the first record for MemberNo 1, change the Zip to **64153** using the new combo box. Notice that the City and State fields automatically change to Blue Springs, MO to reflect the zip code choice.

   g. Save and close the Member Entry Form.

6. Add a combo box to find records.

   a. Open the Names Main Form in Design View.

   b. Use the Combo Box Wizard to add to the right side of the Form Header section a new combo box that finds records in the form.

   c. Select the First and Last fields, make sure that each column is wide enough to view all values, and label the combo box **FIND THIS MEMBER**

   d. Widen the new combo box to be about 2" wide, change the label text to white, save the Names Main form, then view it in Form View.

   e. Use the FIND THIS MEMBER combo box to find the Benjamin Martin record. Notice that the entries in the combo box are not alphabetized on last name.

   f. Return to Form Design View, and use the Row Source property for the combo box to add an ascending sort order to the Last field. Close the Query Builder, saving changes. View the Names Main Form in Form View, and find the record for Sherry Walker. Note that the entries in the combo box list are now sorted in ascending order by the Last field.

   g. Find the record for Micah Zecharius using the combo box, change the record to your own first and last names, print only that record, then save and close the Names Main Form. (*Hint*: To print only one record, choose the Selected Record(s) option in the Print dialog box.)

7. Add option groups.

   a. Open the Member Entry Form in Design View, then delete the Dues text box and label in the main form.

   b. Using the Option Group Wizard, add the Dues field back to the form just below the Birthday text box.

   c. Enter **$25** and **$50** as the label names, then accept $25 as the default choice.

   d. Change the values to **25** and **50** to correspond with the labels.

▼ SKILLS REVIEW (CONTINUED)

e. Store the value in the Dues field, choose Option buttons with an Etched style, type the caption **Annual Dues**, then click Finish.

f. Move and resize the new Dues option group and other controls as needed, save the Member Entry Form, display it in Form View, use the combo box to find the record with your name, then change the Annual Dues to **$25**.

8. Add command buttons.

a. Open the Member Entry Form in Design View.

b. Use the Command Button Wizard to add a command button to the right side of the Form Header section.

c. Choose the Print Record action from the Record Operations category.

d. Display the text **Print Current Record** on the button, then name the button **PrintButton**.

e. Save the form, display it in Form View, then print the record for yourself. The final form should look similar to Figure G-22.

f. Navigate to the record with your own name, change the month and day of the Birthday entry to your own, then print the record using the new Print Current Record command button.

g. Save, then close the Member Entry Form.

h. Close the Membership-G.accdb database.

FIGURE G-22

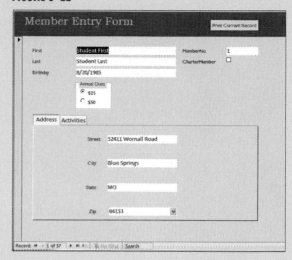

▼ INDEPENDENT CHALLENGE 1

As the manager of a music store's instrument rental program, you have created a database to track instrument rentals to schoolchildren. Now that several rentals have been made, you want to create a form/subform to make it easy for users to enter a new rental record.

a. Start Access, then open the database **MusicRentals-G.accdb** from the drive and folder where you store your Data Files. Enable content if prompted.

b. Using the Form Wizard, create a new form based on all of the fields in the Customers and Rentals tables.

c. View the data by Customers, choose a Datasheet layout for the subform and an Opulent style, then accept the default form titles of Customers for the main form and Rentals Subform for the subform.

d. Add another record to the rental subform for Amanda Smith by typing **888335** as the SerialNo entry and **5/1/10** as the RentalDate entry. (*Hint*: If the RentalDate field isn't visible, press [Tab] to move to it.) Note that no entries are necessary in the RentalNo field because it is an AutoNumber field nor the CustNo field as it is the foreign key field that connects the main form to the subform and is automatically populated when the forms are in this arrangement.

e. Save and close the Customers form.

f. Open the Rentals Subform in Form Design View and change the subform to show only the SerialNo, Date, and the Description for the instrument. You don't need to see the RentalNo or CustNo fields in the subform.

g. Delete the RentalNo and CustNo fields, open the Field List, and drag the Description field from the Field List (*Hint*: Look in the Instruments related table) to just under the Date field. Remember that the subform is in a datasheet layout so precise positioning of the controls in Form Design View is not necessary.

h. Save and close the Rentals Subform, then open the Customers main form in Form View.

i. Resize the columns in the subform so that all fields are visible.

j. In Form Design View, add a combo box to the right side of the Form Header to find records based on the data in the FirstName and LastName fields. Label the combo box FIND CUSTOMER: and change the label text to white so that it is visible on the dark background.

k. Use the Row Source property of the combo box to sort the list in ascending order on LastName, and widen the control.

l. Open the Customers main form in Form View and search for the record Kris Joy. Change that name to your own, and print only this record. (*Hint*: To print only one record, choose the Selected Record(s) option in the Print dialog box.)

m. Save and close the Customers form, close the MusicRentals-G.accdb database, then exit Access.

▼ INDEPENDENT CHALLENGE 2

As the manager of a music store's instrument rental program, you have created a database to track instrument rentals to schoolchildren. You add command buttons to a form to make it easier to use.

a. Start Access, then open the database **InstrumentRentals-G.accdb** from the drive and folder where you store your Data Files. Enable content if prompted.

b. Using the Form Wizard, create a form/subform using all the fields of both the Customers and Schools tables.

c. View the data by Schools, use a Datasheet layout for the subform, then choose a Northwind style.

d. Accept the default names of Schools for the main form and Customers Subform for the subform.

e. Resize the subform columns to view all of the data in Form View. Use Form Design View to delete the SchoolNo field from the subform, and to resize the subform as necessary to display all columns.

f. In Form Design View, add a command button to the middle of the Form Header. The action should print the current record and display the text **Print School Record**. Name the button **PrintButton**.

Advanced Challenge Exercise

- Add a second command button to the right of the Print School Record button using the Command Button Wizard. The action should add a new record and display the text **Add New School**. Name the button **AddButton**.
- Add a third command button to the right side of the Form Header section using the Command Button Wizard. The action should close the form and display the text **Close**. Name the button **CloseButton**.
- Align the top edges of all three buttons.
- Open the Property Sheet for the Form Header and give the Display When property the **Screen Only** value. Close the Property Sheet, then save the Schools form.
- Display the form in Form View, click the Add New School button, add the name of your high school to the SchoolName field, allow the SchoolNo to increment automatically, then add the information of a friend as the first record within the subform. Note that the CustNo and SchoolNo fields in the subform will be entered automatically.

g. Use the Print School Record button to print only this new school record.

h. Close the Schools form, close the InstrumentRentals-G.accdb database, then exit Access.

▼ INDEPENDENT CHALLENGE 3

As the manager of an equipment rental program, you have created a database to track equipment rentals. Now that the users are becoming accustomed to forms, you add a combo box and option group to make the forms easier to use.

a. Start Access, then open the database **Equipment-G.accdb** from the drive and folder where you store your Data Files. Enable content if prompted.

b. Using the Form Wizard, create a form/subform using all the fields of both the Equipment and Rentals tables.

c. View the data by Equipment, use a Datasheet layout for the subform, and choose a Concourse style.

d. Enter the name **Equipment Main Form** for the main form and **Rentals Subform** for the subform. In Form View, resize the columns of the subform so that all data is clearly visible.

e. In Form Design View of the Equipment Main Form, delete the Deposit text box and label.

f. Add the Deposit field as an option group to the right side of the main form using the Option Group Wizard.

g. Enter the Label Names as **$0**, **$50**, and **$100**. Do not specify a default option. The corresponding values for the option buttons should be **0**, **50**, and **100**.

h. Store the value in the Deposit field. Use Option buttons with an Etched style.

i. Caption the option group **Deposit**, save the form, then view it in Form View. Resize and move controls as necessary.

j. Specify a **$50** deposit for each of the first three records (Weed Eater, Weed Whacker, and Mulching Mower). Save and close the Equipment Main Form.

Advanced Challenge Exercise

- In Table Design View of the Equipment table, add a field named **Condition** with a Text data type. This field will record the condition of the instrument as Excellent, Good, Fair, or Poor.
- Start the Lookup Wizard for the Condition field, and choose the "I will type in the values that I want" option button.
- Enter **Excellent**, **Good**, **Fair**, and **Poor** as the four possible values, and accept the name **Condition** as the label for the lookup column. Save and close the Equipment table.
- In Form Design View of the Equipment Main Form, open the Field List and add the Condition field to just below the WeeklyRate text box. Note that the Condition field is automatically added as a combo box control due to the Lookup properties it was given in Table Design View of the Equipment table where it is defined.
- Save the form then display it in Form View. Move through the records, selecting Excellent as the Condition value choice for the first two records and Good for the third record.

k. In Design View, add a command button to the Form Header section that prints the current record. Use the text **Print** on the button and give it the meaningful name of PrintButton. Add your own name as a label under the Equipment Main Form label.

l. Print only the record for the Weed Eater.

m. Save and close the Equipment Main Form, close the Equipment-G.accdb database, and then exit Access.

▼ REAL LIFE INDEPENDENT CHALLENGE

One way to use Access in your real life is in a community service project. People in schools and nonprofit agencies often inherit databases created by others and need help extracting information from them. Suppose you're working with the local high school guidance counselor to help her with an Access database she inherited that is used to record college scholarship opportunities. You can help her keep the database updated by creating some easy to use forms.

a. Start Access and open the **Scholarships-G.accdb** database from the drive and folder where you store your Data Files. Enable content if prompted.

b. Create a split form for the Scholarships table. Save and name the form **Scholarships**.

c. Move and resize controls as necessary to expand the size of the Description field as shown in Figure G-23.

FIGURE G-23

d. Add a combo box to find a scholarship by name to the Form Header section with the label FIND SCHOLARSHIP:. Widen the control as necessary and change its List Rows property to **50**.

e. Modify the Row Source property of the combo box so that the scholarships are sorted in ascending order based on the scholarship name.

f. Use the combo box to find the Patrick Charnon Scholarship. Change "Patrick Charnon" to your name in both the ScholarshipName text box as well as the Description field, then print only that record by using the Selected Record(s) option on the Print dialog box.

g. Save and close the Scholarship form, close the Scholarships-G.accdb database, then exit Access.

Access 2007

▼ VISUAL WORKSHOP

Open the RealEstate-G.accdb database from the drive and folder where you store your Data Files. Enable content if prompted. Use the Form Wizard to create a new form. Select all the fields from the Agencies, Agents, and Listings tables. View the data by Agencies which will create two subforms as one agency has many agents and one agent has many listings. Use a datasheet layout for each subform, and Equity style for the main form, and accept the default names for the forms. Resize the columns in the datasheets to show more fields, and also resize the subforms themselves to better use the width of the form. In Form View, navigate to the Camden and Camden Realtors agency in the main form, navigate to Shari Duncan in the Agents subform as shown in Figure G-24, then change Shari's name to your own. Use the Selected Record(s) option button in the Print dialog box to print that record.

FIGURE G-24

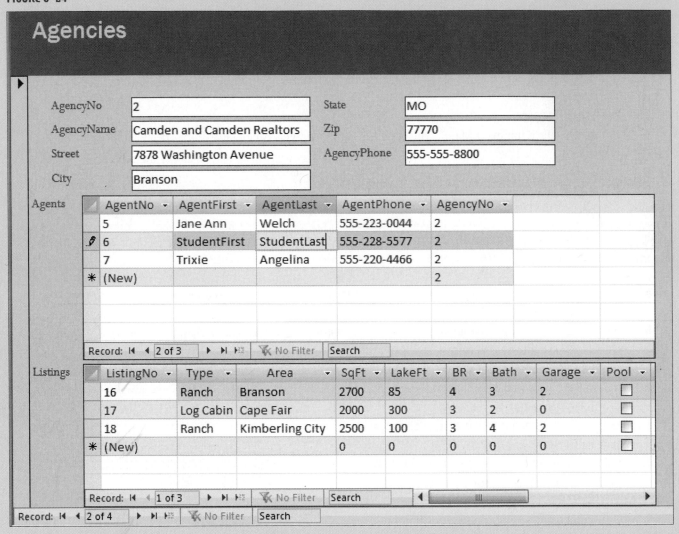

Analyzing Data with Reports

Although you can print data in forms and datasheets, **reports** give you more control over how data is printed and greater flexibility in presenting summary information. To create a report, you use bound controls, such as text boxes, to display data and unbound controls, such as lines, graphics, and labels, to clarify the data. 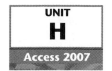 Using additional report design skills, such as building summary reports and parameter reports and applying conditional formatting, you can create reports that not only present but also analyze and clarify the information.

OBJECTIVES

Create summary reports

Create parameter reports

Apply conditional formatting

Add lines

Use the Format Painter and AutoFormats

Add subreports

Modify section properties

Use domain functions

Creating Summary Reports

Summary reports are reports that show statistics on groups of records. As the amount of data in your database grows over time, you probably become more interested in summary statistics that analyze groups of records rather than details about the specific data in each record. You create summary reports by using Access functions such as Sum, Count, or Avg in expressions that calculate the desired statistic. These expressions are entered in text boxes in report group header or footer sections. Therefore, you need to understand report sections and calculated expressions so you can create summary reports effectively. Table H-1 reviews report sections. The Group Footer section is most commonly used to calculate statistics on groups of records. ▆▆▆▆ Mark Rock asks for a report to summarize the revenue for each tour category. You can create a summary report to satisfy this request.

1. **Start Access, open the** Quest-H.accdb **database from the drive and folder where you store your Data Files, enable content if prompted, click the** Create tab, **click the** Report Design button, **then maximize the report window**

    The first step in building a report from scratch in Report Design View is to select the fields you want for the report. You do this by setting the report's Record Source property.

2. **Double-click the** report selector button ■ **to open the Property Sheet, click the** Data tab, **click the** Record Source Build button [...], **double-click** Tours, **double-click** Sales, **then click** Close

3. **Scroll down and double-click** Category **in the Tours field list, then double-click** Revenue **in the Sales field list**

    The Revenue field represents what was actually charged at the time of the sale. Tours are sometimes discounted for various reasons.

4. **Click the** Close button **on the Query Tools Design tab, click** Yes **to save changes, click the** Property Sheet button **on the Design tab to close the Property Sheet, then click the** Group & Sort button **if the Group, Sort, and Total pane is not open**

    With the fields selected for the report, the next step is to specify the Category field as the grouping field.

5. **Click the** Add a group button **in the Group, Sort, and Total pane, then click** Category

    The Category Header section appears in Report Design View. To identify each new tour category, you add the Category field to this report section.

6. **Click the** Add Existing Fields button **on the Design tab, then drag the** Category field **to the left side of the Category Header section**

    To sum the revenue for each category, you need to add an expression to a text box that subtotals the Revenue for each Category. You use the Access Sum function.

7. **Click the** Text Box button [ab] **on the Design tab, click to the** right of the Category control **in the Category Header section, click** Unbound **in the new text box, type** =Sum([Revenue]), **press [Enter], then change, move, resize, and align the controls as shown in Figure H-1**

    A summary report doesn't need a Detail section, so you can close the Detail section.

    TROUBLE
    You must scroll down in order to see the bottom edge of the Detail section.

8. **Close the Group, Sort, and Total pane, drag the** top edge of the Page Footer section up **to completely close the Detail section, click the** Home tab, **click the** View button arrow, **then click** Print Preview

    The summarized revenue for each category is shown in the one-page summary report in Figure H-2.

9. **Close Print Preview, save the report with the name** Category Revenue Summary, **then close it**

FIGURE H-1: Design View of summary report

Group & Sort button

Add Existing Fields button

Text Box button

New expression to subtotal Revenue

Group on Category field

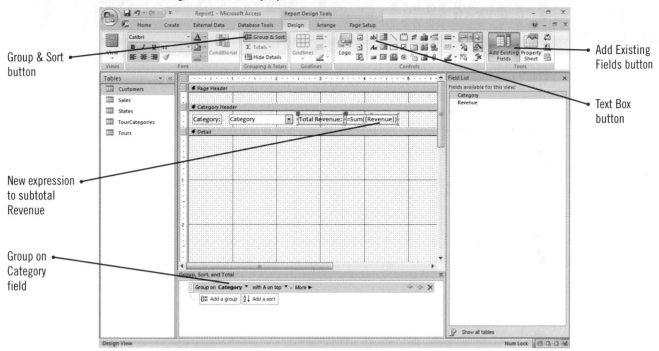

FIGURE H-2: Print Preview of summary report

Each row represents many records for each category

Total revenue subtotaled by category

TABLE H-1: Review of report sections

section	where does this section print?	what is this section most commonly used for?
Report Header	At the top of the first page of the report	To print a title or logo
Page Header	At the top of every page (but below the Report Header on page one)	To print titles, dates, or page numbers at the top of every page
Group Header	Before every group of records	To identify the value of the grouping field
Detail	Once for every record	To display data for every record in the report
Group Footer	After every group of records	To calculate summary statistics on groups of records
Page Footer	At the bottom of every page	To print dates or page numbers at the bottom of every page

Creating Parameter Reports

A **parameter report** prompts you for criteria to determine the records to use for the report. To create a parameter report, you base the report on a parameter query by setting the report's Record Source property to the name of the parameter query. ~~Mark Rock~~ Mark Rock requests a report that shows all tour sales for a given period. You use a parameter query to prompt the user for the dates, then build the report on that query.

STEPS

1. **Click the** Create tab, **click the** Query Design button, **double-click** Customers, **double-click** Sales, **double-click** Tours, **click** Close, **then maximize the query window**

   You want fields from all three tables in the report, so you add them to the query that will supply the report's records.

2. **Double-click** FName, LName, SaleDate, Revenue, **and** TourName

   To select only those tours sold in a given period, you add parameter prompts to the SaleDate field.

3. **Click the** Criteria cell for the SaleDate field, **type** Between [Enter start date] and [Enter end date], **then widen the** SaleDate column **to see the entire entry as shown in Figure H-3**

   To test the query, run it and enter dates in the parameter prompts.

   > **QUICK TIP**
   > You can shorten date criteria by entering only two digits for the year, as in 6/1/10.

4. **Click the** View button **on the Design tab to run the query, type** 6/1/2010 **in the Enter start date box, click** OK, **type** 6/30/2010 **in the Enter end date box, then click** OK

   Twenty-five records are displayed in the datasheet, each with a SaleDate value in June 2010. To create a parameter report, you use the Report Wizard to build a report on this query.

5. **Click the** Save button 🖫 **on the Quick Access toolbar, type** SalesParameter **as the new query name, click** OK, **then close the query**

   You use the Report button on the Create tab to quickly build a report on the SalesParameter query.

6. **Click the** SalesParameter query **in the Navigation Pane, click the** Create tab, **click the** Report button, **type** 7/1/2010 **in the Enter start date box, click** OK, **type** 7/31/2010 **in the Enter end date box, then click** OK

   The report is displayed in Layout View with records in July 2010. You decide to preview and save the report.

7. **Click the** View button arrow **on the Format tab, click** Print Preview, **click the** One Page button **on the Print Preview tab to view an entire page, then maximize the window as shown in Figure H-4**

8. **Close Print Preview, save the report with the name** SalesParameter, **then close it**

FIGURE H-3: Creating parameter criteria in a query

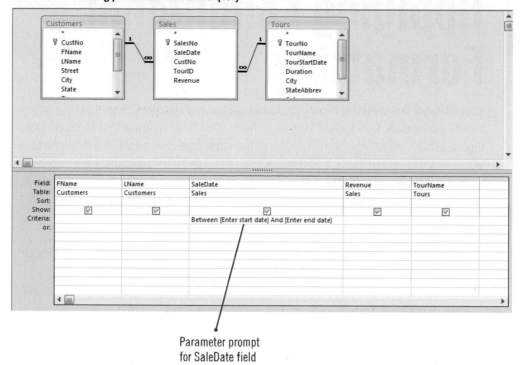

Parameter prompt
for SaleDate field

FIGURE H-4: Previewing the parameter report

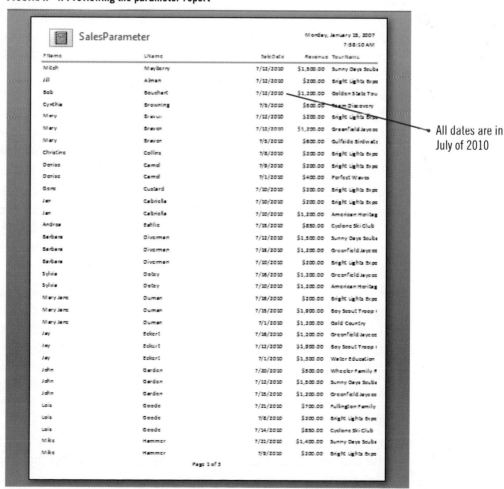

All dates are in
July of 2010

Applying Conditional Formatting

Conditional formatting allows you to change the appearance of a control on a form or report based on criteria you specify. Conditional formatting helps you highlight important or exceptional data on a form or report. When formatting several controls at the same time, you might find it helpful to group the controls. When you **group controls**, a formatting choice you make for any control in the group is applied to every control in the group. 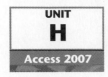 You want to apply conditional formatting to the SalesParameter report to emphasize different revenue levels as well as make other formatting modifications.

1. **Right-click the** SalesParameter report **in the Navigation Pane, click** Design View, **close the Field List, then maximize the report**

   You notice that you don't need as much room on the report for the FName or LName fields, but that the TourName field needs more space. First, you can resize these controls to better display the data.

2. **Use your resizing skills to resize the** text box controls **in the Detail section as shown in Figure H-5, making sure that the right edge of the report is aligned with the 8-inch mark on the ruler**

   Notice that when you resize FName or LName, **group selection handles** surround the text box and its associated label in the Page Header section, so resizing any control in the group resizes *every* control in the group. Click the Remove button on the Arrange tab if you want to remove this grouping effect, but in this case, the grouped controls allowed you to resize the controls more productively. Make sure that the right edge of a report is no greater than 8 inches on the vertical ruler so the printout fits on one 8.5 x 11-inch sheet of paper with .25-inch left and right margins.

3. **Click the** Revenue text box **in the Detail section, then click the** Conditional button **on the Design tab**

   The Conditional Formatting dialog box opens, asking you to define the conditional formatting rules. You want Revenue values between 500 and 1000 to be formatted in bold text, and values equal to or greater than 1000 to be formatted with both bold text and a light green fill/back color.

4. **Click the** text box to the right of the between arrow, **type** 500, **press [Tab], type** 999, **click the Bold button** B, **click the Add button to add Condition 2, click the** between list arrow, **click** greater than or equal to, **press [Tab], type** 1000, **click** B **for Condition 2, click the** Fill/Back Color button arrow **for Condition 2, then click a** light green box

   The Conditional Formatting dialog box should look like Figure H-6.

5. **Click** OK **in the Conditional Formatting dialog box, click the** View button arrow **on the Design tab, click** Print Preview, **type** 8/1/10 **in the Enter start date box, click** OK, **type** 8/31/10 **in the Enter end date box, click** OK, **then click the** Zoom pointer ⊕ **as necessary to zoom into the top portion of the report as shown in Figure H-7**

   Conditional formatting made the Revenue value for two tours bold because the values are between 500 and 1000. It made the Revenue for the Broadway workshops appear bold and with a light green fill color because the value is greater than 1000. Default formatting was applied to the Revenue value for the Japanese California Connection tour because it does not meet any of the conditions.

6. **Click the** Close Print Preview button **on the Print Preview tab, click the** Label button Aa **on the Design tab, click** to the right of the SalesParameter label, **then type** your name

7. **Save, print, then close the** SalesParameter **report**

FIGURE H-5: Design View of SalesParameter report after controls and report are resized

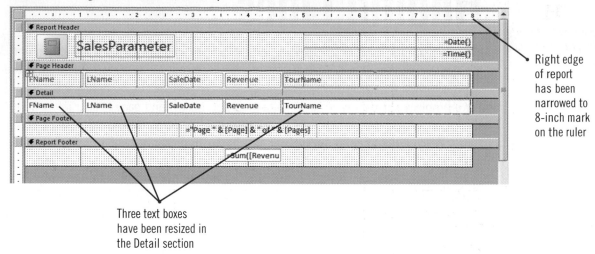

Right edge
of report
has been
narrowed to
8-inch mark
on the ruler

Three text boxes
have been resized in
the Detail section

FIGURE H-6: Conditional Formatting dialog box

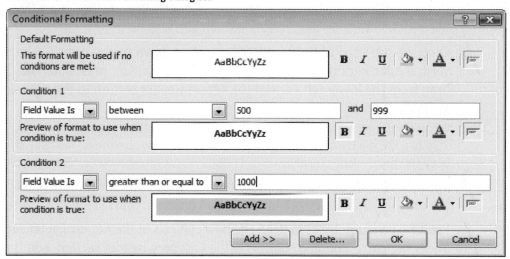

FIGURE H-7: Conditional formatting applied to SalesParameter report

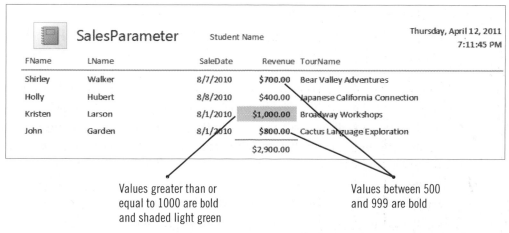

Values greater than or
equal to 1000 are bold
and shaded light green

Values between 500
and 999 are bold

Access 2007

Adding Lines

Unbound controls such as labels, lines, and rectangles can enhance the clarity of a report. When you create a report with the Report Wizard, it often creates line controls at the top or bottom of the report sections to visually separate the sections on the report. You can add, delete, or modify lines to best suit your needs. For example, you might want to separate the report header and page header information from the rest of the report with a line, or use lines to call attention to totals.  Mark Rock likes the data on the Category Revenue Summary report, but he asks you to enhance the report with labels, formatting, and a grand total. You plan to add lines to separate report sections and to indicate subtotals and grand totals.

STEPS

1. Right-click the Category Revenue Summary report in the Navigation Pane, click Design View, then maximize the report

Your first step is to create a report title. Because you want the title to print at the top of only the first page, you need to open the Report Header section.

2. Click the Arrange tab, click the Report Header/Footer button ▦ in the Show/Hide group, click the Design tab, click the Label button A𝒶, click the left side of the Report Header section, type Category Revenue Summary Report, then press [Enter]

You're ready to add a line to separate the Report Header from the rest of the report.

3. Drag the top edge of the Page Header section down to about the 0.5-inch mark on the vertical ruler, click the Line button ╲ on the Design tab, press and hold [Shift], then drag from the lower-left edge of the Report Header section to the right edge as shown in Figure H-8

Pressing [Shift] while drawing a line makes sure that the line stays in a perfectly horizontal position. You also want to add a grand total to the Report Footer section to total all revenue. You can copy and paste the text box with the calculation from the Category Header to the Report Footer section to accomplish this task.

4. Click the =Sum([Revenue]) text box in the Category Header section, press [Ctrl][C] to copy the control, click the Report Footer section bar, then press [Ctrl][V] to paste the control

5. Press [→] enough times to align the new controls in the Report Footer section directly under the corresponding controls in the Category Header section, edit the label in the Report Footer section to read Grand Total:, then drag the bottom edge of the Report Footer section down to about the 0.5-inch mark on the ruler

With the Report Footer section resized, it is tall enough to add lines to help identify the grand total figure.

6. Click the Line button ╲, press and hold [Shift], drag from just above the left edge of the text box with the calculation in the Report Footer section to the right edge of the text box, press [Ctrl][C] to copy the line, press [Ctrl][V] twice to paste the line twice, then move the two copies of the line to just under the text box as shown in Figure H-9

The single line above the calculation in the Report Footer section indicates that the numbers in the column above it are being added. Double lines under a calculation indicate a grand total. One other quick formatting change that can improve the report is to apply a Currency format to the calculations.

QUICK TIP
Double-clicking a property label toggles through the choices for that property.

7. Select the =Sum([Revenue]) text box in the Category Header section and the =Sum([Revenue]) text box in the Report Footer section, click the Property Sheet button on the Design tab, click the Format tab, click the Format property list arrow, click Currency, double-click the Decimal Places property to set it to 0, click the View button arrow on the Design tab, then click Print Preview

The final Category Revenue Summary report is shown in Figure H-10.

8. Close Print Preview, then save and close the Category Revenue Summary report

FIGURE H-8: New line added to Report Header section

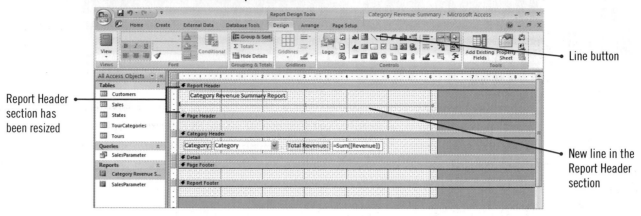

Report Header section has been resized

Line button

New line in the Report Header section

FIGURE H-9: New lines added to Report Footer section

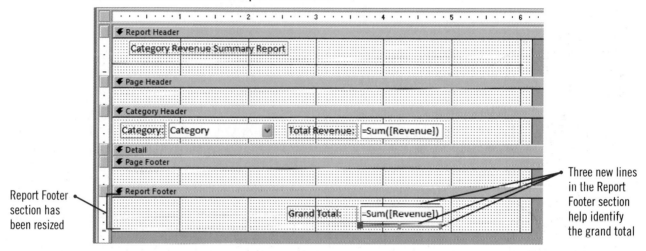

Report Footer section has been resized

Three new lines in the Report Footer section help identify the grand total

FIGURE H-10: Final Category Revenue Summary Report

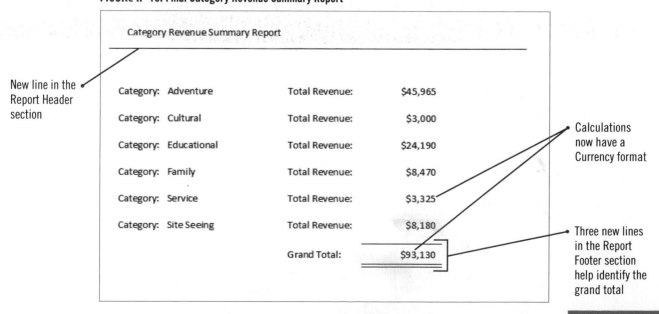

Category Revenue Summary Report

New line in the Report Header section

Category:	Adventure	Total Revenue:	$45,965
Category:	Cultural	Total Revenue:	$3,000
Category:	Educational	Total Revenue:	$24,190
Category:	Family	Total Revenue:	$8,470
Category:	Service	Total Revenue:	$3,325
Category:	Site Seeing	Total Revenue:	$8,180
		Grand Total:	$93,130

Calculations now have a Currency format

Three new lines in the Report Footer section help identify the grand total

Access 2007

Using the Format Painter and AutoFormats

The **Format Painter** is a tool used to copy multiple formatting properties from one control to another in Form or Report Design View. **AutoFormats** are predefined formats that you apply to a form or report to set all of the formatting enhancements such as font, color, and alignment. Access provides several AutoFormats that you can use. You think the Category Revenue Summary report can be improved with a few formatting embellishments. You can use the Format Painter to quickly change the characteristics of selected labels in the Category Revenue Summary report, then apply an AutoFormat.

STEPS

1. **Right-click the Category Revenue Summary report in the Navigation Pane, click Design View, close the Property Sheet, then maximize the report**

   Because you don't have any controls in either the Page Header or Page Footer sections, you decide to remove those sections from Report Design View. You also want to change the font size and color of the label in the Report Header section before using the Format Painter and an AutoFormat.

2. **Click the Arrange tab, then click the Page Header/Footer button 🖼 in the Show/Hide group to toggle those sections off**

   You can make other formatting changes in Layout View.

3. **Click the Home tab, click the View button arrow, click Layout View, click the Category Revenue Summary Report label, click the Font Size list arrow 10, click 18, and move the line in the Report Header section down as needed so that it doesn't touch the edge of the label**

   Next, you can apply an AutoFormat to see how it affects the report.

4. **Click the AutoFormat button arrow, then click the Solstice AutoFormat (fourth row, fifth column)**

   The Solstice AutoFormat gives the Report Header section a tan background. If there were controls in the Detail section of this report, more formatting changes would be applied. You decide to bold and change the color of the values in all of the Revenue text boxes. You also want to make sure the values in these text boxes are right-aligned.

5. **Click the Grand Total: label, click the Bold button B on the Format tab, click $45,965 to select all the Total Revenue values, click B, click the Font Color button arrow A·, click the Green box in the top row of the Standard Colors, then click the Align Text Right button ≡**

   The Format Painter will help you quickly copy these three formatting embellishments from one control to another.

6. **Click the Format Painter button ✓ on the Format tab, then click the Grand Total value**

   Report Layout View should look like Figure H-11. Now view the report in Print Preview.

7. **Click the View button arrow, then click Print Preview**

   The formatted report should look like Figure H-12.

8. **Close Print Preview, then save and close the Category Revenue Summary report**

   You can also press [Esc] to release the Format Painter.

FIGURE H-11: Report Design View of formatted Category Revenue Summary report

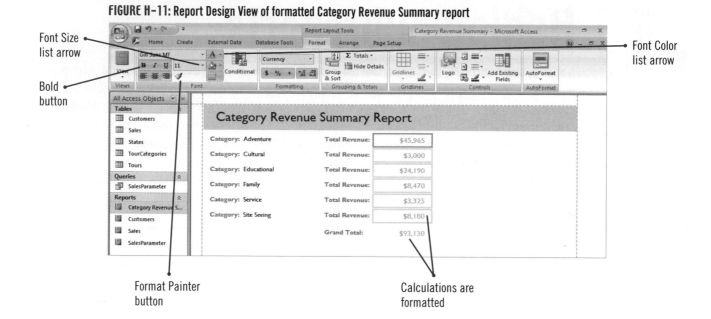

Font Size list arrow

Bold button

Format Painter button

Font Color list arrow

Calculations are formatted

FIGURE H-12: Print Preview of formatted Category Revenue Summary report

Category Revenue Summary Report

Category:	Adventure	Total Revenue:	$45,965
Category:	Cultural	Total Revenue:	$3,000
Category:	Educational	Total Revenue:	$24,190
Category:	Family	Total Revenue:	$8,470
Category:	Service	Total Revenue:	$3,325
Category:	Site Seeing	Total Revenue:	$8,180
		Grand Total:	$93,130

Line troubles

Sometimes lines are difficult to find in Report Design View because they are placed against the edge of a section or the edge of other controls. To find lines that are positioned next to the edge of a section, drag the section bar to expand it to expose the line. Recall that to draw a perfectly horizontal line, you hold [Shift] while creating or resizing it. Also note that it is easy to accidentally widen a line beyond the report margins, thus creating extra unwanted pages in your printout. To fix this problem, narrow any controls that extend beyond the margins of the printout and drag the right edge of the report to the left. Also note that the default left and right margins for an 8.5 x 11-inch sheet of paper are often .25 inches each, so a report in portrait orientation must be no wider than 8 inches and a report in landscape orientation must be no wider than 10.5 inches.

Adding Subreports

A **subreport** control displays a report within another report. The report that contains the subreport control is called the **main report**. You use the subreport control when you want to link two reports together to automate printing. You also use a subreport control when you want to change the order in which information automatically prints. For example, if you want report totals (generally found in the Report Footer section, which prints on the last page) to print on the first page, you could use a subreport to present the grand total information, and place it in the main report's Report Header section, which prints first. You want the Category Revenue Summary report to automatically print at the end of a similar report that shows all of the sales revenue detail. You use a subreport to accomplish this.

STEPS

1. **Click the** Create tab, **click the** Report Wizard button, **click the** Tables/Queries list arrow, **click Table: Sales, double-click** SaleDate, **double-click** Revenue, **click the** Tables/Queries list arrow, **click Table: Tours, double-click** TourName, **double-click** Category, **then click** Next

   With the fields selected for the detailed report, you continue working through the Report Wizard.

2. **Click by Sales (if not already selected), click** Next, **double-click** Category **as a grouping level, click** Next, **click the** first sort list arrow, **click** SaleDate, **click** Next, **accept a Stepped layout and Portrait orientation by clicking** Next, **click** Solstice **for the style, click** Next, **then click** Finish

   The report opens in Print Preview.

3. **Click the** Next Page button ▶ **on the navigation bar to observe the detail records grouped by Category, click the** Close Print Preview button **on the Print Preview tab to switch to Report Design View, then maximize the window**

   You want the Category Summary Revenue report to print as the first page of this report, so you add it as a subreport control to the Report Header.

4. **Click the** Sales label **in the Report Header section, press [Delete], click the** Subform/ Subreport button 🖾 **on the Design tab, click the** left side of the Report Header section, **click the** Category Revenue Summary report **in the SubReport Wizard, click** Next, **click** None **when asked how you want the reports to be linked, click** Next, **then click** Finish **to accept the default label**

   Report Design View now looks like Figure H-13. The Report Header section contains the Category Revenue Summary report, which will now print as the first page of the Sales report.

5. **Click the** View button arrow **on the Design tab, then click** Print Preview

   The report appears in Print Preview, and you notice that the entire value for the first category, "Adventure," isn't completely displayed in the main report. You decide to modify the report to widen the Category text box and to add your name as a label to the Page Footer section.

6. **Click the** Close Print Preview button **on the Print Preview tab, widen the** Category text box **in the Category Header section, click the** Label button 🗚, **click in the** Page Footer section above the =Now() expression, **type your name, then move or resize any controls as needed**

7. **Click the** View button arrow **on the Design tab, click** Print Preview, **then click the** One Page Zoom button **on the Print Preview tab as shown in Figure H-14**

8. **Close Print Preview, then save and close the** Sales **report**

Analyzing Data with Reports

FIGURE H-13: Subreport in Report Design View

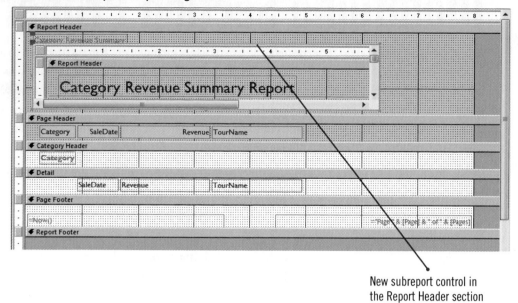

New subreport control in
the Report Header section

FIGURE H-14: Subreport in Print Preview

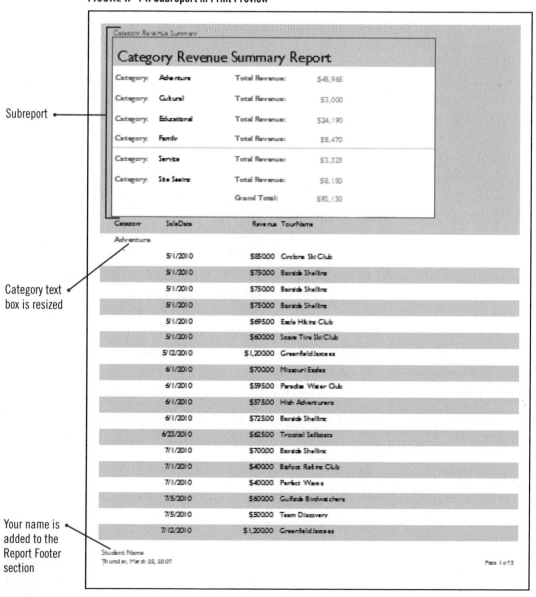

Subreport

Category text
box is resized

Your name is
added to the
Report Footer
section

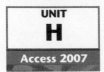
Modifying Section Properties

Report **section properties**, the characteristics that define each section, can be modified to improve report printouts. For example, you might want each new Group Header to print at the top of a new page. Or, you might want to modify section properties to format that section with a background color. ▄▄▄▄▄ Mark Rock asks you to modify the Sales report so that each new category prints at the top of a new page. You also decide to make the detail records more readable by alternating the background color of each row. You make these section property changes in Report Design View.

1. **Right-click the Sales report, click Design View, then maximize the report**

   To force each new category to print at the top of a new page, you modify the Category Header using its property sheet.

2. **Double-click the Category Header bar, click the Format tab, then double-click the Force New Page property to change the value to Before Section**

   The second change you want to make is to modify the back color of alternating rows in the Detail section. You could make this change in the Detail section's property sheet, or use the Alternate Fill/Back Color button ⊞ on the Design tab.

3. **Click the Detail section bar to display the properties for this section in the Property Sheet, click the Alternate Fill/Back Color button arrow ⊞▾, then click the Light Gray 2 box (first column, third row of the Standard Colors palette)**

   Design View for the report now looks like Figure H-15. Note that the **Back Color** and **Alternate Back Color** property are specified with a **hexadecimal** number (numbers that consist of numbers 0-9 as well as letters A-H). If you know that number, you can enter it directly in the Property Sheet. Both the Back Color and Alternate Back Color properties provide a Build button to select or mix a color from a palette of choices.

4. **Click the View button arrow on the Design tab, click Print Preview, click the One Page button on the Print Preview tab, then click the Next Page button ▶ on the navigation bar several times to observe that all categories after the first (Adventure) start printing at the top of a new page**

   Although alternating gray and white as the background colors for the detail records makes them easier to follow across the page, you want to change the background color of the Report Header and Page Header.

5. **Click the Close Print Preview button on the Print Preview tab to switch to Report Design View, click the Page Header section to display the Page Header properties, select #E7DEC9 in the Back Color property, press [Ctrl][C] to copy the hexadecimal number, click the Detail section to display its properties, select #D8D8D8 in the Alternate Back Color property, press [Ctrl][V] to paste #E7DEC9 into this property**

   With the matching alternate back color, you're ready to preview and print the report.

   TROUBLE
   If the alternating color of the Detail section doesn't match the Report and Page Header color, make sure that you modified the Detail section's Alternate Back Color property in Report Design View.

6. **Click the View button arrow on the Design tab, click Print Preview, click the One Page button on the Print Preview tab, click the Last Page button ▶▌ on the navigation bar, click the Print button on the Print Preview tab, click the From box, type 8, click the To box, type 8, then click OK**

   The last page of the Sales report is shown in Figure H-16.

7. **Save the report, then close it**

FIGURE H-15: Specifying section properties in Report Design View

Alternate Fill/Back Color button

Report Selector button

Report Selector button for subform

Detail section bar is selected

Hexadecimal number

Alternate Back Color property

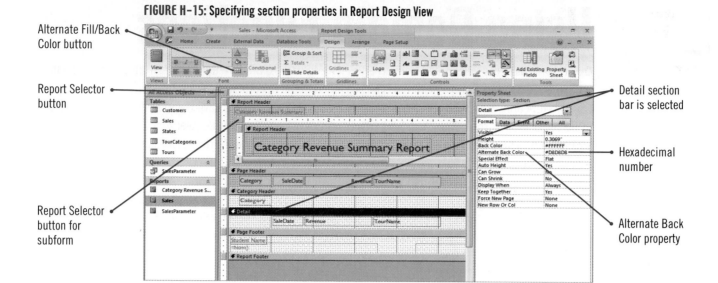

FIGURE H-16: Viewing section properties in Print Preview

Alternate Fill/Back Color of Detail section matches the back color of the Category Header section

Each new category is starting at the top of a new page

Page 8 of 8

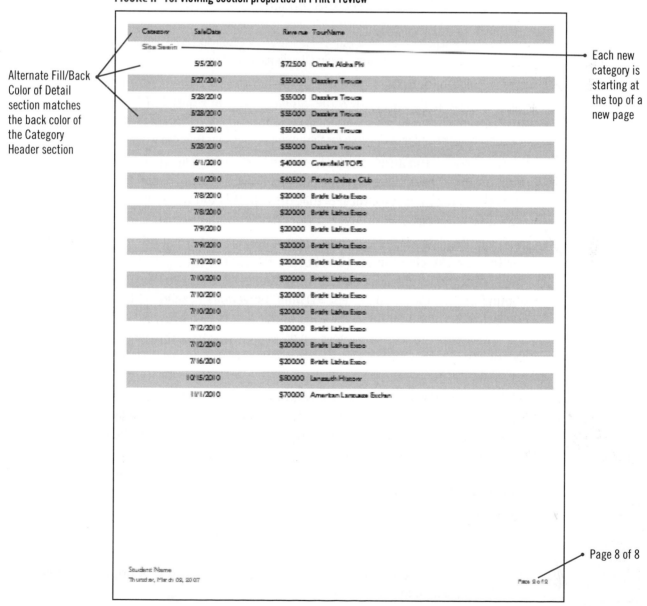

Using Domain Functions

Domain functions, also called domain aggregate functions, are functions that can display a calculation on a form or a report using a field that is not included in the Record Source property for the form or report. Domain functions start with a "D" for "domain" such as DSum, DAvg, DMin, and DMax, and perform the same calculation as their Sum, Avg, Min, Max, and Count counterparts. Regular functions require only one argument, the field that is to be used for the calculation such as =Sum([Price]). Domain functions have two required arguments: the field that is to be used for the calculation and the domain name. The **domain** is the recordset (table or query) that contains the field used in the calculation. A third optional argument allows you to select given records for the calculation based on criteria you specify. 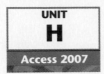 Mark Rock asks you to build a report listing all of the customers and including a subtotal of the money they have spent on Quest tours as recorded by the Revenue field in the Sales table. You decide to create a basic report on the Customers table, and then use a domain function to calculate the maximum revenue value.

STEPS

1. **Click the Customers table in the Navigation Pane, click the Create tab, click the Report button, close the Property Sheet, then maximize the report**

   The report opens in Layout View, which allows you to see data while making changes such as resizing controls. Because the report exceeds the width of a regular sheet of paper, you decide to narrow the fields and switch to landscape orientation before adding the domain function.

2. **For each column, drag the right edge to the left to resize the fields to be as narrow as possible yet wide enough to view the data as shown in Figure H-17**

   With the columns narrowed, you can switch the page orientation to landscape to fit all of the columns on a single sheet of paper and provide room for the revenue calculation you plan to add to the report.

3. **Click the View button arrow on the Format tab, click Print Preview, click the One Page button on the Print Preview tab, click the Landscape button on the Print Preview tab, then click OK if a message indicates that the report is too wide for the paper**

   You can make other formatting changes in Report Design View when you add the revenue calculation.

QUICK TIP
The arguments for domain functions are string expressions, so they must be enclosed in quotation marks.

4. **Close Print Preview, click the View button arrow on the Format tab, click Design View, scroll to the right, click the Text Box button ⎇, click to the right of the FirstContact control, click the label that is created with the new text box, press [Delete], click Unbound in the new text box, type =DSum("[Revenue]", "Sales", "[CustNo] ="&[CustNo]), then drag the right edge of the report to narrow it**

   The expression sums the Revenue field found in the Sales domain (Sales table) for every CustNo in the Sales table that is equal to the CustNo in this report. You are now ready to format the new text box, then preview and print the report.

5. **Click the new text box, click the Property Sheet button on the Design tab, click the Format tab, click the Format property list arrow, click Currency, double-click the Decimal Places property to change it to 0, click the Label button ⎇, click in the Report Footer section, then type your name**

   With the DSum expression and your name as a label in place and the width of the report narrowed, you're ready to preview and print the report for the last time.

6. **Click the View button arrow on the Design tab, click Print Preview, click the One Page button on the Print Preview tab, then print both pages of the report**

   The first page of the printout should look like Figure H-18.

7. **Save the report with the name Customers, close the Customers report, close the Quest-H.accdb database, and exit Access**

FIGURE H-17: Resizing fields in Report Layout View

Each column has been narrowed

Drag right edge of each column to the left

FIGURE H-18: Viewing the DSum function in Print Preview

CustNo	FName	LName	Street	City	State	Zip	Phone	FirstContact	
1	Mitch	Mayberry	52411 Oakmont Rd	Kansas City	Missouri	64144	(555) 444-1234	Friend	$2,075
2	Jill	Alman	2505 McGee St	Des Moines	Iowa	50288	(555) 111-6931	Friend	$1,550
3	Bob	Bouchart	5200 Main St	Kansas City	Missouri	64105	(555) 111-3081	Mail	$2,620
4	Cynthia	Browning	8206 Marshall Dr	Lenexa	Kansas	66214	(555) 222-9101	Mail	$2,900
5	Mary	Braven	600 Elm St	Olathe	Kansas	66031	(555) 222-7002	Friend	$2,000
6	Christine	Collins	520 W 52nd St	Kansas City	Kansas	64105	(555) 222-3602	Radio	$3,750
7	Denise	Camel	66020 King St	Overland Park	Kansas	66210	(555) 222-8402	Internet	$600
8	Gene	Custard	66900 College Rd	Overland Park	Kansas	66210	(555) 222-5102	Radio	$2,705
9	Jan	Cabriella	52520 W. 505 Ter	Lenexa	Kansas	66215	(555) 333-9871	Internet	$1,900
10	Andrea	Eahlie	56 Jackson Rd	Kansas City	Missouri	64145	(555) 333-0401	Mail	$1,650
11	Barbara	Diverman	466 Lincoln Rd	Kansas City	Missouri	64105	(555) 333-0401	Friend	$2,900
12	Sylvia	Dotey	96 Lowell St	Overland Park	Kansas	66210	(555) 444-4404	Internet	$4,750
13	Mary Jane	Duman	525 Ambassador Dr	Kansas City	Missouri	64145	(555) 444-8844	Mail	$3,300
14	Jay	Eckert	903 East 504th St.	Kansas City	Kansas	64131	(555) 444-7414	Radio	$4,795
15	John	Garden	305 W. 99th St	Lenexa	Kansas	66215	(555) 566-4344	Radio	$5,750
16	Lois	Goode	900 Barnes St	West Des Moines	Iowa	50265	(555) 666-1324	Mail	$3,900
17	Mike	Hammer	624 Richmond Ter	Clive	Iowa	50266	(555) 666-0865	Mail	$3,800
18	Jeff	Hopper	4435 Main St	Greenfield	Iowa	50849	(555) 777-8774	Internet	$2,650
19	Holly	Hubert	2345 Grand Blvd	Kansas City	Kansas	64108	(555) 888-6004	Friend	$2,200
20	Traci	Kalvert	7066 College Rd	Overland Park	Kansas	66211	(555) 999-7154	Internet	$1,400
21	Brad	Lang	5253 Duck Creek Dr	Iowa City	Iowa	52240	(555) 999-8777	Friend	$2,250
22	Kristen	Larson	3966 Woodland St	West Des Moines	Iowa	50266	(555) 222-8908	Internet	$2,825

Page 1 of 2

Results of expression using the DSum function for each customer

Practice

If you have a SAM user profile, you may have access to hands-on instruction, practice, and assessment of the skills covered in this unit. Log in to your SAM account (http://sam2007.course.com/) to launch any assigned training activities or exams that relate to the skills covered in this unit.

▼ CONCEPTS REVIEW

Identify each element of the Report Design View shown in Figure H-19.

FIGURE H-19

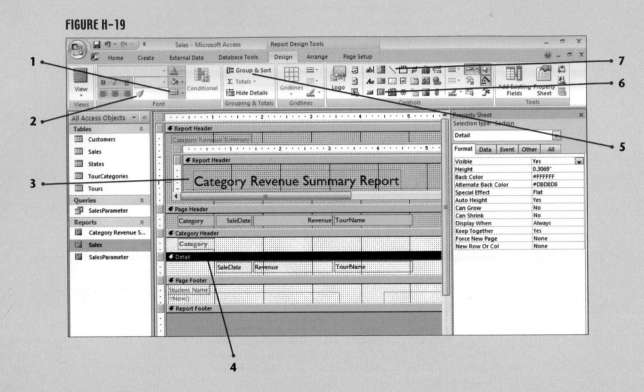

Match each term with the statement that best describes its function.

8. **Summary reports**
9. **Parameter report**
10. **Conditional formatting**
11. **Format Painter**
12. **Domain**

a. Prompts the user for the criteria by which the records for the report are selected
b. A way to change the appearance of a control on a form or report based on criteria you specify
c. Used to show statistics on groups of records
d. The recordset (table or query) that contains the field used in the calculation
e. Used to copy multiple formatting properties from one control to another in Report Design View

Select the best answer from the list of choices.

13. **Which control would you use to visually separate groups of records on a report?**
   a. Option group
   b. Image
   c. Bound Object Frame
   d. Line
14. **Which of the following is *not* a Detail section property?**
   a. Alternate Back Color
   b. Force New Page
   c. Display When
   d. Calculate

15. What feature allows you to apply the formatting characteristics of one control to another?
- **a.** AutoContent Wizard
- **b.** AutoFormat
- **c.** Report Layout Wizard
- **d.** Format Painter

16. Which key do you press when creating a line to make it perfectly horizontal?
- **a.** [Shift]
- **b.** [Alt]
- **c.** [Ctrl]
- **d.** [Home]

17. If you want to apply the same formatting characteristics to several controls at once, you might consider _____ them.
- **a.** AutoFormatting
- **b.** AutoPainting
- **c.** Grouping
- **d.** Exporting

18. In a report, an expression used to calculate values is entered in which type of control?
- **a.** Text Box
- **b.** Label
- **c.** Combo Box
- **d.** Command Button

19. The Page Header/Footer and Report Header/Footer buttons are found on which tab of the Ribbon?
- **a.** Home
- **b.** Create
- **c.** Design
- **d.** Arrange

20. What button allows you to change the appearance of a control in every other record on the report?
- **a.** Font Color
- **b.** Alternate Fill/Back Color
- **c.** Conditional
- **d.** Group & Sort

▼ SKILLS REVIEW

1. Create summary reports.
- **a.** Open the **RealEstate-H.accdb** database from the drive and folder where you store your Data Files and enable content if prompted.
- **b.** Create a new report in Report Design View. Include the AgencyName from the Agencies table and the Asking field from the Listings table in the Record Source property. (*Hint*: Include the Agents table in the query builder as well to properly link the Agents table to the Listings table.)
- **c.** Add AgencyName as a grouping field, then add the AgencyName field to the AgencyName Header section.
- **d.** Add a text box to the right side of the AgencyName Header section and enter the following expression into the text box: **=Sum([Asking])**
- **e.** Modify the label to read **Subtotal of Asking Price:**
- **f.** Move, resize, and align the tops of all controls in the AgencyName Header section so that they are clearly visible.
- **g.** Apply a Currency format and change the Decimal Places property to **0** for the new text box that contains the expression.
- **h.** Completely close the Detail section.
- **i.** Add a label to the Page Header section that reads **Subtotal of Asking Prices by Agency.**
- **j.** Add a label to the Page Footer section with your name. Preview the report. Continue to modify, resize, and move controls as needed in order to see all data.
- **k.** Save the report with the name **Asking Price Summary Report**, then close it.

2. Create parameter reports.
- **a.** Create a query in Query Design View, including the AgentFirst, AgentLast, and AgentPhone fields from the Agents table. Include the Type, Area, SqFt, and Asking field from the Listings table.
- **b.** In the Asking field, include the following parameter criteria: **<[Enter maximum asking price]**
- **c.** Save the query as **AskingParameter**, then close it.
- **d.** Click the AskingParameter query in the Navigation Pane, then click Report on the Create tab. Enter **200000** in the Enter maximum asking price box, then click OK.
- **e.** Work in Layout View to narrow each column to be only as wide as necessary.
- **f.** In Report Design View add a label with your name to the Report Header section and make sure the report is no wider than 8 inches.
- **g.** Preview the report again, entering **200000** in the prompt, then print it.
- **h.** Save the report with the name **AskingParameter**, then close it.

3. Apply conditional formatting.

   a. Open the AskingParameter report in Report Design View, then add a calculated field to the right of the Asking text box with the expression =[Asking]/[SqFt]. Delete the label associated with the new text box. Format the new calculation with a Currency format and 0 for the Decimal Places property.

   b. Add a label to the Page Header section above the new calculation with the caption Cost per Sq Ft.

   c. Move, resize, and align controls as necessary to keep the report within the 8-inch mark of the ruler.

   d. Conditionally format the new calculated text box so that values less than or equal to 50 are formatted with bold, green text, and values greater than or equal to 100 are formatted with bold, red text.

   e. Test the report in Print Preview, entering a value of 150000 when prompted.

4. Add lines.

   a. Open the AskingParameter report in Design View, then use the Group, Sort, and Total pane to add a sort order. Order the fields in descending (largest to smallest) order on the Asking field.

   b. Add a text box to the Report Footer section directly below the Asking text box in the Detail section with the expression =Sum([Asking]).

   c. Modify the label to read Grand Total:.

   d. Draw one short horizontal line just above the =Sum([Asking]) calculation, then copy and paste it twice and move the second and third copy of the short lines below the =Sum([Asking]) calculation to indicate a grand total.

   e. Modify the Asking text box and the =Sum([Asking]) text box to be formatted with a Currency format and Decimal Places property of 0.

   f. Save the report, then preview the changes using a value of 125000 when prompted. Move, resize, and align any controls as needed to improve the report.

5. Use the Format Painter and AutoFormats.

   a. Open the AskingParameter Report in Layout View using a value of 175000 when prompted.

   b. Change the AskingParameter label to Asking Price Analysis.

   c. Click the AutoFormat arrow button, then click the Foundry option (first column, third row). If labels overlap in the Report Header section, reduce the font size of the label with your name so that all labels are clearly visible.

   d. Use the Format Painter to copy the format from the Asking text box in the Detail section to the =Sum([Asking]) text box and label in the Report Footer section.

   e. Move, resize, and align the text boxes and label as needed to improve the report.

   f. Save the report, then preview the changes. Return to Design View and change the color of the three lines in the Report Footer section to black using the Line Color button on the Design tab.

6. Add subreports.

   a. Expand the vertical size of the Report Header section so it is about 2 inches in vertical height.

   b. Insert the Asking Price Summary Report as a subreport using the SubReport Wizard. Specify None for the link between the main report and subreport, and accept the default name Asking Price Summary Report for the subreport.

   c. Save and preview the report using 225000 when prompted. Return to Report Design View, and resize and move the subreport control as needed to clearly see all of the data.

7. Modify section properties.

   a. In Report Design View of the Asking Price Analysis report, modify the Detail section so that alternating rows have a Light Gray 1 shade.

   b. Save and preview the report using 275000 when prompted. The top of the first page of the final report is shown in Figure H-20. Your fonts and colors might be slightly different depending on how Access 2007 was installed on your computer.

   c. Print the Asking Price Analysis report, then close it.

8. Use domain functions.

   a. Create a new table named StandardText with two new fields: Disclaimer, with a Memo data type, and DisclaimerID, with an AutoNumber data type. The DisclaimerID field should be set as the primary key field.

b. Add one record to the table with the following entry in the Disclaimer field:

The realtor makes no warranty or representation with respect to the accuracy of the listing.

c. Close the StandardText table.

d. Create a new report in Report Design view, and specify StandardText in the Record Source property for the report. Open the Report Footer section, then enter the following expression in a new text box in the Report Footer section:
=DLookup("[Disclaimer]", "StandardText","[DisclaimerID] ="&1)

e. Delete the label associated with the new text box, then resize the text box so it is 6.25 inches wide.

FIGURE H-20

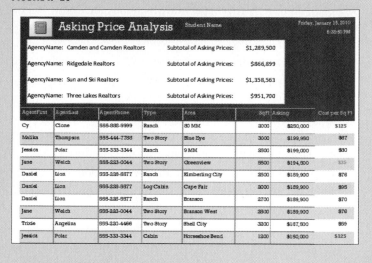

f. Add your name to the Report Header section, close the Detail section, save the report with the name StandardReport, then print and close the report. In the future, you could use a domain function in this way to add standard disclaimers to various reports.

g. Close the RealEstate-H.accdb database, and exit Access.

▼ INDEPENDENT CHALLENGE 1

As the manager of a music store's instrument rental program, you created a database to track instrument rentals to schoolchildren. Now that several instruments have been purchased, you need to create a report listing the rental transactions for each instrument.

a. Start Access, open the database MusicRentals-H.accdb from the drive and folder where you store your Data Files, and enable content if needed.

b. Use the Report Wizard to create a report based on the FirstName and LastName fields in the Customers table, the RentalDate field from the Rentals table, and the Description and MonthlyFee fields from the Instruments table.

c. View the data by Instruments, do not add any more grouping levels, sort the data in ascending order by RentalDate, use a Block layout and Portrait orientation, use an Urban style, and title the report Instrument Rental Report.

d. Open the report in Design View, then change the first grouping level from SerialNo to Description, and open the Description Footer section.

e. Enter the expression =Count([MonthlyFee]) to a new, unbound control in the text box in the Description Footer section and change the label to Times Rented:

f. Add your name as a label to the Report Header section.

g. Save and preview the report as shown in Figure H-21. (Your colors and fonts might look slightly different.)

h. Move, resize, and align controls as needed, then print the report.

i. Save and close the Instrument Rental Report, close the MusicRentals-H.accdb database, then exit Access.

FIGURE H-21

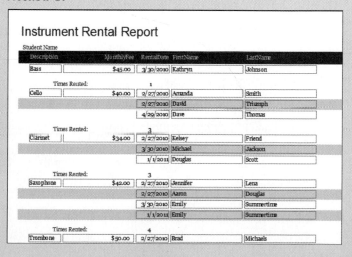

▼ INDEPENDENT CHALLENGE 2

As the manager of a music store's instrument rental program, you have created a database to track instrument rentals to schoolchildren. Now that the rental program is underway, you need to create a summary report that shows how many instruments have been rented by each school.

a. Start Access, open the database **InstrumentRentals-H.accdb** from the drive and folder where you store your Data Files, and enable content if needed.

b. Use Report Design View to create a summary report. Use the Record Source property to add the SchoolName field from the Schools table and the RentalDate field from the Rentals table to the query. (*Hint*: Include the Customers table to build the proper relationships between the Schools and the Rentals table.)

c. Close the Query Builder window and save the changes.

d. Add SchoolName as a grouping field, and add the SchoolName field to the left side of the SchoolName Header section.

e. Add a text box with the following expression to the right side of the SchoolName Header section:
   =Count([RentalDate]).

f. Modify the caption of the new label to read **Number of rentals for this school:**.

g. Move, resize, and align the controls in the SchoolName Header section so that all controls are clearly visible, and completely close the Detail section.

h. Preview the report and continue to modify the controls in the SchoolName Header section as necessary.

i. Add a label to the Page Header section with your name.

j. Save the report with the name **School Summary Report**.

k. Apply a Trek AutoFormat as shown in Figure H-22. (Your colors and fonts might look slightly different.)

l. Print then close the School Summary Report, close the InstrumentRentals-H.accdb database, then exit Access.

FIGURE H-22

Student Name			
SchoolName:	CPA Elementary	Number of rentals for this school:	2
SchoolName:	Lincoln Elementary	Number of rentals for this school:	4
SchoolName:	Naish Middle School	Number of rentals for this school:	3
SchoolName:	South High School	Number of rentals for this school:	3
SchoolName:	Thomas Jefferson Elementary	Number of rentals for this school:	6

▼ INDEPENDENT CHALLENGE 3

As the manager of an equipment rental program, you have created a database to track rentals. You need to build a parameter report for this database.

a. Start Access, open the database **Equipment-H.accdb** from the drive and folder where you store your Data Files, and enable content if prompted.

b. Create a query with the RentalDate field from the Rentals table; the Description, DailyRate, WeeklyRate, Deposit, and Condition fields from the Equipment table; and the FirstName and LastName fields from the Customers table.

c. Enter the parameter criteria **Between [Enter start date] And [Enter end date]** for the RentalDate field.

d. Save the query with the name **RentalParameter** and close it.

e. Use the Report Wizard to create a report on all fields in the RentalParameter query. View the data by Equipment, do not add any more grouping or sorting levels, and use an Outline layout and a Landscape orientation. Use a Flow style. Title the report **Equipment Rental Report**.

f. To respond to the prompts, enter **3/1/10** for the start date and **3/31/10** for the end date.

g. Change the text color to black for all controls in the Description Header section except for the RentalDate, FirstName, and LastName labels.

h. Add your name as a label to the Report Header section. Format it with a color and size so that it is clearly visible.

▼ INDEPENDENT CHALLENGE 3 (CONTINUED)

Advanced Challenge Exercise

- Add spaces between all words in the labels in the Description Header section so that, for example, DailyRate becomes Daily Rate. Be careful to add spaces to the *label* controls and not the *text box* controls.
- Modify the Record Source property so that the records are sorted in ascending order on the Description field.
- Move and resize controls so they are within an 8-inch width and improve the report's appearance, then change the page orientation to portrait.
- Close up any extra space in the Report Header and Description Header sections.

FIGURE H-23

i. Display the report for RentalDates 3/1/10 through 3/31/10, then print it. If you completed all of the Advanced Challenge Exercise steps, your printout should look similar to Figure H-23. (Your background colors and fonts might look slightly different.)

j. Save and print the Equipment Rental Report, close the Equipment-H.accdb database, then exit Access.

▼ REAL LIFE INDEPENDENT CHALLENGE

One way to use Access in your real life is in a community service project. People in schools and nonprofit agencies often inherit databases created by others and need help extracting information from them. Suppose you're working with the local high school guidance counselor to help her with an Access database she inherited that is used to record college scholarship opportunities. You can help her analyze scholarships by building a report with conditional formatting.

a. Start Access and open the Scholarships-H.accdb database from the drive and folder where you store your Data Files. Enable content if necessary.

b. Use the Report Wizard to create a report based on the Scholarships table. Include all of the fields. Add Amount as the grouping level, then click the Grouping Options button in the Report Wizard. Choose 10000s (ten thousands) as the Grouping interval. Sort the records by DueDate in a descending order. Use a Stepped layout and a Landscape orientation. Use a None style, and title the report Scholarship Listing.

c. Preview the report, then add your name as a label next to the report title.

d. In Report Layout View, narrow most of the text boxes in the Detail section so that you can widen the Description field on the right side of the report and give the field as much room as possible.

e. Center the values in the ID and Amount fields.

Advanced Challenge Exercises

- In Report Design View, click the Report Selector button, then use the Record Source property and Query Builder to select all of the fields in the Scholarships table. Enter the following parameter criteria in the DueDate field: Between [Enter start date] and [Enter end date].
- Close and save the Query Builder.
- Apply the Equity AutoFormat to the report.

FIGURE H-24

f. Preview the report using 1/1/10 and 1/31/10 dates, then print it. If you completed all of the Advanced Challenge Exercises, the report should look like Figure H-24. (Your background colors and fonts might look slightly different.) Close the report and the Scholarships-H.accdb database.

▼ VISUAL WORKSHOP

Open the Training-H.accdb database from the drive and folder where you store your Data Files. Enable content if necessary. Use the Report Wizard to create the report shown in Figure H-25. Select the First, Last, and Location fields from the Employees table and the Description and Hours fields from the Courses table. View the data by Employees, do not add any more grouping levels, sort in ascending order by Description, and use the Summary Options to sum the hours. Use the Stepped, Portrait, and Module style options. Title the report **Employee Education Report**. In Report Design View, enter your name as a label in the Report Header section in a font and color that is easily visible. Use Layout View to widen text boxes to display all values clearly. In Report Design View, delete the long calculated field and the Sum label in the SSN Footer section, and add conditional formatting so that the =Sum([Hours]) field appears in bold with a bright yellow background if the value is greater than or equal to 100. (*Hint*: The =Sum([Hours]) calculation is in a text box on the right side of the SSN Footer and Report Footer sections, but they may not be visible depending on how the text boxes are currently sized. Click the ruler to the left of the SSN Footer section or the left of the Report Footer section to find and select small controls.) Add a black, horizontal subtotal line above the =Sum([Hours]) field in the SSN Footer section, and add two lines to indicate a grand total below the =Sum([Hours]) field in the Report Footer section. Make other changes as necessary so that the first page of your report looks like Figure H-25. (Your background colors and fonts might look slightly different.)

FIGURE H-25

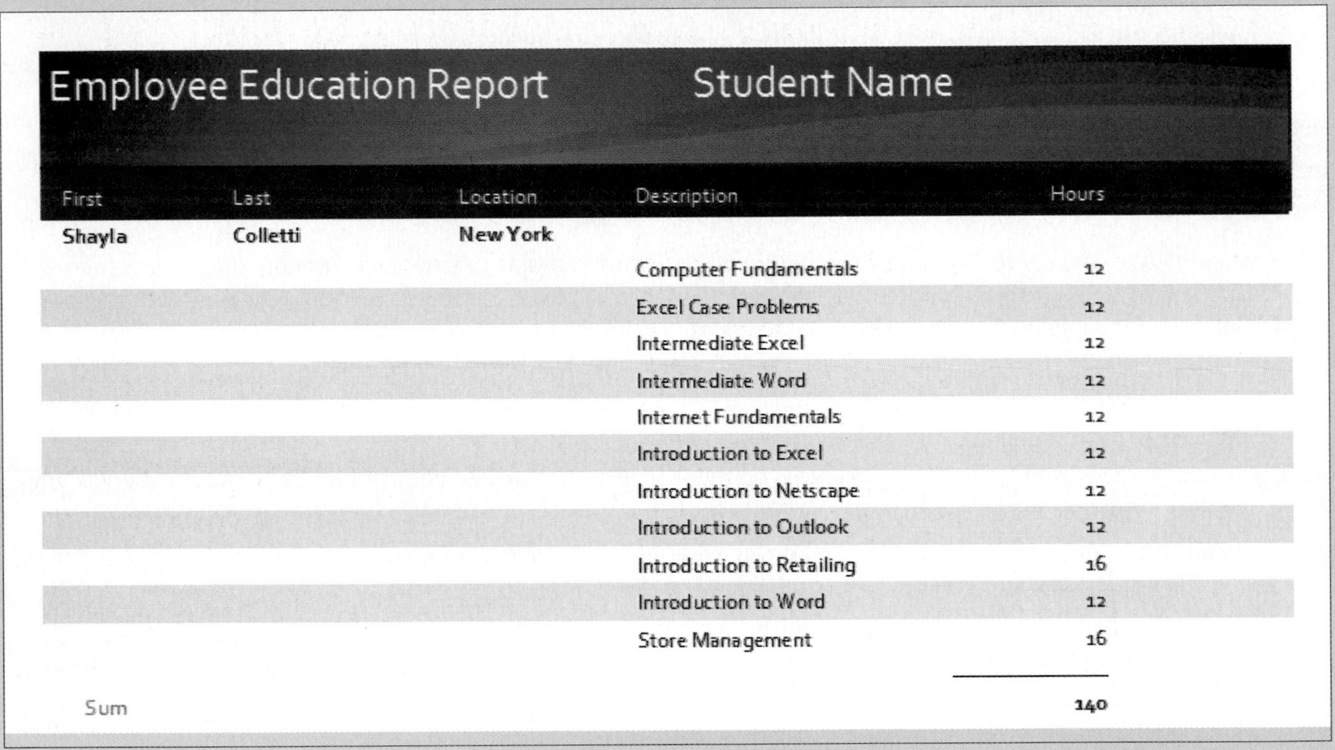

First	Last	Location	Description	Hours
Shayla	Colletti	New York		
			Computer Fundamentals	12
			Excel Case Problems	12
			Intermediate Excel	12
			Intermediate Word	12
			Internet Fundamentals	12
			Introduction to Excel	12
			Introduction to Netscape	12
			Introduction to Outlook	12
			Introduction to Retailing	16
			Introduction to Word	12
			Store Management	16
Sum				140

Employee Education Report — Student Name

Importing and Exporting Data

Files You Will Need

Education-I.accdb

DepartmentData.xlsx

CourseMaterials.xlsx

Machinery-I.accdb

MachineryEmployees.
xlsx

Vendors.xlsx

Basketball-I.accdb

Languages-I.accdb

Access can share data with many other Microsoft Office programs. This capability is important because you may want to use data stored in one type of Microsoft Office file in another Office program. For example, you might want to use Excel's "what-if" analysis and charting features to analyze and chart data that is currently stored in an Access database. Or, you may want to merge records selected by an Access query into a Word document to create a mass mailing. Fortunately, Microsoft provides many tools to share data between Microsoft Office programs. At Quest Specialty Travel, you have been asked to develop an Access database that tracks professional staff continuing education for Julia Rice, director of staff development. You need to share Access data with other software programs so that each Quest department can have the necessary data in a format they can use.

OBJECTIVES

Use database templates

Use table templates

Import data from Excel

Link data

Export data to Excel

Analyze data with Excel

Publish data to Word

Merge data with Word

Using Database Templates

A **database template** is a tool that can be used to quickly create a new database based on a particular subject such as assets, contacts, events, or projects. When you install Access 2007 on your computer, Microsoft provides many database templates for you to use. Additional templates are available from Microsoft Office Online, where they are organized by category such as business, personal, and education. 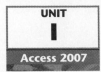 Julia Rice, director of staff development, asks you to develop a new Access database to track the continuing education of Quest employees. You use a database template to help you get started.

STEPS

1. **Start Access, and on the Getting Started with Microsoft Office Access page, click** Local Templates **in the Template Categories list**

   As shown in Figure I-1, **local templates** are stored on your hard drive, whereas **online templates** are available to download from the Microsoft Office Online Web site. The database you want to create should track employees and the continuing education courses they have completed. You start by using the Students template.

2. **Click** Students, **click the** Browse icon [icon]**, navigate to the drive and folder where you store your Data Files, click** OK, **then click** Create

   The template builds a new database named Students that includes several tables, queries, forms, and reports. You can use or modify these objects to meet your needs. To better understand all that the template has created, you decide to review the objects of the new Students database.

3. **If the Security Warning appears, click the** Options button, **click** Enable this content, **click** OK, **then click the** Shutter Bar Open/Close button [icon] **to expand the Navigation Pane as shown in Figure I-2**

   The objects in the database are presented as shortcuts in the Navigation Pane; they are organized in three groups: Students, Guardians, and Supporting Objects. A **group** in the Navigation Pane is a custom category that organizes the objects that belong to that category. **Shortcuts** are pointers to the actual object and are identified as shortcuts by the small black arrow in the lower-left corner. You double-click a shortcut icon to open that object.

4. **Double-click the** Student Details form shortcut **in the Navigation Pane to open the form**

   Objects created by database templates are rich in functionality and can be modified or analyzed to learn more about Access. For now, however, you want to view all of the objects in the Navigation Pane that the Students template created.

5. **Close the** Student Details form, **click the** Students Navigation list arrow [icon]**, then click** Object Type

   The 15 objects that were created by the Students template (two tables, two queries, three forms, and eight reports) are now listed in the Navigation Pane by object type.

FIGURE I-1: Local Templates

Local Templates link

Online template categories

Local Templates

Students template

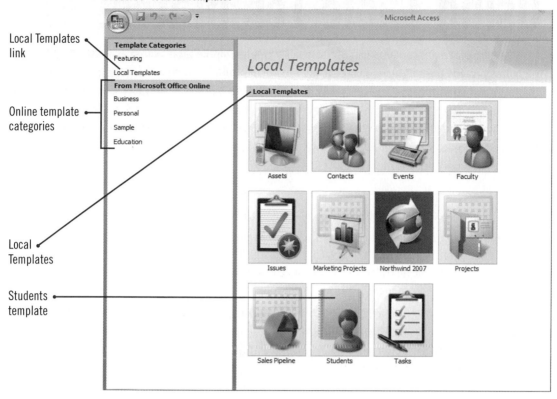

FIGURE I-2: Using the Navigation Pane

Shutter Bar Open/Close button

Students group

Student Details form shortcut

Guardians group

Report shortcut

Table shortcut

Query shortcut

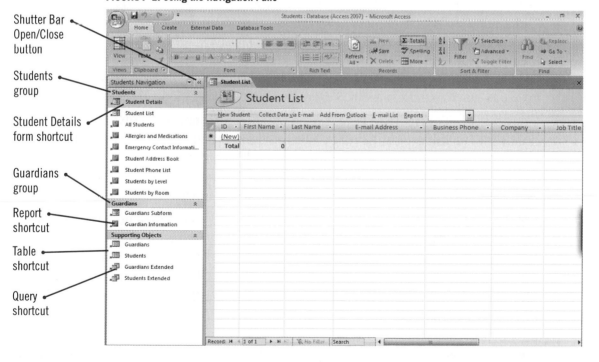

Access 2007

Using Table Templates

A **table template** is a tool you can use to quickly create a single table within an existing database. Table templates provide a set of fields that describe a particular subject, such as contacts or tasks, which can be used or modified to meet your needs. 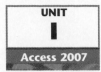 In addition to information about students, the database you create for Julia Rice to track professional development courses at Quest must include data on the courses taken. Many of the fields you want to track, such as course title, location, and description, are similar to the fields needed to describe an event. Therefore, you decide to use the Events table template to add this new table to the Students database.

STEPS

1. **Click the Create tab, click the Table Templates button, then click Events**

   Access creates a new table named Table1 from the Events template. The new table already contains several fields that describe an event: ID, Title, Start Time, End Time, Location, Description, and Attachments field. You can use the same fields for the Courses table you are creating, with a couple of minor modifications. Use Table Design View to change the fields to meet your needs.

2. **Click the Home tab, click the Design View button, type Courses, then click OK**

   The Courses table opens in Table Design View. Instead of tracking the start and end times of an event, you want to track the date and hours of the course taken. You can modify the Start Time and End Time fields to meet this need.

3. **Select the Start Time field name, type CourseDate, select the End Time field name, type Hours, press [Tab], type n to select the Number data type, then press [Tab]**

   One more consideration for the Courses table is how it should participate in the relational database. One student can take many courses, so the Courses table needs a foreign key field to connect it in a one-to-many relationship with the Students table. The primary key field of the Students table is also an AutoNumber field named ID. To create a foreign key field in the Courses table that connects to an AutoNumber field in a one-to-many relationship, you use the Number data type.

4. **Click the blank Field Name cell below the Attachments field, type StudentIDFK (for student ID foreign key) as the field name, press [Tab], click the Data Type list arrow, then click Number**

   The updated Courses table should look like Figure I-3. With the tables and linking fields in place, you need to close all open objects to connect the Students and Courses tables in the Relationships window.

5. **Right-click the Courses tab, click Close on the shortcut menu, click Yes to save changes, right-click the Student List tab, click Close on the shortcut menu, click the Database Tools tab on the Ribbon, then click the Relationships button**

   Currently, the Relationships window displays only two tables: the Students table and the Guardians table. The database template created both tables and the relationship between them.

QUICK TIP

Expanding a field list to show all of its fields removes the scroll bars from the field list window.

6. **Click the Show Table button, double-click Courses, click Close, then drag the bottom edge of the field lists down to display as many fields in each table as possible**

   After adding the Courses table field list to the Relationships window and expanding the field lists, you're ready to connect the Courses table to the Students table so that it can participate in the relational database.

7. **Drag the ID field from the Students table to the StudentIDFK field of the Courses table, click the Enforce Referential Integrity check box in the Edit Relationships dialog box, then click Create**

   The screen should look like Figure I-4. Currently, the Students table participates in two one-to-many relationships. One student can be linked to many records in the Guardians table, and one student can be linked to many records in the Courses table.

8. **Close the Relationships window, click Yes to save changes, then close the Students.accdb database and Access**

Importing and Exporting Data

FIGURE I-3: Design View of updated Courses table

CourseDate field

Hours field with Number data type

StudentIDFK field with Number data type

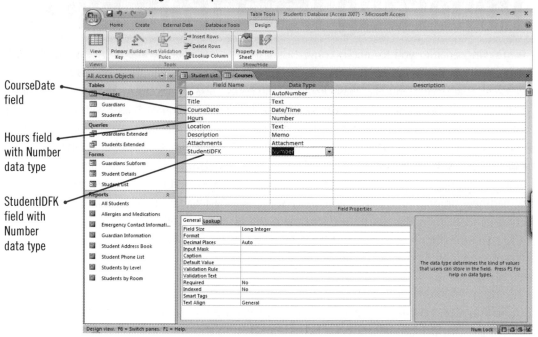

FIGURE I-4: Creating a relationship between Students and Courses

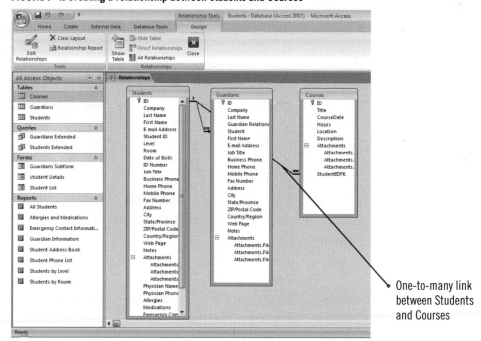

One-to-many link between Students and Courses

Referential integrity cascade options

When connecting tables in one-to-many relationships, apply referential integrity whenever possible. This feature prevents orphan records from being created in the database and also provides access to the cascade options. **Cascade Update Related Fields** means that if a value in the primary key field (the field on the "one" side of a one-to-many relationship) is modified, all values in the foreign key field (the field on the "many" side of a one-to-many relationship) are automatically updated as well. **Cascade Delete Related Records** means that if a record in the "one" side of a one-to-many relationship is deleted, all related records in the "many" table are also deleted. Because both of these options automatically change or delete data in the "many" table behind the scenes, they should be used carefully. Often these features are not employed as standard options, but are used temporarily to correct a problem in the database.

Importing Data from Excel

Importing enables you to quickly convert data from an external file into an Access database. You can import data from one Access database to another—or from many other data sources such as files created by Excel, SharePoint, Outlook, dBase, Paradox, and Lotus 1-2-3 or text files in an HTML, XML, or delimited text file format. A **delimited text file** typically stores one record on each line, with the field values separated by a common character such as a comma, tab, or dash. A delimited text file might be called a **CSV (comma-separated values)** file. An **XML file** is a text file that contains **Extensible Markup Language (XML)** tags that identify field names and data. However, the most common file format from which to import data to an Access database is probably a Microsoft Office Excel spreadsheet. **Excel** is the spreadsheet program in the Microsoft Office suite. 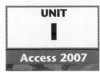 Julia Rice gives you an Excel spreadsheet that contains supplemental materials used for various courses such as study guides and assessment quizzes. She asks if you can import and then use the information in the new database to track continuing education.

STEPS

1. **Open the Education-I.accdb database from the drive and folder where you store your Data Files, enable content if prompted, click the External Data tab, click the Excel button in the Import group, click the Browse button in the Get External Data – Excel Spreadsheet dialog box, navigate to the drive and folder where you store your Data Files, double-click CourseMaterials.xlsx, then click OK**

   The Import Spreadsheet Wizard dialog box opens, as shown in Figure I-5.

2. **Click Next, click the First Row Contains Column Headings check box, click Next, click Next to accept the default field options, click Next to allow Access to add a primary key field, type Materials in the Import to Table box, click Finish, then click Close**

   The information in the CourseMaterials.xls Excel spreadsheet is imported into the Education-I database as the table named Materials. You review the records in the Materials table, then link it up to the Courses table in a one-to-many relationship. One course record can be related to many records in the Materials table.

   You can quickly repeat the import process by saving the import steps when prompted by the last dialog box in the Import Wizard. Run the saved import process using the **Saved Imports** button on the External Data tab or by running an Outlook task.

   QUICK TIP
   You can also copy and paste data from Excel to Access.

3. **Double-click the Materials table to view the datasheet containing four fields and 45 records, right-click the Materials tab, then click Design View to view the data types for the four fields**

   Note that the ID field is the primary key field for this table. CourseID serves as the foreign key field to link this table to the Courses table.

4. **Type MaterialID to replace the ID field name, right-click the Materials tab, click Close, then click Yes to save the changes**

   Now that you've examined the data and structure of the Materials table, you're ready to link it in a one-to-many relationship with the Courses table.

5. **Click the Database Tools tab, click the Relationships button, click the Show Table button, double-click Materials, click Close, drag the CourseID field in the Courses table to the CourseID field in the Materials table, click the Enforce Referential Integrity check box, then click Create**

   The final Relationships window should look similar to Figure I-6. One employee record is related to many enrollments. One course record is related to many enrollments and to many materials.

6. **Click the Close button, then click Yes to save the changes to the database relationships**

FIGURE I-5: Import Spreadsheet Wizard

External Data tab

Excel button

Import group

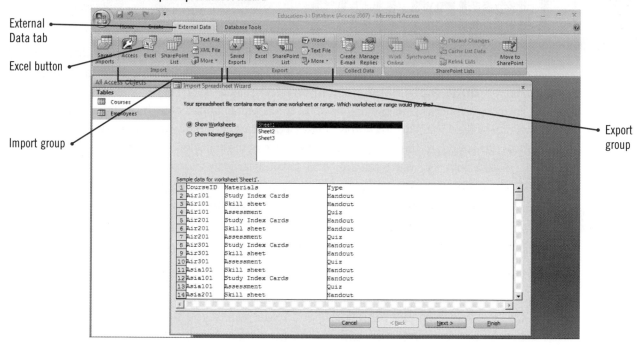

Export group

FIGURE I-6: Relationships window with imported Materials table

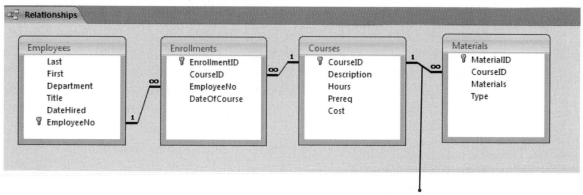

One-to-many relationship between the Courses and Materials tables with referential integrity enforced

Linking Data

Linking connects an Access database to data in an external file such as another Access, dBase, or Paradox database; an Excel or Lotus 1-2-3 spreadsheet; a text file; an HTML file; an XML file; or other data sources that support **ODBC (open database connectivity)** standards. Linking is different from importing in that linked data is not copied into the database as it is with imported data. If you link, data is only stored in the original file. Importing, in contrast, makes a duplicate copy of the data as a new table in the Access database, so changes to either the original data source or the imported Access copy have no effect on the other. 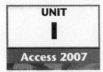 Julia Rice has created a small spreadsheet with information about the departments at Quest. She wants to use the information in the Education-I database while maintaining it in Excel. She asks you to help create a link to this Excel file from the Education-I database.

STEPS

1. **Click the External Data tab, then click the Excel button in the Import group**
   The Get External Data-Excel Spreadsheet dialog box opens, as shown in Figure I-7. This dialog box allows you to choose whether you want to import (default), append, or link to the data source.

2. **Click Browse, navigate to the drive and folder where you store your Data Files, double-click DepartmentData.xlsx, click Link to the data source by creating a linked table, click OK, click Next to accept the default range selection, click Next to accept the default column headings, type DepartmentData as the linked table name, click Finish, then click OK**
   The Link Spreadsheet Wizard guides you through the process of linking to a spreadsheet. The linked DepartmentData table appears in the Navigation Pane with a linking Excel icon, as shown in Figure I-8. Like any other table, in order for the linked table to function with the rest of a database, a one-to-many relationship between it and another table should be created.

3. **Click the Database Tools tab, click the Relationships button, click the Show Table button, double-click DepartmentData, then click Close**
   The Department field in the DepartmentData table creates the one-to-many relationship with the Department field in the Employees table

4. **Drag the Department field in the DepartmentData table to the Department field in the Employees table, then click Create in the Edit Relationships dialog box**
   Your Relationships window should look like Figure I-9. A one-to-many relationship is established between the DepartmentData and Employees tables, but because referential integrity is not enforced, the one and many symbols do not appear on the link line. You cannot establish referential integrity when one of the tables is a linked table, but now that the linked DepartmentData table is related to the rest of the database, it can participate in queries, forms, pages, and reports that use fields from multiple tables.

5. **Click the Close button, then click Yes when prompted to save changes**
   You work with a linked table in a query just as you work with any other table. The data in a linked table can be edited through either the source program (in this case, Excel) or in the Access database, even though the data is only physically stored in the original source file.

6. **Click the Create tab, click the Query Design button in the Other group, double-click Employees, double-click Department Data, then click Close**
   The relationships you established in the Relationships window appear in the upper portion of the Query Design window. You want fields from both tables in the query.

7. **Double-click Last, First, and Department in the Employees field list, double-click Office and Extension in the DepartmentData field list, then click the Datasheet View button**
   Data from both the Employees and DepartmentData tables are presented in the same query datasheet.

8. **Click the Save button 🖫 on the Quick Access toolbar, type DepartmentListing as the query name, click OK, then close the query window**

FIGURE I-7: Get External Data—Excel Spreadsheet dialog box

Your path
might
differ

Import

Append

Link

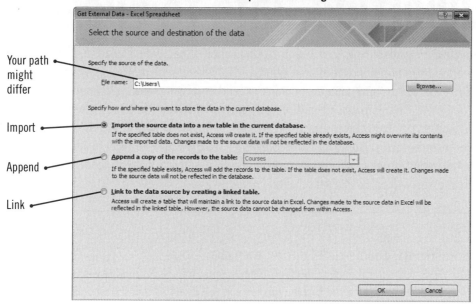

FIGURE I-8: DepartmentData table is linked from Excel

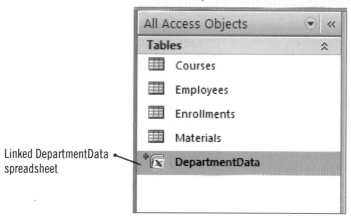

Linked DepartmentData
spreadsheet

FIGURE I-9: Relationships window with linked DepartmentData table

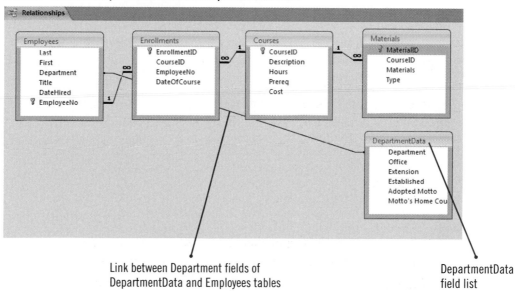

Link between Department fields of
DepartmentData and Employees tables

DepartmentData
field list

Exporting Data to Excel

Exporting is a way to copy Access information to another database, spreadsheet, or file format. Exporting is the opposite of importing. You can export data from an Access database to other file types, such as those used by Excel, Lotus 1-2-3, dBase, and Paradox, and in several general file formats including HTML, XML, and various text file formats. Given the popularity of analyzing numeric data in Excel, it is common to export Access data to an Excel spreadsheet for further analysis. 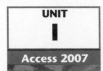 The Finance Department asks you to export some Access data to an Excel spreadsheet so they can use Excel to analyze how increases in the cost of the courses would affect departments. You can gather the fields needed in an Access query, then export the query to an Excel spreadsheet.

STEPS

1. **Click the Create tab, click the Query Design button, double-click Employees, double-click Enrollments, double-click Courses, then click Close**

   The fields you want to export to Excel—Department and Cost—are in the Employees and Courses tables. You also need to include the Enrollments table in this query so that the records in the Employees table are linked correctly to the records in the Courses table.

2. **Double-click Department in the Employees field list, double-click Cost in the Courses field list, click the Sort cell for the Department field, click the Sort cell list arrow, click Ascending, then click the Datasheet View button to display the query datasheet**

   The resulting datasheet is shown in Figure I-10. You can now save the query with a meaningful name.

3. **Click the Save button 🔲 on the Quick Access toolbar, type DepartmentCosts, then click OK**

   Close the DepartmentCosts query so that you can export it to Excel.

QUICK TIP

If you export the same data on a regular basis, you can save the export steps to help automate the export process.

4. **Click the DepartmentCosts query in the Navigation Pane (if it is not already selected), click the External Data tab, click the Excel button in the Export section, click Browse, navigate to the drive and folder where you store your Data Files, click Save, click OK, then click Close**

   The data in the DepartmentCosts query has now been exported to an Excel spreadsheet file. Other file formats that Access can import from and export to are listed in Table I-1. You can save and then repeat the export process by saving the export steps when prompted by the last dialog box in the Export Wizard. Run the saved export process using the **Saved Exports** button on the External Data tab or by running an Outlook task.

FIGURE I-10: New query selects fields to be exported

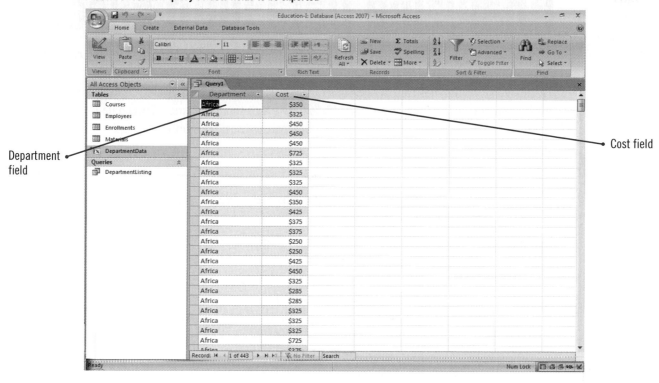

Department field

Cost field

TABLE I-1: File formats that Access can link, import, and export

file format	allows you to:
Access	Link one Access table to another database and import or export any Access object (tables, queries, forms, reports, macros, modules) to another Access database
Excel	Link, import, and export Excel spreadsheets with an Access database
SharePoint Site	Link, import, and export SharePoint Site lists with an Access database
Text file	Link, import, and export structured text files such as comma-delimited files with an Access database
XML file	Link, import, and export XML files with an Access database
XPS file	Export to an XPS format. XML Paper Specification (XPS) is a fixed-layout electronic file format that preserves document formatting and enables file sharing. The XPS format ensures that when the file is viewed online or printed, it retains exactly the format that you intended, and that data in the file cannot be easily changed.
ODBC Database	Link, import, and export ODBC Database data such as that from an SQL Server database with an Access database
HTML Document	Link, import, and export structured HTML data, such as data in an HTML table, to an Access database
Outlook Folder	Import or link structured Outlook data to an Access database
dBASE	Link, import, and export dBASE data to an Access database
Paradox	Link, import, and export Paradox data to an Access database
Lotus 1-2-3	Link, import, and export Lotus 1-2-3 spreadsheets with an Access database
Word	Export Access data including tables, queries, forms, and reports to a Word document or you may use an Access table or query with a Word mail merge process

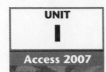
Analyzing Data with Excel

Excel is an excellent tool for projecting and graphing numeric trends. For example, you can analyze the impact of a price increase on budget or income projections by applying several assumptions. This reiterative analysis is sometimes called **"what-if"** analysis. Excel's superior graphing tools allow you to quickly display numeric information as a chart. ▰▰▰▰ Now that the DepartmentCosts data has been exported to Excel, the Finance Department has asked you to use Excel to graphically display the costs for each department.

STEPS

1. **Start Excel, then open the DepartmentCosts.xlsx file from the drive and folder where you store your Data Files**

   The data you exported from the DepartmentCosts query now appears in the Excel spreadsheet. Because the export process makes a copy of the data, any changes you make to either copy of the data does not affect the other.

2. **Widen columns A and B by double-clicking the column separator between columns A and B and between columns B and C, click the Data tab, click the Subtotal button, click OK, then click the 2 outline button**

   The spreadsheet now looks like Figure I-11. With the departmental data subtotaled, it's easy to create a chart to graphically display this data in Excel.

   > **TROUBLE**
   >
   > Be sure to select only the department data and not the Grand Total row data.

3. **Drag to select from cell A1 to the cell containing 10,655.00 (the Cost for the USA Total), click the Insert tab, click the Column button in the Charts group, then click the first button in the first row to create a clustered column chart**

   The spreadsheet now looks like Figure I-12. The cost subtotals for each department are graphically displayed in the spreadsheet. Although Access does have some charting capabilities, Excel is a superior graphing tool, so it is not uncommon to export data to Excel for this purpose.

4. **Click any cell on the spreadsheet to remove the selection, then preview and print the spreadsheet in landscape orientation**

   By moving the focus back to the spreadsheet and changing the paper orientation to landscape, you can print both the data and the chart on one sheet of paper.

5. **Save and close the workbook, then exit Excel**

FIGURE I-11: DepartmentCosts data subtotaled in Excel

2 outline button

Separator line between columns A & B

Data tab

Subtotal button

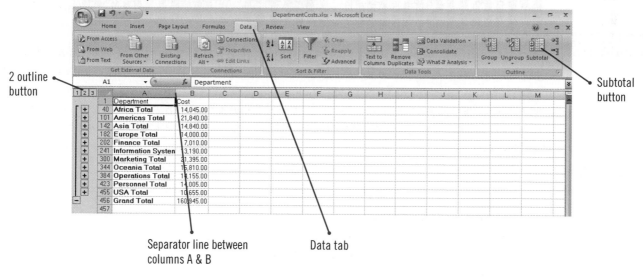

Insert tab

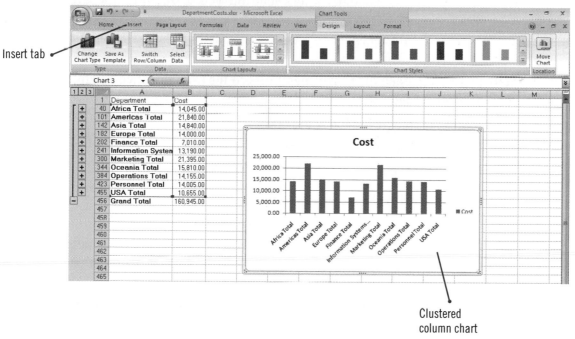

Clustered column chart

FIGURE I-12: Department cost data presented as a column chart

Access 2007

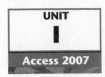

Publishing Data to Word

Microsoft Office Word, the word-processing program in the Microsoft Office suite, is a premier program for entering, editing, and formatting text, especially in long documents. You can easily export data from an Access table, query, form, or report into a Word document. This is helpful when you want to use Word's superior text editing features to combine explanatory paragraphs with Access data or if you want to insert Access data into an existing Word report. 🔳🔳 You have been asked to write a memo to the management committee describing departmental costs for continuing education. You can create a query that describes the data you want to present, then export it to Word to finish the memo.

STEPS

1. **Double-click the DepartmentCosts query to open its datasheet (if it is not already open), click the Home tab, then click the Design View button**

   Rather than exporting each record to Word, you use the subtotaling features within Access to subtotal the costs by department and then export those subtotals.

2. **Click the Totals button in the Show/Hide group, click Group By for the Cost field, click the list arrow, click Sum, then click the Datasheet View button**

   The summarized costs per department are shown in Figure I-13. Note that these values are exactly the same as the subtotals created earlier by Excel. The products within the Microsoft Office suite have overlapping features. The product you choose for each task should depend on which product is best suited to give you the results you want. In this case, Word cannot provide these subtotals, so you must create them in Access before exporting the data to Word.

3. **Click the External Data tab, click the Word button in the Export group, click Browse, navigate to the drive and folder where you store your Data Files, click Save, click OK, then click Close**

   The data in the DepartmentCosts query is exported as an **RTF (Rich Text Format)** file, which can be opened and edited in Word.

4. **Start Word, then open the DepartmentCosts.rtf file from the drive and folder where you store your Data Files**

5. **Press [Enter], then type the following text:**

To:	Management Committee
From:	Your Name
Re:	Analysis of Continuing Education Courses
Date:	Today's date

   The following information shows the overall cost for continuing education subtotaled by department. The information shows that the Americas and Marketing departments are the highest consumers of continuing education.

6. **Proofread your document, which should now look like Figure I-14, then preview and print it**

   The **word wrap** feature in Word determines when a line of text extends into the right margin of the page and automatically forces the text to the next line without you needing to press Enter. This allows you to enter and edit large paragraphs of text in Word very efficiently.

7. **Save and close the document, then exit Word**

   In addition to exporting data, Table I-2 lists other techniques you can use to copy Access data to other applications.

FIGURE I-13: Summarized costs by department

Department field ●—

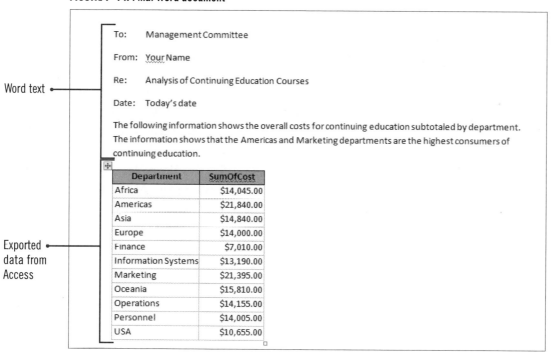

DepartmentCosts	
Department	SumOfCost
Africa	$14,045.00
Americas	$21,840.00
Asia	$14,840.00
Europe	$14,000.00
Finance	$7,010.00
Information System:	$13,190.00
Marketing	$21,395.00
Oceania	$15,810.00
Operations	$14,155.00
Personnel	$14,005.00
USA	$10,655.00

—● SumOfCost field summarizes costs per department

FIGURE I-14: Final Word document

To: Management Committee

From: Your Name

Word text ●—   Re: Analysis of Continuing Education Courses

Date: Today's date

The following information shows the overall costs for continuing education subtotaled by department. The information shows that the Americas and Marketing departments are the highest consumers of continuing education.

Department	SumOfCost
Africa	$14,045.00
Americas	$21,840.00
Asia	$14,840.00
Europe	$14,000.00
Finance	$7,010.00
Information Systems	$13,190.00
Marketing	$21,395.00
Oceania	$15,810.00
Operations	$14,155.00
Personnel	$14,005.00
USA	$10,655.00

Exported data from Access ●—

Access 2007

TABLE I-2: Techniques to copy Access data to other applications

technique	button or menu option	description
Office Clipboard	Copy and Paste	Click the Copy button to copy selected data to the Office Clipboard. The Office Clipboard can hold up to 24 different items. Open a Word document or Excel spreadsheet, click where you want to paste the data, then click the Paste button.
Export	Use the buttons on the Export section of the External Data tab.	Copy information from an Access object into a different file format.
Drag and drop	Resize Access window so that the target location (Word or Excel, for example) can also be seen on the screen.	With both windows visible, drag the Access table, query, form, or report object icon from the Access window to the target (Excel or Word) window.

Merging Data with Word

Another way to export Access data is to merge it to a Word document as the data source for a mail merge process. In a **mail merge**, data from an Access table or query is combined into a Word form letter, label, or envelope to create mass mailing documents. Julia Rice wants to send the Quest employees a letter announcing two new continuing education courses. You use the Access merge to Word feature to customize a standard form letter to each employee whose name and department data is stored in the Employees table.

1. **If the DepartmentCosts query is still open, close and save it, click the Employees table in the Navigation Pane, click the External Data tab, click the More button in the Export group, then click Merge it with Microsoft Office Word**

   The Microsoft Word Mail Merge Wizard starts, requesting information about the merge process. Because you have not started the letter that describes the two new courses yet, you choose the second option in the first dialog box.

2. **Click the Create a new document and then link the data to it option button, click OK, then maximize the Word window**

   Word starts and opens the **Mail Merge task pane**, which steps you through creating a mail merge, on the right side of the Word window and selects the Mailings tab on the Ribbon. You can use either or both tools to help you with the mail merge process. Before you merge the Access data with the Word document, you must create the **main document**, the document used to determine how the letter and Access data are combined. This is the standard text that will be consistent for each letter created in the mail merge process.

3. **Type the standard text shown in Figure I-15, click the Next: Starting document link in the bottom of the Mail Merge task pane to create merged letters, click the Next: Select recipients link to use the current document, click the Next: Write your letter link to use the existing list of names (the one you just exported from Access), press [Tab] after To: in the letter, then click the More items link in the Mail Merge task pane**

   The Insert Merge Field dialog box lists all of the fields in the original data source, the Employees table. You use the Insert Merge Field dialog box to insert **merge fields**, codes that are replaced with the values in the field that the code represents when the mail merge is processed.

4. **Double-click First, double-click Last, click Close, click between the First and Last codes, then press [Spacebar] to insert a space between the codes as shown in Figure I-16**

   You must use the Insert Merge Field dialog box to add merge fields to a Word document—you cannot type them directly from the keyboard. You can, however, insert the same merge field into one letter multiple times. With the main document and merge fields inserted, you are ready to complete the mail merge.

5. **Click the Next: Preview your letters link in the Mail Merge task pane, click the Next: Complete the merge link to complete the merge, click the Edit individual letters link to view the letters on the screen, then click OK to complete the merge**

   The mail merge process combines field values from the Employees table with the main document, creating a letter for each record in the Employees table. The first letter is to Ron Dawson, as shown in Figure I-17. "Ron" is the field value for the First field in the first record, and "Dawson" is the field value for the Last field in the first record. The status bar of the Word document shows that this document contains 23 pages, one page for each of the 23 records in the Employees table.

6. **Press [Page Down] several times to view several pages of the final merged document**

   Each page is a separate letter to a different employee.

7. **Print only the first page, close Word without saving any documents, then close the Education-I.accdb database and exit Access**

FIGURE I-15: Creating the main document in Word

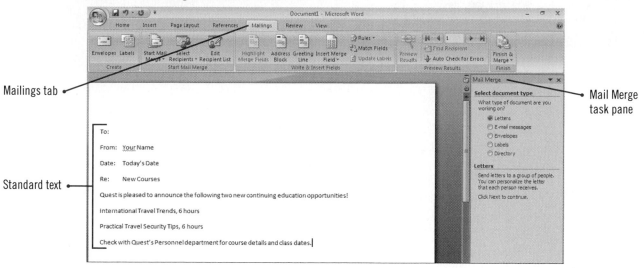

Mailings tab

Standard text

Mail Merge task pane

FIGURE I-16: Inserting merge fields

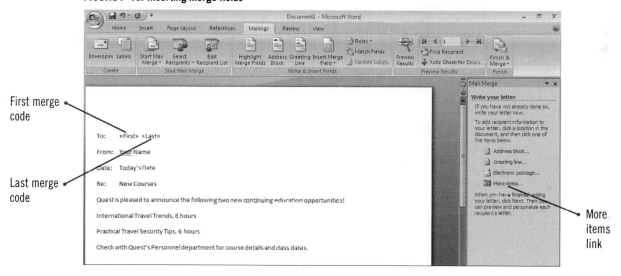

First merge code

Last merge code

More items link

FIGURE I-17: Merged letters

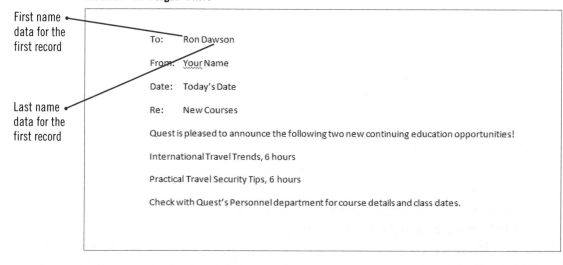

First name data for the first record

Last name data for the first record

Practice

▼ CONCEPTS REVIEW

Identify each element of the database window as shown in Figure I-18.

FIGURE I-18

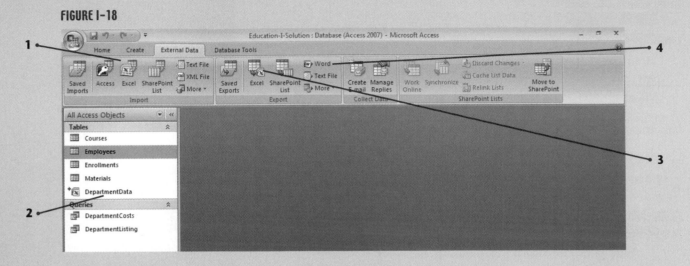

Match each term with the statement that best describes its function.

5. **Database template**
6. **Exporting**
7. **Main document**
8. **Linking**
9. **Delimited text file**
10. **Mail Merge**
11. **Importing**
12. **Table template**

  a. A tool used to quickly create a single table within an existing database

  b. A file used to determine how the letter and Access data will be combined

  c. A file that stores one record on each line, with the field values separated by a common character such as a comma, tab, or dash

  d. A way to copy Access information to another database, spreadsheet, or file format

  e. The process of converting data from an external source into an Access database

  f. A way to connect to data in an external source without copying it

  g. A tool used to quickly create a new database based on a particular subject such as assets, contacts, events, or projects

  h. To combine data from an Access table or query into a Word form letter, label, or envelope to create mass mailing documents

Select the best answer from the list of choices.

13. **Which of the following is *not* true about templates?**
    a. They create multiple database objects.
    b. They analyze the data on your computer and suggest database applications.
    c. They cover a wide range of subjects including assets, contacts, events, or projects.
    d. Microsoft provides online templates in areas such as business and personal database applications.

14. **Which of the following is *not* true of exporting?**
    a. Access data can be exported to Word.
    b. Exporting retains a link between the original and target data files.
    c. Exporting creates a copy of data.
    d. Access data can be exported into Excel.

15. **Which of the following is *not* a file format that Access can import?**
    a. Excel
    b. HTML
    c. Access
    d. Word

16. **Which of the following software products would most likely be used to analyze the effect on future sales and profits based on the change to several different assumptions?**
    a. Word
    b. PowerPoint
    c. Access
    d. Excel

17. **Which of the following is *not* the subject of a local database template?**
    a. Assets
    b. Contacts
    c. Events
    d. Accounts Receivable

18. **Which is *not* true about enforcing referential integrity?**
    a. It is required for all one-to-many relationships.
    b. It prevents records from being deleted in the "one" side of a one-to-many relationship that have matching records on the "many" side.
    c. It prevents records from being created in the "many" side of a one-to-many relationship that do not have a matching record on the "one" side.
    d. It prevents orphan records.

19. **Which of the following is *not* true about linking?**
    a. Linking copies data from one data file to another.
    b. Access can link to data in an Excel spreadsheet.
    c. Access can link to data in an HTML file.
    d. You can edit linked data in Access.

20. **During a mail merge, what is the purpose of a main document?**
    a. It is the same thing as the final merged document.
    b. It stores all of the data available for the mail merge.
    c. It stores the merge fields that you may insert into letters, envelopes, or labels.
    d. It contains the standard text that you want each merged letter to display.

▼ SKILLS REVIEW

1. **Use database templates.**
    a. Use the Assets database template in the Business category from Microsoft Office Online templates to build a new Access database. Save the database with the name Assets-I.accdb in the drive and folder where you store your Data Files. (*Hint*: This step might require that you are connected to the Internet to download online templates.)
    b. Enable content if prompted, close any forms that open automatically, expand the Navigation Pane to view all of the objects created by the Assets database template, and make sure the Navigation Pane menu displays the objects by All Access Objects rather than by Tables and Related Views.
    c. View the database relationships to better understand how the Assets and Contacts tables are related.
    d. Double-click the one-to-many link line between Assets and Contacts, click the Join Type button in the Edit Relationships dialog box, click option 1, click OK, and click OK to change the relationship from one that shows all Assets records even if there is no matching record in the Contacts table to the default one-to-many relationship that only selects Assets records that have one or more matching records in the Contacts table.
    e. Save and close the Relationships window.
    f. Explore the other queries, forms, and reports in the Assets database template, then close all objects.

2. **Use table templates.**
    a. Use the Issues table template to create a new table in the Assets-I.accdb database.
    b. Close the table, saving it as Issues.
    c. In Table Design View of the Issues table, rename the ID field as IssueID.
    d. In Table Design View of the Issues table, add a new field named AssetID with a Number data type and Foreign key field to connect Issues to Assets as the Description, then save and close the Issues table.
    e. In Table Design View of the Assets table, rename the ID field to AssetID then save and close the Assets table.

f. In the Relationships window, add the Issues table, then connect the Assets table to the Issues table in a one-to-many relationship using the common AssetID field. Enforce referential integrity on the relationship.

g. Print the relationships for the Assets-I.accdb database, save and close the Relationships window, then close the Assets-I.accdb database.

3. Import data from Excel.

a. Open the Machinery-I.accdb database from the drive and folder where you store your Data Files. Enable content if prompted.

b. Import the MachineryEmployees.xlsx spreadsheet from the drive and folder where you store your Data Files, using the Import Spreadsheet Wizard to import the data. Make sure that the first row is specified as the column headings.

c. Choose the EmployeeNo field as the primary key, and import the data to a table named Employees.

d. In Table Design View for the Employees table, change the Data Type of the EmployeeNo field to Number, specifying Double for the Field Size. Save and close the Employees table.

4. Link data.

a. Link to the Vendors.xlsx Excel file stored on the drive and folder where you store your Data Files.

b. In the Link Spreadsheet Wizard, specify that the first row contains column headings.

c. Name the linked table Vendors.

d. Open the Relationships window, and display all five field lists in the window. Link the tables together with one-to-many relationships, as shown in Figure I-19. Be sure to enforce referential integrity whenever possible.

e. Save and close the Relationships window.

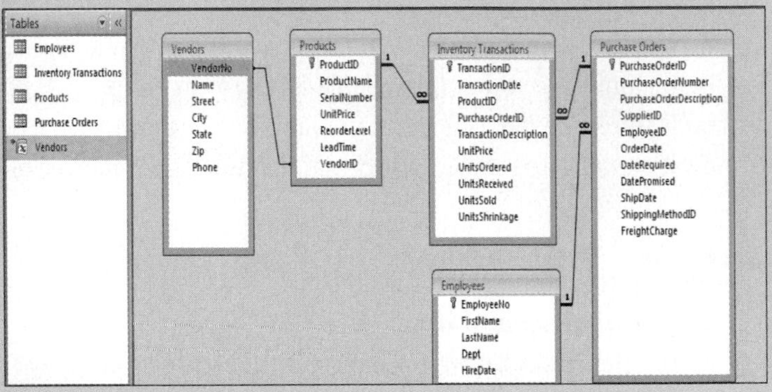

5. Export data to Excel.

a. Open the Products table to view the datasheet, then close it.

b. Export the Products table data to an Excel spreadsheet named Products.xlsx. Save the spreadsheet to the drive and folder where you store your Data Files. Do not save the export steps.

FIGURE I-19

6. Analyze data with Excel.

a. Start Excel and open the Products.xlsx spreadsheet from the drive and folder where you store your Data Files.

b. Widen each column so that all of the data can be easily viewed.

c. Select all of the product names (cells B1 through B11), press and hold the [Ctrl] key to select all unit price values (cells D1 through D11) including the column labels, click the Insert tab, then insert a clustered column chart.

d. Drag the column chart so that it is positioned below the data, click any cell on the spreadsheet, then preview and print the spreadsheet. It should print on one piece of paper.

e. Save and close the Products.xlsx spreadsheet.

7. Publish data to Word.

a. In the Machinery-I.accdb database, export the Products table to a Word document named Products.rtf. Save the Products.rtf file in the drive and folder where you store your Data Files.

b. Start Word, open the Products.rtf document from the drive and folder where you store your Data Files. Press [Enter] twice, press [Ctrl][Home] to return to the top of the document, then type the following text:

INTERNAL MEMO

From: Your Name

To: Sales Staff

Date: Today's date

Do not forget to mention the long lead times on the Back Hoe, Thatcher, and Biodegrader to customers. We usually do not keep these expensive items in stock.

c. Proofread the document, then save and print it. Close the document, then exit Word.

8. **Merge data with Word.**

a. In the Machinery-I.accdb database, merge the data from the Employees table to a Word document.

b. Use the "Create a new document and then link the data to it" option in the Microsoft Word Mail Merge Wizard dialog box. In the Word document, enter the following text as the main document for the mail merge.

Date: February 9, 2010

To:

From: Your Name

Re: CPR Training

The annual CPR Training session will be held on Friday, February 26, 2010. Please sign up for this important event in the lunchroom. Friends and family over 18 years old are also welcome.

c. To the right of To:, press [Tab] to position the insertion point at the location for the first merge field.

d. Move to step 4 of 6 of the Mail Merge task pane, click the More items link, then use the Insert Merge Field dialog box to add the FirstName and LastName fields to the main document.

e. Close the Insert Merge Field dialog box, and insert a space between the <<FirstName>> and <<LastName>> merge codes.

f. Complete the mail merge process to merge all records in the Employees table to the letter.

g. Print the last page of the merged document, the letter to Don Balch, then exit Word without saving any documents.

▼ INDEPENDENT CHALLENGE 1

As the manager of a women's college basketball team, you have created a database called Basketball-I that tracks the players, games, and player statistics. You want to link to an Excel file that contains information on the player's course load. You also want to export a report to a Word document in order to add a paragraph of descriptive text.

a. Open the database **Basketball-I.accdb** from the drive and folder where you store your Data Files. Enable content if prompted.

b. In the Relationships window, connect the Games and Stats tables with a one-to-many relationship based on the common GameNo field. Connect the Players and Stats tables with a one-to-many relationship based on the common PlayerNo field. Be sure to enforce referential integrity on both relationships. Save and close the Relationships window.

c. Export the Player Statistics report to Word with the name **Player Statistics.rtf**. Save the Player Statistics.rtf document in the drive and folder where you store your Data Files. Do not save the export steps.

d. Start Word and open the Player Statistics.rtf document.

e. Press [Enter] three times, then press [Ctrl][Home] to position the insertion point at the top of the document.

f. Type your name on the first line of the document, enter today's date as the second line, then write a sentence or two that explains the Player Statistics data that follows. Save, print, and close the Player Statistics document.

g. Exit Word. Close the Basketball-I.accdb database, then exit Access.

▼ INDEPENDENT CHALLENGE 2

As the manager of a women's college basketball team, you have created a database called Basketball-I that tracks the players, games, and player statistics. You want to export some information in the Basketball-I database to an Excel worksheet to analyze and graph the data.

a. Open the database **Basketball-I.accdb** from the drive and folder where you store your Data Files. Enable content if prompted.

b. If the relationships haven't already been established, in the Relationships window connect the Games and Stats tables with a one-to-many relationship based on the common GameNo field. Connect the Players and Stats tables with a one-to-many relationship based on the common PlayerNo field. Be sure to enforce referential integrity on both relationships. Save and close the Relationships window.

c. Export the Field Goal Stats query to Excel. Save the file with the name **Field Goal Stats.xlsx** in the drive and folder where you store your Data Files.

▼ INDEPENDENT CHALLENGE 2 (CONTINUED)

Advanced Challenge Exercise

- Start Excel, then open the Field Goal Stats.xlsx file.
- Click any cell in column A that contains the player names, click the Sort & Filter button, then click Sort A to Z.
- On the Data tab, click the Subtotal button, click the FG check box to add a subtotal to that field as well as the FGA field, then click the 2 outline button.
- Widen column A to view all of the data in the column, select all of the data, including column labels, except for the Grand Total row, click the Insert tab, click the Column button, then click the Clustered Column option.
- Position the clustered column chart beside the data, as shown in Figure I-20, then click any cell to deselect the chart. The spreadsheet and graph should fit on one page if printed in landscape orientation.

FIGURE I-20

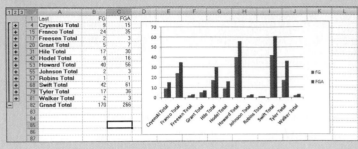

d. Save and close the Field Goal Stats.xlsx workbook, then exit Excel. Close the Basketball-I.accdb database, then exit Access.

▼ INDEPENDENT CHALLENGE 3

This Independent Challenge requires an Internet connection.

You have been asked by a small private school to build a database to track library books. You decide to explore Microsoft database templates to see if there is a tool that could help you get started.

a. Create a new database using the Lending library database template from the Personal category of online templates. Enable content if prompted. Name the database **Lending Library.accdb**, and store it in the drive and folder where you store your Data Files.

FIGURE I-21

b. Review the Relationships window. Rearrange the field lists as shown in Figure I-21, then print the Relationships report. Close the report without saving it.

c. Display all Access objects in the Navigation Pane, then enter two records in the Contacts table. Enter fictional but reasonable data for each field, but do not enter anything for the Notes or Attachments fields. Close the Contacts table.

d. Enter two records in the Assets table that represent automobiles. Enter fictional but reasonable data for each field, using the default field values for the Category and Condition fields. Do not enter anything for the Comments, ID Number, Attachments, or Retired Date fields, but do select one of the two records you entered in the Contacts table for the Owner field. Close the Assets table.

Advanced Challenge Exercise

- In Design View of the Assets table, select the Category field, then review the Lookup properties.
- Change the Row Source property to **"(1) Automobile";" (2) Motorcycle";" (3) Boat"**
- Select the Location field, then review the Lookup properties.
- Change the Row Source property to **"(1) West";" (2) East";" (3) Midwest"**

- Save the table, then return to Datasheet View.
- For both records, modify the Category field to correctly classify the two automobiles you entered, modify the Location field to best classify your location, then close the Assets table.
- Explore the forms and reports created by the Lending Library database template, then answer these questions on a separate sheet of paper:
- Identify a form that provides features you have not used before. Of what value is this form to the database?
- Identify a report that provides features you have not used before. Of what value is this report to the database?
- Review the Relationships window. Why does the Contacts table have a one-to-many relationship with both the Transactions and Assets tables?

e. Close the Lending Library.accdb database, then exit Access.

▼ REAL LIFE INDEPENDENT CHALLENGE

Learning common phrases in a variety of foreign languages is valuable if you travel and is a hallmark of a well-educated adult. One way to increase your knowledge of foreign languages is to have regular contact with non-English speakers, such as by volunteering with the foreign student exchange program at your college. Suppose the director of the program asks you to help find ways to welcome new foreign exchange students. To overcome the language barrier, you have created a database that documents the primary and secondary languages used by foreign countries. The database also includes a table of common words and phrases that you can use to practice basic conversation skills.

a. Open the **Languages-I.accdb** database from the drive and folder where you store your Data Files. Enable content if prompted.

b. Open the datasheets for each of the three tables to familiarize yourself with the fields and records. The Language1 and Language2 fields in the Countries table represent the primary and secondary languages for that country.

c. Open the Relationships window and create a one-to-many relationship between the Languages and Countries table using the LanguageID field in the Languages table and the Language1 field in the Countries table. Enforce referential integrity on the relationship.

d. Create a one-to-many relationship between the Languages and Countries tables using the LanguageID field in the Languages table and the Language2 field in the Countries table. Click No when prompted to edit the existing relationship, and enforce referential integrity on the new relationship. The field list for the Languages table will appear twice in the Relationships window with Languages_1 as the title for the second field list, as shown in Figure I-22. The Words table is used for reference and does not have a direct relationship to the other tables.

e. View the Relationship report in Design View.

f. Add a label to the Report Header section with your name as the caption, then print and close the report without saving it.

g. Save and close the Relationships window.

h. Connect to the Internet and go to *www.ask.com*, *www.about.com*, or any search engine. Your goal is to find a Web site that translates English to other languages, and to print the home page of that Web site.

FIGURE I-22

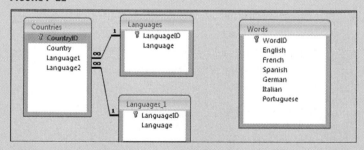

i. Add three new words or phrases to the Words table, making sure that the translation is made in all five of the represented languages: French, Spanish, German, Italian, and Portuguese. If you have an interest in another language, add a field for that language and enter the representative words or phrases.

j. Print the updated datasheet for the Words table, close the Words table, close the Languages-I.accdb database, then exit Access.

▼ VISUAL WORKSHOP

Start Access and open the **Basketball-I.accdb** database from the drive and folder where you store your Data Files. Enable content if prompted. Merge the information from the Players table to a form letter. The final page of the merged document is shown in Figure I-23. Notice that the player's first and last names have been merged to the first line and that the player's first name is merged a second time in the first sentence of the letter. Print the last page of the merged document, then close both documents without saving them.

FIGURE I-23

To:	Jamie Johnson
From:	Your Name
Date:	Current Date
Re:	Big 13 Champions!

Congratulations, Jamie, for an outstanding year at Central College! Your hard work and team contribution have helped clinch the Big 13 Championship for Central College for the third year in a row

Thank you for your dedication!

Keep the faith,

Coach

Analyzing Database Design Using Northwind

Access databases are unlike other Microsoft Office files in that, once they are created, the same database file can be used every day for several years. Over time, hundreds of hours are often spent designing and modifying Access database files as users discover new ways to analyze and apply the data. One of the best ways to teach yourself advanced database skills is to study a well-developed database. Microsoft provides a fully developed database example called **Northwind**, which illustrates many advanced database techniques that you can apply to your own development needs. You work with Julia Rice, director of staff development at Quest Specialty Travel, to examine the Microsoft Northwind database and determine what features and techniques could be applied to improve the Education database.

OBJECTIVES

Normalize data

Analyze relationships

Evaluate tables

Improve fields

Use subqueries

Analyze queries

Analyze forms

Analyze reports

Normalizing Data

Normalizing data means to structure it for a relational database. A normalized database reduces inaccurate and redundant data, reduces storage requirements, improves database performance (speed), and simplifies overall database maintenance. It also enhances your ability to create queries, forms, and reports. **Database normalization** defines an extensive set of rules about how to structure data into a well-defined relational database. ▓▓▓▓ Julia Rice asks you to study the Northwind database to see how its structure might help you improve the Education-J database.

STEPS

1. **Start Access, open the Northwind.mdb database from the drive and folder where you store your Data Files, enable content if prompted, then click OK if the Welcome to Northwind Traders window opens**

   Northwind.mdb is a database in the Access 2000 file format, and was provided by Microsoft with Access 2000, Access 2002, and Access 2003 to help you learn about relational databases and Access.

QUICK TIP
Foreign key values should be repeated to provide a link between "many" records in a table and the "one" record in a related table.

2. **Double-click the Categories table in the Navigation Pane, press [Tab] to move from one field to another, note the number of records in the Current Record box, close the datasheet, then open and close each of the seven other table datasheets**

   The Customers table, for example, contains 11 fields and 91 records. A clue that data might need to be better normalized is repeating data in any field. The tables of the Northwind database contain few fields with unnecessary repeating data. You look for repeating data in the fields of the Education-J database.

3. **Start a second session of Access, then open the Education-J.accdb database from the drive and folder where you store your Data Files, enabling content if prompted**

4. **Double-click the Employees table in the Navigation Pane**

   The Department and Title fields contain repeating data. You decide to further normalize the Department data by creating a Departments table that uses a one-to-many relationship to link to the Department field of the Employees table. (The Department field of the Employees table will become a foreign key field.) This change will help Quest users manage and enter accurate and consistent department data in the Employees table.

5. **Close the Employees datasheet, click the Create tab, click the Table Design button in the Tables group, type Department as the field name, click the Primary Key button, save the table with the name Departments, then close it**

6. **Double-click the new Departments table in the Navigation Pane, then enter the values shown in Figure J-1**

7. **Save and close the Departments datasheet, right-click the Employees table in the Navigation Pane, then click Design View**

   You can use the Lookup Wizard to establish the Department field in the Employees table as the foreign key field linked to the Department field in the Departments table.

8. **Click the Department field in the Data Type column, click the list arrow in the Text Data Type cell, click Lookup Wizard, click Next to look up values in a table, click Table:Departments, click Next, double-click Department as the selected field, click Next, click the first sort arrow, click Department, click Next, click Next, click Finish, then click Yes**

9. **Click the View button on the Design tab, click any record in the Department field, then click the field list arrow as shown in Figure J-2**

   The Department field of the Employees datasheet is linked to the Department field of the Departments table, which provides the valid choices for that field. Now data entry for the field will be faster, more consistent, and more accurate.

FIGURE J-1: Departments datasheet

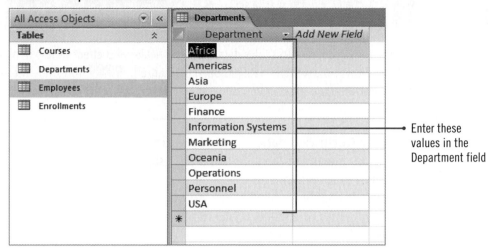

Enter these values in the Department field

FIGURE J-2: Department field of the Employees datasheet

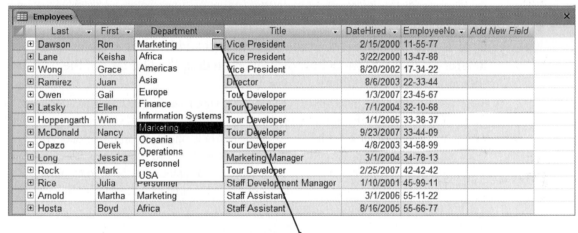

Click the field list arrow to display the values in the Department field

Understanding third normal form

The process of normalization can be broken down into degrees, which include **first normal form (1NF)**, a single two-dimensional table with rows and columns; **second normal form (2NF)**, where redundant data in the original table is extracted, placed in a new table, and related to the original table; and **third normal form (3NF)**, where calculated fields (also called derived fields) such as totals or taxes are removed. In an Access database, calculated fields can be created "on the fly" using a query, which means that the information in the calculation is automatically produced and is always accurate based on the latest updates to the database. Strive to create databases that adhere to the rules of third normal form.

Analyzing Relationships

The relationships between tables determine the health and effectiveness of a database. The Relationships window shows how well the data has been normalized. You study the Relationships window of the Northwind database to see if you can apply its techniques to the Education-J database.

QUICK TIP

Move field lists by dragging their title bars.

1. **In the Northwind database window, click the Database Tools tab, click the Relationships button, maximize the window, then resize and move the field lists so that all fields are visible as shown in Figure J-3**

   Notice that all of the relationships between the tables are one-to-many relationships with referential integrity enforced. Recall that referential integrity helps prevent orphan records—records in the "many" (child) table that do not link to a matching record in the "one" (parent) table.

2. **Switch to the Education-J database window, close the Employees datasheet, click the Database Tools tab, click the Relationships button, then maximize the window**

   You need to add the relationship you just created between the Departments and Employees tables using the Lookup Wizard to the Relationships window.

QUICK TIP

Click the All Relationships button to display all relationships created since the last time the Relationships window was saved.

3. **Click the Show Table button on the Design tab, double-click Departments, then click Close**

   The Relationships window now shows the Departments table and the one-to-many relationship between it and the Employees table, but relationships created through the Lookup Wizard are not created with referential integrity. You can enforce referential integrity on any existing relationship provided that orphan records do not exist in the "many" table.

QUICK TIP

Click the Relationship Report button to create a printout of the Relationships window.

4. **Double-click the link between the Departments and Employees tables, click the Enforce Referential Integrity check box, click OK, then drag the title bars of the field lists as shown in Figure J-4**

   Most relationships between tables are "one-to-many." **One-to-one relationships** are rare and occur when the primary key field of the first table is related to the primary key field of a second table. In other words, one record in the first table can be related to one and only one record in the second table. An example of when a one-to-one relationship would be appropriate is when you want to separate sensitive information such as medical facts from a table that stores basic demographic data about an employee. One employee record might be linked to one medical record stored and secured in another table. The Northwind database also has good examples of many-to-many relationships.

5. **Click the Save button 🖫 on the Quick Access toolbar, close the Education-J database, then switch to the Northwind database window**

   A many-to-many relationship cannot be created directly between two tables in Access. However, two tables have a many-to-many relationship when they are both related to the same intermediate table with one-to-many relationships. Note that the Employees and Shippers tables have a many-to-many relationship, as do the Employees and Customers tables in the Northwind database. Also note that the Order Details table has a **multi-field primary key** that consists of the OrderID and ProductID fields. In other words, an OrderID value can be listed multiple times in the Order Details table, and a ProductID value can be listed multiple times in the Order Details table. But the combination of a particular OrderID value plus a ProductID value should be unique for each record.

FIGURE J-3: Northwind.mdb relationships

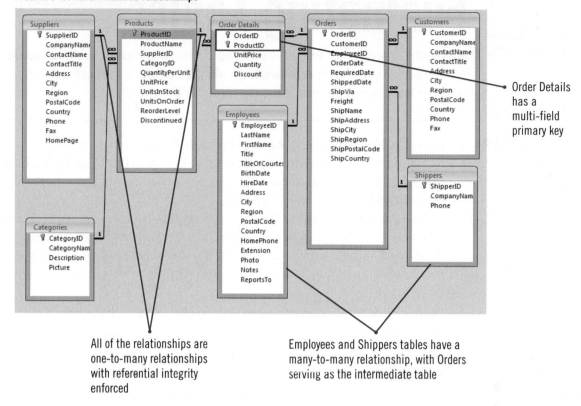

Order Details has a multi-field primary key

All of the relationships are one-to-many relationships with referential integrity enforced

Employees and Shippers tables have a many-to-many relationship, with Orders serving as the intermediate table

FIGURE J-4: Education-J.accdb relationships

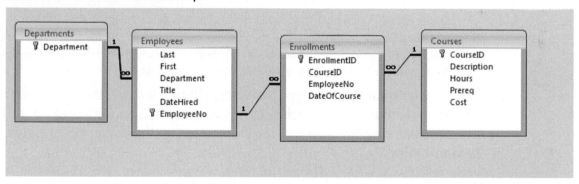

Copying database objects

Microsoft provides the Northwind database and other database templates to help you understand and develop a new database. To use a Northwind object such as a table in another database, right-click the table in the Navigation Pane, click Copy, switch to the database window where you want to paste the object, right-click the Navigation Pane, then click Paste. If you are copying a table, you are asked if you want to paste the structure only, to paste the structure and data, or to append the data to an existing table.

Evaluating Tables

Access 2007 offers several new table features that make analyzing existing data and producing results, such as datasheet subtotals, much easier and faster. You review the tables of the Northwind database to examine new Access 2007 features and to study table properties.

STEPS

QUICK TIP

To move to a specific record, enter that number in the Current Record box.

1. **Close the Northwind Relationships window, double-click the Products table in the Navigation Pane, click the Totals button in the Records group on the Home tab, scroll to the Units in Stock field, click the Total cell for the Units in Stock field, click the list arrow, then click Sum as shown in Figure J-5**

   A subtotal of the units in stock, 3119, appears in the Total cell for the Units in Stock field. As shown in the Totals list, a numeric field allows you to calculate the Average, Sum, Count, Maximum, Minimum, Standard Deviation, or Variance statistic for the field. If you were working in the Totals cell of a Text field, you could choose only the Count statistic. Notice that the Current Record box displays the word "Totals" to indicate that you are working in the Total row.

2. **Double-click Totals in the Current Record box, type 6, then press [Enter]**

   Access moves the focus to the Units in Stock field of the sixth record.

3. **Click the record selector button of the sixth record to select the entire record, then press [Delete]**

   Working with a well-defined relational database with referential integrity enforced on all relationships, you are prevented from deleting a record in a "one" (parent) table if the record is related to many records in a "many" (child) table. In this case, the sixth record in the Products table is related to several records in the Order Details table, and therefore it cannot be deleted. Next, you examine table properties.

4. **Click OK, close the Products table, click Yes to save changes to the layout, right-click the Employees table, click Design View, then click the Property Sheet button to open the Property Sheet for the table (if it's not already open) as shown in Figure J-6**

   The Property Sheet for a table controls characteristics for the entire table object, such as an expanded description of the table, default view, and validation rules that use more than one field. In this case, you can prevent data-entry errors by specifying that the HireDate field value is greater than the BirthDate field value. Because two fields are used in the Validation Rule expression, you should enter the rule in the table Property Sheet instead of in the Validation Rule property of an individual field.

5. **Click the Validation Rule box, type [HireDate]>[BirthDate], click the Validation Text box, type Hire date must be greater than birth date, click the Save button 🖫 on the Quick Access toolbar, click Yes, then click the View button on the Design tab to switch to Datasheet View**

   Test the new table validation rule by entering a birth date greater than the hire date for the first record.

6. **Tab to the Birth Date field, type 5/5/2010, then press [Tab]**

   A dialog box opens, displaying the text entered in the Validation Text property.

7. **Click OK, then press [Esc] to remove the incorrect birth date entry for the first record**

FIGURE J-5: Products datasheet with Total row

Record selector button

Totals button

Total row

Sum

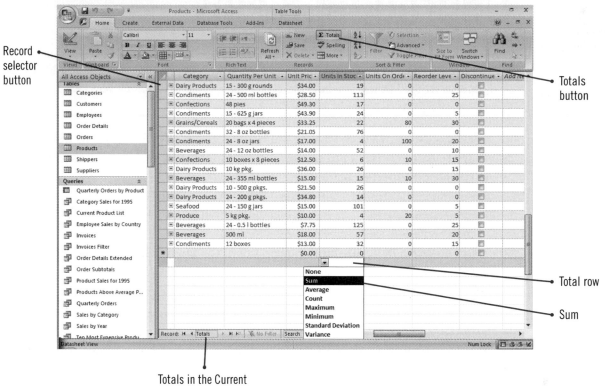

Totals in the Current Record box

FIGURE J-6: Property Sheet for Employees table

Property Sheet button

Validation Rule

Validation Text

Your Property Sheet might be docked instead of floating

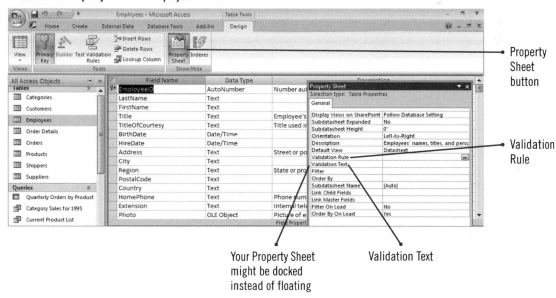

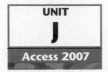
Improving Fields

To improve and enhance database functionality, the Northwind database also employs several useful field properties, such as Caption, Allow Zero Length, and Index. You review the Northwind database to study how lesser-used field properties have been implemented in the Employees table.

1. **Click the Design View button on the Home tab, click the EmployeeID field, then press [▼] to move through the fields of the Employees table while observing the Caption property in the Field Properties pane**

   The Northwind database uses the Caption property on all fields that consist of two words, such as HireDate, to separate the words with a space, as in Hire Date. The **Caption** property text is displayed as the default field name at the top of the field column in datasheets as well as in labels that describe fields on forms and reports.

2. **Select Reports To in the Caption property of the ReportsTo field, then type Manager**

   The Caption property doesn't have to match the field name. Use the Caption property any time you want to clarify or better describe a field for the users, but prefer not to change the actual field name.

3. **Click the HireDate field, then change the Indexed property to Yes (Duplicates OK)**

   An **index** keeps track of the order of the values in the indexed field as data is being entered and edited. Therefore, if you often sort on a field, the Index property should be set to Yes so that Access can sort and present the data faster. The Index property improves database performance when a field is often used for sorting by creating the index for the sort order as data is being entered, rather than requiring the database to build the index from scratch when the field is used for sorting purposes. Fields that are not often used for sort orders should have their Index property set to No because creating and maintaining indexes is a productivity drain on the database. Remember, you can sort on any field at any time, whether the Index property is set to Yes or No.

4. **Click the HomePhone field and examine the Allow Zero Length property**

   Currently, the **Allow Zero Length** property is set to No, meaning zero-length strings ("") are not allowed. A zero-length string is an *intentional* "nothing" entry (as opposed to a **null** entry, which also means that the field contains nothing, but doesn't indicate intent). Zero-length strings are valuable when you want to show that the "nothing" entry is on purpose. For example, some employees might not want to provide a home phone number. In those instances, a zero-length string entry is appropriate. Note that you query for zero-length strings using "" criteria, whereas you query for null values using the operator **Is Null**.

5. **Double-click the Allow Zero Length property to switch the choice from No to Yes as shown in Figure J-7**

   With the field changes in place, you test them in Datasheet View.

6. **Click the Datasheet View button on the Design tab, click Yes to save the table, tab to the Home Phone field, enter "", tab to the Extension field, enter "", press [Tab], click OK to acknowledge the error message indicating that you cannot enter a zero-length string in the Extension field, press [Esc], press [Tab] three more times to observe the Manager caption for the ReportsTo field, then close the Employees table**

FIGURE J-7: Changing field properties in the Employees table

HomePhone field is selected

Caption property

Allow Zero Length property

Indexed property

Using Memo fields

Use Memo fields when you need to store more than 256 characters in a field, which is the maximum Field Size value for a Text field. Fields that store comments, reviews, notes, or other ongoing conversational information are good candidates for the Memo data type. The Append Only property is available for Memo fields in Access 2007 databases. When enabled, the **Append Only** property allows you to add data to a Memo field, but not change or remove existing data.

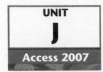

Using Subqueries

The Northwind database contains several interesting queries that demonstrate advanced query techniques, such as grouping on more than one field, using functions in calculated fields, and developing subqueries, which you might not have studied yet. ⬛⬛⬛⬛ You work in the Northwind database to study how to use advanced query techniques, including subqueries.

1. **Double-click the Product Sales for 1995 query to view the datasheet**

   This query summarizes product sales by product name for the year 1995. The datasheet includes 77 records, and each record represents one product name. The third column summarizes product sales for the product name. To analyze the construction of the query, switch to Design View.

2. **Click the Design View button on the Home tab, close the Property Sheet, then resize the Query Design View window to better view the data as shown in Figure J-8**

   Several interesting techniques have been used in the construction of this query. A calculated field, ProductSales, is computed by first multiplying the UnitPrice field from the Order Details table by the Quantity field, then subtracting the Discount, converting the result to a currency value with the **CCur** function, and finally summing the values in all of the records in the ProductName field using the Sum function. In addition, criteria has been added to the ShippedDate field so that only those sales between the dates of 1/1/1995 and 12/31/1995 are selected. Finally, the records are grouped by both the CategoryName and the ProductName fields.

3. **Close the Product Sales for 1995 query, saving changes if prompted, then double-click the Category Sales for 1995 query in the Navigation Pane to open the query datasheet**

   This query contains only eight records because the sales are summarized (grouped) by the Category field and there are only eight unique categories. The Category Sales field summarizes total sales by category. To see how this query was constructed, switch to Design View.

4. **Click the Design View button on the Home tab, then resize the query window to display all of the fields**

   Note that the field list for the query is based on the Product Sales for 1995 query, as shown in Figure J-9. When a query is based on another query's field list, the field list is called a **subquery**. In this case, the Category Sales for 1995 query used the Product Sales for 1995 as its subquery to avoid having to re-create the long Product Sales calculated field.

5. **Close the Category Sales for 1995 query, then click No if you are asked to save changes**

Analyzing Database Design Using Northwind

FIGURE J-8: Design View of the Product Sales for 1995 query

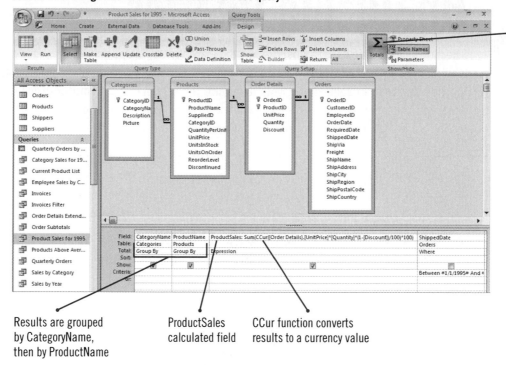

Totals button opens the Total row in the query design grid

Results are grouped by CategoryName, then by ProductName

ProductSales calculated field

CCur function converts results to a currency value

FIGURE J-9: Using the Product Sales for 1995 query as a subquery

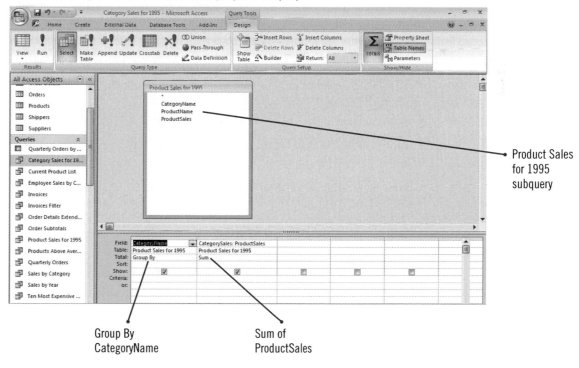

Product Sales for 1995 subquery

Group By CategoryName

Sum of ProductSales

Analyzing Queries

Selecting the right fields for a query seems to be an obvious task, but when the field name is the same in two different tables, how do you know which field to choose for the query? The field you select does affect the query results. In some cases, you can refine the results by including both fields in the query. The Northwind database contains several queries that demonstrate this and other advanced query-building techniques. 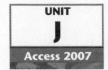 You work in the Northwind database to analyze queries.

STEPS

1. **Click the Create tab, click the Query Design button, double-click Employees, double-click Orders, then click Close**

   In this query, you want to identify employee, freight, and shipper values for each order.

2. **Double-click the EmployeeID, LastName, and FirstName fields in the Employees table, then double-click the EmployeeID, ShipVia, and Freight fields in the Orders table**

   In this query, the EmployeeID field in the Employees table is the primary key field for the table. It cannot be modified if related records are linked to it (unless the Cascade Update Related Fields option is checked in the Edit Relationships dialog box in the Relationships window). Changing the EmployeeID field in the Orders table, however, simply changes which employee is associated with the order.

3. **Click the Datasheet View button on the Design tab, type 2 in the EmployeeID field, read the message in the status bar indicating that the field cannot be edited, press [Tab] three times to move the Employee column, type 2, then press [Tab]**

   The datasheet should look like Figure J-10. Notice that when the foreign key field was changed from EmployeeID 1 (Nancy Davolio) to EmployeeID 2, the First Name and Last Name field values selected from the Employees table changed as well to reflect EmployeeID 2, Andrew Fuller. Sometimes you need to add a field list to Query Design View twice in order to relate a table to itself.

4. **Click the Design View button on the Home tab, right-click the Orders field list, click Remove Table, click the Show Table button on the Design tab, double-click the Employees table, click Close, right-click the Employees_1 field list, click Properties, select Employees_1 in the Alias text box, type Supervisors, press [Enter], then close the Property Sheet**

   In this case, the Employees table relates to itself through the EmployeeID and ReportsTo fields because each employee record reports to another employee whose EmployeeID value has been entered in the ReportsTo field.

5. **Drag the EmployeeID field in the Supervisors field list to the ReportsTo field in the Employees field list**

6. **Double-click the Last Name field in the Supervisors field list so that Query Design View looks like Figure J-11**

7. **Click the Datasheet View button on the Design tab**

   The datasheet shows that five employees report to Fuller and three report to Buchanan.

8. **Save the query as SupervisorList, close the query, then close the Northwind database**

   Studying the objects in the Northwind database is a great way to teach yourself additional Access skills.

FIGURE J-10: Using the foreign key field

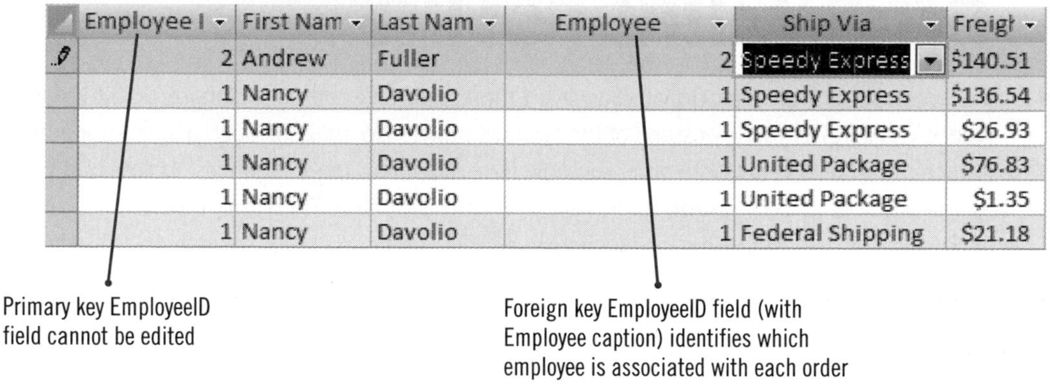

Employee I ▾	First Nam ▾	Last Nam ▾	Employee ▾	Ship Via ▾	Freigl ▾
2	Andrew	Fuller	2	Speedy Express ▾	$140.51
1	Nancy	Davolio	1	Speedy Express	$136.54
1	Nancy	Davolio	1	Speedy Express	$26.93
1	Nancy	Davolio	1	United Package	$76.83
1	Nancy	Davolio	1	United Package	$1.35
1	Nancy	Davolio	1	Federal Shipping	$21.18

Primary key EmployeeID
field cannot be edited

Foreign key EmployeeID field (with
Employee caption) identifies which
employee is associated with each order

FIGURE J-11: Relating a table to itself

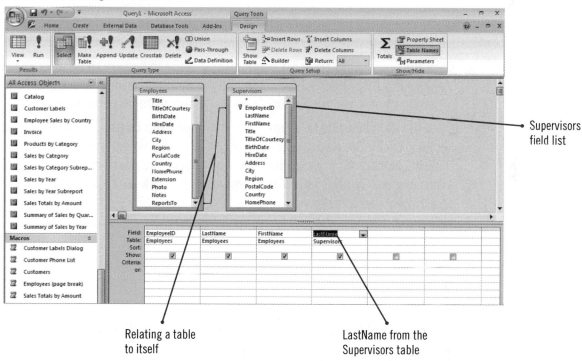

Supervisors
field list

Relating a table
to itself

LastName from the
Supervisors table

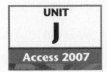
Analyzing Forms

In Access 2007, Microsoft provides an even more extensive sample database called **Northwind 2007**. Northwind 2007 showcases some of the features new to Access 2007 such as the Attachment field. Recall that the Attachment field can store multiple files, including .jpg image files. Access 2003 could not store .jpg image files nor did it have the Attachment field data type. Therefore, if your database needs to store image files, Access 2007 is a superior choice. ▰▰▰▱▱ You decide to examine the Northwind 2007 database to improve your skills with forms and Attachment fields.

STEPS

1. **On the Getting Started with Microsoft Office Access page, click the** Sample link **in the From Microsoft Office Online area, click the** Northwind 2007 Sample database, **click the** Browse button 🗁, **navigate to the drive and folder where you store your Data Files, click OK, click Download, then click** Continue **if prompted**

   Access downloads the Northwind 2007.accdb database from the Microsoft Web site, then opens an Access Help window introducing the database.

2. **Close the** Northwind 2007 Access Help window, **enable content if prompted in the Northwind 2007 database window, click** Login **to log on to the database as Andrew Cencini, then expand the Navigation Pane as shown in Figure J-12**

   The Northwind 2007.accdb database is even more fully developed than the Northwind.mdb database. Not only does it contain more traditional tables, such as Purchase Orders and Inventory Transactions, the interface has been expanded to recognize and automatically display different information and forms based on employee information. You decide to explore the Home form that was automatically loaded when the database was opened.

3. **Click the** Northwind Traders Chocolate link **in the Inventory to Reorder section of the form**

   The Product Details form opens, providing two tabs of information on this product. You will use the Attachment field to add files associated with this product to the inventory record.

4. **Click the** Attachments field box, **click the** Paper Clip button 📎 **on the Attachments toolbar, click** Add, **navigate to the drive and folder where you store your Data Files, double-click** BoxCandy.jpg, **click** Add **and repeat the portions of the step to add** Coins.jpg **and** Truffles.jpg **as attachments, then click** OK **to add all three pictures as attachments to this record**

   Only one attachment is shown at a time, but you can scroll through the attachments using the Attachments toolbar.

5. **Click the image of** box candy, **then click the** Next button 🔘 **twice on the Attachments toolbar to scroll through the images**

   See Figure J-13. You can also export attachments using the Attachments dialog box.

6. **Double-click the** candy image **to open the Attachments dialog box, click** Coins.jpg, **click** Save As, **navigate to the drive and folder where you store your Data Files, type** ChocolateCoins.jpg **as the filename, then click** Save

   If you want to delete an attachment, you can remove it using the Attachments dialog box.

7. **Click** Coins.jpg, **click** Remove, **click** OK, **then click the** Close link **in the upper-right corner of the Product Details form**

FIGURE J-12: Home form of the Northwind 2007 database

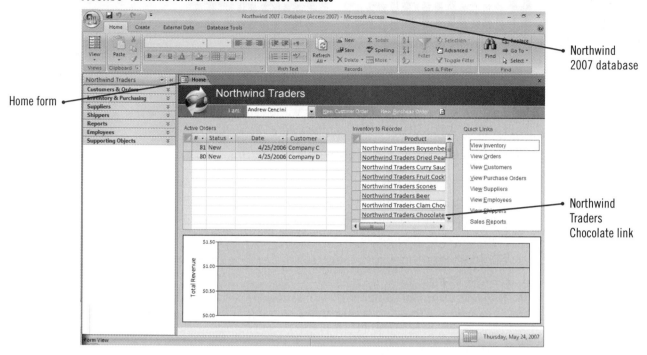

Home form •

Northwind 2007 database

Northwind Traders Chocolate link

FIGURE J-13: Attachments in the Northwind Traders Chocolate record

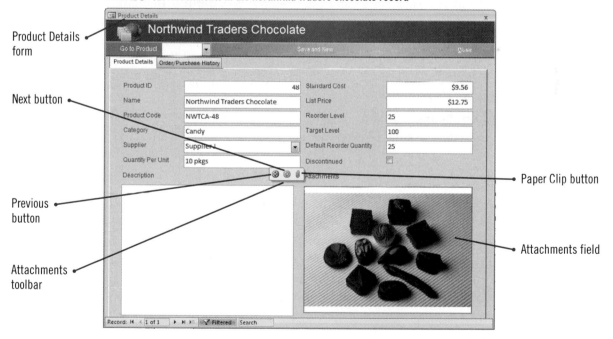

Product Details form

Next button •

Previous button •

Attachments toolbar

Paper Clip button

Attachments field

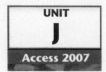

Analyzing Reports

Both the Northwind.mdb and Northwind 2007.accdb databases offer many examples of reports and other objects that you can study and apply to your own unique databases. One of the best ways to get an overview of everything a database has to offer is to spend time opening and viewing objects. Then use Design View to see exactly how an object was created. ▰▰▰▰ You decide to study the reports in the Northwind 2007 database to pick up new ideas and skills.

STEPS

1. **Click the Reports bar in the Navigation Pane, then double-click Top Ten Biggest Orders**

   The report lists the ten orders with the highest sales amounts from highest to lowest, as shown in Figure J-14. You might wonder how the report can select the top ten sales items and sort them from the highest sales value to the lowest. To find these answers, you switch to Report Design View to study the construction of the report.

2. **Click View button arrow, click Design View, then click the Group & Sort button on the Design tab**

   The Group, Sort, and Total pane shows that the SaleAmount field was used in the report as the first and only sort order, from largest to smallest. This explains the order in which the records appear on the report. But how does the report select only the top ten sales? The number of fields and records displayed in a report depends on the Record Source of the report, which is accessed through the report's Property Sheet.

3. **Click the Property Sheet button, click the Data tab, click Top Ten Orders by Sales Amount, then click the Build button [...]**

   The Query Builder opens, showing you which fields have been selected and which field lists participate in the query. The query selects the first ten records when sorted in descending order based on the SaleAmount field because of sort order and Top Values options set in the query, as shown in Figure J-15.

4. **Click 10 in the Return (Top Values) text box, type 10%, click the Close button on the Design tab, click Yes to save the changes, edit the Top 10 Biggest Orders label in the Report Header to be Top 10% Biggest Orders, save the report, then preview it**

   The report now shows only four records because the Northwind 2007 database has only about 40 total sales records. As the number of orders grows, however, this report will show more top sales because the number of records returned by the query in the Record Source property is based on a percentage of the total sales records, not a fixed number.

5. **Close the report, then close the Northwind 2007.accdb database and exit Access 2007**

   The Northwind.mdb and Northwind 2007.accdb databases provide many sample objects to learn from. As you become more familiar with these sample databases, you can analyze their advanced techniques and apply them to your own unique Access applications.

Analyzing Database Design Using Northwind

FIGURE J-14: Preview Top 10 Biggest Orders report

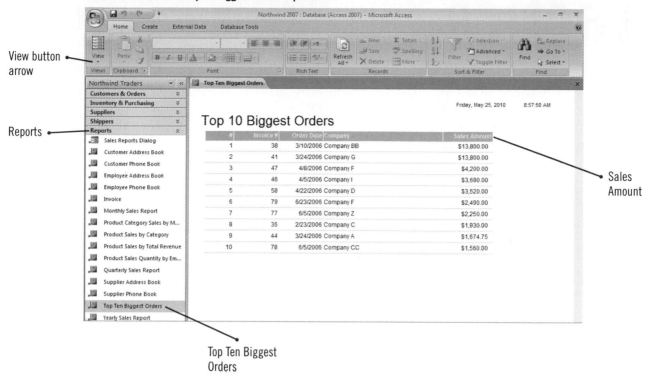

View button arrow

Reports

Sales Amount

Top Ten Biggest Orders

FIGURE J-15: Query Builder for Top Ten Orders report

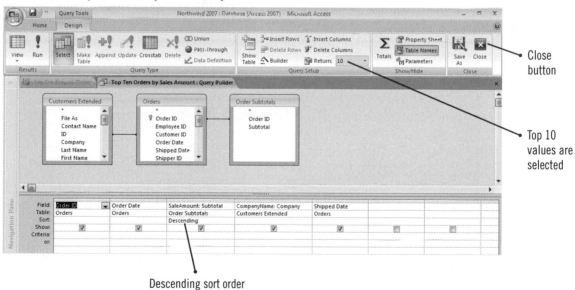

Close button

Top 10 values are selected

Descending sort order

Practice

If you have a SAM user profile, you may have access to hands-on instruction, practice, and assessment of the skills covered in this unit. Log in to your SAM account (http://sam2007.course.com/) to launch any assigned training activities or exams that relate to the skills covered in this unit.

▼ CONCEPTS REVIEW

Identify each element of the Access options dialog box in Figure J-16.

FIGURE J-16

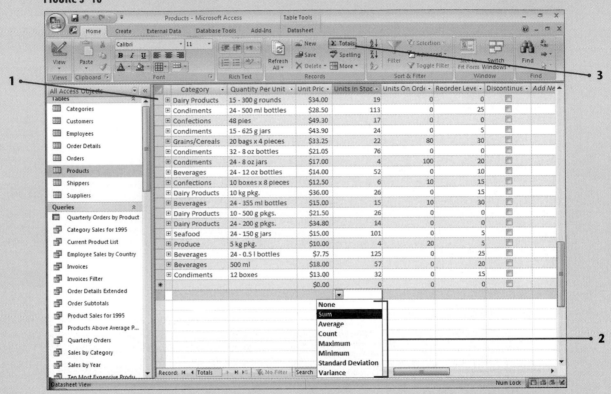

Match each term with the statement that best describes its function.

4. **Zero-length string**

5. **Normalization**

6. **Caption**

7. **Index**

8. **Subquery**

a. An *intentional* "nothing" entry

b. Displayed as the default field name at the top of the field column in datasheets as well as in labels that describe fields on forms and reports

c. Keeps track of the order of the values in the indexed field as data is entered and edited

d. A query based on another query's field list

e. The process of structuring data into a well-formed relational database

Analyzing Database Design Using Northwind

Select the best answer from the list of choices.

9. **Which of the following is *not* a benefit of a well-designed relational database?**
   a. Is easier to create than a single-table database
   b. Reduces redundant data
   c. Improves reporting flexibility
   d. Has lower overall storage requirements

10. **First normal form can be described as:**
    a. Any collection of data in any form.
    b. A single two-dimensional table with rows and columns.
    c. A well-functioning, fully developed relational database.
    d. A series of queries and subqueries.

11. **Which of the following activities occurs during the creation of second normal form?**
    a. Calculated fields are removed from tables.
    b. Additional calculated fields are added to tables.
    c. Redundant data is removed from one table, and relationships are created.
    d. One-to-one relationships are examined and eliminated.

12. **Which of the following activities occurs during the creation of third normal form?**
    a. Calculated fields are removed from tables.
    b. Additional calculated fields are added to tables.
    c. Redundant data is removed from one table, and relationships are created.
    d. One-to-one relationships are examined and eliminated.

13. **One-to-one relationships occur when:**
    a. The foreign key field of the first table is related to the primary key field of a second table.
    b. The foreign key field of the first table is related to the foreign key field of a second table.
    c. The primary key field of the first table is related to the foreign key field of a second table.
    d. The primary key field of the first table is related to the primary key field of a second table.

14. **A multi-field primary key consists of:**
    a. one field.
    b. two or more fields.
    c. an AutoNumber field.
    d. a primary key field that also serves as a foreign key field.

15. **Which of the following is *not* true for the Caption property?**
    a. It is the default field name at the top of the field column in datasheets.
    b. The value of the Caption property is the default label that describes a field on a report.
    c. The value of the Caption property is the default label that describes a field on a form.
    d. It is used instead of the field name when you build expressions.

16. **Which of the following fields would be the most likely to be used for an index?**
    a. MiddleName
    b. State
    c. ApartmentNumber
    d. FirstName

17. **Which of the following phrases best describes the need for both null values and zero-length strings?**
    a. They look different on a query datasheet.
    b. Having two different choices for "nothing" clarifies data entry.
    c. Null values speed up calculations.
    d. They represent two different conditions.

18. **Which Memo field property allows you to add data but not change or remove existing data?**
    a. Indexed
    b. New Values
    c. Add
    d. Append Only

19. **Which function is used to convert a value to currency?**
    a. CCur
    b. ConvertCur
    c. ConvertCurrency
    d. CurrencyConvert

20. **The Northwind 2007 database is available from Microsoft as a(n):**
    a. template.
    b. online tutorial.
    c. Help manual lesson.
    d. Attachment field.

▼ SKILLS REVIEW

1. Normalize data.

   a. Start Access 2007, then open the Basketball-J.accdb database from the drive and folder where you store your Data Files, enabling content if prompted.

   b. Double-click the Players table to view its datasheet. Notice the repeated data in the Year, Position, and HomeState fields. Close the Players datasheet. You will build a lookup table to better describe and manage the values in the Year field.

   c. Click the Create tab, click Table Design, then create a two-field table with the field names YearDescription and YearAbbrev. Both fields should have a Text data type. Set YearAbbrev as the primary key field. Save the table with the name Years, and enter the data in the datasheet shown in Figure J-17. Save and close the Years table when you are finished.

FIGURE J-17

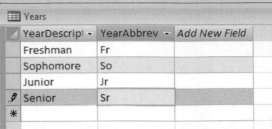

   d. Open the Players table in Design View, click the Year field, then choose Lookup Wizard using the Data Type list arrow.

   e. Choose the "I want the lookup column to look up the values..." option, choose Table:Years, choose both fields, do not choose any sorting orders, do not hide the key column, choose YearAbbrev as the field that uniquely identifies the row, accept the Year label, finish the Lookup Wizard, then click Yes to save the table.

   f. Close Table Design View for the Players table, open the Relationships window, click the All Relationships button, double-click the link between the Years and Players table, click the Enforce Referential Integrity check box, then click OK. (If you were unable to enforce referential integrity, it means you've made a data-entry error in the Years table. Open the Years table in Datasheet View and check your data against the values in Figure J-17, then redo step f.)

   g. In the Players table, click the Year field list arrow to verify that the field now provides a list for selecting a year, then close the Players table.

   h. Save and close the Relationships window, then close the Basketball-J.accdb database.

2. Analyze relationships.

   a. Start Access 2007, then open the Northwind 2007.accdb database from the drive and folder where you store your Data Files. If you have not created the Northwind 2007.accdb database in a previous step, choose the Northwind 2007 sample database from the Microsoft Office Online template section to save and download the Northwind 2007 sample database. If you are downloading the database for the first time, save it in the drive and folder where you store your Data Files. When the database opens, enable content when prompted.

   b. Close the Login dialog box, click the Database Tools tab, then click the Relationships button to view the relationships in the Northwind 2007.accdb database. These relationships are more complex than those in the Northwind.mdb database because Northwind 2007.accdb contains more small lookup tables. You can hide the lookup tables to examine only the core tables in the relational database.

   c. Right-click the Privileges table, click Hide Table, and repeat this process for the Employee Privileges, Orders Status, Order Details Status, Orders Tax Status, Inventory Transaction Types, Purchase Order Status, Invoices, Suppliers, Purchase Orders, Inventory Transactions, and Purchase Order Details tables.

d. Move and resize the remaining field lists so that your Relationships window looks like Figure J-18, then use the Relationship Report button to preview and print this view, changing the report orientation to landscape if necessary to print it on one page. While this presentation of the database relationships is not an exhaustive look at the database, by isolating a few key tables and then printing and studying relationship reports, you can focus on various parts of the database.

FIGURE J-18

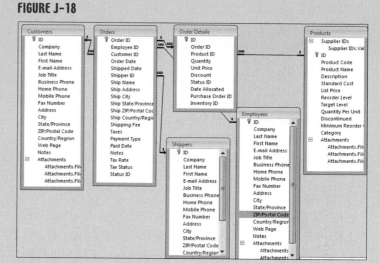

e. Close the Relationships report without saving it.

f. Save and close the Relationships window.

3. Evaluate tables.

a. Expand the Supporting Objects group in the Navigation Pane.

b. Double-click the Products table to open its datasheet.

c. Tab to the Standard Cost field, then click the Totals button to open the Total row on the datasheet.

d. Use the Total row to find the Average Standard Cost and Average List Price values for all of the records in the Products table. Based on these two values, what is the average markup percentage? (*Hint*: Divide the difference between the average list price and the average standard cost by the average standard cost.)

4. Improve fields.

a. Switch to Design View for the Products table.

b. Change the Caption property for the ID field to **Automatic ID**.

c. Change the value for the Allow Zero Length property of the Description field to Yes.

d. Change the value for the Indexed property of the Product Name field to Yes (No Duplicates).

e. Save the table, then display it in Datasheet View to observe the new caption for the ID field (second column).

f. Close the Products table datasheet.

5. Use subqueries.

a. Click the Create tab, then click the Query Design button.

b. Double-click Orders, Order Details, and Products, then click Close.

c. Double-click the Order Date field in the Orders table, the Quantity and Unit Price fields in the Order Details table, and the Product Name field in the Products table.

d. Double-click the relationship link between Orders and Order Details, and choose option 1. You want to see only orders where there are order details, not orders that have been entered but do not have any associated order details. Click OK.

e. In the fifth column, enter the following calculated field: **GrossRevenue:[Quantity]*[Unit Price]**

f. Save the query with the name **GrossRevenue**, then close it.

g. Click the Create tab, then click the Query Design button.

h. Click the Queries tab in the Show Table dialog box, double-click GrossRevenue, then click Close.

i. Double-click the Product Name and GrossRevenue fields, then click the Totals button.

j. Change Group By in the GrossRevenue field to Sum, click the Property Sheet button, change the Format property to Currency, then view and print the resulting datasheet.

k. Save the query with the name **GrossRevenueByProduct**, then close it.

Access 2007

6. **Analyze queries.**

   a. Open the Employees table in the Supporting Objects group in Table Design View.

   b. After the Attachments field, enter a field named **Manager** with a Number data type. Save and close the Employees table.

   c. Open the Employees table in Datasheet View, then tab to the Manager field. Every value in the Manager field should be 5 (all Sales Representatives report to the Sales Manager, Steven Thorpe, whose ID is 5), except for two. The Manager value for the fifth record should be 2 because Employee ID 5 in record 5 (Steven Thorpe) reports to the Vice President, Andrew Cencini, whose ID is 2. The Manager value for the second record should be null because Employee ID 2 in record 2 (Andrew Cencini) doesn't report to any other employee in this database. Close the Employees datasheet.

   d. Click the Create tab, click the Query Design button, double-click the Employees table twice, then click the Close button.

   e. Right-click the Employees_1 title bar, click Properties, then change the Alias property value from Employees_1 to Managers.

   f. Drag the ID field from the Managers field list to the Manager field in the Employees field list.

   g. Double-click First Name and Last Name in the Employees field list, then double-click First Name and Last Name from the Managers field list. Display and print the resulting datasheet.

   h. Save the query with the name **Employees-Supervisors**, then close it.

7. **Analyze forms.**

   a. Open the Product Details form in the Inventory & Purchasing group, then navigate to the Northwind Traders Marmalade record, Product ID 20.

   b. Click the Attachments field, click the Paper Clip button on the Attachments toolbar, then click the Add button. Add the Cherry.wmf and Strawberry.wmf files as attachments, then click OK in the Attachments dialog box.

   c. Close Product Details form.

8. **Analyze reports.**

   a. In the Reports group of the Navigation Pane, double-click the Customer Address Book report to preview it. You will use Report Design View to learn how the first letter of the last name was calculated to introduce each new group of records.

   b. Open the Customer Address Book report in Report Design View, then open the Group, Sort, and Total pane.

   c. Expand the text box in the File As Header section so that you can read the entire expression, =UCase(Left(Nz([File As]),1))

   d. Using Microsoft Help, research the functions that were used in this expression (UCase, Left, and Nz). On a sheet of paper, write a brief description of each.

   e. To determine how the File As field was created, you need to open the Record Source for the report. Open the Property Sheet for the report, click the Data tab, click Customers Extended in the Record Source property, then click the Build button.

   f. Right-click the File As field, then click Zoom to read the entire expression, which uses three nested IIF functions as well as the IsNull criterion. On your paper, write a nontechnical explanation of how the expression determines the value of the File As field.

   g. Cancel the Zoom dialog box, close the Customers Extended query, then close the Customer Address Book report.

   h. Close the Northwind 2007 database and exit Access 2007.

▼ INDEPENDENT CHALLENGE 1

As the manager of a basketball team, you have created an Access database called Basketball-J.accdb to track players, games, and statistics. You have recently learned how to create lookup tables to better control the values of a field that contains repeated data and further apply the skills to your database.

a. Start Access 2007, then open the **Basketball-J.accdb** database from the drive and folder where you store your Data Files, enabling content if prompted.

b. Double-click the Players table to view its datasheet. Notice the repeated data in the Year, Position, and HomeState fields. Close the Players datasheet. You will build a lookup table to better describe and manage the values in the Position field.

c. Click the Create tab, click Table Design, then create a two-field database with the field names **PositionDescription** and **PositionID**. Both fields should have a Text data type. Set PositionID as the primary key field. Save the table with the name **Positions**, and enter the data in the datasheet shown in Figure J-19.

d. Open the Players table in Design View, click the Position field, then choose Lookup Wizard using the Data Type list arrow.

e. Choose the "I want the lookup column to look up the values..." option, choose Table:Positions, choose both fields, do not choose any sorting orders, do not hide the key column, choose PositionID as the field that uniquely identifies the row, accept the Position label, finish the Lookup Wizard, then click Yes to save the table.

f. Close Table Design View for the Players table, open the Relationships window, click the All Relationships button, double-click the link between the Positions and Players table, click the Enforce Referential Integrity check box, then click OK. (If you were unable to enforce referential integrity, it means you've made a data-entry error in the Positions table. Open the Positions table in Datasheet View and check your data entry against the values in Figure J-19, then redo step f.)

g. Open the Players table in Datasheet View, click the Position field list arrow to verify that the field now provides a list for selecting a position, then close the Players table.

h. Save and close the Relationships window.

FIGURE J-19

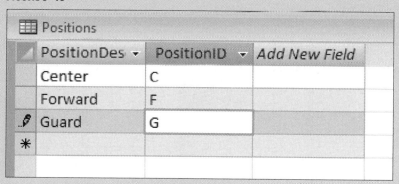

Advanced Challenge Exercise

- Repeat steps c through f, creating a States table instead of a Positions table using the data shown in Figure J-20. The final Relationships window should look like Figure J-21.

i. Print the final Relationship report for the Basketball-J.accdb database, then close the Relationship report without saving it.

j. Close the Basketball-J.accdb database, then exit Access.

FIGURE J-20

StateName	State2	Add New Field
Iowa	IA	
Illinois	IL	
Kansas	KS	
Minnesota	MN	
North Dakota	ND	
Nebraska	NE	
Texas	TX	
Wisconsin	WI	

FIGURE J-21

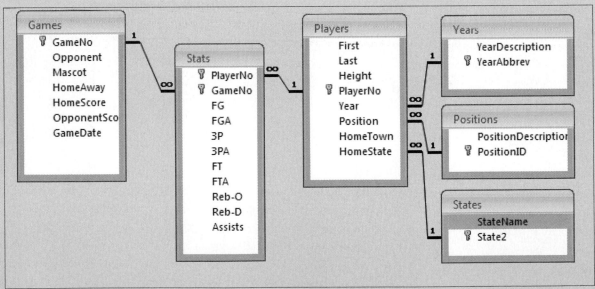

▼ INDEPENDENT CHALLENGE 2

You have been hired to help the foreign exchange program at your school organize information about languages and common phrases for different countries. You want to build a form that displays the information about various countries, including the flag of each country. You'll use an Attachment data type to display .jpg pictures of the country's flag.

a. Open the **Languages-J.accdb** database from the drive and folder where you store your Data Files, and enable content if prompted.

b. Right-click the Countries table in the Navigation Pane, click Design View, click the field name cell below Language, type **Flag** as the new field name, and specify the Attachment data type. Save and close the Countries table.

c. Click the Create tab, click the Countries table in the Navigation Pane, then click Split Form. You want to resize some controls in the upper portion of the form, so you will have space to add the country's flag to the right side.

d. In Layout View, click any text box in the upper part of the form, then narrow the controls to about half of their previous size.

e. Click the Arrange tab, select all the controls, click the Remove button to remove control grouping, then drag the Flag control to the right half of the form. Resize the Flag control (not the label) so it is about twice as high.

f. Switch to Design View, right-click the Language control, point to Change To, and then click Combo Box.

g. Click the Home tab, then click the View button to view the form in Form View.

h. Starting with the first record, click the Flag attachment placeholder, click the Paper Clip button on the Attachments toolbar, click the Add button, navigate to the drive and folder where you store your Data Files, then add the appropriate .jpg file for that country. Repeat step g until all nine countries in the database display the correct flag.

i. Save the form with the name **Countries** as shown in Figure J-22, close the Countries form, close the Languages-J.accdb database, then close Access.

FIGURE J-22

Access 2007

▼ INDEPENDENT CHALLENGE 3

The Northwind 2007.accdb database contains many tables, but you have noticed repeating data in the Category field of the Products table and decide to separate the field values into a Categories table that is linked back to the Products table with a one-to-many relationship. This modification will help improve data accuracy and consistency.

a. Start Access 2007, then open the **Northwind 2007.accdb** database from the drive and folder where you store your Data Files. If you have not created the Northwind 2007.accdb database in a previous exercise, choose the Northwind 2007 sample database from the Microsoft Office Online template section to save and download the Northwind 2007 sample database. If you are downloading the database for the first time, save it in the drive and folder where you store your Data Files. When the database opens, enable content when prompted.

b. Close the Welcome to Northwind form if it opens, open the Products datasheet in the Supporting Objects group of the Navigation Pane, tab to the Category field, then click the Sort Ascending button. With all of the category values displayed together in ascending order, it will be easier to determine what field values should be added to the linking Categories table.

c. Click the Create tab, click Table Design, type **CategoryName** as the field name, choose Text as the data type, and set the CategoryName field as the primary key field.

d. Save the table with the name **Categories**, then display it in Datasheet View.

e. Click the Products tab, right-click the Category column heading, click Copy, click the Categories tab, right-click the CategoryName field, click Paste, click OK when prompted that you can't create duplicate values in a primary key field, click Yes when prompted to suppress error messages, click Yes when asked if you want to paste 16 records, then click OK when informed about the Paste Errors table.

f. Close the Categories datasheet, scroll down to the Unassigned Objects group in the Navigation Pane, then double-click the Paste Errors table to see what it contains (the duplicate category name values).

g. Close the Paste Errors table, right-click the Paste Errors table in the Navigation Pane, click Delete on the shortcut menu, then click Yes.

h. Open the Products table in Design View, click Text for the Category field, click the Data Type list arrow, then click Lookup Wizard.

i. Choose the "I want the lookup column to look up the values in a table or query" option button, click Next, click Table:Categories, click Next, double-click CategoryName, click Next three times, click Finish, then click Yes.

j. Open the Products table in Datasheet View, tab to the Category field, then test the lookup list. It should contain all of the unique values in the CategoryName field of the Categories table, which will help you more quickly and consistently enter data in the Category field of the Products table.

k. Close the Products datasheet.

Advanced Challenge Exercise

- Open the Relationships window, click the All Relationships button, then find the relationship between the Products table and the newly created Categories table.
- Double-click the link between the Products and Categories tables, enforce referential integrity, click OK in the Edit Relationships dialog box, then close the Relationships window. (If you are unable to enforce referential integrity it means that there is a data-entry problem in the Categories table. Carefully check each CategoryName entry to make sure it matches the values in the Category field of the Products table.)
- Save the changes to the Relationships window, then close the Relationships window.

l. Close the Northwind 2007.accdb database, then exit Access.

▼ REAL LIFE INDEPENDENT CHALLENGE

Mastering the use of Access requires curiosity and perseverance. In this exercise, you will work in the Northwind.mdb database, independently examining different object types and looking for new knowledge and skills in your pursuit of becoming a self-sufficient Access database consultant.

    a. Start Access and open the Northwind.mdb database from the drive and folder where you store your Data Files. Enable content if prompted.

    b. Close the Welcome to Northwind form if it is presented, then group the objects in the Navigation Pane by Object Type if they are not already grouped in that manner.

    c. Double-click each table, query, form, and report object, observing it in Datasheet, Form, or Print Preview. For each object type, pick one object that presents something new or interesting to you, then examine the object in Design View.

    d. On a sheet of paper, list each object type, the Northwind object you chose to study further, and what you learned from that object. Use the Print Screen key to capture an image of each object you chose to the Windows Clipboard, then paste each image in a document.

    e. Close the Northwind.mdb database, then exit Access 2007.

▼ VISUAL WORKSHOP

Use the Northwind 2007.accdb database to create the following Relationships report by removing field lists from the Relationships window that are not shown on this report. (*Note*: Do not permanently delete relationships.) Save the Relationships report with the name **Customers-Orders-Products-Invoices**, then print and close the report. Close the Northwind 2007.accdb database, then exit Access 2007.

FIGURE J-23

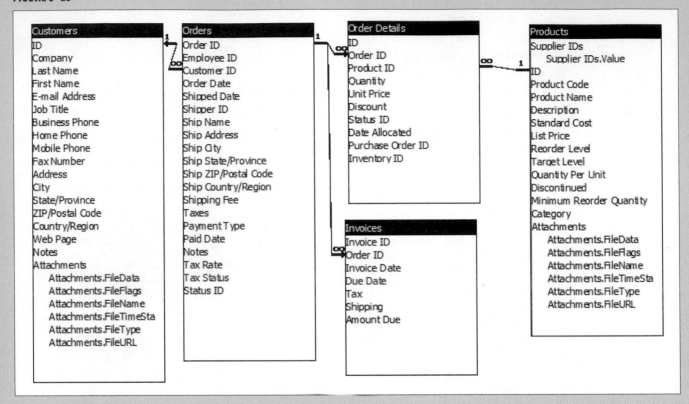

Analyzing Database Design Using Northwind

Creating Advanced Queries

Files You Will Need

Education-K.accdb
Seminar-K.accdb
Basketball-K.accdb
Chocolate-K.accdb

Queries are database objects that answer questions about the data. The most common query is the **select query**, which selects fields and records that match specific criteria and displays them in a datasheet. Other types of queries, such as top value, parameter, and action queries, are powerful tools for displaying, analyzing, and updating data. An **action query** changes all of the selected records when it is run. Access provides four types of action queries: delete, update, append, and make table.  You use advanced queries to help Julia Rice handle the requests for information about data stored in the Education database.

OBJECTIVES

Query for top values

Create a parameter query

Modify query properties

Create a make table query

Create an append query

Create a delete query

Create an update query

Specify join properties

Find unmatched records

Querying for Top Values

After you enter a large number of records into a database, you rarely query for all of the records, but often list only the most significant records by choosing a subset of the highest or lowest values from a sorted query. Use the **Top Values** feature in Query Design View to specify a number or percentage of sorted records that you want to display in the query's datasheet.  Employee attendance at continuing education classes has grown recently as employees want to expand their employment options in the rapidly changing world of tourism. To help plan future classes, Julia Rice wants to print a datasheet listing the names of the top five classes, sorted by number of students per class. You can create a summarized select query to find the total number of attendees for each class, then use the Top Values feature to find the five most attended classes.

STEPS

1. **Start** Access, **open the** Education-K.accdb **database, enable content if prompted, click the** Create **tab, then click the** Query Design **button in the Other group**

   You need fields from both the Enrollments and Courses tables.

TROUBLE

If you add a table's field list to Query Design View twice by mistake, click the title bar of the extra field list, then press [Delete].

2. **Double-click** Enrollments, **double-click** Courses, **then click** Close **in the Show Table dialog box**

   Query Design View displays the field lists of the two related tables in the upper portion of the query window.

3. **Double-click** EnrollmentID **in the Enrollments field list, double-click** Description **in the Courses field list, then click the** Datasheet View **button on the Design tab**

   The datasheet shows 443 total records. You want to know how many people took each course, so you need to group the records by the Description field and count the EnrollmentID field.

4. **Click the** Design View **button on the Home tab, click the** Totals **button in the Show/Hide group, click** Group By **for the EnrollmentID field, click the** Group By **list arrow, then click** Count

   Sorting helps you further analyze the information and prepare for finding the top values.

QUICK TIP

Click the Datasheet View button as you design a query to view the datasheet at that point in development.

5. **Click the** EnrollmentID **field Sort cell, click the** EnrollmentID **field Sort list arrow, then click** Descending

   Your screen should look like Figure K-1. Choosing a descending sort order lists the courses with the highest count value (the most attended courses) at the top of the datasheet.

6. **Click the** Top Values **list arrow on the Design tab**

   The number or percentage specified in the Top Values list box determines which records the query displays, starting with the first one on the sorted datasheet. See Table K-1 for more information on how to use the Top Values feature.

7. **Click** 5, **then click the** Datasheet View **button on the Design tab**

   Your screen should look like Figure K-2. The datasheet shows the three most attended continuing education courses. (More than one course has the same number of attendees.) The USA Biking I course has 21 attendees, three courses have 19 attendees, and two courses have 18 attendees. This query displayed all the top values, even though more than five records have those values.

8. **Click the** Save **button** 🖫 **on the Quick Access toolbar, type** TopFive, **click** OK, **then close the datasheet**

   As with all queries, if you enter additional enrollment records into this database, the count statistics change. The TopFive query always selects the most up-to-date data each time it is displayed.

Creating Advanced Queries

FIGURE K-1: Designing a summary query for top values

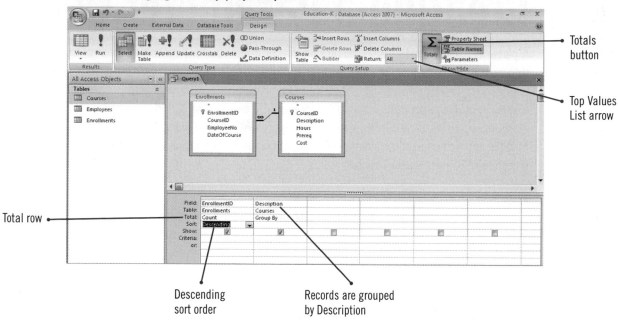

Total row ●

Descending
sort order

Records are grouped
by Description

Totals
button

Top Values
List arrow

FIGURE K-2: Top Values datasheet

CountOfEnrollmentID
field counts the
records in each group

Records are sorted in
descending order

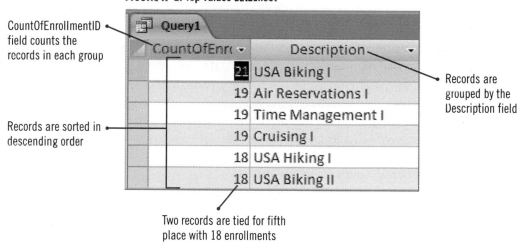

CountOfEnr ▾	Description ▾
21	USA Biking I
19	Air Reservations I
19	Time Management I
19	Cruising I
18	USA Hiking I
18	USA Biking II

Records are
grouped by the
Description field

Two records are tied for fifth
place with 18 enrollments

TABLE K-1: Top Values options

action	displays
Click 5, 25, or 100 from the Top Values list	Top 5, 25, or 100 records
Enter a number, such as 10, in the Top Values text box	Top 10, or whatever value is entered, records
Click 5% or 25% from the Top Values list	Top 5 percent or 25 percent of records
Enter a percentage, such as 10%, in the Top Values text box	Top 10%, or whatever percentage is entered, of records
Click All	All records

Creating a Parameter Query

A **parameter query** displays a dialog box that prompts you for field criteria. Your entry in the dialog box determines which records appear on the final datasheet, similar to criteria entered directly in the query design grid. You can also build a form or report based on a parameter query. Then, when you open the form or report, the parameter dialog box opens. The entry in the dialog box determines which records the query selects in the recordset for the form or report. ▰▰▰▰ You want to enhance the TopFive query to display the top five courses for a department that you specify each time you run the query. To do so, you add parameter prompts to the TopFive query.

1. **Right-click the TopFive query in the Navigation Pane, click Design View on the shortcut menu, click the Show Table button in the Query Setup group on the Design tab, double-click Employees, then click Close**

    The Employees table contains the Department field needed for this query.

2. **Drag the title bar of the Courses field list to the left, then drag the Enrollments field list to the right so that the relationship lines do not cross behind a field list**

    You are not required to rearrange the field lists of a query, but doing so can help clarify the relationships between them.

3. **Double-click the Department field in the Employees field list, click the Top Values list arrow on the Design tab, click All, then click the Datasheet View button on the Design tab**

    The query now counts the EnrollmentID field for records grouped by Description as well as Department. Because you only want to query for one department at a time, however, you need to add parameter criteria to the Department field.

To enter a long criterion, right-click the Criteria cell, then click Zoom.

4. **Click the Design View button on the Home tab, click the Department field Criteria cell, type [Enter department:], then click the Datasheet View button on the Design tab**

    Your screen should look like Figure K-3. In Query Design View, you must enter parameter criteria within [square brackets]. The parameter criterion you entered appears as a prompt in the Enter Parameter Value dialog box. The entry you make in the Enter Parameter Value box is used as the final criterion for the field that contains the parameter criterion. You can combine logical operators such as > (greater than) or < (less than) as well as wildcard characters such as * (asterisk) with parameter criteria to create flexible search options. See Table K-2 for more examples of parameter criteria.

Query criteria are not case sensitive, so "marketing" is the same as "Marketing".

5. **Type Marketing in the Enter department: text box, then click OK**

    Only those records with "Marketing" in the Department field are displayed, as shown in Figure K-4. The records are still sorted in descending order by the CountOfEnrollmentID field, and they are grouped by both the Description and the Department fields.

6. **Click the Office button 🔘, click Save As, type DepartmentParameter, then click OK**

    The new query appears as an object in the Navigation Pane.

7. **Close the datasheet**

FIGURE K-3: Using parameter criteria for the Department field

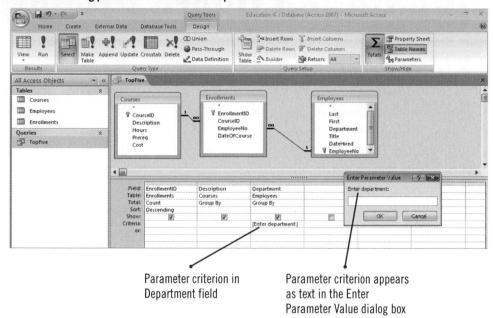

Parameter criterion in
Department field

Parameter criterion appears
as text in the Enter
Parameter Value dialog box

FIGURE K-4: Datasheet for parameter query when Department equals Marketing

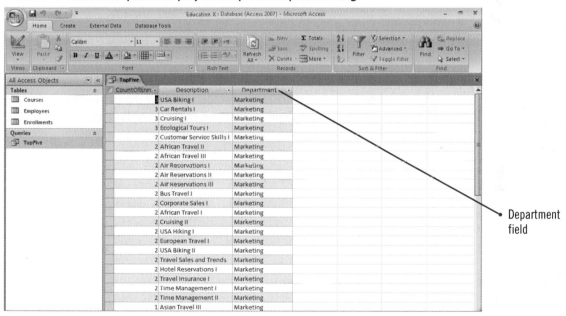

Department
field

TABLE K-2: Examples of parameter criteria

field data type	parameter criteria	description
Date/Time	>=[Enter start date:]	Searches for dates on or after the entered date
Date/Time	>=[Enter start date:] and <=[Enter end date:]	Prompts you for two date entries and searches for dates on or after the first date and on or before the second date
Text	LIKE [Enter the first character of the last name:] & "*"	Searches for any name that begins with the entered character
Text	LIKE "*" & [Enter any character(s) to search by:] & "*"	Searches for words that contain the entered characters anywhere in the field

Modifying Query Properties

Properties are characteristics that define the appearance and behavior of items in the database such as objects, fields, sections, and controls. You can view the properties for an item by opening its property sheet. **Field properties**, those that describe a field, can be changed in either Table Design View or Query Design View. If you change field properties in Query Design View, they are modified for that query only (as opposed to changing the field properties in Table Design View, which affects that field's characteristics throughout the database). Queries themselves also have properties that you might want to modify to better describe or protect the information they present. 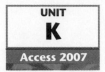 You want to modify the query and field properties of the DepartmentParameter query to better describe and present the data.

STEPS

1. **Right-click the DepartmentParameter query in the Navigation Pane, then click Object Properties**

   The DepartmentParameter Properties dialog box opens, providing information about the query and a text box where you can enter a description for the query.

2. **Type Counts enrollments per course description, prompts for Department, click OK, right-click All Access Objects in the Navigation Pane title bar, point to View By, click Details, then drag the right edge of the Navigation Pane to the right as shown in Figure K-5**

   The Date Created, Date Modified, and Description property you entered appears below each object in the Navigation Pane.

   > **QUICK TIP**
   > The title bar of the Property Sheet always indicates which item's properties are shown. If it shows "Field Properties" instead of "Query Properties," click a blank spot below the query grid, resizing the panes in Query Design View as necessary.

3. **Right-click the DepartmentParameter query in the Navigation Pane, click Design View on the shortcut menu, right-click in a blank spot below the query grid, then click Properties on the shortcut menu**

   The Property Sheet opens, as shown in Figure K-6. Viewing the query Property Sheet from within Query Design View gives a complete list of the query's properties including the Description property that you modified earlier. The **Recordset Type** property determines if and how records displayed by a query are locked. **Snapshot** locks the recordset (which prevents it from being updated). **Dynaset** is the default value and allows updates to data. Because a summary query's datasheet summarizes several records, you cannot update the data, but for regular select queries, you can modify the Recordset Type property to give users read (but not write) access to data.

   To change the field name for the CountOfEnrollmentID field in this query to something more readable, you modify the field's **Caption** property. When you click a property in a Property Sheet, a short description of the property appears in the status bar. Press [F1] to open Microsoft Office Access Help for a longer description of the selected property.

   > **QUICK TIP**
   > You can also click the Property Sheet button on the Design tab to open or close the Property Sheet.

4. **Click the EnrollmentID field, click the Caption property, type Total Enrollment, click the Datasheet View button on the Design tab, type Marketing, then click OK**

   The Total Enrollment field now appears in the datasheet, but the numbers are not formatted in a way that makes them easy to read. You need to work with the field's Property Sheet to change the way the numbers are formatted.

5. **Double-click the column separator between the first and second columns to view the entire caption for the first field**

   Your screen should look like Figure K-7. The first field now has a descriptive caption as specified in the field's Property Sheet.

6. **Save and close the DepartmentParameter query**

7. **Right-click All Access Objects in the title bar of the Navigation Pane, point to View By, click List, then drag the right edge of the Navigation Pane to the left**

   The Navigation Pane should be sized large enough to identify all of the objects, but small enough to retain screen space that shows as much of the current database objects as possible.

Creating Advanced Queries

FIGURE K-5: Details of each object in the Navigation Pane

Date Created

Date Modified

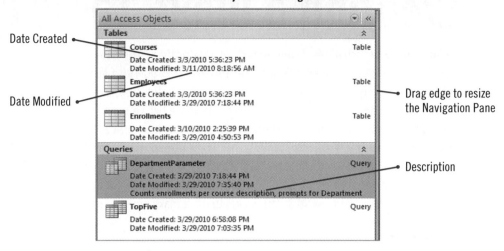

Drag edge to resize
the Navigation Pane

Description

FIGURE K-6: Query Property Sheet

EnrollmentID field

Query
properties

Recordset Type
property

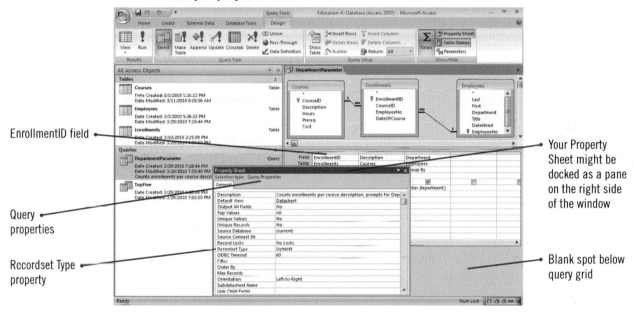

Your Property
Sheet might be
docked as a pane
on the right side
of the window

Blank spot below
query grid

FIGURE K-7: Final DepartmentParameter datasheet

Total Enrollment
is the Caption
property for the
first field

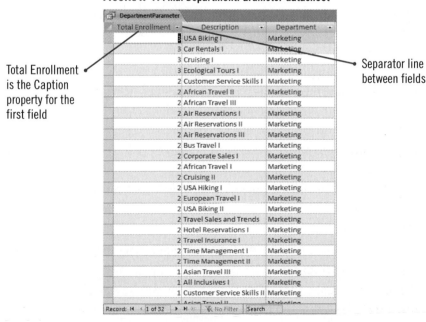

Separator line
between fields

Creating Advanced Queries

Creating a Make Table Query

An **action query** changes many records in one process. The four types of action queries are delete, update, append, and make table. In order for an action query to complete its action, you must run the action query using the Run button on the Design tab. Because you cannot undo an action query, it is always a good idea to create a backup of the database before running the query. See Table K-3 for more information on action queries. A **make table query** creates a new table of data based on the recordset defined by the query. The make table query works like an export feature in that it creates a copy of the selected data and pastes it into a new table in a database specified by the query. The location of the new table can be the current database or any other Access database. Sometimes a make table query is used to back up a subset of data. ▓▓▓▓ You decide to use a make table query to archive the first quarter's records for the year 2010 that are currently stored in the Enrollments table.

STEPS

1. **Click the Create tab, click the Query Design button, double-click Enrollments in the Show Table dialog box, click Close, then close the Property Sheet if it is open**

2. **Double-click the * (asterisk) at the top of the Enrollments table's field list**

   Adding the asterisk to the query design grid includes all of the fields in that table in the grid. Later, if you add new fields to the Enrollments table, they are also added to this query.

   QUICK TIP

   Access automatically adds pound signs (#) around the date criteria in the DateOfCourse field.

3. **Double-click the DateOfCourse field to add it to the second column of the query grid, click the DateOfCourse field Criteria cell, type >=1/1/2010 and <=3/31/2010, click the DateOfCourse field Show check box to uncheck it, then use the ✛ pointer to widen the DateOfCourse column to view the entire Criteria entry**

   Your screen should look like Figure K-8. Before changing this select query into a make table query, it is always a good idea to view the selected data.

4. **Click the Datasheet View button on the Design tab, click any entry in the DateOfCourse field, then click the Descending button 🖽 on the Home tab**

   Sorting the records in descending order based on the values in the DateOfCourse field allows you to confirm that no records after the first quarter, January through March of 2010, appear in the datasheet.

5. **Click the Design View button on the Home tab, click the Make Table button on the Design tab, type ArchiveEnrollments in the Table Name text box, then click OK**

   The make table query is ready, but the new table has not yet been created. Action queries do not change data until you click the Run button on the Design tab. All action query icons include an exclamation point to warn you that they change data when you run them. Use the Datasheet View button to view the datasheet, reserving use of the Run button to when you want to run action queries.

6. **Click the Run button on the Design tab, click Yes when prompted that you are about to paste 180 rows, then close the query without saving it**

   When you run an action query, Access prompts you with an "Are you sure?" message before actually updating the data. The Undo button cannot undo changes made by action queries.

7. **Double-click ArchiveEnrollments in the Navigation Pane to view the new table's datasheet**

   All 180 records are pasted into the new table, as shown in Figure K-9.

8. **Close the ArchiveEnrollments table**

FIGURE K-8: Using the asterisk in the query grid

Query Type buttons

Make Table button

Asterisk in the query grid

Criteria to select first quarter's records

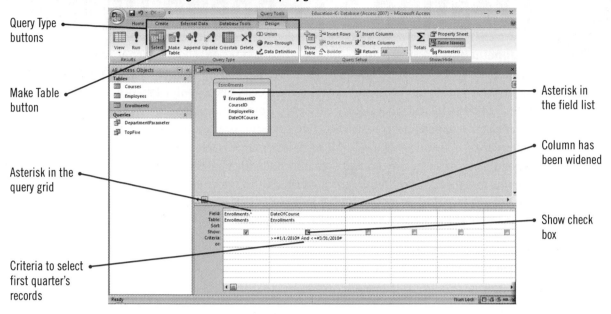

Asterisk in the field list

Column has been widened

Show check box

FIGURE K-9: ArchiveEnrollments datasheet

ArchiveEnrollments table

180 records

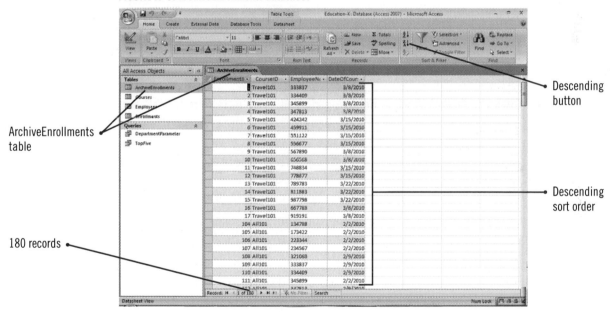

Descending button

Descending sort order

TABLE K-3: Action queries

action query	query icon	description	example
Delete	×!	Deletes a group of records from one or more tables	Remove products that are discontinued or for which there are no orders
Update	⁄!	Makes global changes to a group of records in one or more tables	Raise prices by 10 percent for all products
Append	+!	Adds a group of records from one or more tables to the end of another table	Append the employee address table from one division of the company to the address table from another division of the company
Make Table	!	Creates a new table from data in one or more tables	Export records to another Access database or make a back-up copy of a table

Creating an Append Query

An **append query** adds selected records to an existing table called the **target table**. The append query works like an export feature because the records are copied from one location and a duplicate set is pasted within the target table. The target table can be in the current database or in any other Access database. The most difficult thing about an append query is making sure that all of the fields you have selected in the append query match fields with similar characteristics in the target table. For example, you cannot append text data to a Number field. If the target table has more fields than those you want to append, the append query adds the data in the matching fields and ignores the other fields. If you attempt to append a field to an incompatible field in the target table (for example, if you attempt to append a Text field to a Number field in the target table) an error message appears allowing you to cancel and correct the append query.  You decide to use an append query to append April's records to the ArchiveEnrollments table.

1. **Click the** Create tab, **click the** Query Design button, **double-click** Enrollments **in the Show Table dialog box, then click** Close

2. **Double-click the** title bar **in the Enrollments table's field list, then drag the** highlighted fields **to the first column of the query design grid**
    Double-clicking the title bar of the field list selects all of the fields, allowing you to add them to the query grid very quickly. To successfully append records to a table, you need to identify how each field in the query is connected to an existing field in the target table. Therefore, the technique of adding all of the fields to the query grid by using the asterisk does not work when you append records, because using the asterisk doesn't list each field in a separate column in the query grid.

3. **Click the** DateOfCourse field Criteria cell, **type** Between 4/1/10 and 4/30/10, **widen the DateOfCourse field column as needed to view the criteria, then click the** Datasheet View button **on the Design tab**
    The datasheet should show 111 records with an April date in the DateOfCourse field. **Between...and** criteria select all records between the two dates, including the two dates. Between...and criteria work the same way as the >= and <= operators you used in the make table query.

4. **Click the** Design View button **on the Home tab, click the** Append button **in the Query Type group, click the** Table Name list arrow **in the Append dialog box, click** ArchiveEnrollments, **then click** OK
    Your screen should look like Figure K-10. The Append To row now appears in the query design grid to show how the fields in the query match fields in the target table, ArchiveEnrollments. You can now click the Run button to append the selected records to the table.

5. **Click the** Run button **on the Design tab, click** Yes **to indicate that you want to append 111 rows, then close the query without saving the changes**

6. **Double-click** ArchiveEnrollments **in the Navigation Pane, click any entry in the DateOfCourse field, then click the** Descending button
    The 111 April records are appended to the ArchiveEnrollments table, which previously had 180 records and now has a new total of 291 records, as shown in Figure K-11.

7. **Close the** ArchiveEnrollments table **without saving changes**

FIGURE K-10: Creating an append query

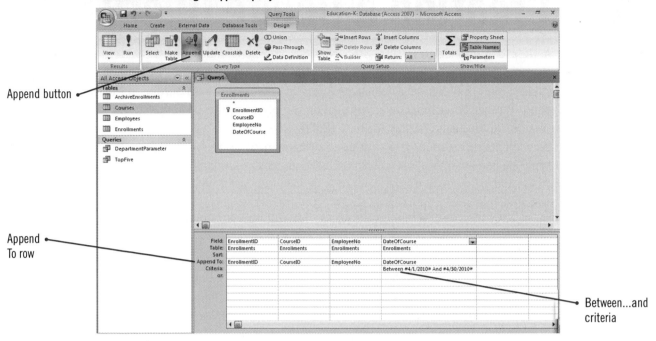

Append button

Append To row

Between...and criteria

FIGURE K-11: Updated ArchiveEnrollments table with appended records

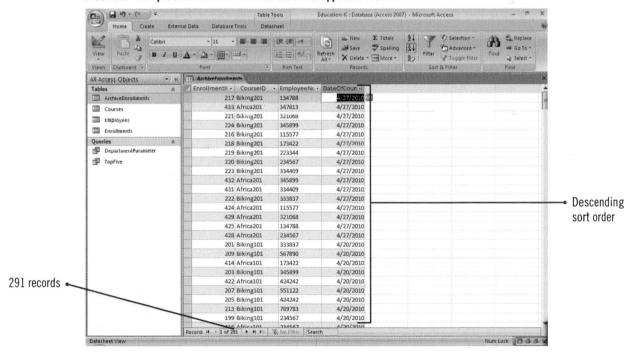

Descending sort order

291 records

1900 versus 2000 dates

If you type only two digits of a date, Access assumes that the digits 00 through 29 are for the years 2000 through 2029. If you type 30 through 99, Access assumes the years refer to 1930 through 1999. If you want to specify years outside these ranges, you must type all four digits of the year.

Creating a Delete Query

A **delete query** deletes a group of records from one or more tables. Delete queries delete entire records, not just selected fields within records. If you want to delete a field from a table, you open Table Design View, click the field name, then click the Delete Rows button on the Design tab. As in all action queries, you cannot reverse the action completed by the delete query by clicking the Undo button 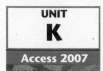 on the Quick Access toolbar. Now that you have archived the first four months of Enrollments records for 2010 in the ArchiveEnrollments table, you want to delete the same records from the Enrollments table. You can use a delete query to accomplish this task.

STEPS

1. **Click the Create tab, click the Query Design button, double-click Enrollments in the Show Table dialog box, then click Close**

2. **Double-click the * (asterisk) at the top of the Enrollments table's field list, then double-click the DateOfCourse field**

   Using the asterisk adds all fields from the Enrollments table to the first column of the query design grid. You add the DateOfCourse field to the second column of the query design grid so you can enter limiting criteria for this field.

3. **Click the DateOfCourse field Criteria cell, type Between 1/1/10 and 4/30/10, then widen the DateOfCourse field column as needed to view the criteria**

   Before you run a delete query, check the selected records to make sure that you have selected the same 291 records that you added to the ArchiveEnrollments table.

4. **Click the Datasheet View button on the Design tab to confirm that the datasheet has 291 records, click the Design View button on the Home tab, then click the Delete button on the Design tab**

   Your screen should look like Figure K-12. The Delete row now appears in the query design grid. You can delete the selected records by clicking the Run button.

5. **Click the Run button on the Design tab, click Yes to confirm that you want to delete 291 rows, then close the query without saving the changes**

6. **Double-click the Enrollments table in the Navigation Pane, click any entry in the DateOfCourse field, then click the Ascending button 🔼 on the Home tab if the records are not already sorted in this order**

   The records should start in May, as shown in Figure K-13. The delete query deleted all records from the Enrollments table with dates between 1/1/2010 and 4/30/2010.

7. **Close the Enrollments datasheet without saving changes**

Creating Advanced Queries

FIGURE K-12: Creating a delete query

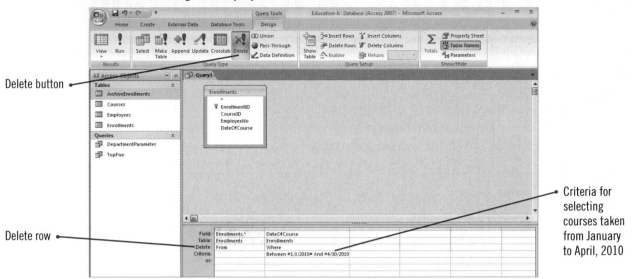

Delete button

Delete row

Criteria for selecting courses taken from January to April, 2010

FIGURE K-13: Enrollments table after deleting 291 records

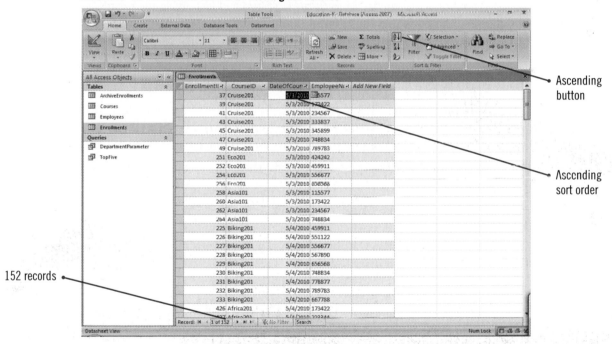

Ascending button

Ascending sort order

152 records

Reviewing referential integrity

Recall that you can establish, or enforce, **referential integrity** between two tables when joining tables in the Relationships window. Referential integrity applies a set of rules to the relationship that ensures that no orphaned records currently exist, are added to, or are created in the database. Only the table on the "many" side of a one-to-many relationship may contain an orphan record. A table has an **orphan record** when information in the foreign key field of the "many" table doesn't have a matching entry in the primary key field of the "one" table. The term "orphan" comes from the analogy that the "one" table contains **parent records**, and the "many" table contains **child records**. Referential integrity means that a child record cannot be created without a corresponding parent record. Also, referential integrity means that a delete query would not be able to delete records in the "one" (parent) table that has related records in the "many" (child) table.

Creating an Update Query

An **update query** is a type of action query that updates the values in a field. For example, you might want to increase the price of a product in a particular category by 5 percent. Or you might want to update information such as assigned sales representative, region, or territory for a subset of customers. 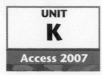 Julia Rice has just informed you that the cost of continuing education is being increased by $10 across the board to cover the costs of producing training CDs for each course. You can create an update query to quickly calculate and update the new course costs.

1. **Click the Create tab, click the Query Design button, double-click Courses in the Show Table dialog box, then click Close**

2. **Double-click CourseID in the Courses field list, double-click Description, then double-click Cost**

   Every action query starts as a select query. Always review the datasheet of the select query before initiating any action that changes data to double-check which records are affected.

3. **Click the Datasheet View button on the Design tab, note that the values in all three of the Africa courses are $450, then click the Design View button on the Home tab**

   After confirming the initial values in the Cost field and identifying the records the query selects, you're ready to change this select query into an update query.

4. **Click the Update button on the Design tab**

   The Update To row appears in the query design grid. To update the values in the Cost field by $10, you need to enter the appropriate expression in the Update To cell for the Cost field to add $10 to the current Cost field value.

5. **Click the Update To cell for the Cost field, then type [Cost]+10**

   Your screen should look like Figure K-14. The Cost field is not updated until you run the query.

   > **TROUBLE**
   > Be sure to enter the [Cost]+10 update criterion for the Cost field, *not* for the CourseID or Registration fields.

6. **Click the Run button on the Design tab, then click Yes to indicate that you want to update 32 rows**

   To view the updates to the Cost field, you can change this query back into a select query, then view the datasheet.

7. **Click the Select button on the Design tab, then click the Datasheet View button**

   Your screen should look like Figure K-15.

8. **Close the query without saving the changes**

   Often, you do not need to save action queries, because after the data has been updated, you don't need the query object anymore. If you double-click an action query from the Navigation Pane, you run the query (as opposed to double-clicking a select query, which opens its datasheet). Therefore, don't save any action queries unless you are sure you need to run them on a regular basis.

FIGURE K-14: Creating an update query

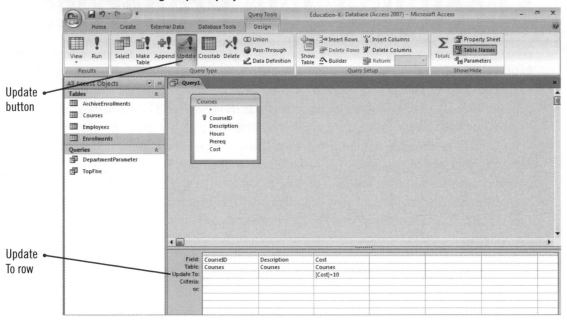

Update button

Update To row

FIGURE K-15: Updated Cost values

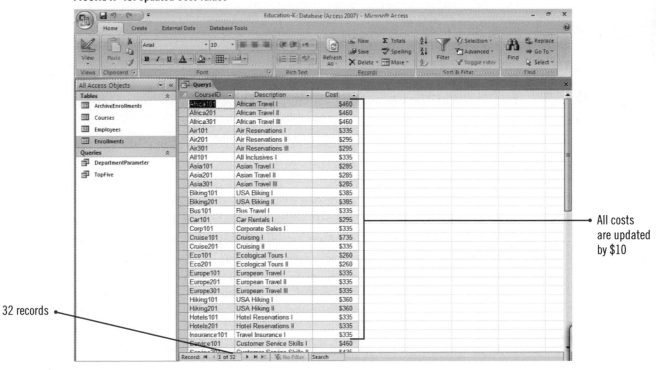

All costs are updated by $10

32 records

Specifying Join Properties

When you use more than one table's field list in a query, the tables are joined as defined in the Relationships window for the database. If referential integrity is enforced on a relationship, a "1" appears next to the field that serves as the "one" side of the one-to-many relationship, and an infinity symbol (∞) appears next to the field that serves as the "many" side. The "one" field is usually the primary key field for its table, and the "many" field is always called the foreign key field. If no relationships have been established, Access automatically creates join lines in Query Design View if the linking fields have the same name and data type in two tables. You can edit table relationships for a query in Query Design View by double-clicking the join line. You want to create a query to find out which courses have never been attended. As you create a query, you can modify the join properties between the Enrollments and Courses table to find this answer.

STEPS

1. **Click the Create tab, click the Query Design button, double-click Courses, double-click Enrollments, then click Close**

   Because the Courses and Enrollments tables have already been related with a one-to-many relationship with referential integrity enforced in the Relationships window (one course can have many enrollments), the join line appears, linking the two tables using the CourseID field common to both.

> **TROUBLE**
> Double-click the middle portion of the join line, not the "one" or "many" symbols, to open the Join Properties dialog box.

2. **Double-click the one-to-many join line between the field lists**

   The Join Properties dialog box opens and displays the characteristics for the join, as shown in Figure K-16. The dialog box shows that option 1 is selected, the default join type, which means that the query displays only records where joined fields from *both* tables are equal. In SQL (structured query language), this is called an **inner join**. This means that if the Courses table has any records for which there are no matching Enrollments records, those courses do not appear in the resulting datasheet.

> **QUICK TIP**
> To view the Relationships window from within Query Design View, right-click to the right of the field lists, then click Relationships.

3. **Click the 2 option button**

   By choosing option 2, you are specifying that you want to see *all* of the records in the Courses table (the "one," or parent table), even if the Enrollments table (the "many," or child table) does not contain matching records. In SQL, this is called a **left join**. Option 3 selects all records in the Enrollments (the "many," or child table) even if there are no matches in the Courses table. In SQL, this is called a **right join**. Because referential integrity is enforced on this relationship, however, it is impossible to have orphan records, which means that options 1 (inner join) and 3 (right join) produce the exact same results.

4. **Click OK**

   The join line's appearance changes, as shown in Figure K-17.

5. **Double-click CourseID in the Courses field list, double-click Description in the Courses field list, double-click EnrollmentID in the Enrollments field list, click the Criteria cell for the EnrollmentID, type Is Null, then click the Datasheet View button on the Design tab**

   The query finds 17 courses that currently have no matching records in the Enrollments table, as shown in Figure K-18. These courses contain a null (nothing) value in the EnrollmentID field. Changing the join property between the tables to include *all* records from the Courses table selects these records because the default join type, the inner join, requires a matching record in both tables to display a record in the resulting datasheet.

6. **Save the query with the name Courses-NoEnrollments, then close it**

FIGURE K-16: Join Properties dialog box

Default join property

Selects parent records even if they have no matching child records

Selects child records even if they have no matching parent records

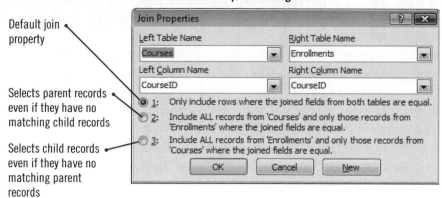

FIGURE K-17: The join line changes when properties are changed

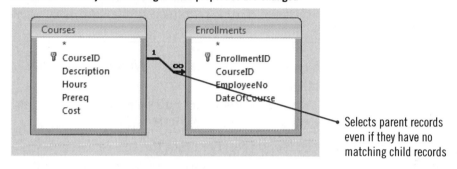

Selects parent records even if they have no matching child records

FIGURE K-18: Courses with no matching enrollments

Courses with no matching enrollment records

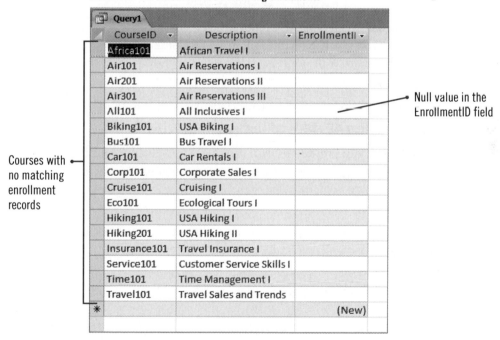

Null value in the EnrollmentID field

Null and zero-length string values

The term **null** describes a field value that does not exist because it has never been entered. In a datasheet, null values look the same as a zero-length string value but have a different purpose. A **zero-length string** value is a *deliberate* entry that contains no characters. You enter a zero-length string by typing two quotation marks ("") with no space between them. A null value, on the other hand, indicates *unknown* data. By using null and zero-length string values appropriately, you can later query for the records that match one or the other condition. To query for zero-length string values, enter two quotation marks ("") as the criterion. To query for null values, use **Is Null** as the criterion. To query for another value other than a null value, use **Is Not Null** as the criterion.

Finding Unmatched Records

Another way to find records in one table that have no matching records in another is to use the **Find Unmatched Query Wizard**. A **find unmatched query** is a query that finds records in one table that do not have matching records in a related table. When referential integrity is enforced on a relationship before you enter data into a database, orphan records cannot be created. Therefore, with referential integrity enforced, the only unmatched records that could possibly exist in a database are those in the "one" (parent) table. Sometimes, though, you inherit a database in which referential integrity was not imposed from the beginning, and unmatched records already exist in the "many" table, which are orphans. You could use your knowledge of join properties and null criteria to find unmatched records in either the "one" or "many" tables of a one-to-many relationship. Or you could use the Find Unmatched Query Wizard to structure the query for you. Julia Rice wonders if any employees have never enrolled in a class. You can use the Find Unmatched Query Wizard to create a query to answer this question.

STEPS

1. **Click the** Create tab, **click the** Query Wizard button, **click** Find Unmatched Query Wizard, **then click** OK

   The Find Unmatched Query Wizard starts, prompting you to select the table or query that may contain no related records.

2. **Click** Table: Employees, **then click** Next

   You want to find which employees have no enrollments, so the Enrollments table is selected as the related table.

3. **Click** Table: Enrollments, **then click** Next

   The next question asks you to identify which field is common to both tables. Because the Employees table is already related to the Enrollments table in the Relationships window via the EmployeeNo field, those fields are already selected as the matching fields, as shown in Figure K-19.

4. **Click** Next

   Now you must select the fields from the Employees table that you want to display in the query datasheet.

5. **Click the** Select All Fields button [>>]

6. **Click** Next, **type** Employees-NoEnrollments, **then click** Finish

   The final datasheet is shown in Figure K-20. One employee who was recently hired has never enrolled in a class. To complete any further study or to modify this query, you could work in Query Design View, just like a query created from scratch.

7. **Save and close the** Employees-NoEnrollments **query, then close the** Education-K.accdb **database**

FIGURE K-19: Using the Find Unmatched Query Wizard

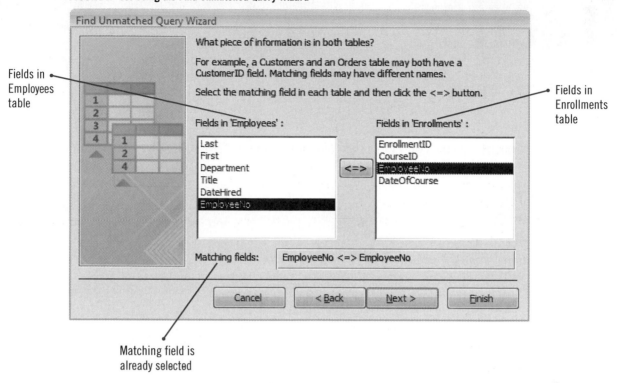

Fields in Employees table

Fields in Enrollments table

Matching field is already selected

FIGURE K-20: Employees without matching enrollment records

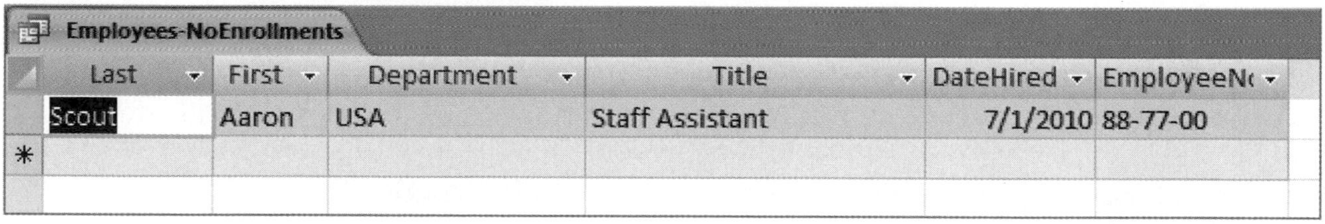

Employees-NoEnrollments

Last	First	Department	Title	DateHired	EmployeeN(
Scout	Aaron	USA	Staff Assistant	7/1/2010	88-77-00
*					

Find Duplicates Query Wizard

The Find Duplicates Query Wizard is another query wizard that is only available from the New Query dialog box. As you would suspect, the **Find Duplicates Query Wizard** helps you find duplicate values in a field, which can assist in finding and correcting potential data entry errors. For example, if you suspect that the same customer has been entered with two different names in your Customers table, you could use the Find Duplicate Query Wizard to find records with duplicate values in the Street or Phone field. After you isolated the records with the same value in one of these fields, you could then edit or delete incorrect or redundant data.

Practice

If you have a SAM user profile, you may have access to hands-on instruction, practice, and assessment of the skills covered in this unit. Log in to your SAM account (http://sam2007.course.com/) to launch any assigned training activities or exams that relate to the skills covered in this unit.

▼ CONCEPTS REVIEW

Identify each element of the Query Design View shown in Figure K-21.

FIGURE K-21

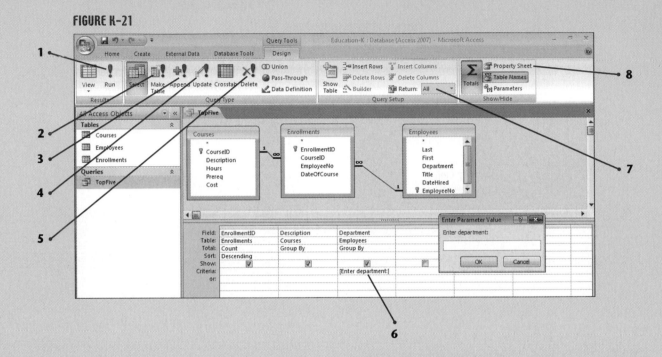

Match each term with the statement that best describes its function.

9. Action query
10. Inner join
11. Properties
12. Null
13. Parameter
14. Top Values query

a. Characteristics that define the appearance and behavior of items within the database
b. Displays only a number or percentage of records from a sorted query
c. Displays a dialog box prompting you for criteria
d. Means that the query displays only records where joined fields from both tables are equal
e. Makes changes to data
f. A field value that does not exist

Select the best answer from the list of choices.

15. Which join type selects all records from the "one" (parent) table?

   a. Inner

   b. Central

   c. Left

   d. Right

16. Which of the following is a valid parameter criterion entry in the query design grid?

   a. >=(Type minimum value here:)

   b. >=Type minimum value here:

   c. >={Type minimum value here: }

   d. >=[Type minimum value here:]

17. You *cannot* use the Top Values feature to:

   a. Display a subset of records.

   b. Show the top 30 records.

   c. Update a field's value by 5 percent.

   d. Select the bottom 10 percent of records.

18. Which of the following is *not* an action query?

   a. Make table query

   b. Delete query

   c. Append query

   d. Union query

19. Which of the following precautions should you take before running a delete query?

   a. Check the resulting datasheet to make sure the query selects the right records.

   b. Have a current backup of the database.

   c. Understand the relationships between the records you are about to delete in the database.

   d. All of the above

20. When querying tables in a one-to-many relationship with referential integrity enforced, which records appear (by default) on the resulting datasheet?

   a. All records from the "one" table, and only those with matching values from the "many" side

   b. Only those with matching values in both tables

   c. All records from the "many" table, and only those with nonmatching values from the "one" side

   d. All records from both tables will appear at all times.

▼ SKILLS REVIEW

1. Query for top values.

   a. Start Access, then open the Seminar-K.accdb database from the drive and folder where you store your Data Files. Enable content if prompted.

   b. Create a new select query in Query Design View with the EventName field from the Events table and the RegistrationFee field from the Registration table.

   c. Add the RegistrationFee field a second time, then click the Totals button. In the Total row of the query grid, Group By the EventName field, Sum the first RegistrationFee field, then Count the second RegistrationFee field.

   d. Sort in descending order by the summed RegistrationFee field.

   e. Enter 2 in the Top Values list box to display the top two seminars in the datasheet, then view the datasheet.

   f. Save the query as TopRevenue, then close the datasheet.

2. Create a parameter query.

   a. Create a new select query in Query Design View with the AttendeeLastName field from the Attendees table, the RegistrationDate field from the Registration table, and the EventName field from the Events table.

   b. Add the parameter criteria Between [Enter Start Date:] and [Enter End Date:] in the Criteria cell for the RegistrationDate field.

    c. Specify an ascending sort order on the RegistrationDate field.

    d. Click the Datasheet View button, then enter 5/1/10 as the start date and 5/31/10 as the end date to find everyone who has attended a seminar in May 2010. You should view six records.

    e. Save the query as **RegistrationDateParameter**, then close it.

3. Modify query properties.

    a. Click the Navigation Pane title bar, then click All Access Objects.

    b. Right-click the RegistrationDateParameter query, click Object Properties, then add the following description: **Prompts for a starting and ending registration date.**

    c. Close the RegistrationDateParameter Properties dialog box, then open the RegistrationDateParameter query in Query Design View.

    d. Right-click the RegistrationDate field, then click Properties on the shortcut menu to open the Field Properties dialog box. Enter **Date of Registration** for the Caption property, change the Format property to Medium Date, then close the Field Properties dialog box.

    e. View the datasheet for records between 5/1/10 and 5/31/10 to view the caption on the date field.

    f. Change Skorija to your own last name, then print, save, and close the datasheet.

4. Create a make table query.

    a. Create a new select query in Query Design View, and select all the fields from the Registration table by double-clicking the Registration field list's title bar and dragging the selected fields to the query design grid.

    b. Enter <=3/31/2010 in the Criteria cell for the RegistrationDate field to find those records in which the RegistrationDate is on or before 3/31/2010.

    c. View the datasheet. It should display 22 records.

    d. In Query Design View, change the query into a make table query that creates a new table in the current database. Give the new table the name **BackupRegistration**.

    e. Run the query to paste 22 rows into the BackupRegistration table.

    f. Close the make table query without saving it, open the BackupRegistration table, view the 22 records, then close the table.

5. Create an append query.

    a. Create a select query and select all the fields from the Registration table by double-clicking the Registration field list's title bar and dragging the selected fields to the query design grid.

    b. Enter >=4/1/10 and <=4/30/10 in the Criteria cell for the RegistrationDate field to find those records in which the RegistrationDate is in April 2010.

    c. View the datasheet, which should display one record.

    d. In Query Design View, change the query into an append query that appends records to the BackupRegistration table.

    e. Run the query to append the row into the BackupRegistration table.

    f. Close the append query without saving it.

    g. Open the BackupRegistration table to confirm that it now contains the additional record, then close the table.

6. Create a delete query.

    a. Create a select query and select all the fields from the Registration table by double-clicking the Registration field list's title bar and dragging the selected fields to the query design grid.

    b. Enter <5/1/2010 in the Criteria cell for the RegistrationDate field to find those records in which the RegistrationDate is before May 1, 2010.

    c. View the datasheet, which should display 23 records.

    d. In Query Design View, change the query into a delete query.

    e. Run the query to delete 23 records from the Registration table.

    f. Close the query without saving it.

    g. Open the Registration table in Datasheet View to confirm that it contains only six records, then close the table.

7. **Create an update query.**
   a. Create a select query in Query Design View and select all the fields from the Registration table by double-clicking the Registration field list's title bar and dragging the selected fields to the query design grid.
   b. View the datasheet, which should display six records. Note the values in the RegistrationFee field.
   c. In Query Design View, change the query to an update query, then enter **[RegistrationFee]+20** in the RegistrationFee field Update To cell to increase each value in that field by $20.
   d. Run the query to update the six records.
   e. Change the query back to a select query, then view the datasheet to make sure that the RegistrationFee fields were updated properly.
   f. Close the datasheet without saving the query.

8. **Specify join properties.**
   a. Create a select query in Query Design View with the following fields: AttendeeFirstName and AttendeeLastName from the Attendees table, and EventID and RegistrationFee from the Registration table.
   b. Double-click the link between the Attendees and Registration tables to open the Join Properties dialog box. Click the option button to include *all* records from Attendees and only those records from Registration where the joined fields are equal.
   c. View the datasheet, add your own first and last name as the last record, but do not enter anything in the EventID or RegistrationFee fields for your record.
   d. In Query Design View, add Is Null criteria to either field from the Registration table to select only those names who have never registered for an event.
   e. Save this query as **PeopleWithoutRegistrations**, then view, print, and close the query.

9. **Create find unmatched queries.**
   a. Start the Find Unmatched Query Wizard.
   b. Indicate that you want to find the events that have no related records in the Registration table.
   c. Specify that the two tables are related by the EventID field.
   d. Select all of the fields from the Events table in the query results.
   e. Name the query **EventsWithoutRegistrations**, then view the results. Change one of the entries in the Location field to a high school or convention center in your area, as shown in Figure K-22.
   f. Print the EventsWithoutRegistrations query, then close the query, close the Seminar-K.accdb database, and exit Access.

FIGURE K-22

Event I	Event Name	Location	Start Date	Available Sp
5	Wealth Management	Millen Civic Center	5/5/2010	25
6	Planning for College	Student's High School	5/6/2010	25
7	Live Debt Free	Wells Fargo Center	5/7/2010	75
(New)				

▼ INDEPENDENT CHALLENGE 1

As the manager of a college women's basketball team, you want to create several queries using the Basketball-K database.

a. Start Access, then open the Basketball-K.accdb database from the drive and folder where you store your Data Files. Enable content if prompted.

b. Create a query in Query Design View with the First and Last fields from the Players table, the FG (field goal), 3P (three pointer), and FT (free throw) fields from the Stats table, and the Opponent and GameDate fields from the Games table.

c. Enter **Between [Enter start date:] and [Enter end date:]** in the Criteria cell for the GameDate field.

d. View the datasheet for all of the records between **12/1/2010** and **12/31/2010**. It should display 24 records.

e. Save the query with the name **ParameterStats**, change Lindsey Swift's name to your own, then print the datasheet.

f. In Query Design View of the ParameterStats query, insert a new calculated field named TotalPoints between the FT and Opponent field with the expression **TotalPoints:[FG]*2+[3P]*3+[FT]**, then sort the records in descending order on the TotalPoints field.

g. Apply the 25% Top Values option, and view the datasheet for all of the records between 12/1/2010 and 12/31/2010. It should display six records.

h. Save the revised query as **ParameterStatsTop25%**. Print and close the datasheet.

i. Create a new query in Query Design View with the Opponent, Mascot, HomeScore, and OpponentScore fields from the Games table, then add a new calculated field as the last field with the following field name and expression:

Win%:[HomeScore]/[OpponentScore].

FIGURE K-23

Opponent	Mascot	HomeScore	OpponentSc	Win%
Iowa	Hawkeyes	81	65	125%
Creighton	Bluejays	106	60	177%
Northern Illinoi:	Huskies	65	60	108%
Louisiana Tech	Red Raiders	69	89	78%
Drake	Bulldogs	80	60	133%
Northern Iowa	Panthers	38	73	52%
Buffalo	Bulls	50	55	91%
Oklahoma	Sooners	53	60	88%
Texas	Longhorns	57	60	95%
Kansas	Jayhawks	74	58	128%
Colorado	Buffaloes	90	84	107%
Texas A&M	Aggies	77	60	128%
Clemson	Lady Tigers	72	81	89%
Nebraska	Cornhuskers	79	58	136%
Missouri	Tigers	80	54	148%
Oklahoma State	Cowgirls	76	42	181%
Kansas State	Wildcats	63	70	90%
Baylor	Lady Bears	68	70	97%
Oregon	Ducks	85	70	121%
Georgia	Bulldogs	91	89	102%
Connecticut	Huskies	64	58	110%
Soutwest Texas	Bobcats	97	48	202%
*		0	0	

j. View the datasheet to make sure that the Win% field calculates properly, and widen the column as necessary to see all of the data. Because the home score is generally greater than the opponent score, most values are greater than 1.

Advanced Challenge Exercise

- In Query Design View, change the Format property of the Win% field to Percent and the Decimal Places property to 0.
- View the datasheet as shown in Figure K-23.

k. Save the query as **WinPercentage**, change the first opponent's name (Iowa) and mascot to your own name and a mascot of your choice, then print and close the datasheet.

l. Close the Basketball-K.accdb database, then exit Access.

▼ INDEPENDENT CHALLENGE 2

As the manager of a college women's basketball team, you want to enhance the Basketball-K database by creating several action queries.

a. Start Access, then open the Basketball-K.accdb database from the drive and folder where you store your Data Files. Enable content if prompted.

b. Create a new select query in Query Design View, and select all the fields from the Stats table by double-clicking the field list's title bar and dragging the selected fields to the query design grid.

c. Add criteria to find all of the records with the GameNo field equal to 1, 2, or 3, then view the datasheet. It should display 26 records.

d. In Query Design View, change the query to a make table query to paste the records into a table in the current database called Games1-3.

e. Run the query to paste the 26 rows, then close the query without saving it.

f. Open the datasheet for the Games1-3 table to confirm that it contains 26 records, then close it.

g. In Query Design View, create another new select query that includes all of the fields from the Stats table by double-clicking the field list's title bar and dragging the selected fields to the query design grid.

h. Add criteria to find all of the statistics for those records with the GameNo field equal to 4 or 5, then view the datasheet. It should display 12 records.

i. In Query Design View, change the query to an append query to append the records to the Games1-3 table.

j. Run the query to append the 12 rows, then close the query without saving it. (In the Append To row, check each field name before running the query. If a field name appears in brackets such as [3P], change it to the actual field name, 3P.)

k. Right-click the Games1-3 table to rename it to Games1-5-YourName, then open the datasheet to make sure it contains 38 records.

l. Resize each of the columns to be only as wide as needed, then print and close the table.

m. Close the Basketball-K.accdb database, then exit Access.

▼ INDEPENDENT CHALLENGE 3

As the manager of a college women's basketball team, you want to query the Basketball-K database to find specific information about each player.

a. Start Access, then open the **Basketball-K.accdb** database from the drive and folder where you store your Data Files. Enable content if prompted.

b. Create a select query in Query Design View using the Players and Stats tables.

c. Double-click the linking line to open the Join Properties dialog box, then change the join properties to include *all* records from Players and only those from Stats where the joined fields are equal.

d. Add the First and Last fields from the Players table and the Assists field from the Stats table.

e. Type **is null** in the Criteria cell for the Assists field, as shown in Figure K-24, then view the datasheet to find those players who have never recorded an Assist value in the Stats table. It should display one record.

f. Change the last name to your own last name.

g. Print the datasheet, save the query as **NoAssists**, then close the datasheet.

h. Close Basketball-K.accdb, then exit Access.

FIGURE K-24

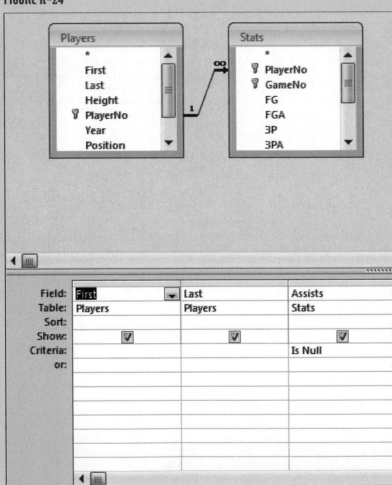

▼ REAL LIFE INDEPENDENT CHALLENGE

One way to use Access to support your personal interests is to track the activities of a club or hobby. For example, suppose you belong to a culinary or cooking club. The club might collect information on international chocolate factories and museums and ask you to help build a database to organize the information.

   a. Start Access, then open the Chocolate-K.accdb database from the drive and folder where you store your Data Files. Enable content if prompted.

   b. Open the Countries table, then add two more country records, allowing the CountryID field to automatically increment because it is an AutoNumber data type.

   c. Create a query in Query Design View with the Country field from the Countries table, and the PlaceName, City, and State fields from the ChocolatePlaces query.

   d. Name the query PlacesOfInterest, double-click the link line between the Countries and ChocolatePlaces tables, then choose the option that includes *all* records from the Countries table. See Figure K-25.

   e. View, save, print, then close the PlacesOfInterest query.

   f. Close Chocolate-K.accdb, then exit Access.

FIGURE K-25

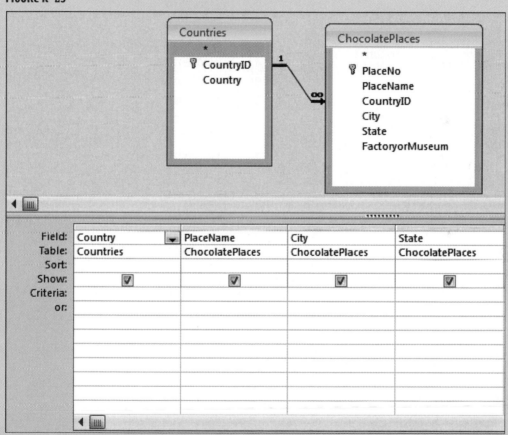

▼ VISUAL WORKSHOP

As the manager of a college women's basketball team, you want to create a query from the **Basketball-K.accdb** database with the fields from the Players, Stats, and Games tables as shown. The query is a parameter query that prompts the user for a start and end date using the GameDate field from the Games table. Figure K-26 shows the datasheet where the start date of 11/1/2010 and end date of 11/30/2010 are used. Save and name the query **Defense**, then print the datasheet. Be sure to change one player's name to your own if you haven't previously done this to identify your printout.

FIGURE K-26

First	Last	Reb-O	Reb-D	GameDate
Sydney	Freesen	2	3	11/17/2010
StudentFirst	StudentLast	1	2	11/14/2010
StudentFirst	StudentLast	2	2	11/17/2010
StudentFirst	StudentLast	2	1	11/24/2010
Ellyse	Howard	1	2	11/14/2010
Ellyse	Howard	3	3	11/17/2010
Ellyse	Howard	4	3	11/24/2010
Amy	Hodel	5	3	11/14/2010
Amy	Hodel	1	4	11/17/2010
Amy	Hodel	1	4	11/24/2010
Theresa	Grant	1	3	11/14/2010
Theresa	Grant	3	3	11/17/2010
Sandy	Robins	0	1	11/17/2010
Abbey	Walker	2	4	11/17/2010
Kristen	Czyenski	2	2	11/14/2010
Kristen	Czyenski	3	2	11/17/2010
Denise	Franco	2	3	11/14/2010
Denise	Franco	5	3	11/17/2010
Denise	Franco	5	3	11/24/2010
Megan	Hile	1	2	11/14/2010
Megan	Hile	1	5	11/17/2010
Megan	Hile	2	2	11/24/2010
Morgan	Tyler	4	6	11/14/2010
Morgan	Tyler	3	6	11/17/2010
Morgan	Tyler	3	4	11/24/2010
Jamie	Johnson	0	1	11/14/2010

Record: I ◄ 1 of 26 ► ►I ►✱ ☒ No Filter Search

Creating Advanced Reports

Characteristics of advanced reports cover a wide variety of enhancements such as formatting, print layout, and charting. In this unit you will learn techniques to make sure that the data in your report is printed logically, clearly, and in a way that makes the best use of paper. You will also learn how to graphically display data in a variety of chart types such as pie, bar, and line charts. Julia Rice, coordinator of training at Quest Specialty Travel, wants to enhance existing reports to more professionally and clearly present the information in the Education-L database.

OBJECTIVES

Apply advanced formatting

Group controls

Set advanced print layout

Create charts

Modify charts

Apply chart types

Create multi-column reports

Create mailing labels

Applying Advanced Formatting

Each type of control on a report has formatting properties such as Font Name, Font Size, Fore Color, and Border Style that you can modify. For example, if the control is a text box bound to a date field, the Format property provides several ways to format the date (19-Jun-10, 6/19/2010, or Friday, June 19, 2010). If the text box is bound to a numeric field, the number can be displayed in a variety of numeric formats such as Currency ($77.25), Percent (52%), or Scientific Notation (3.46E + 03). ▓▓▓▓ Julia Rice has asked you to review the Departmental Summary Report and identify formatting problems.

STEPS

1. **Start Access, open the Education-L.accdb database from the drive and folder where you store your Data Files, enable content if prompted, double-click DeptSummary in the Navigation Pane, then scroll down so your screen looks like Figure L-1**

   The report opens in Report View. Some of the information is not displayed correctly and subtotals are not formatted properly. You will work in Report Design View to tackle these problems.

2. **Right-click the report, click Design View, drag the left edge of the Date label in the Page Header section to the 4" mark to widen that control, click the View button arrow, click Print Preview, then click OK to respond to the message about section width**

   The report opens in Print Preview. Although the date is now displayed properly, the report is too wide to fit on a single sheet of paper.

3. **Click the Next Page button ▶ on the navigation bar several times**

   Every other page is a blank page, the result of designing a report wider than the physical width of a page in portrait orientation, 8.5 inches. You need to narrow the report in Report Design View.

4. **Right-click the report, click Design View, scroll to the right edge of the report, then drag the right edge of the report as far left as possible**

   You also want to change the subtotal fields so that they align directly under the columns they represent (Hours or Cost), and so that the Cost subtotals are formatted as currency values (with dollar signs).

TROUBLE
If a control is already right-aligned and you click the Align Text Right button, you might change its alignment. Click the Align Text Right button a second time.

5. **Click the 7.75" mark on the horizontal ruler to select all controls in the Cost column (see Figure L-2), click the Align Text Right button 📄 on the Design tab, click the Arrange tab, then click the Align Right button**

   To properly align controls, you can align values within a control (using buttons such as the Align Text Right button on the Design tab) and the edges of controls (using buttons such as the Align Right button on the Arrange tab). To format the text boxes with the same currency format, first deselect the Cost label.

6. **Press and hold [Shift], click the Cost label in the Page Header section, click the Design tab, click the Property Sheet button, click the Format tab, click the Format list arrow, click Currency, click the Decimal Places box, then type 0**

7. **Click the 7" mark on the horizontal ruler to select all controls in the Hours column, click 📄 on the Design tab, click the Arrange tab, click the Align Right button, press and hold [Shift], click the Hours label in the Page Header section, click the Format tab on the Property Sheet, click the Format list arrow, click Standard, click the Decimal Places box, then type 0**

8. **Click the View button arrow on the Design tab, then click Print Preview**

   The dates should all appear clearly in the Date column, Access no longer indicates that the report is too wide, and the numbers in both the Hours and Cost columns are aligned and formatted properly.

Creating Advanced Reports

FIGURE L-1: Previewing the Departmental Summary Report

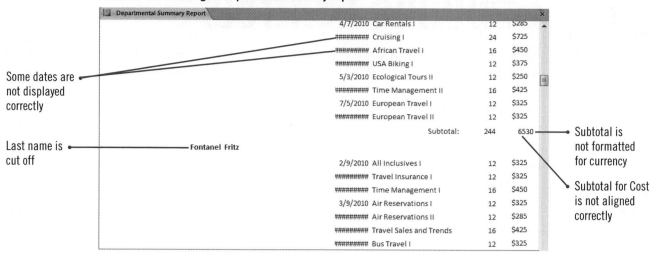

Some dates are not displayed correctly

Last name is cut off

Subtotal is not formatted for currency

Subtotal for Cost is not aligned correctly

FIGURE L-2: Aligning and formatting controls in Report Design View

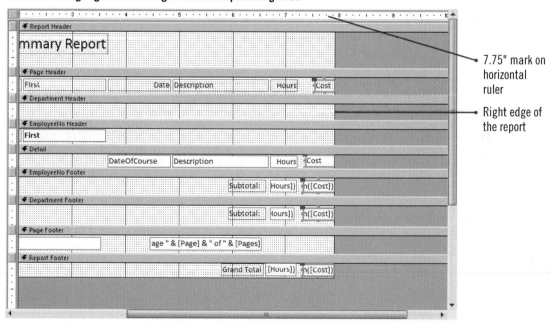

7.75" mark on horizontal ruler

Right edge of the report

Grouping Controls

"Grouping" has two meanings in Access. Grouping records on a report means to sort them plus provide a group header or group footer section before and after that group of records. **Grouping controls** refers to connecting them as a set so that when you move or resize them in Form or Report Design View, the action you take on one control applies to all controls in the group. When you create a report using the Report Wizard, many of the controls are automatically grouped together. To productively work in Report Design View, you need to know how to ungroup existing controls and create new groups for your own purposes. 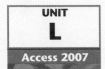 The Departmental Summary Report is almost finished, but you still need to widen the Last text box to clearly display the entire contents of the last name field.

1. **Right-click the report, click Design View, close the Property Sheet, click the Last label in the Page Header section, then drag the right sizing handle to the right to the 2.5" mark on the horizontal ruler, as shown in Figure L-3**

   Because the controls are grouped, changes to the sizing of one control affect other controls. In this case, the Hours label and text box were resized, though only the Last text box needs resizing. To correct this, undo your last action, and ungroup the Last label and text box in order to work with them individually.

2. **Click the Undo button 🔄 on the Quick Access toolbar, click in the vertical ruler to the left of the Page Header section to select all labels, click the Arrange tab, then click the Remove button in the Control Layout group to remove the layout applied to the controls**

   Now that none of the controls are grouped, each one moves individually, without affecting others. This means that as you widen or resize one control, another control will not be resized to accommodate the change.

3. **Click the report background to deselect the controls, click the First label in the Page Header section, press and hold [Shift] while clicking the First text box in the EmployeeNo Header section, then drag the left edge of the First controls to resize them to about half of their original size**

4. **Click the Department label in the Page Header section, press and hold [Shift] while clicking the Department text box in the Department Header section, then drag the Department controls as far to the left edge of the report as possible**

   With more space available on each side of the Last label and text box, you have room to expand that control.

5. **Click the Last label in the Page Header section, press and hold [Shift] while clicking the Last text box in the EmployeeNo Header section, drag the left edge of the Last controls to the left, then drag the right edge of the Last controls to the right to widen them**

   See Figure L-4. With the controls moved and repositioned, you're ready to preview the report in Print Preview.

6. **Click the Home tab, click the View button arrow, click Print Preview, then page through the report**

   Be sure that long last names such as Fontanelle and Hoppengarth are clearly visible. All dates should be displayed properly and the Hours and Cost fields should be aligned. You might also notice other formatting embellishments you can make at a later time. Advanced formatting, aligning, and grouping skills are at the heart of report design.

FIGURE L-3: Resizing grouped controls in Report Design View

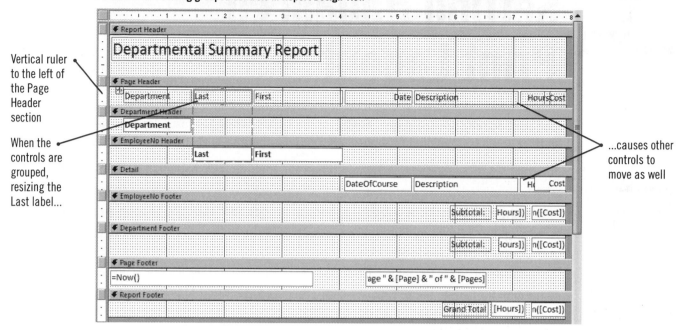

Vertical ruler to the left of the Page Header section

When the controls are grouped, resizing the Last label...

...causes other controls to move as well

FIGURE L-4: Ungrouping controls in Report Design View

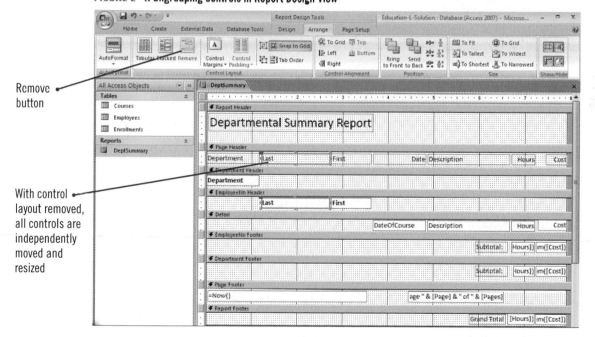

Remove button

With control layout removed, all controls are independently moved and resized

Setting Advanced Print Layout

Setting advanced print layout in a report means controlling print options such as page breaks, margins, and printing only selected pages. ░░░░░ In the Departmental Summary Report, Julia asks you to print each person's information on a separate report and to repeat the Department Header information at the top of each page.

1. **Right-click the report, click Design View, double-click the Department Header section bar to open its Property Sheet, then double-click the Repeat Section box to change the property from No to Yes**

   The controls in the Department Header section will now repeat at the top of every page.

2. **Click the EmployeeNo Footer section bar, click the Force New Page property list arrow, then click After Section as shown in Figure L-5**

   Access will format the report with a page break after each EmployeeNo Footer. This means each employee's records print on a separate sheet of paper.

3. **Click the View button arrow on the Design tab, click Print Preview, right-click the report, enter 85% in the Zoom magnification box, press [Enter], then scroll to the second page**

   Your screen should look like Figure L-6. To print only page 2 of the report, you use the Print dialog box.

4. **Click the Print button, click the From box, enter 2, click the To box, enter 2, then click OK**

   Only page 2 of a 24 page report is sent to the printer.

5. **Save and close the report**

FIGURE L-5: Report Design View of Departmental Summary Report

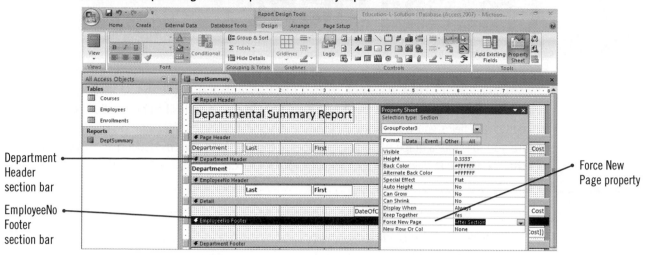

Department Header section bar

EmployeeNo Footer section bar

Force New Page property

FIGURE L-6: Print Preview of Departmental Summary Report

Department name repeats at the top of each page

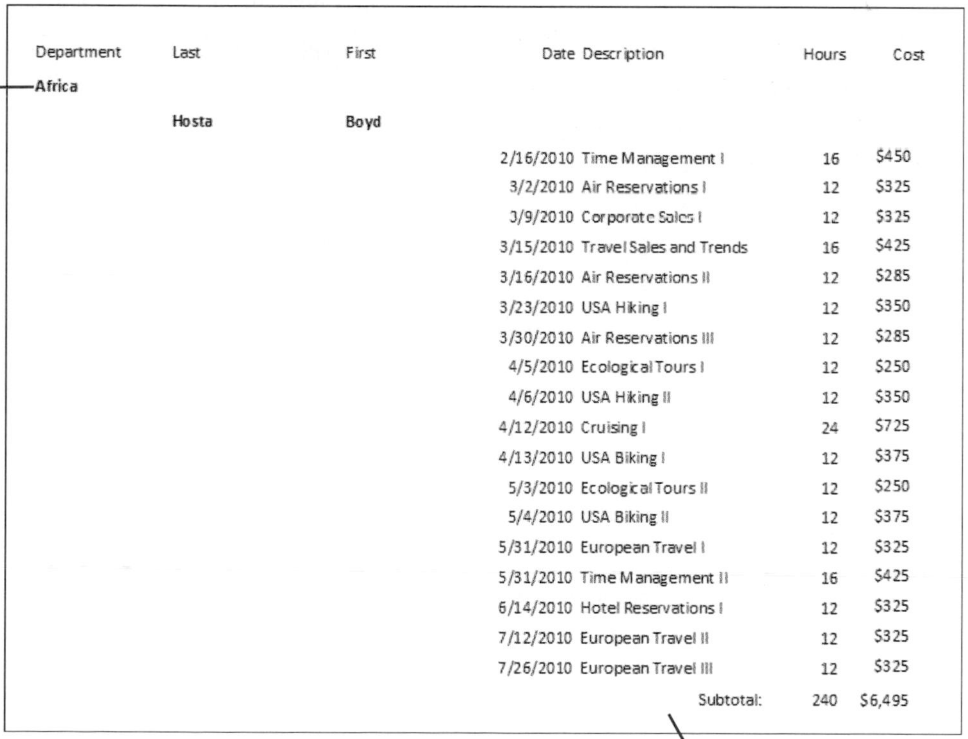

Department	Last	First	Date	Description	Hours	Cost
Africa						
	Hosta	Boyd				
			2/16/2010	Time Management I	16	$450
			3/2/2010	Air Reservations I	12	$325
			3/9/2010	Corporate Sales I	12	$325
			3/15/2010	Travel Sales and Trends	16	$425
			3/16/2010	Air Reservations II	12	$285
			3/23/2010	USA Hiking I	12	$350
			3/30/2010	Air Reservations III	12	$285
			4/5/2010	Ecological Tours I	12	$250
			4/6/2010	USA Hiking II	12	$350
			4/12/2010	Cruising I	24	$725
			4/13/2010	USA Biking I	12	$375
			5/3/2010	Ecological Tours II	12	$250
			5/4/2010	USA Biking II	12	$375
			5/31/2010	European Travel I	12	$325
			5/31/2010	Time Management II	16	$425
			6/14/2010	Hotel Reservations I	12	$325
			7/12/2010	European Travel II	12	$325
			7/26/2010	European Travel III	12	$325
				Subtotal:	240	$6,495

Page break is inserted after EmployeeID Footer section prints

Creating Charts

Charts, also called graphs, are visual representations of numeric data that help users see comparisons, patterns, and trends in data. Charts can be inserted on a form or report. Access provides a **Chart Wizard** that helps you create the chart. Before using the Chart Wizard, however, you should determine what data you want the graph to show and what chart type you want to use. As with all report creation, it's a good practice to gather the fields you want the chart to show in a query and base the report on that query. ▓▒▓▒▒ Julia wants you to create a graph of the total number of course registrations by department. This requires a count of the EnrollmentID field in the Enrollments table when the records are grouped by Department, a field included in the Employees table.

STEPS

1. **Click the** Create **tab, click the** Query Design **button in the Other group, double-click** Employees, **double-click** Enrollments, **click** Close, **then close the Property Sheet if it is open**
   The first step in creating a chart is to select the data that the chart will graph.

2. **Double-click** Department **in the Employees field list, double-click** EnrollmentID **in the Enrollments field list, save the query with the name** DepartmentEnrollments, **then close it**
   With the two fields collected in a query that you want the chart to present, you're ready to build the chart. Charts can be added to forms or reports.

3. **Click the** Create **tab, click the** Report Design **button, click the** Insert Chart **button** 📊 **on the Design tab, then click in the** Detail **section of the report**
   The Chart Wizard starts by asking which table or query holds the fields you want to add to the chart.

4. **Click the** Queries **option button, click** Next **because the DepartmentEnrollments query is selected, click the** Select All Fields **button** >>, **click** Next, **then click** Column Chart **(first column, first row if it isn't already selected) as shown in Figure L-7**
   With the chart type selected, the next question asks you how you want to structure the data. You can always change this later, but using the wizard to choose the best layout for your fields improves your productivity.

5. **Click** Next, **then drag the** EnrollmentID **field from the Series area to the Data area as shown in Figure L-8**
   The **Data area** determines what data the chart graphs. When you drag the EnrollmentID field (or any other Text or AutoNumber field) to the Data area, the Chart Wizard automatically counts the values in that field. If you drag a Number or Currency field to the Data area, the Chart Wizard sums the values in the field. See Table L-1 for more information on chart layout.

6. **Click** Next, **type** Department Enrollment Totals **as the chart title, then click** Finish
   When charts are displayed in Design View or Layout View, they appear as a generic Microsoft chart placeholder. Preview the report to see the actual data.

7. **Click the** View **button arrow on the Design tab, then click** Print Preview
   The chart should look similar to Figure L-9. The number of labels on the x-axis depends on the size of the chart.

TABLE L-1: Chart areas

chart area	description
Data	Determines what field the bars (lines, wedges, so forth) on the chart represent
Axis	The x-axis (horizontal axis) on the chart
Series	Displays the legend when multiple series of data are graphed

FIGURE L-7: Choosing a chart type

Column Chart

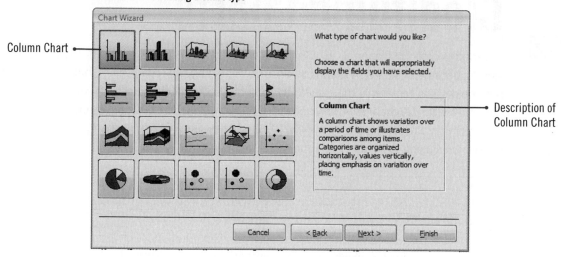

Description of Column Chart

FIGURE L-8: Choosing the chart areas

Drag EnrollmentID from Series area to Data area

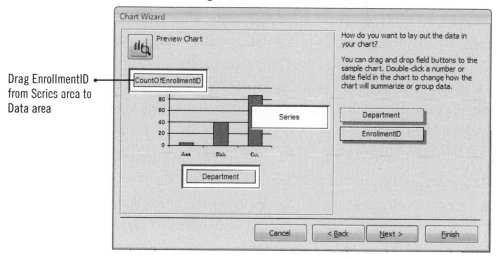

FIGURE L-9: Department Enrollment Totals column chart

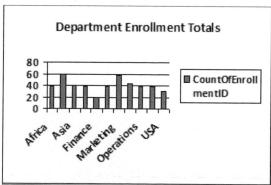

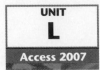
Modifying Charts

You modify charts in Design View of the form or report that contains the chart. Modifying a chart is challenging because Design View doesn't always show you the actual chart values, but instead, displays a chart placeholder that represents the embedded chart object. To modify the chart, you modify the chart placeholder. To view the changes as they apply to the real data you are charting, return to either Form View for a form or Print Preview for a report. You want to resize the chart, change the color of the bars, and remove the legend to better display the values on the x-axis.

STEPS

1. **Right-click the** report, **click** Design View, **then drag the** corner sizing handles of the chart **so it's about 5 inches wide and 3.75 inches tall**

   To make changes to chart elements, you open the chart in edit mode by double-clicking it. Use **edit mode** to select and modify individual chart elements such as the title, legend, bars, or axes. If you double-click the *edge* of the chart placeholder, you open the Property Sheet for the chart instead of opening the chart itself in edit mode.

   > **TROUBLE**
   > If placeholder data appears instead of the data shown in Figure L-10, continue with the steps.

2. **Double-click the** chart

   The hashed border of the chart placeholder control indicates that the chart is in edit mode, as shown in Figure L-10. The Standard and Formatting Chart toolbars also appear when the chart is in edit mode.

   > **TROUBLE**
   > If you make a mistake, use the Undo button on the Quick Access toolbar.

3. **Click the** legend **on the chart, then press [Delete] to remove it**

   By removing the legend, you provide more room for the x-axis labels to be displayed clearly. With only one series of data, a legend isn't necessary anyway. The data can be clearly identified in the chart title.

4. **Click any** periwinkle bar **to select all bars of that color**

   Clicking any bar selects all bars in that data series as evidenced by the sizing handle in each of the bars.

5. **Right-click any** periwinkle bar, **click** Format Data Series, **click the** bright green sample box, **then click** OK

   The bars change to bright green in the chart placeholder. Finally, you notice that shortening the "Information Systems" x-axis label would create more vertical room for the graph to show the bars. If you make this change to the data itself, it automatically updates the chart.

6. **Click** outside the hashed border **to return to Report Design View, double-click the** Employees table, **change the two instances of** Information Systems **to** IS **in the** Department field, **then close the datasheet**

   Preview the updated chart.

7. **Save the report as** DepartmentChart, **click the** View button arrow **on the Home tab, then click** Print Preview

   The final chart is shown in Figure L-11.

FIGURE L-10: Editing the chart

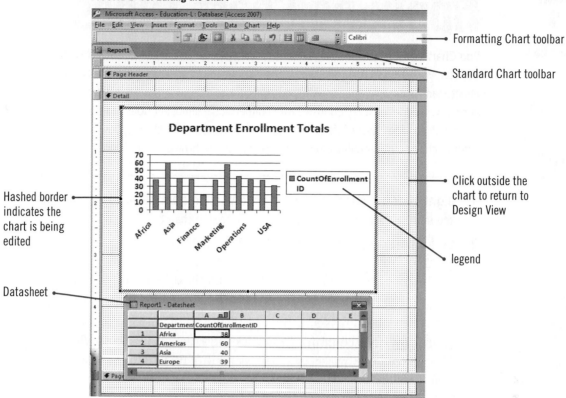

Formatting Chart toolbar

Standard Chart toolbar

Hashed border indicates the chart is being edited

Click outside the chart to return to Design View

legend

Datasheet

FIGURE L-11: Final Department Enrollment Totals column chart

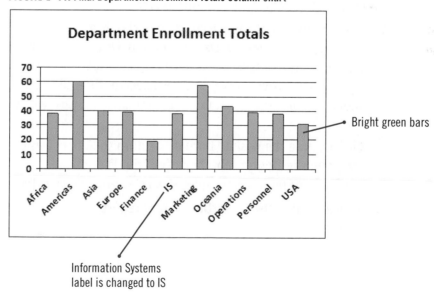

Bright green bars

Information Systems label is changed to IS

Applying Chart Types

The Chart Wizard provides 20 different chart types for creating a chart. While column charts are the most popular, you can also use line, area, and pie charts to effectively show some types of data. Three-dimensional effects can be used to enhance the chart, but those effects can make it difficult to compare the sizes of bars, lines, and wedges, so only choose a three-dimensional effect if it does not detract from the point of the chart. Table L-2 provides more information on the most common chart types.  You change the existing column chart to other chart types and subtypes to see how the data is presented.

STEPS

1. **Right-click the** chart, **click** Design View, **then double-click the** chart placeholder
   You must open the chart in edit mode to change the chart type.

2. **Click** Chart **on the menu bar, then click** Chart Type
   The Chart Type dialog box opens as shown in Figure L-12. All major chart types plus many chart sub-types are displayed. A button is available to preview any choice before applying that chart sub-type.

   TROUBLE
   If a sample of the 3-D Column chart doesn't appear, continue with step 4.

3. **Click the** Clustered column with a 3-D visual effect button (second row, first column), **click the** Press and Hold to View Sample button, **click the** 3-D Column button (third row, first column), **then click the** Press and Hold to View Sample button
   A Sample box opens, presenting a rough idea of what the final chart will look like. While 3-D charts appear more interesting than 2-D chart types, the samples do not show the data more clearly, so you decide to preview other 2-D chart types.

4. **Click the** Bar Chart **type, click the** Press and Hold to View Sample button, **click the** Line Chart **type, click the** Press and Hold to View Sample button, **click the** Pie Chart **type, click the** Press and Hold to View Sample button, **click the** Default formatting check box, **then click the** Press and Hold to View Sample button
   Because this chart only has one set of values that represent 100% of all enrollments, the data fits a pie chart. The more slices the pie supports, however, the less it can differentiate the color and sizes of the wedges. Other chart options help you enhance pie charts.

5. **Click** OK **to accept the pie chart type, click the** chart, **click** Chart **on the menu bar, click** Chart Options, **click the** Data Labels tab, **click the** Percentage check box, **click the** Titles tab, **click the** Chart title box, **type** Enrollment % by Dept, **click the** Legend tab, **click the** Show legend check box **if it is not selected, then click** OK
   With the modifications made to change the chart into a pie chart, you view it in Print Preview to see the final result.

6. **Click** outside the hashed border **to return to Report Design View, click the** View button arrow **on the Design tab, then click** Print Preview
   The same departmental data, expressed as a pie chart, is shown in Figure L-13.

7. **Save and close the** DepartmentChart **report**

Creating Advanced Reports

FIGURE L-12: Chart Type dialog box

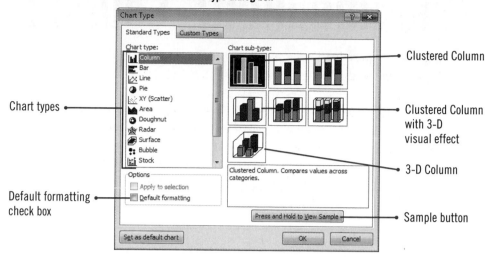

Chart types •————

Default formatting • check box

————• Clustered Column

————• Clustered Column with 3-D visual effect

————• 3-D Column

————• Sample button

FIGURE L-13: Department Enrollment Totals pie chart

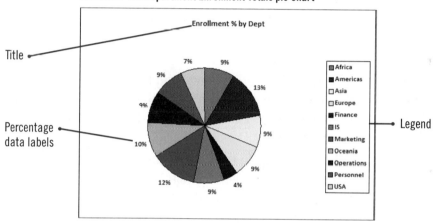

Title •————

Percentage • data labels

————• Legend

<!-- side bar -->
Access 2007

TABLE L-2: Common chart types

chart type	chart icon	used to show most commonly	example
Column		Comparisons of values (vertical bars)	Each vertical bar represents the annual sales for a different product for the year 2010
Bar		Comparisons of values (horizontal bars)	Each horizontal bar represents the annual sales for a different product for the year 2010
Line		Trends over time	Each point on the line represents monthly sales for one product for the year 2010
Pie		Parts of a whole	Each slice represents total quarterly sales for a company for the year 2010
Area		Cumulative totals	Each section represents monthly sales by representative, stacked to show the cumulative total sales effort for the year 2010

Creating Advanced Reports

Access 301

Creating Multi-Column Reports

A **multi-column report** repeats information in more than one column on the page. When creating multi-column reports only one column is displayed at a time in Report Design View. To set the report to present multiple columns, you use options in the Page Setup dialog box to specify the columns. 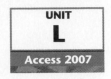 Julia asks you to create a report that shows employee names sorted in ascending order for each course. A report with only a few fields is a good candidate for a multi-column report.

1. **Click the** Create tab, **click the** Report Wizard button, **click the** Tables/Queries list arrow, **click** Table:Courses, **double-click** Description, **click the** Tables/Queries list arrow, **click** Table: Employees, **double-click** First, **double-click** Last, **click** Next, **click** Next **to view the data by Description, click** Next **to bypass adding any more grouping levels, click the** first sort list arrow, **click** Last, **click** Next, **click** Stepped, **click** Landscape, **click** Next, **click** Flow, **click** Next, **type** Attendance List **for the title, then click** Finish

   The initial report is shown in Figure L-14. The Description field needs to be widened to show the entire course description. This report would work well as a multi-column report because only two fields of data are reported for each class, First and Last. You also decide to combine the names into a single expression with the employee's full name.

2. **Right-click the** report, **click** Design View, **drag the** right edge of the Description text box **to about the 3" mark on the horizontal ruler, then delete the** Last and First controls

   With the Description text box widened, you add a new text box to the Detail section with an expression that contains both the first and last names.

3. **Click the** Text Box button ⓐ **in the Controls group on the Design tab, click at about the 1" mark of the Detail section, then** delete the accompanying label

4. **Click** Unbound **in the text box, type** =[Last]&", "&[First], **press [Enter], widen the new control to the 3" mark on the horizontal ruler, click the** View button arrow **on the Design tab, then click** Print Preview

   With the information clearly presented in a single column, you're ready to specify that the report print multiple columns. First you need to modify the report in Design View to only be one column wide.

5. **Right-click the** report, **click** Design View, **click the** Now expression **in the Page Footer, resize it so it's 3 inches wide, click the long** Page expression **in the Page Footer, press [Delete], then** drag the right edge of the report **to the 3" mark on the horizontal ruler**

   With the report only 3 inches wide, you can specify that three columns print across a landscape piece of paper with plenty of room for 1-inch margins.

6. **Click the** Office Button ⓐ, **click** Print, **click** Setup **in the Print dialog box, click the** Left margin box, **type** 1, **click the** Right margin box, **type** 1, **click the** Columns tab, **click the** Number of Columns box, **type** 3, **then click the** Down, **then** Across option button **as shown in Figure L-15**

   The content of the report is now set to print in three newspaper-style columns.

7. **Click** OK, **click** Cancel **(so the report won't print), click the** View button arrow **on the Design tab, then click** Print Preview

   By specifying that the report is three columns wide, it is reduced from over 20 pages to 7–8 pages.

8. **Save and close the** Attendance List **report**

FIGURE L-14: Initial Attendance List report

Last and First fields could be combined

Description is cut off

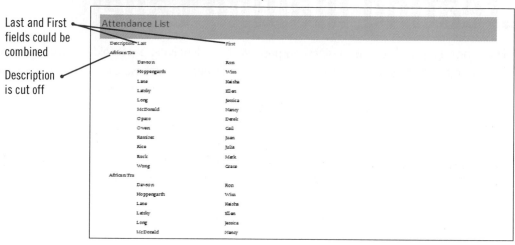

FIGURE L-15: Page Setup dialog box

Number of Columns = 3

Down, then Across option button

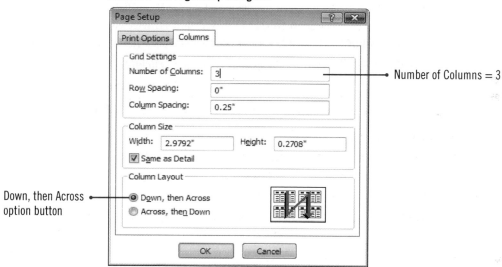

FIGURE L-16: Attendance List report in three columns

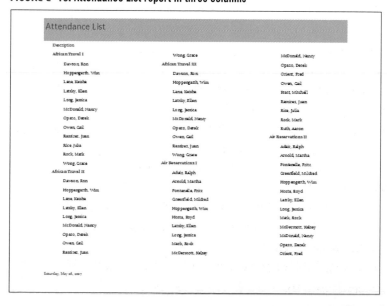

Creating Mailing Labels

Mailing labels are used for many business purposes such as identifying paper folders, creating name tags, and providing addresses for envelopes. Any data in your Access database can be converted into labels using the **Label Wizard**, a special report wizard. Julia asks you to create name tag labels for all employees for an upcoming meeting.

1. **Click the Employees table in the Navigation Pane, click the Create tab, click the Labels button in the Reports group, then scroll the Product number list and click 5390 (Avery 5390) as shown in Figure L-17**

   Avery is a common label manufacturer, so Microsoft has preloaded all of their product numbers into the Label Wizard. The best way to determine what product number you need to specify is to check the box of labels for the number before you start this wizard and especially before you send the labels to the printer.

2. **Click Next, click the Font size list arrow, click 14, click Next, click the First field, click the Select Single Field button ⟩ , press [Spacebar], click the Last field, then click ⟩**

   The **prototype label** previews the fields and punctuation that will appear on the final label as shown in Figure L-18. It does not show you the font, size, or color selected in the previous dialog box. If you needed to print multiline labels such as address labels, you'd press [Enter] and continue adding fields to new lines.

3. **Click Next, double-click Last as the sort field, click Next, then click Finish**

   The final report formatted for Avery 5390 labels is shown in Figure L-19.

4. **Save and close the Labels Employees report, close the Education-L.accdb database, then exit Access**

FIGURE L-17: Label Wizard – choosing the label type

5390 •⎯⎯⎯

Dimensions •⎯⎯⎯

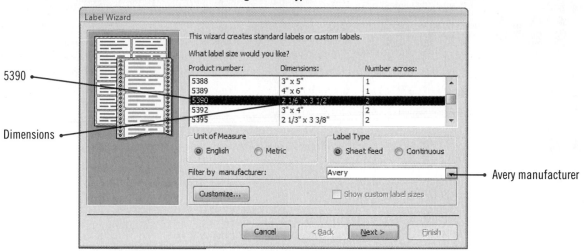

•⎯⎯ Avery manufacturer

FIGURE L-18: Label Wizard – setting up the prototype label

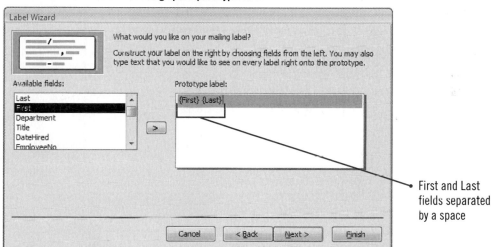

•⎯⎯ First and Last
fields separated
by a space

FIGURE L-19: Labels Employees report

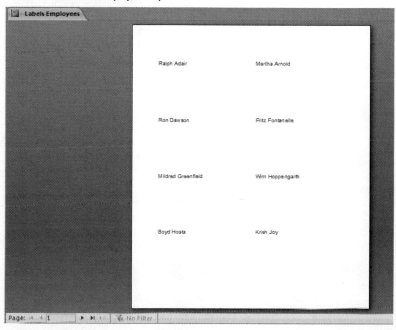

Access 2007

Practice

If you have a SAM user profile, you may have access to hands-on instruction, practice, and assessment of the skills covered in this unit. Log in to your SAM account (http://sam2007.course.com/) to launch any assigned training activities or exams that relate to the skills covered in this unit.

▼ CONCEPTS REVIEW

Identify each element of the Report Design View shown in Figure L-20.

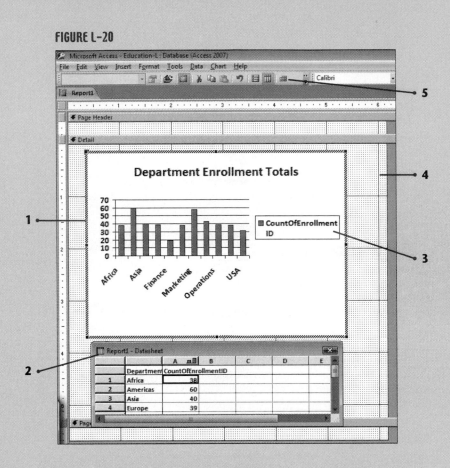

FIGURE L-20

Match each term with the statement that best describes its function.

6. Charts
7. Grouping controls
8. Prototype label
9. Data area
10. Edit mode

a. Connects them as a set so that the action you take on one control applies to all
b. Used to select and modify individual chart elements such as the title, legend, bars, or axes
c. Determines what data is graphed on the chart
d. Shows you the fields and punctuation that will appear on the final label
e. Visual representations of numeric data

Select the best answer from the list of choices.

11. **Which button aligns the edges of two or more selected controls?**
    - **a.** Align Right button on the Arrange tab
    - **b.** Align Right button on the Design tab
    - **c.** Align Text Right button on the Design tab
    - **d.** Align Text Right button on the Arrange tab

12. **The Label Wizard is what type of wizard?**
    - **a.** Table
    - **b.** Query
    - **c.** Form
    - **d.** Report

13. **Which would *not* be a use for the Label Wizard?**
    - **a.** identifying paper folders
    - **b.** creating name tags
    - **c.** providing addresses for mailing labels
    - **d.** calculating subtotals

14. **Which dialog box allows you to specify the number of columns you want to view in a report?**
    - **a.** Print
    - **b.** Page Setup
    - **c.** Columns
    - **d.** Property Sheet

15. **Which type of chart is best to show an upward sales trend over several months?**
    - **a.** Column
    - **b.** Line
    - **c.** Pie
    - **d.** Scatter

16. **Which task can be performed on a chart *without* being in edit mode?**
    - **a.** Modifying the title
    - **b.** Changing bar colors
    - **c.** Deleting the legend
    - **d.** Resizing the chart

17. **Which chart area determines the field that the bars (lines, wedges, so forth) on the chart represent?**
    - **a.** Data
    - **b.** Category
    - **c.** X-axis
    - **d.** Legend

18. **Which chart area is used to identify the legend?**
    - **a.** Data
    - **b.** Category
    - **c.** X-axis
    - **d.** Series

19. **Which chart type is best at showing cumulative totals?**
    - **a.** Column
    - **b.** Bar
    - **c.** Area
    - **d.** Pie

20. **Which chart type is best at showing parts of a whole?**
    - **a.** Column
    - **b.** Bar
    - **c.** Area
    - **d.** Pie

▼ SKILLS REVIEW

1. **Apply advanced formatting.**
    - **a.** Start Access, then open the RealEstate-L.accdb database from the drive and folder where you store your Data Files. Enable content if prompted.
    - **b.** Preview the AgencyListings report, noting the format for the SqFt and Asking fields.
    - **c.** In Report Design View, change the Format property for the SqFt text box in the Detail section to Standard and change the Decimal Places property to 0.
    - **d.** In Report Design View, change the Format property for the Asking text box in the Detail section to Currency and change the Decimal Places property to 0.
    - **e.** Preview the report to make sure your SqFt values appear with commas, the Asking values appear with dollar signs, and neither shows any digits to the right of the decimal place.

2. **Group controls.**
    - **a.** Open the AgencyListings report in Design View.
    - **b.** Open the Group, Sort, and Total pane and add an AgencyName Footer section.
    - **c.** Add a text box in the AgencyName Footer under the SqFt text box in the Detail section with the expression =Sum([SqFt]).

d. Add a text box in the AgencyName Footer under the Asking text box in the Detail section with the expression =Sum([Asking])

e. Modify a label to the AgencyName Footer section to have the caption Subtotals:. Delete the extra label in the AgencyName Footer section.

f. Format and align the text boxes under the fields they subtotal so that Print Preview looks similar to Figure L-21, removing the layout as needed to move controls and resizing the report width to 8 inches.

FIGURE L-21

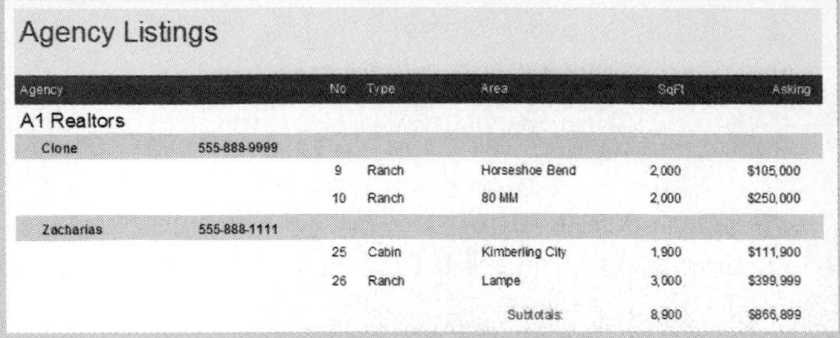

3. Set advanced print layout.

a. Open the AgencyListings report in Design View.

b. Modify the AgencyName Footer section to force a new page after that section prints.

c. Preview the report to make sure each of the four agencies prints on its own page.

d. Close and save the AgencyListings report.

4. Create charts.

a. Open the Inventory query in Query Design View, then add criteria to select only the Ranch (in the Type field) records.

b. Click the Office button, then click Save As. Save the query as RanchHomes, then close it.

c. Start a new report in Report Design View.

d. Insert a chart in the Detail section based on the RanchHomes query.

e. Choose the AgentLast and Asking fields for the chart, choose a Column Chart, then make sure the Asking field appears in the Data area and move the AgentLast field to the Series area.

f. Title the chart Revenue by Agent.

g. Preview the report to view the chart.

5. Modify charts.

a. Close Print Preview, double-click the chart to open it in edit mode, then remove the legend.

b. Double-click the y-axis values to open the Format Axis dialog box, click the Number tab, then choose a Currency format from the Category list, entering 0 for the Decimal places.

c. Change the color of the periwinkle bars to bright red.

d. Return to Report Design View, then switch to Print Preview. Print the report. (*Hint*: Add your name as a label in the Report Footer section if you need to identify it on the printout.)

6. Apply chart types.

a. Save the report with the name AgentRevenue.

b. Open the chart in edit mode, then change the chart type to a Clustered column with a 3-D visual effect.

c. In Design View, resize the chart so it is about 5.5 inches wide and 4 inches tall. Preview the report then print it.

d. Compare the printouts from the 2-D column chart and the 3-D column chart. On a piece of paper answer these questions: Which one is more interesting? Why? Which one presents the values in a clearer manner? Why?

e. Save and close the AgentRevenue report.

7. Create multi-column reports.

a. Use the Report Wizard to create a report with the AgencyName field from the Agencies table, the AgentFirst and AgentLast fields from the Agents table, and the Type field from the Listings table.

b. View the data by Listings, add AgencyName as the grouping level, sort the records in ascending order by AgentLast, use a Stepped layout and a Landscape orientation, and use the Trek style.

c. Use Listings as the report title.

d. In Report Design View, delete the AgentLast and AgentFirst controls and widen the AgencyName control so that it is about 2 inches wide.

e. Delete the page expression in the Page Footer section, narrow the =Now() expression in the Page Footer section to be no wider than 3 inches, narrow the Type field in the Detail section so that the right edge is within the 3-inch mark, and drag the right edge of the report to the 3-inch mark on the ruler.

f. Add a new text box to the left side of the Detail section with the following expression: =[AgentLast]&", "&[AgentFirst]

FIGURE L-22

g. Delete the label for the new text box, then widen the =[AgentLast]&", "&[AgentFirst] text box in the Detail section to be about 2 inches wide.

h. Use the Page Setup dialog box to set the Number of Columns setting to 3 and the column layout to Down, then Across.

i. Preview the report. It should look like Figure L-22.

j. Save and close the Listings report.

8. Create labels.

a. Use the Label Wizard to create Avery 5160 labels based on the Inventory query. Use the default font size and color.

FIGURE L-23

b. Add the fields to the prototype label using the pattern shown in Figure L-23.

c. Sort by the AgentLast field, and name the report **InventoryLabels**. Click OK if prompted, then print the report.

d. Save and close the InventoryLabels report.

e. Close the RealEstate-L.accdb database and exit Access 2007.

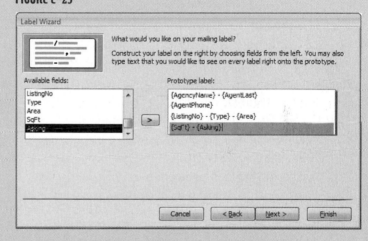

▼ **INDEPENDENT CHALLENGE 1**

As the manager of a college women's basketball team, you want to enhance a form within the Basketball-L.accdb database to chart the home versus visiting team scores. You will build on your report creation skills to do so.

a. Start Access, then open the database **Basketball-L.accdb** from the drive and folder where you store your Data Files. Enable content if prompted.

b. Open then maximize the GameInfo form. Page down through several records observing the Home and Visitor scores.

c. Open the form in Form Design View, then insert a chart on the right side of the form based on the Games table. Choose the HomeScore and OpponentScore fields for the chart. Choose a Column Chart type.

d. Add both the HomeScore and OpponentScore fields to the Data area, double-click the SumOfHomeScore field, select None as the summarize option, double-click the SumOfOpponentScore field, then select None as the summarize option.

e. Click Next and choose GameNo as the Form Field and as the Chart Field so that the chart changes from record to record showing the HomeScore versus the OpponentScore in the chart.

FIGURE L-24

f. Title the chart **Scores**, and do not display a legend.

g. Open the form in Form View and print the record for GameNo 10 as shown in Figure L-24. If you need your name on the printout, add it as a label to the Form Header section. (*Hint*: If the graph doesn't appear automatically, press F5 to refresh the screen.)

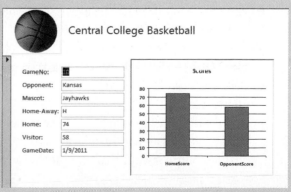

h. Save the GameInfo form, close it, close the Basketball-L.accdb database and exit Access 2007.

Access 2007

▼ INDEPENDENT CHALLENGE 2

As the manager of a college women's basketball team, you want to build a report that shows a graph of total points per player per game.

a. Start Access, then open the database Basketball-L.accdb from the drive and folder where you store your Data Files. Enable content if prompted.

b. Open the PlayerStatistics report and study the structure. Notice that this report has the total points per player you want to graph per game in the last column. Open the PlayerStatistics report in Report Design View.

c. Double-click the far right text box in the Detail section and click the Data tab in the Property Sheet to study the Control Source property. The expression =[FT]+([fg]*2)+([3p]*3) adds one-point free throws [FT] to two-point field goals [fg] to three-point three-pointers [3p] to find the player's total contribution to the score. You will calculate the total point value in the underlying query instead of on the report to make it easier to graph.

d. Click the report selector button, then click the Build button for the Record Source property, which currently displays the PlayerStats query. In the final column add a new field with the following expression:
TotalPts:[FT]+([fg]*2)+([3p]*3).

e. Save and close the PlayerStats query, then open the Property Sheet for the GameNo Footer section. On the Format tab, change the Force New Page property to After Section.

f. Expand the height of the GameNo Footer section, then insert a chart just below the existing controls.

g. In the Chart Wizard, choose the PlayerStats query to create the chart, choose the Last and TotalPts fields for the chart, and choose the Column Chart type.

h. Use SumOfTotalPts in the Data area and the Last field in the Axis area (which should be the defaults). Choose <No Field> for both the Report Fields and Chart Fields, and title the chart Player Total Points.

i. Widen the chart to be about 6 inches wide in Report Design View, then save and preview the report.

j. Save the PlayerStatistics report, print the first page, then close the report.

k. Close the Basketball-L.accdb database and exit Access 2007.

▼ INDEPENDENT CHALLENGE 3

As the manager of a college women's basketball team, you want to create a multi-column report from the Basketball-L.accdb database to summarize total points per game per player.

a. Start Access, then open the database Basketball-L.accdb from the drive and folder where you store your Data Files. Enable content if prompted.

b. Open the PlayerStats query in Design View. In the final column add a new field with the following expression (if it has not already been added): TotalPts:[FT]+([fg]*2)+([3p]*3).

c. Save and close the PlayerStats query.

d. Create a new report using the Report Wizard from the PlayerStats query with the fields Opponent, GameDate, Last, and TotalPts. View the data by Games, do not add any more grouping levels, then sort the records in descending order by TotalPts.

e. Click the Summary Options button and click the Sum check box for the TotalPts field.

f. Choose a Stepped layout and a Landscape orientation. Choose an Aspect style, title the report Point Production, and preview it.

g. In Report Design View remove the long Summary calculated field in the GameNo Footer section. Widen the GameDate text box to be about twice its current width.

h. Remove the layout applied to both the Last and TotalPts fields, then delete the Last and TotalPts labels from the Page Header section.

i. Delete the page expression in the Page Footer section, narrow the =Now() expression to be no wider than 3 inches, then move the Last and TotalPts text boxes in the Detail section to the left. Move any other text boxes to the left so that no control is wider than the 3-inch mark on the horizontal ruler.

j. Drag the right edge of the report to the left, so that it is no wider than 3 inches, then right-align the TotalPts text box with the subtotal for total points in the GameNo Footer and the Report Footer sections. Both right-align the values within their respective controls as well as right-align the right edges of the controls.

k. In the Page Setup dialog box, set the report to 3 columns and specify that the column layout go down, then across.

Advanced Challenge Exercise

- In Design View, improve the report by adding a line at the bottom of the GameNo Footer section to separate the records from game to game.
- Change the GameNo Footer Back Color and Alternate Back Color property for the Opponent Footer section to the same as the Report Header section, #E3DED1.
- Add other formatting improvements as desired.

l. Preview the Point Production report. It should structurally look like Figure L-25. Print the first page of the report, adding your name as a label to the Report Header section if needed for the printout.

m. Close the Point Production report, close the Basketball-L.accdb database, then exit Access.

FIGURE L-25

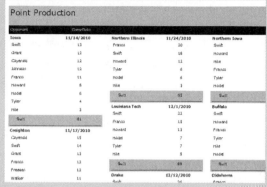

▼ REAL LIFE INDEPENDENT CHALLENGE

In your quest to become an Access database consultant, you want to know more about the built-in Microsoft Access templates, and what you can learn about report design from these samples. In this exercise, you'll explore the reports of the Sales pipeline template.

a. Start Access 2007, then select the Sales pipeline template. Specify the drive and folder where you store your Data Files as the location to save Sales pipeline.accdb, then click Download.

b. Close the Access Help window that automatically appears, then expand the Navigation Pane to review the objects in the database.

c. Briefly open then close each object in the Opportunities, Employees, and Customers navigation sections to study the structure of the available forms and reports.

d. Open the Customers table in the Supporting Objects section, and enter your own name with other fictitious data as the first customer. Close the Customers table.

e. Open the Employees table in the Supporting Objects section, and enter a friend's name with other fictitious data as the first employee. Close the Employees table.

f. Open the Opportunities table in the Supporting Objects section, and enter a record with the title **Big Sale** choosing yourself as the customer and your friend as the employee. Enter appropriate values in all fields. Enter $15,000 in the Est Revenue field. Add two more records to the Opportunities table choosing yourself as the customer, your friend as the employee, but varying the Category, Rating, Probability, and Est Revenue values. Close the Opportunities datasheet.

g. Open the Forecast Tracking Charts form in the Opportunities section to see how the information is being tracked. Click the Assigned To list arrow, then choose your friend's name (as the employee this project was assigned to). Click each of the four tabs in the lower part of the form.

h. Click the Opportunities by Category "For printed reports" command button, then print that page. (*Hint:* If you didn't choose more than one category option when you were entering the three opportunities in step f, the pie chart will be one single color. Go back to step f and choose at least two different Category values to create different wedges in this pie chart before printing it.)

i. Close the Forecast Tracking Charts form, close the Sales pipeline.accdb database, and exit Access 2007.

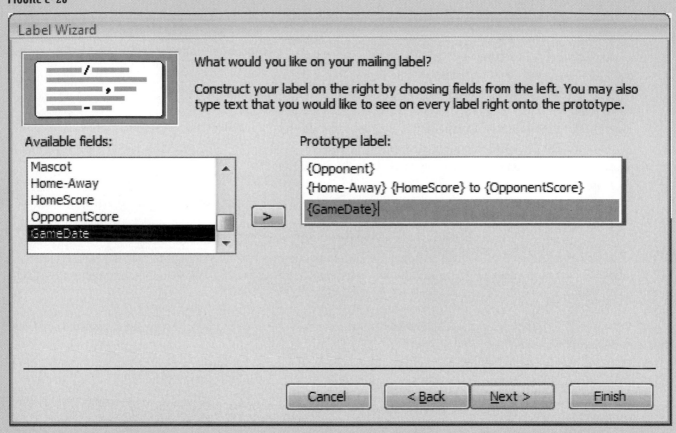

▼ VISUAL WORKSHOP

As the manager of a college women's basketball team, you need to create folders to store paper contracts for each game. You use the Label Wizard to create labels to identify these folders. Select the Games table, start the Label Wizard, choose the Avery 5160 label type, choose a Rockwell 12-point, Normal, black font, and set up the prototype label as shown in Figure L-26. Sort by GameDate, and name the report **GameLabels**. Click OK if prompted, print the first page, then save and close the report, close the Basketball-L.accdb database and exit Access 2007.

FIGURE L-26

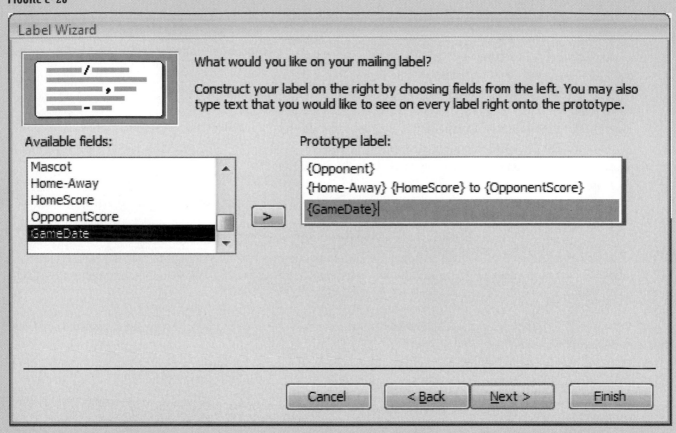

Managing Database Objects

Files You Will Need

Technology-M.accdb

Basketball-M.accdb

RealEstate-M.accdb

Baltic-M.accdb

As your database grows in size and functionality, the number of objects (especially queries and reports) grows as well. As it does, you need to manage the database, which involves finding, renaming, deleting, and documenting objects, as well as making the database easier to use. ▰▰▰ Wilbur Young is the network administrator at Quest corporate headquarters. You have helped Wilbur develop a database to document Quest computer equipment. The number of objects in the database makes it increasingly difficult to find and organize information. You will use Access tools and create navigational forms to manage the growing database and make it easier to use.

OBJECTIVES

Work with objects

Use the Documenter

Group objects

Modify shortcuts and groups

Create a dialog box

Create a pop up form

Create a switchboard

Modify a switchboard

Working with Objects

Working with Access objects is similar to working with files in Windows Explorer. For example, you can use **View By options** (Details, Icon, List) on the Navigation Pane title bar shortcut menu to arrange the objects in three different ways, just as you arrange files within Windows Explorer. Similarly, you can right-click an object within Access to open, copy, delete, or rename it.  Wilbur Young asks you to make several queries easier to find. You decide to delete, rename, sort, and add descriptions to the queries.

STEPS

1. **Start Access, open the Technology-M.accdb database from the drive and folder where you store your Data Files, enable content if prompted, right-click the Navigation Pane title bar, point to View By, then click Icon**

   The Navigation Pane displays the objects as icons. By default, objects are categorized by object type, but you can also group them by created date, modified date, or by their relationship to each table.

   QUICK TIP
   Right-click the Navigation Pane title bar, point to Sort By, then click Name, Type, Created Date, or Modified Date.

2. **Right-click the Navigation Pane title bar, point to Category, click Tables and Related Views, then click OK when prompted**

   Each table is now listed in the Navigation Pane, followed by queries, forms, and reports that contain fields from the table, as shown in Figure M-1. An object such as the Africa query is listed four times because it contains fields from four different tables: PCSpecs, Employees, Assignments, and Equipment. Another way to view the relationships between objects is to view object dependencies.

3. **Click the PCSpecs table, click the Database Tools tab, click the Object Dependencies button, then click OK if prompted**

   The Object Dependencies task pane opens, as shown in Figure M-2. Option buttons allow you to view either the objects that depend on the selected object or objects that the selected object itself depends on.

4. **Click the expand button ⊞ to the left of the Africa query in the Object Dependencies task pane**

   Expanding the Africa query reveals that the Africa report is dependent on the Africa query. Another way to organize and manage objects is to determine whether you want to view open objects as overlapping windows or with tabs. To see which option is applied to this database, open two objects.

5. **Double-click the Africa report, then double-click the Americas report in the Navigation Pane**

   Because you do not see the tabs in this database, you know that database options are set to show open objects as overlapping windows. To view object tabs for open objects, you need to change the database options.

6. **Click the Office button ⬤, click the Access Options button, click Current Database, click the Tabbed Documents option button, click OK, then click OK**

   You must close the database and reopen it to see the change in the presentation of open objects.

7. **Close the Technology-M database, reopen the Technology-M database enabling content if necessary, and then reopen the Africa report and Americas report**

   Tabbed objects appear as shown in Figure M-3.

FIGURE M-1: Viewing objects by table

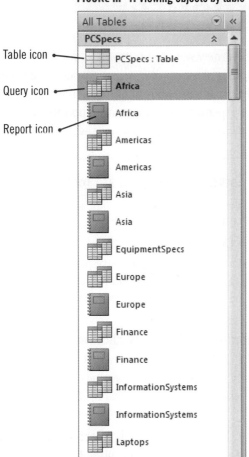

Table icon

Query icon

Report icon

FIGURE M-2: Object Dependencies task pane

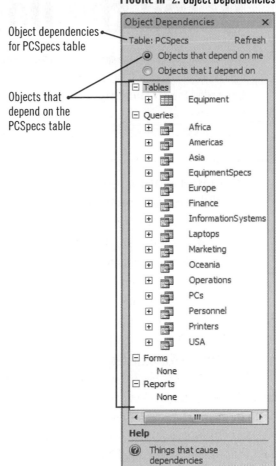

Object dependencies for PCSpecs table

Objects that depend on the PCSpecs table

FIGURE M-3: Tabs for open objects

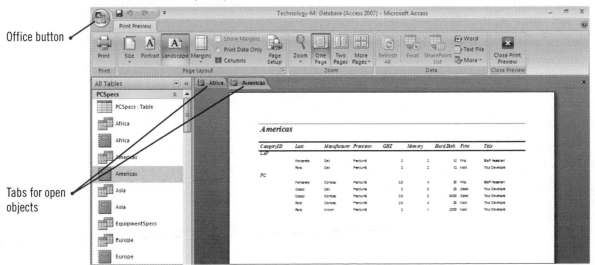

Office button

Tabs for open objects

Using the Documenter

As your Access database grows, users will naturally request new ways to use the data. Your ability to modify a database depends on your understanding of existing database objects. Access provides an analysis feature called the **Documenter** that creates reports on the properties and relationships among the objects in a database. ▧▧▧▧ You use the Documenter to create paper documentation to support the database for other Quest employees.

STEPS

1. **Close the Africa report, close the Americas report, click the Database Tools tab, then click the Database Documenter button**

   The Documenter dialog box opens, displaying tabs for each object type.

2. **Click the Tables tab, then click Options in the Documenter dialog box**

   The Print Table Definition dialog box opens. See Figure M-4. This dialog box gives you some control over what type of documentation you will print for the table. The documentation for each object type varies slightly. For example, the documentation on forms and reports also includes information on controls and sections.

3. **Click the Names, Data Types, and Sizes option button for fields, click the Nothing option button for indexes, then click OK**

   Be careful before you select the option to print property values for each field because it creates a long printout. You can select or deselect individual objects by clicking check boxes, or you can click the Select All button to quickly select all objects of that type.

4. **Click Select All to select all of the tables, click the Forms tab, click Select All to select all of the forms, click OK, then click the 🔍 pointer on the report preview to zoom in**

   The Documenter creates a report for all of the table objects in the Technology-M.accdb database and displays it as an Access report, as shown in Figure M-5. The first page contains information about the first table in the database, the Assignments table.

5. **Click the Last Page button ▶│ in the navigation bar, then click the Previous Page button ◀**

   The last part of the report contains information about the forms in the database. The properties for each control on the form are listed in two columns. Because most form controls have approximately 50 properties, the documentation to describe a form can be quite long. You can print the report, or send it to a Word document using the Word button, but you cannot modify a Documenter report in Report Design View or save it as an object within this database.

6. **Click Close Print Preview on the Print Preview toolbar**

FIGURE M-4: Print Table Definition dialog box

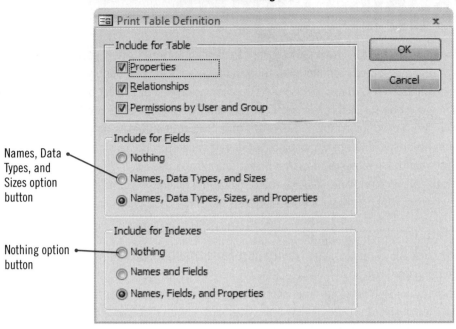

Names, Data Types, and Sizes option button

Nothing option button

FIGURE M-5: Object Definition report

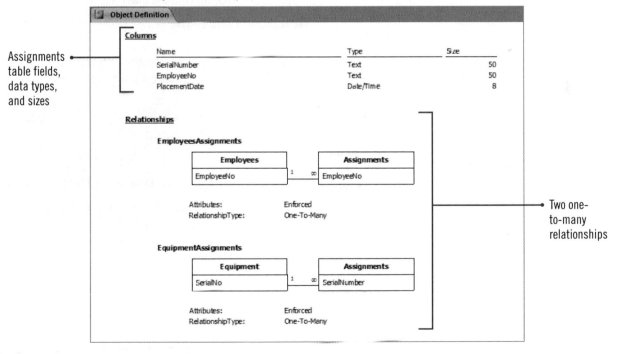

Assignments table fields, data types, and sizes

Two one-to-many relationships

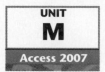

Grouping Objects

Viewing every object in the Navigation Pane can be cumbersome when your database contains many objects. Sometimes object-naming conventions are used to help identify and organize objects, as described in Table M-1. **Groups** are also used to organize objects by subject or purpose. For example, you might create a group for each department so that the forms and reports used by a department are presented as a set. A group consists of **shortcuts** (pointers) to the objects that belong to a specific group. These shortcuts are used to open the object but do not affect the original location of the object. More than one shortcut can be created to the same object and placed in several groups. You can add and display groups on the Navigation Pane. You organize the objects in your database by creating groups for two different departments: Travel and Operations.

STEPS

1. **Right-click** All Tables **on the Navigation Pane title bar, click** Navigation Options, **then click** Custom Groups

   The Navigation Options dialog box opens, as shown in Figure M-6. One custom group that you can modify is Favorites, or you can create your own custom groups. Objects that have not been placed in a custom group remain in the Unassigned Objects group.

2. **Click the** Add Group **button, type** Travel, **click the** Add Group **button, type** Operations, **then click** OK

   With the new groups in place, you're ready to organize objects within them.

3. **Right-click** All Tables **on the Navigation Pane title bar, point to** Category, **click** Custom Groups, **then scroll to the top of the** Navigation Pane

   Dragging an object to a group icon places a shortcut to that object within the group. A shortcut icon looks different from the actual object because it has a small black arrow in the lower-left corner.

4. **Drag the** Africa query icon **in the Navigation Pane to the Travel group, then drag the** Africa report icon **to the Travel group**

   Your screen should look like Figure M-7, with two shortcut icons representing the Africa query and African report in the Travel group. You can open or design an object by accessing it through a shortcut icon. You can also create multiple shortcuts to the same object.

5. **Click the** Travel group bar **twice**

   Click a group bar to collapse or expand that section of the Navigation Pane.

6. **Click the** Operations group bar **twice**

   No objects have yet been added to the Operations group, so it doesn't expand or collapse to show or hide any icons when it is clicked.

Naming objects

Object names can be 64 characters long and can include any combination of letters, numbers, spaces, and special characters except a period (.), exclamation point (!), accent (`), or brackets ([ ]). It is helpful to keep the names as short, yet as descriptive, as possible. Short names make objects easier to reference in other places in the database, such as in the Record Source property for a form or report.

FIGURE M-6: Navigation Options dialog box

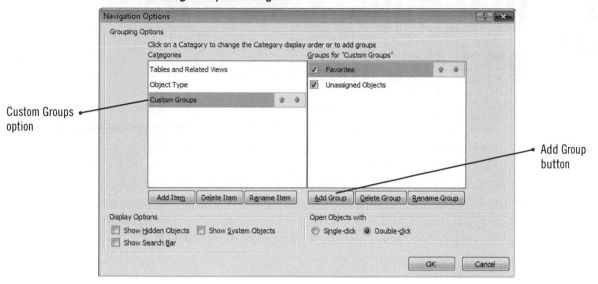

Custom Groups
option

Add Group
button

FIGURE M-7: Navigation Pane with custom Travel group

Travel group bar

Africa query shortcut

Africa report shortcut

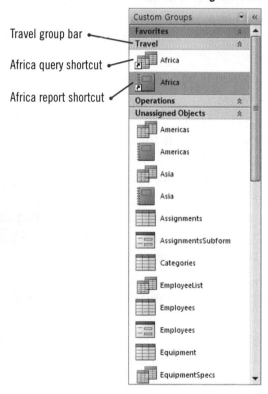

TABLE M-1: Naming conventions

object type	prefix	object name example
Table	tbl	tblProducts
Query	qry	qrySalesByRegion
Form	frm	frmProducts
Report	rpt	rptSalesByCategory
Macro	mcr	mcrCloseInventory
Module	bas	basRetirement
Module	mdl	mdlCheckCredit

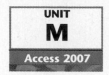
Modifying Shortcuts and Groups

Once groups are created and object shortcuts are added to them, you work with the shortcut as if you were working directly with the original object. Any changes you make to an object by accessing it through a shortcut are saved with the object, just as if you had opened that object without using the shortcut. You can delete, rename, or copy a shortcut by right-clicking it and choosing the appropriate command from the shortcut menu. The biggest difference between working with shortcuts and actual objects is that if you delete a shortcut, you delete only that pointer; the original object it references is not affected. If you delete an object, however, it is, of course, permanently deleted, and any shortcuts that reference it no longer function properly. You can also rename or delete entire groups. ▓▓▓▓▓ You modify groups and shortcuts to clarify your database.

STEPS

1. **Right-click the Africa query shortcut in the Travel group, click Rename Shortcut on the shortcut menu, type Africa Query, then press [Enter]**

   A shortcut does not have to use the same name as the object that it points to, but shortcuts should be clearly named. You can also rename groups.

2. **Right-click the Operations group bar, click Rename on the shortcut menu, type Internal Reports, then press [Enter]**

   The Navigation Pane should look like Figure M-8.

3. **Double-click Africa Query, then change the entry in the Last field from Hosta to Hoffman**

   Because Boyd Hosta, now Boyd Hoffman, is listed in this query twice, both records automatically change. Editing data through a query shortcut is the same as editing data in a query or table datasheet. You want to close the Africa Query and restore the Navigation Pane to its default settings.

4. **Close the Africa Query, right-click Custom Groups on the Navigation Pane title bar, point to Category, then click Object Type**

   To display more objects without scrolling, change the default view of the icons in the Navigation Pane from icons to list.

5. **Right-click All Access Objects on the Navigation Pane title bar, point to View By, then click List**

   Your Navigation Pane should look like Figure M-9.

6. **Click the Tables group bar if you need to expand the group, double-click the PCSpecs table to open its datasheet, click the Find button on the Home tab, type JK123FL3 in the Find What text box, press [Enter], then click Cancel**

   The Memory field for the JK123FL3 record contains the value 4.

7. **Close the PCSpecs datasheet**

FIGURE M-8: Modifying shortcuts and groups

FIGURE M-9: Default Navigation Pane

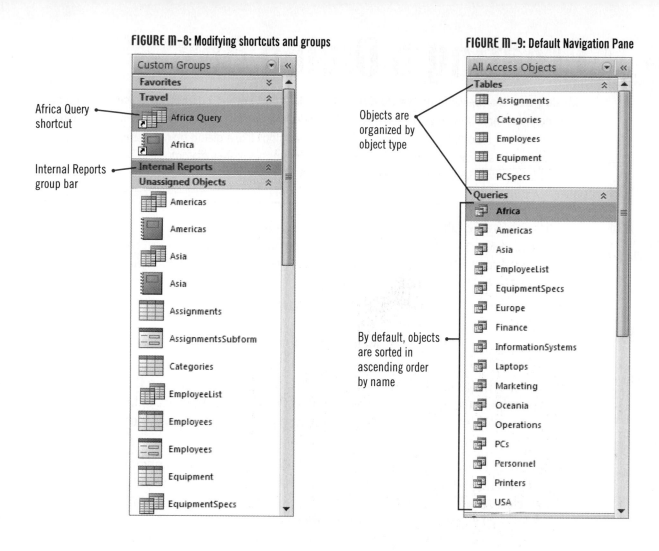

Africa Query shortcut

Internal Reports group bar

Objects are organized by object type

By default, objects are sorted in ascending order by name

Creating a Dialog Box

A **dialog box** is a special form used to display information or prompt a user for a choice. Creating dialog boxes help to simplify the Access interface. For example, you might create a dialog box to give the user an easy-to-use list of reports to view or print. To make a form look like a dialog box, you modify form properties that affect its appearance and borders. ▰▰▰▱▰ You want to create a dialog box to provide an easy way for users to print various reports.

STEPS

1. **Click the Create tab, then click the Form Design button**
   A dialog box form is not bound to an underlying table or query, and therefore doesn't use the form's Record Source property. You place unbound controls, such as labels and command buttons, on a dialog box to offer the user information and choices.

2. **Click the Button button on the Design tab, then click in the upper-middle section of the form**
   The **Command Button Wizard** shown in Figure M-10 organizes over 30 of the most common command button actions within six categories.

3. **Click Report Operations in the Categories list, click Preview Report in the Actions list, click Next, click Africa as the report choice, click Next, click the Text option button, press [Tab], type Africa, click Next, type AfricaButton as the button name, then click Finish**
   The command button appears in Form Design View.

4. **Click the Button button on the Design tab, click below the first command button, click Report Operations in the Categories list, click Preview Report in the Actions list, click Next, click Americas, click Next, click the Text option button, press [Tab], type Americas, click Next, type AmericasButton, then click Finish**
   With the command buttons in place, you modify form properties to make the form look like a dialog box.

5. **Double-click the Form Selector button ▨ to open the form's Property Sheet, click the Format tab, then double-click the Border Style property to change it from Sizable to Dialog**
   The **Border Style** property determines the appearance of the outside border of the form. The **Dialog** option indicates that the form will have a thick border and may not be maximized, minimized, or resized. A dialog box does not need a record selector or navigation buttons, so you want to remove them from this form using the Records Selector and Navigation Buttons properties.

6. **Double-click the Records Selectors property to change it from Yes to No, then double-click the Navigation Buttons property to change it from Yes to No as shown in Figure M-11**

7. **Close the Property Sheet, drag the lower-right corner of the form up and to the left so it is approximately 3 inches wide by 2 inches tall, save the form with the name ReportsDialogBox, then click the Form View button on the Design tab**
   The dialog box should look similar to Figure M-12.

8. **Click the Americas command button**
   Clicking the Americas command button displays the Americas report, which shows the technology assignments to employees in the Americas department. Given more time, you'd want to add command buttons for all departmental reports to this dialog box form.

9. **Close the Americas report, then save and close the ReportsDialogBox form**

FIGURE M-10: Command Button Wizard

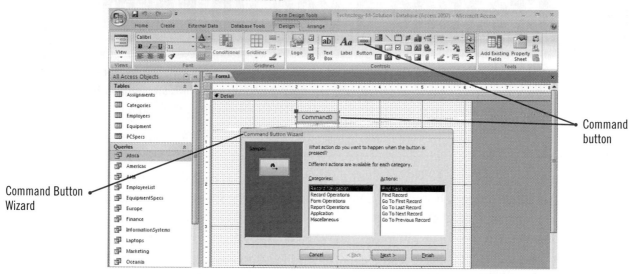

Command Button Wizard

Command button

FIGURE M-11: Modifying form properties

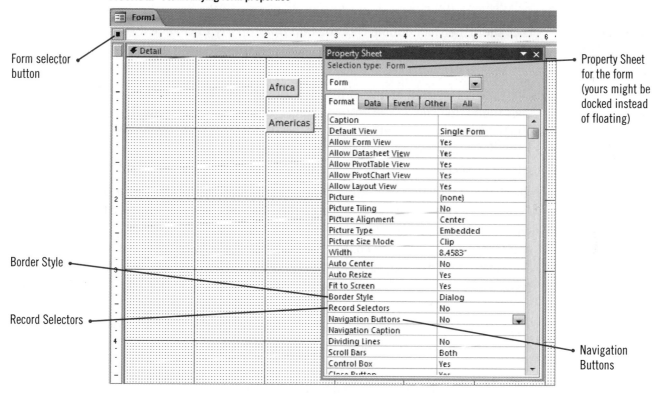

Form selector button

Border Style

Record Selectors

Property Sheet for the form (yours might be docked instead of floating)

Navigation Buttons

FIGURE M-12: ReportsDialogBox in Form View

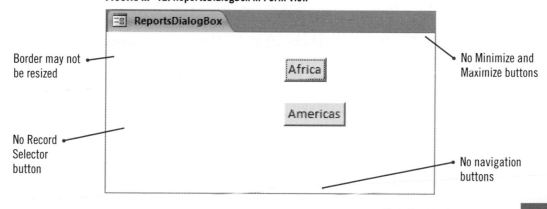

Border may not be resized

No Record Selector button

No Minimize and Maximize buttons

No navigation buttons

Creating a Pop Up Form

A **pop up form** is a form that stays on top of other open forms, even when another form is active. For example, you might want to create a pop up form to give the user easy access to reference lists such as phone numbers or e-mail addresses. You can open a pop up form with a command button. You create a pop up form to access employee department information. You add a command button to the ReportsDialogBox form to open the pop up form.

STEPS

1. **Click the Create tab, click the Form Design button, click the Property Sheet button on the Design tab, click the Data tab in the Property Sheet, click the Record Source list arrow, then click Employees**

   You want to add three fields to the pop up form, First, Last, and Department.

   > **QUICK TIP**
   > If the field list is in the way, drag its title bar to move it or click the Add Existing Fields button on the Design tab to toggle it off.

2. **Close the Property Sheet, click the Add Existing Fields button on the Design tab, double-click First, double-click Last, double-click Department, then close the Field List**

   You change a regular form into a pop up form by changing its Pop Up property.

3. **Double-click the Form Selector button ▢ to reopen the Property Sheet for the form, click the Other tab, double-click the Pop Up property to change it from No to Yes as shown in Figure M-13**

   Now you can save and close the form.

4. **Drag the lower-right corner of the form to size it to about 4 inches wide by 2 inches tall, click the Format tab in the Property Sheet, double-click the Default View property to change the value to Continuous Forms, close the Property Sheet, save the form with the name EmployeePopup, then close it**

   Add a command button to the right side of the ReportsDialogBox form to open the EmployeePopup form.

   > **TROUBLE**
   > You may need to drag the right edge of the form to the right to widen the form.

5. **Right-click the ReportsDialogBox form, click Design View, click the Button button on the Design tab, click to the right of the existing buttons on the form, click the Form Operations category, click the Open Form action, click Next, click EmployeePopup, click Next, click Next to show all of the records, click the Text option button, press [Tab], type Employee Departments, click Next, type EmployeeDeptButton, then click Finish**

   Pop up forms are often used to display reference information. They can be used just like any other form. You need to test your pop up form.

6. **Save the form, click the Form View button on the Design tab, click the Employee Departments command button, then move and resize the EmployeePopup form so that it is positioned on the right side of the window**

7. **Click the Africa command button on the ReportsDialogBox form**

   The EmployeePopup form stayed "on top" even though you opened a report, as shown in Figure M-14. Given more time, you'd want to resize the pop up form to be as small as possible, yet still show all of the information in the form.

8. **Close the EmployeePopup form, close the Africa report, then close the ReportsDialog Box form**

FIGURE M-13: Building a pop up form

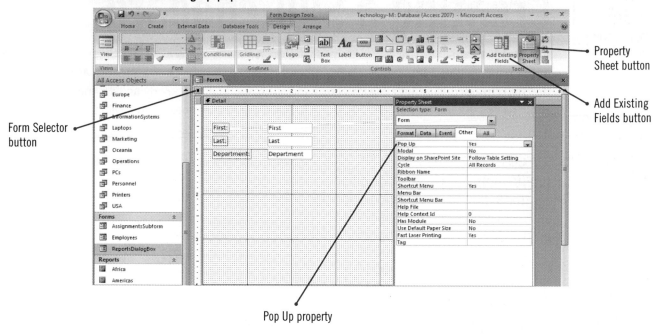

Form Selector button

Property Sheet button

Add Existing Fields button

Pop Up property

FIGURE M-14: Viewing a pop up form

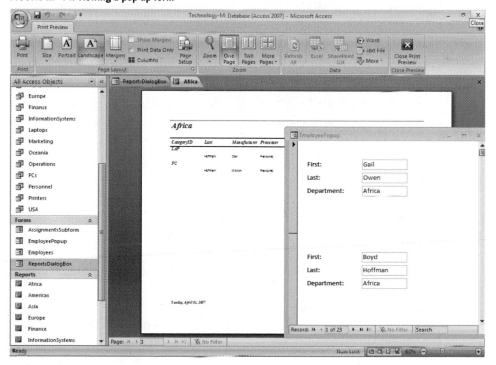

Creating a Switchboard

A **switchboard** is a special Access form that uses command buttons to provide an easy-to-use and secure database interface. Switchboards are created and modified by using a special Access tool called the **Switchboard Manager**, which allows you to create the form quickly and without programming skills. You create a switchboard form to make your database easier to navigate.

1. **Click the** Database Tools tab, **click the** Switchboard Manager button, **then click** Yes **when prompted to create a switchboard**

   The Switchboard Manager dialog box opens and presents the options for the first switchboard page. Depending on how you want to organize switchboard options, you can create multiple switchboard pages for various audiences or subjects and link them together. One switchboard page must be designated as the **default switchboard**, which is used to link to additional switchboard pages as needed. Your switchboard page will start with two command buttons, which you add to the default switchboard page.

2. **Click** Edit

   The Edit Switchboard Page dialog box opens. At this point, the switchboard page does not contain any items. You add items using the New button.

3. **Click** New

   The Edit Switchboard Item dialog box opens, prompting you for three pieces of information: Text (a label on the switchboard form that identifies the corresponding command button), Command (which corresponds to a database action), and Switchboard (an option that changes depending on the command and further defines the command button action).

4. **Type** Open Employees Form **in the Text text box, click the** Command list arrow, **click** Open Form in Edit Mode, **click the** Form list arrow, **then click** Employees

   The Edit Switchboard Item dialog box should look like Figure M-15. Opening a form in **Edit Mode** allows you to edit records, whereas **Add Mode** only allows you to add new records.

5. **Click** OK **to add the first command button to the switchboard, click** New, **type** Select Reports **in the Text text box, click the** Command list arrow, **click** Open Form in Edit Mode, **click the** Form list arrow, **click** ReportsDialogBox, **then click** OK

   The Edit Switchboard Page dialog box should look like Figure M-16. Each entry in this dialog box represents a command button that will appear on the final switchboard.

6. **Click** Close **to close the Edit Switchboard Page dialog box, then click** Close **to close the Switchboard Manager dialog box**

7. **Double-click the** Switchboard form **in the Navigation Pane**

   The finished switchboard opens in Form View, as shown in Figure M-17.

8. **Click the** Open Employees Form command button **on the Switchboard, close the** Employees form, **click the** Select Reports command button, **then close the** ReportsDialogBox form

   Switchboard forms provide a fast and easy way to help users work with just those objects they need in a database. Given more time, you'd want to add more buttons to the switchboard to access more database objects.

FIGURE M-15: Adding an item to a switchboard page

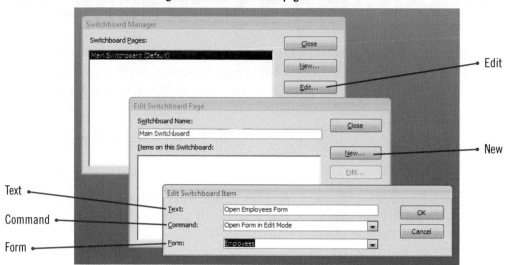

Edit

New

Text

Command

Form

FIGURE M-16: Edit Switchboard Page dialog box

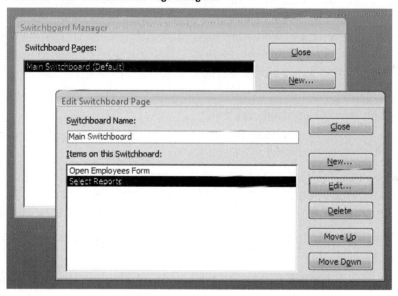

FIGURE M-17: Switchboard form

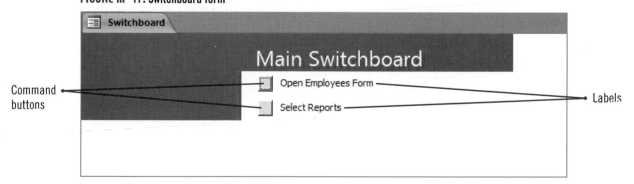

Command
buttons

Labels

Modifying a Switchboard

Always use the Switchboard Manager to add, delete, move, and edit the command buttons and labels on a switchboard form. Use Form Design View to make formatting modifications such as changing form colors, adding clip art, or changing the switchboard title. Wilbur Young is pleased with the steps you've taken to make the database easier to use, but he suggests changing the title, colors, and order of the command buttons to improve the switchboard. You use Form Design View to make the formatting changes and the Switchboard Manager to change the order of the buttons.

STEPS

1. **Right-click the Switchboard tab, click Design View, then click the teal rectangle on the left of the Detail section**

   The teal areas on the left and top portion of the Switchboard are rectangles. You can modify their color or shape just as you would modify any drawn object.

2. **Click the Fill/Back Color button arrow ⬛⏷ on the Design tab, click the yellow box in the last row, click the teal rectangle in the Form Header section, click ⬛⏷, then click the red box in the last row**

3. **Click the Label button 𝘈𝘢 on the Design tab, click the left side of the Form Header section, type your name, then press [Enter]**

   Your Switchboard should look like Figure M-18. You use Form Design View to modify colors, clip art, and labels. Notice that neither the command buttons nor the text describing each command button appears in Form Design View. You use the Switchboard Manager to modify the command buttons on a switchboard.

4. **Save and close the Switchboard form, click the Database Tools tab, click the Switchboard Manager button, then click Edit**

   Use the Switchboard Manager to add, delete, or modify the command buttons on the switchboard, including the text labels that describe them.

5. **Click Select Reports, click Edit, click between "Select" and "Reports" in the Text text box, type Departmental, press [Spacebar], then click OK**

   You can also change the order of the command buttons from the Edit Switchboard Page dialog box.

6. **Click Move Up to make Select Departmental Reports the first item in the switchboard, click Close, then click Close**

7. **Double-click the Switchboard form in the Navigation Pane to open it in Form View, save, print, and close the switchboard, then exit Access**

   The final switchboard should look like Figure M-19.

FIGURE M-18: Modifying a Switchboard in Form Design View

Fill/Back
Color
button

Label
button

New label

Rectangle in
Detail section

Rectangle in Form
Header section

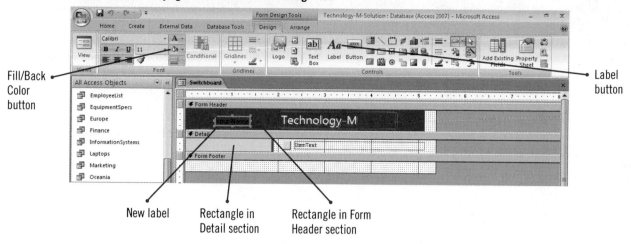

FIGURE M-19: Final Switchboard in Form View

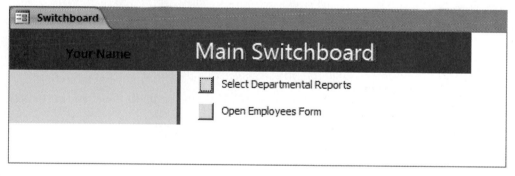

Practice

▼ CONCEPTS REVIEW

Identify each element of the database window shown in Figure M-20.

FIGURE M-20

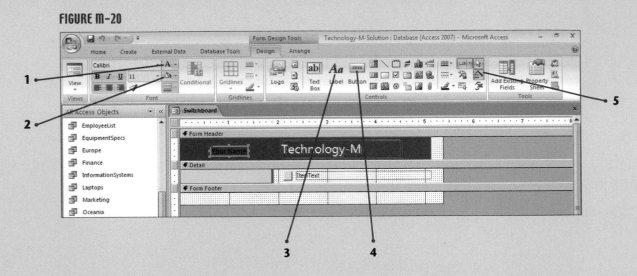

Match each term with the statement that best describes its function.

6. **Dialog box**
7. **Pop up form**
8. **Switchboard**
9. **Shortcut**
10. **Command Button Wizard**
11. **Documenter**

a. Creates reports on the properties and relationships among the objects in your database
b. Pointer to a database object
c. Stays on top of other open forms, even when another form is active
d. Uses command buttons to simplify access to database objects
e. Used to display information or prompt a user for a choice
f. Organizes over 30 of the most common command button actions within six categories

Select the best answer from the following list of choices.

12. **Which View option do you use to display the date that an object was created?**
   a. Small Icons
   b. List
   c. Details
   d. Date
13. **Which feature helps organize objects in the Navigation Pane?**
   a. Documenter
   b. Renamer
   c. Groups
   d. Switchboard Manager
14. **If you wanted to add a command button to a switchboard, which view or tool would you use?**
   a. Form Design View
   b. Report Design View
   c. Switchboard Analyzer
   d. Switchboard Manager

15. **Which item would *not* help you organize the Access objects that the Human Resources (HR) Department most often uses?**
   a. A report that lists all HR employees
   b. A switchboard that provides command buttons to the appropriate HR objects
   c. A dialog box with command buttons that reference the most commonly used HR forms and reports
   d. An HR group with shortcuts to the HR objects

16. **A dialog box is which type of object?**
   a. Form
   b. Table
   c. Report
   d. Macro

17. **A switchboard is which type of object?**
   a. Form
   b. Table
   c. Report
   d. Macro

18. **If you want to modify the text that identifies each command button on the switchboard, which view or tool do you use?**
   a. Form Design View
   b. Table Design View
   c. Documenter
   d. Switchboard Manager

19. **If you want to change color of a switchboard, which view or tool do you use?**
   a. Form Design View
   b. Form View
   c. Switchboard Documenter
   d. Switchboard Manager

20. **Which is *not* a valid name for an Access object?**
   a. tblEmployees
   b. Employees table
   c. E1-E2
   d. E1!E2

▼ SKILLS REVIEW

1. **Work with objects.**
   a. Start Access, open the Basketball-M.accdb database from the drive and folder where you store your Data Files, and enable content if prompted.
   b. Using the Navigation Pane, change the view to Details.
   c. Using the Navigation Pane, change the category grouping to Tables and Related Views.
   d. Using the Navigation Pane, make sure the objects are sorted by type.
   e. Press the [PrtSc] (Print Screen) key to capture the current Access window and copy it to the Windows Clipboard.
   f. Open Word or PowerPoint, then click the Paste button to paste a copy of the Access window to the document.
   g. Add your name to the document, print it, then close it without saving changes.

2. **Use the Documenter.**
   a. Use the Database Documenter tool to document all tables and the form in the database.
   b. Print the first two pages and the last two pages of the report.
   c. On the printout, circle the field list for the Games table, the one-to-many relationship between the Games and Stats table, and three different color properties for the Year_Label.
   d. Close the report created by Documenter without saving it.

3. **Group objects.**
   a. Use Navigation Pane options to create one new group named Forwards and another named Guards.
   b. In the Navigation Pane, change the category grouping to Custom.
   c. Create shortcuts for the ForwardFieldGoals query and the ForwardFieldGoals report in the Forwards group.
   d. Create shortcuts for the GuardFieldGoals query and GuardFieldGoalStats report in the Guards group.

4. **Modify shortcuts and groups.**
   a. Rename the ForwardFieldGoals report shortcut in the Forwards group to Forward FG.
   b. Rename the GuardFieldGoalStats report shortcut in the Guards group to Guard FG.

5. **Create a dialog box.**
   a. Create a new form in Form Design View.
   b. Add a command button to the upper-left corner of the form using the Command Button Wizard. Select Report Operations from the Categories list, select Preview Report from the Actions list, then select the GamesSummaryReport.
   c. Type **Preview Games Summary Report** as the text for the button, then type **GamesReportButton** for the button name.
   d. Add a second command button below the first to preview the PlayerFieldGoalStats report.
   e. Type **Preview Player FG Report** as the text for the button, then type **PlayerFGButton** for the button name.
   f. Below the two buttons, add a label to the form with your name.
   g. In the Property Sheet for the form, change the Border Style property of the form to Dialog, the Record Selectors property to No, and the Navigation Buttons property to No.
   h. Close the Property Sheet, then size the buttons to be the same size and aligned on their left edges.
   i. Resize the form and Form Design View window until it is approximately 3 inches wide by 3 inches tall, then save the form as **TeamReports**.
   j. Open the TeamReports form in Form View, test the buttons, close the reports, then print the form. Your TeamReports form should be similar to Figure M-21.
   k. Close the TeamReports form.

FIGURE M-21

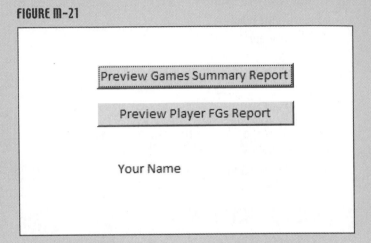

6. **Create a pop up form.**
   a. In Form Design View, create a form with the following fields from the Players table: First, Last, and PlayerNo.
   b. Save the form with the name **PlayerPopup**.
   c. Open the Property Sheet for the PlayerPopup form, change the Pop Up property to Yes, change the Default View property to Continuous Forms, then close the Property Sheet.
   d. Resize the PlayerPopup form to be as small as possible yet show all three text boxes.
   e. Save, then close the PlayerPopup form.
   f. Open the TeamReports form in Form Design View, then add a command button below your name using the Command Button Wizard.
   g. In the Command Button Wizard, select the Form Operations category, the Open Form action, and the PlayerPopup form to open. The form should be opened to show all of the records.
   h. Type **Open Player Pop up** as the text for the button, then name the button **PlayerPopup**.
   i. Save the TeamReports form, then open it in Form View. Click the Open Player Pop up command button to test it. Test the other buttons as well. The PlayerPopup form should stay on top of all other forms and reports until you close it.
   j. Save, then close all open forms and reports.

7. **Create a switchboard.**
   a. Start the Switchboard Manager, and click Yes to create a new switchboard.
   b. Click Edit to edit the Main Switchboard, then click New to add the first item to it.
   c. Type **Select a Team Report** as the Text entry for the first command button, select Open Form in Add Mode for the Command, select TeamReports for the Form, then click OK to add the first command button to the switchboard.
   d. Click New to add a second item to the switchboard. Type **Open Player Entry Form** as the Text entry, select Open Form in Add Mode for the Command, select PlayerEntryForm for the Form, then click OK to add the second command button to the switchboard.

e. Close the Edit Switchboard manager dialog box, then close the Switchboard Manager dialog box. Open the Switchboard form and click both command buttons to make sure they work. Notice that when you open the Player Entry Form in Add Mode (rather than using the Open Form in Edit Mode action within the Switchboard Manager), the navigation buttons indicate that you can only add a new record, and not edit an existing one.

f. Close all open forms, including the Switchboard form.

8. Modify a switchboard.

a. Open the Switchboard Manager, then click Edit to edit the Main Switchboard.

b. Click the Open Player Entry Form item, then click Edit.

c. Select Open Form in Edit Mode for the Command, select PlayerEntryForm for the Form, then click OK.

d. Move the Open Player Entry Form item above the Select a Team Report item, then close the Switchboard Manager.

e. In Form Design View of the Switchboard form, add a label with the name of your favorite team as well as a label with your own name to the Form Header section of the form. Format the labels with a color and size that make them easy to read in Form View.

f. View the modified switchboard in Form View, as shown in Figure M-22, then test the buttons. Notice the difference in the Open Player Entry Form button (the Player Entry Form opens in Edit Mode versus Add Mode).

FIGURE M-22

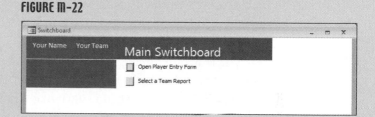

g. Save, print, then close the Switchboard form.

h. Close the Basketball-M.accdb database, then exit Access.

▼ INDEPENDENT CHALLENGE 1

As the manager of a real estate office, you have created a database to track local real estate agencies, agents, and property listings. You want to create a group to organize the database objects used by the realtors. You also want to document the database's relationships.

a. Start Access, open the database **RealEstate-M.accdb** from the drive and folder where you store your Data Files, and enable content if prompted.

b. Create a new custom group named **Agents**.

c. View the objects in the Navigation Pane by Custom Groups, then add the following shortcuts to the Agents group: AgencyInformation form, ListingsEntryForm, AgentList report, and PropertyList report.

d. Test all of the shortcuts to make sure that they open the object they point to, then close all open objects.

e. Start the Documenter. On the Current Database tab, click the Relationships check box, then click OK.

f. Print the Documenter's report, then close it. Write your name on the printout.

Advanced Challenge Exercise

■ Create a switchboard form with the following four command buttons in the following order:

Text	Command	Form or Report
Open Agency Information Form	Open Form in Edit Mode	AgencyInformation
Open Listings Entry Form	Open Form in Edit Mode	ListingsEntryForm
Open Agent List Report	Open Report	AgentList
Open Property List Report	Open Report	PropertyList

▼ INDEPENDENT CHALLENGE 1 (CONTINUED)

- Open the Switchboard, and insert a label that reads **Your Name's Real Estate Agency** in the Form Footer section.
- Save, print, then close the switchboard form. It should look like Figure M-23.

g. Close the RealEstate-M.accdb database, then exit Access.

FIGURE M-23

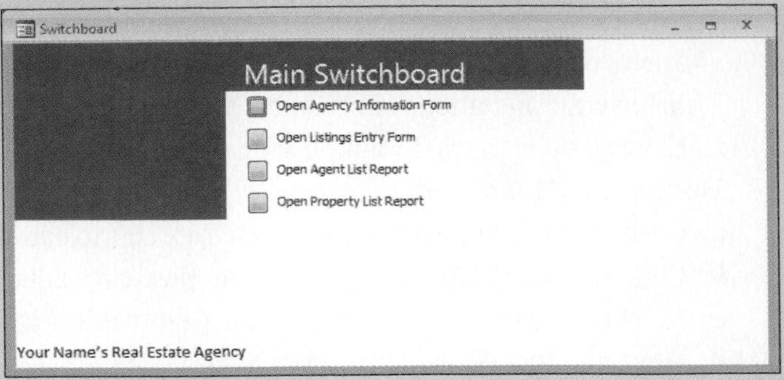

▼ INDEPENDENT CHALLENGE 2

As the manager of a real estate office, you have created a database to track local real estate agencies, agents, and property listings. You want to create a new dialog box to make it easier to preview the reports within your database.

a. Start Access, then open the database **RealEstate-M.accdb** from the drive and folder where you store your Data Files. Enable content if prompted.

b. Start a new form in Form Design View.

c. Using the Command Button Wizard, add a command button to the form. Select Report Operations from the Categories list, select Preview Report from the Actions list, then select the AgentList report.

d. Type **Agent List** as the text for the button, then type **AgentListButton** for the button name.

e. Using the Command Button Wizard, add a second command button under the first. Select Report Operations from the Categories list, select Preview Report from the Actions list, then select the PropertyList report.

f. Type **Property List** as the text for the button, then type **PropertyListButton** for the button name.

g. Using the Command Button Wizard, add a third command button under the second. Select Form Operations from the Categories list, and select Close Form from the Actions list.

h. Use the Exit Doorway picture on the button, then type **CloseButton** as the meaningful name for the button.

i. Add a label to the form with your name and any other formatting enhancements you desire.

j. Open the Property Sheet for the form, change Border Style property to Dialog, the Record Selectors property to No, and the Navigation Buttons property to No.

k. Close the Property Sheet, size the form so it is approximately 3 inches wide by 3 inches tall, then save the form as **ReportDialogBox**.

l. Open the ReportDialogBox form in Form View, test the buttons, then print the form. It should look similar to Figure M-24.

m. Close the ReportDialogBox form, close the RealEstate-M.accdb database, then exit Access.

FIGURE M-24

▼ INDEPENDENT CHALLENGE 3

As the manager of a real estate office, you have created a database to track local real estate agencies, agents, and property listings. You want to create a pop up form to provide agent information. You want to add a command button to the ListingsEntryForm to open the pop up form.

a. Start Access, then open the database **RealEstate-M.accdb** from the drive and folder where you store your Data Files.

b. Use the Form Wizard to create a form with the AgentNo, AgentFirst, AgentLast, and AgentPhone fields from the Agents table.

c. Use a Tabular layout, an Aspect style, and type **Agent Popup** for the form title.

d. Open the Property Sheet for the form, then change the Pop Up property to Yes.

▼ INDEPENDENT CHALLENGE 3 (CONTINUED)

e. Save, then close the Agent Popup form. Rename it to **AgentPopup** in the Navigation Pane.

f. In Form Design View of the ListingsEntryForm, open the Form Header section about 0.5", then use the Command Button Wizard to create a command button on the right side of the Form Header.

g. Select Form Operations from the Categories list, select Open Form from the Actions list, select the AgentPopup form, then open the form and show all of the records.

h. Type **Agent Popup** as the text for the button, then type **AgentsButton** for the button name.

i. Add a label to the left side of the Form Header with your name.

j. Save the ListingsEntryForm, open it in Form View, then click the Agent Popup command button. Drag the title bars of the two open forms to view them.

k. Move through the records of the ListingsEntryForm. The AgentPopup form should stay on top of all other forms.

Advanced Challenge Exercise

- Create a second pop up form using the Form Wizard with all of the fields of the Agencies table except for AgencyNo.
- Use a Tabular layout, an Apex style, and title the form **Agency Popup**.
- Change the form's Pop Up property to Yes, then save and close the form. Rename it **AgencyPopup** in the Navigation Pane.
- In Design View of the ListingsEntryForm, add another command button just under the Agent Popup command button in the Form Header section to open the AgencyPopup form and show all of the records.
- Type **Agency Popup** as the text for the button, then type **AgencyPopupButton** for the button name.
- Move, resize, and align the controls in the Form Header as needed.
- Open the form in Form View, and test both command buttons.

l. Close any open pop up forms, then print the first record in the ListingsEntryForm.

m. Save and close all open forms, close the RealEstate-M.accdb database, then exit Access.

▼ REAL LIFE INDEPENDENT CHALLENGE

The larger your database becomes, the more important it is to document it properly so that others can also work with it successfully. Many companies require that you use an adopted set of naming standards when you create new fields, objects, and controls so that other database developers can more readily understand and modify a database they have not created. In this Real Life Independent Challenge, you will search for and report on database naming standards.

a. Connect to the Internet, go to *www.google.com*, *www.yahoo.com*, or your own favorite search engine, then search for Web sites with the key words **Access naming conventions**. You might also try searching for the **Leszynski Naming Convention**, **object naming convention**, or **database naming convention**.

b. Find and print two different reference pages that describe naming conventions for fields, objects, or controls.

c. Find and print two different discussions of the advantages of adopting a common naming convention for all database development for your company.

Advanced Challenge Exercise

- Call two local businesses and contact a programmer in the Information Systems department who would be willing to answer questions about naming conventions. Ask whether their business employs standardized naming conventions in database development. Ask what types of database software they use. Ask what types of challenges they face in database development, maintenance, and standards. Finally, ask what type of advice they have for a future database developer. Be sure to thank them for their time and advice.

d. Write a two-page paper summarizing your findings. If using references or information from articles or interviews, be sure to reference those sources of information properly, in accordance with class instructions.

▼ VISUAL WORKSHOP

As the manager of a tourism company that promotes travel to European countries, you have created an Access database called **Baltic-M.accdb** that tracks events at various European cities. Create a switchboard form to give the Baltic-M users an easy-to-use interface, as shown in Figure M-25. All command buttons on the switchboard access a report for the country they reference. Be sure to add your own name as a label to the switchboard, and include any other formatting improvements that you desire. Print the switchboard.

FIGURE M-25

Creating Macros

A macro is a database object that stores Access actions. When you run a macro, you execute the stored set of actions. Actions are the tasks that you want the macro to perform. Access provides about 50 actions from which to choose when creating a macro. A repetitive Access task, such as printing a report, opening a form, or exporting data, is a good candidate for a macro. Automating routine and complex tasks by using macros builds efficiency, accuracy, and flexibility into your database.  Wilbur Young, the network administrator at Quest Specialty Travel, has identified several Access tasks that are repeated on a regular basis. He has asked you to help him automate these processes with macros.

OBJECTIVES

Understand macros

Create a macro

Modify actions and arguments

Create a macro group

Set conditional expressions

Work with events

Assign a macro to a
    command button

Troubleshoot macros

Understanding Macros

A macro object may contain one or more actions, the tasks that you want Access to perform. Actions are entered in the **Macro Builder**, the window in which you build and modify macros. Each action has a specified set of arguments. **Arguments** provide additional information on how to carry out the action. For example, the OpenForm action contains six arguments, including Form Name (identifies which form to open) and View (determines whether the form should be opened in Form View or Design View). After choosing the macro action you want from a list, the associated arguments for the action automatically appear in the lower pane of the Macro Builder. You decide to study the major benefits of using macros, macro terminology, and the components of the Macro Builder before building your first macro.

The major benefits of using macros include:

- Saving time by automating routine tasks
- Increasing accuracy by ensuring that tasks are executed consistently
- Improving the functionality and ease of use of forms by using macros connected to command buttons
- Ensuring data accuracy in forms by using macros to respond to data entry errors
- Automating data transfers such as exporting data to an Excel workbook
- Creating your own customized environment by using macros to customize toolbars and menus

Macro terminology:

- A **macro** is an Access object that stores a series of actions to perform one or more tasks.
- Each task that you want the macro to perform is called an **action**. Each macro action occupies a single row in the Macro Builder.
- The Macro Builder is the window in which you create a macro, as shown in Figure N-1. See Table N-1 for a description of the Macro Builder components.
- Arguments are properties of an action that provide additional information on how the action should execute.
- A **macro group** is an Access macro object that stores more than one macro. The macros in a macro group run independently of one another, but are grouped together to organize multiple macros that have similar characteristics. For example, you may want to put all of the macros that print reports in one macro group.
- An **expression** is a combination of values, fields, and operators that result in a value.
- A **conditional expression** is an expression resulting in either a true or false answer that determines whether a macro action will execute. For example, if the Country field contains a null value (nothing), you may want the macro to execute an action that sends the user a message to enter a value for that field.
- An **event** is something that happens on a form, window, toolbar, or datasheet—such as the click of a command button or an entry in a field—that can be used to initiate the execution of a macro.

FIGURE N-1: Macro Builder of a macro group

Run button
Conditions button
Macro Names button
Macro Name column
Arguments button
Condition column

Action column
Comment column
Action list arrow

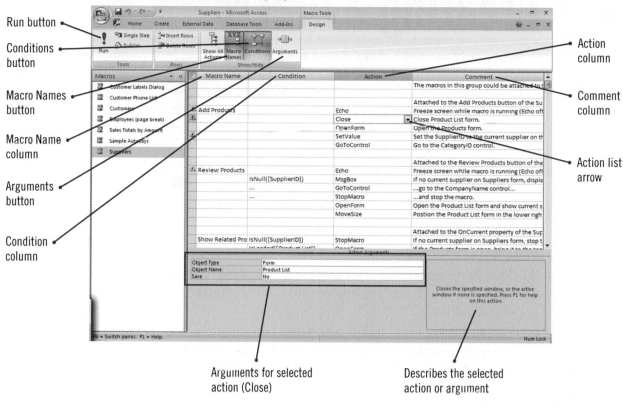

Arguments for selected action (Close)

Describes the selected action or argument

TABLE N-1: Macro Builder components

component	description
Macro Name column	Contains the names of individual macros within a macro group. If the macro object contains only one macro, it isn't necessary to use this column because you can run the macro by referring to it by the macro object's name. View this column by clicking the Macro Names button. The Macro Names button works as a toggle to open and close the Macro Name column.
Condition column	Contains conditional expressions that are evaluated either true or false. If true, the macro action on the row is executed. If false, the macro action on the row is skipped. View this column by clicking the Conditions button on the Macro Tools Design tab. The Conditions button works as a toggle to open and close the Condition column.
Action column	Contains the actions, or the tasks, that the macro executes when it runs.
Comment column	Contains optional explanatory text for each row.
Action Arguments pane	Displays the arguments for the selected action. Indicates which row is currently selected.

Creating a Macro

In Access, you create a macro by choosing a series of actions in the Macro Builder that accomplishes the job you want to automate. Therefore, to become proficient with Access macros, you must be comfortable with macro actions. Access provides more than 50 macro actions. Some of the most common actions are listed in Table N-2. In some programs, such as Microsoft Word or Microsoft Excel, you create a macro by using a "macro recorder" to save the keystrokes and mouse clicks used to perform a task. Another difference between Access and the other Microsoft Office products is that when you create a macro in Word or Excel, you create Visual Basic for Applications (VBA) statements. In Access, macros do not create VBA code, but after a macro is created, you can convert it to VBA if desired. ▰▰▰▰ Wilbur observes that users want to open the AllEquipment report from the Employees form, so he asks you to create a macro to automate this task.

STEPS

1. **Start Access, open the Technology-N.accdb database from the drive and folder where you store your Data Files, enable content if prompted, click the Create tab, then click the Macro button**

   The Macro Builder opens, ready for you to choose your first action. The Macro Name and Condition columns may be visible, and can be toggled on and off by clicking their buttons on the Macro Tools Design tab. They are only needed if you are creating multiple macros in the same macro object or using conditional expressions.

2. **Click the first row's Action list arrow, type o to quickly scroll to the actions that start with the letter "o", then click OpenReport**

   The OpenReport action is chosen for the first line, and the arguments that further define the OpenReport action appear in the next column as well as in the **Action Arguments pane** in the lower half of the Macro Builder. The OpenReport action has three required arguments: Report Name, View, and Window Mode. View and Window Mode have default values that you can modify. The Filter Name and Where Condition arguments are optional.

3. **Click the Report Name argument in the Action Arguments pane, click the Report Name list arrow, then click AllEquipment**

   All of the report objects in the Technology-N.accdb database appear in the Report Name argument list.

4. **Click View argument in the Action Arguments pane, click the View list arrow, then click Print Preview**

   Your screen should look like Figure N-2. Macros can be one or many actions long. In this case, the macro is only one action long and has no conditional expressions.

5. **Click the Save button 🖫 on the Quick Access toolbar, type PreviewAllEquipmentReport in the Macro Name text box, click OK, then close the Macro Builder**

   The Navigation Pane lists the PreviewAllEquipmentReport object in the Macros group.

6. **Double-click the PreviewAllEquipmentReport macro in the Navigation Pane to run the macro**

   The AllEquipment report opens in Print Preview.

7. **Close the AllEquipment preview window**

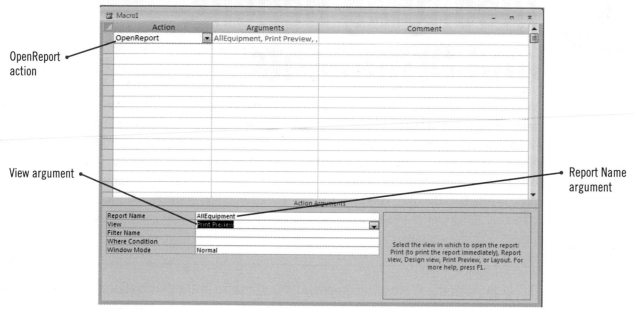

TABLE N-2: Common macro actions

subject area	macro action	description
Handling data in forms	ApplyFilter	Restricts the number of records that appear in the resulting form or report by applying limiting criteria
	FindRecord	Finds the first record that meets the criteria
	GoToControl	Moves the focus (where you are currently typing or clicking) to a specific field or control
	GoToRecord	Makes a specified record the current record
Executing menu options	RunCode	Runs a Visual Basic function (a series of programming statements that do a calculation or comparison and return a value)
	RunCommand	Carries out a specified menu command
	RunMacro	Runs a macro or attaches a macro to a custom menu command
	StopMacro	Stops the currently running macro
Importing/ exporting data	TransferDatabase, TransferSpreadsheet, TransferText	Imports, links, or exports data between the current Microsoft Access database and another database, spreadsheet, or text file
Manipulating objects	Close	Closes a window
	Maximize	Enlarges the active window to fill the Access window
	OpenForm	Opens a form in Form View, Design View, Print Preview, or Datasheet View
	OpenQuery	Opens a select or crosstab query in Datasheet View, Design View, or Print Preview; runs an action query
	OpenReport	Opens a report in Design View or Print Preview, or prints the report
	OpenTable	Opens a table in Datasheet View, Design View, or Print Preview
	PrintOut	Prints the active object, such as a datasheet, report, form, or module
	SetValue	Sets the value of a field, control, or property
Miscellaneous	Beep	Sounds a beep tone through the computer's speaker
	MsgBox	Displays a message box containing a warning or an informational message
	SendKeys	Sends keystrokes directly to Microsoft Access or to an active Windows application

Access 2007

Modifying Actions and Arguments

Macros can contain as many actions as necessary to complete the process that you want to automate. Each action is evaluated in the order in which it appears in the Macro Builder, starting at the top. A macro stops executing actions when it encounters a blank row in the Macro Builder or a new macro name in the Macro Name column. While some macro actions open, close, preview, or export data or objects, others are used only to make the database easier to use. **MsgBox** is a useful macro action because it displays an informational message to the user. ░░░░░ You decide to add an action to the PrintAllEquipmentReport macro to clarify for the user what is happening when the macro runs. You add a MsgBox action to the macro to display a descriptive message.

STEPS

1. **Right-click the** PreviewAllEquipmentReport **macro in the Navigation Pane, then click** Design View **on the shortcut menu**

   The PreviewAllEquipmentReport macro opens in the Macro Builder.

QUICK TIP
Press [F1] to display Help text for the action and argument currently selected.

2. **Click the** Action cell **for the second row, click the** Action list arrow, **type m to quickly scroll to the actions that start with the letter "m", then click** MsgBox

   Each action has its own arguments that further clarify what the action does.

3. **Click the** Message argument text box **in the Action Arguments pane, then type** Click the Print button to print this report

   The Message argument determines what text appears in the message box. By default, the Beep argument is set to "Yes" and the Type argument is set to "None".

4. **Click the** Type argument text box **in the Action Arguments pane, read the description in the lower-right corner of the Macro Builder, click the** Type list arrow, **then click** Information

   The Type argument determines which icon appears in the dialog box that is created by the MsgBox action.

5. **Click the** Title argument text box **in the Action Arguments pane, then type** To print this report. . .

   Your screen should look like Figure N-3. The Title argument specifies what text is displayed in the title bar of the resulting dialog box. If you leave the Title argument empty, the title bar of the resulting dialog box displays "Microsoft Office Access."

6. **Save the macro, then click the** Run button **on the Design tab**

   If your speakers are turned on, you should hear a beep, then the message box should appear, as shown in Figure N-4.

7. **Click** OK **in the dialog box, close the AllEquipment report, then close the Macro Builder**

FIGURE N-3: New MsgBox action in the Macro Builder

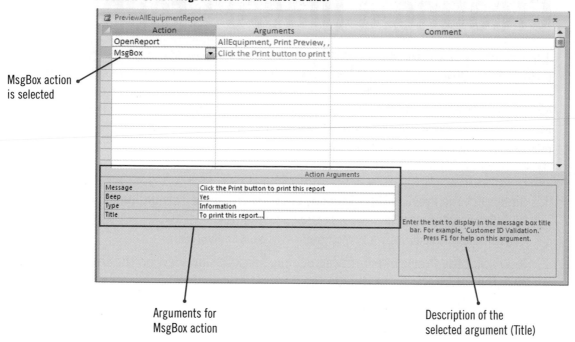

MsgBox action is selected

Arguments for MsgBox action

Description of the selected argument (Title)

FIGURE N-4: Dialog box created by MsgBox action

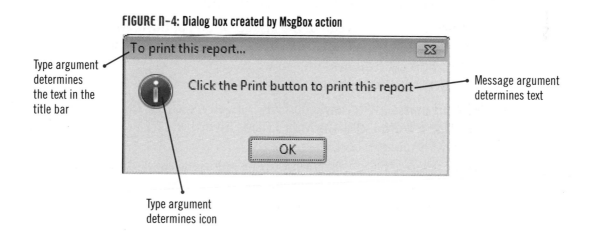

Type argument determines the text in the title bar

Message argument determines text

Type argument determines icon

Creating a Macro Group

A **macro group** is a macro object that stores more than one macro. Macro groups are used to organize multiple macros that have similar characteristics, such as all the macros that print reports or all the macros that are used by the same form. When you put several macros in the same macro object to create a macro group, you must enter a unique name for each macro in the Macro Name column of the first action in that macro to identify where each macro starts. ▆▆▆ You add a macro to the existing macro object that prints the Personnel report, thereby creating a macro group.

STEPS

1. **Right-click the PreviewAllEquipmentReport macro in the Navigation Pane, click Rename, type PreviewReportsMacroGroup, then press [Enter]**
   Object names should identify the object contents as clearly as possible.

2. **Right-click the PreviewReportsMacroGroup, click Design View on the shortcut menu, click the Macro Names button on the Design tab, type PreviewAllEquipment in the first Macro Name cell, then press [Enter]**
   An individual macro in a macro group must be given a name in the Macro Name column.

3. **Click the Macro Name cell in the fourth row, type PreviewPersonnelReport, drag the column divider between the Macro Name and Action columns to the right using the ✛ pointer, then press [Enter]**
   An individual macro in a macro group stops when it encounters a blank row, or when a new macro name is entered in the Macro Name column. Therefore, a blank row between macros is not required, but it helps clarify where macros start and stop even when the Macro Name column is not visible.

4. **Click the Action list arrow, scroll and click OpenReport, click in the Report Name argument in the Action Arguments pane, click the Report Name list arrow, click Personnel, click the View argument, click the View list arrow, then click Print Preview**
   Your screen should look like Figure N-5. One benefit of creating several macros in one macro group is that you can copy and paste actions from one macro to another.

5. **Right-click the row selector of the MsgBox action of the PreviewAllEquipment macro, click Copy on the shortcut menu, right-click the row selector for the fifth row, then click Paste on the shortcut menu**
   Your screen should look like Figure N-6. Test the second macro.

6. **Save the macro as PreviewReportsMacroGroup, click the Database Tools tab, click the Run Macro button, click the Macro Name list arrow, click PreviewReportsMacroGroup. PreviewPersonnelReport, then click OK**
   Separating a specific macro within a macro group with a period is called **dot notation**. Dot notation is also used when developing modules with Visual Basic programming code.

7. **Close the Personnel report and the Macro Builder**
   The PreviewReportsMacroGroup now contains two macros.

Creating Macros

FIGURE N-5: Creating a macro group

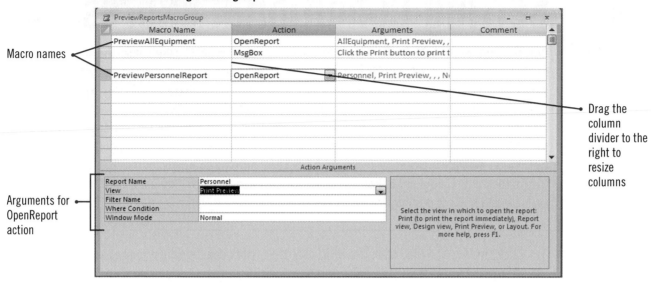

Macro names

Arguments for
OpenReport
action

Drag the
column
divider to the
right to
resize
columns

FIGURE N-6: Creating the PreviewPersonnelReport macro

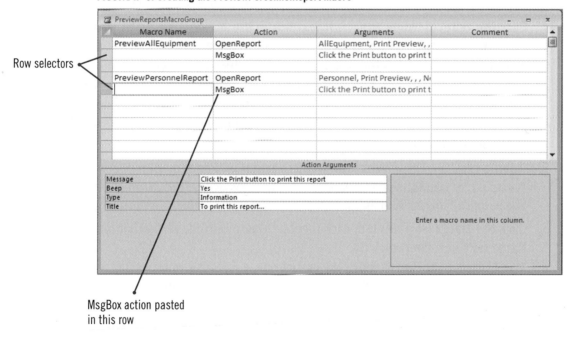

Row selectors

MsgBox action pasted
in this row

Assigning a macro to a key combination

You can assign a key combination (such as [Ctrl][L]) to a macro by creating a macro group with the name **AutoKeys**. Enter the key combination in the Macro Names column for the first action of the associated macro. Any key combination assignments you make in the AutoKeys macro override those that Access has already specified.

Therefore, be sure to check the Keyboard Shortcuts information in the Microsoft Access Help system to make sure that the AutoKey assignment that you are creating doesn't override an existing Access quick keystroke that may be used for another purpose.

Setting Conditional Expressions

Conditional expressions are expressions that result in a true or false value and are entered in the Condition column of the Macro Builder. If the condition evaluates true, the action on that row is executed. If the condition evaluates false, the macro skips that row. When building a conditional expression that refers to a value in a control on a form or report, use the following syntax: [Forms]![*formname*]![*controlname*] or [Reports]![*reportname*]![*controlname*]. Separating the object type (Forms or Reports) from the object name and from the control name by using [square brackets] and exclamation points (!) is called **bang notation**. ▨▨▨ At Quest, everyone who has been with the company longer than five years is eligible to take their old PC equipment home as soon as it has been replaced. You use a conditional macro to help evaluate and present this information in a form.

STEPS

QUICK TIP

You can also right-click the Condition cell, then click Zoom to open the Zoom dialog box to enter long expressions.

1. **Click the Create tab, click the Macro button, click the Conditions button, type [Forms]![Employees]![DateHired]<Date()-(5*365), then widen the Conditions column so that the expression is clearly visible**

   The conditional expression shown in Figure N-7 says, "Check the value in the DateHired control on the Employees form and evaluate true if the value is earlier than five years from today. Evaluate false if the value is not earlier than five years ago."

2. **Click the Action list arrow, then scroll and click SetProperty**

   The SetProperty action has three arguments: Control Name, Property, and Value.

QUICK TIP

In order for this step to work, the Name property of the label on the form must be spelled exactly as entered in the Control Name argument.

3. **Click the Control Name argument text box in the Action Arguments pane, type LabelPCProgram, click the Enabled Property argument, click the Property argument list arrow, click Visible, click the Value Property argument, then type –1**

   Your screen should look like Figure N-8. The lower-right corner displays a short description of the current argument. For the Value argument, it explains you should enter 0 for False and –1 for True.

4. **Save the macro with the name 5PC, then close the Macro Builder**

   Test the macro using the Employees form.

TROUBLE

Be sure Juan Ramirez with a hire date of 8/6/2000 is the current record.

5. **Double-click the Employees form in the Navigation Pane to open it**

   The record for Juan Ramirez, hired 8/6/2000, appears. You use the 5PC macro to determine whether the Eligible for PC Program! label should be displayed.

6. **Click the Database Tools tab, click the Run Macro button, verify that 5PC is in the Macro Name text box, then click OK**

   After evaluating the date of this record and determining that this employee has been working at Quest longer than five years, the "Eligible for PC Program!" label's Visible property was set to true, as shown in Figure N-9.

7. **Navigate through several records, and note that the label remains visible for each employee even though the hire date may not be longer than five years ago**

   Because the macro only ran once, when the DateHired field value is more than five years ago, the label's Visible property remains true. You need a way to rerun or trigger the macro to turn the label's Visible property true or false as you move from record to record.

8. **Close the Employees form**

FIGURE N-7: Creating a conditional expression

Form name

Control name

Today's date

5 years times
365 days
per year

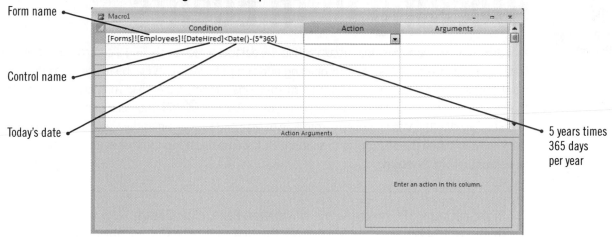

FIGURE N-8: Completing the action arguments

Arguments for
SetProperty
action

SetProperty
action

Short description of current
argument, Value

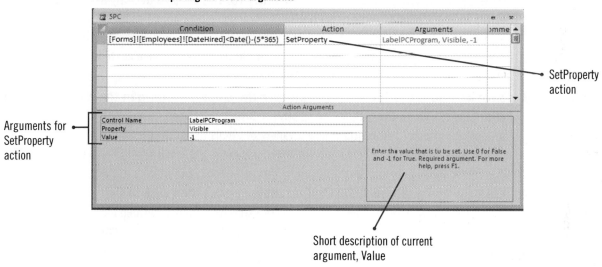

FIGURE N-9: Running the 5PC macro

LabelPCProgram
Visible property is
set to true

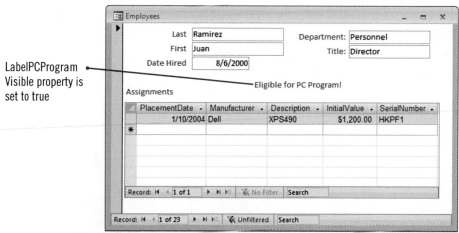

Working with Events

An **event** is a specific activity that occurs within the database, such as clicking a command button, moving from record to record, editing data, or opening or closing a form. Events can be triggered by the user or by the database itself. By assigning a macro to an appropriate event, rather than running the macro from the Tools menu, you further automate and improve your database. ████████ You need to modify the 5PC macro so that it switches the Visible property from true to false and back again as the DateHired field is evaluated. Then you can attach the 5PC macro to an event on the Employees form so that it automatically runs as you move from record to record.

1. **Right-click the 5PC macro in the Navigation Pane, click Design View on the shortcut menu, right-click the row selector for the first row, click Copy, right-click the row selector for the second row, then click Paste**

   With the action copied and pasted, you can now edit the second copy to change the label's Visible property back to false should the hire date be less than five years ago.

2. **Click the Condition entry in the second row, change the < (less than symbol) to be > (greater than symbol), click the Value entry for the second action, then change the -1 entry in the Value argument to be 0**

   Your screen should look like Figure N-10. With the second action edited, the macro will now turn the label's Visible property to true or false, depending on how the expression is evaluated. Now attach the macro to the event on the form that triggers each time you move from record to record.

3. **Save and close the 5PC macro, right-click the Employees form in the Navigation Pane, click Design View, then click the Property Sheet button**

   All objects, sections, and controls have a variety of events to which macros can be attached. Most event names are self-explanatory for a particular item, such as the **On Click** event (which occurs when that item is clicked).

   QUICK TIP

   A short description of the current property appears in the status bar. Press [F1] for more help on that property.

4. **Click the Event tab, click the On Current list arrow, then click 5PC**

   Your screen should look like Figure N-11. The **On Current** event occurs when focus moves from one record to another, therefore the 5PC macro will automatically run as you move from record to record in the form.

5. **Click the Form View button on the Design tab, then click the Next record button ▶ in the navigation bar for the main form several times while observing the Eligible for PC Program! label**

   For every DateHired value that is earlier than five years before today's date, the Eligible for PC Program! label is visible.

6. **Save and close the Employees form**

Creating Macros

FIGURE N-10: Adding a second action to the 5PC macro

less than symbol (<)
changed to greater
than symbol (>)

Value property
set to 0, False

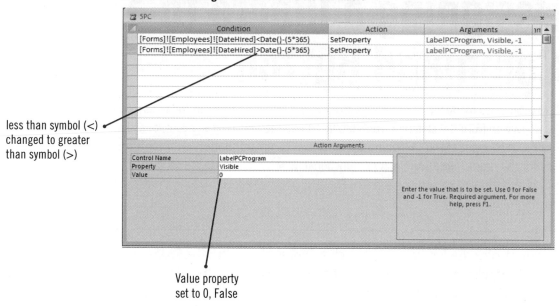

FIGURE N-11: Assigning a macro to an event

Form property
sheet

On Current
event

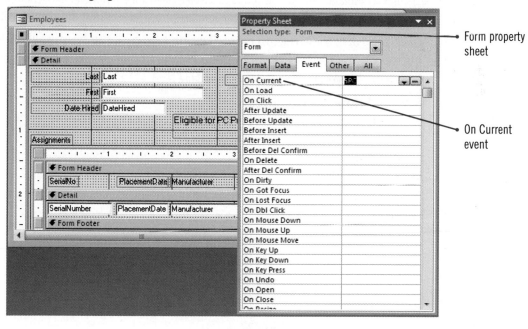

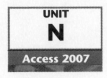

Assigning a Macro to a Command Button

Access provides many ways to run a macro: clicking the Run button in the Macro Builder, clicking the Run Macro button from the Database Tools tab, assigning the macro to an event, or assigning the macro to the Ribbon or shortcut menu. Assigning a macro to a command button on a form provides a very intuitive way for the user to access the macro's functionality. ▰▰▰▰ You decide to modify the Employees form to include a command button that runs the PreviewPersonnelReport macro in the PreviewReportsMacroGroup macro group.

STEPS

1. **Right-click the** Employees **form, click** Design View, **click the** Property Sheet **button to close it, click the** Button **button, then click just below the** Title **text box**
   The Command Button Wizard starts. The Miscellaneous category contains an action that allows you to run an existing macro.

2. **Click** Miscellaneous **in the Categories list, click** Run Macro **in the Actions list, click** Next, **click** PreviewReportsMacroGroup.PreviewPersonnelReport, **click** Next, **click the** Text **option button, select** Run Macro, **type** Personnel Report, **then click** Next
   The next question posed by the Command Button Wizard asks you to give the button a meaningful name. The meaningful name is used in behind-the-scenes VBA (Visual Basic for Applications) and is not the same thing as the text entered in the previous dialog box that sets the command button's caption.

3. **Type** PersonnelReportButton, **compare your screen to Figure N-12, then click** Finish
   The new command button that runs a macro has been added to the Employees form in Form Design View. To make sure that it works, you view the form in Form View and test the command button.

4. **Click the** Form View **button on the Design tab, click the** Personnel Report **command button on the form, click** OK **in the message box, then close the Personnel report**
   The final Employees form should look like Figure N-13.

5. **Save and close the Employees form**

FIGURE N-12: Adding a new command button to run a macro

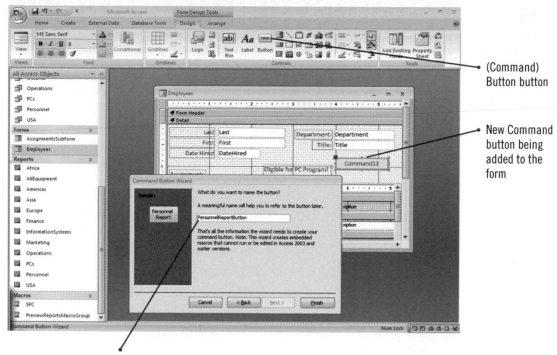

(Command) Button button

New Command button being added to the form

Command Button Wizard asks for a meaningful name

FIGURE N-13: Final Employees form with new command button

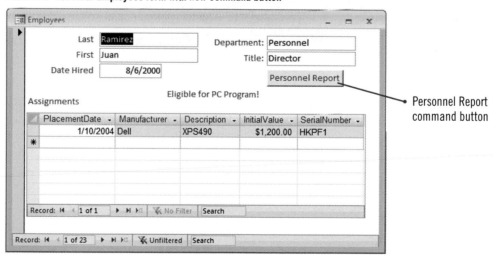

Personnel Report command button

Access 2007

Troubleshooting Macros

When macros don't execute properly, Access supplies several tools to debug them. **Debugging** means determining why the macro doesn't run correctly. It usually involves breaking a dysfunctional macro down into small pieces that can be individually tested. For example, you can **single step** a macro, which means to run it one line (one action) at a time to observe the effect of each specific action in the Macro Single Step dialog box. Another debugging technique is to disable a particular macro action(s) by entering false in the Condition cell for the action(s) that you want to temporarily skip. 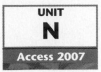 You use the PreviewReportsMacroGroup to learn debugging techniques.

STEPS

1. **Right-click PreviewReportsMacroGroup, click Design View on the shortcut menu, click the Single Step button on the Design tab, then click the Run button**

   The screen should look like Figure N-14, with the Macro Single Step dialog box open. This dialog box displays information including the macro's name, the action's name, the action arguments, and whether the current action's condition is true. From the Macro Single Step dialog box, you can step into the next macro action, halt execution of the macro, or continue running the macro without single stepping.

2. **Click Step in the Macro Single Step dialog box**

   Stepping into the second action lets the first action execute, and pauses the macro at the second action. The Macro Single Step dialog box now displays information about the second action.

3. **Click Step**

   The second action, the MsgBox action, executes, displaying the message box.

4. **Click OK, then close the AllEquipment report**

   You can use the Condition column to temporarily ignore an action while you are debugging a macro.

5. **Click the Design tab, click the Single Step button to toggle it off, click the Conditions button, click the Condition cell for the first row, then type False**

   Your screen should look like Figure N-15.

6. **Save the macro, then run it**

   Because the Condition value is False for the OpenReport action, it did not execute.

7. **Click OK, double-click False in the Condition cell, then press [Delete]**

   You must delete a value to remove a condition; merely hiding the Condition column does not delete or change the values stored in that column.

8. **Save and close the PreviewReportsMacroGroup, close the Technology-N.accdb database, then exit Access**

FIGURE N-14: Single stepping through a macro

Single Step button

Macro Single Step dialog box

Step

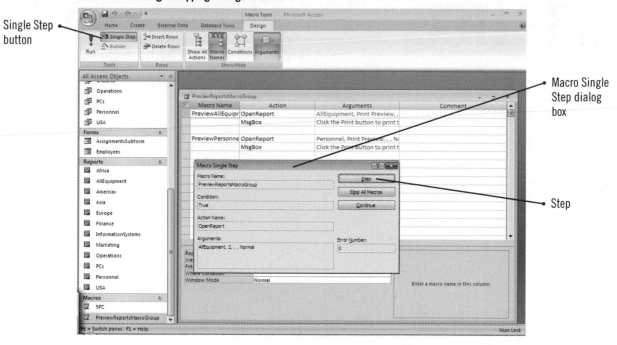

FIGURE N-15: Using a false condition

False condition

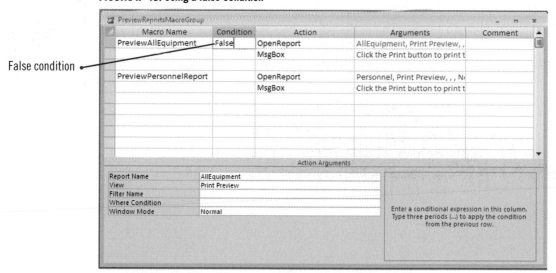

Access 2007

Practice

▼ CONCEPTS REVIEW

Identify each element of the Macro Builder shown in Figure N-16.

FIGURE N-16

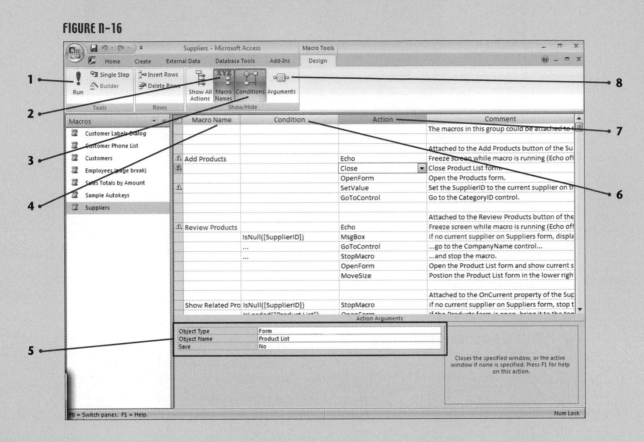

Match each term with the statement that best describes its function.

9. **Action**

10. **Event**

11. **Debugging**

12. **Argument**

13. **Conditional expression**

14. **Macro**

a. Determines why a macro doesn't run properly

b. Specific action that occurs within the database, such as clicking a button or opening a form

c. Evaluates as either true or false, which determines whether Access executes that action or not

d. Individual step that you want the Access macro to perform

e. Access object that stores one or more actions that perform one or more tasks

f. Provides additional information to define how an Access action will perform

Select the best answer from the list of choices.

15. Which of the following is *not* a major benefit of using a macro?

    a. To redesign the relationships among the tables of the database

    b. To ensure consistency in executing routine or complex tasks

    c. To save time by automating routine tasks

    d. To make the database more flexible or easy to use

16. Which of the following best describes the process of creating an Access macro?

    a. Use the macro recorder to record clicks and keystrokes as you complete a task.

    b. Use the Macro Wizard to determine which tasks are done most frequently.

    c. Open the Macro Builder and add actions, arguments, and conditions to accomplish the desired task.

    d. Use the single-step recorder to record clicks and keystrokes as you complete a task.

17. Which of the following would *not* be a way to run a macro?

    a. Assign the macro to a command button on a form.

    b. Assign the macro to an event of a control on a form.

    c. Double-click the macro action within the Macro Builder window.

    d. Click the Run button on the Database Tools tab.

18. Which of the following is *not* a reason to run a macro in single-step mode?

    a. You want to run only a few of the actions of a macro.

    b. You want to observe the effect of each macro action individually.

    c. You want to change the arguments of a macro while it runs.

    d. You want to debug a macro that isn't working properly.

19. Which of the following is *not* a reason to use conditional expressions in a macro?

    a. Conditional expressions allow you to skip over actions when the expression evaluates as false.

    b. Conditional expressions give the macro more power and flexibility.

    c. You can enter "False" in the Conditions column for an action to skip it.

    d. More macro actions are available when you are also using conditional expressions.

20. Which example illustrates the proper syntax to refer to a specific control on a form?

    a. {Forms} ! {*formname*} ! (*controlname*)   **c.** Forms ! *formname. controlname*

    b. (Forms) ! (*formname*) ! (*controlname*)   **d.** [Forms] ! [*formname*] ! [*controlname*]

21. Which event executes every time you move from record to record in a form?

    a. New Record   **c.** On Current

    b. On Move   **d.** Next Record

▼ SKILLS REVIEW

1. Understand macros.

    a. Start Access, then open the Basketball-N.accdb database from the drive and folder where you store your Data Files. Enable content if prompted.

    b. Open the PrintMacroGroup in the Macro Builder, then record your answers to the following questions on a sheet of paper:

      • How many macros are in this macro group?

      • What are the names of the macros in this macro group?

      • What actions does the first macro in this macro group contain?

      • What arguments does the first action contain? What values were chosen for these arguments?

      • Point to the warning symbol to the left of each macro name. What popup message is presented?

    c. Close the Macro Builder for the PrintMacroGroup object.

2. Create a macro.

    a. Start a new macro in the Macro Builder.

    b. Add the OpenQuery action to the first row.

    c. Select ScoreDelta as the value for the Query Name argument.

    d. Select Datasheet for the View argument.

    e. Select Edit for the Data Mode argument.

    f. Save the macro with the name **ViewScoreDelta**.

    g. Run the macro to make sure it works, close the ScoreDelta query, then close the ViewScoreDelta macro.

3. Modify actions and arguments.

    a. Open the ViewScoreDelta macro in the Macro Builder.

    b. Add a MsgBox action in the second row of the Macro Builder.

    c. Type **We had a great season!** for the Message argument.

    d. Select Yes for the Beep argument.

    e. Select Warning! for the Type argument.

    f. Type **Iowa State Cyclones** for the Title argument.

    g. Save the macro, then run it to make sure the MsgBox action works as intended.

    h. Click OK in the dialog box created by the MsgBox action, then close the ScoreDelta query and the ViewScoreDelta macro.

4. Create a macro group.

    a. Rename the ViewScoreDelta macro, changing it to **QueryMacroGroup**.

    b. Open QueryMacroGroup in the Macro Builder.

    c. Open the Macro Name column, then enter **ViewScoreDelta** as the name for the first macro.

    d. Start another macro by typing **ViewForwardFG** in the Macro Name cell of the fourth row.

    e. Add an OpenQuery action for the first action of the ViewForwardFG macro.

    f. Select ForwardFieldGoals for the Query Name argument of the OpenQuery action, and use the default entries for the other two arguments.

    g. Add a MsgBox action for the second action of the ViewForwardFG macro.

    h. Type **Forward Field Goals** as the Message argument for the MsgBox action.

    i. Select Yes for the Beep argument of the MsgBox action.

    j. Select Critical for the Type argument of the MsgBox action.

    k. Type **Big 12 Conference** for the Title argument of the MsgBox action, then save the macro.

    l. Run the ViewForwardFG macro from the Database Tools tab.

    m. Click OK, close the query datasheet, then close the QueryMacroGroup.

5. Set conditional expressions.

    a. Start a new macro in the Macro Builder.

    b. Open the Condition column.

    c. Enter the following condition in the Condition cell of the first row:
       [Forms]![GameSummaryForm]![HomeScore]>[OpponentScore]. (*Hint*: Use the Zoom dialog box or widen the column to more clearly view the entry.)

    d. Add the SetProperty action to the first row.

    e. Type **VictoryLabel** in the Control Name argument value for the SetProperty action.

    f. Select **Visible** for the Property argument for the SetProperty action.

    g. Enter **–1** for the Value argument for the SetProperty action to indicate True.

    h. Copy the first row of the macro with the SetProperty action, then paste it to the second row.

    i. Modify the Condition to change the > (greater than sign) to a < (less than sign) for the second SetProperty action so the condition reads: [Forms]![GameSummaryForm]![HomeScore]<[OpponentScore]

    j. Modify the Value property from –1 to **0** for the second SetProperty action.

    k. Save the macro with the name **VictoryCalculator**, then close the Macro Builder.

6. Work with events.

    a. Open the GameSummaryForm in Form Design View.

    b. Open the Property Sheet for the form.

    c. Assign the VictoryCalculator macro to the On Current event of the form.

    d. Close the Property Sheet, save the form, then open the GameSummaryForm in Form View.

e. Navigate through the first four records. The Victory label should be marked for the first three records, but not the fourth.

f. Add your name as a label in the Form Header section to identify your printouts, print the third and fourth records, then save and close the GameSummaryForm.

7. Assign a macro to a command button.

a. In Design View of the PlayerEntryForm, use the Command Button Wizard to add a command button on the bottom of the form that runs the ViewForwardFG macro in the QueryMacroGroup.

b. The text, or caption, on the button should read View Forward Field Goals.

c. The meaningful name for the button should be ViewForwardButton.

d. Test the command button, as shown in Figure N-17, then click OK in the message box, and close the ForwardFieldGoals query.

e. Save and close the PlayerEntryForm.

8. Troubleshoot macros.

a. Open the PrintMacroGroup in the Macro Builder.

b. Click the Single Step button, then click the Run button.

c. Click Step twice to step through the two actions of the first macro in this macro group, GamesSummary, then click OK in the resulting message box.

d. Open the Condition column if it's not already open.

e. Enter the value **False** as a condition to the first row, the OpenReport action of the GamesSummary macro.

f. Save the macro, then single step through the macro again.

g. This time the GamesSummary report should *not* be printed. Click OK when prompted with the information created by the MsgBox action.

h. Delete the False condition in the first row, save the macro, then click the Single Step button to toggle it off.

i. Save and close the PrintMacroGroup macro, close the Basketball-N.accdb database, then exit Access.

FIGURE N-17

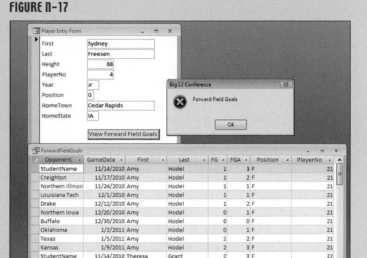

▼ INDEPENDENT CHALLENGE 1

As the manager of a doctor's clinic, you have created an Access database called Patients-N.accdb to track insurance claim reimbursements. You use macros to help automate the database.

a. Start Access, then open the database **Patients-N.accdb** from the drive and folder where you store your Data Files. Enable content if prompted.

b. Open the Macro Builder of the CPT Form Open macro. (CPT stands for Current Procedural Terminology, which is a code that describes a medical procedure.) If the Single Step button is toggled on, click it to toggle it off.

c. On a separate sheet of paper, identify the macro actions, arguments for each action, and values for each argument.

d. In two or three sentences, explain in your own words what tasks this macro automates.

e. Close the CPT Form Open macro.

f. Open the Claim Entry Form in Form Design View. Maximize the window.

g. In the footer of the Claim Entry Form are several command buttons. (*Hint*: Scroll the main form to see these buttons.) Open the Property Sheet of the Add CPT Code button, then click the Event tab.

h. On your paper, write the event to which the CPT Form Open macro is assigned.

i. Open the Claim Entry Form in Form View, then click the Add CPT Code button in the form footer.

j. On your paper, write the current record number that is displayed for you.

k. Find the record for CPT Code 99243. Write down the RBRVS value for this record, then close the CPT form and Claim Entry form. (RBRVS stands for Resource-Based Relative Value System, a measurement of relative value between medical procedures.)

l. Close the Patients-N.accdb database, then exit Access.

▼ INDEPENDENT CHALLENGE 2

As the manager of a doctor's clinic, you have created an Access database called Patients-N.accdb to track insurance claim reimbursements. You use macros to help automate the database.

a. Start Access, then open the database **Patients-N.accdb** from the drive and folder where you store your Data Files. Enable content if prompted.

b. Start a new macro in the Macro Builder, then open the Macro Name column. If the Single Step button is toggled on, click it to toggle it off.

c. Type **Preview DOS Denied** as the first macro name, then add the OpenReport macro action in the first row.

d. Select Date of Service Report - Denied for the Report Name argument, then select Print Preview for the View argument of the OpenReport action.

e. In the third row, type **Preview DOS Fixed** as a new macro name, then add the OpenReport macro action in the third row.

f. Select Date of Service Report - Fixed for the ReportName argument, then select Print Preview for the View argument of the second OpenReport action.

g. Save the object with the name **Preview Group**, then close the Macro Builder.

h. Using the Run Macro button on the Database Tools tab, run the Preview DOS Denied macro to test it, then close Print Preview.

i. Using the Run Macro button on the Database Tools tab, run the Preview DOS Fixed macro to test it, then close Print Preview.

Advanced Challenge Exercise

■ In Preview Group, create two more macros, one that previews Monthly Claims Report - Denied and the other that previews Monthly Claims Report - Fixed. Name the two macros **Preview MCR Denied** and **Preview MCR Fixed**.

■ In Design View of the Claim Entry Form, add four separate command buttons on the right side of the Form Header to run the four macros in Preview Group. Use appropriate captions, as shown in Figure N-18.

j. Close the Patients-N.accdb database, then exit Access.

FIGURE N-18

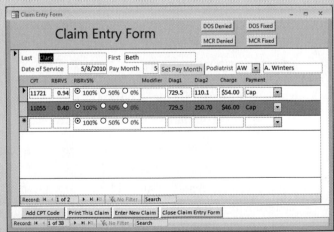

▼ INDEPENDENT CHALLENGE 3

As the manager of a doctor's clinic, you have created an Access database called Patients-N.accdb to track insurance claim reimbursements. You use macros to help automate the database.

a. Start Access, then open the **Patients-N.accdb** database from the drive and folder where you store your Data Files.

b. Start a new macro in the Macro Builder, then open the Condition column. If the Single Step button is toggled on, click it to toggle it off.

▼ INDEPENDENT CHALLENGE 3 (CONTINUED)

c. Enter the following in the Condition cell of the first row: [Forms]![CPT Form]![RBRVS]=0.

d. Select the SetProperty action for the first row.

e. Enter the following arguments for the SetProperty action: Control Name: **ResearchLabel**, Property: **Visible**, and Value: **-1**

f. Enter the following in the Condition cell of the second row: [Forms]![CPT Form]![RBRVS]<>0.

g. Select the SetProperty action for the second row.

h. Enter the following arguments for the SetProperty action: Control Name: **ResearchLabel**, Property: **Visible**, and Value: **0**

i. Save the macro with the name **Value Research**, close the Macro Builder, then click the Value Research macro object to select it.

j. Open the CPT Form in Form Design View, and open the Property Sheet for the form.

k. Assign the Value Research macro to the On Current event of the form.

l. Close the Property Sheet, save the form, then open the CPT Form in Form View.

m. Use the Next Record button to move quickly through all 64 records in the form. Notice that the macro displays Research! only when the RBRVS value is equal to zero.

Advanced Challenge Exercise

- Open the Claim Entry Form in Form Design View.
- Select the Add CPT Code command button in the Form Footer section, then open the Property Sheet.
- Click the Event tab to observe the 12 events that are associated with the command button.
- Using the information provided by the status bar when you click a property or Microsoft Office Access Help, write a short description for 6 of the 12 events used by the command button. Which of these events do you think is used most often? Why?

n. Save and close the CPT Form, then close the Patients-N.accdb database.

▼ REAL LIFE INDEPENDENT CHALLENGE

Suppose your culinary club is collecting information on international chocolate factories, museums, and stores, and asks you to help build a database to organize the information. You can collect some information on the World Wide Web to enter into the database, then tie the forms together with macros attached to command buttons.

a. Open the **Chocolate-N.accdb** database from the drive and folder where you store your Data Files, enable content if prompted, then open the Countries form in Form View.

b. Click the New (blank) Record button for the main form, then type **Canada** in the Country text box.

c. In the subform for the Canada record, enter **Godiva Boutique** in the Name field, **S** in the Type field (S for store), **5500 Main** in the Street field, **Toronto** in the City field, and **Ontario** in the StateProvince field.

d. Open the Macro Builder for a new macro, then add the Maximize action to the first row. Save the macro with the name **Maximize**, then close it.

e. Add the Maximize macro to the On Load event of the Countries form, then open the Countries form in Form View to test it.

f. Save and close the Countries form.

g. Add the Maximize macro to the On Load event of the Places of Interest report, then open the Places of Interest report in Print Preview to test it.

h. Save and close the Places of Interest report.

i. Close the Chocolate-N.accdb database, then exit Access.

As the manager of a doctor's clinic, you have created an Access database called **Patients-N.accdb** to track insurance claim reimbursements. Develop a new macro called **QueryGroup** with the actions and argument values shown in Figure N-19 and Table N-3. Run both macros to test them, and debug them if necessary. Print the macro by clicking File on the menu bar. Click Print, and then click OK in the Print Macro Definition dialog box.

TABLE N-3

macro name	action	argument	argument value
Denied	OpenQuery	Query Name	Monthly Query - Denied
		View	Datasheet
		Data Mode	Edit
	Maximize		
	MsgBox	Message	These claims were denied
		Beep	Yes
		Type	Information
		Title	Denied
Fixed	OpenQuery	Query Name	Monthly Query - Fixed
		View	Datasheet
		Data Mode	Edit
	Maximize		
	MsgBox	Message	These claims were fixed
		Beep	Yes
		Type	Information
		Title	Fixed

FIGURE N-19

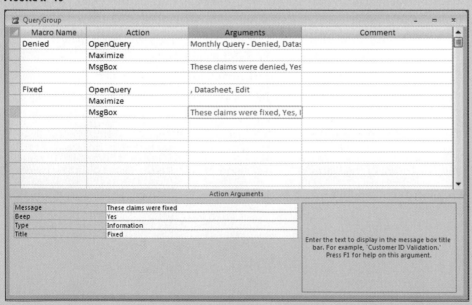

Creating Modules and VBA

Access is a robust and easy-to-use relational database program. Access provides user-friendly tools, such as wizards and Design Views, to help users quickly create reports and forms that previously took programmers hours to build. You may, however, want to automate a task or create a new function that goes beyond the capabilities of the built-in Access tools. Within each program of the Microsoft Office suite, a programming language called **Visual Basic for Applications (VBA)** is provided to help you extend the program's capabilities. In Access, VBA is stored within modules. ▓▓▓▓ You want to learn about VBA and create modules to enhance the capabilities of the Technology-O database.

OBJECTIVES

Understand modules and VBA

Compare macros and modules

Create functions

Use If statements

Document procedures

Examine class modules

Create sub procedures

Troubleshoot modules

Understanding Modules and VBA

A **module** is an Access object that stores Visual Basic for Applications (VBA) programming code. VBA is written in the **Visual Basic Editor Code window (Code window)**, shown in Figure O-1. The components and text colors of the Code window are described in Table O-1. An Access database has two kinds of modules. **Class modules** contain VBA code used only within a form or report and store the code within the form or report object itself. **Standard modules** contain global code that can be executed from anywhere in the database. Standard modules are displayed as module objects in the Navigation Pane. ▰▰▰▰ Before working with modules, you ask some questions about VBA.

The following questions and answers introduce the basics of Access modules:

- **What does a module contain?**

  A module contains VBA programming code organized in procedures. A procedure contains several lines of code, each of which is called a **statement**. Modules can also contain **comments**, text that helps explain and document the code.

- **What is a procedure?**

  A **procedure** is a series of VBA statements that performs an operation or calculates an answer. VBA has two types of procedures: functions and subs. **Declaration statements** precede procedure statements and help set rules for how the statements in the module are processed.

- **What is a function?**

  A **function** is a procedure that returns a value. Access supplies many built-in statistical, financial, and date functions—such as Sum, Pmt, and Now—that can be used in an expression in a query, form, or report to calculate a value. You might want to create a new function, however, to help perform calculations unique to your database. For example, you might create a new function called StockOptions to calculate the date an employee is eligible for stock options within your company.

- **What is a sub?**

  A **sub** (also called **sub procedure**) performs a series of VBA statements, but it does not return a value and cannot be used in an expression like a function procedure. You use subs to manipulate controls and objects. They are generally executed when an event occurs, such as when a command button is clicked or a form is opened.

- **What are arguments?**

  Arguments are constants, variables, or expressions passed to a procedure that the procedure needs in order to execute. For example, the full syntax for the Sum function is Sum (*expr*), where *expr* represents the argument for the Sum function, the field that is being summed. In VBA, arguments are declared in the first line of the procedure. They are specified immediately after a procedure's name and are enclosed in parentheses. Multiple arguments are separated by commas. For example, in the first VBA statement used to create the StockOptions function, Function StockOptions (*Salary, StartDate*), the two arguments Salary and StartDate are declared.

- **What is an object?**

  In VBA, an **object** is any item that can be identified or manipulated, including the traditional Access objects (table, query, form, report, macro, module) as well as other items that have properties such as controls, sections, and existing procedures.

- **What is a method?**

  A **method** is an action that an object can perform. Procedures are often written to invoke methods in response to user actions. For example, you could invoke the GoToControl method to move the focus to a specific control on a form.

FIGURE O-1: Visual Basic Editor Code window for a standard module

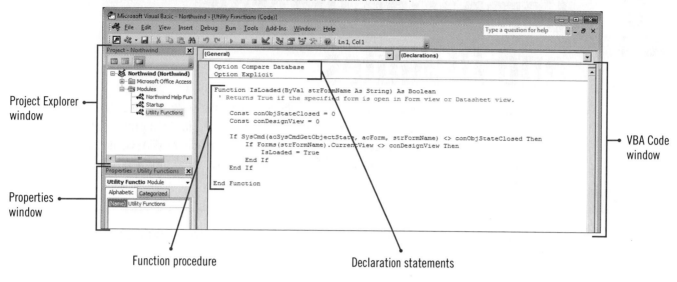

Project Explorer window

Properties window

Function procedure

Declaration statements

VBA Code window

TABLE O-1: Components and text colors for the Visual Basic window

component or color	description
Visual Basic Window	Comprises the entire Microsoft Visual Basic program window that contains smaller windows, including the Code window and Project Explorer window
Code window	Contains the VBA for the project selected in the Project Explorer window
Project Explorer window	Displays a hierarchical list of the projects in the database; a project can be a module itself or an object that contains class modules, such as a form or report
Procedure View button	Shows the statements that belong only to the current procedure
Full Module View button	Shows all the lines of VBA (all of the procedures) in the current module
Declaration statements	Includes statements that apply to every procedure in the module, such as declarations for variables, constants, user-defined data types, and external procedures in a dynamic link library
Object list	In a class module, lists the objects associated with the current form or report
Procedure list	In a standard module, lists the procedures in the module; in a class module, lists events (such as Click or Dblclick)
Blue	Indicates keyword text; blue words are reserved by VBA and are already assigned specific meanings
Black	Indicates normal text; black words are the unique VBA code developed by the user
Red	Indicates syntax error text; a line of code in red indicates that it will not execute correctly because of a syntax error (perhaps a missing parenthesis or a spelling error)
Green	Indicates comment text; any text after an apostrophe is considered documentation and is therefore ignored in the execution of the procedure

Comparing Macros and Modules

Macros and modules help run your database more efficiently and effectively. Creating a macro or a module requires some understanding of programming concepts, an ability to follow a process through its steps, and patience. Some tasks can be accomplished by using an Access macro or VBA. Guidelines can help you determine which tool is best for the task. ▰▰▰ You learn how Access macros and modules compare by asking more questions.

DETAILS

The following questions and answers provide guidelines for using macros and modules:

- **For what types of tasks are macros best suited?**

  Macros are an easy way to handle repetitive, simple tasks such as opening and closing forms, showing and hiding toolbars, and printing reports. Any process that can be automated through a macro action is probably easier to create using macro actions than by writing equivalent VBA statements.

- **Which is easier to create, a macro or a module, and why?**

  Macros are generally easier to create because you don't have to know any programming syntax. The hardest part of creating a macro is choosing the correct action. (Access presents a limited list of about 50 actions from which you can choose.) Once the action is chosen, the arguments associated with that action are displayed in the Action Arguments pane, eliminating the need to learn any special programming syntax. To create a module, however, you must know a robust programming language, VBA, as well as the correct **syntax** (rules) for each VBA statement. In a nutshell, macros are simpler to create, but VBA is far more powerful.

- **When must I use a macro?**

  You must use macros to make global, shortcut key assignments. You can also use an automatic macro that executes when the database first opens.

- **When must I use a module?**

  You must use modules to create unique functions. Macros cannot create functions. For instance, you might want to create a function called Commission that calculates the appropriate commission on a sale using your company's unique commission formula.

  Access error messages can be confusing to the user. But using VBA procedures, you can detect the error when it occurs and display your own message. Macros cannot be used to detect errors.

  You can't use a macro to accomplish many tasks outside Access, but VBA code stored in modules works with other products in the Microsoft Office suite.

  VBA code can contain nested If statements, Case statements, and other programming logic, which makes them much more powerful and flexible than macros. Some of the most common VBA keywords, including If...Then, are shown in Table O-2. VBA keywords appear blue in the Code window. The only logic available to a macro is executing a macro action based on whether an expression entered in the Condition column evaluates true or false.

  VBA code may declare **variables**, which are used to store data that can be used, modified, or displayed during the execution of the procedure. Macros cannot declare variables.

  Class modules, like the one shown in Figure O-2, are stored as part of the form or report object in which they are created. If you develop forms and reports in one database and copy them to another, class module VBA automatically travels with the object that stores it.

Creating Modules and VBA

FIGURE O-2: Code window for a class module

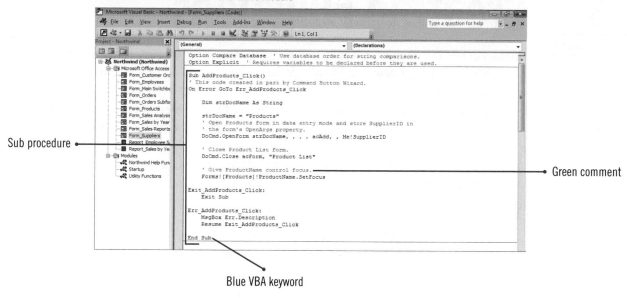

Sub procedure

Green comment

Blue VBA keyword

TABLE O-2: Common VBA keywords

statement	explanation
Function	Declares the name and arguments that create a new function procedure
End Function	When defining a new function, the End Function statement is required as the last statement to mark the end of the VBA code that defines the function
Sub	Declares the name for a new sub procedure; **Private Sub** indicates that the sub is accessible only to other procedures in the module where it is declared
End Sub	When defining a new sub, the End Sub statement is required as the last statement to mark the end of the VBA code that defines the sub
If...Then	Executes code (the code follows the Then statement) when the value of an expression is true (the expression follows the If statement)
End If	When creating an If...Then statement, the End If statement is required as the last statement
Const	Declares the name and value of a **constant**, an item that retains a constant value throughout the execution of the code
Option Compare Database	A declaration statement that determines the way string values (text) will be sorted
Option Explicit	A declaration statement that specifies that you must explicitly declare all variables used in all procedures; if you attempt to use an undeclared variable name, an error occurs at **compile time**, the period during which source code is translated to executable code
Dim	Declares a **variable**, a named storage location that contains data that can be modified during program execution
On Error GoTo	Upon an error in the execution of a procedure, the On Error GoTo statement specifies the location (the statement) where the procedure should continue
Select Case	Executes one of several groups of statements called a **Case** depending on the value of an expression; use the Select Case statement as an alternative to using **ElseIf** in **If...Then...Else** statements when comparing one expression to several different values
End Select	When defining a new Select Case group of statements, the End Select statement is required as the last statement to mark the end of the VBA code

Creating Functions

Access supplies hundreds of functions such as Sum, Count, Ilf, First, Last, Date, and Hour. However, you might need to create a new function to calculate a value based on unique business rules used by your company. You would store the VBA used to create the new function in a standard module so that it can be used in any query, form, or report in the database. ▰▰▰▰▰ Quest Specialty Travel started a program that allows employees to purchase computer equipment when it is replaced. Equipment that is less than a year old will be sold to employees at 75 percent of its initial value, and equipment that is more than a year old will be sold at 50 percent of its initial value. Wilbur Young, network administrator, asks you to use VBA to create a new function called EmployeePrice that determines the employee purchase price of replaced computer equipment.

STEPS

QUICK TIP

The Option Explicit statement appears if the Require Variable Declaration option is checked. To view the default settings, click Options on the VBA Tools menu.

1. **Start Access, open the Technology-O.accdb database from the drive and folder where you store your Data Files, enable content if prompted, click the Create tab, click the Macro button arrow, click Module, then maximize the Code window**

   Access automatically inserts the Option Compare Database declaration statement in the Code window. This statement is used to determine the way string values (text) will be sorted. Your new function won't sort text, but leaving the statement in the Code window doesn't create any problems.

2. **Type Function EmployeePrice(StartingValue), then press [Enter]**

   This statement creates a new function, EmployeePrice, and states that it contains one argument, StartingValue. VBA automatically adds the **End Function** statement, a required statement to mark the end of the code that defines the new function. Because both Function and End Function are VBA keywords, they are blue. The insertion point is positioned between the statements so that you can further define how the new EmployeePrice function will calculate using more VBA statements.

3. **Press [Tab], type EmployeePrice = StartingValue * 0.5, then press [Enter]**

   Your screen should look like Figure O-3. The second statement explains how the EmployeePrice function will calculate. The function will return a value that is calculated by multiplying the StartingValue by 0.5. It is not necessary to indent statements, but indenting code between matching Function/End Function, Sub/End Sub, or If/End If statements enhances the program's readability. Also, it is not necessary to enter spaces around the equal sign and an asterisk used as a multiplication sign, but when you press [Enter], Access adds spaces as appropriate to enhance the readability of the statement.

4. **Click the Save button 🖫 on the Standard toolbar, type Functions in the Save As dialog box, then click OK**

   You can use the new function, EmployeePrice, in a query, form, or report.

5. **Close the Visual Basic window, right-click the EmployeePricing query in the Navigation Pane, then click Design View on the shortcut menu**

   Now you can use the EmployeePrice function in the query to determine the employee purchase price of replaced computer equipment.

QUICK TIP

Field names used in expressions are not case sensitive, but they must exactly match the spelling of the field name as defined in Table Design View.

6. **Click the blank Field cell to the right of the InitialValue field, type Price:EmployeePrice([InitialValue]), click the Datasheet View button, then maximize the datasheet**

   Your screen should look like Figure O-4. In this query, you created a new field called Price that uses the EmployeePrice function. The value in the InitialValue field is used for the StartingValue argument of the new EmployeePrice function. The InitialValue field is multiplied by 0.5 to create the new Price field.

7. **Save the EmployeePricing query, then close the datasheet**

FIGURE O-3: Creating the EmployeePrice function

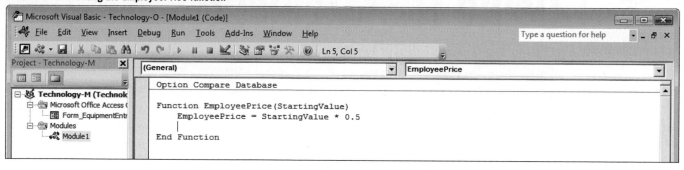

```
Option Compare Database

Function EmployeePrice(StartingValue)
    EmployeePrice = StartingValue * 0.5

End Function
```

FIGURE O-4: Using the EmployeePrice function in a query

Last	Manufacture	Description	PlacementDat	InitialValue	Price
Joy	Micron	Transtrek4000	7/8/2010	$2,000.00	1000
Joy	Micron	Transtrek4000	7/8/2011	$2,000.00	1000
Dawson	Micron	Prosignet403	7/15/2010	$1,800.00	900
Rock	Micron	Prosignet403	7/31/2010	$1,800.00	900
McDermott	Micron	Prosignet403	7/31/2010	$1,800.00	900
Mark	Micron	Prosignet403	7/31/2010	$1,800.00	900
Rice	Micron	Prosignet403	1/9/2010	$1,700.00	850
Hosta	Micron	Prosignet403	8/14/2010	$1,700.00	850
McDonald	Micron	Prosignet403	8/14/2011	$1,700.00	850
Long	Micron	Prosignet403	8/14/2010	$1,700.00	850
Orient	Compaq	Centuria9099	6/14/2011	$1,500.00	750
Greenfield	Compaq	Centuria9099	6/14/2011	$1,500.00	750
Lane	Micron	Transtrek4000	8/31/2010	$1,900.00	950
Adair	Micron	Transtrek4000	12/31/2009	$1,900.00	950
Hoppengarth	Micron	Transtrek4000	8/31/2010	$1,800.00	900
Latsky	Micron	Transtrek4000	8/31/2011	$1,800.00	900
Pratt	Micron	Transtrek4000	8/31/2010	$1,750.00	875

Price field uses the EmployeePrice function to create the calculation

Using If Statements

If...**Then**...**Else** logic allows you to test logical conditions and execute statements only if the conditions are true. If...Then...Else code can be composed of one or several statements, depending on how many conditions you want to test, how many possible answers you want to provide, and what you want the code to do based on the results of the tests. 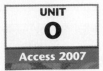 You need to add an If statement to the EmployeePrice function to test the age of the equipment, and then calculate the answer based on that age. Right now, the calculation multiplies the StartingValue argument by 50 percent. You want to modify it so that if the equipment is less than one year old, the function multiplies the StartingValue argument by 75 percent.

STEPS

1. **Scroll down and right-click the** Functions module **in the Navigation Pane, then click** Design View

   To determine the age of the equipment, the EmployeePrice function needs another argument, the purchase date of the equipment.

2. **Click just before the** right parenthesis **in the Function statement, type** , **(a comma), press** [Spacebar], **then type** PurchaseDate

   Now that you established another argument, you can use the argument in the function.

QUICK TIP
Indentation doesn't affect the way the function works, but does make the code easier to read.

3. **Click to the right of the** right parenthesis **in the Function statement, press** [Enter], **press** [Tab], **then type** If (Now()–PurchaseDate) >365 Then

   The expression compares whether today's date, represented by the Access function **Now()**, minus the PurchaseDate argument value is greater than 365 days. If true, this indicates that the equipment is older than one year.

4. **Indent and type the rest of the statements exactly as shown in Figure O-5**

   The **Else** statement is executed only if the expression is false (if the equipment is less than 365 days old). The **End If** statement is needed to mark the end of the If block of code.

QUICK TIP
If a compile or syntax error appears, open the Visual Basic window, check your function against Figure O-5, then correct any errors.

5. **Click the** Save button 💾 **on the Standard toolbar, close the Visual Basic window, right-click the** EmployeePricing **query in the Navigation Pane, then click** Design View **on the shortcut menu**

   Now that you've modified the EmployeePrice function to include two arguments, you need to modify the Price field expression so it calculates correctly.

6. **Right-click the** Price field **in the query design grid, click** Zoom **on the shortcut menu, click between the** right square bracket **and** right parenthesis, **then type** ,[PlacementDate]

   Your Zoom dialog box should look like Figure O-6. Both of the arguments used to calculate the EmployeePrice function are field names, so they must be typed exactly as shown and surrounded by square brackets. Commas separate multiple arguments in the function.

7. **Click** OK **in the Zoom dialog box, then click the** Datasheet View button

QUICK TIP
The new calculated Price field is based on the current date on your computer, so your results may vary.

8. **Click any entry in the** PlacementDate field, **then click the** Ascending button ⬇️ **on the Home tab**

   The EmployeePrice function now calculates two ways, depending on the age of the equipment determined by the date in the PlacementDate field, as shown in Figure O-7.

9. **Save, then close the** EmployeePricing **query**

Creating Modules and VBA

FIGURE O-5: Using an If...Then...Else statement

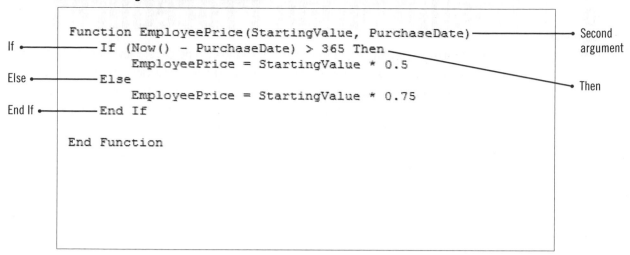

```
Function EmployeePrice(StartingValue, PurchaseDate)
    If (Now() - PurchaseDate) > 365 Then
        EmployeePrice = StartingValue * 0.5
    Else
        EmployeePrice = StartingValue * 0.75
    End If

End Function
```

If ●
Else ●
End If ●

Second argument
Then

FIGURE O-6: Zoom dialog box is used for long expressions

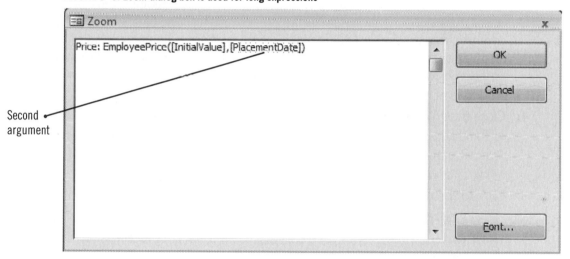

Second argument ●

Price: EmployeePrice([InitialValue],[PlacementDate])

OK

Cancel

Font...

FIGURE O-7: Price field is calculated two ways based on If statements in the EmployeePrice function

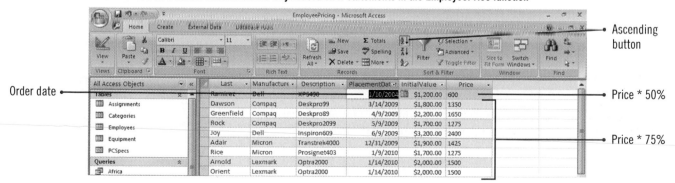

Order date ●

Ascending button

Price * 50%

Price * 75%

Last	Manufacture	Description	PlacementDat	InitialValue	Price
Ramirez	Dell	XPS490	1/10/2004	$1,200.00	600
Dawson	Compaq	Deskpro99	3/14/2009	$1,800.00	1350
Greenfield	Compaq	Deskpro89	4/9/2009	$2,200.00	1650
Rock	Compaq	Deskpro2099	5/9/2009	$1,700.00	1275
Joy	Dell	Inspiron609	6/9/2009	$3,200.00	2400
Adair	Micron	Transtrek4000	12/31/2009	$1,900.00	1425
Rice	Micron	Prosignet403	1/9/2010	$1,700.00	1275
Arnold	Lexmark	Optra2000	1/14/2010	$2,000.00	1500
Orient	Lexmark	Optra2000	1/14/2010	$2,000.00	1500

Documenting Procedures

Comment lines are statements in the code that document the code; they do not affect how the code runs. At any time, if you want to read or modify existing code, you can write the modifications much more quickly if the code is properly documented. Comment lines start with an apostrophe and are green in the Code window. 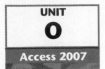 You decide to document the EmployeePrice function in the Functions module with descriptive comments. This will make it easier for you and others to follow the purpose and logic of the function later.

STEPS

1. **Right-click the Functions module in the Navigation pane, then click Design View**
   The Code window for the Functions module opens.

QUICK TIP

You can also create comments by starting the statement with Rem (for remark).

2. **Click the blank line between the Option Compare Database and Function statements, press [Enter], type 'This function is called EmployeePrice and has two arguments, then press [Enter]**
   As soon as you move to another statement, the comment statement becomes green in the Code window.

TROUBLE

Be sure to use an ' (apostrophe) and not a " (quotation mark) to begin the comment line.

3. **Type 'Created by Your Name on Today's Date, then press [Enter]**
   Your screen should look like Figure O-8. You can also place comments at the end of a line by entering an apostrophe to mark that the next part of the statement is a comment. Closing the Project Explorer window gives you more room for the Code window. (You use the **Project Explorer window** to switch between open projects, objects that can contain VBA code. The **utility project** contains VBA code that helps Access with certain activities such as presenting the Zoom dialog box. It automatically appears in the Project Explorer window when you use the Access features that utilize this code.)

4. **Close the Project Explorer and Properties windows, click to the right of Then at the end of the If statement, press [Spacebar], then type 'Now() returns today's date**
   This comment explains that the Now() function is today's date. All comments are green, regardless of whether they are on their own line or at the end of an existing line.

5. **Click to the right of 0.5, press [Spacebar], then type 'If > 1 year, value is 50%**

6. **Click to the right of 0.75, press [Spacebar], then type 'If < 1 year, value is 75%**
   Your screen should look like Figure O-9. Each comment will turn green as soon as you move to a new statement. Table O-3 provides more information about the Standard toolbar buttons in the Visual Basic window.

7. **Click the Save button 🔘 on the Standard toolbar, click File on the menu bar, click Print, then click OK**

8. **Click File on the menu bar, then click Close and Return to Microsoft Office Access**

FIGURE O-8: Adding comments to the Code window

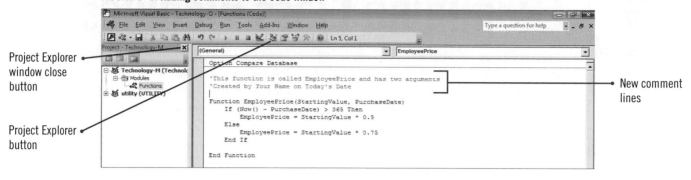

Project Explorer window close button

Project Explorer button

New comment lines

FIGURE O-9: Adding comments at the end of a statement

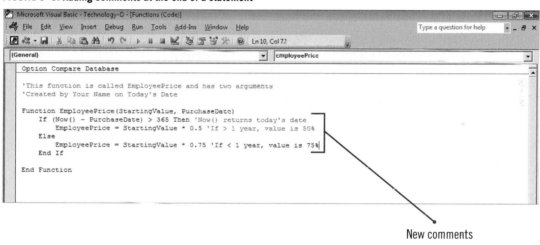

New comments

TABLE O-3: Standard toolbar buttons in the Visual Basic window

button name	button	description
View Microsoft Office Access		Switches from the active Visual Basic window to the Access window
Insert Module		Opens a new module or class module Code window, or inserts a new procedure in the current Code window
Run Sub/UserForm		Runs the current procedure if the insertion point is in a procedure, or runs the UserForm if it is active
Break		Stops the execution of a program while it's running, and switches to break mode, the temporary suspension of program execution in which you can examine, debug, reset, step through, or continue program execution
Reset		Resets the procedure
Project Explorer		Displays the Project Explorer, which displays a hierarchical list of the currently open projects (set of modules) and their contents
Object Browser		Displays the Object Browser, which lists the defined modules and procedures as well as available methods, properties, events, constants, and other items that you can use in the code

Examining Class Modules

Class modules are contained and executed within specific forms and reports. Class modules most commonly contain sub procedures and execute in response to an **event**, which is a specific action that occurs as the result of a user action. Clicking a command button, editing data, or closing a form are examples of common events. You examine an existing class module to understand and create sub procedures that are connected to events that occur on the form.

STEPS

1. Right-click the EquipmentEntry form in the Navigation Pane, click Design View on the shortcut menu, then maximize the form window

The form has three command buttons. Two of the command buttons are connected to sub procedures that are executed when the button is clicked (when the On Click event of the command button occurs). These procedures are stored in a class module within the form. You access these procedures through the Property Sheet.

2. Click the Delete This Record button, click the Property Sheet button on the Design tab, then click the Event tab

As shown in Figure O-10, the On Click property shows that it is connected to a sub procedure with the words **[Event Procedure]** (a procedure that is triggered by this event, also called an **event handler procedure**). Note the **Name property** of the control, which is displayed in the control list box and entered in the Name property text box (on the Other tab). To see the VBA code triggered by the On Click event, you need to open the Code window.

3. Click the Build button [...] for the On Click property

The Microsoft Visual Basic editor window opens, with your insertion point on the line immediately below the first line of the event procedure that is connected to the current control, the DeleteThisRecordButton. Note that the sub's name, DeleteThisRecordButton_Click contains both the name of the control as well as the control's event that triggers the procedure. You can add a new event procedure by typing it directly into the Visual Basic editor, or use the Property Sheet to help build the first and last lines of the procedure.

TROUBLE

Be sure to type a period (.) after DoCmd to see the list of available methods.

4. Close the Visual Basic window, click the Add New Record button, click [...] for the On Click property, click Code Builder in the Choose Builder dialog box, then click OK

The Visual Basic window opens and automatically adds the first and last lines, the **stub**, of a new event handler procedure.

QUICK TIP

Erase the DoCmd statement, and then redo steps 5 and 6, watching the screen closely to learn more about how IntelliSense helps you enter a VBA statement.

5. Type DoCmd. (including the period)

DoCmd is a VBA object that supports many methods to run common Access commands such as closing windows, opening forms, previewing reports, navigating records, and setting the value of controls. As you write a VBA statement, visual aids that are part of **IntelliSense technology** help you complete it. For example, when you press the period (.) after the DoCmd object, a list of available methods appears. Watching the VBA window carefully and taking advantage of all IntelliSense clues as you complete a statement can greatly improve your accuracy and productivity in writing VBA.

6. Select GoToRecord in the methods list, press [Spacebar], type ,,(two commas), select acNewRec in the IntelliSense list, then press [Enter]

Your screen should look like Figure O-11. IntelliSense helped you fill out the rest of the statement, indicating the order of arguments needed for the method to execute (the current argument is listed in bold), and whether the argument is required or optional (optional arguments are listed in [square brackets]). Optional arguments can be skipped by typing a comma (,). Optional arguments at the end of a statement can be ignored.

TROUBLE

If the VBA code window appears with a yellow line, it means the code cannot be run successfully. Click the Reset button, then compare your VBA to Figure O-11.

7. Close the Visual Basic window, save the EquipmentEntry form, click the Form View button on the Design tab, then click the Add New Record button to test it

The Current Record box in the record navigation buttons should read 49 of 49, indicating that you are ready to enter a new record.

Creating Modules and VBA

FIGURE O-10: Examining event procedures in class modules

Property Sheet

Control Name

Delete This
Record button

Build button

[Event
Procedure]

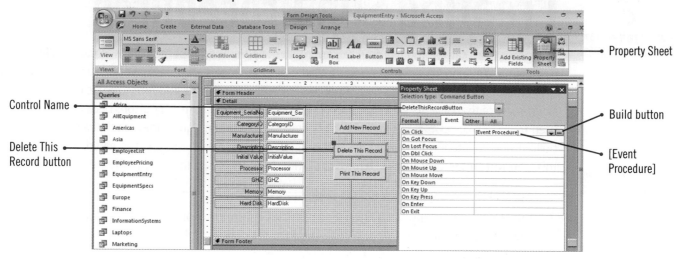

FIGURE O-11: Creating an event handler procedure in a class module

New Event
Handler
Procedure

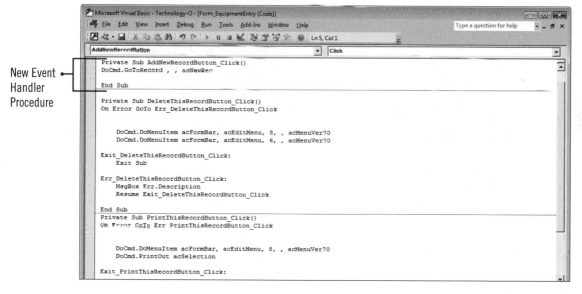

Access 2007

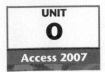

Creating Sub Procedures

Sub procedures can be triggered on any event identified in the Property Sheet such as **On Dbl Click** (on double-click) or After Update (after a field is updated). Not all items have the same set of event properties. For example, a text box control has both a Before Update and After Update event property, but neither of these events exists for unbound controls such as command buttons because they are not used to update data. ▟▟▟▟▟ Quest Specialty Travel programming guidelines ask that all forms include built-in documentation to identify the author and the date that the form was created. To accomplish this, you write a sub procedure in a form class module triggered by the On Dbl Click event of the form.

STEPS

1. **Right-click the** Equipment Entry Form, **click** Design View **on the shortcut menu, click the Form Selector button** ▣ **then click the** Property Sheet **button if the Property Sheet is not open**

    Forms have a large number of event properties that are not available for controls on the form such as On Current (triggers when focus moves from one record to another), On Load (triggers when the form is loaded), and On Close (triggers when the form is closed).

2. **Click the** Event tab, **click the** On Dbl Click text box, **click the Build button** ▣, **click** Code Builder, **then click OK**

    The class module opens the stub of the new procedure. The name of the new procedure is Form_DblClick. The name of the new sub references both the object and the event that will trigger the procedure. This event handler will display an Access message box with the documentation requested by Quest. As you type the statement, be sure to watch the screen carefully for IntelliSense programming support.

3. **Type** MsgBox ("Created by Your Name on Today's Date") **as the single statement for the Form_DblClick sub, then save the procedure**

    Your screen should look like Figure O-12. Use the Object list to add a new procedure based on any object in the form. Use the Procedure list to change the event that triggers the procedure.

4. **Close the Visual Basic window, close the Property Sheet, click the** Form View **button on the Design tab, then double-click the** record selector **to the left of the record**

    The MsgBox statement in the Form_DblClick sub creates the dialog box, as shown in Figure O-13.

5. **Click OK in the message box, then save and close the** EquipmentEntry **form**

    VBA is as robust and powerful as Access itself. It takes years of experience to appreciate the vast number of objects, events, methods, and properties that are available. With only modest programming skills, however, you can create basic sub procedures.

FIGURE O-12: Creating the Form_DblClick procedure

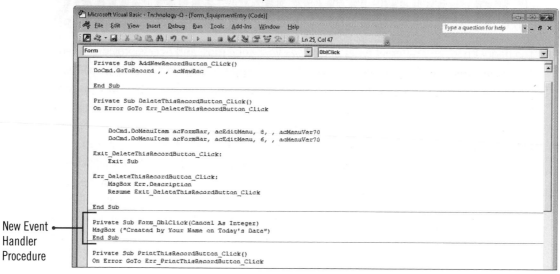

New Event
Handler
Procedure

FIGURE O-13 Message box created with MsgBox statement

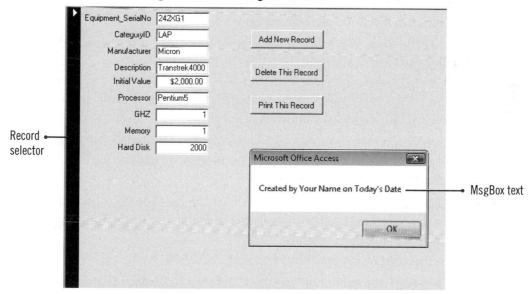

Record
selector

MsgBox text

Troubleshooting Modules

You might encounter different types of errors as your code runs, and Access provides several techniques to help you **debug** (find and resolve) them. A **syntax error** occurs immediately as you are writing a VBA statement that cannot be read by the Visual Basic Editor. This is the easiest type of error to identify because your code turns red as the syntax error occurs. **Compile-time errors** occur as a result of incorrectly constructed code and are detected as soon as you run your code or select the Compile option on the Debug menu. For example, you may have forgotten to write an End If statement following an If clause. **Run-time errors** occur as incorrectly constructed code runs and include attempting an illegal operation such as dividing by zero or moving focus to a control that doesn't exist. When you encounter a run-time error, VBA will stop executing your procedure at the statement in which the error occurred and highlight the line with a yellow background in the Visual Basic Editor. **Logic errors** are the most difficult to troubleshoot because they occur when the code runs without obvious problems, but the procedure still doesn't produce the desired result. ▄▄▄▄▄▄ You study debugging techniques using the Functions module.

STEPS

1. **Right-click the Functions module in the Navigation Pane, click Design View, click to the right of the End If statement, press the [Spacebar], type your name, then press [↓]**

   Because the End If your name statement cannot be resolved by the Visual Basic Editor, it immediately turns red.

2. **Click OK in the Compile error message box, delete your name, then click anywhere in another statement**

   Another VBA debugging tool is to set a **breakpoint**, a bookmark that suspends execution of the procedure at that statement to allow you to examine what is happening.

3. **Click anywhere in the If statement, click Debug on the menu bar, then click Toggle Breakpoint**

   Your screen should look like Figure O-14.

4. **Click the View Microsoft Office Access button 🖼 on the Standard toolbar, then double-click the EmployeePricing query in the Navigation Pane**

   When the EmployeePricing query opens, it immediately runs the EmployeePrice function. Because you set a breakpoint at the If statement, the statement is highlighted, as shown in Figure O-15, indicating that the code has been suspended at that point.

5. **Click View on the menu bar, click Immediate Window, type ? PurchaseDate, then press [Enter]**

   Your screen should look like Figure O-16. The **Immediate window** is an area where you can determine the value of any argument at the breakpoint.

6. **Click Debug on the menu bar, click Clear All Breakpoints, click the Continue button ▷ on the Standard toolbar to execute the remainder of the function, then save, print, and close the Functions module**

   The EmployeePricing query's datasheet should be visible.

7. **Close the EmployeePricing datasheet, close the Technology-O.accdb database, then exit Access**

FIGURE O-14: Setting a breakpoint

View Microsoft Office Access button

Breakpoint

Debug menu

Reset button

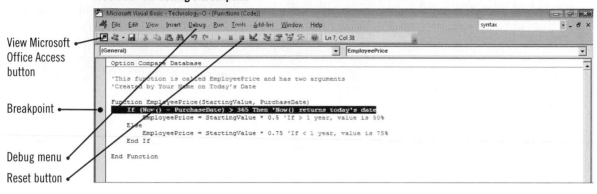

FIGURE O-15: Stopping execution at a breakpoint

Execution stopped at breakpoint

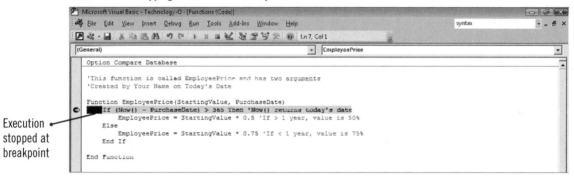

FIGURE O-16: Using the Immediate window

Continue button

Immediate window

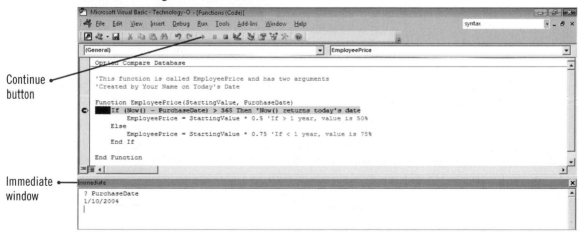

Practice

If you have a SAM user profile, you may have access to hands-on instruction, practice, and assessment of the skills covered in this unit. Log in to your SAM account (http://sam2007.course.com/) to launch any assigned training activities or exams that relate to the skills covered in this unit.

▼ CONCEPTS REVIEW

Identify each element of the Visual Basic window shown in Figure O-17.

FIGURE O-17

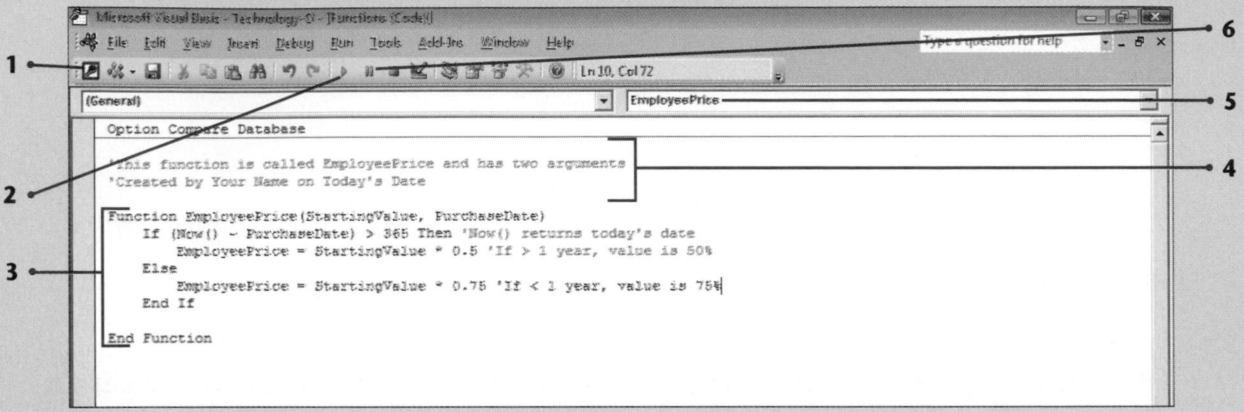

Match each term with the statement that best describes its function.

7. **Visual Basic for Applications (VBA)**

8. **Debugging**

9. **If...Then...Else statement**

10. **Breakpoint**

11. **Function**

12. **Module**

13. **Procedure**

14. **Arguments**

15. **Class modules**

a. Allows you to test a logical condition and execute commands only if the condition is true

b. The programming language used in Access modules

c. A line of code that automatically suspends execution of the procedure

d. A procedure that returns a value

e. Constants, variables, or expressions passed to a procedure to further define how it should execute

f. Stored as part of the form or report object in which they are created

g. The Access object where VBA code is stored

h. A series of VBA statements that perform an operation or calculate a value

i. A process to find and resolve programming errors

Select the best answer from the list of choices.

16. **A module contains VBA programming code organized in units called:**
    a. Breakpoints.
    b. Arguments.
    c. Procedures.
    d. Macros.

17. **Which type of procedure returns a value?**
    a. Function
    b. Sub procedure
    c. Sub
    d. Class module

18. **Which of the following is *not* a reason to use modules rather than macros?**
    a. Modules are used to create unique functions.
    b. Modules contain code that can work with other Microsoft Office programs.
    c. Modules are usually easier to write than macros.
    d. Modules can contain procedures that mask error messages.

19. **Which of the following is *not* a type of VBA error?**
    a. Class action
    b. Run time
    c. Logic
    d. Compile time

20. **Which of the following is a specific action that occurs on or to an object, and is usually the result of a user action?**
    a. Argument
    b. Event
    c. Function
    d. Sub

▼ SKILLS REVIEW

1. **Understand modules.**
   a. Start Access, then open the **Basketball-O.accdb** database from the drive and folder where you store your Data Files.
   b. Open the Code window for the ShotStatistics module.
   c. Record your answers to the following questions on a sheet of paper.
      - What is the name of the function defined in this module?
      - What are the names of the arguments defined in this module?
      - What is the purpose of the If statement?
      - What is the purpose of the End Function statement?
      - Why is the End Function statement in blue?
      - Why are some of the lines indented?

2. **Compare macros and modules.**
   a. If not already opened, open the Code window for the ShotStatistics module.
   b. Record your answers to the following questions on a sheet of paper.
      - Why was a module rather than a macro used to create this function?
      - Why is code written in the ShotStatistics Code window generally more difficult to create than a macro?
      - Identify each of the keywords or keyword phrases, and explain the purpose for each.

3. Create functions.

  a. If not already opened, open the Code window for the ShotStatistics module.

  b. Create a function called Contribution below the End Function statement of the TotalShotPercentage function by typing the VBA statements shown in Figure O-18.

FIGURE O-18

```
Function Contribution(fg, threept, ft, offreb, defreb, assists)
    Contribution = (fg * 2 + threept * 3 + ft + offreb * 2 + defreb + assists * 2)

End Function
```

  c. Save the ShotStatistics module, then close the Visual Basic window.

  d. Use Query Design View to create a new query using the First and Last fields from the Players table and all of the fields from the Stats table.

  e. Create a calculated field named **Rank** in the first available column by carefully typing the Contribution function as follows: **Rank: Int(Contribution([FG], [3P], [FT], [Reb-O], [Reb-D], [Assists]))** (*Note*: The Int function converts the result to an integer rather than text for later sorting purposes.)

  f. Sort the query in ascending order on the GameNo field.

  g. View the datasheet, change PlayerNo 51 to your first and last name, then print the first page of the datasheet in landscape orientation.

  h. Save the query with the name **Rankings**, then close the Rankings datasheet.

4. Use If statements.

  a. Open the Code window for the ShotStatistics module, click to the right of the Function Contribution statement, press [Enter], then modify the function with the statements shown in Figure O-19. The new function tests to see whether the player contributed any points (field goals plus three pointers plus free throws), and if not, divides their total contribution by 2. It also tests to see whether the player had any rebounds (rebounds on offense plus rebounds on defense), and if not, divides their total contribution by 3. (*Hint*: You can use copy and paste to copy repeating statements, then edit for the differences.)

FIGURE O-19

```
Function Contribution(fg, threept, ft, offreb, defreb, assists)
    If fg + threept + ft = 0 Then
        Contribution = (fg * 2 + threept * 3 + ft + offreb * 2 + defreb + assists * 2) / 2
    ElseIf offreb + defreb = 0 Then
        Contribution = (fg * 2 + threept * 3 + ft + offreb * 2 + defreb + assists * 2) / 3
    Else
        Contribution = (fg * 2 + threept * 3 + ft + offreb * 2 + defreb + assists * 2)
    End If
End Function
```

  b. Save the ShotStatistics module, then close the Visual Basic window.

  c. Open the Rankings datasheet, then print the first page in landscape orientation. You should see the Rank calculated value go down for those players who did not score any points or who did not have any rebounds.

  d. Close the datasheet.

5. Document procedures.

  a. Open the Code window for the ShotStatistics module, and edit the Contribution function to include the five comment statements shown in Figure O-20.

  b. Save the changes to the ShotStatistics module, print the module, then close the Visual Basic window.

FIGURE O-20

```
Function Contribution(fg, threept, ft, offreb, defreb, assists)
'If no field goals, 3 pointers, or free throws were made
    If fg + threept + ft = 0 Then
'Then the Contribution statistic should be divided by 2
        Contribution = (fg * 2 + threept * 3 + ft + offreb * 2 + defreb + assists * 2) / 2
'If no offensive or defensive rebounds were grabbed
    ElseIf offreb + defreb = 0 Then
'Then the Contribution statistic should be divided by 3
        Contribution = (fg * 2 + threept * 3 + ft + offreb * 2 + defreb + assists * 2) / 3
    Else
        Contribution = (fg * 2 + threept * 3 + ft + offreb * 2 + defreb + assists * 2)
    End If
End Function
'This function was created by Your Name on Today's Date
```

6. Examine class modules.

  a. Open the PlayerEntryForm in Form Design View.

  b. On the right side of the form, select the Print Current Record button.

  c. Open the Property Sheet for the button, click the Event tab, click the On Click property, then click the Build button to open the class module.

  d. Edit the comment on the last line to show your name and the current date. Save and print the module, then close the Visual Basic window.

7. Create sub procedures.

a. Open the PlayerEntryForm in Form Design View, if it's not already opened.

b. Click the form selector button, open the Property Sheet for the form if it is not already open, click the Event tab, click the On Mouse Move property text box, then click the Build button.

c. Enter the following statement between the Private Sub and End Sub statements:

[First].ForeColor = 255

d. Enter the following comment below the statement you just created:

'When the mouse moves, the First text box will become red.

e. Save, then close the Visual Basic window.

f. Close the Property Sheet, save, then open the PlayerEntryForm in Form View.

g. Move the mouse over the record selector (the left edge) of the form. The color of the First text box should turn red.

h. Save, then close the PlayerEntryForm.

8. Troubleshoot modules.

a. Open the Code window for the ShotStatistics module.

b. Click anywhere in the If fg + threept + ft = 0 statement.

c. Click Debug on the menu bar, then click the Toggle Breakpoint option to set a breakpoint at this statement.

d. Save and close the Visual Basic window, then return to Microsoft Access.

e. Open the Rankings query datasheet. Navigate through the second record. This action will use the Contribution function, which will stop and highlight the statement where you set a breakpoint.

f. Click View on the menu bar, click Immediate Window (if not already visible), type ?fg, then press [Enter]. On a sheet of paper, write the current value of the fg variable.

g. Type ?offreb, then press [Enter]. On a sheet of paper, write the current value of the offreb variable.

h. Click Debug on the menu bar, click Clear All Breakpoints, then click the Continue button on the Standard toolbar.

i. Return to the Rankings query in Datasheet View. Using both Query Design View and Query Datasheet View, answer the following questions:

- When calculating the Rank field, what field is used for the fg argument?
- When calculating the Rank field, what field is used for the offreb argument?
- What is the value of the fg argument for the first record?
- What is the value of the offreb argument for the first record?

j. Close the Rankings query, close the Basketball-O.accdb database, then exit Access.

▼ INDEPENDENT CHALLENGE 1

As the manager of a doctor's clinic, you have created an Access database called Patients-O.accdb to track insurance claim reimbursements and general patient health. You want to modify an existing function within this database.

a. Start Access, then open the Patients-O.accdb database from the drive and folder where you store your Data Files.

b. Open the BodyMassIndex module in Design View, then record your answers to the following questions on a sheet of paper:

- What is the name of the function in the module?
- What are the function arguments?
- How many comments are in the function?

c. Edit the BMI function by adding a comment at the end of the code with your name and today's date.

d. Edit the BMI function by adding a comment above the Function statement with the following information:

'A healthy BMI is in the range of 21-24.

e. Edit the BMI function by adding an If clause that checks to make sure the height argument is not equal to 0. The final BMI function code should look like Figure O-21.

f. Save and print the module, then close the Visual Basic window.

FIGURE O-21

```
'A healthy BMI is in the range of 21-24.
Function BMI(weight, height)
    If height = 0 Then
        BMI = 0
    Else
        BMI = (weight * 0.4536) / (height * 0.0254) ^ 2
    End If
End Function
'Your Name and today's date
```

g. Create a new query that includes the following fields from the Patients table: PtLastName, PtFirstName, Weight, Height.

h. Create a calculated field with the following field name and expression: **BMINumber: bmi([weight], [height])**

i. Save the query as **BMI**, view the BMI query datasheet, then test the If statement by entering **0** in the Height field for the first record. Press [◄] to move to the Weight field, and the BMICalculation field should recalculate to 0.

j. Edit the first record to contain your first and last name, print the record, save the query with the name **BMI**, then close the BMI datasheet.

k. Close the Patients-O.accdb database, then exit Access.

▼ INDEPENDENT CHALLENGE 2

As the manager of a doctor's clinic, you have created an Access database called Patients-O.accdb to track insurance claim reimbursements. You want to study the existing sub procedures stored as class modules in the Claim Entry Form.

a. Start Access, then open the **Patients-O.accdb** database from the drive and folder where you store your Data Files.

b. Open the Claim Entry Form in Form Design View.

c. Open the Visual Basic Editor window to view this class module, then record your answers to the following questions on a sheet of paper:

- What are the names of the sub procedures in this class module? (*Hint*: Be sure to scroll the window to see the complete contents.)
- What Access functions are used in the PtFirstName_AfterUpdate sub?
- How many arguments do the functions in the PtFirstName_AfterUpdate sub have?
- What do the functions in the PtFirstName_AfterUpdate sub do? (*Hint*: You may have to use the Visual Basic Help system if you are not familiar with the functions.)
- What is the purpose of the On Error command? (*Hint*: Use the Visual Basic Help system if you are not familiar with this command.)

Advanced Challenge Exercise

- Use the Property Sheet of the form to create an event handler procedure based on the On Load property. The statement will be one line using the Maximize method of the VBA DoCmd object, which will maximize the form each time it is loaded.
- Save and close the VBA Editor window and the Claim Entry Form, then open the Claim Entry Form in Form View to test the new event handler.

d. Close the Visual Basic window, save and close the Claim Entry Form, close the Patients-O.accdb database, then exit Access.

▼ INDEPENDENT CHALLENGE 3

As the manager of a doctor's clinic, you have created an Access database called Patients-O.accdb to track insurance claim reimbursements that are fixed (paid at a predetermined fixed rate) or denied (not paid by the insurance company). You want to enhance the database with a class module.

a. Start Access, then open the **Patients-O.accdb** database from the drive and folder where you store your Data Files.

b. Open the CPT Form in Form Design View.

c. Maximize the window, then expand the width of the CPT Form to about the 5" mark on the horizontal ruler.

d. Use the Command Button Wizard to add a command button in the Form Header section. Choose the Add New Record action from the Record Operations category.

e. Accept **Add Record** as the text on the button, then name the button **AddRecordButton**.

f. Use the Command Button Wizard to add a command button in the Form Header section to the right of the existing Add Record button. (*Hint*: Move and resize controls as necessary to put two command buttons in the Form Header section.)

g. Choose the Delete Record action from the Record Operations category.

h. Accept **Delete Record** as the text on the button, and name the button **DeleteRecordButton**.

i. Save and view the CPT Form in Form View, then click the Add Record command button.

j. Add a new record (it will be record number 65) with a CPTCode value of **999** and an RBRVS value of **1.5**.

k. To make sure that the Delete Record button works, click the record selector for the new record you just entered, click the Delete Record command button, then click Yes to confirm the deletion.

Advanced Challenge Exercise

- In Form Design View, open the Property Sheet for the Delete Record command, click the Event tab, then click the Build button beside [Embedded Macro].

- Click the Save As button on the Macro Tools Design tab, enter **CPT Form Macros** as the macro name, then click OK. Save and close Design View of the CPT Form Macros, then save and close the CPT Form.

- Click CPT Form Macros in the Navigation Pane, click the Database Tools tab, click Convert Macros to Visual Basic, then click Convert and OK.

- Close the VBA Editor window, right-click the Converted Macro-CPT Form Macros module, then click Design View.

- Add a comment as the last line of code in the Code window with your name and the current date, save, print, then close the Visual Basic window.

l. Close the Patients-O.accdb database, then exit Access.

▼ REAL LIFE INDEPENDENT CHALLENGE

Learning a programming language is sometimes compared to learning a foreign language. Imagine how it would feel to learn a new software program or programming language if English wasn't your primary language, or if you had another type of accessibility challenge? Advances in technology are helping to break down many barriers to those with vision, hearing, mobility, cognitive, and language impairments. In this challenge, you explore the Microsoft Web site for resources to address these issues.

a. Go to *www.microsoft.com/enable*, then print that page. Explore the Web site.

b. Go back to *www.microsoft.com/enable*, point to the Guides by Impairment menu, then click the Language or Speech link.

c. After exploring the Web site (you might want to print some pages as well, but be careful as some articles are quite long), write a one-page, double-spaced paper describing some of the things that you learned about how Microsoft products accommodate people with language and speech impairments.

d. Go back to *www.microsoft.com/enable*, click the International link near the top of the window, then explore the sites for other languages such as Chinese and Japanese. You may be prompted to install a language pack in order to display these languages. Write down the languages for which the Microsoft Accessibility Web site is available.

▼ VISUAL WORKSHOP

As the manager of a college basketball team, you are helping the coach build meaningful statistics to compare the relative value of the players in each game. The coach has stated that one offensive rebound is worth as much to the team as two defensive rebounds, and would like you to use this rule to develop a "rebounding impact statistic" for each game. Open the Basketball-O.accdb database and use Figure O-22 to develop a new function called ReboundImpact in a new module called Rebound Statistic to calculate this statistic. Include your name and the current date as a comment in the last row of the function. Print the function.

FIGURE O-22

```
Function ReboundImpact(offense, defense)
    ReboundImpact = (offense * 2) + defense
End Function


'Your Name, current date
```

Managing the Database

Access databases are unlike the other Microsoft Office files, such as Word documents or Excel spreadsheets, in that they are typically used by more people and for extended periods. Therefore, spending a few hours to secure a database and improve its performance is a good investment. **Database administration** involves the task of making the database faster, easier, more secure, and more reliable. ▓▓▓▓ You work with Wilbur Young, network administrator at Quest Specialty Travel, to examine several administrative issues such as setting passwords, changing startup options, and analyzing database performance to protect, improve, and enhance the database.

OBJECTIVES

Back up a database

Convert a database

Encrypt a database and set a password

Change Access and startup options

Analyze database performance

Analyze table performance

Split a database

Compact and repair a database

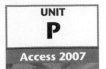

Backing Up a Database

Backing up a database refers to making a copy of it in a secure location. Because the cost of large hard drives has dropped dramatically over the past few years, most backups are saved on an external hard drive or the hard drive of a second computer. Several years ago, portable backup technology such as tape drives or compact discs (CDs) were used. Because most users are familiar with saving and copying files to hard drives, the new technology streamlines the effort of backing up a database. ▚▚▚▚ Wilbur Young asks you to review the methods of backing up the database.

STEPS

1. **Start Access, then open the** Technology-P.accdb **database from the drive and folder where you store your Data Files, enabling content if prompted**

   One way to back up an Access database is to use the Save As option on the Office Button menu.

2. **Click the** Office Button ⊕ **on the Quick Access toolbar, point to** Save As, **then click** Access 2007 Database

   The Save As dialog appears, as shown in Figure P-1. Obviously, your drive list reflects the physical drives on your computer and does not match the figure. Your folder and file list reflects the folders and files on your computer, which are also different.

3. **Use the Folders list in the Navigation Pane to navigate to the drive and folder where you want to create the backup, then click** Save

   A copy of the Technology-P.accdb database is saved in the location you selected for the backup. Previous versions of Microsoft Office Access did not let you use a Save As command to save a database. Another way to make a backup copy of an Access database file, or any file, is to use your Windows skills to copy and paste the database file in a folder.

FIGURE P-1: Save As dialog box used to back up a database

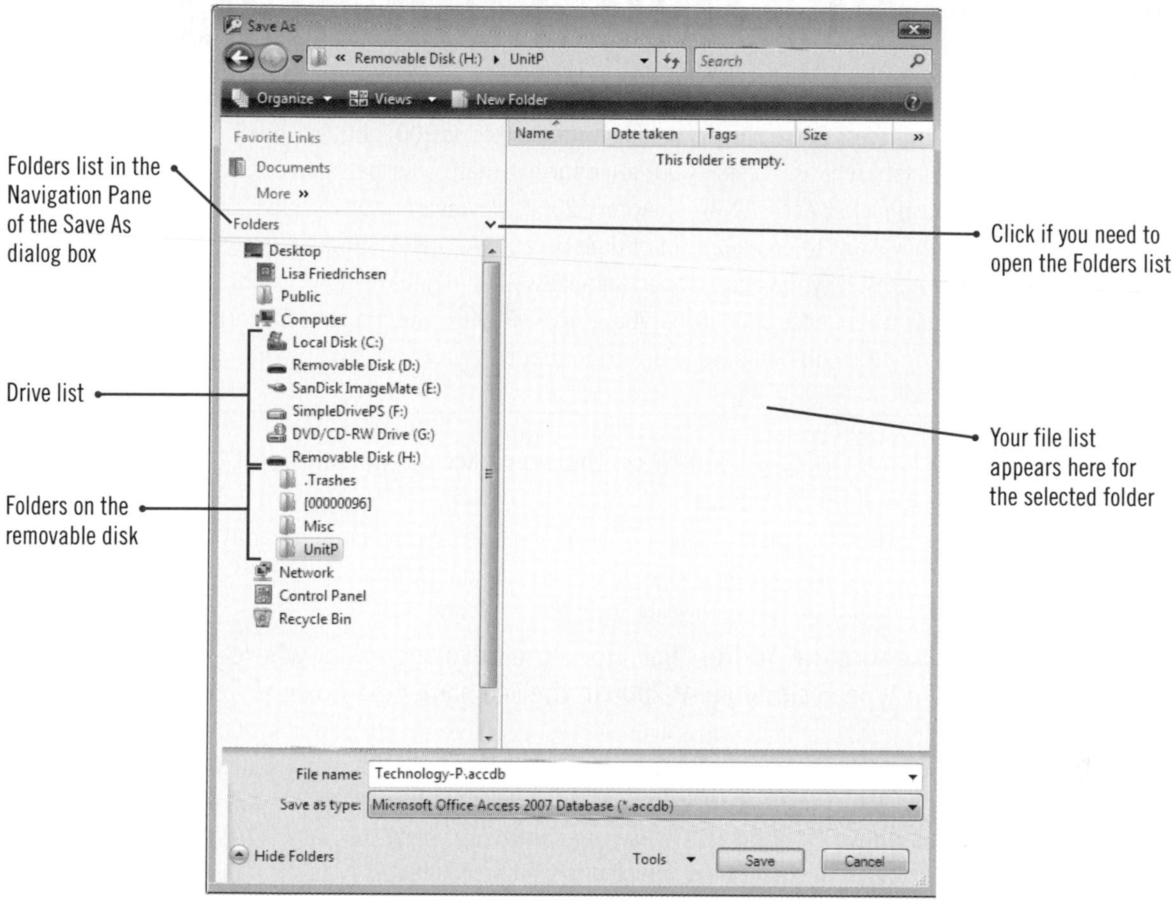

Folders list in the Navigation Pane of the Save As dialog box

Drive list

Folders on the removable disk

Click if you need to open the Folders list

Your file list appears here for the selected folder

Using portable storage media

Technological advancements continue to make it easier and less expensive to store large files on portable storage devices. A few years ago, 3.5-inch disks with roughly 1 **MB** (megabyte, a million bytes) of storage capacity were common. Today, 3.5-inch disks have been replaced by a variety of inexpensive, high-capacity storage media that work with digital devices such as digital cameras, cell phones, and Personal Digital Assistants (PDAs). **Secure digital (SD) cards** are quarter-sized devices that slip directly into a computer and typically store around 256 MB. **CompactFlash (CF) cards** are slightly larger, about the size of a matchbook, and store more data, around 1 **GB** (gigabyte, 1000 MB). **USB (Universal Serial Bus) drives** (which plug into a computer's USB port), are also popular. USB drives are also called thumb drives, flash drives, and travel drives. USB devices typically store 1 GB to 10 GB of information. Larger still are **external hard drives**, sometimes as small as the size of a cell phone, that store anywhere from 20 to 200 GB of information and connect to a computer using either a USB or FireWire port.

Converting a Database

When you **convert** a database, you change the file into one that can be opened in another version of Access. In Access 2007, the default file format is Access 2007, but in Access 2003, the default file format for a new database was Access 2000, a file format that could be seamlessly opened in Access 2000, Access 2002 (also called Access XP), or Access 2003. However, Access users must now consider the version of Access they want to create ahead of time because Access 2007 databases cannot be opened in earlier versions of Access. If you want to open an Access 2007 database in Access 2000, 2002, or 2003, you need to convert it to an Access 2000 database first. ▄▄▄▄▄ The Training Department asks you to convert the Technology-P.accdb database to a version that they can open and use in Access 2003 for a training class.

STEPS

1. **Click the** Office Button ⊙ **on the Quick Access toolbar, point to** Save As, **then click** Access 2000 Database

   To convert a database, you must make sure that no other users are currently working with it. Because you are the sole user of this database, you can start the conversion process. The Save As dialog box opens, prompting you for the name of the database.

2. **Make sure the Address bar shows the drive and folder where you store your Data Files, then type** Technology-P-2000 **in the File name text box**

   Your screen should look like Figure P-2. Because Access 2000, 2002, and 2003 all work with Access 2000 databases equally well, allowing for maximum backward compatibility, you decide to convert this database to an Access 2000 version database. Recall that Access 2007 databases have an **.accdb** file extension, but Access 2000 and 2002-2003 databases have the **.mdb** file extension. Therefore, it is helpful to identify the version of Access in the filename if you plan to work with multiple versions of the same database file on the same computer.

3. **Click** Save, **then click** OK

   A copy of the database with the name Technology-P-2000.mdb is saved to the drive and folder you specified. You can open and use Access 2000 and 2002-2003 databases in Access 2007 without modification. To view the database files, use Windows Explorer or any folder window.

4. **Right-click the** Start button ⊕ **on the taskbar, click** Explore **on the shortcut menu, then scroll and locate your Data Files in the Folders list**

5. **Click** Views **on the toolbar, then click** Details

   Your screen should look similar to Figure P-3. By choosing Details view, the folder window displays columns of details about the files. You can right-click any column heading in the file list to change the details and display the Size, Type, and Date Modified columns, for example, to display the size in KB, file type, and date the file was last modified. Notice that the list includes Technology-P-2000.mdb, the database you just created by converting the Technology-P.accdb Access 2007 database to an Access 2000 version database. The filename Technology-P-2000.mdb appears twice, however, both with an .mdb and an .ldb extension. The **.ldb** file is a temporary file that keeps track of record-locking information when the database is open. It helps coordinate the multiuser capabilities of an Access database so that several people can read and update the same database at the same time.

6. **Close the folder window**

TROUBLE
If you do not see the extensions on the filenames, click Organize on the toolbar, click Folder and Search Options, click the View tab, then uncheck the Hide file extensions for known file types check box.

FIGURE P-2: Save As dialog box used to convert a database

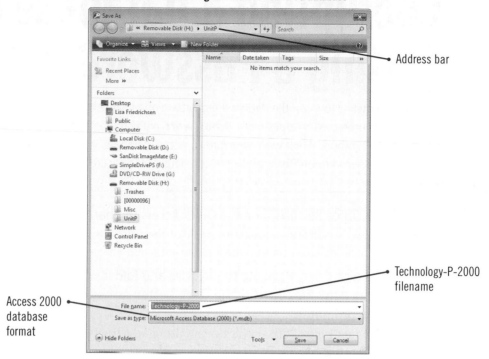

Address bar

Technology-P-2000
filename

Access 2000
database
format

FIGURE P-3: Viewing database files in Windows Explorer

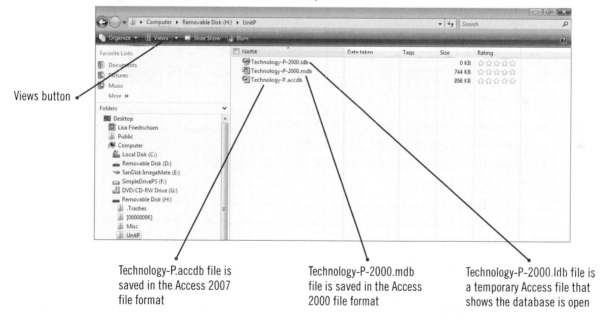

Views button

Technology-P.accdb file is
saved in the Access 2007
file format

Technology-P-2000.mdb
file is saved in the Access
2000 file format

Technology-P-2000.ldb file is
a temporary Access file that
shows the database is open

Access 2000 versus Access 2002–2003 file formats

Microsoft Office Access 2003 provided some new features such as smart tags (which help you update properties and find errors), ways to view object dependency information, better backup tools, and expanded XML support. Access database files themselves, however, did not dramatically change from the Access 2000 to the Access 2002–2003 file format. Therefore, use the default Access 2000 file format for databases you want to convert from Access 2007. By using the 2000 file format, you preserve seamless forward and backward compatibility with Access 2000, 2002, and 2003 software users.

Encrypting a Database and Setting a Password

Encryption means to make the data in the database unreadable by tools other than the Access database itself, which is protected by a password. A **password** is a combination of uppercase and lowercase letters, numbers, and symbols. Other ways to secure an Access database are listed in Table P-1. ▓▓▓▓ You apply a database password to the Technology-P.accdb database to secure its data.

STEPS

QUICK TIP
It's always a good idea to back up a database before creating a database password.

1. **Click the Office Button 🔘 on the Quick Access toolbar, then click Close Database**

   The Technology-P-2000.mdb database closes, but the Access application window remains open. To set a database password, you must open the database in Exclusive mode.

2. **Click 🔘, click Open, navigate to the drive and folder where you store your Data Files, click Technology-P.accdb, click the Open button arrow, click Open Exclusive, then enable content if prompted**

   Exclusive mode means that you are the only person who has the database open, and others cannot open the file during this time.

3. **Click the Database Tools tab on the Ribbon, then click the Encrypt with Password button in the Database Tools group**

   The Set Database Password dialog box opens, as shown in Figure P-4. If you lose or forget your password, it cannot be recovered. For security reasons, your password does not appear as you type; for each keystroke, an asterisk appears instead. Therefore, you must enter the same password in both the Password and Verify text boxes to make sure you haven't made a typing error. Passwords are case sensitive, so Cyclones and cyclones are different.

QUICK TIP
Check to make sure the Caps Lock light is not on before entering a password.

4. **Type Cy!34567!Clones in the Password text box, press [Tab], type Cy!34567!Clones in the Verify text box, then click OK**

   Passwords should be easy to remember, but not as obvious as your name, the word "password," the name of the database, or the name of your company. **Strong passwords** are longer than eight characters and use the entire keyboard including uppercase and lowercase letters, numbers, and symbols. Microsoft provides an online tool (currently at *www.microsoft.com/athome/security/privacy/password_checker.mspx*) to check the strength of your password.

5. **Close, then reopen Technology-P.accdb**

   The Password Required dialog box opens, as shown in Figure P-5.

6. **Type Cy!34567!Clones, then click OK**

   The Technology-P.accdb database opens, giving you full access to all of the objects. To remove a password, you must exclusively open a database, just as you did when you set a database password.

7. **Click 🔘, click Close Database, click 🔘, click Open, navigate to the drive and folder where you store your Data Files, click Technology-P.accdb, click the Open button arrow, click Open Exclusive, type Cy!34567!Clones in the Password Required dialog box, then click OK**

8. **Click the Database Tools tab, click the Decrypt Database button in the Database Tools group, type Cy!34567!Clones, then click OK**

FIGURE P-4: Set Database Password dialog box

Enter the new password •———

Retype the password to confirm it •———

FIGURE P-5: Password Required dialog box

TABLE P-1: Methods to secure an Access database

method	description
Password	Restricts access to the database, and can be set at the database, workgroup, or VBA level
Encrypting	Makes the data indecipherable to other programs
Startup options	Hides or disables certain functions when the database is opened
Show/hide objects	Shows or hides objects in the Navigation Pane; a simple way to prevent users from unintentionally deleting objects is to hide them in the database window by checking the Hidden property in the object's property sheet
Split a database	Separates the back-end data and the front-end objects (such as forms and reports) into two databases that work together; splitting a database allows you to give each user access to only those front-end objects they need as well as add additional security measures to the back-end database that contains the data

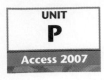

Changing Access and Startup Options

Access options are default settings that control a wide variety of features within Access. **Startup options** are a series of commands that execute when the database is opened. You manage the default Access and startup options using the **Access Options dialog box**; its categories are summarized in Table P-2. More startup options are available through the use of **command-line options**, a special series of characters added to the end of the pathname (for example, C:\My Documents\Quest.accdb /excl), which execute a special command when the file is opened. See Table P-3 for information on common startup command-line options. You want to view and set database properties and then specify that the Employees form opens when the Technology-P.accdb database does.

STEPS

1. **Click the** Office Button **on the Quick Access toolbar, then click** Access Options

   The Access Options dialog box opens. The most popular options are presented first.

2. **Click the** Current Database **category, click the** Application Title text box, **then type** Quest Specialty Travel

   The Application Title database property value appears in the title bar instead of the database filename.

3. **Click the** Display Form list arrow, **then click** Employees

   See Figure P-6. You test the Application Title and Display Form database properties.

4. **Click** OK, **click** OK, **close the** Technology-P.accdb **database, then reopen the** Technology-P.accdb **database and enable content if prompted**

   The Technology-P.accdb database opens, followed by the Employees form, with the new application title, as shown in Figure P-7. If you want to open an Access database and bypass startup options, press and hold [Shift] while the database opens.

5. **Close the** Employees **form**

TABLE P-2: Default database settings managed in the Access Options dialog box

category	description
Popular	Changes the most popular options in Access such as default file format, default database folder, and user name
Current Database	Manages the options for the current database such as application title, compact on close, and document window options (overlapping windows versus tabbed documents)
Datasheet	Sets the default color, font, gridlines, cell effects, and other datasheet options
Object Designers	Customizes options for creating and modifying database settings in Access such as default field type, query design font, default form template, and error checking preferences
Proofing	Determines which dictionaries and rules are used for the spell check feature, and which AutoCorrect options are applied
Advanced	Sets the defaults for editing, presenting, and printing data such as navigation rules, default margins, displayed confirmation messages, and advanced record-level locking options
Customize	Allows you to customize the Quick Access toolbar with icons representing the commands of your choice
Add-ins	Lets you view and manage Microsoft Office add-ins
Trust Center	Provides settings to help keep your computer and documents secure and error-free
Resources	Provides links to find online resources, run diagnostics, and contact Microsoft

FIGURE P-6: Access Options dialog box—Current Database category

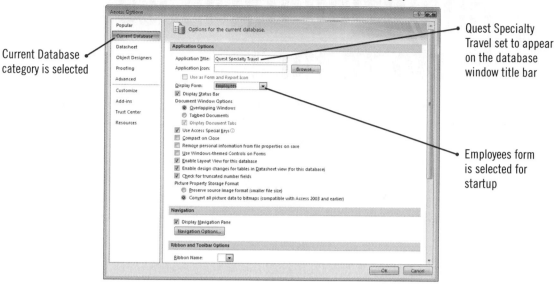

Current Database category is selected

Quest Specialty Travel set to appear on the database window title bar

Employees form is selected for startup

FIGURE P-7: Property changes applied when the database opens

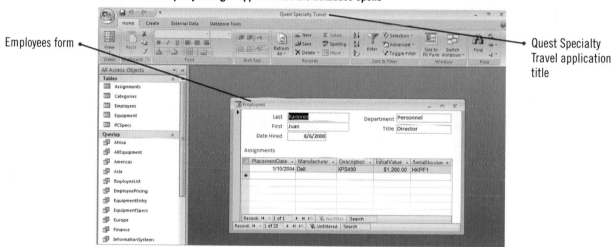

Employees form

Quest Specialty Travel application title

TABLE P-3: Startup command-line options

option	effect
/excl	Opens the database for exclusive access
/ro	Opens the database for read-only access
/pwd *password*	Opens the database using the specified *password* (applies to Access 2002–2003 and earlier version databases only)
/repair	Repairs the database (in Access 2000 and 2002, compacting the database also repairs it; if you choose the Compact on Close command, you don't need the /repair option)
/convert *target database*	Converts a previous version of a database to an Access 2000 database with the *target database* name
/x *macro*	Starts Access and runs the specified *macro*
/wrkgrp *workgroup information file*	Starts Access using the specified *workgroup information file* (applies to Access 2002–2003 and earlier version databases only)

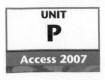

Analyzing Database Performance

Access provides a tool called the **Performance Analyzer** that studies the structure and size of your database and makes a variety of recommendations on how you can improve its performance. With adequate time and Access skills, you can alleviate many performance bottlenecks by using software tools and additional programming techniques to improve database performance. You can often purchase faster processors and more memory to accomplish the same goal. See Table P-4 for tips on optimizing the performance of your computer. You use the Database Performance Analyzer to see whether Access provides any recommendations on how to easily maintain peak performance of the Technology-P.accdb database.

STEPS

1. **Click the Database Tools tab, click the Analyze Performance button in the Analyze group, then click the All Object Types tab**

   The Performance Analyzer dialog box opens, as shown in Figure P-8. You can choose to analyze selected tables, forms, other objects, or the entire database.

2. **Click Select All, then click OK**

   The Performance Analyzer examines each object and presents the results in a dialog box, as shown in Figure P-9. The key shows that the analyzer gives four levels of advice regarding performance: recommendations, suggestions, ideas, and items that were fixed.

3. **Click each item in the Analysis Results area, then read each description in the Analysis Notes area**

   The light bulb icon next to an item indicates that this is an idea. The Analysis Notes section of the Performance Analyzer dialog box gives you additional information regarding the specific item. All of the Performance Analyzer's ideas should be considered, but they are not as important as recommendations and suggestions.

4. **Click Close to close the Performance Analyzer dialog box**

FIGURE P-8: Performance Analyzer dialog box

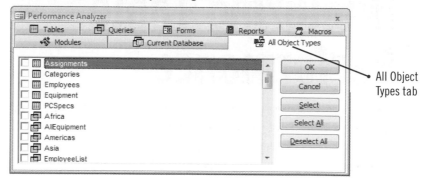

All Object Types tab

FIGURE P-9: Performance Analyzer results

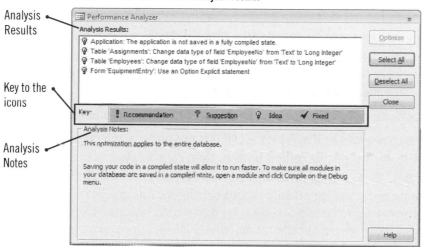

Analysis Results

Key to the icons

Analysis Notes

TABLE P-4: Tips for optimizing performance

degree of difficulty	tip
Easy	To free memory and other computer resources, close all applications that you don't currently need
Easy	If they can be run safely only when you need them, eliminate memory-resident programs such as complex screen savers, e-mail alert programs, and virus checkers
Easy	If you are the only person using a database, open it in Exclusive mode
Easy	Use the Compact on Close feature to regularly compact and repair your database
Easy	Convert the database to the Access 2000 file format
Moderate	Add more memory to your computer; once the database is open, memory is generally the single most important determinant of overall performance
Moderate	If others don't need to share the database, load it on your local hard drive instead of the network's file server (but be sure to back up local drives regularly, too)
Moderate	Split the database so that the data is stored on the file server, but other database objects are stored on your local (faster) hard drive
Moderate to difficult	If you are using disk compression software, stop doing so or move the database to an uncompressed drive
Moderate to difficult	Run Performance Analyzer on a regular basis, examining and appropriately acting on each recommendation, suggestion, and idea
Moderate to difficult	Make sure that all PCs are running the latest versions of Windows and Access; this might involve purchasing more software or upgrading hardware to properly support these robust software products

Analyzing Table Performance

Another Access database performance analysis tool, called the **Table Analyzer Wizard**, looks for duplicate information in one table that should be separated and stored in its own table. Storing duplicate data in one table wastes space and causes database accuracy errors, yet it is a very common table design problem. The Table Analyzer Wizard also recommends how to relate any tables that you should separate into two tables. The best time to analyze tables is when you initially design the database, because you might need to edit a query, form, or report that relies on fields from a particular table that has been redesigned when you reorganize the tables. ▨▨▨▨▨ You use the Table Analyzer Wizard to examine the Employees table.

STEPS

QUICK TIP

Click the Show me an example buttons to study the concepts more closely.

1. **Click the Database Tools tab, then click the Analyze Table button**

   The Table Analyzer Wizard starts, as shown in Figure P-10. The first dialog box describes the problems caused by storing duplicate data in one table. The **Show me an example** buttons give you more information by using a common example to explain the problem.

2. **Click Next, read about solving the redundant data problem, then click Next**

TROUBLE

You might need to resize the field lists to view all of the fields in each list.

3. **Click Employees in the Tables list (if it is not already selected), click Next, click the Yes, let the wizard decide option button, then click Next**

   The Table Analyzer Wizard evaluates the Employees table and finds redundant data in both the Department and Title fields. See Figure P-11. It suggests breaking the data into two separate **lookup tables**, tables that contain one record for each field value. For example, the lookup table for the Department field should contain one record for each department and be related to the original Employees table through a common field, which the Table Analyzer Wizard suggests should be a generated unique ID number (in other words, an AutoNumber field). By using a lookup table, users can't unintentionally enter the same department two or more ways (Human Resources and HR, for example).

4. **Click Table3, click the Rename Table button 🖽, type QuestTitles, click OK, click Table2, click 🖽, type QuestDepartments, click OK, click Table1, click 🖽, type QuestEmployees, then click OK**

   The wizard prevents you from using the names of existing tables so you do not replace any data.

5. **Click Next, click the QuestEmployees table (if it is not already selected), click the Add Generated Key button 🔲, then click Next**

   The QuestEmployees table doesn't contain a primary key field (shown in bold), so you added one. Your database does not have any errors, so you choose the (Leave as is) option.

6. **Click the Correction list arrow, click (Leave as is), click Next, click the Correction list arrow, click (Leave as is), click the second row in the Correction column, click its list arrow, click (Leave as is), click Next, then click Finish**

   The wizard creates an Employees query with fields from three new tables—QuestDepartments, QuestEmployees, and QuestTitles—to simulate the old Employees table, which has been renamed Employees_OLD. Doing so reduces typographical errors and data storage requirements.

7. **Close the Access Help window, open the Relationships window, add the QuestEmployees, QuestDepartments, and QuestTitles field lists to the Relationships window, link the ID field in the QuestEmployees table to the EmployeeNo field in the Assignments table to create a one-to-many relationship without enforcing referential integrity, then save and close the window**

   Any time you split tables for better performance, you might need to reestablish database relationships.

FIGURE P-10: Table Analyzer Wizard

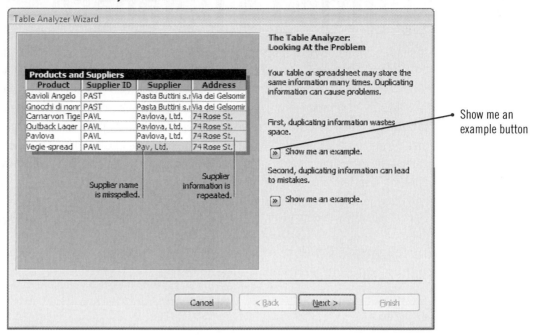

Show me an example button

FIGURE P-11: Table Analyzer Wizard suggestion

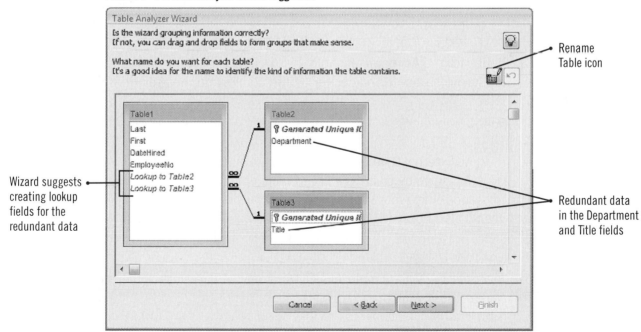

Rename Table icon

Wizard suggests creating lookup fields for the redundant data

Redundant data in the Department and Title fields

Access 2007

Splitting a Database

As your database grows, more people will want to use it, which creates the need for higher levels of database connectivity. **Local area networks (LANs)** are installed to link multiple PCs so they can share hardware and software resources. After a LAN is installed, a shared database can be moved to a **file server**, a centrally located computer from which every user can access the database via the network. The more users share the same database, however, the slower it responds. To improve the performance of a database shared among several users, you might want to split the database into two files: the **back-end database**, which contains the actual table objects and is stored on the file server, and the **front-end database**, which contains the other database objects (forms and reports, for example), and links to the back-end database tables. You copy the front-end database for as many users as needed because the front-end database must be located on each user's PC. You can also customize the objects contained in each front-end database. Therefore, front-end databases not only improve performance but also add a level of customization and security. ▰▰▰▰ You split the Technology-P.accdb database into two databases in preparation for the new LAN being installed in the Information Systems Department.

STEPS

1. **Close the Employees query, click the Office Button ▣ on the Quick Access toolbar, point to Save As, click Access 2007 Database, navigate to the drive and folder where you store your Data Files, enter Technology-P-FrontEnd.accdb in the File name text box, then click Save**

   To create a front-end or back-end database, you start by creating a copy of the original database. The copy can serve as either the front-end or back-end database, and therefore the name you give the database helps you remember which role it serves.

2. **Enable content if prompted, then close the Employees form**

   You are now working with the front-end database, which will contain all of the Access objects except for the tables. Therefore, you need to delete the existing physical tables and link to the tables in the original database, which will serve as the back-end database.

3. **Right-click the Assignments table, click Delete, click Yes, click Yes, then continue repeating this process until you delete all of the tables and their relationships in the front-end database**

   In the current front-end database, you need to create links to the physical tables in the original database, which is now serving as the back-end database.

4. **Click the External Data tab, click the Access button in the Import group, click the Link to the data source by creating a linked table option button, click Browse, navigate to the drive and folder where you store your Data Files, click Technology-P.accdb in the File Open dialog box, click Open, then click OK**

   The Link Tables dialog box opens, as shown in Figure P-12. This allows you to select those tables in the back-end database that you want to link to in the front-end database.

5. **Click Select All, click Employees_OLD in the list to deselect it, then click OK**

   You do not need to link to Employees_OLD, because it was replaced by the QuestDepartments, QuestEmployees, and QuestTitles tables. You might want to delete the Employees_OLD table when you are confident that the new database structure works well. The linked tables in the front-end database look like Figure P-13.

6. **Double-click the QuestEmployees linked table icon**

   Linked tables work just like regular physical tables, even though the data is physically stored in another database. If you completed splitting the database, you could delete the objects except for tables from the back-end database.

7. **Close the QuestEmployees datasheet**

Managing the Database

FIGURE P-12: Link Tables dialog box

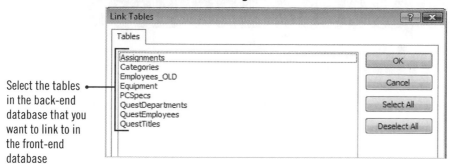

Select the tables in the back-end database that you want to link to in the front-end database

FIGURE P-13: Tables are linked in the front-end database

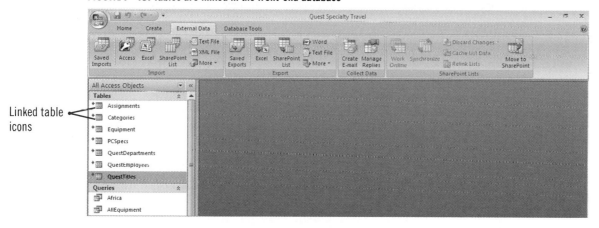

Linked table icons

Databases and client/server computing

Splitting a database into a front-end and back-end database that work together is an excellent example of client/server computing. **Client/server computing** can be defined as two or more information systems cooperatively processing to solve a problem. In most implementations, the **client** is defined as the user's PC and the **server** is defined as the shared file server, mini, or mainframe computer. The server usually handles corporate-wide computing activities such as data storage and management, security, and connectivity to other networks. Within Access, client computers generally handle those tasks specific to each user, such as storing all of the queries, forms, and reports used by a particular user. Effectively managing a vast client/server network in which many front-end databases link to a single back-end database is a tremendous task, but the performance and security benefits are worth the effort.

Compacting and Repairing a Database

Compacting and repairing a database refers to a process that Access 2007 uses to reorganize the pieces of the database to eliminate wasted space on the disk storage device, which also helps prevent data integrity problems. You can compact and repair a database at any time, or you can set a database option to automatically compact and repair the database when it is closed. ██████ Because you recently deleted the tables from the front-end database, you should compact and repair it to use space more efficiently. You also decide to set database options to automatically compact and repair the database when it is closed.

STEPS

1. **Click the Office Button 🖲 on the Quick Access toolbar, point to Manage, then click Compact and Repair Database**

   The database is automatically closed, the compact and repair process is completed, and the database is reopened.

2. **Enable content if prompted, then close the Employees form**

   Compacting and repairing a database that has not yet been compacted can reduce the size of the database by 10, 50, or even 75 percent because the space occupied by deleted objects and data is not reused until the database is compacted. Therefore, it's a good idea to set up a regular schedule to compact and repair a database or to change Access options to automatically compact and repair the database when it is closed.

3. **Click 🖲, then click Access Options**

   The Compact on Close feature is in the Current Database category.

4. **Click the Current Database category, then click the Compact on Close check box**

   Your screen should look like Figure P-14. Now, every time the database is closed, Access will also compact and repair it. This helps you keep the database as small and efficient as possible, and protects your database from potential corruption. For other database threats and solutions, see Table P-5.

5. **Click OK, click OK, then close the Technology-P-FrontEnd.accdb database and exit Access**

FIGURE P-14: Setting the Compact on Close option

Current Database category

Compact on Close check box

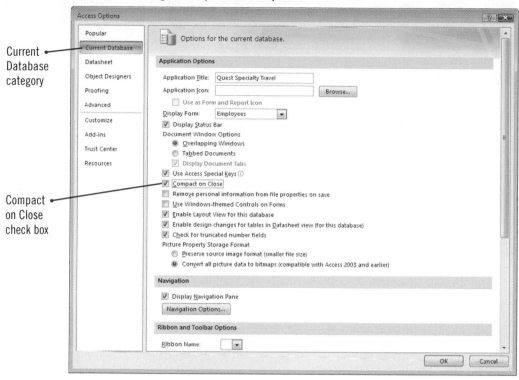

TABLE P-5: Database threats

incident	what can happen	appropriate actions
Virus	Viruses can cause a wide range of harm, from profane messages to corrupted files	Purchase the leading virus-checking software for each machine, and keep it updated
Power outage	Power problems such as construction accidents, **brown-outs** (dips in power often causing lights to dim) and **spikes** (surges in power) can damage the hardware, which may render the computer useless	Purchase a **UPS** (Uninterruptible Power Supply) to maintain constant power to the file server (if networked) Purchase a **surge protector** (power strip with surge protection) for each end user
Theft or intentional damage	Computer thieves or other scoundrels steal or vandalize computer equipment	Place the file server in a room that can be locked after hours
		Use network drives for user data files, and back them up on a daily basis
		Use off-site storage for backups
		Set database passwords and encode the database so that files that are stolen cannot be used; use computer locks for equipment that is at risk, especially laptops

Practice

▼ CONCEPTS REVIEW

Identify each element of the Access Options dialog box in Figure P-15.

FIGURE P-15

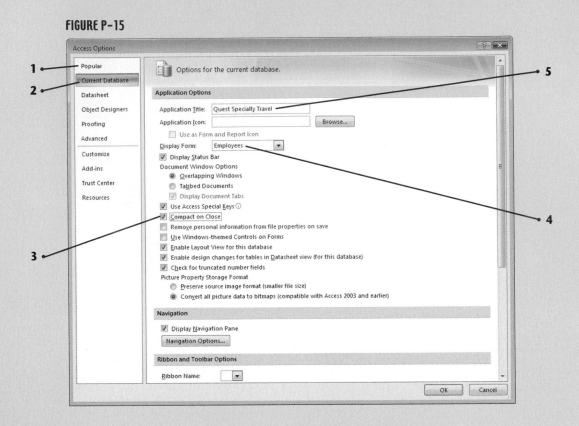

Match each term with the statement that best describes its function.

6. **Table Analyzer Wizard**
7. **Back-end database**
8. **Encrypting**
9. **Database Performance Analyzer**
10. **Exclusive mode**

a. Means that no other users can have access to the database file while it's open
b. Scrambles data so that it is indecipherable when opened by another program
c. Studies the structure and size of your database, and makes a variety of recommendations on how you can improve its speed
d. Contains database tables
e. Looks for duplicate information in one table that should be separated and stored in its own table

Select the best answer from the list of choices.

11. **Changing a database file so that a previous version of Access can open it is called:**
    a. Splitting.
    b. Analyzing.
    c. Encrypting.
    d. Converting.

12. **Which is *not* a strong password?**
    a. password
    b. 5Matthew14?
    c. Lip44Balm*!
    d. 1234$College=6789

13. **Power outages can be caused by which of the following?**
    a. Surges
    b. Construction accidents
    c. Spikes
    d. All of the above

14. **Which character precedes a command-line option?**
    a. /
    b. @
    c. !
    d. ^

▼ SKILLS REVIEW

1. **Back up a database.**
   a. Start Access, then open the **Basketball-P.accdb** database from the drive and folder where you store your Data Files. Enable content if prompted.
   b. Click the Office Button, point to Save As, and save the database backup as an Access 2007 database with the name **Basketball-P-Backup.accdb** in the drive and folder where you store your Data Files.

2. **Convert a database.**
   a. Click the Office Button, point to Save As, and save the database backup as an Access 2000 database with the name **Basketball-P-2000.mdb** in the drive and folder where you store your Data Files.
   b. Start Windows Explorer, then navigate to the drive and folder where you store your Data Files. The folder should contain the original Basketball-P.accdb database, the Basketball-P-Backup.accdb database, the converted Basketball-P-2000.mdb database, and the Basketball-P-2000.ldb temporary file because Basketball-P-2000.mdb is currently open.
   c. Close Explorer, then close the Basketball-P-2000.mdb database.

3. **Encrypt a database and set a password.**
   a. Open the **Basketball-P.accdb** database in Exclusive mode.
   b. Set the database password to **b*i*g*1*2**. (*Hint*: Check to make sure the Caps Lock light is not on because passwords are case sensitive).
   c. Close the Basketball-P.accdb database, but leave Access open.
   d. Reopen the **Basketball-P.accdb** database in Exclusive mode. Type **b*i*g*1*2** as the password.
   e. Unset the database password.
   f. On a sheet of paper, explain why it was necessary for you to open the database in Exclusive mode in Steps a and d.

4. Change Access and startup options.

   a. Open the Access Options dialog box.

   b. Type **Iowa State Cyclones** in the Application Title text box, click the Display Form list arrow, click the GameSummaryForm, then apply the changes. Notice the change in the Access title bar.

   c. Close the Basketball-P.accdb database, then reopen it to check the startup options.

   d. Close the GameSummaryForm that automatically opened when the database was opened.

   e. On a sheet of paper, identify one reason for changing each of the two startup options modified in Step b.

5. Analyze database performance.

   a. On the Database Tools tab, click the Analyze Performance button.

   b. On the All Object Types tab, select all objects, then click OK. Close the Visual Basic Editor window if it opens.

   c. Read each of the ideas and descriptions, and summarize the ideas on another sheet of paper. Close the Analysis Results window.

6. Analyze table performance.

   a. On the Database Tools tab, click the Analyze Table button.

   b. Step through the wizard, choosing the Players table to analyze. Choose the No, I want to decide option button when prompted.

   c. Drag the Position field from Table1 to a blank spot in the Table Analyzer Wizard dialog box to create a new lookup table named **Positions**.

   d. Rename Table1 to **TeamMembers** so that the Table Analyzer Wizard dialog box looks like Figure P-16.

FIGURE P-16

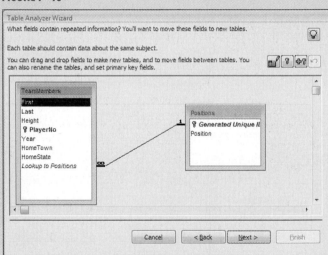

   e. For the Position field that equals "C" (Center), choose the (Leave as is) correction, which might initially appear as the first, blank option. In this database, a Position field value of F stands for Forward and a Position field value of G stands for Guard.

   f. Do not choose to create the query, then finish the Table Analyzer Wizard.

   g. Close the Access Help window if it opens, and close any datasheets that open.

7. Split a database.

   a. Use the Save As command to save a copy of the Basketball-P.accdb database, and name it **Basketball-P-FE.accdb** (FE for FrontEnd).

   b. Delete the five table objects and all of their relationships in the Basketball-P-FE.accdb file.

   c. In the Basketball-P-FE.accdb file, create links to the Games, Positions, Stats, and TeamMembers tables in the Basketball-P.accdb file.

8. Compact and repair a database.

   a. Open Windows Explorer, navigate to the drive and folder where you store your Data Files, and then record the size for the Basketball-P-FE.accdb file. (*Hint*: In Details view, right-click a column heading, then click Size to view file sizes.)

   b. Set database options in the Basketball-P-FE.accdb database to compact on close, then close the database.

   c. Return to the folder window, press F5 to refresh the window, and record the size for the Basketball-P-FE.accdb file.

▼ INDEPENDENT CHALLENGE 1

As the manager of a doctor's clinic, you have created an Access database called Patients-P.accdb to track insurance claims. You want to set a database password and encrypt the database as well as set options to automatically compact the database when it is closed.

a. Start Access. Open **Patients-P.accdb** in Exclusive mode from the drive and folder where you store your Data Files. Enable content if prompted.

b. Encrypt the database with a password.

c. Enter **4-your-health** in the Password text box and the Verify text box, then click OK.

d. Close the Patients-P.accdb database, but leave Access running.

e. Reopen the Patients-P.accdb database, enter **4-your-health** as the password, then click OK.

f. In the Access Options dialog box, check the Compact on Close option.

g. Close the database and Access.

▼ INDEPENDENT CHALLENGE 2

As the manager of a doctor's clinic, you have created an Access database called Patients-P.accdb to track insurance claims. You want to analyze database performance.

a. Open the **Patients-P.accdb** database from the drive and folder where you store your Data Files, and enable content if prompted.

b. Enter **4-your-health** as the password if prompted, then close the Claim Entry Form if it opens.

c. Use the Performance Analyzer tool on the Database Tools tab to analyze all objects. Close the VBA Editor window if it opens.

d. Click each item in the Performance Analyzer results window, and record the idea on another sheet of paper.

Advanced Challenge Exercise

- Implement each of the ideas in the Performance Analyzer results window. Apply each suggestion to the database.
- Rerun the Analyze Performance tool until there are no more suggestions, indicating that all ideas have been applied. After converting the macros to modules, delete the macros.
- Eventually you end up with only one suggestion: to save the application as an MDE file. To implement this suggestion, use the Make ACCDE button on the Database Tools tab to save the database as Patients-P.accde in the drive and folder where you store your Data Files.

e. Close the Patients-P.accde database, then close Access.

▼ INDEPENDENT CHALLENGE 3

As the manager of a community service club, you have created an Access database called Membership-P.accdb to track community service hours. You want to convert the database to an Access 2007 database and analyze table performance.

a. Start Access, then open the database **Membership-P.mdb** from the drive and folder where you store your Data Files.

b. Convert the database to an Access 2007 database with the name **Membership-P-2007.accdb**.

c. Analyze table performance for all three tables, letting the wizard decide whether the table needs to be split. This requires you to use the table analyzer three times.

d. After letting the wizard make recommendations for all three tables, analyze table performance for the Zips table again, choosing the "No, I want to decide" option button.

e. Drag the State field from Table1, calling the table **States**.

f. Rename Table1 to **Zipcodes**.

g. Do not create the query, finish the wizard, and close the Access Help window and any datasheets that open. Open the Navigation Pane.

Advanced Challenge Exercise

- Delete the Zips table and its relationships to other tables in the database.
- Add the Zipcodes and States tables to the Relationships window.
- Link the Names and Zipcodes tables using the common Zip field. Enforce referential integrity on the relationship. The Relationships window should look like Figure P-17.
- Save and close the Relationships window.

h. Close the Membership-P-2007.accdb database, then exit Access.

FIGURE P-17

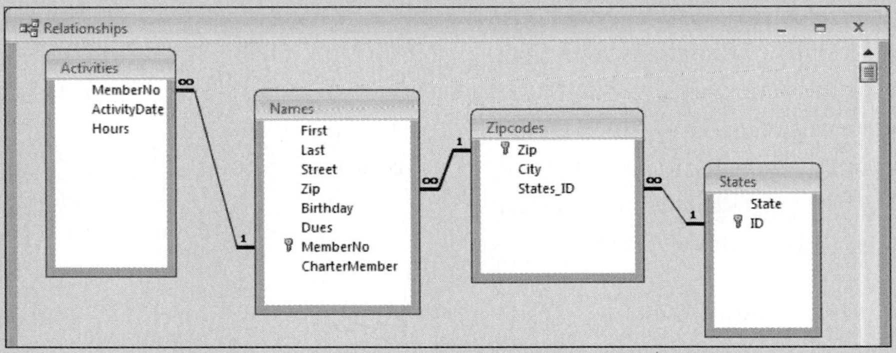

▼ REAL LIFE INDEPENDENT CHALLENGE

Microsoft provides extra information, templates, files, and ideas at a Web site called Tools on the Web. You have been given an opportunity to intern with an Access consultant and are considering this type of work for your career. As such, you know that you need to be familiar with all of the resources on the Web that Microsoft provides to help you work with Access. In this exercise, you'll explore the Tools on the Web services.

a. Start Access, but do not open any databases.

b. Click the Microsoft Office Access Help button.

c. Explore the Access Help and How-to pages at your own pace. You might want to print some articles, but preview them first because some articles are quite long. Click the Access Demos link.

d. Play the demo "Find what you need faster with the redesigned Office Online." Write a one-page paper with the following structure.

- In paragraph one, describe your previous experiences with the Microsoft Help system. Has it been positive, negative, or both? Explain why.

- In paragraph two, identify and describe a new feature about Access 2007 Office Online help that you were previously unaware of until after watching the demo.

- In paragraph three, identify any feature of Access 2007, such as designing tables, creating calculated fields, or adding subtotals to reports, and research it with the Access Help system. Describe the clarity of the information you received.

- In paragraph four, summarize your overall impressions of the Microsoft Help system.

Advanced Challenge Exercise

- Play the demo "Up to speed with Access 2007." Write two paragraphs describing two new features of Access 2007 that you were either unaware of before watching the demo, or which you want to explore more.

- Play the demo "Windows Vista and the 2007 Office system—better together." Write a one-page paper with the following structure. Write two paragraphs describing two new features of Access 2007 that you were either unaware of before watching the demo, or which you want to explore further.

e. Close Access and any other open windows.

▼ VISUAL WORKSHOP

As the manager of a doctor's clinic, you have created an Access database called **MusicStore-P.accdb** that tracks musical instrument rentals to schoolchildren. Use the Performance Analyzer to generate the results shown in Figure P-18 by analyzing all object types.

FIGURE P-18

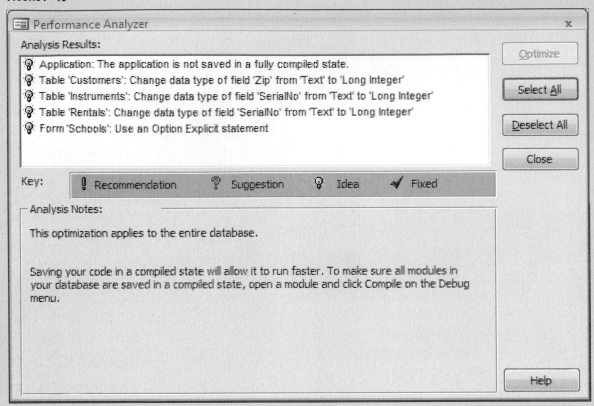

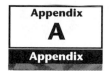
Restoring Defaults in Windows Vista and Disabling and Enabling Windows Aero

Windows Vista is the most recent version of the Windows operating system. An operating system controls the way you work with your computer, supervises running programs, and provides tools for completing your computing tasks. After surveying millions of computer users, Microsoft incorporated their suggestions to make Windows Vista secure, reliable, and easy to use. In fact, Windows Vista is considered the most secure version of Windows yet. Other improvements include a powerful new search feature that lets you quickly search for files and programs from the Start menu and most windows, tools that simplify accessing the Internet, especially with a wireless connection, and multimedia programs that let you enjoy, share, and organize music, photos, and recorded TV. Finally, Windows Vista offers lots of visual appeal with its transparent, three-dimensional design in the Aero experience. This appendix explains how to make sure you are using the Windows Vista default settings for appearance, personalization, security, hardware, and sound and to enable and disable Windows Aero. For more information on Windows Aero, go to *www.microsoft.com/windowsvista/experiences/aero.mspx*.

OBJECTIVES

Restore the defaults in the Appearance and Personalization section

Restore the defaults in the Security section

Restore the defaults in the Hardware and Sound section

Disable Windows Aero

Enable Windows Aero

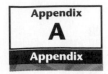
Restoring the Defaults in the Appearance and Personalization Section

The following instructions require a default Windows Vista Ultimate installation and the student logged in with an Administrator account. All of the following settings can be changed by accessing the Control Panel.

STEPS

- To restore the defaults in the Personalization section

  1. Click Start, and then click Control Panel. Click Appearance and Personalization, click Personalization, and then compare your screen to Figure A-1

  2. In the Personalization window, click Windows Color and Appearance, select the Default color, and then click OK

  3. In the Personalization window, click Mouse Pointers. In the Mouse Properties dialog box, on the Pointers tab, select Windows Aero (system scheme) in the Scheme drop-down list, and then click OK

  4. In the Personalization window, click Theme. Select Windows Vista from the Theme drop-down list, and then click OK

  5. In the Personalization window, click Display Settings. In the Display Settings dialog box, drag the Resolution bar to 1024 by 768 pixels, and then click OK

FIGURE A-1

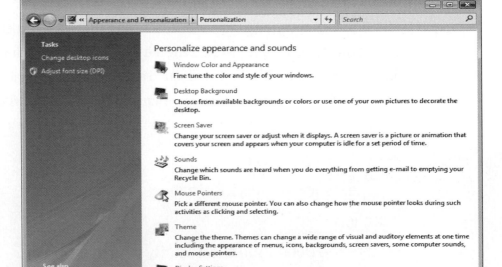

- To restore the defaults in the Taskbar and Start Menu section

  1. Click Start, and then click Control Panel. Click Appearance and Personalization, click Taskbar and Start Menu, and then compare your screen to Figure A-2

  2. In the Taskbar and Start Menu Properties dialog box, on the Taskbar tab, click to select all checkboxes except for "Auto-hide the taskbar"

  3. On the Start Menu tab, click to select the Start menu radio button and check all items in the Privacy section

  4. In the System icons section on the Notification Area tab, click to select all of the checkboxes except for "Power"

  5. On the Toolbars tab, click to select Quick Launch, none of the other items should be checked

  6. Click OK to close the Taskbar and Start Menu Properties dialog box

- To restore the defaults in the Folder Options section

  1. Click Start, and then click Control Panel. Click Appearance and Personalization, click Folder Options, and then compare your screen to Figure A-3

  2. In the Folder Options dialog box, on the General tab, click to select Show preview and filters in the Tasks section, click to select Open each folder in the same window in the Browse folders section, and click to select Double-click to open an item (single-click to select) in the Click items as follows section

  3. On the View tab, click the Reset Folders button, and then click Yes in the Folder views dialog box. Then click the Restore Defaults button

  4. On the Search tab, click the Restore Defaults button

  5. Click OK to close the Folder Options dialog box

- To restore the defaults in the Windows Sidebar Properties section

  1. Click Start, and then click Control Panel. Click Appearance and Personalization, click Windows Sidebar Properties, and then compare your screen to Figure A-4

  2. In the Windows Sidebar Properties dialog box, on the Sidebar tab, click to select Start Sidebar when Windows starts. In the Arrangement section, click to select Right, and then click to select 1 in the Display Sidebar on monitor drop-down list

  3. Click OK to close the Windows Sidebar Properties dialog box

FIGURE A-2

FIGURE A-3

FIGURE A-4

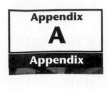

Restoring the Defaults in the Security Section

The following instructions require a default Windows Vista Ultimate installation and the student logged in with an Administrator account. All of the following settings can be changed by accessing the Control Panel.

STEPS

- To restore the defaults in the Windows Firewall section

  1. Click Start, and then click Control Panel. Click Security, click Windows Firewall, and then compare your screen to Figure A-5

  2. In the Windows Firewall dialog box, click Change settings. If the User Account Control dialog box appears, click Continue

  3. In the Windows Firewall Settings dialog box, click the Advanced tab. Click Restore Defaults, then click Yes in the Restore Defaults Confirmation dialog box

  4. Click OK to close the Windows Firewall Settings dialog box, and then close the Windows Firewall window

- To restore the defaults in the Internet Options section

  1. Click Start, and then click Control Panel. Click Security, click Internet Options, and then compare your screen to Figure A-6

  2. In the Internet Properties dialog box, on the General tab, click the Use default button. Click the Settings button in the Tabs section, and then click the Restore defaults button in the Tabbed Browsing Settings dialog box. Click OK to close the Tabbed Browsing Settings dialog box

  3. On the Security tab of the Internet Properties dialog box, click to uncheck the Enable Protected Mode checkbox, if necessary. Click the Default level button in the Security level for this zone section. If possible, click the Reset all zones to default level button

  4. On the Programs tab, click the Make default button in the Default web browser button for Internet Explorer, if possible. If Office is installed, Microsoft Office Word should be selected in the HTML editor drop-down list

  5. On the Advanced tab, click the Restore advanced settings button in the Settings section. Click the Reset button in the Reset Internet Explorer settings section, and then click Reset in the Reset Internet Explorer Settings dialog box

  6. Click Close to close the Reset Internet Explorer Settings dialog box, and then click OK to close the Internet Properties dialog box

FIGURE A-5

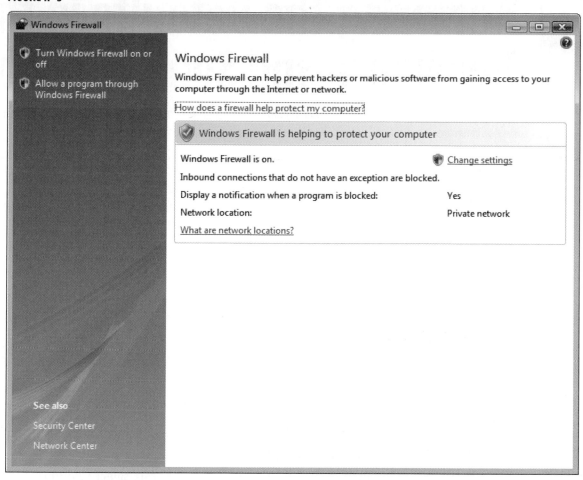

FIGURE A-6

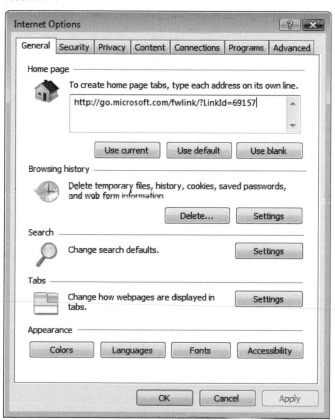

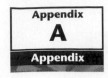

Restoring the Defaults in the Hardware and Sound Section

The following instructions require a default Windows Vista Ultimate installation and the student logged in with an Administrator account. All of the following settings can be changed by accessing the Control Panel.

- To restore the defaults in the Autoplay section
  1. Click Start, and then click Control Panel. Click Hardware and Sound, click Autoplay, and then compare your screen to Figure A-7. Scroll down and click the Reset all defaults button in the Devices section at the bottom of the window, and then click Save

- To restore the defaults in the Sound section
  1. Click Start, and then click Control Panel. Click Hardware and Sound, click Sound, and then compare your screen to Figure A-8
  2. In the Sound dialog box, on the Sounds tab, select Windows Default from the Sound Scheme drop-down list, and then click OK

- To restore the defaults in the Mouse section
  1. Click Start, and then click Control Panel. Click Hardware and Sound, click Mouse, and then compare your screen to Figure A-9
  2. In the Mouse Properties dialog box, on the Pointers tab, select Windows Aero (system scheme) from the Scheme drop-down list
  3. Click OK to close the Mouse Properties dialog box

FIGURE A-7

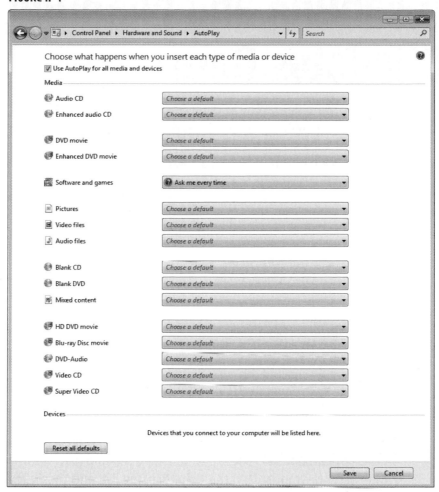

FIGURE A-8

FIGURE A-9

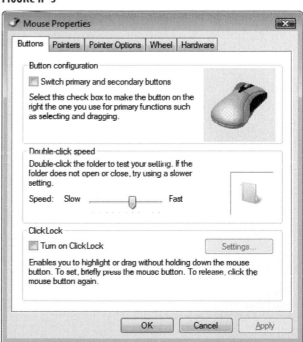

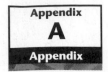
Disabling and Enabling Windows Aero

Unlike prior versions of Windows, Windows Vista provides two distinct user interface experiences: a "basic" experience for entry-level systems and more visually dynamic experience called Windows Aero. Both offer a new and intuitive navigation experience that helps you more easily find and organize your applications and files, but Aero goes further by delivering a truly next-generation desktop experience.

Windows Aero builds on the basic Windows Vista user experience and offers Microsoft's best-designed, highest-performing desktop experience. Using Aero requires a PC with compatible graphics adapter and running a Premium or Business edition of Windows Vista.

The following instructions require a computer capable of running Windows Aero, with a default Windows Vista Ultimate installation and student logged in with an Administrator account.

STEPS

- **To Disable Windows Aero**

We recommend that students using this book disable Windows Aero and restore their operating systems default settings (instructions to follow).

1. **Right-click the desktop, select** Personalize**, and then compare your screen in Figure A-10. Select** Window Color and Appearance**, and then select** Open classic appeareance properties for more color options**. In Appearance Settings dialog box, on the Appearance tab, select any non-Aero scheme (such as** Windows Vista Basic **or** Windows Vista Standard**) in the Color Scheme list, and then click OK. Figure A-11 compares Windows Aero to other color schemes. Note that this book uses Windows Vista Basic as the color scheme**

- **To Enable Windows Aero**

1. **Right-click the desktop, and then select** Personalize**. Select** Window Color and Appearance**, then select** Windows Aero **in the Color scheme list, and then click OK in the Appearance Settings dialog box**

FIGURE A-10

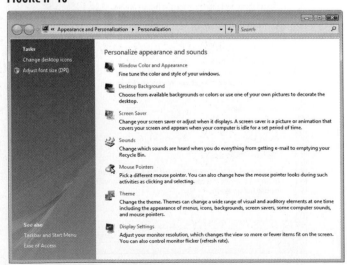

Select other color schemes

FIGURE A-11

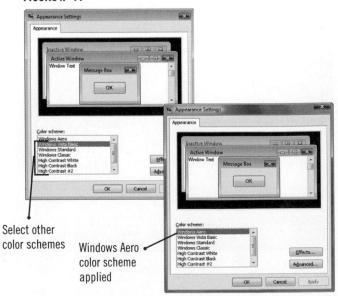

Windows Aero color scheme applied

Glossary

.accdb The file extension that usually means the database is an Access 2007 format database.

.ldb The file extension for a temporary file that keeps track of record-locking information when the database is open. It helps coordinate the multi-user capabilities of an Access database so that several people can read and update the same database at the same time.

.mdb The file extension for Access 2000 and 2002-2003 databases.

Access option One of the default settings that control a wide variety of features within Access.

Access Options dialog box The Access dialog box that manages default and startup options.

Accessories Simple programs to perform specific tasks that come with Windows Vista, such as the Calculator for performing calculations.

Action Each task that you want a macro to perform.

Action Arguments pane The lower half of the Macro Builder window.

Action query A query that changes all of the selected records when it is run. Access provides four types of action queries: delete, update, append, and make table.

Active The currently available document, program, or object; on the taskbar, the button of the active document appears in a darker shade while the buttons of other open documents are dimmed.

Active window The window you are currently using.

Add Mode When creating a switchboard, an option you can specify so that users can only add new records to an object, such as a form.

Address Bar A horizontal box near the top of a window that shows your current location in the computer's file hierarchy as a series of links separated by arrows; used to navigate to other locations on your computer.

Aggregate function A function such as Sum, Avg, and Count used in a summary query to calculate information about a group of records.

Alignment command A command used in Layout or Design View for a form or report to either left-, center-, or right-align a value within its control, or to align the top, bottom, right, or left edge of the control with respect to other controls.

Allow Value List Edits A property you specify to determine whether the Edit List Items button is active in a combo box list.

Allow Zero Length A field property that does not allow zero-length strings (""), which are intentional "nothing" entries, such as a blank Phone Number field for an employee who does not provide a home phone number.

Alternate Back Color A property that determines the color that alternates with white in the background of a report section.

AND criteria Criteria placed in the same row of the query design grid. All criteria on the same row must be true for a record to appear on the resulting datasheet.

Append Only A field property available for Memo fields in Access 2007 databases. When enabled, the property allows users to add data to a Memo field, but not change or remove existing data.

Append query A query that adds selected records to an existing table, and works like an export feature because the records are copied from one location and a duplicate set is pasted within the target table.

Argument Part of a macro that provides additional information on how to carry out an action. In VBA, a constant, variable, or expression passed to a procedure that the procedure needs in order to execute.

Attachment field A field that allows you to attach an external file such as a Word document, PowerPoint presentation, Excel workbook, or image file to a record.

AutoFormat A predefined format that you can apply to a form or report to set the background picture, font, color and alignment formatting choices.

AutoKeys A macro group that is designed to be assigned a key combination (such as [Ctrl][L]).

Autonumber A field data type in which Access enters a sequential integer for each record added into the datasheet. Numbers cannot be reused even if the record is deleted.

Avg function Built-in Access function used to calculate the average of the values in a given field.

Back Color property A property that determines the background color of the selected control or section in a form or report.

Back-end database Part of a split database that contains the actual table objects and is stored on a file server.

Backup A duplicate copy of a file that is stored in another location.

Backward-compatible Software feature that enables documents saved in an older version of a program to be opened in a newer version of the program.

Bang notation A format that separates the object type from an object name and from a control name by using [square brackets] and exclamation points (!).

Between...and Criteria that selects all records between the two dates, including the two dates. Between...and criteria work the same way as the >= and <= operators.

Binding The field binding determines the field to which a bound control in a form or report is connected.

Boolean filter A word or symbol for locating programs, folders, and files by specifying criteria so that you have a greater chance of finding what you need.

Booting A process that Windows steps through to get the computer up and running.

Border Style A form property that determines the appearance of the outside border of the form.

Bound control A control used in either a form or report to display data from the underlying field; used to edit and enter new data in a form.

Breakpoint A VBA debugging tool that works like a bookmark to suspend execution of the procedure at that statement so you can examine what is happening.

Brown-out A power problem caused by a dip in power, often making the lights dim.

Byte One character of storage space on disk or in RAM.

Calculated field A field created in Query Design View that results from an expression of existing fields, Access functions, and arithmetic operators. For example, the entry Profit: [RetailPrice]-[WholesalePrice] in the field cell of the query design grid creates a calculated field called Profit that is the difference between the values in the RetailPrice and WholesalePrice fields.

Calculation A new value that is created by entering an expression in a text box on a form or report.

Calendar icon An icon you can click to select a date from a pop-up calendar.

Calendar picker A pop-up calendar from which you can choose dates for a date field.

Caption A field property that determines the default field name at the top of the field column in datasheets as well as in labels that describe fields on forms and reports.

Cascade Delete Related Records A relationship option that means that if a record in the "one" side of a one-to-many relationship is deleted, all related records in the "many" table are also deleted.

Cascade Update Related Fields A relationship option that means that if a value in the primary key field (the field on the "one" side of a one-to-many relationship) is modified, all values in the foreign key field (the field on the "many" side of a one-to-many relationship) are automatically updated as well.

Case In VBA, a programming structure that executes one of several groups of statements depending on the value of an expression.

Category axis On a PivotChart, the horizontal axis. Also called the x-axis.

CCur A function that converts the result of a calculation to a currency value.

Chart A visual representation of numeric data that helps users see comparisons, patterns, and trends in data. Also called a graph.

Chart Field List A list of fields in the underlying record source for a PivotChart.

Chart Wizard A wizard that guides you through the steps of creating a chart in Access.

Check box A box that turns an option on when checked or off when unchecked.

Child record A record contained in the "many" table in a one-to-many relationship.

Class module An Access module that is contained and executed within specific forms and reports.

Click To quickly press and release the left button on the pointing device; also called single-click.

Client In client/server computing, the user's PC.

Client/server computing Two or more information systems cooperatively processing to solve a problem.

Clipboard Temporary storage area in Windows.

Collapse button A button that shrinks a portion of a dialog box to hide some settings.

Column separator The thin line that separates the field names to the left or right.

Combo box A bound control used to display a list of possible entries for a field in which you can also type an entry from the keyboard. It is a "combination" of the list box and text box controls.

Combo Box Wizard A bound control used to display a list of possible entries for a field in which you can also type an entry from the keyboard.

Command An instruction to perform a task

Command button A button that completes or cancels an operation. In Access, an unbound control used to provide an easy way to initiate an action.

Command Button Wizard A wizard that organizes over 30 of the most common command button actions within six categories.

Command-line option A special series of characters added to the end of the path to the file (for example, C:\My Documents\Quest.accdb /excl), and execute a special command when the file is opened.

Comma-separated values (CSV) A text file where fields are delimited, or separated, by commas.

Comment Text in a module that helps explain and document the code.

Comment line In VBA, a statement in the code that documents the code; it does not affect how the code runs.

Compact and repair To reorganize the pieces of the database to eliminate wasted space on the disk storage device, which also helps prevent data integrity problems.

Compact Flash (CF) card A card about the size of a matchbook that you can plug into your computer to store data.

Compatible The capability of different programs to work together and exchange data.

Compile time The period during which source code is translated to executable code.

Compile-time error In VBA, an error that occurs as a result of incorrectly constructed code and is detected as soon as you run your code or select the Compile option on the Debug menu.

Compress To reduce the size of file so that it takes up less storage space on a disk.

Computer window The window shows the drives on your computer and as well as other installed hardware components.

Conditional expression An expression resulting in either a true or false answer that determines whether a macro action will execute.

Conditional formatting Formatting that is based on specified criteria. For example, a text box may be conditionally formatted to display its value in red if the value is a negative number.

Constant In VBA, an object that retains a constant value throughout the execution of the code.

Contextual tab Tab on the Ribbon that appears when needed to complete a specific task; for example, if you select a chart in an Excel workbook, three contextual Chart Tool tabs (Design, Layout, and Format) appear.

Control Any element on a form or report such as a label, text box, line, or combo box. Controls can be bound, unbound, or calculated.

Control Source property A property of a bound control in a form or report that determines the field to which the control is connected.

Convert To change the database file into one that can be opened in another version of Access.

Copy To make a duplicate copy of a file that is stored in another location.

Criteria Entries (rules and limiting conditions) that determine which records are displayed when finding or filtering records in a datasheet or form, or when building a query.

Criteria syntax Rules by which criteria need to be entered. For example, text criteria syntax requires that the criteria are surrounded by quotation marks (" "). Date criteria are surrounded by pound signs (#).

Crosstab query A query that presents data in a cross-tabular layout (fields are used for both column and row headings), similar to PivotTables in other database and spreadsheet products.

Crosstab Query Wizard A wizard used to create crosstab queries and which helps identify fields that will be used for row and column headings, and fields that will be summarized within the datasheet.

Crosstab row A row in the query design grid used to specify the column and row headings and values for the crosstab query.

Current record The record that has the focus or is being edited.

Data area When creating a chart, the area in the Chart Wizard that determines what data the chart graphs.

Data type A required property for each field that defines the type of data that can be entered in each field. Valid data types include AutoNumber, Text, Number, Currency, Date/Time, OLE Object, and Memo.

Database administration The task of making a database faster, easier, more secure, and more reliable.

Database designer The person responsible for building and maintaining tables, queries, forms, and reports.

Database normalization An extensive set of rules about how data can be structured into a well-defined relational database.

Database template A tool that can be used to quickly create a new database based on a particular subject such as assets, contacts, events, or projects.

Datasheet A spreadsheet-like grid that displays fields as columns and records as rows.

Datasheet View A view that lists the records of the object in a datasheet. Tables, queries, and most form objects have a Datasheet View.

Date function Built-in Access function used to display the current date on a form or report; enter the Date function as Date().

Debug To determine why a macro doesn't run correctly.

Declaration statement A type of VBA statement that precedes procedure statements and helps set rules for how the statements in the module are processed.

Default A setting that is built into a program that is used by that program until you change the setting.

Default View property A form property that determines whether a subform automatically opens in Datasheet or Continuous Forms view.

Delete To remove a folder or file.

Delete query A query that deletes a group of records from one or more tables.

Delimited text file A text file that typically stores one record on each line, with the field values separated by a common character such as a comma, tab, or dash.

Design View A view in which the structure of the object can be manipulated. Every Access object has a Design View.

Desktop The graphical user interface (GUI) displayed on your screen after you start Windows that you use to interact with Windows and other software on your computer.

Details Pane A pane located at the bottom of a window that displays information about the selected disk, drive, folder, or file.

Device A hardware component in your computer system.

Dialog A Border Style option that indicates a form will have a thick border and cannot be maximized, minimized, or resized.

Dialog box In Access, a special form used to display information or prompt a user for a choice. In Windows, a type of window in which you specify how you want to complete an operation.

Dialog box launcher An icon available in many groups on the Ribbon that you can click to open a dialog box or task pane, offering an alternative way to choose commands.

Display When property A control property that determines whether the control appears only on the screen, only when printed, or at all times.

DoCmd A VBA object that supports many methods to run common Access commands such as closing windows, opening forms, previewing reports, navigating records, and setting the value of controls.

Document window The portion of a program window that displays all or part of an open document.

Documenter An Access analysis feature that creates reports on the properties and relationships among the objects in a database.

Documents folder The folder on your hard drive used to store most of the files you create or receive from others.

Domain The recordset (table or query) that contains the field used in a domain function calculation.

Domain function A function used to display a calculation on a form or report using a field that is not included in the Record Source property for the form or report. Also called domain aggregate function.

Dot notation A format that separates a specific macro within a macro group with a period.

Double-click To quickly click the left button on the pointing device twice.

Drag To point to an object, press and hold the left button on the pointing device, move the object to a new location, and then release the left button.

Drag and drop To use a pointing device to move or copy a file or folder to a new location.

Drive A physical location on your computer where you can store files.

Drive name A name for a drive that consists of a letter followed by a colon, such as C: for the hard disk drive.

Drop area A position on a PivotChart or PivotTable where you can drag and place a field. Drop areas on a PivotTable include the Filter field, Row field, Column field, and Totals or Detail field. Drop areas on a PivotChart include the Filter field, Category field, Series field, and Data field.

Drop-down list button A button that opens a list with one or more options from which you can choose.

Dynaset A query property that allows updates to data in a recordset.

Edit To make changes to a file.

Edit List Items button A button you click to add items to the combo box list in Form View.

Edit mode When working with Access records, the mode in which Access assumes you are trying to edit a particular field, so keystrokes such as [Ctrl][End], [Ctrl][Home], [↑], and [↓] move the insertion point within the field. When working with charts, a mode that lets you select and modify individual chart elements such as the title, legend, bars, or axes. When creating a switchboard, an option you can specify so that users can open an object, such as a form, for editing records.

Edit record symbol A pencil-like symbol that appears in the record selector box to the left of the record that is currently being edited in either a datasheet or a form.

Else In VBA, a statement that is executed only if the expression is false.

Enabled property A control property that determines whether the control can have the focus in Form View.

Encryption To make the data in the database unreadable by tools other than opening the Access database itself, which is protected by a password.

End Function In VBA, a required statement to mark the end of the code that defines the new function.

End If In VBA, a statement needed to mark the end of the If block of code.

Error Indicator button A smart tag that helps identify potential design errors in Report or Form Design View.

Event A specific activity that happens in a database, such as the click of a command button or an entry in a field, that can be used to initiate the execution of a macro.

Event procedure A procedure that is triggered by an event. Also called an event handler procedure.

Exclusive mode A mode indicating that you are the only person who has the database open, and others cannot open the file during this time.

Expand button A button that extends a dialog box to display additional settings.

Export To copy Access information to another database, spreadsheet, or file format.

Expression A combination of values, fields, and operators that result in a value.

Extensible Markup Language (XML) A programming language in which data can be placed in text files and structured so that most programs can read the data.

External hard drive A device that plugs into a computer and stores more data than a typical USB drive, anywhere from 20 to 200 GB of information and connect to a computer using either a USB or FireWire port.

Field list A list of the available fields in the table or query that the field list represents.

Field name The name given to each field in a table.

Field property A property that describes a field.

Field selector The button to the left of a field in Table Design View that indicates which field is currently selected. Also the thin gray bar above each field in the query grid.

File An electronic collection of stored data that has a unique name, distinguishing it from other files.

File extension Additional characters assigned by a program added to the end of a filename to identify the type of file.

File hierarchy The structure for organizing folders and files; describes the logic and layout of the folder structure on a disk.

File management A strategy for organizing folders and files.

File server A centrally located computer from which every user can access the database by using the network.

Filename A unique, descriptive name for a file that identifies the file's content. A filename can be no more than 255 characters, including spaces, and can include letters, numbers, and certain symbols.

Filter By Form A way to filter data that allows two or more criteria to be specified at the same time.

Filter By Selection A way to filter records for an exact match.

Find Duplicates Query Wizard A wizard that guides you to create a query that finds duplicate values in one or more fields.

Find unmatched query A type of query that finds records in one table that do not have matching records in a related table.

Find Unmatched Query Wizard A wizard used to create a query that finds records in one table that doesn't have related records in another table.

First normal form (1NF) The first degree of normalization, in which a table has rows and columns with no repeating groups.

Focus The property that indicates which field would be edited if you were to start typing.

Folder A container for a group of related files. A folder may contain subfolders for organizing files into smaller groups.

Folder name A unique, descriptive name for a folder that identifies what you store in that folder.

Foreign key field In a one-to-many relationship between two tables, the foreign key field is the field in the "many" table that links the table to the primary key field in the "one" table.

Form An Access object that provides an easy-to-use data entry screen that generally shows only one record at a time.

Form View View of a form object that displays data from the underlying recordset and allows you to enter and update data.

Form Wizard An Access wizard that helps you create a form.

Format To enhance or improve the appearance of a document.

Format bar A toolbar in the WordPad window that displays buttons for formatting, or enhancing, the appearance of a document.

Format Painter A tool you can use when designing and laying out forms and reports to copy formatting characteristics from one control to another.

Format property A field property that controls how information is displayed and printed.

Front-end database Part of a split database that contains the database objects other than tables (forms, reports, so forth), and links to the back-end database tables.

Function A procedure that returns a value. Access supplies many built-in statistical, financial, and date functions—such as Sum, Pmt, and Now—that can be used in an expression in a query, form, or report to calculate a value.

Gadget A mini-program on the Windows Sidebar for performing an every day task, such as the Clock gadget for viewing the current time.

Gallery A collection of choices you can browse through to make a selection. Often available with Live Preview.

Gigabyte (GB or G) One billion bytes (or one thousand megabytes).

Graphic image *See* Image.

Group *(noun)* In the Navigation Pane, a custom category that organizes the objects that belong to that category. On the Ribbon, a set of related commands on a tab.

Group *(verb)* To sort records in a particular order, plus provide a section before and after each group of records. Also a way to organize database objects by subject or purpose in the Navigation Pane.

Group controls To allow you to identify several controls as a group to quickly and easily apply the same formatting properties to them.

Group selection handles Selection handles that surround grouped controls.

Hard copy A paper copy of a file.

Hard disk A built-in, high-capacity, high-speed storage medium for all the software, folders, and files on a computer.

Hexadecimal Numbers that consist of numbers 0-9 as well as letters A-H.

Icon A small image on the desktop or in a window that represents a tool, resource, folder, or file you can open and use.

If...Then...Else In VBA, a logical structure that allows you to test logical conditions and execute statements only if the conditions are true. If...Then...Else code can be composed of one or several statements, depending on how many conditions you want to test, how many possible answers you want to provide, and what you want the code to do based on the results of the tests.

Image A nontextual piece of information such as a picture, piece of clip art, drawn object, or graph. Because images are graphical (and not numbers or letters), they are sometimes referred to as graphical images.

Immediate window In the Visual Basic Editor, a pane where you can determine the value of any argument at the breakpoint.

Import To quickly convert data from an external file into an Access database. You can import data from one Access database to another—or from many other data sources such as files created by Excel, SharePoint, Outlook, dBase, Paradox, and Lotus 1-2-3 or text files in an HTML, XML, or delimited text file format.

Inactive window An open window you are not currently using.

Index A field property that keeps track of the order of the values in the indexed field as data is being entered and edited. Therefore, if you often sort on a field, the Index property should be set to Yes as this theoretically speeds up the presentation of the sorted data later (because the index has already been created).

Infinity symbol The symbol that indicates the "many" side of a one-to-many relationship.

Inner join A type of relationship in which a query displays only records where joined fields from *both* tables are equal. This means that if a parent table has any records for which there are no matching records in the child table, those records do not appear in the resulting datasheet.

Input Mask property A field property that provides a visual guide for users as they enter data.

Insertion point A blinking, vertical bar that indicates where the next character you type will appear.

Instant Search A Windows tool you use to quickly find a folder or file on your computer.

Integrate To incorporate a document and parts of a document created in one program into another program; for example, to incorporate an Excel chart into a PowerPoint slide, or an Access table into a Word document.

IntelliSense technology In VBA, visual aids that appear as you write a VBA statement to help you complete it.

Interface The look and feel of a program; for example, the appearance of commands and the way they are organized in the program window.

Is Not Null A criterion that finds all records in which any entry has been made in the field.

Is Null A criterion that finds all records in which no entry has been made in the field.

Join line The line identifying which fields establish the relationship between two related tables.

JPEG Acronym for Joint Photographic Experts Group, which defines the standards for the compression algorithms that allow image files to be stored in an efficient compressed format.

Junction table A table created to establish separate one-to-many relationships to two tables that have a many-to-many relationship.

Key field combination Two or more fields that as a group contain unique information for each record.

Keyboard shortcut A key or a combination of keys that you press to perform a command.

Keyword A descriptive word or phrase you enter to obtain a list of results that include that word or phrase.

Kilobyte (KB or K) One thousand bytes.

Label Wizard A report wizard that guides you through the steps of creating labels, such as mailing labels.

Landscape orientation A way to print or view a page that is 11 inches wide by 8.5 inches tall.

Launch To open or start a program on your computer.

Layout The general arrangement in which a form displays the fields in the underlying recordset. Layout types include Columnar, Tabular, Datasheet, Chart, and PivotTable. Columnar is most popular for a form, and Datasheet is most popular for a subform.

Layout View An Access view that lets you make some design changes to a form or report while you are browsing the data.

Left function An Access function that returns a specified number of characters, starting with the left side of a value in a Text field.

Left join A type of relationship in which a query displays all of the records in the parent table, even if the child table does not contain matching records.

Like operator An Access comparison operator that allows queries to find records that match criteria that include a wildcard character.

Limit to List A combo box control property that allows you to limit the entries made by that control to those provided by the combo box list.

Link To connect an Access database to data in an external file such as another Access, dBase, or Paradox database; an Excel or Lotus 1-2-3 spreadsheet; a text file; an HTML file; or an XML file. In Windows, a shortcut for opening a Help topic or a Web site.

Link Child Fields A subform property that determines which field serves as the "many" link between the subform and main form.

Link Master Fields A subform property that determines which field serves as the "one" link between the main form and the subform.

List box In Access, a bound control that displays a list of possible choices for the user. Used mainly on forms. In Windows, a box that displays a list of options from which you can choose (you may need to scroll and adjust your view to see additional options in the list).

Live Preview A feature that lets you point to a choice in a gallery or palette and see the results in the document without actually clicking the choice.

Live taskbar thumbnails A Windows Aero feature that displays a small image of the content within open, but not visible windows, including live content such as video.

Live view A file icon that displays the actual content in a file on the icon.

Local area network (LAN) A type of network installed to link multiple PCs together so they can share hardware and software resources.

Local template A database template stored on your hard drive.

Lock To lock your user account, then display the Welcome screen.

Lock button A Start menu option that locks your computer.

Lock menu button A Start menu option that displays a list of shut-down options.

Locked property A control property that specifies whether you can edit data in a control on Form View.

Log Off To close all windows, programs, and documents, then display the Welcome screen.

Logic error In VBA, an error that occurs when the code runs without obvious problems, but the procedure still doesn't produce the desired result.

Logical view The datasheet of a query is sometimes called a logical view of the data because it is not a copy of the data, but rather, a selected view of data from the underlying tables.

Lookup field A field that has lookup properties. Lookup properties are used to create a drop-down list of values to populate the field.

Lookup properties Field properties that allow you to supply a drop-down list of values for a field.

Lookup table A table that contains one record for each field value.

Lookup Wizard A wizard used in Table Design View that allows one field to "look up" values from another table or entered list. For example, you might use the Lookup Wizard to specify that the Customer Number field in the Sales table display the Customer Name field entry from the Customers table.

Macro An Access object that stores a series of actions to perform one or more tasks.

Macro Builder An Access window in which you build and modify macros.

Macro group An Access macro object that stores more than one macro. The macros in a macro group run independently of one another, but are grouped together to organize multiple macros that have similar characteristics.

Mail merge A way to export Microsoft Office Access data by merging it to a Word document as the data source for a mail merge process, in which data from an Access table or query is combined into a Word form letter, label, or envelope to create mass mailing documents.

Mail Merge task pane A tool in Microsoft Office Word that steps you through creating a mail merge.

Main document In a mail merge, the document used to determine how the letter and Access data are combined. This is the standard text that will be consistent for each letter created in the mail merge process.

Main form A form that contains a subform control.

Main report A report that contains a subreport control.

Make table query A query that creates a new table of data based on the recordset defined by the query. The make table query works like an export feature in that it creates a copy of the selected data and pastes it into a new table in a database specified by the query.

Many-to-many relationship The relationship between two tables in an Access database in which one record of one table relates to many records in the other table and vice versa. You cannot directly create a many-to-many relationship between two tables in Access. To relate two tables with such a relationship, you must establish a third table called junction table that creates separate one-to-many relationships with the two original tables.

Maximized window A window that fills the desktop.

Megabyte (MB or M) One million bytes (or one thousand kilobytes).

Menu A list of related commands.

Menu bar A horizontal bar in a window that displays menu names categories of related commands.

Merge field A code in the main document of a mail merge that is replaced with the values in the field that the code represents when the mail merge is processed.

Method An action that an object can perform. Procedures are often written to invoke methods in response to user actions.

Microsoft Office Excel The spreadsheet program in the Microsoft Office suite.

Microsoft Office Word The word-processing program in the Microsoft Office suite.

Microsoft Windows Vista An operating system.

Minimized window A window that shrinks to a button on the taskbar.

Module An Access object that stores Visual Basic for Applications (VBA) programming code that extends the functions of automated Access processes.

Move To change the location of a file by physically placing it in another location.

MsgBox A macro action that displays an informational message to the user.

Multi-column report A report that repeats the same information in more than one column across the page.

Multi-field primary key A primary key that is composed of two or more fields. For example, an OrderID value can be listed multiple times in the Order Details table, and a ProductID value can be listed multiple times in the Order Details table. But the combination of a particular OrderID value plus a ProductID value should be unique for each record.

Multitask To perform several tasks at the same time.

Multivalued field A field that allows you to make more than one choice from a drop-down list.

Name property In the Visual Basic Editor window, a property that displays the name of an object.

Navigation buttons Buttons in the lower-left corner of a datasheet or form that allow you to quickly navigate between the records in the underlying object as well as add a new record.

Navigation mode A mode in which Access assumes that you are trying to move between the fields and records of the datasheet (rather than edit a specific field's contents), so keystrokes such as

[Ctrl][Home] and [Ctrl][End] move you to the first and last field of the datasheet.

Navigation Pane In Access, a pane in the Access program window that provides a way to move between objects (tables, queries, forms, reports, macros, and modules) in the database. In Windows, a pane on the left side of a window that contains links to your personal folders, including the Documents, Pictures, and Music folders.

Normalize To structure data for a relational database.

Northwind 2007 In Access 2007, an extensive sample database provided by Microsoft to showcase some of the new features of Access such as the Attachment field.

Northwind.mdb A fully developed database example in the Access 2000 file format that illustrates many advanced database techniques you can apply to your own development needs.

Notification area An area on the right side of the taskbar that displays the current time as well as icons for open programs, connecting to the Internet, and checking problems identified by Windows Vista.

Now() An Access function that displays today's date.

Null A field value that means that a value has not been entered for the field.

Null entry The state of "nothingness" in a field. Any entry such as 0 in a numeric field or a space in a text field is not null. It is common to search for empty fields by using the Null criterion in a filter or query. The Is Not Null criterion finds all records where there is an entry of any kind.

Object In VBA, any item that can be identified or manipulated, including the traditional Access objects (table, query, form, report, macro, module) as well as other items that have properties such as controls, sections, and existing procedures.

ODBC *See* open database connectivity

OLE object A field data type that stores pointers that tie files, such as pictures, sound clips, or spreadsheets, created in other programs to a record.

On Click An event that occurs when an item is clicked.

On Current An event that occurs when focus moves from one record to another.

On Dbl Click An Access event that is triggered by a double-click.

One-to-many line The line that appears in the Relationships window and shows which field is duplicated between two tables to serve as the linking field. The one-to-many line displays a "1" next to the field that serves as the "one" side of the relationship and displays an infinity symbol next to the field that serves as the "many" side of the relationship when referential integrity is specified for the relationship. Also called the one-to-many join line.

One-to-many relationship The relationship between two tables in an Access database in which a common field links the tables together. The linking field is called the primary key field in the "one" table of the relationship and the foreign key field in the "many" table of the relationship.

One-to-one relationship A relationship in which the primary key field of the first table is related to the primary key field of a second table. In other words, one record in the first table can be related to one and only one record in the second table.

Online collaboration The ability to incorporate feedback or share information across the Internet or a company network or intranet.

Online template A database template available to download from the Microsoft Office Online Web site.

Open database connectivity (ODBC) A collection of standards that govern how Access connects to other sources of data.

Operating system Software that manages the complete operation of your computer.

Option button In Access, a bound control used to display a limited list of mutually exclusive choices for a field, such as "female" or "male" for a gender field in form or report. In Windows, a small circle you click to select only one of two or more related options.

Option group A bound control placed on a form that is used to group together several option buttons that provide a limited number of values for a field.

OR criteria Criteria placed on different rows of the query design grid. A record will appear in the resulting datasheet if it is true for any single row.

Orphan record A record in the "many" table of a one-to-many relationship that doesn't have a matching entry in the linking field of the "one" table.

Page orientation Printing or viewing a page of data in either a portrait (8.5 inches wide by 11 inches tall) or landscape (11 inches wide by 8.5 inches tall) direction.

Parameter query A query that displays a dialog box to prompt users for field criteria. The entry in the dialog box determines which records appear on the final datasheet, similar to criteria entered directly in the query design grid.

Parameter report A report that prompts you for criteria to determine the records to use for the report.

Parent record A record contained in the "one" table in a one-to-many relationship.

Password A combination of uppercase and lowercase letters, numbers, and symbols that should be kept confidential.

Performance Analyzer An Access tool that studies the structure and size of your database and makes a variety of recommendations on how you can improve its performance.

PivotChart A graphical presentation of the data in a PivotTable.

PivotChart View The view in which you build a PivotChart.

PivotTable An arrangement of data that uses one field as a column heading, another as a row heading, and summarizes a third field, typically a Number field, in the body.

PivotTable View The view in which you build a PivotTable.

Pixel (picture element) One pixel is the measurement of one picture element on the screen.

Point To position the tip of the pointer over an object, option, or item.

Pointer A small arrow or other symbol on the screen that moves in the same direction as the pointing device.

Pointing device A hardware device, such as a mouse, trackball, touch pad, or pointing stick, or an onscreen object for interacting with your computer and the software you are using.

Pop up form A form that stays on top of other open forms, even when another form is active.

Portrait orientation A way to print or view a page that is 8.5 inches wide by 11 inches tall.

Power button A Start menu option that puts your computer to sleep (your computer appears off and uses very little power).

Preview Pane A pane on the right side of a window that shows the actual contents of a selected file without opening a program. Preview may not work for some types of files.

Primary key field A field that contains unique information for each record. A primary key field cannot contain a null entry.

Print Preview A full-page view of a document that you can use to check its layout before you print.

Private Sub A statement that indicates a sub procedure is accessible only to other procedures in the module where it is declared.

Procedure A series of VBA statements that performs an operation or calculates an answer. VBA has two types of procedures: functions and subs.

Program tab Single tab on the Ribbon specific to a particular view, such as Print Preview.

Project Explorer window In the Visual Basic Editor, a window you use to switch between open projects, objects that can contain VBA code.

Property A characteristic that defines the appearance and behavior of items in the database such as objects, fields, sections, and controls. You can view the properties for an item by opening its Property Sheet.

Property sheet A window that displays an exhaustive list of properties for the chosen control, section, or object within the Form Design View or Report Design View.

Prototype label A sample label that previews the fields and punctuation that will appear on the final label.

Query An Access object that provides a spreadsheet-like view of the data, similar to that in tables. It may provide the user with a subset of fields and/or records from one or more tables. Queries are created when the user has a "question" about the data in the database.

Query Datasheet View The view of a query that shows the selected fields and records as a datasheet.

Query design grid The bottom pane of the Query Design View window in which you specify the fields, sort order, and limiting criteria for the query.

Query Design View The window in which you develop queries by specifying the fields, sort order, and limiting criteria that determine which fields and records are displayed in the resulting datasheet.

Quick Access toolbar Customizable toolbar that includes buttons for common Office commands, such as saving a file and undoing an action.

Quick Launch toolbar A toolbar on the left side of the taskbar; includes buttons for showing the desktop when it is not currently visible, switching between windows, and starting the Internet Explorer Web browser.

RAM (random access memory) The physical location used to temporarily store open programs and documents.

Read-only An object property that indicates whether the object can read and display data, but cannot be used to change (write to) data.

Record Source property In a form or report, the property that determines which table or query object contains the fields and records that the form or report will display. It is the most important property of the form or report object. A bound control on a form or report has a Control Source property. In this case, the Control Source property identifies the field to which the control is bound.

Recordset Type A property that determines if and how records displayed by a query are locked.

Recycle Bin A desktop object that stores folders and files you delete from your hard drive(s) and that enables you to restore them.

Referential integrity A set of Access rules that govern data entry and help ensure data accuracy.

Relational database software Software such as Access that is used to manage data organized in a relational database.

Removable storage Storage media that you can easily transfer from one computer to another, such as DVDs, CDs, or flash drives.

Report An Access object that creates a professional printout of data that may contain such enhancements as headers, footers, and calculations on groups of records.

Report View An Access view that maximizes the amount of data you can see on the screen.

Report Wizard An Access wizard that helps you create a report.

Resize bar A thin gray bar that separates the field lists from the query design grid in Query Design View.

Resizing button A button that you use to adjust the size of a window, such as Maximize, Restore Down, and Minimize.

Restart To shut down your computer, then start it again.

Ribbon Area that displays commands for the current Office program, organized into tabs and groups.

Rich Text Format (RTF) A file format for exporting data to a text file that can be opened and edited in Word.

Right join A type of relationship in which a query selects all records in the child table even if there are no matches in the parent table.

Right-click To quickly press and release the right button on the pointing device.

Row selector The small square to the left of a field in Table Design View or the Tab Order dialog box. Called the record selector in Datasheet View and Form View.

Row Source The Lookup property that defines the list of values for the Lookup field.

RTF *See* Rich Text Format.

Ruler In Access, a vertical or horizontal guide that both appear in Form and Report Design View to help you position controls. In Windows, a horizontal bar in the WordPad window that marks a document's width in 1/8ths of an inch (also shows one-inch marks).

Run a query To open a query and view the fields and records that you have selected for the query presented as a datasheet.

Run-time error In VBA, an error that occurs as incorrectly constructed code runs and include attempting an illegal operation such as dividing by zero or moving focus to a control that doesn't exist. When you encounter a run-time error, VBA will stop executing your procedure at the statement in which the error occurred and highlight the line with a yellow background in the Visual Basic Editor.

Saved Exports An option provided in Microsoft Office Access that lets you save export steps.

Saved Imports An option provided in Microsoft Office Access that lets you quickly repeat the import process by saving the import steps.

Screen capture A snapshot of your screen, as if you took a picture of it with a camera, which you can paste into a document.

Scroll To adjust your view in a window.

Scroll arrow button A button at each end of a scroll bar for adjusting your view in small increments in that direction.

Scroll bar A vertical or horizontal bar that appears along the right or bottom side of a window when there is more content than can be displayed within the window so that you can adjust your view.

Scroll box A box in a scroll bar that you can drag to display a different part of a window.

Search criteria One or more pieces of information that helps Windows identify the program, folder, or file you want to locate.

Second normal form (2NF) The second degree of normalization, in which redundant data from an original table is extracted, placed in a new table, and related to the original table.

Section A location of a form or report that contains controls. The section in which a control is placed determines where and how often the control prints.

Section properties Characteristics that define each section in a report.

Secure digital (SD) card A small device that slips directly into a computer, and typically stores around 256 MB.

Select query The most common type of query that retrieves data from one or more linked tables and displays the results in a datasheet.

Server In client/server computing, the shared file server, mini, or mainframe computer. The server usually handles corporate-wide computing activities such as data storage and management, security, and connectivity to other networks.

Shortcut In Access, a pointer to the actual database object that is identified as a shortcut by the small black arrow in the lower-left

corner of the icon. You double-click a shortcut icon to open that object. In Windows, a link that gives you quick access to a particular folder, file, or Web site.

Shortcut menu A menu of common commands for an object that opens when you right-click that object.

Show me an example A button that gives you more information on the subject at hand by using a common example to explain the issue.

Shut Down To completely shut down your computer.

Sidebar A Windows Vista desktop component that displays gadgets.

Simple Query Wizard A wizard used to create a select query.

Single step To run a macro one line (one action) at a time to observe the effect of each specific action in the Macro Single Step dialog box.

Single-click *See* Click.

Sizing handles Small squares at each corner of a selected control in Access. Dragging a handle resizes the control. Also known as handles.

Sleep To save your work, turn off the monitor, then reduce power consumption to all the hardware components in your computer so it appears off; press any key to use your computer again.

Slider A shape you drag to select a setting that falls within a range, such as between Slow and Fast.

Smart tag A button that provides a small menu of options and automatically appears under certain conditions to help you work with a task, such as correcting errors. For example, the AutoCorrect Options button, which helps you correct typos and update properties, and the Error Indicator button, which helps identify potential design errors in Form and Report Design View, are smart tags.

Snapshot A query property that locks the recordset (which prevents it from being updated).

Sort To reorder records in either ascending or descending order based on the values of a particular field.

Spike A surge in power, which can cause damage to the hardware, and can render the computer useless.

Spin box A text box with up and down arrows; you can type a setting in the text box or click the arrows to increase or decrease the setting.

Split form A form that shows you two views of the same data at one time: a traditional form and a datasheet view.

SQL (Structured Query Language) A language that provides a standardized way to request information from a relational database system.

Standard module A type of Access module that contains global code that can be executed from anywhere in the database. Standard modules are displayed as module objects in the Navigation Pane.

Start button The button on the left side of the taskbar that opens the Start menu to start programs, find and open files, access Windows Help and Support, and more.

Startup option One of a series of commands that execute when the database is opened.

Statement A single line of code within a VBA procedure.

Status bar A horizontal bar at the bottom of a window that displays simple Help information and tips.

Strong password A password longer than eight characters that uses a combination of uppercase and lowercase letters, numbers, and symbols.

Stub In the Visual Basic window, the first and last lines of an event handler procedure.

Sub (sub procedure) A procedure that performs a series of VBA statements, but it does not return a value and cannot be used in an expression like a function procedure. You use subs to manipulate controls and objects. They are generally executed when an event occurs, such as when a command button is clicked or a form is opened.

Subfolder A folder within another folder for organizing sets of related files into smaller groups.

Subform A form placed within a form that shows related records from another table or query. A subform generally displays many records at a time in a datasheet arrangement.

Subform/Subreport control A control you use to start the Subform Wizard, which guides you through adding the subform to the main form in Form Design View

Subquery A query based on another query's field list.

Subreport A report placed as a control in another report.

Suite A group of programs that are bundled together and share a similar interface, making it easy to transfer skills and program content among them.

Sum function A mathematical function that totals values in a field.

Summary query A query used to calculate and display information about records grouped together.

Summary report A report that calculates and displays information about records grouped together.

Surge protector A power strip with surge protection,

Switch User To lock your user account and display the Welcome screen so another user can log on.

Switchboard A special Access form that uses command buttons to provide an easy-to-use and secure database interface.

Switchboard Manager An Access tool that help you create and modify switchboards.

Syntax Rules that govern how to write programming statements so that they execute properly.

Syntax error In VBA, an error that occurs immediately as you are writing a VBA statement that cannot be read by the Visual Basic Editor.

Tab A set of commands on the Ribbon related to a common set of tasks or features. Tabs are further organized into groups of related commands. Also a sheet within a dialog box that contains a group of related settings.

Tab control An unbound control used to create a three-dimensional aspect to a form so that other controls can be organized and shown in Form View by clicking the "tabs."

Tab order The sequence in which the controls on the form receive the focus when the user presses [Tab] or [Enter] in Form view.

Tab stop In Access, this refers to whether you can tab into a control when entering or editing data; in other words, whether the control can receive the focus.

Table A collection of records for a single subject, such as all of the customer records.

Table Analyzer Wizard An Access tool that looks for duplicate information in one table that should be separated and stored in its own table.

Table Design View The view in which you can add, delete, or modify fields and their associated properties.

Table template A tool you can use to quickly create a single table within an existing database by providing a set of fields that describe a particular subject, such as contacts or tasks, which can be used or modified to meet your needs.

Tag A word or phrase assigned to a file that reminds you of a file's content.

Target table The table to which an append query adds records.

Taskbar The horizontal bar at the bottom of the desktop; displays the Start button, the Quick Launch toolbar, and the Notification area.

Template A sample file, such as a database provided within the Microsoft Access program.

Terabyte (TB or T) One trillion bytes (or one thousand gigabytes).

Text box A box in which you type text.

Themes Predesigned combinations of colors, fonts, and formatting attributes you can apply to a document in any Office program.

Third normal form (3NF) The third degree of normalization, in which calculated fields (also called derived fields) such as totals or taxes are removed. Strive to create databases that adhere to the rules of third normal form.

Thumbnail A smaller image of the actual contents of a file.

Title bar The top border of a window that displays the name of the window, folder, or file and the program name.

Toolbar A set of buttons you can click to open menus or select common commands that are also available from a menu bar, such as saving and printing.

ToolTip A label that appears and identifies the purpose of an object when you point to it.

Top Values A feature in Query Design View that lets you specify a number or percentage of sorted records that you want to display in the query's datasheet.

Total row Row in the query design grid used to specify how records should be grouped and summarized with aggregate functions.

Touch pointer A pointer on the screen for performing pointing operations with a finger if touch input is available on your computer.

Translucency The transparency feature of Windows Aero that enables you to locate content by seeing through one window to the next window.

Unbound control A control that does not change from record to record and exists only to clarify or enhance the appearance of the form, using elements such as labels, lines, and clip art.

Update query A type of action query that updates the values in a field.

UPS (Uninterruptible Power Supply) A device that provides constant power to other devices, including computers.

USB (Universal Serial Bus) drive A device that plugs into a computer's USB port to store data. USB drives are also called thumb drives, flash drives, and travel drives. USB devices typically store 1 GB to 10 GB of information.

User The person primarily interested in entering, editing, and analyzing the data in the database.

User interface A collective term for all the ways you interact with a software program.

Utility project A VBA project containing code that helps Access with certain activities such as presenting the Zoom dialog box. It automatically appears in the Project Explorer window when you use the Access features that use this code.

Validation Rule A field property that helps eliminate unreasonable entries by establishing criteria for an entry before it is accepted into the database.

Validation Text A field property that determines what message appears if a user attempts to make a field entry that does not pass the validation rule for that field.

Value axis On a PivotChart, the vertical axis. Also called the y-axis.

Value field A numeric field, such as Cost, that can be summed or averaged.

Variable In VBA, an object used to store data that can be used, modified, or displayed during the execution of the procedure.

View By options Navigation Pane options (Details, Icon, List) that let you arrange database objects in different views.

Views Display settings that show or hide selected elements of a document in the document window, to make it easier to focus on a certain task, such as formatting or reading text.

Visual Basic Editor Code window (**Code window**) The window where you write VBA code.

Visual Basic for Applications (VBA) A programming language provided with each program of the Microsoft Office suite to help you extend the program's capabilities. In Access, VBA is stored within modules.

Wallpaper The image that fills the desktop background.

Welcome screen An initial startup screen that displays icons for each user account on the computer.

What-if analysis Reiterative analysis you can perform using tools such as Microsoft Office Excel.

Wildcard A special character used in criteria to find, filter, and query data. The asterisk (*) stands for any group of characters. For example, the criteria I* in a State field criterion cell would find all records where the state entry was IA, ID, IL, IN, or Iowa. The question mark (?) wildcard stands for only one character.

Window A rectangular-shaped work area that displays a program or file, folders and files, or Windows tools.

Windows *See* Microsoft Windows Vista.

Windows 3-D Flip A Windows Aero feature that allows you to display stacked windows at a three-dimensional angle to see even more of the content of all open windows and select the window you want to use.

Windows Aero A Windows Vista feature supported in some editions (or versions) of Windows Vista that enhances the transparency (or translucency) of the Start menu, taskbar, windows, and dialog boxes; enables live taskbar thumbnails, Windows Flip, and Windows 3-D Flip.

Windows Flip A Windows Aero feature that allows you to display a set of thumbnails, or miniature images, of all open windows so that you can select and switch to another window.

Word wrap A feature in word processing programs that determines when a line of text extends into the right margin of the page and automatically forces the text to the next line without you needing to press Enter.

XML file A text file that contains XML tags that identify field names and data. *See also* Extensible Markup Language (XML).

Zooming in A feature that makes a document appear bigger but shows less of it on screen at once; does not affect actual document size.

Zooming out A feature that shows more of a document on screen at once but at a reduced size; does not affect actual document size.

Index

Ext - Monday
Spl 11

Desiree 1978

Anaheim 1